Silver Level
Handbook Edition

Upper Saddle River, New Jersey
Needham, Massachusetts

Handbook Edition

Copper
Bronze
Silver
Gold
Platinum
Ruby
Diamond

ISBN 0-13-037548-9

2 3 4 5 6 7 8 9 10 07 06 05 04

Use iText *Writing and Grammar*, the interactive textbook!

Includes every grammar exercise in this book!

- instant feedback on interactive grammar exercises
- interactive writing tools and writing tutorials
- access to e-rater™, the electronic essay-scoring tool

iText is also available on CD-ROM.

Go on-line to get instant help on the Writing and Grammar Web site!

- additional grammar practice opportunities
- scoring rubrics with scored student models for different modes of writing

Here's how to use the Writing and Grammar Web site:

Look for these Web Codes in your book:

eck-8001
eck-8002

Here's how to use Web Codes:

1. Go on-line. Enter URL: PHSchool.com
2. If you want instant feedback on interactive grammar exercises, enter Web Code: eck-8002
   Choose the appropriate chapter from the menu that appears.
3. If you want to review writing rubrics and scored student models, enter Web Code: eck-8001
   Choose the appropriate chapter from the menu that appears.

Program Authors

The program authors guided the direction and philosophy of *Prentice Hall Writing and Grammar: Communication in Action*. Working with the development team, they contributed to the pedagogical integrity of the program and to its relevance to today's teachers and students.

Joyce Armstrong Carroll

In her forty-year career, Joyce Armstrong Carroll, Ed.D., has taught on every grade level from primary to graduate school. In the past twenty years, she has trained teachers in the teaching of writing. A nationally known consultant, she has served as president of TCTE and on NCTE's Commission on Composition. More than fifty of her articles have appeared in journals such as *Curriculum Review, English Journal, Media & Methods, Southwest Philosophical Studies, Ohio English Journal, English in Texas*, and the *Florida English Journal*. With Edward E. Wilson, Dr. Carroll co-authored *Acts of Teaching: How to Teach Writing* and co-edited *Poetry After Lunch: Poems to Read Aloud*. Beyond her direct involvement with the writing pedagogy presented in this series, Dr. Carroll guided the development of the Hands-on Grammar feature. She co-directs the New Jersey Writing Project in Texas.

Edward E. Wilson

A former editor of *English in Texas*, Edward E. Wilson has served as a high-school English teacher and a writing consultant in school districts nationwide. Wilson has served on the Texas Teacher Professional Practices Commission and on NCTE's Commission on Composition. With Dr. Carroll, he co-wrote *Acts of Teaching: How to Teach Writing* and co-edited the award-winning *Poetry After Lunch: Poems to Read Aloud*. In addition to his direct involvement with the writing pedagogy presented in this series, Wilson provided inspiration for the Spotlight on Humanities feature. Wilson's poetry appears in Paul Janeczko's anthology *The Music of What Happens*. Wilson co-directs the New Jersey Writing Project in Texas.

Gary Forlini

Gary Forlini, a nationally known education consultant, developed the grammar, usage, and mechanics instruction and exercises in this series. After teaching in the Pelham, New York, schools for many years, he established Research in Media, an educational research agency that provides information for product developers, school staff developers, media companies, and arts organizations, as well as private-sector corporations and foundations. Mr. Forlini was co-author of the *S.A.T. Home Study* program and has written numerous industry reports on elementary, secondary, and post-secondary education markets.

National Advisory Panel

The teachers and administrators serving on the National Advisory Panel provided ongoing input into the development of *Prentice Hall Writing and Grammar: Communication in Action.* Their valuable insights ensure that the perspectives of teachers and students throughout the country are represented within the instruction in this series.

Dr. Pauline Bigby-Jenkins
Coordinator for Secondary English Language Arts
Ann Arbor Public Schools
Ann Arbor, Michigan

Lee Bromberger
English Department Chairperson
Mukwonago High School
Mukwonago, Wisconsin

Mary Chapman
Teacher of English
Free State High School
Lawrence, Kansas

Jim Deatherage
Language Arts Department Chairperson
Richland High School
Richland, Washington

Luis Dovalina
Teacher of English
La Joya High School
La Joya, Texas

JoAnn Giardino
Teacher of English
Centennial High School
Columbus, Ohio

Susan Goldberg
Teacher of English
Westlake Middle School
Thornwood, New York

Jean Hicks
Director, Louisville Writing Project
University of Louisville
Louisville, Kentucky

Karen Hurley
Teacher of Language Arts
Perry Meridian Middle School
Indianapolis, Indiana

Karen Lopez
Teacher of English
Hart High School
Newhall, California

Marianne Minshall
Teacher of Reading and Language Arts
Westmore Middle School
Columbus, Ohio

Nancy Monroe
English Department Chairperson
Bolton High School
Alexandria, Louisiana

Ken Spurlock
Assistant Principal
Boone County High School
Florence, Kentucky

Cynthia Katz Tyroff
Staff Development Specialist and Teacher of English
Northside Independent School District
San Antonio, Texas

Holly Ward
Teacher of Language Arts
Campbell Middle School
Daytona Beach, Florida

Grammar Review Team

The following teachers reviewed the grammar instruction in this series to ensure accuracy, clarity, and pedagogy.

Kathy Hamilton
Paul Hertzog
Daren Hoisington
Beverly Ladd
Karen Lopez
Dianna Louise Lund
Sean O'Brien

CONTENTS IN BRIEF

Chapters 1–13

Part 1: Writing 1

Part 2: Grammar, Usage, and Mechanics 190

Chapters 28–31

Part 3: Academic and Workplace Skills 484

Resources

CONTENTS
PART 1: WRITING

Chapter 4

Narration

Autobiographical Writing 32

Student Work IN PROGRESS

Featured Work:
"Zermatt or Bust!"
by Evan Twohy
Prospect Sierra School
El Cerrito, California

INTEGRATED SKILLS

Chapter 5

Narration

Student Work IN PROGRESS

Featured Work:
"A Tear and a Smile"
by Robin Myers
Maplewood Middle School
Maplewood, New Jersey

INTEGRATED SKILLS

Chapter 6

Description 66

Student Work IN PROGRESS

Featured Work:
"My Home Sweet Wet Home"
by Victoria Kilinskis
St. Francis Xavier School
La Grange, Illinois

INTEGRATED SKILLS

Chapter 7

Persuasion

Persuasive Essay 82

Student Work IN PROGRESS

Featured Work:
"I Will Be Drug Free"
by Ryan Caparella
Chain of Lakes Middle School
Orlando, Florida

INTEGRATED SKILLS

Chapter 8 Exposition: *Comparison-and-Contrast Essay* 100

Student Work IN PROGRESS

Featured Work:
"Small Town, Big City"
by Mindy Glasco
Los Alamos Middle School
Los Alamos, New Mexico

INTEGRATED SKILLS

Chapter 9

Exposition

Cause-and-Effect Essay 114

Student Work IN PROGRESS

Featured Work:
"The Dust Bowl"
by Emily Meade
Ingersoll Middle School
Canton, Illinois

INTEGRATED SKILLS

Chapter 10

Exposition

How-to Essay 130

Student Work IN PROGRESS

Featured Work:
"How to Groom a Dog"
by Katherine Ann Roshani Stewart
Villa Duchesne School
St. Louis, Missouri

INTEGRATED SKILLS

Chapter 11

Research

Research Report 146

Student Work IN PROGRESS

Featured Work:
"Ben Franklin: Man of Many Talents"
by Joseph Hochberger
Gotha Middle School
Windermere, Florida

INTEGRATED SKILLS

Chapter 12

Response to Literature 162

Student Work IN PROGRESS

Featured Work:
"A Response to 'Christmas Day in the Morning' by Pearl S. Buck"
by Stacy Osborn
Gilmer Independent School District
Gilmer, Texas

INTEGRATED SKILLS

Chapter 13

Writing for Assessment

Student Work IN PROGRESS

Featured Work:
"A Letter to His Majesty, King George III"
by Paul Keller
Roosevelt Middle School
Oceanside, California

INTEGRATED SKILLS

PART 2: GRAMMAR, USAGE, AND MECHANICS

Chapter 14

Chapter 15

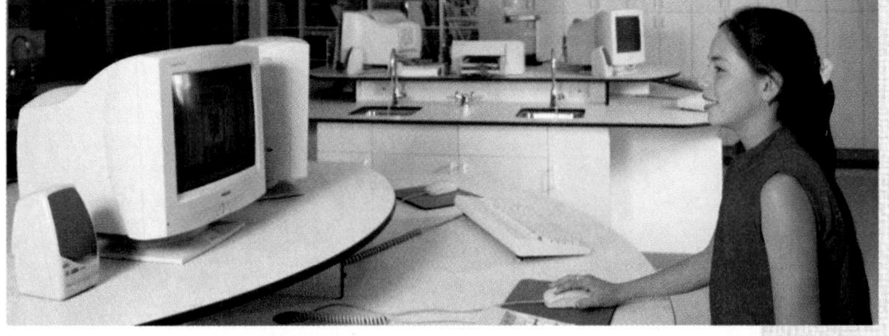

Chapter 19

Basic Sentence Parts 264

Chapter 20

Phrases and Clauses 294

CP Rail

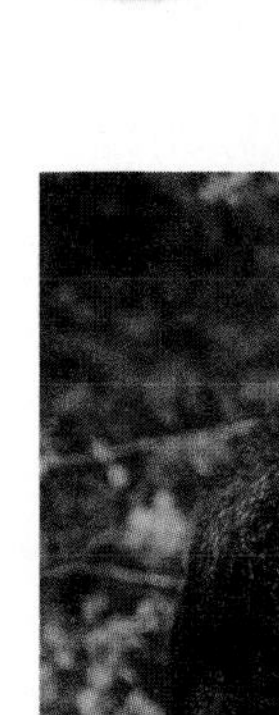

PART 3: ACADEMIC AND WORKPLACE SKILLS

Chapter 30

Reading Skills

Chapter 31

Study, Reference, and Test-Taking Skills

Resources

PART 1

Writing

Orange Sweater, 1955, Elmer Bischoff, San Francisco Museum of Modern Art, San Francisco, California

Chapter 1 The Writer in You

▲ **Critical Viewing** For what purpose do you think this boy might be writing? **[Speculate]**

Writing in Everyday Life

A writer writes—it's as simple as that. Every time you use a pen or type on a keyboard, you are a writer. There is no big mystery about being a writer. However, being an effective and powerful writer takes time, practice, and self-awareness.

You have already grown a great deal as a writer. You have advanced from writing your name, using newly learned alphabet letters, to composing thoughtful essays for school. Today, you use writing for a wide variety of important daily tasks. Your writing takes many forms: phone messages, a journal, business letters, e-mail, stories, reports, invitations, and more. Sometimes, you write a quick note or a sign in just a few minutes. Other times, you take weeks to plan and complete a larger project, such as a persuasive essay or a short story.

What Are the Qualities of Good Writing?

Ideas Many writers choose the same topics to write about—but each writer has his or her own ideas about each topic. Your ideas are what will make your writing different from the writing of others. Don't simply offer readers information they already have; share your unique ideas and insights.

Organization If writing is to be effective, it must be understood. Organize your writing so that readers can follow its internal structure. Give information in the right amount and in the right order.

Voice When you call friends on the telephone, many of them probably recognize your voice even before you identify yourself. As a writer, too, you have a distinctive voice. Learn to develop your writing voice. Let your personality show in the way you express yourself, while still observing the conventions of written English.

Word Choice If you just asked a waiter to "bring food," you could end up with any one of a wide variety of dishes. You are probably more precise when you order something to eat—you use precise words with precise meanings. As a writer, help your readers understand exactly what you mean by using the most precise word for your purpose. Consider the connotations, or associations, of words as well as their denotations, or dictionary meanings.

Sentence Fluency Good writing contains a variety of sentence patterns and lengths. Sentence variety creates a flow that sounds smooth and polished.

Conventions When people share a language, certain rules or conventions make it possible for everyone to communicate effectively. When you write, follow the conventions for English—the rules of grammar, usage, and mechanics.

Reflecting on Your Writing

As you review your writing portfolio, or before you begin a new project, spend some time thinking about your accomplishments and goals. Ask yourself these questions:

- Of what piece of writing am I the most proud? Why?
- What specific types of writing would I like to try?
- Did I ever feel intimidated by a blank piece of paper? How did I conquer my fear? What strategy might I try next time?

You may find it useful to share your responses with a partner and to note your ideas in your writer's journal.

Chapter 2 A Walk Through the Writing Process

▲ **Critical Viewing** How do your writing habits reflect the type of writing you do? **[Connect]**

The **writing process**—a systematic approach to writing—can help you achieve your writing goals. From prewriting through publishing and presenting, understanding the stages of the writing process will help you to be a better writer.

Types of Writing

Writing can be categorized in terms of **modes,** the form or shape that the writing takes. The chart at right shows the modes you'll encounter in this book.

Writing may also be divided into two broader categories: *reflexive* and *extensive,* according to the inspiration and intended audience of your work. When you write **reflexively,** you choose the subject and the format and you decide whether to share your writing with others. Reflexive writing—such as a journal or diary entry—is *for* you and *from* you. In contrast, when you write **extensively,** you follow guidelines set by others. This type of writing, which includes a report or an essay assigned in school, is *for* others and *from* others.

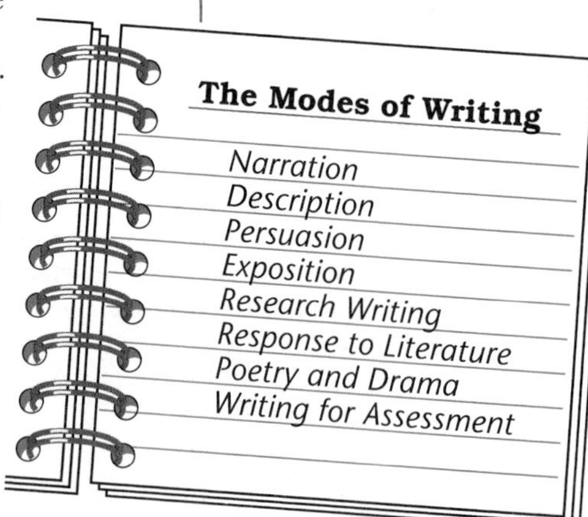

The Modes of Writing

Narration
Description
Persuasion
Exposition
Research Writing
Response to Literature
Poetry and Drama
Writing for Assessment

The Process of Writing

These are the stages of the writing process:

- **Prewriting** is the process of freely exploring ideas, choosing a topic, and gathering and organizing details before you write.
- **Drafting** is a way to get your ideas down on paper in roughly the format you intend.
- **Revising** gives you the opportunity to correct any errors and improve your writing's form and content.
- **Editing and Proofreading** let you polish your writing, fixing errors in grammar, spelling, and mechanics.
- **Publishing and Presenting** allow you to share your writing.

These steps may seem to suggest a progression from one to the next, but writers often return to earlier writing stages as they work. For example, when you are drafting, you may discover that you need to do some additional investigation of your topic. When you are revising, you may decide to include more information from your prewriting stage.

A Guided Tour

You can use this chapter as an introduction to the stages of the writing process. Look closely at the steps of the process presented here. Consider some of the strategies used by effective writers, and experiment with them in your own writing. By applying these strategies to your own writing process, you can improve the quality of your final draft.

2.1 What Is Prewriting?

All writers can experience moments of uncertainty when faced with a blank sheet of paper. Often, writers are not sure what to write about or how much to write. The prewriting stage provides preparation for writing by helping you flex and stretch your creative muscles. Prewriting consists of routines and strategies for getting started; it's a mental warm-up for writing. Each writing chapter will offer you several techniques for getting started, including choosing a topic, narrowing a topic, considering audience and purpose, and gathering details before you draft.

For additional Prewriting strategies suited to specific writing tasks, see Chapters 4–13.

Choosing Your Topic

In order to write, you must first choose a topic. You'll find that you do your best writing when you address a topic that you find meaningful. Prewriting strategies allow you to explore issues, ideas, and experiences that are significant to you. Try the sample strategies to help generate a topic for writing.

SAMPLE STRATEGY

Reviewing Newspapers and Magazines To find a topic that is contemporary and interesting, flip through articles and advertisements in newspapers and magazines. For each subject or image that catches your eye, write a key word that summarizes what you found. Then, using this key word to direct your thinking, jot down a few ideas for writing. Review your notes to find a topic.

In this example, the writer found several compelling subjects and images in a newsmagazine. After reading an article on family reunions, the writer decided to write an essay about her aunt and uncle.

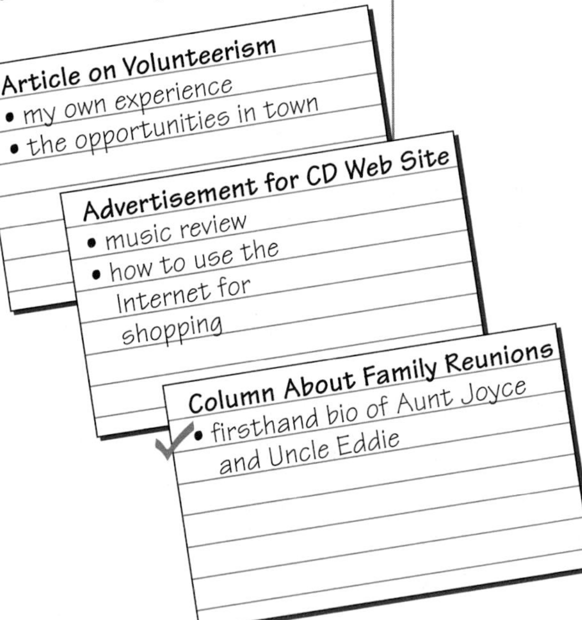

Narrowing Your Topic

Once you have chosen a topic to write about, make sure it is not so general or broad that it becomes unmanageable. For example, in a short paper, it would be difficult to address the benefits of all competitive sports. However, by narrowing your focus to show the benefits of joining a school soccer team, you will be able to treat the subject thoroughly. Look at these sample broad and narrowed topics:

BROAD:	Pets
NARROW:	Bringing a new pet home
NARROWER:	How to house-train a puppy

BROAD:	Cities
NARROW:	Hollywood
NARROWER:	Spotting celebrities in the city of stars

SAMPLE STRATEGY

Using a Topic Web One way to narrow a topic that is too broad is to create a topic web. Start by placing a broad topic at the top of the web. Next, divide the broad topic into two or more subtopics. Then, divide each subtopic into even narrower topics, drawing lines to connect each topic with its subtopics. The following model shows how you might narrow the broad topic "Television Shows" by using this strategy.

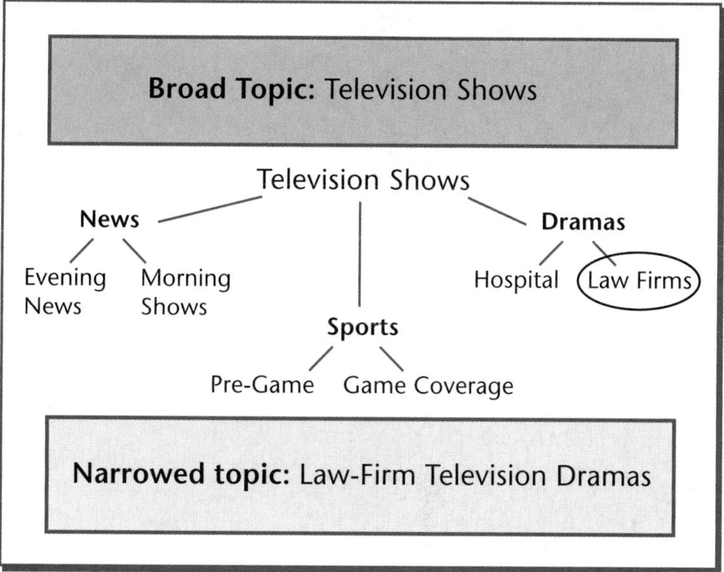

2.1

Considering Your Audience and Purpose

To increase the effectiveness of your writing, analyze your audience, or the people you hope to reach. Then, refine your purpose by focusing on your reason for writing.

Considering Your Audience Before you begin to draft, consider the audience you want your writing to reach. For example, teenagers have different concerns from those of business executives; writers should take such differences into account when writing for a particular audience. A profile like the one shown here can help you identify the interests and knowledge level of your readers. Use your answers to guide the language and details you include in your writing.

AUDIENCE PROFILE

- What is the average age of my audience?
- What do they know about my topic?
- What details will be most interesting to my audience?
- What background do I need to provide?

Considering Your Purpose Your purpose, or your reason for writing, will influence the kinds of details you include. If you want to praise a restaurant for its varied menu, include examples of the range of dishes available. In contrast, if you want to entertain readers with a description of the bumbling service, include humorous examples that re-create your dining experience. Consider these tips for achieving specific purposes:

- **To inform—**include facts, details, and examples that show your subject in a new light.
- **To reflect—**summarize an experience, but focus on showing what you have learned from it.
- **To persuade—**include reasons and arguments to support a position.

Gathering Details

Just as a gardener gathers seeds, bulbs, gloves, and tools before planting, you must gather the details and materials you will need before you write your first draft. Collecting relevant ideas and facts at this stage makes writing easier.

SAMPLE STRATEGY

Preparing a Parts-of-Speech Word Web A parts-of-speech word web can help you gather the right words to describe your subject. In this example, a writer identifies details to describe a rainstorm.

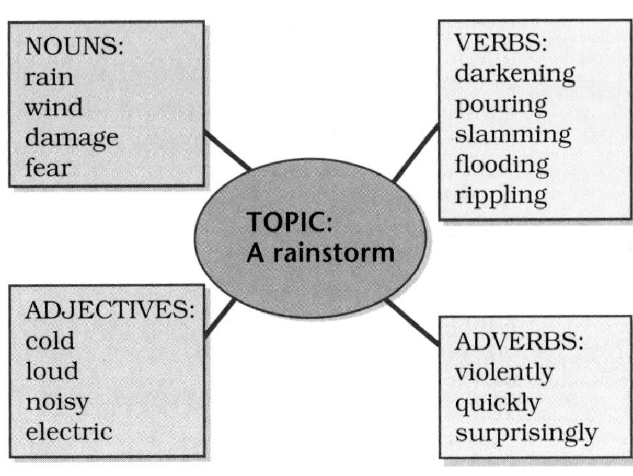

SAMPLE STRATEGY

Using Hexagonal Writing The hexagonal writing technique can be helpful for writing about literature. Hexagonal writing allows you to focus on different aspects of a piece of literature and to prepare to write an organized, thorough analysis. Complete each side of a hexagon according to the directions in the sample shown.

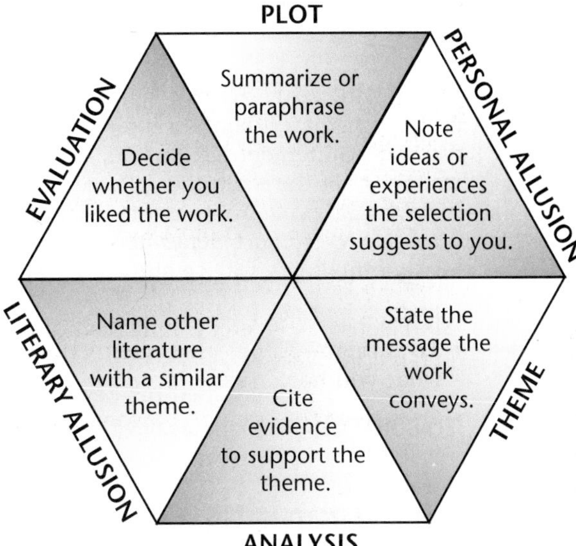

DIRECTIONS FOR USING A HEXAGON

APPLYING THE PREWRITING STRATEGIES

1. Find three magazine articles or images that interest you. For each, identify a potential writing topic.
2. Narrow the subject "Leisure Time" into a topic that you would be able to address in an essay.
3. Create two different audience profiles for a report you might write about bicycles. Identify two unique audiences.
4. Create a parts-of-speech word web to describe your best friend.
5. Complete a hexagon for a short story you have recently read.

2.2 What Is Drafting?

Shaping Your Writing

Focusing on the Form Readers bring expectations to every type of writing they encounter. They expect persuasion to convince, narration to tell a story, and comparison-and-contrast writing to show similarities and differences. Keep these expectations in mind as you draft.

Pulling Readers In With an Enticing Lead Your opening sentences should introduce your topic, show off your writing style, and encourage your audience to keep reading. Start with a compelling quotation or a vivid description. Then, link your opening sentences to your topic and main idea.

Providing Elaboration

Whether you are writing a letter of complaint or a short story, the details and explanations you include can enhance your writing. Add facts and descriptions to help readers imagine the action or understand your ideas. The SEE method is one strategy that can help you strengthen your writing.

SAMPLE STRATEGY

Using the SEE Method You strengthen your writing by providing greater depth of information when you use the SEE method—Statement, Extension, Elaboration. Start with a statement of the main idea. Then, write an extension by restating or explaining the first sentence. Elaborate further by providing even more detail about the main idea. Think of the SEE method as a way to shed more light on your subject:

STATEMENT:	After a long day, Andy was ready to leave.
EXTENSION:	At eleven o'clock, he cleared his desk and grabbed his keys.
ELABORATION:	As he walked out, he waved to the night guard and headed for the deserted parking lot.

APPLYING THE DRAFTING STRATEGIES

1. Write an interest-grabbing lead for a description of a busy train station.
2. Complete the sentences below. Then, using the SEE method, elaborate on each one.
   (a) My favorite season is __?__.
   (b) __?__ played an important role in history.

2.3 What Is Revising?

Revision can be a challenging process, especially when you are looking at several aspects of your writing at once. To make the task easier, use a system called **ratiocination** (rash´ ē äs ə nā´ shen). This method of applying logical thinking to your writing helps you focus on one element at a time. For example, by marking your draft with brackets, highlighting, circles, or other clues, you can make informed decisions about revising. The revision sections of each writing chapter provide strategies to guide your analysis of structure, paragraphs, sentences, and word choice.

Writers in ACTION

"After a lifetime of writing, I still revise every sentence many times and still worry that I haven't caught every ambiguity; I don't want anyone to have to read a sentence of mine twice to find out what it means."

—*William Zinsser*

Revising Your Overall Structure

Whether you are revising a story, a response to literature, or another type of writing, a logical first step in revision is to review the overall structure of your writing. Make sure your draft is well-organized and that your main idea is clearly communicated. Here is one technique to focus your evaluation:

SAMPLE STRATEGY

REVISION STRATEGY
Scanning the Sequence

Review the sequence of ideas in your draft to be sure the organization is logical. Using an index card for each paragraph in your writing, jot down a summarizing word or phrase to identify the main idea developed. Then, review your cards and evaluate their sequence. If the presentation of ideas does not support your main idea effectively, consider reordering the paragraphs. Move the cards until you find an order that works. You might also add transitional words, phrases, or sentences to make the writing flow more smoothly. In the model shown here, the writer reorders her essay on baseball.

EVALUATING SEQUENCE

Main idea: Baseball is popular for many reasons.

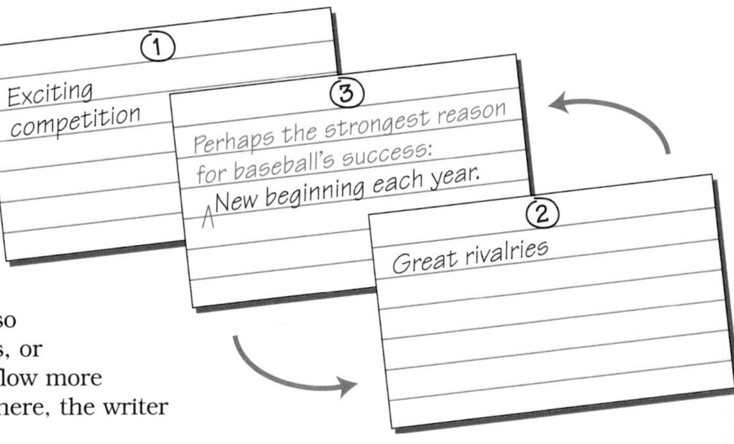

2.3

Revising Your Paragraphs

Take a closer look at each paragraph in your writing. To allow each part of your writing to contribute successfully to the draft, you may need to change some of your paragraphs.

SAMPLE STRATEGY

REVISION STRATEGY
Comparing Body Paragraphs to Purpose

To be sure your draft achieves the purpose you had planned, write your specific purpose on a sticky note. As you review each paragraph in your draft, slide the note down the paper. Highlight details that address your purpose. If you notice that some paragraphs do not have highlights, add or revise a sentence to strengthen your work.

COMPARING PARAGRAPH TO PURPOSE

My aunt went to college to study nursing. ^This was a good career choice for her because she has a caring personality and likes to make people feel at ease. Later, she married my uncle and started to work at Barnabas Hospital, where she worked steadily for twenty years. Everyone who meets her at the hospital is struck by her good humor. She always tells patients jokes or finds the humor in a situation.

Aunt Elaine finds ways to spend time with my brothers and sisters . . .

Purpose: to praise

Revising Your Sentences

When you focus on your writing at the sentence level, try to enliven it by breaking repetitive patterns. One way to do this is to take a closer look at the lengths of the sentences in your draft.

SAMPLE STRATEGY

REVISION STRATEGY
Tracking Sentence Lengths

To reveal problems with sentence length in any writing you do, track a word count. For each sentence in your draft, count the words and note the number in the side margin. Use these tips for revision.

Evaluate	Revise
• Do you notice a series of short or long sentences?	• Break the pattern by combining short sentences or breaking down long ones.

Revising Your Word Choice

Get the most mileage out of the words you use by taking a closer look at the language in your draft. Every complete sentence has a verb, so verbs are a good candidate for your review.

SAMPLE STRATEGY

REVISION STRATEGY
Circling "Be" Verbs

Verbs are the action words and state-of-being words that bring a sentence to life. Using a red pen, circle the *be* verbs in your draft. Locate every use of *am, is, are, was, were, be, being,* and *been.* While you may occasionally need to use a verb that expresses being, challenge yourself to eliminate some of these verbs by replacing them with precise action verbs. Look at the example at right.

EVALUATING "BE" VERBS

As one of the most famous dance teams, Fred Astaire and Ginger Rogers ~~are an~~ [danced their way into] American legend. They ~~were~~ [starred] in ten films together, and their graceful style made it look so easy!

Peer Review

When you invite other people to respond to your writing, you get the chance to see your work from a reader's point of view. Use these ideas to take advantage of a classmate's perspective.

Focusing Peer Review	
Purpose	**Ask**
Evaluate description	What words helped you see the subject I described?
Analyze organization Summarize the main idea	Which details seemed unrelated to my main idea?

Evaluate the Feedback You have the authority to say what your final draft will include. Consider your reviewers' suggestions, and ask further questions to get more specific directions. Then, decide how you want to revise your work.

APPLYING THE REVISION STRATEGY

Choose a recent draft you have written, and try the revision strategies shown here. Then, identify and explain four improvements you have made.

2.4 What Are Editing and Proofreading?

All forms of writing—from a letter to a friend to a research paper—are more effective when they are error-free. Once you are satisfied with the content of your writing, polish the grammar, usage, and mechanics.

Focusing on Proofreading

Challenge yourself to learn and apply the skills of proofreading to everything you write. While the writing chapters in this book offer a specific focus to help you develop these skills, review your writing carefully to find and correct all errors. These are the broad categories that should direct your proofreading work:

Check Your Spelling Check every word in your draft and consult a dictionary to confirm any spelling of which you are unsure. Be especially mindful of the presentation of the names of people, places, and organizations.

Check Your Grammar and Usage Use a dictionary and a usage handbook to correct problems in language and grammatical structures. For example, review subject-verb agreement, check that you have not included sentence fragments unintentionally, and confirm the usage of such problem word pairs as *further* and *farther, accept* and *except*, and *can* and *may*.

Review Capitalization and Punctuation Review your draft to be sure you've begun each sentence with a capital letter and used proper end punctuation.

Double-Check the Facts When your writing includes facts gathered from outside sources or makes claims that you believe are true, take the time to confirm the accuracy of your work. Consult reference material to double-check these items:

- names
- dates
- statistics
- direct quotations

APPLYING THE EDITING AND PROOFREADING STRATEGIES

To focus your proofreading on the types of errors you make, start a list of the mistakes you often make. Compare your list with that of a partner, and discuss techniques for finding and correcting these errors. Keep the list in your portfolio, and use it to guide your proofreading this year.

Learn More

For extensive instruction on grammar, usage, and mechanics issues that affect your writing, see Chapters 14–27.

2.5 What Are Publishing and Presenting?

Moving Forward

This chapter has provided you with an introduction to the techniques and strategies you can use at every stage of the writing process. Each of the writing chapters in this book will teach you specific strategies to help you write in the mode or type of writing discussed. Take note of the ones that are especially effective for you, and apply them to other writing you complete.

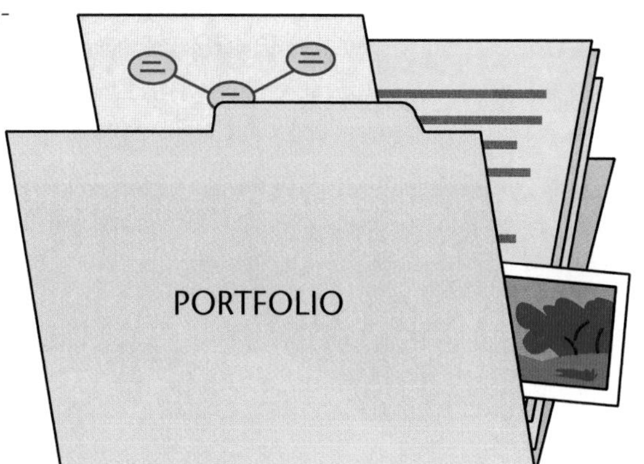

Building Your Portfolio Keep your finished writing products in an organized container, such as a folder, a binder, or a box. This portfolio can help you see your progress as a writer. In addition to the final drafts you keep, you may also want to use your portfolio as a place to store drafts, save peer review notes, and keep ideas for future writing projects.

Reflecting on Your Writing To help yourself become a better writer, take the time to learn from each of your writing experiences. In each writing chapter, a *Reflecting on Your Writing* feature provides questions to encourage you to think about your writing process.

Assessing Your Writing All writing should meet standards of clarity; however, each type of writing should also meet requirements unique to its form. For example, descriptive writing should convey a central image, but a narrative should tell a story. Use the *Rubric for Self-Assessment* in each writing chapter to be sure that you address the key features of each writing form you create.

APPLYING THE PUBLISHING AND PRESENTING STRATEGIES

1. The activities you completed during this chapter may serve as inspirations for later writing. Choose one prewriting activity, and save it in your portfolio. Discuss with a partner why you chose the activity you did.
2. To begin reflecting on your writing process, jot down a response to one of the following questions. Add your reflection to your portfolio.
   - Which of the revision strategies or activities did you find most useful? Why?
   - What are your strengths as a writer?

Chapter 3

Sentences, Paragraphs, and Compositions

Structure and Style

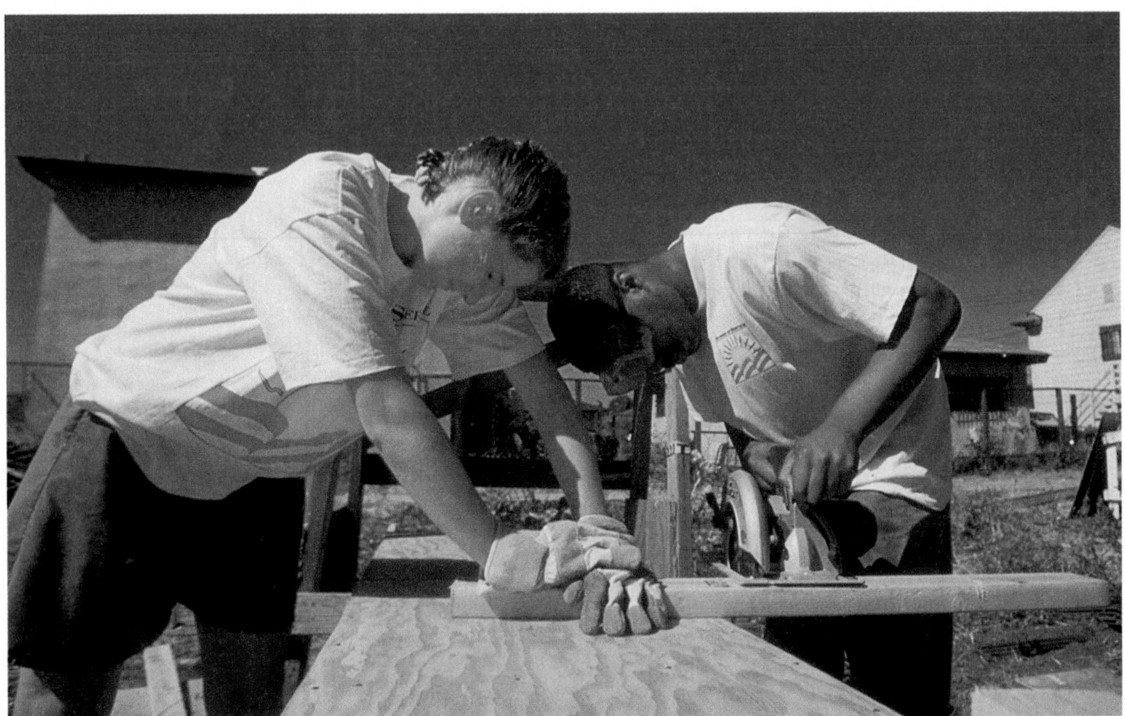

▲ Critical Viewing What skills are the people in this picture using? Compare the skills they are using to the skills needed to "build" a paragraph or composition. [Analyze]

What Are Sentences, Paragraphs, and Compositions?

Like houses, sentences, paragraphs, and compositions are built from pieces that are planned, that fit together logically, and that provide solid support. A **sentence** is a group of words with a subject and a predicate that expresses a complete thought. A **paragraph** is a group of sentences that function as a unit to express a single focus or point. A **composition** is a group of paragraphs that are logically arranged to develop and support a single main idea. Each sentence supports the topic of the paragraph. Each paragraph contributes to the main idea of the composition.

3.1 Sentence Combining

Controlling Your Sentences

You use sentences every day—to ask questions, make statements, express emotion, or share information. In order to hold your reader's interest in your writing, it is necessary to vary your sentence structure. Too many short sentences may make your writing choppy and disconnected. One way to avoid the excessive use of short sentences is to combine sentences—to express two or more related ideas or pieces of information in a single sentence.

Inserting Words and Phrases

Sentences may be combined by changing one of them into a phrase that adds information to the other. (In some cases, the information may be added with the insertion of just one word.) Sometimes, you may have to change the form of words and use additional punctuation.

EXAMPLE: In 1848, gold was discovered at Sutter's Mill in California. James Marshall found the gold.

COMBINED: In 1848, gold was discovered **by James Marshall** at Sutter's Mill in California.

EXAMPLE: San Francisco grew from a village to a city as a result of the Gold Rush. San Francisco was the port closest to Sutter's Mill.

COMBINED: San Francisco**, the port closest to Sutter's Mill,** grew from a village to a city as a result of the Gold Rush.

Exercise 1 **Combining With Words and Phrases** Combine each pair of sentences by inserting key information from one sentence into the other. Add commas as necessary.

1. More than 80,000 people rushed to California in 1849. They were known as *forty-niners.*
2. Some early miners were able to dig for gold with a knife. The gold was near the surface.
3. Some miners made fortunes in a few weeks. They were lucky.
4. Miners came from the United States, Mexico, and Canada. They traveled overland or by sea.
5. Sacramento became a mining center in 1849. Sacramento is now the capital of California.

Using Compound Subjects, Verbs, and Objects

Two or more short sentences may have elements in common—they may have the same subject, verb, or object. Such sentences may be combined into a single sentence that uses a compound subject, a compound verb, or a compound object.

COMMON VERB AND OBJECT:	Trading ships spread the news of the gold strike in California. Newspapers spread the news of the gold strike, too.
COMPOUND SUBJECT:	**Trading ships and newspapers** spread the news of the gold strike in California.
COMMON SUBJECT:	People walked to the gold fields. People rode in covered wagons to the gold fields. People traveled by ship to the gold fields.
COMPOUND VERB:	People **walked, rode** in covered wagons, or **traveled** by ship to the gold fields.
COMMON SUBJECT AND VERB:	The forty-niners discovered hardships in California. They also discovered disease and loneliness.
COMPOUND OBJECT:	The forty-niners discovered **hardships, disease,** and **loneliness** in California.

Learn More

For additional information about compound subjects and verbs, see Section 19.3.

Exercise 2 **Using Compound Subjects, Verbs, and Objects** Combine each pair of sentences by creating compound subjects, compound verbs, or compound objects.

1. The miners needed food. They also needed housing.
2. Sam Brannan bought all the carpet tacks in California. He sold them for huge amounts of money to the miners.
3. Samuel Clemens came to California during the Gold Rush. He wrote for the *San Francisco Call.*
4. Samuel Clemens, who wrote under the name Mark Twain, became a famous author. His boss at the *Call,* Bret Harte, became a famous author, too.
5. During the Gold Rush, Levi Strauss started a business that later had nationwide success. During the Gold Rush, John Studebaker also started a business that later had nationwide success.

Critical Viewing ▼ Using a compound subject, write a sentence that describes this picture. **[Apply]**

Forming Compound Sentences

You can combine two sentences by rewriting each as an independent clause in a **compound sentence.** An **independent clause** is a group of words that contains a subject and verb and can stand on its own. Independent clauses may be combined by using a comma and a coordinating conjunction such as *and, but, or,* or *nor* or by using a semicolon.

EXAMPLE: Georgia became a state in 1788. Atlanta became the capital in 1868.

COMPOUND SENTENCE: Georgia became a state in 1788, **and** Atlanta became the capital in 1868.

EXAMPLE: New York is called the Empire State. Georgia is called the Empire State of the South.

COMPOUND SENTENCE: New York is called the Empire State**;** Georgia is called the Empire State of the South.

Note that each conjunction expresses a different relationship between ideas. For example, *and* indicates similarity or addition, *but* indicates contrast, and *or* indicates an alternative.

Learn More

For additional information about compound sentences, see Section 20.2

▼ **Critical Viewing** Write a compound sentence describing how a gold seeker might have reacted to nuggets in his or her pan, such as those shown. **[Speculate]**

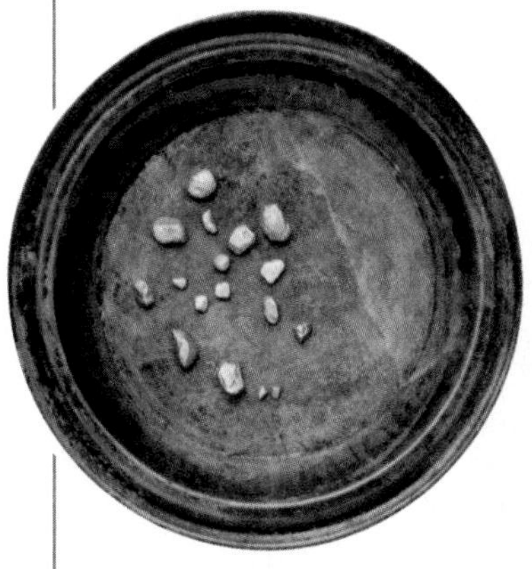

Exercise 3 **Forming Compound Sentences** Combine each pair of sentences in a compound sentence by using a comma and a coordinating conjunction or by using a semicolon.

1. The Okefenokee Swamp is located in southeastern Georgia. It covers 700 square miles.
2. In 1540, Hernando de Soto led a group of explorers through Georgia in search of gold. They did not find any.
3. In colonial times, England and Spain could not peacefully settle their disagreements about the border between Georgia and Florida. They went to war.
4. Georgia was the last of the original thirteen colonies founded. It became the fourth state in 1788.
5. Settlers were eager to move into Georgia's western regions. Land companies were eager to sell them land there.
6. In the 1795 Yazoo Fraud, land companies used bribery to gain lands from the state. The outraged citizens of Georgia voted to stop them.
7. Northern Georgia was the site of a gold rush that began in 1828. This gold rush was not as extensive as the one in California in 1849.
8. Much of the gold was located on Cherokee land. The government forced the relocation of the Cherokees soon after the discovery.
9. In the 1800's, cotton was the state's main product. In the 1870's, industry in the state began to grow.
10. I might write my paper about Georgia in colonial times. I might change my mind and write about Georgia after the Revolutionary War.

3.1

Using Subordination

You can combine two sentences by rewriting one as a subordinate clause and adding it to the other. A **subordinate clause** is a group of words that contains a subject and a verb but does not express a complete thought. One type of subordinate clause is an **adjective clause**—a subordinate clause that begins with *who, whom, whose, which,* or *that.*

EXAMPLE: Jimmy Carter was the thirty-ninth president of the United States. His full name is James Earl Carter, Jr.

COMBINED: Jimmy Carter, **whose full name is James Earl Carter, Jr.,** was the thirty-ninth president of the United States.

You can also combine two sentences by rewriting one as an **adverb clause**—a subordinate clause that begins with a subordinating conjunction such as *although, after, because,* or *until.*

EXAMPLE: Davy Crockett was against the removal of the Cherokees from Georgia. The Indian Removal Act of 1830 was passed.

COMBINED: ***Although* Davy Crockett was against the removal of the Cherokees from Georgia,** the Indian Removal Act of 1830 was passed.

This chart lists a few important subordinating conjunctions.

Time	Cause	Purpose	Condition
after	as	in order that	although
before	because	so that	provided that
until	unless	that	though
when			
while			

Exercise 4 **Combining by Using Clauses** Combine paired sentences by rewriting one as indicated in parentheses.

1. Jimmy Carter was born in Plains, Georgia, in 1924. In 1971, he became governor of Georgia. (adjective clause)
2. Jimmy Carter sold boiled peanuts to passers-by in Plains, Georgia. He was five years old at the time. (adverb clause)
3. In 1942, Jimmy Carter was appointed to the Naval Academy at Annapolis. He entered the Academy in 1943. (adjective clause)
4. Rosalynn Smith was Jimmy's sister's best friend. In 1946, Jimmy Carter married Rosalynn Smith. (adjective clause)
5. In 2002, Jimmy Carter received the Nobel Peace Prize. He left the presidency in 1981. (adverb clause)

Learn More

For additional information about adjective and adverb clauses, see Section 20.2.

3.2 Writing Effective Paragraphs

Main Idea and Topic Sentence

Many of the paragraphs that you will use in compositions are topical paragraphs. *Topical paragraphs* contain a **topic sentence,** a sentence that expresses the key point or main idea of the paragraph. The topic sentence is supported or developed by the facts, details, restatements, and explanations provided in the other sentences in the paragraph.

In some paragraphs, the **main idea** is directly stated. One sentence provides the main idea around which the other sentences are organized. Some paragraphs, however, may have an **implied main idea**—the sentences in the paragraph work together to suggest, without directly stating, the main idea of the paragraph.

WRITING MODELS

from The Trouble with Television

Robert MacNeil

It is difficult to escape the influence of television. If you fit the statistical averages, by the age of 20 you will have been exposed to at least 20,000 hours of television. You can add 10,000 hours for each decade you have lived after the age of 20. The only things Americans do more than watch television are work and sleep.

In this passage, the stated topic sentence is shown in blue italics. This sentence refers to the inescapable influence of television. The rest of the paragraph supports and illustrates the opening sentence.

from Harriet Tubman: Guide to Freedom

Ann Petry

They stumbled along behind her, half-dead for sleep, and she urged them on, though she was as tired and as discouraged as they were. She had never been in Canada but she kept painting wondrous word pictures of what it would be like. She managed to dispel their fear of pursuit, so that they would not become hysterical, panic-stricken. Then she had to bring some of the fear back, so that they would stay awake and keep walking though they drooped with sleep.

In this paragraph, all the sentences work together to support the implied main idea: Tubman must make the slaves feel afraid as well as encouraged. She must not let her group lose hope, and she must urge them on, despite her personal feelings.

Exercise 5 **Identifying a Stated Topic Sentence** Identify the stated topic sentence of the following paragraph.

In the 1920's, New York City's Harlem, which had a large African American population, was a vital social, political, and cultural center. Black artists, writers, and musicians came from all over. The writers wrote poetry and novels, the artists painted, and the musicians played music in Harlem's renowned theaters and clubs. Reminded of the Renaissance in Europe, people called this period the Harlem Renaissance.

Exercise 6 **Identifying an Implied Main Idea** Identify the implied topic sentence of the following paragraph.

I collapse on the towel and remain there, immobilized, like a beached whale. The warmth of the summer sand sinks into my bones. The gulls cry overhead. The sun beats down. The waves lap at the shore. I drift off into a peaceful, mindless slumber.

Writing a Topic Sentence

A topic sentence expresses the main point in a paragraph. As you plan your essay, you will already have some of your main points in mind. Other points may occur to you as you gather details. To write a topic sentence, consider the point you want to make and the details you have or will find. Then, write a single sentence that covers the details and expresses your point.

EXAMPLE:	The lake is icy cold. The shoreline is rocky. A strange film floats on the surface. Snapping turtles have been seen patrolling the murky water.
TOPIC SENTENCE:	The lake is unfit for swimming.

Exercise 7 **Writing Topic Sentences** Write a topic sentence for each group of sentences below.

1. Supplies were low, and the soldiers were discouraged. Although the snow had stopped, the temperature remained below freezing. Across the river was the enemy. As soon as the river froze, the enemy would attack.
2. Max, the main character in the story, always has a plan. No matter what goes wrong, he comes up with an idea for solving the problem. Sometimes, he makes clever gadgets; other times, he just has an idea that no one else has.

Writing Supporting Sentences

A topic sentence, whether stated or implied, contains a paragraph's main idea. The remaining sentences in the paragraph are called **supporting sentences.** They develop, explain, or illustrate the main idea or topic sentence.

You can use one or more of the following strategies to support or develop the main idea:

Use Facts Facts are statements that are provable. They support your main idea by offering proof.

TOPIC SENTENCE: Our soccer team will probably make it to this season's championship game.

SUPPORTING FACT: The team has won all of the games it played this season.

Use Statistics A statistic is a fact, usually stated with numbers.

TOPIC SENTENCE: Our soccer team will probably make it to this season's championship game.

SUPPORTING STATISTIC: The team's record so far is 8–0.

Use Examples, Illustrations, or Instances An example, illustration, or instance is a specific person, thing, or event that demonstrates a point.

TOPIC SENTENCE: Our soccer team will probably make it to this season's championship game.

ILLUSTRATION: The team has beaten all of its opponents, including the Wolverines, who hadn't lost a game in the three previous seasons.

Use Details Details are the specifics—the parts of the whole.

TOPIC SENTENCE: Our soccer team will probably make it to this season's championship game.

DETAIL: In last week's game, there were only seconds left in the final quarter when the striker scored the winning goal.

▲ **Critical Viewing** In what way might this soccer player need support from teammates? **[Connect]**

Exercise 8 **Writing Supporting Sentences** Write two supporting sentences for each of the following topic sentences. Use a variety of types of support.

1. Good nutrition is important for good health.
2. Hiking is a great way to exercise and to get in touch with nature.
3. Life is full of unexpected adventures.
4. Caring for a pet can be a rewarding experience.
5. Playing team sports teaches responsibility and cooperation.

Placing Your Topic Sentence

Often, the most effective placement for your topic sentence is at the beginning of a paragraph, where it introduces the subject of the paragraph. Sometimes, however, you may choose to place your topic sentence in the middle or at the end of a paragraph. You might place the topic sentence in the middle when you need to lead up to it or provide background. You might place the topic sentence at the end to create emphasis or to summarize the details you've provided.

Paragraph Patterns By identifying the function of different sentences within a paragraph, you can analyze the arrangement of sentences and choose the pattern that is most effective. One way to look at the paragraph pattern is through TRI (Topic, Restatement, Illustration). With these basic elements, you "construct" a paragraph.

TOPIC SENTENCE:	State your key idea.
RESTATEMENT:	Interpret your key idea—put it into other words.
ILLUSTRATION:	Support your key idea with an illustration or an example.

After you have identified the basic parts of your paragraph, try variations of the TRI pattern, such as TIR, TII, or ITR, until you are satisfied with the results.

T	It's fun to watch movies on a bleak and rainy weekend.
R	Comedies are especially entertaining and can brighten an otherwise dreary day.
I	Last Saturday it was pouring. We rented two hilarious videos and had a great time watching them with our friends Jake and Rebecca.

Exercise 9 **Placing a Topic Sentence** Arrange the following sentences in a paragraph. First, identify the topic sentence. Next, rearrange the sentences using the TRI pattern. Then, rearrange the sentences in a variation of TRI. Evaluate which arrangement is most effective.

A layer of cheese provides the foundation for a medley of olives, peppers, and onions. These ingredients turn pizza into pizzazz! They add color, texture, and taste to the pie. They turn dough and cheese into a smorgasbord of tasty treats. The key to a good pizza is the toppings.

Maintaining Unity and Coherence

Achieving Unity

A paragraph or composition has **unity** when all of its parts relate to the main idea. Every sentence supports, explains, or develops the main idea of the paragraph. Every paragraph supports or develops the main idea, or **thesis statement,** of the composition. Details that are not related to the main points can undermine the unity of your writing and should be deleted.

In the following paragraph, one sentence is marked for deletion because it interferes with the unity of the paragraph.

The ancient Romans were successful in gaining territory and building an empire for many reasons. First of all, the Romans had a fine military organization. More important, the government of Rome could adapt to new situations. ~~Ancient Roman ruins are fascinating~~. Probably the most important reason of all was that the Romans treated captured people fairly.

Exercise 10 **Revising for Unity** On a separate sheet of paper, copy the following paragraph. Mark for deletion any sentences that interfere with the unity of the paragraph.

Pompeii was an ancient Roman city founded in the eighth century B.C. The city was located less than one mile from Mount Vesuvius, a volcanic mountain. In A.D. 79, Mount Vesuvius erupted violently. Volcanic mountains exist throughout the world. The volcanic eruption showered Pompeii with hot ashes and stones. Pompeii was soon completely buried in ashes. Pompeii remained buried until 1748, when a peasant digging in a vineyard accidentally struck a wall of the city. Italian vineyards are known for their fine grapes. After the chance discovery, archaeologists began to excavate the city. Today, about one fourth of Pompeii is uncovered, and tourists can now walk the ancient streets.

▶ **Critical Viewing** What details from this ruin suggest that it was once part of a unified whole? **[Connect]**

3.2

Establishing Coherence

A paragraph or composition has **coherence** when the ideas are logically connected and the reader can see how one idea is related to another. To establish coherence, choose and maintain a *logical organization* and connect sentences and paragraphs with *transitional words and phrases.*

Organization	Transitional Words and Phrases	Common Purposes
Chronological	first, next, last, then, meanwhile, finally	Process explanations Narratives
Spatial	near, above, below, beyond, next to	Descriptions Directions
Comparison and Contrast	however, on the other hand, likewise, similarly	Comparison-and-contrast essays Evaluations
Cause and Effect	therefore, as a result, due to, because	Cause-and-effect essays Analyses

Exercise 11 **Revising for Coherence** On a separate sheet of paper, rewrite the following paragraph. Establish coherence by reorganizing details with one of the organizational patterns explained above. Use transitional words and phrases to show connections. Add details or make other changes as needed.

The English language contains many words that have been borrowed from other languages. Some words come from French, which had been influenced by the classical languages of Greek and Latin. French was the language of the rulers, so words like *government* and *legal* became part of the language used by the conquered Anglo-Saxons. Early American settlers borrowed some words from Native American languages to name things for which they had no names. In 1066, France invaded England. Modern scientists borrow directly from Latin or Greek to name new discoveries. Prefixes and suffixes that are used in English also come from Greek and Latin. Explorers of the fifteenth and sixteenth centuries who traveled from England to far-off places often incorporated words from the places they visited.

3.3 Paragraphs in Essays and Other Compositions

Understanding the Parts of a Composition

A **composition** is something that consists of—or is put together from—a number of parts. Musical compositions are made up of notes of music. Written compositions are made up of sentences and paragraphs that are organized in a logical order to develop a main idea or thesis. Most compositions have three basic parts, or sections.

Introduction

The **introduction** of a composition indicates the focus of the composition. This focus is expressed in a sentence called the **thesis statement**. The introduction usually serves the additional purpose of capturing readers' interest with a strong **lead.** This lead may take the form of a quotation that is related to the topic or a surprising statement that makes readers curious and eager to read more.

Body Paragraphs

The **body paragraphs** of a composition develop the thesis statement with supporting facts, details, and examples. The paragraphs in the body are organized in a logical order, such as time order, order of importance, or spatial order. The chart on the previous page shows some common methods of organization and the kinds of writing for which they are most often used.

Conclusion

The **conclusion**, as its name suggests, "wraps up," or closes, the composition. In this part of the composition, a few sentences sum up the thesis statement and the overall support. An effective conclusion ends memorably. A memorable ending might be a strong statement, an interesting quotation, or a call to action.

Exercise 12 **Planning a Composition** On a separate sheet of paper, outline the parts of a how-to essay on an activity or skill you know well. Write a lead that will make your readers want to try the activity. Identify the most logical organization for your body paragraphs. Then, select the information you will include in each body paragraph, and write preliminary topic sentences. Finally, decide how you will conclude in a memorable way.

Types of Paragraphs

Topical Paragraphs

A **topical paragraph** consists of a group of sentences containing one main idea or sentence and several sentences that support or illustrate that main idea.

Functional Paragraphs

Functional paragraphs are used for specific purposes. Although a functional paragraph may not contain a topic sentence, it is unified and coherent because the sentences are clearly connected and logically ordered. Functional paragraphs can serve the following purposes:

To Arouse or Sustain Interest A few vivid sentences can work together to capture the reader's attention.

To Indicate Dialogue One of the conventions of written dialogue is that a new paragraph begins each time the speaker changes.

To Make a Transition A short paragraph can help readers move between the main ideas in two topical paragraphs.

WRITING MODEL

from Animal Craftsmen

Bruce Brooks

I scrambled down the ladder, leaping from the third rung and landing in the frosty salad of . . . leaves and windswept grass that collected at the foot of the barn wall. I looked down and saw that my left boot had, by no more than an inch, just missed crushing the very thing I was rushing off to seek. There, lying dry and separate on the leaves, was the wasp house.

I looked up. Yes. I was standing directly beneath the spot where the sphere had hung—it was a straight fall. I picked up the wasp house, gave it a shake to see if any insects were inside, and, discovering none, took it home.

My awe of the craftsman grew as I unwrapped the layers of the nest. Such beautiful paper! It was much tougher than any I had encountered. . . .

This paragraph indicates the transition from the narration of the preceding paragraph to the description in the one that follows.

Paragraph Blocks

Occasionally, you may have too much information about a single idea to include in one manageable paragraph. When this occurs, you can devote several paragraphs to the development of that single idea. These "blocks" of paragraphs all support the same main idea or topic sentence. By separating the contributing ideas into blocks, you make your ideas more understandable.

PARAGRAPH BLOCKS

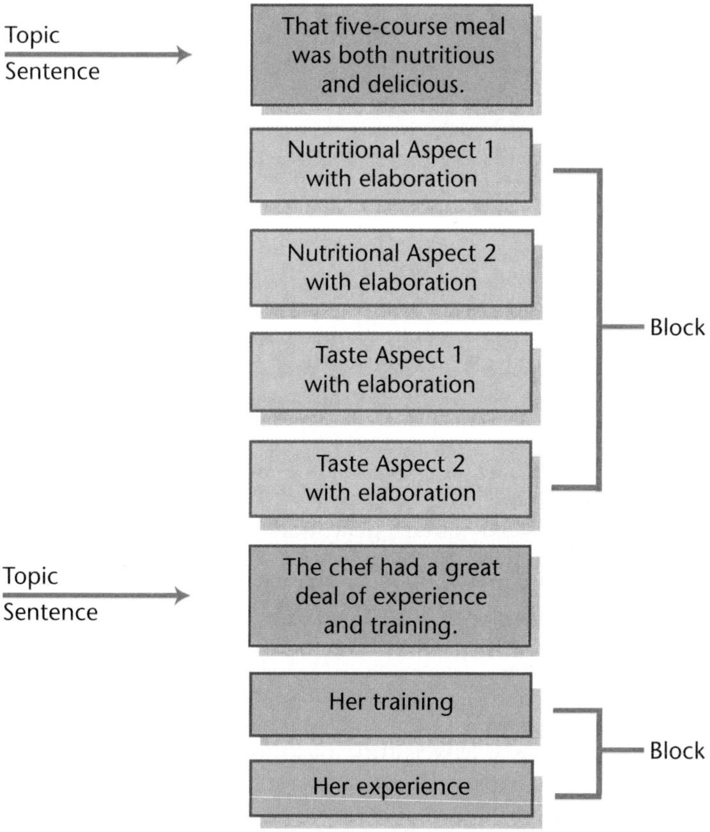

Topic Sentence → That five-course meal was both nutritious and delicious.

- Nutritional Aspect 1 with elaboration
- Nutritional Aspect 2 with elaboration
- Taste Aspect 1 with elaboration
- Taste Aspect 2 with elaboration

(Block)

Topic Sentence → The chef had a great deal of experience and training.

- Her training
- Her experience

(Block)

Exercise 13 **Analyzing Types of Paragraphs** Choose an article from a magazine that focuses on a hobby or interest of yours. Make a photocopy of the article. Then, identify and color-code the different types of paragraphs you find. Draw a box around each topical paragraph and underline the topic sentence. Bracket the margin to show paragraph blocks. Finally, use a red star to indicate functional paragraphs, and note in the margin the function that each performs.

3.4 Writing Style

Developing Your Style

Your clothing, your hairstyle, and the activities you prefer are expressions of your personal style. Style also refers to the way you express yourself in writing. Several qualities that contribute to your writing style are shown below:

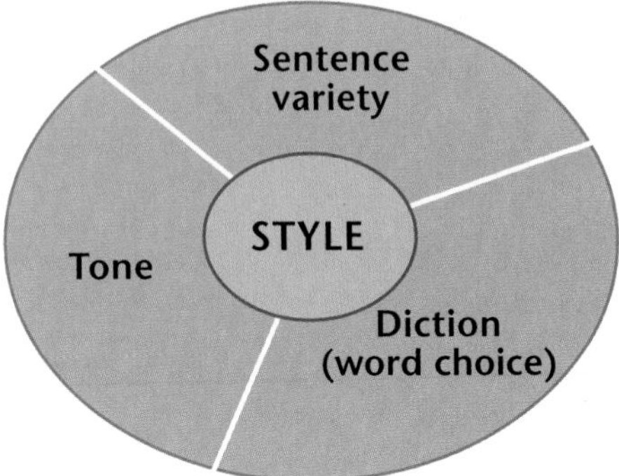

Creating Sentence Variety You have a variety of options to contribute to your writing style as well. When you write a paragraph, try to vary your sentence lengths, types, and structures.

Choosing Words The words you choose add to the style, or overall effect, of a paragraph. Think about your choice of words when planning how to achieve a particular effect. For instance, if you are writing a description, you'll employ vivid details to convey a powerful image. The clarity of your description will be aided when you use specific, rather than general, nouns. The way words sound can also contribute to a paragraph's style.

Setting a Tone Your attitude toward your subject is conveyed in the tone of your writing. You may view your subject in many ways, such as with scorn, appreciation, or awe. The paragraphs of an e-mail to a classmate will probably have a casual tone, while the paragraphs of a cause-and-effect essay assignment will probably have a more serious and formal tone.

Exercise 14 **Choosing a Paragraph Style** Read the two Writing Models on page 21. Study the sentence lengths and structures, the word choice, and the tone of each. Discuss with a partner how the styles of the two paragraphs are similar and different. Then, write a paragraph of your own, modeled on the style of one of the paragraphs you have read. See if your partner can tell which style you used as a model.

Using Formal and Informal English

Standard English can be either formal or informal. Formal English is appropriate for serious and academic purposes. Use informal English for casual writing or when you want your writing to have a conversational tone.

The Conventions of Formal English

Formal English is the standard language of written communication. You will use formal English for most of your school assignments. It is appropriate for reports, speeches, biographies, instructional manuals, articles, presentations, and job and school applications. When writing in formal English, you should observe these conventions:

- Avoid contractions.
- Do not use slang.
- Follow standard English usage and grammar.
- Use a serious tone and sophisticated vocabulary.

▼ Critical Viewing
Would you and your friends use formal or informal English to talk about CD's? **[Connect]**

Informal English

Informal English is the language of everyday speech. You can also use informal English when you write humorous essays, dialogue, letters to friends, personal reminders, journal entries, and some stories. When you use informal English, you can

- use contractions.
- use slang and popular expressions, especially to capture the natural sounds of speech.

FORMAL ENGLISH: He said he will discount the price of the next compact disc that I purchase.

INFORMAL ENGLISH: He said he'll give me a break on the next CD I buy.

Exercise 15 **Using Formal and Informal English** Rewrite the following sentences on a separate sheet of paper. Use formal English for those written in informal English. Use informal English for those written in formal English.

1. That was the coolest movie ever!
2. I thought the director did a superb job.
3. All the actors delivered outstanding performances.
4. The skiing footage was awesome!
5. The final scene was a total shocker—it blew us all away!

Chapter 4

Narration

Autobiographical Writing

▲ **Critical Viewing** What do you think the boy is thinking? What story might he tell of his train ride? **[Speculate]**

Autobiographical Writing in Everyday Life

After you take a difficult test or play in a crucial game or spend a day out sick, people want to know: "So, what happened?!" The answer is a kind of story, a short autobiographical narrative you might create on the spot. These stories about what we did or wish we'd done remind us of who we are. They also bind us closer to others.

In **autobiographical writing,** you set down a story from life on paper, and you can tell it in as much detail as you wish. Don't be surprised, though, if the story changes a little in the telling—if past defeat turns into a kind of victory, or past disappointments become valuable lessons. In this chapter, you will learn ways to strengthen and improve your autobiographical writing.

What Is Autobiographical Writing?

Autobiographical writing tells the story of an event, period, or person in the writer's life. By writing autobiographically, you can share part of your life with others. You can also learn more about yourself. A good autobiographical piece usually includes

- true events from the writer's life presented in logical order and in such a way as to build the reader's interest.
- a central conflict, or problem, that the writer or another person has to resolve, or a shift between the writer's past and present views of events.
- the use of vivid details to give a clear sense of characters and places.

To learn the criteria on which your work may be assessed, see the Rubric for Self-Assessment on page 47.

Writers in ACTION

Rudolfo Anaya is the author of novels, short stories, and articles. He has also translated folk tales that are an important part of Mexican American culture. He understands that telling stories about ourselves is part of life.

"I think people sometimes think that storytelling is a time in our life that we go sit in a certain room and tell a story or write a story, but it's not. Storytelling goes on all day long."

Types of Autobiographical Writing

There are a few types of autobiographical writing:

- **Autobiographical incidents**, which are also called **personal narratives,** recount an event in which the writer played a central role.
- **Reflective essays** tell of an experience and give the writer's thoughts on its meaning.
- **Autobiographical narratives** relate memorable experiences, and frequently include information about the writer's early life and personal qualities.
- **Memoirs** are recollections of the writer's relationship with a particular person, place, animal, or thing.

To tell a story from your own life, use the strategies and tips in this lesson. You will follow the prewriting, drafting, and revising techniques used by Evan Twohy, who attends Prospect Sierra School in El Cerrito, California, to develop his autobiographical essay, "Zermatt or Bust!"

4.2 Prewriting

Choosing Your Topic

The first step in autobiographical writing is deciding on a topic. Think of incidents in your life that have special meaning for you—funny times, moving times, exciting times. Use the following strategies to select a topic you would like to develop:

Strategies for Generating a Topic

1. **Freewriting** Grab a pen, and start writing about special times in your life. Focus on getting down as many ideas as you can. After five minutes, read what you've written. Choose one of these memories as a topic.
2. **Blueprinting** Draw and label a blueprint of a place that is meaningful to you, such as your room, a friend's house, or the park. Then, study your map. List special incidents you associate with each area. Choose one as your topic.
3. **Writing Round** Form a group with classmates. Write a sentence in which you tell something about yourself. Pass the paper around until each person has added at least one new sentence connected to the previous ones. At the end, read the sentences aloud. Choose a topic suggested in the writing round.

Try it out! Use the interactive Blueprinting activity in **Section 4.2,** on-line or on CD-ROM.

Student Work IN PROGRESS

Name: Evan Twohy
Prospect Sierra School
El Cerrito, CA

Holding a Writing Round

Evan chose his topic—a family vacation—from his notes on a writing round.

Evan: I am a big baseball fan.

Rita: Me, too! Last year, I visited my aunt who lives in New York, and she took me to the Baseball Hall of Fame in Cooperstown.

Harold: I went to New York once on vacation with my family, but we didn't go to Cooperstown. We stayed in New York City and had a great time. We even saw a Broadway play.

Evan: We did something different last summer, too—we went to the Alps!

Topic: My family's trip to the Alps.

TOPIC BANK

If you're having trouble finding a topic, consider the following possibilities:

1. **Remember When We . . . ?** Think of an unforgettable experience you shared with a friend. Tell the story of this experience, reflecting on your reactions to it then and now.
2. **Dream On** Think of a place other than the one in which you now live. It might be a place you visit occasionally or a place in which you used to live. Write a narrative about this place, telling of a significant incident that occurred there.

Responding to Fine Art

3. Interpret the mood of the woman in this painting, noting the colors used—are they bright and clashing or gentle and harmonious?—and the rhythm of the lines—are they jagged or smooth, straight or curving? Then, write about a time when you shared this mood.

Self-Portrait, 1889 Milly Childers, Leeds Museums and Galleries (City Art Gallery) U.K.

Responding to Literature

4. Read Robert Frost's poem "The Road Not Taken." Think of a time when you faced a choice like that described in the poem. Write a narrative telling the story of your decision. Explain the situation, your reasons for choosing as you did, and how you feel about the "road not taken." You can find Frost's poem in *Prentice Hall Literature: Timeless Voices, Timeless Themes*, Silver.

Cooperative Writing Opportunity

5. **Group Memoir** In a group, list teachers, librarians, custodians, and other school personnel who have helped you and your classmates last year. Each group member should choose one "personality" to write about, recording his or her memories of this person. Group members may also interview the person about whom they are writing to get the subject's viewpoint. Collect the memoirs in a binder, illustrate the collection, and display it in the library.

4.2

Narrowing Your Topic

Narrow your topic by focusing on one strong story. For example, the topic "Growing Up in Brooklyn" would include a whirl of stories about your home, your relatives, and so on. By focusing on "The Day Uncle Sid Thought We Were Being Invaded," you can tell a solid, entertaining story. Use the strategy of looping to narrow your topic.

Use Looping to Narrow a Topic

These are the steps of looping:

1. Write freely on your topic for about five minutes.
2. Read what you've written, and circle the "center of gravity"—the idea you find most interesting or important.
3. Write freely for five minutes on this "center of gravity."
4. Review your writing, and find a new "center of gravity."

If this new "center" will make a focused, interesting topic for a narrative, use it as your narrowed topic. If not, continue looping until you arrive at such a topic.

Student Work IN PROGRESS

Name: Evan Twohy
Prospect Sierra School
El Cerrito, CA

Looping

Evan's topic was a family trip to Switzerland. Using looping, he narrowed his topic to focus on a specific outing.

We did a lot of interesting things in Switzerland, like going to a yodeling contest and watching some craftsmen make clocks. As usual, my sister and I argued a lot, but for the most part we enjoyed ourselves.

One of our worst arguments was on the day we got lost on a hike. I wanted to get back to the hotel to use the amazing pool before it closed. She kept telling me to shut up and enjoy the scenery.

Considering Your Audience and Purpose

Knowing your **audience**—who your readers will be—will lead you to shape your writing in specific ways. For instance, if you are writing a letter to your grandparents about your vacation, you don't have to explain that Muffy is your sister's nickname. If you are writing about your vacation for class, you might have to explain this and other details.

Knowing your **purpose** will also help you shape your work. Before you draft, analyze your purpose.

▲ **Critical Viewing** Imagine that you were part of this scene. What might your purpose in writing about it be? Explain. **[Apply]**

Analyze Your Purpose

To decide on your purpose, ask yourself these questions:

- Is my topic funny, moving, or exciting? Is my purpose to **entertain** the reader?
  If so, focus on the amusing, moving, or adventurous aspects of your story.
- Does my topic involve a lesson I learned? Is my purpose to **instruct** the reader?
  If so, focus on the events that taught you the lesson and draw conclusions from them.
- Am I writing about a particularly interesting person? Can I **capture that character's personality** in words?
  If so, focus on details showing the person as he or she is.

Gathering Details

Once you've narrowed your topic and considered your purpose, gather details—events, descriptions, dialogue—to include in your narrative. If you are writing about an experience you shared with others, consider conducting an interview.

Interview Others

Jot down notes on the events about which you are writing. Then, using a different color for each participant in these events, draw rectangles around events on which a participant might have a special point of view. Circle places where your own memories of events are unclear. Reviewing your circled and boxed notes, make a list of questions for each interviewee.

Arrange to speak with each person for an uninterrupted stretch of time. During the interview, ask your questions and take notes on the interviewee's answers. Make sure your notes are accurate—you can ask the person to repeat himself or herself if necessary.

Technology Tip

Use a word processor to input your questions for your interview. Afterward, you can type in the interviewee's answer directly below each question.

4.3

Drafting

Shaping Your Writing

Any well-told story, even a true one, has a **plot**—a sequence of events retold in a way that will sustain a reader's interest. After you've gathered your details, organize them into a plot.

Order Events

First, take notes on the **conflict** in your story. A conflict appears whenever a character wants something that another character or force stops him or her from getting. You may also create interest by showing how your view of an event changed.

After defining a conflict, organize events around it. In the first part of your story, introduce the characters, setting, and situation. Build to a **climax**—a turning point. End with a resolution that settles the conflict.

Emphasize Tension

Tension in your story keeps your reader turning the pages. To create tension, consider which events in your narrative build to a climax. Refer to the example in this chart:

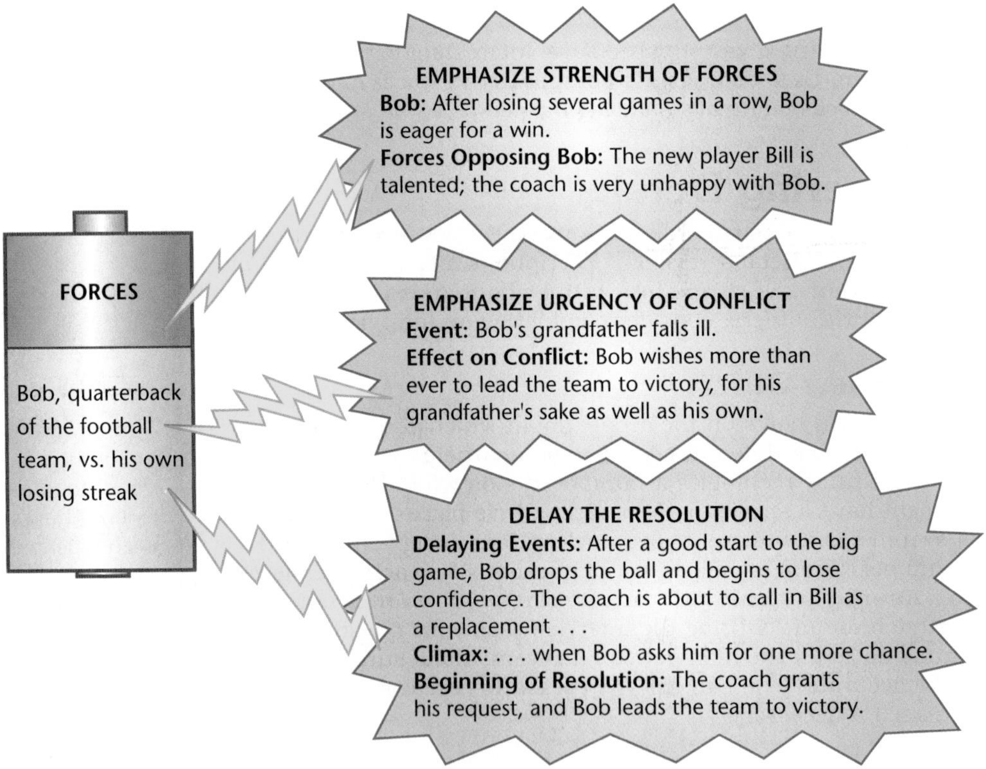

FORCES

Bob, quarterback of the football team, vs. his own losing streak

EMPHASIZE STRENGTH OF FORCES
Bob: After losing several games in a row, Bob is eager for a win.
Forces Opposing Bob: The new player Bill is talented; the coach is very unhappy with Bob.

EMPHASIZE URGENCY OF CONFLICT
Event: Bob's grandfather falls ill.
Effect on Conflict: Bob wishes more than ever to lead the team to victory, for his grandfather's sake as well as his own.

DELAY THE RESOLUTION
Delaying Events: After a good start to the big game, Bob drops the ball and begins to lose confidence. The coach is about to call in Bill as a replacement . . .
Climax: . . . when Bob asks him for one more chance.
Beginning of Resolution: The coach grants his request, and Bob leads the team to victory.

Providing Elaboration

Uncle Ed's twinkling eyes . . . The mall parking lot, as gray, pitted, and lonely as the surface of the moon . . . Details such as these convey the essence of a person or place in just a few words. As you write your autobiographical piece, add such significant details to create colorful, accurate pictures.

Add Significant Details

As you draft, pause at the end of a paragraph. Review it for references introducing an important character or place. For each reference, place a sticky note in the margin. On the note, write your answer to the following questions:

- When I think of the person or place, what feature first comes to mind?
- When I think of the person or place, what feeling first comes to mind?

After you have finished drafting, review your notes. Include any details from them that will enhance the picture you create for readers.

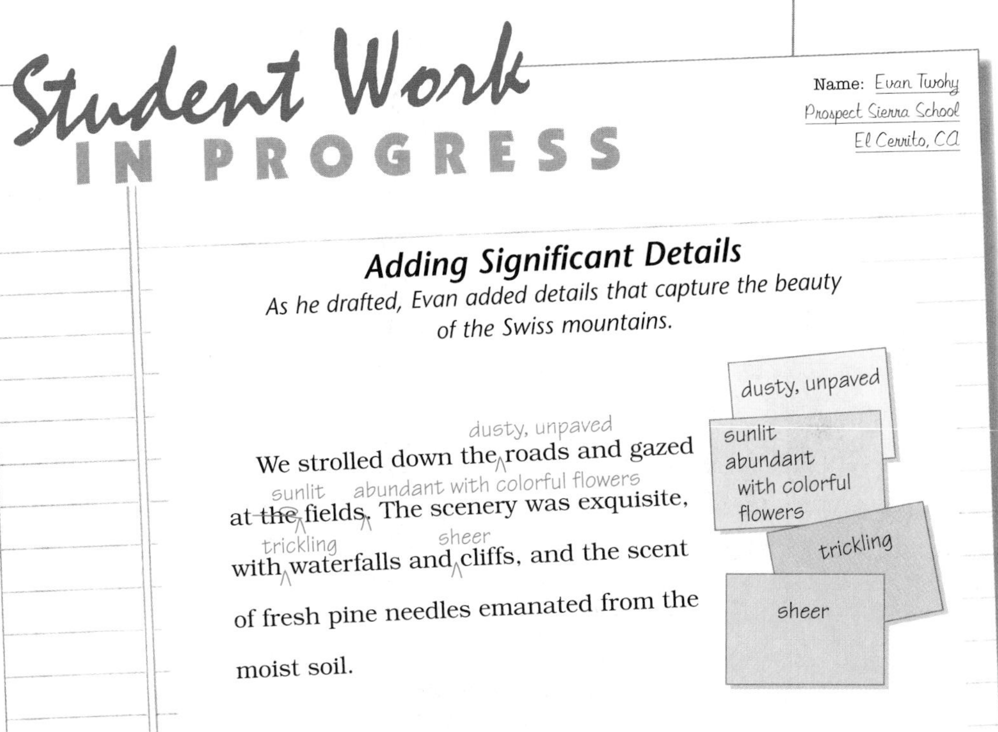

4.4 Revising

Revising Your Overall Structure

Now that you have finished a first draft, your ideas are on the page. Next, make sure they will catch a reader's imagination. Revise to ensure that your opening engages readers and that your story continues to hold their interest.

▲ **Critical Viewing** What question does this photograph raise? What might happen next? **[Interpret]**

Create an Effective Lead

In a narrative, a good first sentence "hooks" the reader, leading him or her to ask, "What will happen next?" or "What's going on?" The next sentence or two should tie this "hook" to the rest of the story, as in this example:

HOOK: A sound like a garbage can full of chains rolling down the stairs woke me in the middle of the night.

TIE TO STORY: It took me a second to remember the "trap" my brother had set for me in the kitchen doorway. It took me another second to remember that my parents usually went straight for the kitchen after an evening out.

To create a good hook, you can use a few kinds of details:

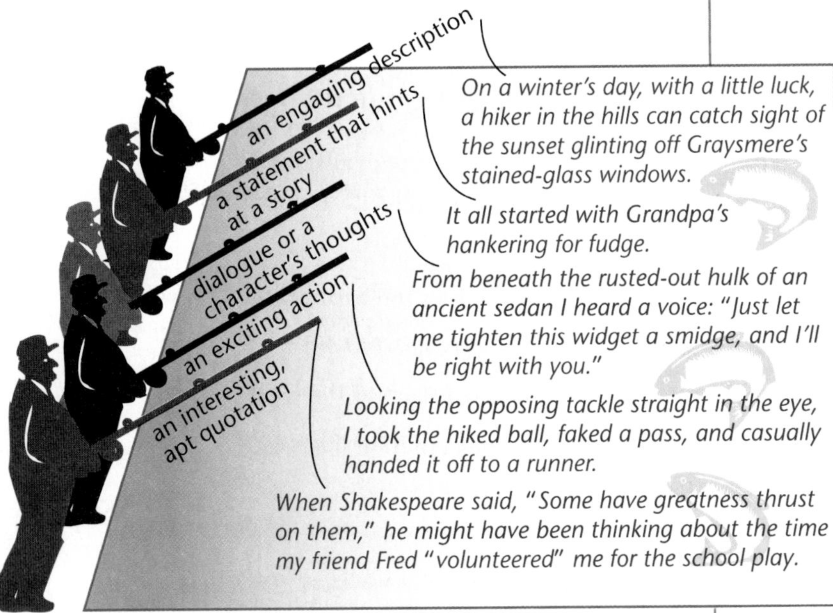

Build Tension

Once you've captured the reader's attention, hold it by building the excitement of your story. Use clues to ensure the tension builds before the climax (the turning point that will decide how the conflict ends).

REVISION STRATEGY
Using Clues to Take Your Story's "Temperature"

Mark the climax of your story with a large red triangle. Starting several paragraphs before the climax, circle each of the following "temperature-raising" details in the color indicated:

YELLOW:	details that establish facts basic to the conflict
ORANGE:	details connecting new events to the conflict
RED:	details adding to the urgency of the conflict

If you find a paragraph near your climax lacking circled details, consider adding details connected with the conflict.

Student Work IN PROGRESS

Name: Evan Twohy
Prospect Sierra School
El Cerrito, CA

Measuring Story "Temperature"

After identifying several "temperature-raising" details before his climax, Evan decided to add a few more.

When we arrived at the place to which the signs were guiding us, it turned out that, "Z'mutt" was approximately four cow sheds and a café, all in a row.

"I knew it," I said. "Now we certainly won't be able to swim."

"Does this mean you'll relax and enjoy the scenery?" laughed my sister.

Evan added his sister's response to relate this event to his conflict with his sister.

A good hour later, after going in the wrong direction more times than the right one, we began following signs for "Z'mutt." ~~"Z'mutt," it turned out, had nothing to do with "Zermatt."~~

Evan replaced this sentence. The new sentence adds urgency to the conflict by creating a contrast between what they found and what they were looking for.

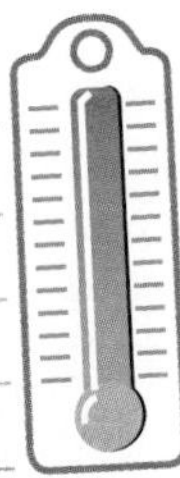

Desperate for our hotel, we sped frantically through the tiny town. We stumbled onto yet another trail and began descending rapidly, until we finally rushed down a small, flat path and ended up, exhausted, in Zermatt.

4.4

Revising Your Paragraphs

Strengthen Coherence

A paragraph is not a dump—don't throw just any old sentence in there! Like the features of a well-laid-out park, each sentence in a paragraph should have a clear relation to the others. Clean up the "litter" in your paragraphs. Check the connection of each sentence to the main idea of the paragraph.

REVISION STRATEGY
Check-Marking for Coherence

Follow these steps to check-mark for coherence.

1. For each paragraph in your draft, identify the main idea.
2. On a sticky note, jot a brief phrase summing up this main idea. Stick the note next to the paragraph.
3. Review each paragraph in your draft. For each sentence in a paragraph, first read the phrase on the sticky note and then read the sentence.
4. Place a check mark over any sentence that seems out of place when you read it after your main idea.
5. After you have finished, review each checked sentence. Eliminate any sentence that does not belong in the paragraph, or rewrite it to make its connection to other sentences clearer.

iText

Get instant help! Use the check-marking tool in the Essay Builder, accessible from the menu bar, on-line or on CD-ROM.

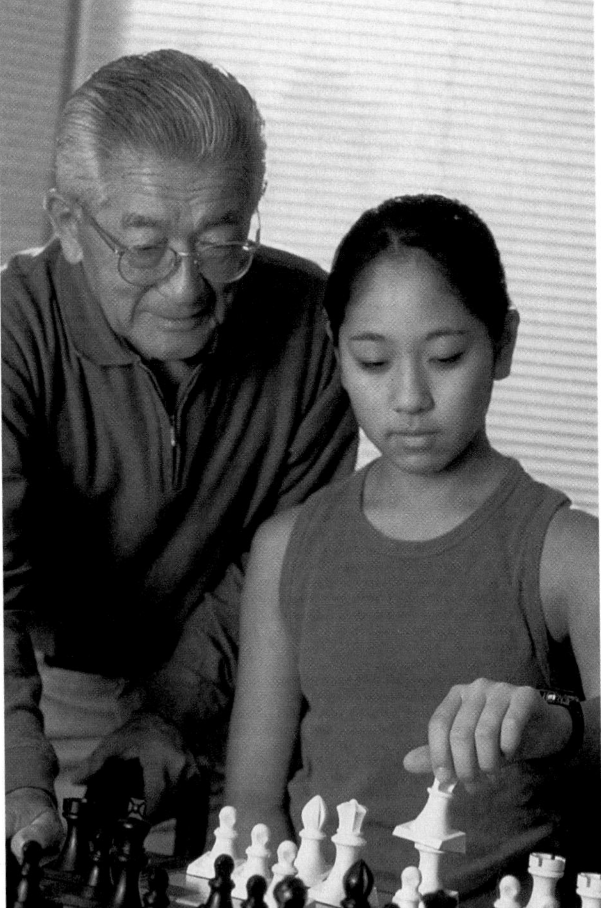

▶ **Critical Viewing**
Write a sentence describing the activity in this photograph. Then, add several related sentences, and organize them in the best order. **[Apply]**

Revising Your Sentences

Vary the Sentence Structure

Even if you build tension, you can still write a dull story. Imagine a story in which every sentence started with *I*: "I did this. I did that. I did something else." This droning beat would put you to sleep! Color-code sentence beginnings to help create an interesting rhythm and vary sentence structure.

REVISION STRATEGY
Color-Coding Sentence Beginnings

Code the first word of each sentence in your draft with a colored shape, as follows:

Articles	include *the*, *a*, and *an*.
Nouns	name a person, place, or thing.
Pronouns	such as *I*, *you*, *he*, *she*, *it*, *we*, and *they* stand in place of nouns.
Adjectives	tell more about something named by a noun. *Blue*, *envious*, and *difficult* are all adjectives.
Adverbs	tell more about a verb, an adjective, or another adverb. *Quickly*, *brightly*, and *less* are adverbs.
Prepositions	show the relationship between things. *In*, *out*, *off*, *on*, *toward*, and *away* are prepositions.

Find groups of circles in the same color. Rewrite sentences in these groups so that some begin with another kind of word.

Collaborative Writing Tip

In a group, read aloud some of the sentences that you want to structure differently. Group members should take turns suggesting other ways in which you might say the same thing.

Student Work IN PROGRESS

Name: Evan Twohy
Prospect Sierra School
El Cerrito, CA

Color-Coding Sentence Beginnings

When Evan saw the number of red rectangles in this paragraph, he rewrote several sentences so that they began with different kinds of words.

As our car rattled out of the little log station,

We peered excitedly out the blue plastic windows ~~as our car rattled out of the little log station~~. Despite the fact that it was almost impossible to see through the white scratches on the pane, my mom snapped photo after photo. We were looking forward to an enjoyable afternoon on the mountain. ~~We planned~~ Our plan was to do some hiking and then return to Zermatt. . . .

4.4

Revising Your Word Choice

Use Precise Nouns

The story you tell unfolds for readers as a series of pictures in their imagination. The more precise your words, the clearer the pictures your readers will form. For instance, if you are writing about a vehicle, the precise word *minivan or hatchback* will give your readers a clearer picture than *car.* A single precise noun also has more impact than a lengthy, though precise, explanation. For example, "person who likes biking" is not as effective as "cyclist."

Highlight nouns to help you use precise words.

REVISION STRATEGY
Highlighting Nouns

Highlight the first five and the last five nouns in your draft. For each, ask yourself:

- What picture do I want to paint with this noun?
- Does my reader need more information to form this picture?
- What precise noun, used by itself, will provide most of this information?

Replace nouns that do not paint a clear picture, or that need additional explanation, with precise nouns.

Research Tip

Use a thesaurus to help you find precise nouns to replace vague or general ones. Always check the meaning of an unfamiliar word in a dictionary before using it.

Student Work IN PROGRESS

Name: Evan Twohy
Prospect Sierra School
El Cerrito, CA

Highlighting Nouns

After reviewing nouns in his draft, Evan replaced a few general nouns with precise nouns to help the reader envision Zermatt.

... Zermatt is a quaint ^town ~~place~~ that consists of a ^chapel ~~small church~~, a pathetic mini golf course, a children's cemetery, an old-fashioned ^bakery ~~store~~, many tourist shops, and more than fifteen ^chalets ~~hotels~~ . . .

Grammar in Your Writing

General and Specific Nouns

A **noun** is a word that names a person, place, or thing. Nouns can be more or less specific. The most general nouns include a wide variety of persons, places, or things. For instance, the word *animal* can be used for giraffes, zebras, turtles, and ants. The more specific the noun, the smaller the variety of things it includes. For instance, the word *apes* names a group of animals that are similar to one another. The word *chimp* is even more specific. **Proper nouns**—nouns naming an individual person, place, or thing—are quite specific. Here are some examples of general and specific nouns:

People		Places		Things	
General:	child	General:	building	General:	clothes
Specific:	infant	Specific:	skyscraper	Specific:	overalls
	toddler		factory		suit
General:	relative	General:	beach	General:	feeling
Specific:	brother	Specific:	seashore	Specific:	tenderness
	Aunt Sue		boardwalk		frustration

Find It in Your Reading Review a short story you have read recently. Find three examples of specific nouns, and describe the picture each creates.

Find It in Your Writing Find three general nouns in your draft. For each, determine whether it captures the precise picture you mean to give readers or whether you should replace it with a more specific noun.

To learn more about nouns, see Chapter 14.

Peer Review

"Say Back"

In a group of four or five students, read your whole story aloud while the others listen closely. Pause briefly, and then read it again. This time, listeners should quickly jot down (1) what they liked and (2) what they want to know more about. Afterward, listeners will "say back" to you what they've jotted down. Use their comments to guide you as you work on your final revision.

4.5 Editing and Proofreading

Errors in your narrative can distract readers. Proofread carefully for errors in spelling, punctuation, and grammar.

Focusing on Commas

Check your work for the incorrect use of commas. Make sure you have included a comma after every introductory clause.

Proofreading in Pairs

Exchange drafts with another student for proofreading. Correct all the errors you find with an erasable red or blue pencil.

Grammar in Your Writing

Using Commas After Introductory Elements

A **phrase** is a group of words that work together like a single word to modify a word in a sentence. A **clause** is a group of words with a subject and a verb. Phrases and clauses can be used to add information at the beginning of a sentence. These introductory elements should be separated from the rest of the sentence by commas, as in these examples:

INTRODUCTORY PHRASES: Humming softly to myself, I walked down the street.
For many reasons, it is a good idea to eat vegetables.

INTRODUCTORY CLAUSES: Before he went to bed, he said "good night" to his hamster.
When I carry an umbrella, I often leave it someplace.

Find It in Your Reading Review an autobiographical narrative or other short work you have read recently. Find three examples of introductory elements followed by commas.

Find It in Your Writing Review your draft, and circle any introductory elements. Make sure that each is separated by a comma from the rest of the sentence. If you do not find any introductory elements, consider rewriting some sentences to begin with an introductory clause.

To learn more about using commas, see Chapter 26.

4.6 Publishing and Presenting

Consider these possibilities for publishing and presenting your work.

Building Your Portfolio

1. **Publish Your Memoirs** Get together with other students to publish a book of memoirs. Work as a team to create a cover and to illustrate the pieces. Finally, write a paragraph that states the purpose of the collection.
2. **Video Collection** Make a video "documentary" in which each member of the class reads his or her narrative, followed by a brief interview with the student about his or her work. Students should take turns introducing and interviewing each other.

Reflecting on Your Writing

Jot down your thoughts on writing autobiographically. Begin by answering the following questions:

- As you wrote about what happened to you, did you gain any fresh insights into yourself?
- How did thinking about the conflict help you structure your work?

Internet Tip

To see autobiographical narratives scored with this rubric, go on-line:
PHSchool.com
Enter Web Code:
eck-8001

Rubric for Self-Assessment

Evaluate your autobiographical narrative using the following criteria:

	Score 4	Score 3	Score 2	Score 1
Audience and Purpose	Contains an engaging introduction; successfully entertains or presents a theme	Contains a somewhat engaging introduction; entertains or presents a theme	Contains an introduction; attempts to entertain or to present a theme	Begins abruptly or confusingly; leaves purpose unclear
Organization	Creates an interesting, clear narrative; told from a consistent point of view	Presents a clear sequence of events; told from a specific point of view	Presents a mostly clear sequence of events; contains inconsistent points of view	Presents events without logical order; lacks a consistent point of view
Elaboration	Provides insight into character; develops plot; contains dialogue	Contains details and dialogue that develop character and plot	Contains details that develop plot; contains some dialogue	Contains few or no details to develop characters or plot
Use of Language	Uses word choice and tone to reveal story's theme; contains no errors in grammar, punctuation, or spelling	Uses interesting and fresh word choices; contains few errors in grammar, punctuation, and spelling	Uses some clichés and trite expressions; contains some errors in grammar, punctuation, and spelling	Uses uninspired word choices; has many errors in grammar, punctuation, and spelling

Chapter 5

Narration

Short Story

Illustration for the poem "Fog" by Carl Sandburg by John English

▲ **Critical Viewing** What kind of story could you tell about this picture? What characters would be in the story? What conflict, or problem, might they face? **[Speculate]**

Short Stories in Everyday Life

Life, you might think, is what *happens* to people, not what they *say* about it. Yet think of your life without stories. No funny stories, like the one about math class you told your friend. No inspiring stories from your family history. No tall tales about why you were late! Without these stories, your life would go on—but what would you make of it? What would you see in it?

A short story is made up, so it probably won't give you many facts about events that have actually *happened*. Instead, it will show you the power of what we *say* about life. Using the right words, a short-story writer can turn life into adventure or comedy or tragedy.

In this chapter, you'll learn to use this power for yourself as you follow the strategies for writing your own short story.

What Is a Short Story?

A **short story** is a brief, creative narrative—a retelling of events arranged to hold a reader's attention. By letting you enter the lives of its characters, a short story pushes you beyond the person you are today, reminding you of all the other possible *you*'s bustling under your skin. Most short stories have

- one or more characters, clearly developed through the course of the story.
- a **conflict,** or problem faced by the main characters.
- a clear structure—with a beginning, middle, and end—which develops the conflict and leads to a **climax** (turning point) and resolution.
- a **theme**, or question about life and human nature, expressed in the events of the story.

To learn the criteria on which your story may be judged, see the Rubric for Self-Assessment on page 62.

Writers in ACTION

Eudora Welty published her first stories as a young woman and won the Pulitzer Prize for Fiction in 1973. On creating characters, she has said:

"I have been told . . . that I seem to love all my characters. What I do in writing of any character is to try to enter into the mind, heart, and skin of a human being who is not myself. Whether this happens to be a man or a woman, old or young, with skin black or white, the primary challenge lies in making the jump itself. It is the act of a writer's imagination that I set most high."

As you write, follow Welty's example: Get "inside" your characters.

Types of Short Stories

There are a few different kinds of short story:

- **Realistic stories** try to reflect the everyday lives of ordinary people.
- **Character studies** reveal a deep truth about a character. They emphasize painting a portrait of the character over telling a series of events.
- **Genre stories,** such as science-fiction stories, detective stories, and horror stories, follow a few basic rules to create a specific effect, such as wonder, suspense, or horror.

PREVIEW Student Work IN PROGRESS

Robin Myers, a student at Maplewood Middle School in Maplewood, New Jersey, wrote a short story called "A Tear and a Smile." In this chapter, you'll see how she used featured strategies to come up with a topic, develop narrative elements, and revise her first draft. At the end of the chapter, you'll read her finished short story.

5.2 Prewriting

Choosing Your Topic

You may already have an idea for a story, but if not, here are a few strategies that might help you come up with a topic:

Strategies for Generating a Topic

1. **Freewriting** Spend five minutes writing down story topics. Focus on getting ideas down rather than on grammar or punctuation. Afterwards, choose one idea as a topic.
2. **Periodical Flip-Through** Flip through a stack of periodicals, and flag photographs, articles, headlines, cartoons, or ads you find intriguing, annoying, or outrageous. Choose a topic from among those suggested by your flagged items.
3. **Writing Round** In a group, have one student write the first sentence of a story. Then, have each student add a sentence. Afterwards, read the story aloud, and choose a topic suggested by it.

Get instant help! Freewrite using the Essay Builder, accessible from the menu bar, on-line or on CD-ROM.

Student Work IN PROGRESS

Name: Robin Myers
Maplewood Middle School
Maplewood, NJ

Choosing a Topic From a Writing Round

These are the notes from a writing round session that helped Robin come up with a topic for her story—a character who discovers a secret.

(John) I knew there was something strange about our next-door neighbors the first day they moved in.

(Wendy) For one thing, why did the moving van arrive in the middle of the night?

(Joseph) The noise woke me up, so I went to the window.

(Heidi) That's when I noticed a man and a woman carrying dozens of large, heavy duffel bags into their new house.

(me) One of the bags was open slightly, and I could see something shiny inside.

My Topic: A character discovers a secret.

TOPIC BANK

If you're having trouble coming up with a topic, consider these possibilities:

1. **An Arduous Journey** Write a story about a teenager who must make a long commute between home and school. (You might model your story after a myth, movie, or video game that involves a hero who faces an arduous journey.)
2. **A Small Tale** A number of stories chronicle the adventures of tiny people—fairy tales like "Tom Thumb," children's books like *The Borrowers*, and movies like *Fantastic Voyage*. Write a story about someone much smaller than his or her surroundings. Explain why this character is so tiny and what mishaps occur as a result.

Responding to Fine Art

3. Write a story based on this painting. Who is the sailor? Where is he going or returning from? Who is waiting for him, at home or at his destination? What is his conflict?

The Dory, Edward Hopper, The Nelson-Atkins Museum of Art, Kansas City, Missouri

Responding to Literature

4. Read the story "The Tell-Tale Heart" by Edgar Allan Poe. Then, write your own story from the point of view of one of the police officers who come to search the murderer's house (have your narrator use the first-person *I*). You can find "The Tell-Tale Heart" in *Prentice Hall Literature: Timeless Voices, Timeless Themes*, Silver.

Cooperative Writing Opportunity

5. **A Group Story** Working with two other students, discuss possible topics and collaborate on a story plan, outlining all of the events for a story and describing all of the characters. Then, have one student write the beginning of the story, another the middle, and one the end. When the first draft is finished, one group member should read it aloud. The group should agree on any changes that need to be made. Using the group's decisions, each writer should then revise his or her part of the story.

5.2

Developing Narrative Elements

Once you've come up with a topic, define your story's basic elements. You need a **main character,** a person you can make vividly real to the reader. Next, you need to involve this character in a conflict. A **conflict** is a struggle between two opposing forces. A character's conflict may be **external,** as when a sheriff fights an outlaw, or **internal,** as when an outlaw struggles with his own conscience. Use the strategy of listing and itemizing to invent a main character and a central conflict.

▲ **Critical Viewing** From this photo, what can you tell about the owner of this room? Explain which details support your conclusions. **[Draw Conclusions]**

List and Itemize

List choices about who your main character might be. Circle your most interesting choice, and create another list of ideas about that circled item. Review this list for the elements you need: a well-defined main character facing a particular conflict. If you do not find these elements, repeat the process.

Student Work IN PROGRESS

Name: Robin Myers
Maplewood Middle School
Maplewood, NJ

Listing and Itemizing

Robin used listing and itemizing to define her main character and conflict. She began with the topic from her writing round: A character discovers a secret.

a kid who uncovers a big mystery or crime
a kid who discovers that her neighbors are secret agents
(a kid who discovers a family secret) ①

kid discovers her parents are secret agents
kid discovers her parents are royalty
(kid discovers something about a parent who died) ②

thirteen-year-old girl (cross between me and Allie)
discovers a note her mom wrote before she died
finds note in the attic (own house? grandmother's?)
doesn't know her mother wrote it
wants to find out who wrote it and why (conflict)

Considering Your Audience and Purpose

An interesting main character and an exciting conflict will keep readers interested. You can't start telling your story, though, until you know your **audience**—who your readers are. Similarly, you need to know your **purpose** in writing. Consider these examples:

If your audience is made up of . . .

- **people like your friends:** You might quickly build a picture of a character by naming the music he or she likes.
- **older people:** If you mention that the character listens to the band Migraine, you should explain what that suggests about your character.

If your purpose is to . . .

- **entertain:** Include funny, moving, or scary details.
- **analyze a character:** Build a complex picture of the person by describing his or her habits, tastes, lifestyle, and motives.
- **present a theme (a question or message about life):** Use events that illustrate this question or message.

Gathering Details

To make characters come to life, you need to get to know them. "Interview" characters to gather details about them.

Interview Your Characters

"Ask" your characters questions, just as you would with someone you are getting to know, and write down what you imagine their answers would be. Start with the list of questions shown.

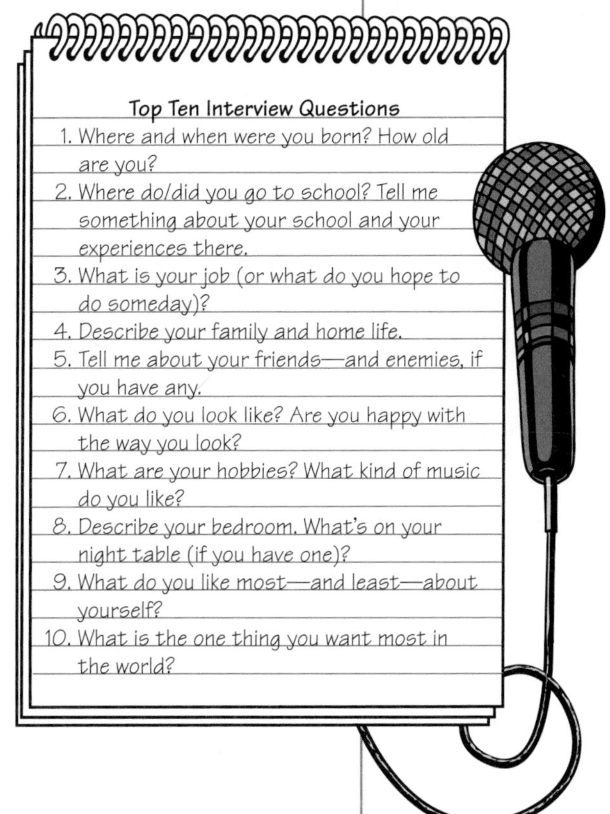

5.3 Drafting

Shaping Your Writing

Now that you've gotten acquainted with your characters, it's time to begin your first draft. Start by mapping out your plot.

Create a Plot

A **plot** is the arrangement of actions and events in a story. In many stories, the plot follows this pattern:

- The **exposition** introduces the main characters and their basic situation, including the central conflict.
- This **conflict** develops during the rising action, leading to
- the **climax** (a high point of suspense, such as a startling revelation, a sudden insight, or a new twist), followed by
- the story's **falling action,** which leads to
- the **resolution,** in which the conflict is resolved in some way.

Using a Plot Diagram Map out the events in your story using a diagram like the one below. Refer to it as you draft.

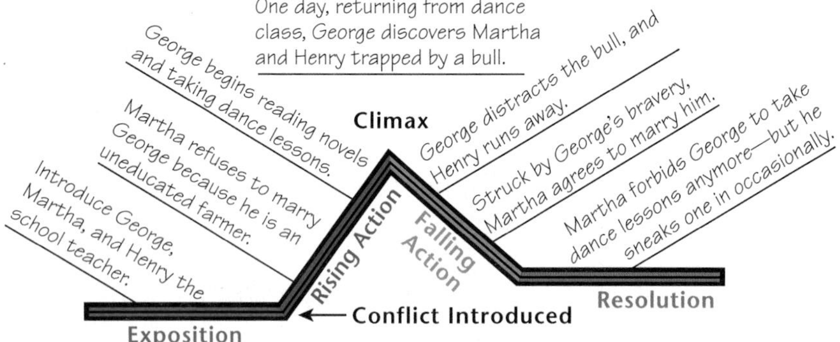

Build to a Climax

As you draft, make sure your plot builds toward the climax. Start by identifying the "setup" and the "payoff." The **setup** is the point at which you give facts that make the resolution possible. For example, you might explain at the beginning that a character speaks French. The **payoff** is the point at which the connection between the setup and the resolution becomes clear. For example, the character might surprise his friends by speaking French to get them out of a jam at the story's climax.

Pace your story effectively by introducing your setup and your payoff at the right times. If the setup is too close to the resolution, the resolution will seem forced. If the payoff comes too early, readers won't care how the story ends.

Providing Elaboration

Use Details to Define Character

A driving plot that roars toward a climax will keep readers reading. Make sure, though, that your readers won't feel like people stuck on a roller coaster. If all you give them is a plot full of twists and turns, they may arrive at the end feeling dizzy and tired. If you give readers reasons to care about your characters, though, they will enjoy the ride.

Show, Don't Tell A character starts out like a stick figure. You can dress up this stick figure a bit by *telling* what the character is like ("Mitch was kind"). Or, you can turn your character into flesh and blood by *showing* what he or she is like. For example, you might describe the gentle tone of Mitch's voice and his quiet way of calming someone. You might also include descriptions of the warm way in which other characters respond to him.

As you draft your story, refer to your prewriting notes on your characters. Add details to your draft that show what each character is like.

Student Work IN PROGRESS

Name: Robin Myers
Maplewood Middle School
Maplewood, NJ

Showing Character

As she drafted, Robin included details showing her main character's thoughtfulness and curiosity, as in this paragraph from her draft.

Main Character: how will she react to an adventure? → she is eager, curious → heart beats fast, takes a deep breath

So here I am now, poised at the door of what could be an incredible adventure. I [take a deep breath,] step onto the landing, shut the heavy oak door with a creak, and ascend the attic stairs, armed with a flashlight and curiosity.

Robin added a physical detail to help readers understand her character.

5.4 Revising

Revising Your Overall Structure

Once you have written a first draft, your story's basic plot—the sequence of actions—is on paper. Now, you must look at the way in which you retell this sequence.

Your story should be more than a list of events. It is an experience that you create for readers. Some short stories are like guided tours of a big city, with a clearly announced stop at each major landmark. Others are like the wild-goose chase on which you lead your brother at the mall while your family is preparing his surprise birthday party.

Your first step in revising your story is to make sure your plot builds toward an exciting climax—an emotional peak.

Create Tension and Surprise

Withholding Information Building to a climax is a matter of revealing information at just the right times. One technique for building to a climax is to create a nearly complete picture of a situation while holding back one crucial piece of information. Reveal the missing piece of information at or after the climax for impact.

One way to create tension as you build to your climax is to plant intriguing clues that will keep readers guessing what will happen next. These clues should hint at events without giving them away.

Hmm, [illegible] as I walked to [illegible] after [illegible]meroom, the halls sure are empty this period. **I wonder where everyone is.** Then I saw Shirley. "Hey, Shirley," I called out, **but when I did, she quickly hid something behind her back.**

[illegible] hi, [illegible] she answered, [illegible] Then she mumbled something about being late and ran

REVISION STRATEGY
Magnifying Your Clues

Look through your draft for places where you've hinted at the story's climax or resolution. Place a check mark in the margin for every clue you find. Next, review each check-marked item. Ask yourself: Will this give too much away? If your answer is yes, consider rephrasing the clue to keep readers guessing.

Next, look for stretches of your draft where there are few check marks. Consider whether you should add hints to these sections. For each spot you choose, draw a magnifying glass in the margin. Afterward, go back and add a clue for each magnifying glass.

Revising Your Paragraphs

Develop Characters Fully

Look for places where you can add more details to flesh out your characters. You want them to seem like real, multifaceted people—not just stick figures with names.

REVISION STRATEGY
Fleshing Out Reactions

Review your draft, circling situations and events to which a character would have a strong reaction. In the margin, jot down a note about the character's reactions. Then, ask yourself: What gestures, words, facial expressions, thoughts, memories, or actions will reflect this reaction? Note these "fleshed-out" reactions in the margin. When you have finished marking up your draft, review these marginal notes and decide which details to include.

Writers in ACTION

"The easiest things to write about are emotions. For a writer, those are what you start with . . . because you start from the inside. You can't start with how people look and speak and behave and come to know how they feel. You must know exactly what's in their hearts and minds before they ever set visible foot on the stage. You must know all, then not tell it all, or not tell too much at once. . . ."

—Eudora Welty

Student Work IN PROGRESS

Name: Robin Myers
Maplewood Middle School
Maplewood, NJ

Fleshing Out Reactions

Robin found a few places to flesh out her narrator's reactions to her adventure—exploring an attic.

Narrator: why does the attic please her?

She likes a mystery.

She likes secrets and Nancy Drew-type mysteries.

At the top, I see that the attic is exactly as I had hoped—the kind of attic in a Nancy Drew mystery, only better, and real.

Revising Your Sentences

Combine Sentences to Show Connections

To show connections between ideas, combine related sentences using words telling *when, why, how,* or *which one:*

CHOPPY: I got home. I ran to my computer to see if I had any e-mail.

COMBINED: **As soon as** I got home, I ran to my computer to see if I had any e-mail.

CHOPPY: I got the dog to stop growling at me. I sang softly to him in my sweetest voice.

COMBINED: I got the dog to stop growling at me **by** singing softly to him in my sweetest voice.

CHOPPY: I gave the package to a man. The man was wearing a gray hooded sweatshirt.

COMBINED: I gave the package to a man **who** was wearing a gray hooded sweatshirt.

Technology Tip

If your computer's word-processing program includes a "track changes" function, turn it on during your revision process. This tool will highlight the inserts and cuts you've made. You can decide later whether you want to "accept" or "reject" these revisions.

REVISION STRATEGY
Coding Clusters to Combine Sentences

Circle clusters of short sentences. Then, draw a square around any sentence in a cluster that explains *when, why, how,* or *which one.* Combine such sentences with the sentences they explain.

Student Work IN PROGRESS

Name: Robin Myers
Maplewood Middle School
Maplewood, NJ

Showing Connections

To show connections between ideas, Robin combined sentences explaining when, why, how, *or* which one *with the sentences they explain.*

This boxed sentence explains how the painting is standing.

This boxed sentence explains why the narrator peers around the back.

Grandie had said that I could touch anything as long as I was careful. The painting is not hung up. [How?] It is propped against the wall with an old iron in front of it to prevent it from sliding. Painstakingly, I ease the painting up higher so that it is vertical. [Then, because] I want to know every inch of it. [Why?] I peer around to the back, still holding it gently by the frame.

Revising Your Word Choice

Use Vivid Verbs

Energize your writing by replacing stale, overused verbs like *said, was, had,* and *went* with colorful, expressive verbs that capture your precise meaning, as in these examples:

OVERUSED:	VIVID:
said	snickered hinted
was	exploded with exuded
went	zigzagged trudged

Technology Tip

Use your word-processing program's "search" or "find" function to locate specific verbs that you've used too often or too many times in a row.

REVISION STRATEGY
Highlighting Verbs

Highlight all the verbs in the last three paragraphs of your story. Use one color for action verbs and another for linking verbs. Then, circle any verbs that sound weak or that you've overused. Consider replacing linking verbs with action verbs. Replace weak verbs with more inventive ones.

Grammar in Your Writing
Identifying Action and Linking Verbs

A **verb** is a word that expresses an action or a state of being. An **action verb** tells what action the subject of the sentence is doing. A **linking verb** connects the subject to a noun, pronoun, or adjective that identifies or describes it later in the sentence. The most common linking verb is *be* in all its forms. Other linking verbs are *feel, look, appear, become, grow, remain, seem, smell, sound, taste, stay, turn,* and *prove.* Notice that some linking verbs can also function as action verbs.

I **looked** at her face carefully. [Subject performs **action.**]
Sucheta *was* the youngest **child** in the family. [**Noun** identifies subject.]
She *looked* **upset** about something. [**Adjective** describes subject.]

Find It in Your Reading Underline three action verbs and circle three linking verbs in a short story you have read.

Find It in Your Writing Underline five action verbs and circle five linking verbs in your story. If you can't find five different action verbs, consider replacing some of your repeated verbs with more vivid or unusual choices.

To learn more about verbs, see Chapter 15.

5.4

Peer Review

After you've finished making major revisions to your story, you've probably read it through a few times. Every word is familiar to you, and you can probably play back the action in your imagination.

It is for this reason—your "closeness" to your own work—that you may benefit by hearing the reactions of your peers. Because they are unfamiliar with the story, their reactions will let you know how your work comes across. They can let you know whether that moment in your story when the ship goes down is as vivid on the page as it is in your imagination. Use the strategy of "say back" to get peer responses.

"Say Back"

Read your revised draft aloud twice to a small group of classmates. After your second reading, ask the group what they liked most about your story and what they wanted to know more about. Think about their comments as you revise.

▼ **Critical Viewing** Compare these two scenes. Which is the more dramatic of the two? Explain which details from the photograph in the background a writer might use to create an exciting description of a ship. **[Analyze]**

5.5 Editing and Proofreading

Proofread your story carefully to catch errors in spelling, punctuation, grammar, and usage. Unless they depict a character's way of speaking, such errors will distract your readers.

Focusing on Dialogue

As you proofread your story, pay close attention to the correct punctuation of dialogue—speech or conversation that you've written as though the character had uttered it.

Grammar in Your Writing

Punctuating and Formatting Dialogue

Dialogue is speech that is presented as though a character had uttered it. Follow these rules for punctuating dialogue:

1. Enclose dialogue in quotation marks:
   "We're never going to get there on time," Elena insisted.
2. Don't use quotation marks to simply report what a character said:
   Elena insisted that they were never going to get there on time.
3. If the dialogue comes after the words announcing speech, use a comma before the quote:
   Brian announced, "I'm going to the park to play basketball."
4. If the dialogue comes before the words announcing speech, use a comma, question mark, or exclamation point (but not a period) before the final quotation mark:
   "I'm going to the park to play basketball," announced Brian.
   "Can I come too?" pleaded his little sister, Rebecca.
   "No, you're not coming with me!" Brian barked at her.
5. Words announcing speech that interrupt the quote should be set off by punctuation marks and go outside the quotation marks:
   "Brian," wailed Rebecca, "you are just the meanest brother!"

Find It in Your Reading Skim a book you have read, and find three examples of dialogue. For each, explain why it is punctuated as it is.

Find It in Your Writing Highlight three instances of "words announcing speech" in your story. Review their punctuation, and correct any errors.

For more on punctuating with quotation marks, see Chapter 26.

5.6

Publishing and Presenting

Building Your Portfolio

Consider these suggestions for sharing your story:

1. **Submit Your Story** Submit your short story to your school's literary magazine, or post it on your school's Web site. Also, consider submitting your story to a national magazine, on-line journal, or contest that publishes student writing. (Ask your teacher or librarian for suggestions.)
2. **Produce an Audiotape** Make a recording of you and several classmates reading your stories aloud. If possible, include background music or sound effects to enhance your performances.

Reflecting on Your Writing

Write down a few thoughts about your experiences writing a short story. You might start off by answering these questions:

- Did you enjoy the writing process? Which part of the process did you like best? Least? Why?
- The next time you write a story, either for school or on your own, what do you think you'll do differently? Why?

Internet Tip

To see short stories scored with this rubric, go on-line: PHSchool.com Enter Web Code: eck-8001

Rubric for Self-Assessment

Evaluate your short story using the following criteria:

	Score 4	Score 3	Score 2	Score 1
Audience and Purpose	Contains an engaging introduction; successfully entertains or presents a theme	Contains a somewhat engaging introduction; entertains or presents a theme	Contains an introduction; attempts to entertain or to present a theme	Begins abruptly or confusingly; leaves purpose unclear
Organization	Creates an interesting, clear narrative; told from a consistent point of view	Presents a clear sequence of events; told from a specific point of view	Presents a mostly clear sequence of events; contains inconsistent points of view	Presents events without logical order; lacks a consistent point of view
Elaboration	Provides insight into character; develops plot; contains dialogue	Contains details and dialogue that develop character and plot	Contains details that develop plot; contains some dialogue	Contains few or no details to develop characters or plot
Use of Language	Uses word choice and tone to reveal story's theme; contains no errors in grammar, punctuation, or spelling	Uses interesting and fresh word choices; contains few errors in grammar, punctuation, and spelling	Uses some clichés and trite expressions; contains some errors in grammar, punctuation, and spelling	Uses uninspired word choices; has many errors in grammar, punctuation, and spelling

5.7 Student Work IN PROGRESS

FINAL DRAFT

House by the Railroad, Edward Hopper, AKG Berlin

◀ **Critical Viewing** Compare the mood of this house with the feelings the narrator associates with her grandmother's house. **[Compare and Contrast]**

A Tear and a Smile

Robin Myers
Maplewood Middle School
Maplewood, New Jersey

The moment I open the attic door and feel the chill whoosh of dusty air, my knees begin to shake and my mouth goes dry. I can't explain why. "Grandie," I had asked my white-haired grandmother just minutes before, "can we go into your attic today?"

I had seen my grandmother infrequently since my mother died and my father and I moved to California ("to get away from sad memories," he'd always told me). But I had longed to visit the dark upstairs room of Grandie's turreted Victorian house ever since I had known what an attic was. I knew there would be something about *her* attic that was special, just like she was. It

In this engaging introduction, Robin draws readers into the story with her use of the present tense, her dramatic description of a "whoosh" of air, and details suggesting her narrator's excitement or fear.

would be dark and dusty and musky, with wonderful ancient things, family things, maybe even secret things, hidden in faded cardboard boxes and trunks. But every time I had asked to go up there, she had simply grinned mysteriously at me and answered, "Not just yet. When you're ready."

The grandmother's mysterious response creates suspense. It also foreshadows the narrator's discovery of something important in the attic.

"Ready for what?" I had always wondered, but I had never had the nerve to ask.

But *this* time, Grandie had pursed her lips, given me a probing, green-eyed stare, and said, "Today I think you are ready, Isabella. I'm a bit tired out, though, so why don't you take a look around while I rest awhile." This was even more thrilling than I had hoped—a chance to explore all by myself! Not that I wouldn't have welcomed Grandie's company and even her wistful memories . . . but sometimes I just prefer being alone with my own thoughts. I thanked her and eagerly ran to the attic door.

The narrator's reaction here reveals something about her character: She enjoys solitude and reflection.

"You can touch anything as long as you're careful!" Grandie had instructed in her slightly tremulous voice. "Some things are quite breakable and very precious." I had nodded solemnly and watched her disappear down the long hallway.

So here I am now, poised at the door of what could be an incredible adventure. I take a deep breath, step onto the landing, shut the heavy oak door with a creak, and ascend the attic stairs, armed with a flashlight and curiosity.

Conflict is created between the narrator's hope that she will make a discovery and the fact that she has no idea what the attic holds.

At the top, I see that the attic is exactly as I had hoped—the kind of attic in a Nancy Drew mystery, only better, and real. I poke around for awhile, finding a beautiful china tea set with delicate roses on it and a box of crinkled photographs ranging in time from when Grandie was three and smiling toothily in a frilly, old-fashioned dress to when she was middle-aged, wearing an elegant business suit and hugging my pony-tailed, bell-bottomed father at his high-school graduation. I find some toy boats, wooden blocks, patchwork quilts, a book of bird pictures, and an antique phonograph. But nothing compares to the painting.

It is taller than my father and wider than I am tall. The background is woods, thick and dark and beautiful, and in front of the woods is a meadow, a velvet green carpet embroidered with thousands of delicate wildflowers. Sitting in the meadow is a red-headed toddler, the center of the painting, playing with a butterfly and laughing. I feel instantly attached to the painting, as if I know the setting, the painter, the child, or all three. I am strangely drawn to it. I pause and think.

▲ **Critical Viewing** What mood does a group of mementos such as these create? **[Infer]**

Grandie had said that I could touch anything as long as I was careful. The painting is not hung up; it is propped against the wall with an old iron in front of it to prevent it from sliding. Painstakingly, I ease the painting up higher so that it is vertical. Then, because I want to know every inch of it, I peer around to the back, still holding it gently by the frame. I notice immediately that there is a rip in the lining of the painting, and somewhere in the ragged folds of brown I see a square of white. I reach my hand carefully into the tear and pull out a yellowed envelope. With cautious fingers, I open it and pull out a letter on a single sheet of paper.

My dear daughter, the letter reads. I smile. Maybe this letter was from a parent who is giving the painting to a child. I check the date on the letter, and it is ten years ago tomorrow. I run my hands through my short auburn hair and read on.

I should start by saying how much I'm going to miss you. Oh, I think, maybe one of them is going on a trip or the daughter's off to college or summer camp. Or maybe the painting has nothing to do with the letter at all.

Please help Daddy, help him get through this . . . This? . . . *and help him raise you into a girl and later a woman we can both be proud of. I know you will. Also, I'd like to tell you how much I love you, which is hard because that's more than I can put into words (I've never been very good with words). And lastly, I'd like to give you this painting of you, which I completed yesterday, my final earthly gift to you.* She's dying, I realize sadly, and think of my own mother, who died . . . ten years ago tomorrow . . . It can't be. I push the thought out of my head and continue reading.

It is to help you remember me, remember us, and to remind you that there is always a part of me you can keep—that I am not leaving you, and won't, I promise, ever. This picture is purely from me to you, and I hope it shows you, better than words could, how much I love you, Bella.

By alternating between passages from the letter and the narrator's thoughts, Robin builds toward her climax—the narrator's realization that the letter is from her mother to her. (Refer to the second paragraph of the story to find Robin's "setup" for this "payoff.")

I jerk my thoughts from the letter, from the swirly script that I realize I know. Bella! That's me—my childhood nickname! The letter is from my mother, a painter, who died when I was nearly three! I begin to tremble and cry.

So much love,

Your mother

P. S. Here are a tear and a smile. I experienced both as I wrote you this letter.

I stare, sobbing, at the two tiny drawings at the end of the letter. Folding the letter carefully with fumbling fingers, I place it back inside the envelope and ease the envelope back into the lining of the painting. I lie down on the dusty attic floor, crying like a three-year-old. But then, through the haze of streaming tears, I begin to smile. I feel as if my mother is here.

The conflict—between hope and the unknown—is resolved. By venturing into the unknown, the narrator discovers something of deep significance to herself.

Chapter 6

Description

Little Blue Horse, 1912, Franz Marc, Giraudon

▲ **Critical Viewing** List five words that would create an image of this painting for a reader. Why do you think the painter "described" this scene using such unnatural colors? **[Apply]**

Description in Everyday Life

Description plays a big part in everyday life. What happened at the end of the football game? Is that new CD any good? How's the food at that new restaurant? The best answers to questions like these are **descriptions**—words that give the listener some idea of how something looks, sounds, smells, tastes, or feels.

If your description is successful, your listener will see, in his or her imagination, what you have experienced in life. By sharing your experience, you show that its value stretches beyond your own life—a powerful reason for writing descriptions. To transform your individual experiences into ones experienced by many, develop your descriptive writing skills.

What Is Descriptive Writing?

Descriptive writing creates a picture of a person, place, thing, or event. A good description works with all of the senses: Passing through hot clouds of steam heavy with cologne and sweat, a description takes you from the locker room to the sudden chill of the court, where sneakers squeak and thump until—swish—the ball flicks through the net! Good descriptive writing includes

- vivid sensory details—details appealing to one or more of the five senses.
- a clear, consistent organization.
- links between sensory details and the feelings or thoughts they inspire.
- a main impression to which each detail adds.

To learn the criteria on which your description will be assessed, see the Rubric for Self-Assessment on page 81.

Writers in ACTION

In her restaurant reviews, Rosie McNulty, a food and restaurant critic, uses strong descriptive writing. She believes her job is to allow a reader to share her experiences as though the reader were at the table with her. "It's your job as a writer to write something that is so vivid and so detailed and so specific . . . that without ever budging from his armchair the reader will feel as if he . . . has had the same wonderful experience without ever tasting a thing."

Types of Descriptive Writing

Your descriptive writing may be one of several types:

- **Descriptions of people or places** portray the physical appearance of a person or place and show readers why the subject is important or special.
- **Remembrances** capture a memorable experience in the writer's life, either a specific moment or a longer period.
- **Observations** describe an event the writer has witnessed.
- **Vignettes** capture a single moment in the writer's life, painting a picture with words.

PREVIEW Student Work IN PROGRESS

Victoria Kilinskis, a student at St. Francis Xavier School in La Grange, Illinois, used a unique point of view to describe her backyard pond. In this chapter, you'll see how she used featured strategies to choose her topic, to gather details, to elaborate, and to revise her work.

6.2 Prewriting

Choosing Your Topic

The following strategies will help you tap into your own experiences to find a good topic for your description:

Strategies for Generating a Topic

1. **Freewriting** Set a timer for five minutes. Then, write about whatever comes to mind. During freewriting, focus more on the flow of ideas than on spelling or punctuation. After five minutes, review your writing and choose something you discussed as the topic for your description.
2. **Blueprinting** Choose a place where you spend time—your home, the park, or a friend's house. Draw a floorplan or diagram of the place you have chosen. List things you associate with each area of the plan. Circle the most interesting items, and choose your topic from among them.

Try it out! Use the interactive Blueprinting activity in **Section 6.2**, on-line or on CD-ROM.

Student Work IN PROGRESS

Name: *Victoria Kilinskis*
St. Francis Xavier School
La Grange, IL

Blueprinting

After Victoria studied her blueprint of her home, she chose the goldfish pond as the subject of her description.

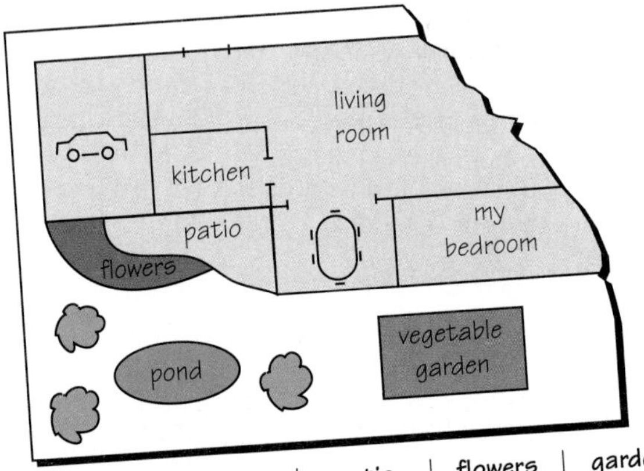

living room
kitchen
patio
flowers
my bedroom
pond
vegetable garden

kitchen	living room	bedroom	patio	flowers	garden	pond
baking pies	television	doll collection	barbecues	tulips I helped plant last year	tomatoes I staked—they're huge	fish
family dinner	hide-and-go-seek	favorite poster				tadpoles
						statue of fish

TOPIC BANK

If you're having trouble finding a topic, consider these possibilities:

1. **Description of a Trip** Think of a memorable trip you have taken somewhere, such as to the beach, a relative's home, a big city—or even to the supermarket. Write a description of the trip and the place you visited.
2. **Remembrance of a Person** Think of the most remarkable person you know. Write a description of him or her. Describe details that show this person's special character, and include your own experiences with him or her.

Van Nuys, Peter Alexander. Courtesy of the artist.

Responding to Fine Art

3. Jot down notes describing the night scene depicted in this painting. Review your notes, and think of your own experiences viewing a city by night. Write a description of one of these experiences, concentrating on the "feel" of a city at night.

Responding to Literature

4. In his book *Woodsong*, Gary Paulsen describes a strange, glowing sight that he comes upon in the woods. It takes him a while to realize what the glow is. Read this description, or another one in the book. Then, write your own description of an experience in the woods. You can find a selection from *Woodsong* in *Prentice Hall Literature: Timeless Voices, Timeless Themes,* Silver.

Cooperative Writing Opportunity

5. **Restaurant Review** Take your cue from Rosie McNulty and review a food experience. With a group of your classmates, decide on three places to review, such as your school cafeteria and two local restaurants. At each dining place, members should each order a different meal, take notes on it, and then write a review. Reviews should describe the service and the atmosphere as well as the food. Compile the reviews in a mini-guide to area eateries.

Narrowing Your Topic

Focus the topic you have chosen so that you can write about it effectively. Consider your perspective on it.

Select a Perspective to Narrow a Topic

A painter looks at a mountain and sees green and gray hues. A climber sees nasty overhangs and handy outcroppings. Each perspective focuses on different details. To find a perspective on your topic, answer these questions:

- What is your strongest impression of your topic?
- Are you interested in a close-up view or in the big picture?
- What interests do you have in your subject? What choices do you have to make related to it?

As you gather details about your topic, focus on those that fit your interests and perspective.

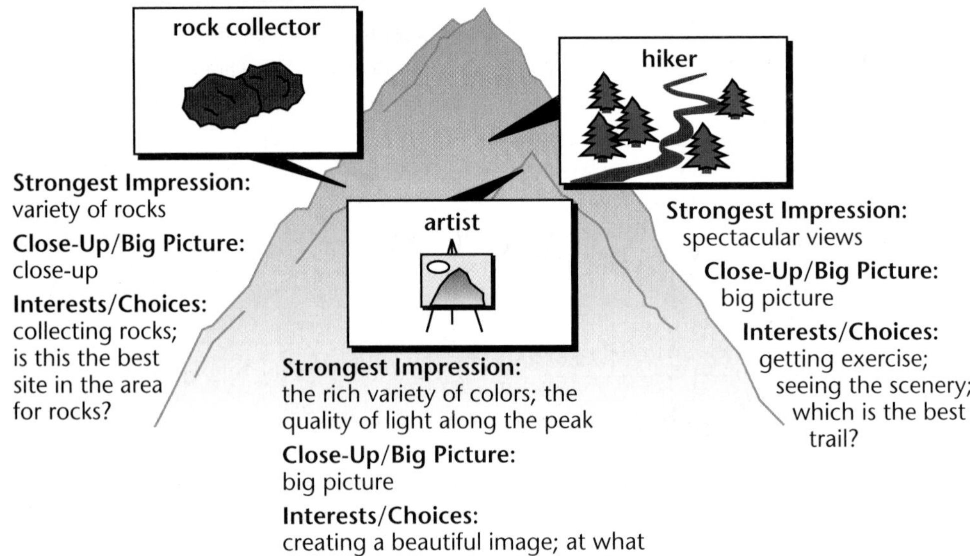

Considering Your Audience and Purpose

Before you draft, think about how familiar your topic is to your **audience**—your readers. If your audience is unfamiliar with your topic, include the most basic details about it. If they are very familiar with your topic, focus on its unique qualities.

Your **purpose** in writing a description is to create a main impression of your subject. The impression may be one of exhilaration, frantic activity, sentimentality—the possibilities are endless. As you gather details, choose those that support this impression.

Gathering Details

To help readers re-create your experiences in their imaginations, use **sensory details**—words capturing the look, smell, sound, feel, or taste of things. Sensory details aren't limited to bare appearances. For instance, you might best capture Uncle Ed's sneeze by comparing it to a volcanic eruption.

Keeping your perspective and your readers' imaginations in mind, "cube" your subject to gather details.

Cubing

To "cube" your subject, follow these steps:

1. **Describe it.** Explain how it looks, sounds, feels, tastes, or smells.
2. **Associate it.** List feelings or stories it calls to mind.
3. **Apply it.** Show how it can be used or what it does.
4. **Analyze it.** Divide it into parts.
5. **Compare or contrast it.** Compare it with a related subject.
6. **Argue for or against it.** Show its good and bad points.

Technology Tip

If you have access to a video camera or a still camera, use it to take pictures of your subject. Try to shoot your pictures from different angles to gain more information that will provide details for your writing.

Student Work IN PROGRESS

Name: Victoria Kilinskis
St. Francis Xavier School
La Grange, IL

Using Cubing

Having decided to describe the pond in her yard from the perspective of a fish, Victoria used cubing to gather details from this perspective.

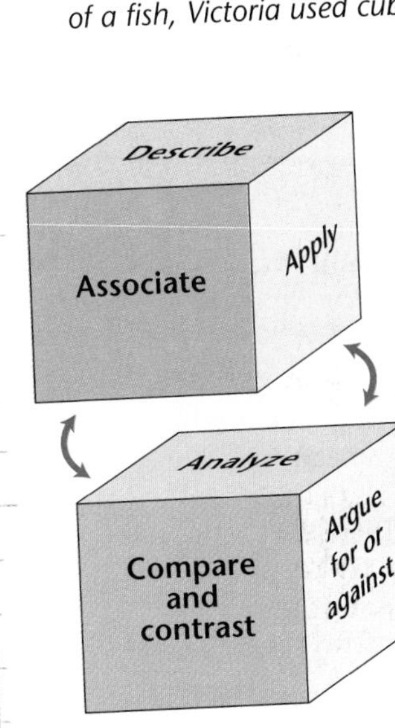

Describe:
thundering water from a giant stone statue
dead leaves floating on the surface

Associate:
peaceful, uneventful days

Apply:
It would be fun to live there.

Analyze:
waterfall at one end
rocks and plants along the bottom

Compare/Contrast:
peaceful day vs. raccoon attack
pond in summer vs. pond in fall

Argue for or against:
Even though life there is quiet, the pond changes with the seasons.

6.3 Drafting

Shaping Your Writing

Once you have gathered details for your description, begin drafting. Your first step is to organize details clearly, so that readers will be able to fit them together into a picture.

Organize Effectively

Following a Basic Organization Choose from the following methods of organization:

Spatial Order

- describes details from front to back, left to right, near to far, and so on.

Chronological Order

- describes what happened first, next, and so on; describes the causes of an event, then the event, and so on.

Order of Importance

- describes the least important details, then the most important details (or vice versa).

Building to a Point Your description should not just "sit there." To make sure it moves in a definite direction, organize details to build to a point. Consider these examples:

3. Conclude with the most significant event.
2. Focus on specific events leading directly to the most significant event.
1. Begin with background events.

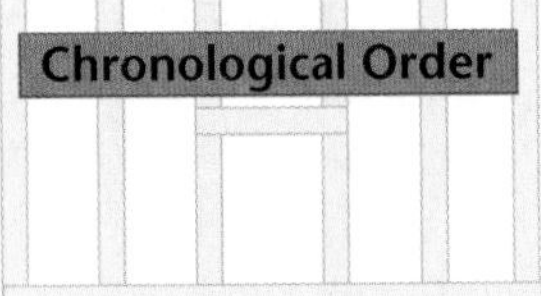

3. Conclude with the most important details.
2. Follow with more important details.
1. Begin with the least important details.

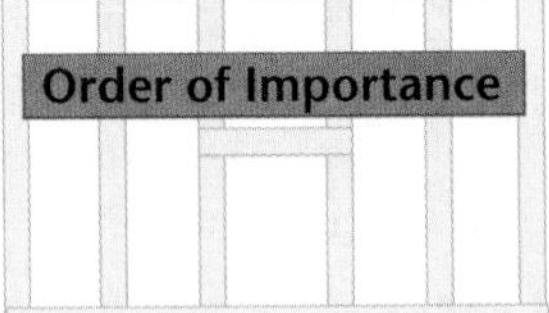

3. Conclude with those details that make the subject unique.
2. Follow with details taken in from close-up.
1. Begin with general details noticeable even at a distance.

Providing Elaboration

Present a Perspective

As you draft, make sure you include details reflecting your particular perspective on your topic. For instance, if you are describing your gymnastics coach from your perspective as her student, include details about how your coach has helped your performance. You might use the following strategy to help you focus your perspective as you draft.

Focusing Your Perspective As you draft, pause occasionally. Review what you have written. Circle any items that are important, given your perspective. For instance, you might circle a detail with which you associate strong feelings or one that influenced a decision you made. Draw arrows from circled items to new lines on the page. For each, write a new sentence reflecting your memories, feelings, or concerns. Then, decide which sentences to include in your final draft.

▶ **Critical Viewing** Describe the perspective of this young woman on the scene in which she is involved. **[Interpret]**

Student Work IN PROGRESS

Name: Victoria Kilinskis
St. Francis Xavier School
La Grange, IL

Focusing Perspective

Victoria wrote her description from the perspective of a fish named Butter. To focus Butter's perspective, she revised the sentence shown below.

Around twilight, just as the muffled chirp and buzz of insects begins, a shadow may fall across the waters. The world grows quiet. Then, with lightning speed, ~~a raccoon shoots his paw into the water and tries to grab me.~~ I swim away from it at top speed, shimmying under the rocks. After a time, the raccoon leaves, and I know it is safe to come out again.

a paw shoots through the water inches in front of me, churning the water into a froth of bubbles.

6.4 Revising

Revising Your Overall Structure

After your first draft is done, it's time to build on the strengths of your description and eliminate weaknesses. Begin by revising your structure.

Analyze Your Organization Plan

Review your draft to make sure you were consistent in using your chosen method of organization. Group related details near each other. Make sure your draft builds to a point, such as an insight or a description of what makes your subject unique. Use cutting and pasting to regroup details as needed.

REVISION STRATEGY
Cutting and Pasting for Order

Make an extra printout or a photocopy of your draft. Reread your work, noting details that concern the same person, place, thing, or idea. If you find related details far apart in your draft, consider putting them together. Cut each misplaced detail out of your photocopied draft and tape it next to the related details with which it belongs.

CUTTING AND PASTING

I remember the first time I met my gymnastics coach. She stood there by the rings, perfectly straight. As the team gathered around her, she said nothing. She waited until we had settled in and grown quiet.

~~At that first meeting~~, Then she ~~spoke~~ began to speak in tones just low enough that we had to listen carefully to hear what she was saying.

At meets, the coach shows few of her reactions. She offers a smile and encouraging words to each gymnast before she performs. She speaks quietly, just like the first time we met her. ~~At that first meeting, she spoke in tones just low enough that we had to listen carefully to hear what she was saying.~~

▲ **Critical Viewing** Write a sentence that this young woman might write in describing her coach. **[Interpret]**

Analyze Perspective

Part of what makes a description effective is a lively, believable perspective. After you have revised the order of details, make sure that you have focused your perspective effectively.

REVISION STRATEGY
Coding Details to Focus Perspective

Follow these steps to focus perspective:

1. On a note card, write your topic.
2. Underneath, briefly describe your perspective.
3. Underneath this description, write the three most important aspects of your topic from your perspective.
4. Run your note card down your draft, stopping at each line.
5. Circle in green details that relate to one of the aspects of your perspective that you have identified.
6. Circle in red details not related to one of those aspects.

If a paragraph has no green circles, consider adding details from your perspective. If many details are circled in red, consider eliminating some or rewriting them to make their connection to your perspective clear.

Student Work IN PROGRESS

Name: Victoria Kilinskis
St. Francis Xavier School
La Grange, IL

Coding Details for Perspective

Victoria coded her draft to focus her perspective.

2 I spend the day drifting in a dream, ~~or~~ exploring among the weeds, or searching for food. ~~The people who own the pond make sure the water stays fresh and clean.~~

The sentence circled in green reflected the watery life of a fish. Victoria decided to build on it by adding a few more details about this life. She deleted the sentence in red, which had little to do with the perspective of a fish.

Topic: my pond at home

Perspective: pond described by a fish who lives there

Three Most Important Aspects of Topic:

1. fish is smaller and more vulnerable than human being
2. water is its home—it eats there, swims there; never leaves
3. fish sees events at surface from below

6.4

Revising Your Paragraphs

Use Functional Paragraphs

A **topical paragraph** develops a main idea, explaining, illustrating, or defending it. A **functional paragraph** emphasizes a point, makes a transition, or adds a special effect, such as dialogue. A functional paragraph may be one sentence or a series of sentences. You can add functional paragraphs to your writing to do various jobs. Here are some examples:

FUNCTIONAL PARAGRAPHS

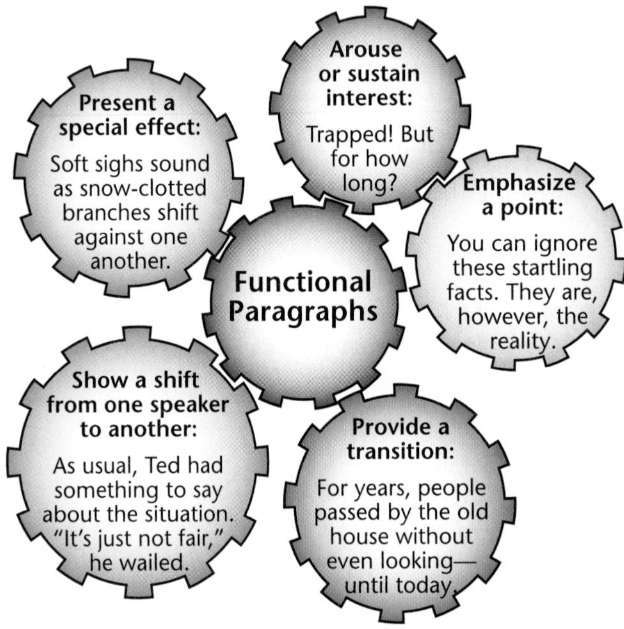

REVISION STRATEGY

Adding Functional Paragraphs

As you reread your draft, look for details of special interest from your chosen perspective. Consider emphasizing your perspective by adding a functional paragraph that comments on, or presents your reaction to, the detail.

Revising Your Sentences

Eliminate Awkward Parallels

It is a mark of a mature writing style to use a coordinating conjunction to link only sentence elements of the same kind —nouns with nouns, phrases with phrases, and clauses with clauses. This sentence style is called **parallelism.**

FAULTY PARALLEL: The colors included **brown**, **patches where it was green**, and **yellow**.

PARALLEL: The colors included **brown spots**, **green patches**, and **yellow streaks**.

FAULTY PARALLEL: I was looking for a cup **with two handles** and **that matched my other cups**.

PARALLEL: I was looking for a cup **that had two handles** and **that matched my other cups**.

Underline coordinating conjunctions (*and, but, for, nor, or, so,* and *yet*) to check parallelism in your draft.

REVISION STRATEGY
Underlining Conjunctions to Find Parallels

Underline the first ten coordinating conjunctions in your draft. Circle the sentence elements each conjunction joins. Balance nouns with nouns, prepositional phrases with prepositional phrases, main clauses with main clauses, and so on.

Student Work IN PROGRESS

Name: Victoria Kilinskis
St. Francis Xavier School
La Grange, IL

Finding Parallels

Notice how Victoria fixed an awkward parallel in her essay.

We would dodge the raccoon together, play hide and seek, and ~~we had~~ have bubble-blowing contests.

Revising Your Word Choice

Replace Vague Modifiers

Check the adjectives and adverbs in your draft to ensure that they are precise. Replace vague modifiers such as *good, big,* and *slowly* with modifers carrying a specific meaning, such as *entertaining, gigantic,* and *cautiously.*

REVISION STRATEGY
Highlighting Adjectives and Adverbs

Highlight the first ten adjectives and the first five adverbs in your draft. For each, ask yourself: "What makes this word apply to what I am describing?" For instance, you might have called your dog "nice" because he is *friendly* or because he is *cuddly.* In the margin, write these modifiers "explaining" your original word choice. If they are more precise than your original modifiers, use the new words in place of your original choices.

Student Work IN PROGRESS

Name: Victoria Kilinskis
St. Francis Xavier School
La Grange, IL

Highlighting Adjectives and Adverbs

Victoria replaced a few vague modifiers in her draft with more precise ones.

One day, though, as I was nibbling at a ~~nice~~ tasty weed growing by a rock, a little ~~dark~~ muddy brown creature scooted by. Its head was huge compared to its slender, leaflike tail. The creature swam ~~fast,~~ frantically darting under rocks and lily pads as it went. I swam after it and caught up easily.

Margin notes:
- tasty, delicious, nutritious
- brown, mud-colored
- big/skinny, flat
- quickly, frantically
- handily, quickly

Grammar in Your Writing

Adjectives and Adverbs

Adjectives add information to the noun and pronoun they modify. They answer the questions *what kind? which one? how many?* or *how much?* **Adverbs** add information to the verb, adjective, or other adverb they modify. They answer the questions *how? where? when?* or *to what extent?*

ADJECTIVES:	**yellow** flower	**many** weeds	**this** rock	**large** meadows
ADVERBS:	flows **swiftly**	runs **underneath**	swims **now**	**very** frothily

Find It in Your Reading Identify two adjectives and two adverbs in an essay you have read recently.

Find It in Your Writing Identify seven nouns and seven verbs in your draft. For each, evaluate whether you should add adjectives or adverbs to clarify its meaning.

For more on adjectives and adverbs, see Chapter 16.

Peer Review

Double Dyad

Exchange descriptions with a partner. Read each other's papers carefully, filling out a sheet like the one below. When you have finished, discuss your papers. Repeat these steps with a new partner. Consider the feedback you received from your partners as you make final revisions to your description.

	Very Well	Okay	Not Very Well
How well does the introduction capture your attention?			
How well does the writer use sensory details and comparisons to create a picture of the subject?			
Does the essay flow?			
Does the writer create a main impression of the subject?			
Does the conclusion leave a memorable impression?			
What is the strongest part of the paper? ______________________________			
What is the weakest part of the paper? ______________________________			

6.5 Editing and Proofreading

Errors in your descriptive writing, such as misplaced or missing commas, may confuse or distract your readers.

Focusing on Commas

Commas signal readers to pause slightly. They are also used to prevent confusion. Color-code your draft to find places where you may need to add commas.

Color-Coding Clues for Commas

Using a colored pencil, draw a box around adjectives wherever you use two or more of them in a row. Read the information below, and then review what you have circled. Add any commas you need.

Grammar in Your Writing

Using Commas With Two or More Adjectives

When two or more adjectives appear in front of the noun they modify, you may need to add a comma between them.

Adjectives of equal rank Adjectives are of equal rank when you can write them in any order before a noun without changing your meaning. Use a comma between adjectives of equal rank.

The energetic, determined fish pushed its way upstream.

The **determined, energetic** fish pushed its way upstream.

Adjectives that must stay in a specific order When adjectives must stay in a specific order, do not put a comma between them.

Many small (never **Small many**) tadpoles turn into large frogs.

Large yellow (rarely **Yellow large**) fish swim in my pool.

Find It in Your Reading Find two or more adjectives used before a noun in an essay you have read. Explain why a comma should or should not be used between them.

Find It in Your Writing Find places in your draft where you use two or more adjectives before a noun. Make sure you have used commas correctly.

To learn more about commas, see Chapter 26.

6.6 Publishing and Presenting

Building Your Portfolio

Consider these ideas for sharing your description:

1. **Submit Your Description** Find an appropriate publication for your description: a local newspaper, the school magazine, or a travel magazine. Submit your description for publication.
2. **Videotape Your Description** If you have described a subject accessible to you, videotape it as you read your description. Plan shots so that viewers will see what you are describing as they listen to you read about it. Rehearse with your assistants before the final taping, and show your final video to the class.

Reflecting on Your Writing

Jot down a few notes on your experience writing a description. To begin, answer these questions:

- As you wrote, what new insights or impressions did you gain about the subject of your description?
- Which strategy for prewriting, drafting, revising, or editing might you use again or recommend to a friend?

Internet Tip

To see descriptive essays scored with this rubric, go on-line:
PHSchool.com
Enter Web Code:
eck-8001

Rubric for Self-Assessment

Use the following criteria to evaluate your description:

	Score 4	Score 3	Score 2	Score 1
Audience and Purpose	Creates a memorable main impression through effective use of details	Creates a main impression through use of details	Contains details that distract from a main impression	Contains details that are unfocused and create no main impression
Organization	Is organized consistently, logically, and effectively	Is organized consistently	Is organized, but not consistently	Is disorganized and confusing
Elaboration	Contains rich sensory language that appeals to the five senses	Contains some rich sensory language	Contains some rich sensory language, but it appeals to only one or two of the senses	Contains only flat language
Use of Language	Uses vivid and precise adjectives; contains no errors in grammar, punctuation, or spelling	Uses some vivid and precise adjectives; contains few errors in grammar, punctuation, and spelling	Uses few vivid and precise adjectives; contains some errors in grammar, punctuation, and spelling	Uses no vivid adjectives; contains many errors in grammar, punctuation, and spelling

Chapter 7

Persuasion

Persuasive Essay

Signing of the Constitution, Howard Chandler Christy

▲ **Critical Viewing** At the Constitutional Convention of 1787, delegates from each state forged the United States Constitution. As this painting of the convention suggests, persuasive words were a major force in building the nation. Explain. **[Infer]**

Persuasion in Everyday Life

Once a word leaves your lips, its journey through the world has just begun. "Please" might end up getting your older brother to drive you to a movie. "Aw, c'mon" might bring your friends to a meeting of the chess club. "Awesome" might send fans in an on-line chat room out to buy a new CD. When you send out words to change people's thinking or to influence their actions, you are using **persuasion**.

Persuasion travels by many roads. Persuasive words roar by in an advertisement on a bus or whisk across your television screen during a commercial break. Along the way, they may unite people in a common action, viewpoint, or lifestyle. By developing your persuasive writing skills, you can have a say in which road people choose.

What Is a Persuasive Essay?

A **persuasive essay** is a written work in which a writer presents a case for or against a particular position. Each logical argument, powerful image, or striking phrase in the essay is like a step on a staircase leading to a window. As readers ascend, they come closer to looking out this "window"—to seeing things from the writer's point of view. A persuasive essay has

- an issue with more than one side.
- a clear organization that builds toward a conclusion.
- a clear statement of the writer's position.
- evidence supporting the writer's position, including arguments, statistics, expert opinions, and personal observations.
- powerful images and language.

To learn the criteria on which your persuasive essay may be assessed, see the Rubric for Self-Assessment on page 96.

Writers in ACTION

Kate Mitchell, a fundraiser, has used persuasion to raise money for an educational program on New York's Hudson River.

"To persuade somebody with your writing is one of the most empowering things that you can do."

Types of Persuasive Writing

Here are a few of the common types of persuasive writing:

- **Editorials** are brief persuasive essays, intended for publication in a newspaper, magazine, or other medium, that state and defend an opinion on a current issue.
- **Political speeches** are persuasive speeches intended to win support for a policy, law, or reform.
- **Public-service announcements** are radio or television commercials written to persuade and educate the public.

PREVIEW Student Work IN PROGRESS

In this chapter, you'll follow the work of Ryan Caparella, a student at Chain of Lakes Middle School, Orlando, Florida. You'll see how Ryan used featured prewriting, drafting, and revising strategies to write a persuasive essay on the dangers of drugs. At the end of the chapter, you can read Ryan's completed essay, "I Will Be Drug Free."

7.2 Prewriting

Choosing Your Topic

Typically, you will do your best job writing a persuasive essay if you choose a topic that is important to you. The following strategies will help you find such a topic:

Strategies for Generating a Topic

1. **Self-Interview** Pretend you're a reporter interviewing yourself. Answer the following questions: (1) What people, groups, places, and things are important in your life? Why? (2) What issues affect these people and things? Review your answers, and choose a topic from among them.
2. **Round Table** With a group of classmates, hold a discussion of issues in your school and community. What problems need solving? What perceptions need changing? Raise as many specific issues as possible. Jot down any that interest you. Select a topic for your essay from your notes.
3. **Media Flip-Through** Every day, the media bring controversies and debates into our living rooms. Over the course of a day or two, read through newspapers or watch the local and national news. Jot down topics that spark your interest, and choose one as a topic for your essay.

Get instant help! Write your Self-Interview questions using the Essay Builder, accessible from the menu bar, on-line or on CD-ROM.

Student Work IN PROGRESS

Name: Ryan Caparella
Chain of Lakes Middle School
Orlando, FL

Using a Media Flip-Through

Over a few days, Ryan flipped through newspapers and watched news programs to find a topic. He jotted down the following ideas and chose one—drug abuse.

Newspapers	TV News
flooding in the Midwest (Small City News)	overexposure to sun increasing, can cause skin cancer (The Nightly News)
city council closes down a park used for youth soccer league (My Town Newspaper)	voter registration declines (The Local Eye)
young people today—dangers and dilemmas—drug abuse (Young Americans Weekly)	baseball teams spend millions to recruit high-school players (The Sports Show)

TOPIC BANK

If you're having trouble finding a topic, consider these possibilities:

1. **Position Paper on Food Science** Giant ears of corn, cows that grow up in no time—these are the results of scientific advances. Some people are concerned, though, about the use of new technologies to produce food. Do research, and write a paper taking a position on a new technology.
2. **Editorial on Freedom** Some argue that freedom of expression ends at the school entrance. Choose an issue involving self-expression, such as school uniforms or the rights of school newspapers. Write an editorial expressing your position on the issue.

Responding to Fine Art

3. This image creates an idea of what happens when people hear the words of others—of leaders, of television commercials, and so on. Write a few notes discussing this idea. Then, choose an issue concerning communication, the media, or authority that could be illustrated by this image. Write a persuasive essay on this topic.

Untitled (Heard), Barbara Kruger, National Museum of American Art, Washington, D.C.

Responding to Literature

4. Read Mario Cuomo's essay "Achieving the American Dream." Write an essay about your own version of the American Dream. You can find the essay in *Prentice Hall Literature: Timeless Voices, Timeless Themes,* Silver.

Cooperative Writing Opportunity

5. **Fitness Advertising Campaign** With a group, investigate teen fitness. Each member can research one aspect of fitness, such as exercise techniques, proper diet, and local exercise programs. Using your research, put together a teen-fitness advertising campaign. One student might create posters, another might write a brochure, and others might illustrate the brochure with photographs and diagrams.

Narrowing Your Topic

Choosing a topic shouldn't mean signing up to write a book! Narrow your topic to make sure you can cover it thoroughly in an essay. For example, your topic might concern fairness in the media. "The media" covers everything from sitcoms to newspaper editorials—it is a topic broad enough for a book. You might narrow your topic to the television news coverage of a particular international situation.

To narrow your topic, use the "reporter's questions"—*Who? What? Where? When? Why?* and *How?*

Use the "Reporter's Questions"

Follow these steps to narrow a topic with the "reporter's questions":

1. Choose a partner, and construct questions about each other's topics using the "reporter's questions."
2. Answer each question as specifically as possible. For instance, your topic might be "television news." Your partner might ask, "What news does television cover?" You may answer, "National, local, and, to a lesser extent, international news."
3. Your partner should jot down your answers.

After answering each other's questions, trade notes. Circle the most interesting issues your answers raise, and choose a narrowed topic from among them.

▲ **Critical Viewing**
Which of the "reporter's questions" might a newspaper photograph answer? **[Analyze]**

Considering Your Audience and Purpose

Your **purpose** in writing a persuasive essay is to convince readers of your opinion. Knowing your **audience**—your readers—will help you find the evidence and language to best achieve this purpose. For example, if you were writing on your school's attendance policy, the arguments you would offer students might differ from those you would use with administrators.

To analyze your audience, answer the following questions:

- What do my readers know about the topic?
- What are their likely opinions or prejudices on the topic?
- About which aspects of the issue might they be most concerned?

Use your answers to help you choose the support for your position that has the best chance of convincing your readers.

Gathering Support

Before you draft, do research in reference books, magazines, and other sources to gather evidence on both sides of your issue.

Provide Support

Types of support include the following:

- **Logical arguments:** *Television news sensationalizes stories. Therefore, viewers get a distorted view of the world.*
- **Statistics:** *Eighty percent of viewers did not know the reasons behind the war.*
- **Expert opinions:** *Psychologist Joseph Lacan argues that the format of the news diminishes viewers' attention span.*
- **Personal observations:** *I watched battle footage on television for a week. I understood what the fighting was about only after I read a magazine article on the war.*

As you do research, complete a T-chart to gather evidence.

Completing a T-Chart Write your issue on a sheet of paper. Divide the sheet into two columns; label one "Pro" and the other "Con." Note support for one side of the issue under "Pro." Note opposing evidence and arguments under "Con."

Research Tip

You can often find the latest evidence about controversial issues in magazines and newspapers. Ask your librarian about on-line and print guides to periodicals.

Student Work IN PROGRESS

Name: Ryan Caparella
Chain of Lakes Middle School
Orlando, FL

Completing a T-Chart

Ryan realized that there was not a "Pro" side to the issue of drug abuse. He adapted a T-chart by labeling one side "Excuses" and the other "Realities."

Drugs Among Young People

Excuses	Realities
Keeping your friends is more important than anything.	Drugs are dangerous and bad for your health.
You have to look "cool."	What you do today will stay with you always.
You should live for today, not tomorrow.	Being responsible for yourself is more important than following your friends.

7.3 # Drafting

Shaping Your Writing

Develop a Thesis Statement

The evidence you have gathered should support your position on your topic. Review your notes, and develop a **thesis statement**—a sentence summing up your argument. Include this statement in your introduction, and organize your essay around it.

Organize to Create Drama

The places in which persuasive argument rings loudest—the courtroom, the pulpit, the Senate floor—are all **dramatic** situations. They set up a contest between two opposing sides. A well-organized persuasive essay can also create a drama. Consider using the following types of organization:

Saving the Best for Last To use **Nestorian Order**, arrange points according to their relative strength. Begin with your second-strongest point. Present other arguments, and end with your strongest point—a dramatic way to conclude.

Facing Your Opponents Challenge yourself to add even more drama to Nestorian Order. State and then knock down an argument against your position.

This form of organization is especially dramatic: The curtain rises to show one of your best arguments. The argument builds and grows—only to meet with a strong opposing argument! After a struggle, the opposing argument is defeated. Finally, your strongest argument arrives, leaving your audience with the impression that your position is invulnerable!

Technology Tip

Use the cut-and-paste feature of your word-processing program to help organize your ideas as you draft.

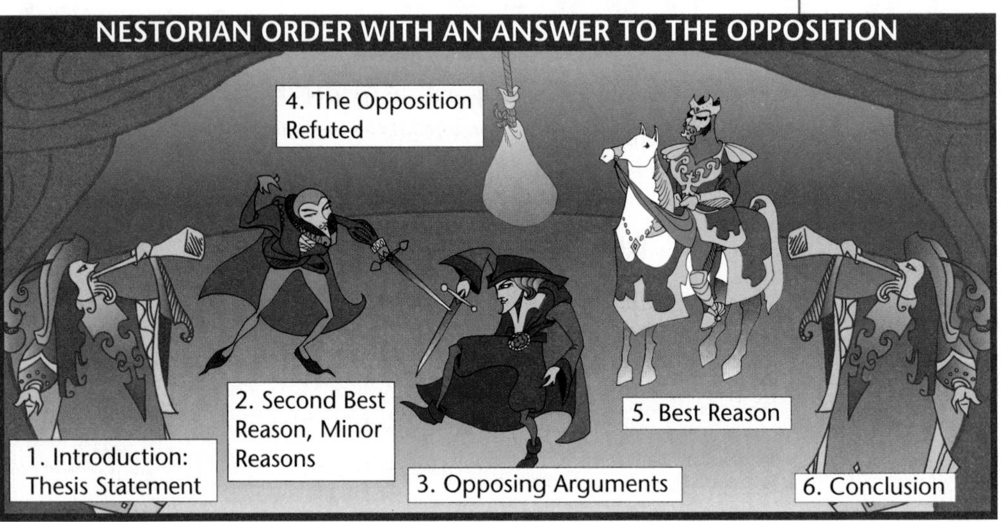

Providing Elaboration

Use a Variety of Persuasive Techniques

As you draft, use these techniques to sway readers:

- **Logical arguments** appeal to most readers. Take your readers step-by-step through your argument, and present accurate evidence to earn their trust.
- **Appeals to basic values** call on ideas that all readers support, but that may be applied in different ways. If you are arguing in favor of a policy, for instance, you might call it *just* (justice is a basic value). If you argue against the policy, you might call it *wasteful* (thrift is also a basic value).
- **Appeals to emotions** may take the form of a brief story or a vivid image. For instance, you might move readers to pity—and win their support—with the story of a young child who suffered because of a certain policy.
- **Repetition and parallelism** (the use of sentences with identical forms) strengthen your presentation. When words fall into a rhythm, it may feel as though each one "had" to be there—and thus, what they *say* is so must *be* so.
- **Charged words** have strong positive or negative connotations. They pack entire arguments into a few syllables. Call a plan *irresponsible*, and you create a scene: The plan is wrong; those who made it were careless, even childish; you (and your reader) are mature enough to see the fault.

Charged words are part of a mature vocabulary. To improve your vocabulary-building skills, see Chapter 29.

Student Work IN PROGRESS

Name: Ryan Caparella
Chain of Lakes Middle School
Orlando, FL

Using a Variety of Techniques

As he drafted his introduction, Ryan included appeals to basic values and to emotions. He also used repetition.

No one wants to be thought of as a criminal. No one wants to go to jail. No one wants to die at a young age, or to lose all of his or her family. Yet a survey shows that in 1996 more than 50 percent of seniors in high school had taken the first step on a road leading to these consequences. They had used an illegal drug.

Ryan's appeals to basic values, such as the desire for respect and for a long life, are shown in red. His use of repetition is shown in green.

7.4 Revising

Revision is the process of shaping and polishing your work to make sure that your ideas are expressed clearly and convincingly. Once you've finished the first draft of your essay, the cast of your persuasive drama—your arguments, examples, and creative phrases—are assembled. To get them ready for their performance, first improve your essay's overall structure. Then, revise paragraphs, sentences, and word choice.

Revising Your Overall Structure

Analyze Main Points and Support

As you reread your draft, look at the way your main points are organized. Are they presented in a logical order? Do they build toward your conclusion?

Your main points are the stars of your argument. To persuade the reader, however, you must present sufficient support and use persuasive devices, such as charged language, to back up each main point.

Code main points and support to help you present your argument effectively.

Technology Tip

Use the highlight and bold features of your word-processing program to make your main ideas stand out.

REVISION STRATEGY

Coding Main Points and Support

Highlight the main points in your essay. Then, rank each point in order according to its relative strength (1 = strongest, 2 = next strongest, and so on). For each of your main points, identify supporting points and devices, using the following symbols:

- ▲ Specific example
- ● Logical argument
- ▬ Measurable fact, such as a statistic
- ■ Expert opinion
- ▼ Personal observation
- ★ Charged language
- * Striking image

Review your main points. Consider rearranging paragraphs to begin with a strong point and end with the strongest. Then, review your support for each main point. If you find places that have just a few symbols for supporting details, consider adding more support.

Enhance Appeals to Your Audience

Reading a list of evidence can have about as much appeal as reading a phone book. Give your readers more than facts and logic. Using the strategy of "image shots," find places to add compelling images and stories to enhance your arguments.

REVISION STRATEGY
Using "Image Shots"

Review your support for each main point. For points that are supported only with logical arguments, statistics, or expert opinions, consider adding a colorful comparison, striking image, or dramatic anecdote. Flag these points with sticky notes on which you jot down a few key reminder words. Afterward, review your notes, and add the appropriate comparison, image, or anecdote. For instance, you might introduce an argument about honesty by telling the story of a child caught telling a lie.

Student Work IN PROGRESS

Name: Ryan Caparella
Chain of Lakes Middle School
Orlando, FL

Using "Image Shots"

After highlighting his main points and identifying the kind of support for each, Ryan saw that he had used a few logical arguments in a row. He used an "image shot" to add interest.

Yet, when you think about it, peer pressure is never a good reason to use drugs. Your friends should want to be your friends because of your personality, not because you ~~imitate~~ reflect everything they do. Being someone's friend doesn't mean turning yourself into a mirror. After all, when people leave the room, a mirror has nothing of its own to show. If anything, a friend sees you for you and tells you straight what he or she sees—the good and, sometimes, the bad.

friendship isn't imitating your friends; you're a person, not somebody's mirror—use image of mirror.

Revising Your Paragraphs

Check Unity

Readers will grow confused unless each of your paragraphs connects logically with the one before it. Think of a play. If actors entered the stage at any point, shouted their lines, and left, the play would make no sense. Instead, actors time their entrances to connect logically with what happened before. Use "Finding the Glue" to check connections between paragraphs.

REVISION STRATEGY

"Finding the Glue" Between Paragraphs

Read the last sentence of each paragraph followed by the opening sentence of the next paragraph. If neither sentence shows the connection between the paragraphs, highlight the space between those paragraphs.

Next, review each place you have highlighted. Add a word, phrase, or sentence to "glue" the two paragraphs together. If you have difficulty finding a good transition, consider moving or deleting one of the paragraphs.

Try it out! Use the "Finding the Glue" activity in **Section 7.4,** on-line or on CD-ROM.

Student Work IN PROGRESS

Name: Ryan Caparella
Chain of Lakes Middle School
Orlando, FL

Adding Transitions by "Finding the Glue"

When Ryan looked for the "glue" between paragraphs, he found that he needed to add a transition sentence to make the connection between these two paragraphs clear.

There is the risk of addiction, which means that you will begin to focus your entire life around getting the drugs you need to keep yourself feeling okay.

These dangers of drug use are all scary, but there is one risk that might be even more dangerous: the risk to your personal integrity.

^ Once you say, "Yes, I will try drugs, because that is what my friends are doing," you are saying, "Yes, I will stop taking responsibility for my own future." In that event, you are less of a person.

By adding this transition sentence, Ryan shows that the second paragraph discusses a different, even scarier danger than those discussed in the first paragraph.

Revising Your Sentences

Construct Parallel Sentences

To make a series of parallel ideas clear, use parallel sentence structures.

PARALLEL IDEAS: After the radio was invented, ham radio enthusiasts flooded the airwaves with news. Citizens today enjoy the freedom of "broadcasting" information over the Internet.

PARALLEL IDEAS IN PARALLEL STRUCTURES: When the radio was invented, ham radio enthusiasts flooded the airwaves with news. When the Internet was created, citizens rediscovered the freedom to "broadcast" information.

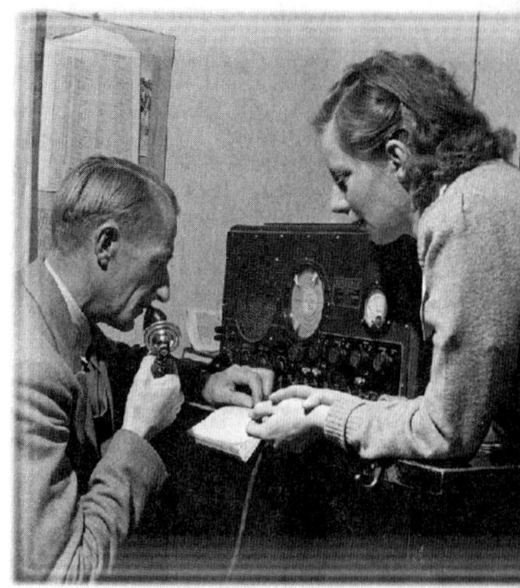

▲ **Critical Viewing** Write two parallel sentences describing this scene. **[Apply]**

REVISION STRATEGY
Coding Parallel Ideas

Circle in red pairs of sentences that express parallel ideas. Then, consider revising these related sentences so that their structures are parallel.

Grammar in Your Writing

Using Complex Sentences

Two complex sentences can make an effective parallel. A **complex sentence** includes one independent clause (often called the main clause) and one or more subordinate clauses. A **subordinate clause** contains a subject and a verb but cannot stand on its own as a sentence.

[Whenever the news is bad,]sub. clause [we tend to blame the messenger.]ind. clause

[Whenever the news is good,]sub. clause [we tend to forget who brought it.]ind. clause

Find It in Your Reading Identify two complex sentences in a persuasive essay you have read.

Find It in Your Writing Review your draft to identify three complex sentences. For each, be sure you have placed a comma after the subordinate clause if it appears at the beginning of the sentence. If you cannot find three examples, consider changing sentences into complex sentences for variety.

For more on complex sentences, see Chapter 20.

7.4

Revising Your Word Choice

Repeat Key Words

Although unnecessary repetition can mar your style, repetition of key words will create emphasis and provide transitions, as in this example:

> Television promised to be a great public resource, like a **park.** The **park** has been stripped, fenced off, and overbuilt. It has been turned into a **wasteland:** a **wasteland** of silly commercials, inane sitcoms, and sensational talk shows.

REVISION STRATEGY

Coding Focus Words

Circle in blue any words that sum up your perspective. Then, circle in green the sentences in which you can repeat one of these words for emphasis. Consider adding the words in blue to these sentences.

Peer Review

"Double Dyad"

For help with revising, use the strategy of the "Double Dyad."

1. Exchange papers with a partner.
2. Use the following grid to rate your partner's paper.
3. Discuss the responses with your partner.
4. Repeat the process with another partner.

	Very Well	Okay	Not Well
How well does the introduction create interest?			
How well does the writer present the main argument?			
Does the essay flow?			
Does the writer prove his or her argument?			
Does the conclusion wrap up the argument?			
What is the strongest part of the paper?			
What is the weakest part of the paper?			

7.5 Editing and Proofreading

Proofread your essay to discover and eliminate errors in spelling, punctuation, grammar, or usage in your essay.

Focusing on Colons and Dashes

As you proofread your persuasive essay, check to make sure that you have used colons and dashes where they are needed.

Grammar in Your Writing

Using Colons and Dashes in Sentences

Colons can be used to separate one part of a sentence from a list of items or from a second independent clause summarizing or illustrating the first. (Notice that if an independent clause follows the colon, the first letter in the clause is capitalized.)

List: Bicycles often come with the following accessories: rear reflector, mudguard, headlight, and handpump. [list]

Illustration: The accessories that come with bicycles are often necessities: You wouldn't want to be stuck cycling at night without a headlight. [ind. clause]

Dashes have several uses. Like a colon, they can be used to separate an independent clause from a list or from an independent clause summarizing or illustrating the first clause. Unlike a colon, a dash suggests an abrupt change of thought or other dramatic shift in focus.

His bicycle has a few accessories—the mudguard he borrowed from me, the reflector he took from Mike, and the headlight he found on the road.

Her bicycle had no accessories—is it any wonder she was stranded?

Find It in Your Reading Find one use each of a colon and a dash in a short story you have read recently, and explain why it is used.

Find It in Your Writing Circle any colons or dashes in your draft. Correct any errors in your use of these marks. If you have not used any colons or dashes in your draft, find places where you could. Consider using them to combine sentences.

For more on using colons and dashes, see Chapter 26.

7.6 Publishing and Presenting

Building Your Portfolio

Consider these ideas for sharing your persuasive essay:

1. **Organize a Forum** Assemble a panel of classmates who have written essays on related topics. Have each student read his or her essay to the class. After each essay, have the class ask questions of the panel members, and ask them to vote on whether they agree or disagree with each paper.
2. **Publish in a Newspaper** Send your persuasive essay, with a cover letter, to a local newspaper. Briefly summarize your essay in the letter, and explain that you wish it to be considered for publication on the editorial page. Share your essay and any response—including a clipping of your published essay—with the class.

Reflecting on Your Writing

Write a few notes describing your experience writing a persuasive essay. Begin by answering the following questions:

- What did you learn about the issue you chose? Did you find your opinions changing as you learned more? Explain.
- What part of the writing process seemed hardest for you? Easiest?

Internet Tip

To see model essays scored with this rubric, go on-line: PHSchool.com
Enter Web Code: eck-8001

Rubric for Self-Assessment

Use the following criteria to evaluate your persuasive essay:

	Score 4	Score 3	Score 2	Score 1
Audience and Purpose	Provides arguments, illustrations, and words that forcefully appeal to the audience and effectively serve the persuasive purpose	Provides arguments, illustrations, and words that appeal to the audience and serve the persuasive purpose	Provides some support that appeals to the audience and serves the persuasive purpose	Shows little attention to the audience or persuasive purpose
Organization	Uses a clear, consistent organizational strategy	Uses a clear organizational strategy with occasional inconsistencies	Uses an inconsistent organizational strategy	Shows a lack of organizational strategy; writing is confusing
Elaboration	Provides specific, well-elaborated support for the writer's position	Provides some elaborated support for the writer's position	Provides some support, but with little elaboration	Lacks support
Use of Language	Uses transitions to connect ideas smoothly; shows few mechanical errors	Uses some transitions; shows few mechanical errors	Uses few transitions; shows some mechanical errors	Shows little connection between ideas; shows many mechanical errors

7.7 Student Work IN PROGRESS

FINAL DRAFT

◀ **Critical Viewing** As part of educational efforts against drugs, boxing champion Sugar Ray Leonard meets with kids, as in this picture. Why might the example of a boxing star like Leonard have great persuasive force among young people? **[Draw Conclusions]**

I Will Be Drug Free

Ryan Caparella
Chain of Lakes Middle School
Orlando, Florida

No one wants to be thought of as a criminal. No one wants to go to jail. No one wants to die at a young age, or to lose all of his or her family. Yet a survey shows that in 1996 more than 50 percent of seniors in high school had taken the first step on a road leading to these consequences. They had used an illegal drug.

Ryan begins his essay with a strong contrast between common-sense ideas and the reality of people's behavior. His effective use of repetition and parallel structure heightens the force of his argument.

Using an illegal drug probably won't ruin your life instantly (although, if used in the wrong amount or combination, many can kill you right away). Using an illegal drug does expose you to risks, though. There is the risk of having a careless accident while you are under the influence and your judgment is impaired. There is the risk of disease from the way some drugs are taken. There is the risk of getting caught in the middle of violence from the dangerous people who sell drugs.

Drug users also take long-term risks. There is the risk that you will grow casual about drug use, so that you don't notice later on when you get into more serious problems. There is the risk of addiction, which means that you will begin to focus your entire life around getting the drugs you need to keep yourself feeling okay.

Ryan begins to make his case against drug abuse by listing facts about its consequences. Then, he makes a transition to the issue of personal integrity.

These dangers of drug use are all scary, but there is one risk that might be even more dangerous: the risk to your personal integrity. Once you say, "Yes, I will try drugs, because that is what my friends are doing," you are saying, "Yes, I will stop taking responsibility for my own future." In that event, you are less of a person.

My own position on these risks is clear: I say no to drugs. In some ways, it's an easy position to take. It's easy to remember. There are no gray areas. And it boosts my self-respect, because I know I am looking out for myself and my future.

None of these ideas that I have presented is original or hard to understand. Everybody knows about these risks. We hear about them all the time in school and in the news. Despite this widespread knowledge, a new generation of young people starts abusing drugs every year. Some even die. The trend seems to be increasing. In 1992, only 40.7 percent of kids had tried drugs by the time they were seniors. Four years later, the percentage had risen to 50.8 percent. Why?

Ryan backs up his argument with statistics.

Kids will give you a couple of reasons. Many kids say they cannot withstand peer pressure. And it's true. Often kids use drugs because they are encouraged to by their friends. After all, it's hard to say no to a friend. And what if people start to think that you're not "cool"? Hey, you might even get a reputation for being out of it!

Ryan shows that he's considered his audience—his classmates—by identifying "reasons" they might have to ignore common sense.

Yet, when you think about it, peer pressure is never a good reason to use drugs. Your friends should want to be your friends because of your personality, not because you reflect everything they do. Being someone's friend doesn't mean turning yourself into a mirror. After all, when people leave the room, a mirror has nothing of its own to show. If anything, a friend sees you for you and tells you straight what he or she sees—the good and, sometimes, the bad.

Ryan uses the transition word yet to connect two paragraphs.

He uses the image of a mirror with nothing to reflect as an effective persuasive device.

When faced with a choice about drugs, some kids will say, "Who cares about tomorrow?" This is a delusion. Even if you think you can avoid tomorrow, it's going to come. And when it gets here, whether you are happy or not depends on what you did today.

Some kids might even say, "Addiction and other drug-related problems may happen to some people, but not to me." Even if you are a clean, alert, attractive person today, if you get strung out on drugs, you can end up on the streets. Just think about this: Nobody whose life was ruined by drugs started out thinking, "I am going to ruin my life." Chances are, they said just what you might say: "That will never happen to me." That didn't protect them from the consequences of drug abuse. It won't protect you either if you start using drugs.

Here, Ryan refutes the opposition.

When I'm an adult, and I have a family of my own, I will want the best for my children. I won't want them to get into trouble, so I will teach them how to avoid drugs. I will be their role model. If they ask me whether I ever did drugs when I was their age, I want to be able to answer that question proudly—no. Each year, thousands of kids choose to begin using drugs. I am not going to make that number one bit higher. I am going to stay drug-free. I say no!

Ryan concludes with his strongest argument—a vision of the kind of parent he can become if he says no to drugs.

Ryan's last sentence is a ringing call to action.

◄ **Critical Viewing** Describe the connections between these family members, using details from the photo. Do you think the children look to their father as a role model? Explain. **[Interpret]**

Chapter 8

Exposition

Comparison-and-Contrast Essay

The Empire of Light, II, René Magritte, The Museum of Modern Art, New York

▲ **Critical Viewing** Compare and contrast the upper and lower halves of this painting. What feelings do their similarities or differences create? **[Compare and Contrast]**

Comparison and Contrast in Everyday Life

If you travel away from home, you might start noticing the things that are different. Look out the window, for instance, and, instead of heaps of snow, you might see flowers. At the same time, you might be surprised by how much the diner down the street reminds you of the diner back home.

Whenever you notice something different, or whenever you are reminded of one thing by another, you have caught yourself in the act of **comparing and contrasting**—the act of noting the similarities and differences between two things.

Comparing and contrasting is a technique for learning more about the world. Comparing your home with a faraway place can show you what is special about your home. If you learn to write an effective comparison-and-contrast essay, you will sharpen your ability to discover things about your world.

What Is a Comparison-and-Contrast Essay?

A **comparison-and-contrast essay** uses factual details to analyze the similarities and differences between two or more persons, places, or things. Comparison-and-contrast essays can help readers look at the things being compared in a new way. Comparison-and-contrast essays include

- a topic involving two or more things that are in some ways similar and in other ways different.
- an introduction that presents the main point of the essay and body paragraphs that include details showing similarities and differences.
- an organization that highlights the points of comparison.

To learn the criteria on which your comparison-and-contrast essay may be assessed, see the Rubric for Self-Assessment on page 113.

Writers in ACTION

Bruce Brooks uses comparisons and contrasts in both his fiction and his nonfiction. His writing is rooted in simple curiosity: "I think curiosity is a writer's greatest tool. . . . I've been very curious all my life, [and] I allow that curiosity to turn into ideas."

Types of Comparison-and-Contrast Essays

There are a variety of specialized comparison-and-contrast essays. These include the following:

- **Product comparisons** compare two or more products and discuss the advantages and disadvantages of each.
- **Comparative reviews** compare books, movies, plays, or television programs and make a recommendation.
- **Comparisons of literary works** analyze similarities and differences between two or more literary works.

PREVIEW Student Work IN PROGRESS

In this chapter, you will follow the progress of Mindy Glasco from Los Alamos Middle School in Los Alamos, New Mexico. As you'll see, Mindy used prewriting, drafting, and revising techniques to develop her comparison-and-contrast essay, "Small Town, Big City."

8.2 Prewriting

Choosing Your Topic

An effective comparison-and-contrast essay begins with a suitable topic. Your topic should

- interest you and your potential readers.
- be something you know about or about which you'd like to learn more.
- involve two or more items that are neither completely alike nor completely different.

Use the following strategies to help you choose your topic.

Strategies for Generating a Topic

1. **Blueprinting** Think of a place you know well, such as a park or your bedroom. Draw a blueprint or map of this place. Include key details such as trees or furniture. Then, write words or phrases on the blueprint that describe objects or activities you associate with this place. Review your blueprint, and choose an item to compare to another, related item.
2. **Personal-Experience Timeline** Every time you outgrow your clothes, you can see how you are changing. These physical changes are fascinating to compare and contrast. So are your changes in attitude. Use a timeline to chart ways you've changed over time. Choose two entries as the basis for a comparison-and-contrast essay.

Try it out! Use the interactive Personal-Experience Timeline in **Section 8.2,** on-line or on CD-ROM.

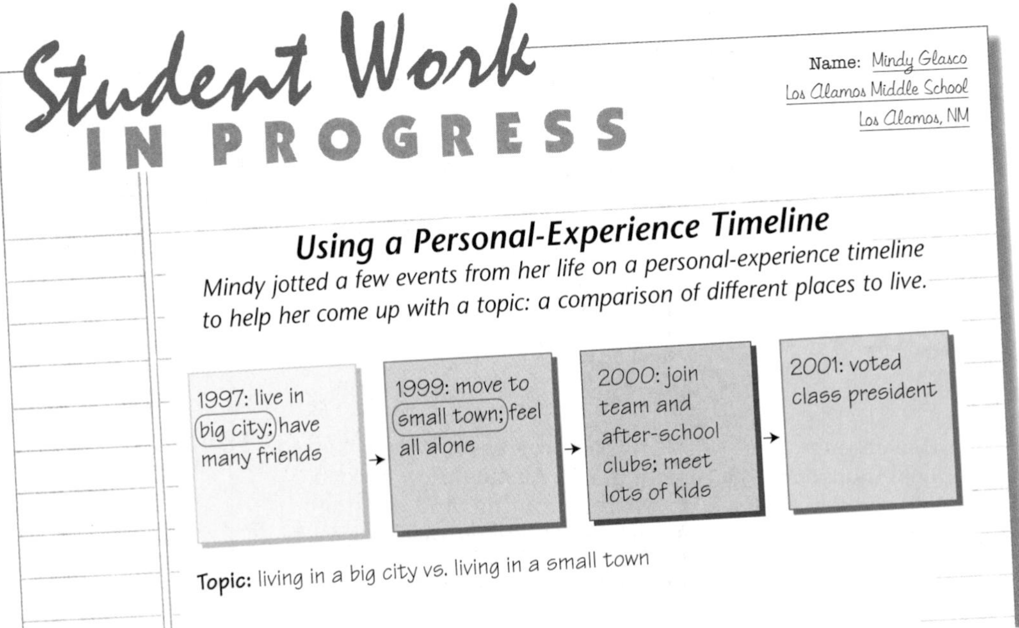

TOPIC BANK

If you're having trouble finding a topic, consider one of the following suggestions:

1. **Comparing Careers** Think about your future. What might your life be like if you became an architect? How would your life differ if you became a landscaper? Choose two professions to compare and contrast.
2. **The Same Song** Compare and contrast two songs on the same subject. Compare styles, rhythms, lyrics, mood, and so on.

Mexican Men With Burro Carrying Sticks, Joan Marron LaRue

3. These two paintings differ in the scenes depicted and in the types of colors and lines used. Write an essay comparing and contrasting the subject and style of each.

Empire State, Tom Christopher, Vicki Morgan Associates

Responding to Literature

4. Compare and contrast "Western Wagons" by Stephen Vincent Benét with "The Other Pioneers" by Roberto Félix Salazar. Analyze the similarities and differences in form, word choice, subject, and viewpoint. Explain how the two poems present different views of a similar subject. You can find these poems in *Prentice Hall Literature: Timeless Voices, Timeless Themes,* Silver.

Cooperative Writing Opportunity

5. **Rating Your Town** Studies are done each year to rate the quality of life in different cities, comparing culture, education, transportation, air quality, safety, and so on. Work with classmates to create a brochure citing the benefits of living in your town or city. Each of you should focus on a single feature. When you have finished your individual assignments, work together to assemble the finished product.

Narrowing Your Topic

Some topics are very broad and are better suited for a long essay—even a whole book. The topic "The Most Exciting Sport," for example, is much too broad to be discussed effectively in a brief essay. You might narrow it to "Football Versus Basketball—Which Is More Exciting?" Divide your topic into separate parts, aspects, or subtopics. Choose one of them as your narrowed topic.

▲ Critical Viewing What sorts of details should you include in a comparison of different basketball shots for this audience? **[Apply]**

Considering Your Audience and Purpose

Before you begin writing, identify your **audience**—the readers of your essay—and your **purpose**—what you hope to accomplish. Both your audience and your purpose will affect your use of language, your choice of details, and the length of your composition. Note the examples in the chart below. Create a similar chart that indicates your audience and purpose and how they will affect your writing.

Audience	Topic	Style	Important Details
teachers	compare history of two cities	formal	dates of founding
parents	compare different places to visit on vacation	formal/informal	places to stay and costs
fellow students	compare what I did on vacation with what I can do at home	informal	the joke we played at my cousin's house
Purpose	**Topic**	**Style**	**Important Details**
instruct	compare businesses in two places	formal	statistics on employees
instruct, persuade	compare museums in two places	formal/informal	school subjects that relate to the museum exhibits
entertain	compare two different amusement park rides	informal	how sick I felt after getting off each ride

Gathering Details

Next, gather details you can use to develop your comparison. Write down as many descriptive details, facts, statistics, and other examples as possible. You don't have to use every detail you think of, but it's better to have too much to work with than not enough to fully develop your essay.

If you don't have a thorough knowledge of your topic, you may find it necessary to conduct research on it. Consider the following sources:

- Reference books
- Newspapers
- Magazines
- Internet sites
- Television documentaries.

Make a note about the source of each piece of outside information you write down. When you write your essay, credit outside sources you have used. See the section on Citing Sources and Preparing Manuscript on page 568 for information on citing sources.

As you gather details, consider using a Venn diagram like the one below to help you organize your information.

Use a Venn Diagram

Draw two overlapping circles, as shown below. Jot down similarities in the center section. Then, note differences in the outside parts of the circles. When you've finished your diagram, study it. Circle the items that seem most vivid and that best show comparisons and contrasts.

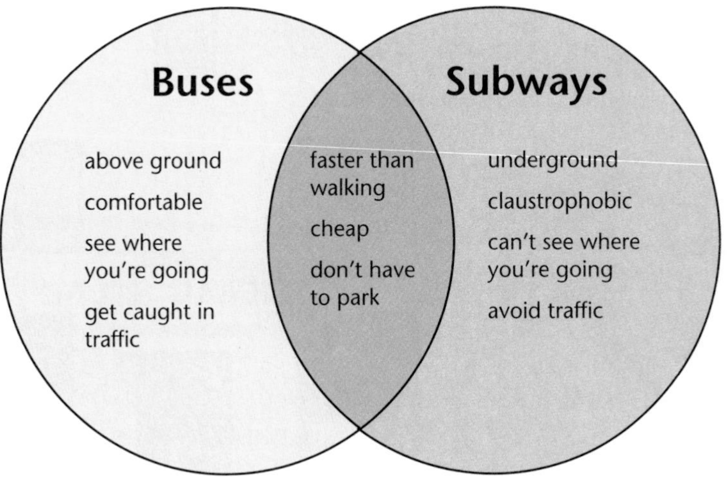

Research Tip

If you are looking for useful data to elaborate your topic, check an almanac. Use the index to see whether there is information about your topic.

8.3 Drafting

Shaping Your Writing

Once you've gathered enough details to include in your first draft, decide how you will organize them.

Select an Effective Organization

There are several ways to organize a comparison-and-contrast essay. Your audience, purpose, and topic will influence the method you choose.

- **Block Method** To use this method, present all of the details about one subject first; then, present details about the second subject, and so on. The block method works well if you are writing about more than two things or if your topic tends to be complicated.
- **Point-by-Point Method** To use this method, discuss one aspect of both subjects, then another aspect, and so on. For example, if you are comparing buses and subways, first discuss the cost of each, then accessibility, and so on.

Find a Theme

A clear organization should not be the only structure guiding your writing. Review your notes for a **theme**—an extended comparison or a lesson involving the overall relationship between the items you are comparing.

For instance, if you were comparing a big supermarket to a tiny Mom-and-Pop grocery, many of your points of comparison might involve size. Yet, you might think the smaller store is the more valuable. You could focus your essay by comparing the grocery to a diamond—small but valuable.

▼ Critical Viewing Write a sentence stating a possible theme for a comparison between these two scenes. **[Analyze]**

Providing Elaboration

A house starts out as a frame. To complete it, you must add layers of wood and siding. Writing an essay is like building a house: You start with an overall structure and layer on details to develop your key points.

As you draft your paper, use the strategy that follows to develop a thorough, detailed comparison.

Layer Ideas Using SEE

To develop the main point of a paragraph, follow these steps:

State the topic of the paragraph.

Extend the idea. Restate it with new emphasis, apply it to a particular case, or contrast it with another point.

Elaborate on your main idea in one or more sentences, giving examples, explanations, supporting facts, or other details about it.

As you elaborate, look for opportunities to connect your main points to the theme of your essay.

Student Work IN PROGRESS

Name: Mindy Glasco
Los Alamos Middle School
Los Alamos, NM

Layering Ideas

Mindy used layering as she drafted this paragraph.

Statement: A small town also has a lot to offer. **Extension:** However, like a shy person, what it has to offer may not be obvious at first. **Elaboration:** After having lived in my town for a while, I can tell you about the great trails right out my back door for hiking, mountain biking, and cross-country skiing in the winter. Our town also has its own downhill ski area, just twenty minutes away.

In the first sentence of her paragraph, Mindy states a new main point.

In extending her main point, Mindy connects it to her theme.

Mindy elaborates on her main idea, listing all that a small town has to offer.

8.4 Revising

Not even the best writers expect a first draft to be perfect. Start revising your draft by reviewing your overall structure.

Revising Your Overall Structure

Check the Organization and Balance

Your essay should follow a consistent organization—either block or point-by-point—and should give a balanced comparison. Use color-coding to check your organization and balance.

REVISION STRATEGY

Color-Coding to Check Organization and Balance

Reread your essay. Use one color to highlight details concerning one of the items you are comparing. Highlight details about the other item in a second color. If you have many more highlights in one color than in the other, add more details on the subject about which you have written less.

Then, note whether your highlighting shows consistent organization. If you see both masses of a single color and places where colors alternate, reorganize your paper—either group together all details on a subject (block method) or alternate details concerning each topic (point-by-point method).

Student Work IN PROGRESS

Name: *Mindy Glasco*
Los Alamos Middle School
Los Alamos, NM

Checking Organization and Balance

When Mindy color-coded, she found a paragraph highlighted in only one color. She revised it to carry through her point-by-point organization consistently.

A good thing about our small town is that the crime rate is low. Most big cities have more than their share of violence. In the city in which my friend lives, it is dangerous to stay out past dark, but in this town it would probably be more dangerous for the criminals than for the kids. There are always people all around who know me and are willing to help.

Mindy realized that she had no details about big cities in this paragraph. For balance, and to maintain her point-by-point organization, she added the sentence shown.

Sharpen Your Theme

An effective comparison-and-contrast essay does not simply list similarities and differences. It has a clear theme—a main idea that unifies all of the details and grows stronger from paragraph to paragraph. For example, an essay comparing buses and subways might drive home the writer's opinion that subways are a more efficient way to travel.

As you revise, eliminate details that do not contribute to your theme, and add details that help strengthen your theme. Use the strategy of circling unfocused details.

Writers in ACTION

Like all professional writers, Bruce Brooks knows that revising is a key step in the writing process: "Revising is something that I regard, really, as a privilege. I think that revision should be regarded as the chance to fix mistakes before they really happen."

REVISION STRATEGY
Circling Unfocused Details

Copy the sentence that most effectively conveys your main theme onto an index card. Run the card down your draft as you read, one line at a time. Circle details that are not clearly related to your main focus. Consider deleting these details or rewriting them to support and develop your main idea. Also, consider adding new details to strengthen the connection of the paragraph to your focus.

Student Work IN PROGRESS

Name: Mindy Glasco
Los Alamos Middle School
Los Alamos, NM

Sharpening the Focus

Notice the changes Mindy made to sharpen the focus of this paragraph.

When I was nine, my three-year-old sister was attacked by a hungry coyote. She would have been dragged off if I hadn't been holding her hand. ~~An event like this would never happen in a big city. Big city people don't realize how predictable and safe their lives actually are.~~ A coyote is as tough as any mugger—maybe tougher.

Mindy's theme is that no place is perfect. The circled sentences shift focus to a criticism of people's perceptions. To emphasize her theme, Mindy replaced them with a new sentence.

Theme:

Towns are like friends: None of them is perfect, but if you concentrate on their good sides, you will be much happier in the end.

8.4

Revising Your Paragraphs

Check Paragraph Structure

Next, focus on each of the paragraphs in your essay. In a comparison-and-contrast essay, nearly every paragraph should contain these elements:

Topic sentence—a sentence that sums up the main idea

Restatement—an expanded version of the idea found in the topic sentence

Illustration—one or more specific facts, statistics, or descriptive details supporting the main idea.

Although all of your body paragraphs should contain these elements, they do not have to appear in the order listed above. Sometimes, you might want to lead with the sentence that provides an illustration, in order to hook your readers. This makes your pattern **ITR**. Or, you might again restate your topic as the final sentence, making your pattern **TRIR**.

REVISION STRATEGY
Marking Paragraph Patterns

Choose four paragraphs in your draft. Mark each sentence in these paragraphs with a *T*, an *R*, or an *I*. If you discover elements missing in any of the paragraphs, add these elements. In addition, if you notice that all four paragraphs follow the same pattern, consider revising one or more to vary the pattern.

Revising Your Sentences

Combine Sentences With Indefinite Pronouns

When comparing and contrasting two things, you may find yourself falling into a "singsong" rhythm, listing one similarity or difference after another. To eliminate this droning rhythm, combine sentences. You can combine some sentences using indefinite pronouns such as *any*, *both*, *each*, *either*, and *neither*.

REPETITIVE:	Subways are fast. Buses are also fast.
POSSIBLE IMPROVEMENTS:	Each of these types of transportation is fast. Neither one of them is slow.

Use the following strategy to eliminate a singsong rhythm.

REVISION STRATEGY
Coding Repetitive Sentences

Read your work aloud slowly and clearly. When you come across two or more sentences that make a singsong rhythm, circle them. Then, review the circled sentences and consider combining them by using indefinite pronouns.

Collaborative Writing Tip

Form a group, and read one another's work. One member should circle the subject of each sentence. Another member should underline all the verbs. Other members should take turns analyzing each sentence, checking for subject-verb agreement.

Grammar in Your Writing

Subject-Verb Agreement With Indefinite Pronouns

Indefinite pronouns refer to persons, places, and things. Some take only one form of a verb, singular or plural; a few can take either singular or plural, as shown below:

SINGULAR:	each	either	much	neither	
PLURAL:	both	few	many	others	several
SINGULAR OR PLURAL:	all	any	more	most	none

To determine which form of the verb to use with an indefinite pronoun that can be either singular or plural, consider whether its **antecedent** (the word it stands for) is singular or plural:

PLURAL: **None** of them [**buses and trains**] are fast.
SINGULAR: **None** of it [**the schedule**] makes sense.

Find It in Your Reading Find an indefinite pronoun used as a subject in a comparison-and-contrast essay you have read. Explain why it agrees with its verb.

Find It in Your Writing Circle each indefinite pronoun used as a subject in your draft. Check for subject-verb agreement, and correct any errors.

For more on subject-verb agreement, see Chapter 24.

Revising Your Word Choice

Avoid Unnecessary Repetition

Finally, check to see that you haven't overused any words.

REVISION STRATEGY
Highlighting Repeated Words

Draw rectangles around words you have used more than once. Evaluate whether the repetition is intentional and creates a desirable effect. If not, replace words you've repeated.

Peer Review

"Say Back"

After you have finished revising on your own, form a group with four classmates. Read your work aloud, pause briefly, and read it again. During the second reading, listeners should jot down (1) what they liked and (2) what they want to know more about. The listeners should then "say back" their comments to you. Use these comments to strengthen your essay.

8.5

Editing and Proofreading

Once you've finished revising, check your essay for errors in spelling, grammar, punctuation, and usage.

Focusing on Pronouns

When pronouns are separated from their antecedents, there may be problems in pronoun-antecedent agreement. Use the chart below to help you check agreement in your writing.

SINGULAR

PERSONAL	POSSESSIVE
I me	my, mine
you	your, yours
he, she, it him, her	his, hers, its

PLURAL

PERSONAL	POSSESSIVE
we us	our, ours
you	your, yours
they them	their, theirs

Grammar in Your Writing

Pronoun-Antecedent Agreement

A pronoun must agree with its antecedent in both person and number. **Person** indicates whether a pronoun refers to the person speaking (**first person**), the person spoken to (**second person**), or the person, place, or thing spoken about (**third person**). **Number** indicates whether a pronoun is singular (referring to one) or plural (referring to more than one).

INCORRECT: A *person* living in a small town should visit a big city. Seeing different lifestyles will broaden **your** perspective. [third person/second person]

INCORRECT: A *person* living in a small town should visit a big city. Seeing different lifestyles will broaden **their** perspective. [singular/plural]

CORRECT: A *person* living in a small town should visit a big city. Seeing different lifestyles will broaden **his or her** perspective. [third person singular/third person singular]

Find It in Your Reading Review a short story you have read. Find two pronouns, and identify the antecedents of each.

Find It in Your Writing Circle in blue three pronouns in your draft. Then, circle the antecedent of each in green. Revise any pronouns that do not agree with their antecedents.

For more on pronouns and their antecedents, see Chapter 24.

8.6 Publishing and Presenting

Building Your Portfolio

Consider the following ideas for sharing your work with a larger audience:

1. **Publish a Local Column** If you compared and contrasted subjects of local interest, such as two restaurants, submit your essay to a local newsletter or newspaper.
2. **Start a Family Tradition** If your essay contains family history, present it at the next family gathering. In the future, you can extend the essay, serving as the family historian.

Reflecting on Your Writing

Now that you have completed your essay, write a few notes about the experience of writing it. Begin by answering these questions:

- What did you enjoy most about writing your comparison-and-contrast essay? What did you like the least? Why?
- If you could begin again, what would you do differently? Explain your answers.

Internet Tip

To read comparison-and-contrast essays scored with this rubric, go on-line: PHSchool.com Enter Web Code: eck-8001

Rubric for Self-Assessment

Evaluate your comparison-and-contrast essay using the following criteria:

	Score 4	Score 3	Score 2	Score 1
Audience and Purpose	Clearly attracts audience interest in the comparison and contrast	Adequately attracts audience interest in the comparison and contrast	Provides a reason for the comparison and contrast	Does not provide a reason for a comparison and contrast
Organization	Clearly presents information in a consistent organization best suited to the topic	Presents information using an organization suited to the topic	Chooses an organization not suited to comparison and contrast	Shows a lack of organizational strategy
Elaboration	Elaborates ideas with facts, details, or examples; links all information to comparison and contrast	Elaborates most ideas with facts, details, or examples; links most information to comparison and contrast	Does not elaborate all ideas; does not link some details to comparison and contrast	Does not provide facts or examples to support a comparison and contrast
Use of Language	Demonstrates excellent sentence and vocabulary variety; includes very few mechanical errors	Demonstrates adequate sentence and vocabulary variety; includes few mechanical errors	Demonstrates repetitive use of sentence structure and vocabulary; includes many mechanical errors	Demonstrates poor use of language; generates confusion; includes many mechanical errors

Chapter 9

Exposition

Cause-and-Effect Essay

▲ **Critical Viewing** How might this batter use knowledge of cause-and-effect relationships to help him hit better? **[Hypothesize]**

Cause-and-Effect Explanations in Everyday Life

A baseball player with a powerful swing hits the ball in just the right spot, launching it over the left-field fence. A teacher announces that there will be a test the next day, leading students to spend their evening studying their textbooks. These stories capture **causes** and **effects**—specific actions and the events or situations that they produce.

Almost anything that happens—from simple daily events to those that affect people all over the world—involve causes and effects. For this reason, analyzing causes and effects helps us better understand our lives and our world.

What Is a Cause-and-Effect Essay?

Expository writing is writing that informs or explains. A **cause-and-effect essay** is a specific type of expository writing that explains the reasons something happened or its results. Effective cause-and-effect essays include

- a clear explanation of how one or more events or situations resulted in another event or situation.
- a thorough presentation of facts, statistics, and other details that support the explanation presented.
- a clear and consistent organization that makes it easy to follow the connections among events and details.

To learn the criteria on which your cause-and-effect essay may be assessed, see the Rubric for Self-Assessment on page 128.

Writers in ACTION

Dutch philosopher Benedict Spinoza (1632–1677) wrote:

"Nothing exists from whose nature some effect does not follow."

However big or small, he thought, everything in the world is linked to other things by causes and effects.

Types of Cause-and-Effect Essays

Following are some of the specific types of writing that explain causes and effects:

- **Historical essays** explain the impact of key events and developments in the past.
- **Scientific reports** explain the results of an experiment or analyze the causes and effects of a natural event.
- **News reports** explain the causes and effects of current events or developments.

PREVIEW Student Work IN PROGRESS

Emily Meade is a student at Ingersoll Middle School in Canton, Illinois. She chose to write about the causes and effects of the Dust Bowl. In this chapter, you will see her work in progress, including her use of featured activities and strategies to develop her topic while writing.

Prewriting

Choosing Your Topic

To begin, choose a topic by thinking of historical or current events, occurrences in nature, and other situations that might have interesting explanations. Use these strategies to help you:

Strategies for Generating a Topic

1. **Browsing** Browse through newspapers and magazines, focusing on headlines and story titles. Jot down headlines and story titles that catch your interest. Review your notes to find an interesting topic that involves causes and effects.
2. **Self-Interview** Ask yourself questions such as those in the example below. Write down your answers. Review your answers to identify those that involve causes and effects. Then, circle the most interesting one and choose it as your topic.

Try it out! Use the interactive Conducting a Self-Interview activity in **Section 9.2,** on-line or on CD-ROM.

Student Work IN PROGRESS

Name: Emily Meade
Ingersoll Middle School
Canton, IL

Conducting a Self-Interview

After looking at her self-interview, Emily decided she wanted to learn more about the causes of the plight of farmers during the Depression.

What is my favorite book?	"Of Mice and Men" by John Steinbeck
What natural or historical events are crucial to the story?	• the Depression • the migration of farmers to the West after their land was destroyed
What interesting facts have I learned in science class?	• Earth's core is made of molten lava. • Redwood trees can live from 500 to 700 years
What political leader do I admire most?	Franklin D. Roosevelt
What was happening in the world at the time of his or her term?	America was in the middle of its worst economic depression.
What invention am I most grateful for?	the Internet

TOPIC BANK

If you're having trouble finding a topic, consider the following possibilities:

1. **Cause-and-Effect Essay About a Historical Event** Think about events you have been studying in your social studies class. Which ones interest you the most? What caused these events? Write a cause-and-effect essay about an event that you find interesting.
2. **Cause-and-Effect Essay About the Weather** What causes snow? What produces hurricanes and tornadoes? Think about various weather conditions. Choose one that especially interests you. Then, write an essay in which you analyze its causes and effects.

Responding to Fine Art

3. Jot down a few notes on what this painting suggests about the effects of industry. Write an essay in which you explore some aspect of the topic of industry—the causes of its growth, for instance, or its economic or social effects on a geographic area.

Pittsburgh, 1927, Elsie Driggs, ©1996: Whitney Museum of American Art, NYC

Responding to Literature

4. In *Life on the Mississippi,* Mark Twain tells us about his experiences learning to become a riverboat pilot. Read an excerpt from *Life on the Mississippi.* Think about a time when you were an apprentice, learning how to do a particular job. What effects did your experience have on you? You can find an excerpt from Twain's work in *Prentice Hall Literature: Timeless Voices, Timeless Themes,* Silver.

Cooperative Writing Opportunity

5. **Success Manual** With a group, brainstorm a list of people in your community whom you would call "successful." Then, brainstorm a list of interview questions on success. Have each member interview your subjects, taking careful notes. Each member should then write an essay on the causes of success based on his or her interview. Assemble the interviews and essays into a "success manual."

9.2

Narrowing Your Topic

Even the most interesting topic can lead to an unsuccessful essay if it is too broad. For example, you couldn't effectively examine all of the causes of poverty in a brief essay. You could, however, explain the impact of a drought on the fortunes of people in a specific country. Use the following strategy to help you narrow your topic.

Use the "Classical Invention" Questions

"Classical Invention" is the name of a questioning strategy used to analyze and refine a topic. To use the strategy, answer the questions that appear below, substituting your topic for Emily's. Review your responses, and circle a series of related events that catch your interest. Come up with one statement that summarizes them, and use this as your narrowed topic.

Student Work IN PROGRESS

Name: Emily Meade
Ingersoll Middle School
Canton, IL

Using "Classical Invention" Questions

Emily answered the "Classical Invention" questions about her topic, circled ideas she intended to use, and summarized them to create a narrowed topic.

General Topic: Farmers During the Depression

- In what group or general category does your topic belong?
  agriculture; historical events
- How is your topic similar to or different from other topics in this category?
  agriculture: the farmers had really bad luck; not only was the economy bad, there was a series of huge storms lasting for years
  historical events: the Depression was totally unexpected; the Depression lasted a long time—almost ten years
- What causes are involved with this topic?
  stock market crash; drought
- What effects are involved in this topic?
  farmers migrated to the West; the government helped farmers; the Great Plains was nicknamed the Dust Bowl
- What came before this event?
  the 1920's, a time of prosperity
- What might come (or came) after this event?
  protection against dust storms

Narrowed Topic
The causes and effects of the Dust Bowl.

Considering Your Audience and Purpose

Appeal to Your Audience

As a writer, you need to think about your **audience**—the people who will read your writing. Unless you plan to send your essay to a specific audience (the school paper, for example), assume that your essay will be shared with your classmates. List two or three ideas for making your thoughts clear and interesting to them.

Define Your Purpose

Before drafting, consider your **purpose**—the goal of your writing. Ask yourself, "What do I want my readers to think or do when they finish reading my essay?" Jot down your answer to this question as a handy reminder while you write.

Gathering Details

Conduct Research

Unless you're already an expert on your topic, you will need to conduct research to gather the facts, examples, and other details you will need to thoroughly illustrate cause-and-effect relationships. Use the Internet or nonfiction sources, such as books and magazines from the library.

Using a K-W-L Chart A K-W-L chart is an excellent tool for planning and guiding your research. In one column, list what you already know about your topic. In a second column, list questions you would like to answer. Fill in a third column with what you learn as you conduct your research.

K-W-L CHART

What I Know	What I Want to Know	What I Learned
Air pollution is increasing.	How can it be reduced?	
Air pollution is dangerous.	What causes it besides cars & factories?	
Polluted air smells bad.	Which countries or cities are the worst?	
Cars & factories cause it.	How can we stop it?	
It hurts people and animals.	What does it do to people? To animals?	

Research Tip

Encyclopedias on CD-ROM make browsing and research especially easy. Many allow you to begin by identifying an area of interest, such as performing arts, science, hobbies, sports, or pets.

9.3 Drafting

Shaping Your Writing

Focus and Organize Your Ideas

Review your information, and circle the main causes and effects. Identify which description below best fits your topic. Then, organize your information accordingly. You may find it helpful to create an outline in which you list the main causes and effects with supporting details.

To learn more about making an outline, see Chapter 31.

Many Causes/Single Effect or Single Cause/Many Effects If your topic has several causes of a single event, develop a paragraph to discuss each cause. Weave its contribution to the overall effect into the paragraph. For one cause with several effects, devote a paragraph to each effect.

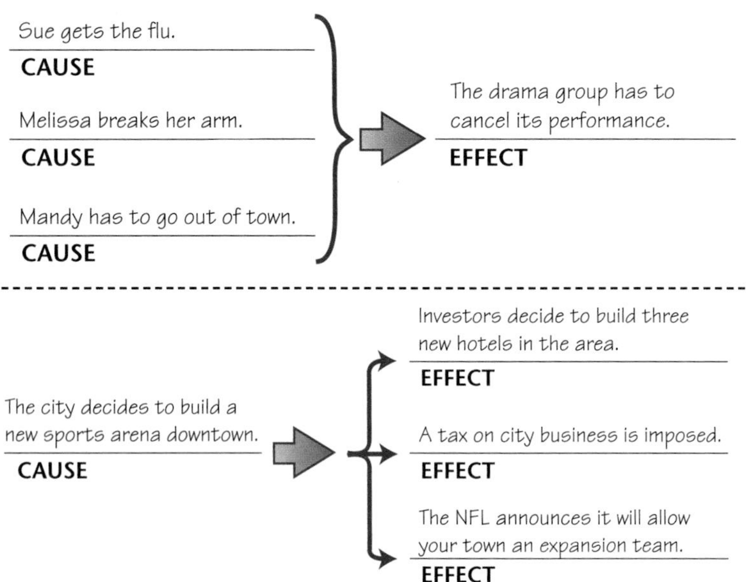

Chain of Causes and Effects If you are presenting a chain of causes and effects, present them in chronological order with transitions to show the connections.

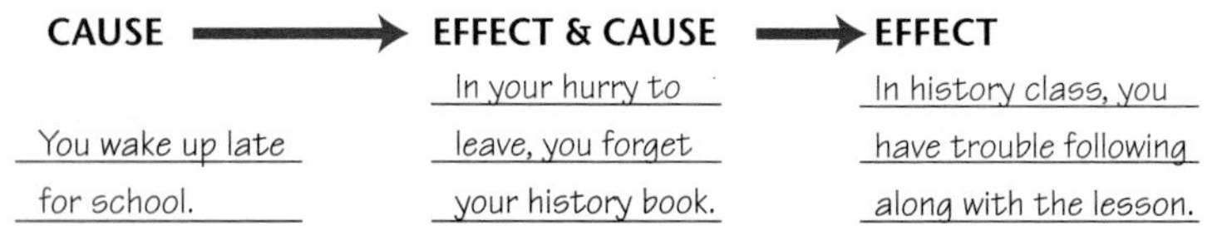

Providing Elaboration

Elaborate on Causal Connections

As you draft, add details that explain the connections between the causes and effects you are discussing. Ties between causes and effects include the following:

Natural Laws Some causes are linked to their effects by natural laws or principles.

EVENTS: Meteors burn up when they enter Earth's atmosphere.

LOGIC: The resistance of the atmosphere creates friction, which produces heat. *(Natural Law: Friction)*

Physical Processes Some cause-and-effect relationships take the form of a regular series of physical events.

EVENTS: Nitrogen-fixing bacteria help plants grow.

LOGIC: Plants need nitrogen to grow, but they can only use it in the form of nitrates. Bacteria produce the nitrates plants need. *(Process: Nitrogen Cycle)*

Motives and Habits Usually, the way people or groups of people behave is explained in terms of motives, habits, or social laws reflecting those motives and habits.

EVENTS: As skilled labor grew more scarce, wages went up.

LOGIC: Employers will pay more if they have trouble finding employees. *(Law: Supply and Demand)*

▲ Critical Viewing What natural phenomenon do you know of that might cause this effect? How might it cause this girl's hair to rise? **[Hypothesize]**

Student Work IN PROGRESS

Name: Emily Meade
Ingersoll Middle School
Canton, IL

Explaining the Logic

As she wrote her essay on the Dust Bowl, Emily explained the logic connecting two events: the destruction of grass and the looseness of the soil. She corrected errors in her draft later.

Plowing by farmers also killed much of the tall prairie grass that covered the Plains. Tall grass had an extremely complex root system, so it held the soil in place very well. With this natural protection gone, the soil was at further risk of being blown away.

By adding this sentence, Emily explains the natural process that links tall grass with the preservation of the soil.

9.4 Revising

Once you've finished your first draft, put your work aside for a day, if time allows. Then, review it carefully with a fresh eye.

Revising Your Overall Structure

Analyze Your Organization

Start your revision process by checking to see whether you have used a consistent organization that suits your topic. You might use the following strategy.

REVISION STRATEGY

Marking Main Causes and Effects

Follow these steps to check your organization.

1. Go through your entire draft, and circle each description of a main cause in one color and each description of a main effect in another. Write the letter *C* above causes and the letter *E* above effects.
2. Look at the order of the portions you have circled.
3. Make sure that all the effects appear *after* the correspon-ding cause(s). If not, you may need to reorganize sentences or paragraphs.
4. Check that you have used an order that fits the type of cause-and-effect relationship you're explaining. For help, review the discussion of the types of relationships on page 192.

▼ **Critical Viewing** Why does this picture make a good model for a sequence of causes and effects? **[Interpret]**

Revising Your Paragraphs

Use Topical Paragraphs

In a cause-and-effect essay, most of your body paragraphs should be topical paragraphs. **Topical paragraphs** develop a single main idea. Typically, a topical paragraph includes a sentence stating this main idea, called the **topic sentence.** The other sentences support or illustrate the topic sentence.

Review your draft to make sure each paragraph has a clear topic sentence. Check to see that each of the other sentences relates to the topic sentence. Eliminate or rewrite any that do not. Then, make sure you have illustrated the topic sentence with sufficient details, using the following strategy.

Learn More

For more on the different types of paragraphs, see Chapter 3.

REVISION STRATEGY
Adding Specific Illustrations

Use a highlighter to mark the topic sentence in each paragraph. Then, check off each sentence in the paragraph that illustrates the topic with facts, statistics, or descriptions to support each explanation. Review paragraphs with few or no checkmarks. Add appropriate illustrations.

Student Work IN PROGRESS

Name: Emily Meade
Ingersoll Middle School
Canton, IL

Adding Specific Illustrations

After coding her essay on the Dust Bowl, Emily realized that this paragraph needed more illustrations.

As a result, when high winds started to blow across the Plains, the dried-up topsoil did not stand a chance. It filled the air ~~as dust~~ in great, black choking clouds and covered farms, fields, and houses in huge drifts. The winds blew on and off for ten years. In 1935, one storm carried twice as much soil as was removed in digging the Panama Canal. Some claim that the wind came through so strongly that dust was blown all the way from Kansas to Albany, New York. In an average year, fifty storms would blow across the Plains, justifying the nickname of the Dust Bowl.

Emily added colorful descriptive language, an impressive fact, and a speculation to illustrate the topic of this paragraph—the effects of the winds on the topsoil of the region.

Revising Your Sentences

Clarify Time Relationships

After strengthening your paragraphs, be sure that you have used verb tenses correctly to indicate the time relationship among events.

REVISION STRATEGY

Circling Events to Analyze Order

Determine the time frame for the events in your paper—the past, the present, or the future. Then, review your paper, circling any events occurring before or after the group of events you're explaining. Also, circle continuing events or conditions, such as natural processes and general truths. Use the information on the next page to choose the correct verb tense to use in these cases.

Student Work IN PROGRESS

Name: Emily Meade
Ingersoll Middle School
Canton, IL

Clarifying Time of Events

Emily circled not only events that happened before other events she discussed but also continuing processes and general truths. She then checked and corrected the tenses that she used to describe these events and truths.

This condition came before and ended before a past event (the farmers plowing). It should be expressed in the past perfect "had covered."

Plowing by farmers also killed much of the tall prairie grass that ^had^ once covered the Plains. Tall grass ~~had~~ ^has^ an extremely complex root system, so it held the soil in place very well. With this natural protection gone, the soil was at further risk of being blown away.

The first part of this sentence expresses a general truth about grass, so Emily changed it to the present tense.

Grammar in Your Writing

Using Perfect Verb Tenses

Using correct verb tense is essential to showing the order of events in a cause-and-effect essay. **Verb tense** refers to changes in the form of a verb to show when the action the verb expresses occurred (or when the condition it expresses was the case).

The **perfect tenses** are used to indicate an action that occurs before another action. The perfect tenses are formed by adding the appropriate tense of *have* to the past participle of the verb:

Use the perfect tense in combination with other tenses to express the sequence of events, as shown below:

Perfect Tenses

Tense	Example	Past Participle +
Present perfect	"I have spoken."	Present form of *have*
Past perfect	"I had spoken."	Past form of *have*
Future perfect	"I will have spoken."	Future form of *have*

One Event Takes Place Before a Present Event = Present Perfect + Present
I **have spoken** to Sarah and Hunter about the meeting, and they **plan** to attend.

One Past Event Takes Place Before Another = Past Perfect + Past
I **had spoken** to Autumn and Greg about the meeting, but they **were** busy on Monday.

One Future Event Takes Place Before Another = Future Perfect + Present
I **will have spoken** to all the club members before they **arrive** to see what they **think** about our fund-raising ideas.

Find It in Your Reading Review an essay you have read recently. On a sheet of paper, list each verb that is used in a paragraph, and identify its tense.

Find It in Your Writing Review your draft, examining any verb in a different tense from the others. If the change in tense is not justified, make the tense consistent with the rest of your draft.

To learn more about verb tenses, see Chapter 22.

9.4

Revising Your Word Choice

Replace Vague Verbs

In addition to presenting time relationships correctly, the verbs you use in a cause-and-effect essay should capture events as precisely as possible. Use the following strategy to strengthen your use of verbs.

▲ Critical Viewing
Use vivid verbs to describe the event pictured here.
[Apply]

REVISION STRATEGY
Underlining Vague Verbs

Read through your draft again. Underline vague verbs—ones that do not create vivid pictures of actions in a reader's mind. Then, go back and replace each verb you've underlined with one that more vividly captures the action. Look at this example:

DRAFT SENTENCE: During the hurricane, the rain fell on houses throughout the village.

REVISED SENTENCE: During the hurricane, the rain **pelted** the houses throughout the village.

Peer Review

Your classmates can help you put the finishing touches on your essay by identifying problems you may have missed. You can get their help using the strategy of "Say Back."

"Say Back"

Read your essay to a group of classmates while they listen. Then, read your essay a second time. Pause for about one minute. During the pause, your classmates should begin making quick notes of things that stood out for them in your essay. Ask reviewers to respond to the following questions:

1. What were the main causes?
2. What were the main effects?
3. Where can I add details to more clearly illustrate causes or effects?

What your classmates tell you about your main causes and effects should match with what you intended to say. If they don't mention an important cause or effect that your essay discusses, consider adding more information about the cause or effect, or even reorganizing your draft to make the connections between events clear.

9.5 Editing and Proofreading

Proofread your essay for errors in spelling, punctuation, and grammar. Take an especially close look at your use of prepositions.

Focusing on Prepositions

Prepositions include words such as *after, before, in, on, of,* and *up*. Whenever possible, try to avoid ending sentences with a preposition. (If you find that revising a sentence to avoid having it end with a preposition makes it sound awkward, consult with your teacher.)

DRAFT SENTENCE: Which credit card are you paying **with**?
REVISED SENTENCE: **With** which credit card are you paying?

Grammar in Your Writing

Prepositions and Prepositional Phrases

A **preposition** is a word that relates the noun or pronoun following it to another word in a sentence. Prepositions indicate relations such as these:

SEQUENCE	LOCATION	DIRECTION	(OTHER)
after	in	around	about
before	near	down	for
during	under	up	of

A **prepositional phrase** consists of a preposition, its object, and any words modifying the object. The object of a preposition is the noun or pronoun following the preposition.

Example: (preposition) **under** the kitchen (object) **table**

(preposition) **against** the thick (object) **wall**

Find It in Your Reading Find three prepositional phrases in an essay you have read recently. For each, identify the object.

Find It in Your Writing Find five prepositional phrases in your essay. Add modifiers where needed to make the objects vivid and specific.

To learn more about prepositional phrases, see Chapter 20.

9.6

Publishing and Presenting

Building Your Portfolio

Consider the following suggestions for publishing and presenting your work:

1. **Post Your Work on the Internet** Search the Internet for Web sites related to your topic, and find out whether the site would be interested in posting your essay.
2. **Organize a Group Reading** Hold a group reading with your classmates in which you take turns reading your essays. Allow time for discussion.

Reflecting on Your Writing

Write a few notes on your experience writing a cause-and-effect essay. Begin by answering the following questions:

- What did you enjoy about analyzing the cause(s) and effect(s) of your topic? What did you learn?
- What was the biggest problem you encountered while writing your essay? How did you resolve it? What did you learn as a result?

Include a copy of these reflections, along with your cause-and-effect essay, in your portfolio.

Internet Tip

To see cause-and-effect essays scored with this rubric, go on-line:
PHSchool.com
Enter Web Code: eck-8001

Rubric for Self-Assessment

Evaluate your cause-and-effect essay using the following criteria:

	Score 4	Score 3	Score 2	Score 1
Audience and Purpose	Consistently targets an audience through word choice and details; clearly identifies purpose in introduction	Targets an audience through most word choice and details; identifies purpose in introduction	Misses a target audience by including a wide range of word choice and details; presents no clear purpose	Addresses no specific audience or purpose
Organization	Presents a clear, consistent organizational strategy to show cause and effect	Presents a clear organizational strategy with occasional inconsistencies to show cause and effect	Presents an inconsistent organizational strategy; creates illogical presentation of causes and effects	Demonstrates a lack of organizational strategy; creates a confusing presentation
Elaboration	Successfully links causes with effects; fully elaborates connections among ideas	Links causes with effects; elaborates connections among most ideas	Links some causes with some effects; elaborates connections among some ideas	Develops and elaborates no links between causes and effects
Use of Language	Chooses clear transitions to convey ideas; presents very few mechanical errors	Chooses transitions to convey ideas; presents few mechanical errors	Misses some opportunities for transitions to convey ideas; presents many mechanical errors	Demonstrates poor use of language; presents many mechanical errors

Connected Assignment

Documentary Video Script

Cause-and-effect explanations make the news every day in news reports and documentaries. These shows analyze how one event or situation leads to another. A **documentary video script** sets down the words that are spoken on a documentary. These words include recorded interviews. as well as narration. A video script also includes directions to the camera operators, sound and lighting engineers, and the editor who will put the video together.

Write a documentary video script. Use the suggestions that follow to guide you.

▲ **Critical Viewing** What narration and sounds might a documentary use with the footage this cameraman is gathering? **[Speculate]**

Prewriting Watch a television newsmagazine show to see how documentary segments are organized. Note how interviews, scenes of events or places, and the reporter's explanations are woven together.

Choose a Topic After taking notes on the structure of documentaries, choose an event or issue that interests you. For instance, you might choose a recent event in your community, such as the opening of a new store.

Gather Details Next, list cause-and-effect questions about your topic. Then, do research in a variety of sources to answer your questions. If possible, conduct interviews with experts, participants, and eyewitnesses. Tape the interviews, using a video recorder if one is available.

Drafting Before you begin writing, organize the facts you have gathered, using an organizer like the one shown. As you draft, follow your organizer. Present the narration of the documentary, including interviews and commentary, indicating in each case who is speaking. For each scene, give directions for camera movements and angles and for sound effects and music.

Title of Documentary: Opening of Hopper's General Store

SHOT 32		SHOT 33	
Visual: Reporter walking toward store; he pauses at door.		**Visual:** Mr. Hopper on ladder patching up walls in his store.	
Camera Angle/ Movement: Camera tracks reporter to door, then cut to Shot 33	→	**Camera Angle/ Movement:** Shot of Mr. Hopper from below.	→
Narration: But while the bank okayed Mr. Hopper's mortgage, . . .		**Narration:** . . . he still faced other obstacles.	
Other Sound: Theme music fades as narration begins.		**Other Sound:** Sound of Mr. Hopper's spackling knife on the walls.	

Revising and Editing Read your script aloud. Mark places where the order of ideas or images grows confused. Add transitions or rearrange elements to improve the flow.

Publishing and Presenting If you have access to video equipment, produce your segment and show it to the class.

Chapter 10

Exposition

How-to Essay

▲ Critical Viewing What do you think was the first step in getting this kite off the ground? Where might you find more information on the subject? **[Speculate]**

How-to Essays in Everyday Life

If you purchase a new computer or CD player, you probably use the how-to instructions in the manual to help you set up your new equipment. Similarly, you might look carefully at the washing instructions on the label of a new outfit you just bought.

How-to instructions are one of the most important types of writing that you encounter in your daily life. They help make it easier to use a wide range of items—from foods to power tools to recreational items such as kites and musical instruments. Learn how to write your own how-to, and share your knowledge with others.

What Is a How-to Essay?

Exposition is writing that informs or explains. A **how-to essay** is a short, focused piece of expository writing that explains how to do or make something. The writer breaks the process down into a series of logical steps and explains them in the order in which the reader should do them. The key features of an effective how-to essay include

- a focused topic that can be fully explained in the length of an essay.
- clear explanations of any terms or materials that may be unfamiliar to readers.
- a series of logical steps explained in chronological, or time, order.
- charts, illustrations, and diagrams as necessary to make complicated procedures understandable.

To learn the criteria on which your essay may be assessed, see the Rubric for Self-Assessment on page 144.

Writers in ACTION

As a television news correspondent, Gary Matsumoto uses expository writing techniques to research, write, and revise the stories that he presents on camera. His writing must be clear and to the point, so he must select only essential facts:

"The only way to make intelligent choices about what facts to include is to think and ask yourself questions. What is important? And why? You can't include every single fact."

Types of How-to Essays

Following are some of the types of how-to essays you might write:

- How to do something ("How to Fly a Kite")
- How to make something ("How to Make a Kite")
- How to improve a skill ("How to Steer and Maneuver a Kite")
- How to achieve a desired effect ("How to 'Paint the Sky' With Kites")

Katherine Ann Roshani Stewart, a student at Villa Duchesne School in St. Louis, Missouri, wrote an essay explaining how to groom a sheepdog. In this chapter, you will see the strategies she used to choose a topic, to gather details, to elaborate, and to revise her overall structure and word choice.

10.2 Prewriting

Choosing Your Topic

To write an effective how-to essay, you need to know your topic well. Choose a process or a type of product with which you are familiar. Make sure it is simple enough for readers to be able to learn how to do it from a brief essay. Following are some strategies you can use to help you settle on a topic:

Strategies for Generating a Topic

1. **Invisible Ink** Put carbon paper between two blank sheets of paper, and "write" on the blank top sheet with a pen that has run dry. Write freely about items you use and activities you enjoy. (As an alternative to using carbon paper, you can write on a computer with the monitor shut off.) Review what has been recorded on the carbon copy, and choose a topic from among the ideas you have jotted down.
2. **Listing** Make a list of people, places, things, and activities that you associate with your home or school. Circle words and draw lines to show connections between items on the lists. These links may suggest a topic.

Get instant help! Create your list using the Essay Builder, accessible from the menu bar, on-line or on CD-ROM.

Student Work IN PROGRESS

Name: *Katherine Ann Roshani Stewart*
Villa Duchesne School
St. Louis, MO

Listing to Discover a Topic

Katherine used listing to find her topic. As she studied her lists, she found links that brought to mind the process of grooming her dog, Biscuit.

Things	Activities	Places
my bicycle	chores	my bedroom
rollerblades	watching TV	the backyard
Biscuit's leash	practicing piano	kitchen
favorite chair	helping Mom with dinner	Biscuit's doghouse
CD collection	walking Biscuit	

Topic: grooming Biscuit

TOPIC BANK

If you're having trouble finding a topic, consider the following possibilities:

1. **How to Make Your Favorite Food** Mmmm . . . It might be brownies, or it might be scrambled eggs. Choose a favorite food, and explain how to prepare it.
2. **How to Make a Craft** You might have a knack for making jewelry, clothing, model cars, or paper airplanes. Or, you might have always wanted to learn how to make something. Choose a craft item, and write a how-to explaining how to make it.

Responding to Fine Art

3. The gentleman in this sculpture appears to be having difficulty—or a very successful game. Write a brief note giving your opinion. Then, think of a pastime in which you have improved. Write a how-to essay giving others tips on improving in the activity.

Strike, 1992, Red Grooms, Marlborough Gallery

Responding to Literature

4. Read "Baseball" by Lionel G. García. Use his explanation to write a how-to essay in which you explain the steps of playing his special version of baseball. You can find "Baseball" in *Prentice Hall Literature: Timeless Voices, Timeless Themes*, Silver.

Cooperative Writing Opportunity

5. **Holiday Celebration Manual** Get together with a group of classmates. Choose a holiday that all of you celebrate. Brainstorm for all the holiday activities. Then, categorize the activities under headings such as food preparation, decorating, and entertainment. Each person should choose a different category and develop a set of how-to instructions related to it. Work together to assemble your completed instructions into a comprehensive manual.

10.2

Narrowing Your Topic

Once you've chosen a topic, evaluate whether you can cover it thoroughly in an essay. Some topics require a great deal of steps or explanation. If this is the case, you will need to narrow your topic. For example, the topic "How to Play Baseball" is probably too broad for a short essay. However, in a short paper you could easily cover a more narrow topic, such as "How to Swing a Bat," "How to Play Shortstop," or "How to Improve Your Fielding."

Divide Your Topic Into Subtopics

To help you evaluate and narrow your topic, divide it into as many subtopics as you can identify. Then, review your list of subtopics. If each one looks as if it will take about a paragraph to explain, your topic is probably narrow enough. If there are several steps or processes within each subtopic, you will probably want to write about a single subtopic.

Considering Your Audience and Purpose

How-to essays have a clearly defined **purpose**—to explain the steps of a process or provide help in using a product. However, they can have many different **audiences**, or potential readers. Identify your audience and consider how it will affect your use of language and choice of details.

Complete an Audience Profile

To help you identify and address the needs of your audience, create an *audience profile*, a note card with information about your audience that you can refer back to as you write. Following are questions to consider in creating your audience profile:

- **Knowledge Level—How much does my audience know about the topic?** Do they need a little or a lot of information? What terms will I need to define?
- **Age—What is the age of my audience?** If you are writing for younger children, use simple vocabulary. If you are writing for adult readers, use more sophisticated terms.
- **Skill Set—What skills do my readers have?** Does my audience understand the basic skills required for the process I am explaining? Should I review those skills as well as cover the specific steps of the procedure?

Get instant help! Create your Audience Profile using the Essay Builder, accessible from the menu bar, on-line or on CD-ROM.

Gathering Details

Use Research

To write an effective how-to essay, you need to be an expert on your topic. If you are not already extremely knowledgeable about your topic, conduct research in the library or on the Internet to make yourself an expert. Follow this strategy:

Creating a K-W-L Chart Use a three-column K-W-L (*K*now–*W*ant to Know–*L*earned) Chart to assess your knowledge of your topic and to guide your research. Fill in the first column with what you know about your topic. List what you want to learn in the second column. Use the information in the second column to guide your research, and fill in the third column with what you learn.

Gather Visual Aids

Remember that your readers may never have attempted the process you are explaining. For this reason, you may want to create or gather visual aids such as the following to help your readers picture the process you're describing:

- photos or illustrations with explanatory captions
- diagrams, charts, or maps.

Research Tip

If you are writing a how-to on cooking or home improvement, watch a television program on the subject for ideas about how to present information.

▲ **Critical Viewing** What more might each of these boys need to know about baseball? What kind of visual aid could help them? **[Apply]**

10.3 Drafting

Shaping Your Writing

Before you begin writing, organize your details. Because most how-to essays describe a process that takes place over time, chronological order is often the most effective organization.

Organize Details in Chronological Order

To help you organize your details in chronological order, you may want to write each detail on a sticky note or note card.

Using Sticky Notes to Organize Details Write each step on an individual sticky note. Arrange the steps in order, and then add or rearrange steps as needed.

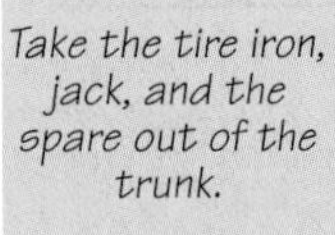

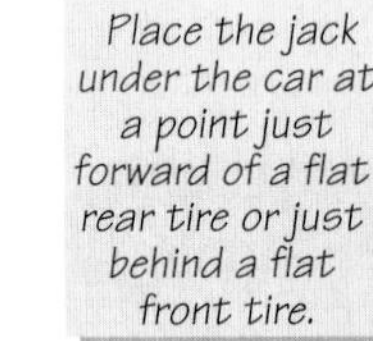

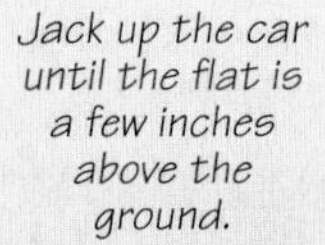

Remove the lug nuts.

Choose the Best Format

In how-to essays, paragraphs are not always the best way to present information. Different readers will have different needs at different times:

- A reader who is considering doing the activity outlined in your how-to essay will want a quick overview of materials and steps.
- A reader who is in the middle of performing your instructions will need to locate a step quickly.
- A reader who is looking for special tips or background information will want additional information.

To meet the needs of each of these readers, consider the following formatting possibilities as you draft:

- Present essential steps as a series of numbered points or in a bulleted list.
- Provide additional information in separate sections, such as boxes inset alongside your main instructions.

Providing Elaboration

As your writing takes shape, you may find that your explanations need more details before your readers will understand exactly what is required. Use the following strategies to make your instructions clear.

Use Graphic Devices

Graphics—photos, diagrams, and drawings—are a great way to help readers follow an explanation. Create or obtain graphics to reinforce your instructions, and place them at the appropriate points in your essay. Follow these guidelines:

- Each graphic must be clear and complete.
- Each graphic must clearly illustrate a step in your essay.
- Each graphic should be accompanied by a label clearly describing it and linking it to your essay.

Add Details by "Exploding the Moment"

Pause after you write each paragraph. Circle any important detail about which readers will need to know: *what kind, how much, how long,* or *to what degree.* Answer these questions on sticky notes and attach them to your draft. Consider adding these details to give readers precise explanations.

Try it out! Use the Exploding the Moment activity in **Section 10.3,** on-line or on CD-ROM.

Student Work IN PROGRESS

Name: Katherine Ann Roshani Stewart
Villa Duchesne School
St. Louis, MO

"Exploding the Moment"

Katherine added details answering the question "what kind?" to make her essay more useful.

Assemble the proper materials to give the dog a bath. When you are buying shampoo, get the (right shampoo) for your dog and the (right brushes.) The towels I gather are thick so they will soak up water quickly.

different types for dogs with long hair and for dogs with short hair

brushes with metal bristles get the tougher tangles

10.4 Revising

Revising Your Overall Structure

After completing a first draft, review your work to find ways to improve it. Begin by looking at the structure of your how-to essay.

Distinguish Main Steps From Substeps

One of the most important parts of a clear how-to is a streamlined set of instructions. Consider how to best organize the steps and substeps in your process, using the following strategy:

REVISION STRATEGY
Highlighting Main Steps and Substeps

Use one color highlighter to mark the main, or most important, steps. Use another color highlighter to mark the substeps within each main step. Review your highlighting and decide whether you should set off any of the substeps in numbered or bulleted lists.

Student Work IN PROGRESS

Name: Katherine Ann Roshani Stewart
Villa Duchesne School
St. Louis, MO

Highlighting Main Steps and Substeps

Katherine highlighted main steps and substeps in her essay in different colors. Then, she made decisions about how to present them in her final draft.

When you groom your dog, the steps include bathing, brushing, and clipping its nails. You will need: shampoo, conditioner, one brush with long metal teeth and one brush with short bristles, towels, a nail clipper, and a restraint.

main step 1

substep 1A
I will make this part of the main step into a bulleted list to help readers.

Before you start, assemble the proper materials to give the dog a bath and brushing. When you are buying shampoo, get the right shampoo for your dog's type of fur. For instance, for a long-haired dog like Biscuit, I buy shampoo for dogs with long hair.

main step 2
I will move this part of the main step before the list of materials.

substep 2A
This substep will just get in the way of the main steps. I will move it to a sidebar box.

◀ Critical Viewing Give some advice to this goalie in three sentences. Use transition words in two of them. **[Apply]**

Revising Your Paragraphs

Identify Paragraph Purpose

Once you're comfortable with the general structure of your paper, carefully focus on each individual paragraph. The purpose of each paragraph will determine which words or phrases you may need to add in order to make your meaning clearer.

REVISION STRATEGY
Using Steps, Stacks, Chains, and Balances

As you analyze each paragraph, decide which of the following descriptions most closely fits its purpose:

- **Steps** If the paragraph explains a step or several related steps for which time order is important, the sequence should be indicated. Use words such as *first, next,* and *finally.*
- **Stacks** If the paragraph explains how one part of a process adds to or contributes to another, point out the connection with words such as *and, furthermore,* and *for instance.*
- **Chains** If the paragraph shows the cause-and-effect relationship between steps, use words such as *so, because,* and *consequently.*
- **Balances** If the paragraph shows choice or contrast, use words or phrases such as *but, however, on the other hand,* and *rather.*

Collaborative Writing Tip

Exchange drafts with a peer. Mark places where the transition from one step to another seems abrupt. Consider your peer's marks when looking for places to add transitions.

10.4

Revising Your Sentences

Vary Sentence Beginnings

After you've revised your paragraphs, look carefully at your sentences. Make sure that you've used a variety of sentence beginnings so your writing flows smoothly.

REVISION STRATEGY
Underlining Sentence Beginnings

Follow these steps to help make sure your sentence beginnings are varied:

1. Choose three paragraphs in your draft. Underline the first few words of each sentence in them.
2. Review underlined words and determine whether most of your sentences begin with the subject of the sentence.
3. If so, look for ways to rewrite or combine sentences to begin with a different word.
4. Also, notice whether you've used transitions at the beginnings of sentences. If not, you may want to use words such as *next, then,* or *now* to help readers follow the progression of steps.

Grammar and Style Tip

One way to vary sentences and clearly show the connections between steps in a process is to use complex sentences. For help combining sentences into complex sentences, see Chapter 21.

Grammar in Your Writing

Adverb Clauses and Adverb Phrases

In many places in your essay, you will want to use words and groups of words that give more information about a step. Adverb phrases and clauses add details that point out *where, why, when, in what manner,* or *to what extent* something is being done.

Where? With the dog facing you, brush its chest.

Why? The towels are thick so they will soak up water quickly.

When? After the shampoo is lathered up, begin rinsing.

In what manner? Dispense the shampoo and lather, rubbing vigorously.

To what extent? Except for its head, immerse the dog completely in water.

Find It in Your Reading Find two adverb phrases or clauses in a how-to essay you have read. Explain what information each one adds.

Find It in Your Writing Find three adverb clauses or phrases that you have used in your how-to essay. If you can't find three of each, consider combining sentences by changing one sentence to an adverb phrase or adverb clause and adding it to another.

To learn more about adverb clauses and adverb phrases, see Chapter 20.

Revising Your Word Choice

Evaluate Repeated Words

For a mature, sophisticated style, varying your word choice is as important as varying your sentence beginnings. Go back through your essay and look for overused words. One way to evaluate whether you have overused any words is to circle those that are repeated.

REVISION STRATEGY
Circling Repeated Words

Go through your essay and circle any nouns, verbs, or adjectives that you have used more than once. After circling repeated words, evaluate each use to determine whether you should replace the word with a synonym or even rephrase the sentence.

Writers in ACTION

Gary Matsumoto values peer review. "It helps to have someone else look at your [writing] because it's another pair of eyes; it's another set of sensibilities. And they can see something that perhaps you didn't see or think of something that you didn't think of. And they can make a contribution. So, never be defensive when someone criticizes [your writing] or makes suggestions, because very often that person can make it better."

Student Work IN PROGRESS

Name: Katherine Ann Roshani Stewart
Villa Duchesne School
St. Louis, MO

Circling Repeated Words

In these steps, Katherine found she had repeated a few words—dog, dry, fur, and towel. She decided that only her repetition of dry was intrusive, and made the changes shown.

1. Little by little, working from the tail up, (dry) each part of your (dog) by squeezing [the water from] the (fur) ~~(dry)~~ with (towels).

2. When the (dog) is [barely damp] ~~mostly (dry)~~, have it sit on a [fresh] ~~(dry)~~ (towel) till its (fur) completely (dries).

Peer Review

Feedback is a useful tool when revising a how-to essay. The purpose of a how-to essay is to explain something to another person. Peer reviewers will be able to help assess how clear your explanation is and whether additional information is needed.

Ask a Group to Try It Out

Read your essay aloud to a small group. Then, read it aloud again, guiding the group through the process you are explaining. The group should go through the motions of each step, taking notes on where they are confused or unsure. After you have finished the second reading, ask reviewers to respond to the following questions:

- Which step or steps could have been explained more clearly?
- What was confusing about those steps?
- In which sections was more or less information needed?
- What other questions or comments do you have?

Use your peers' responses to guide your final revision.

▶ **Critical Viewing** How might you feel if, like this girl, you had to read your draft to a group of peers? **[Relate]**

10.5 Editing and Proofreading

Errors in spelling, punctuation, grammar, or usage can create confusion. Proofread your how-to essay to discover and eliminate errors that might mislead a reader.

Be especially attentive to your use of commas and semicolons. The correct use of these punctuation marks can make your how-to easier to understand. Incorrect use of these marks, though, can lead to confusion—even to your reader's failure to perform your how-to correctly!

Focusing on Commas and Semicolons

Commas and semicolons help you separate steps in a series or materials in a list. By separating descriptions or names of items, commas and semicolons help readers distinguish one description from the next. As you proofread, use the examples below to guide you.

Grammar in Your Writing

Using Commas and Semicolons to Separate Items in a Series

When three or more similar items are listed in a series, punctuation is needed to separate them. Generally, you will use commas to separate words, phrases, or clauses that you list in a series. However, in order to avoid confusion, semicolons are used when some items already contain commas.

The steps of dog grooming include **shampooing**, **rinsing**, and **using conditioner**; **drying**; **brushing**; and **nail clipping**.

Find It in Your Reading Read a how-to essay or set of instructions and find an example of a series of three or more items. Explain how the author punctuates it to aid the reader's understanding.

Find It in Your Writing Look for series of three or more items in your essay. Make sure you have punctuated them correctly with commas or with semicolons, if the items already contain commas.

For more on commas and semicolons, see Chapter 26.

10.6 Publishing and Presenting

Building Your Portfolio

Consider these ideas for sharing your how-to essay:

1. **Give a Demonstration** How-to explanations lend themselves to oral presentation. Demonstrate the steps of your explanation as you present it to the class. Incorporate diagrams you have created listing or illustrating steps.
2. **Make a Video** Tape your how-to explanation with a video camera. Plan out shots. While taping, have a classmate read your essay while you demonstrate the steps that are being explained. Change camera position as necessary to capture the visual details of each step. Show your video to the class.

Reflecting on Your Writing

After you've finished writing, jot down a few notes on your experience. Use these questions to guide you:

- Having written a how-to essay, will you find it easier to follow instructions in the future? Explain.
- As a result of writing a how-to essay, what more did you learn about the activity or skill about which you wrote?

To see how-to essays scored with this rubric, go on-line: PHSchool.com
Enter Web Code: eck-8001

Rubric for Self-Assessment

Use the following criteria to assess your how-to essay:

	Score 4	Score 3	Score 2	Score 1
Audience and Purpose	Clearly focuses on procedures leading to a well-defined end	Focuses on procedures leading to a well-defined end	Includes procedures related to an end, but presents some vaguely	Includes only vague descriptions of procedures and results
Organization	Gives instructions in logical order; subdivides complex actions into steps	Gives instructions in logical order; subdivides some complex actions into steps	For the most part, gives instructions in logical order	Gives instructions in a scattered, disorganized manner
Elaboration	Provides appropriate amount of detail; gives needed explanations	Provides appropriate amount of detail; gives some explanations	Provides some detail; gives few explanations	Provides few details; gives few or no explanations
Use of Language	Shows overall clarity and fluency; uses transitions effectively; contains few mechanical errors	Shows some sentence variety; uses some transitions; includes few mechanical errors	Uses awkward or overly simple sentence structures; contains many mechanical errors	Contains incomplete thoughts and confusing mechanical errors

Connected Assignment Problem-and-Solution Essay

For just about any problem in the world—a park filled with litter, a school schedule that could be more productive, a war that must be ended—people have proposed a solution. These proposals may take the form of a problem-and-solution essay. A **problem-and-solution essay** describes a problem and offers one or more solutions to it. Like a how-to essay, a problem-and-solution essay sets out the steps for achieving an end. An effective problem-and-solution essay

- clearly explains the problem and the proposed solutions.
- defends the solutions using facts and examples.

Prewriting To find a topic, list people, groups, places, and issues that are important to you. For each, list an associated problem. Choose a topic from your list.

Next, do research into the problem and possible solutions. Gather facts, expert opinions, and other evidence to support your solutions. Note the connections between the problem and its solutions in a cause-and-effect diagram like the one shown.

Problem: Homelessness

Causes of Problem →	Solution →	Effect on Problem
not enough affordable housing • little profit for builders; no new housing being built	City should give tax break to builders of affordable housing.	Tax break will encourage builders to build new affordable housing.

Drafting After gathering facts, write an introduction in which you clearly state the problem you will address. Include an overview of the solutions you will propose. In the body of your essay, lay out the background information your readers need to understand the problem. Then, explain your solutions. For each, show specifically how it will solve the problem. Support each with facts, expert opinions, and other evidence.

Revising and Editing Once you have finished your first draft, review it. Focus on these two types of revision:

- Test each solution by considering possible objections. Consider answering these objections.
- Check the support you provide for each main point. If you have not spelled out the reasons for a claim, add sentences to support it.

Finally, proofread your essay to eliminate grammatical and mechanical errors.

Publishing and Presenting Consider sending a version of your essay as a letter to the editor of a local newspaper.

▼ **Critical Viewing** What problem might these teenagers be helping to solve? **[Hypothesize]**

Chapter 11

Research

Research Report

▲ **Critical Viewing** Cite two questions for research suggested by this Civil War photo. **[Question]**

Research in Everyday Life

Where does your world end? It doesn't stop with your nose. It doesn't even stop with the walls of your room. Your world stretches on and on into places you can't even see. Every fact that you know, from the fact that China lies on the other side of the world to the fact that tomorrow is your aunt's birthday, expands the limits of your world.

To stretch your world even further, all you need is to learn new facts. You might ask a relative for facts about your early childhood, or an elderly neighbor for facts about your street. Asking questions like these is a form of **research**. The answers help define your world. When you do research on general topics for a report, you stretch your world even further. Improve your research writing skills, and broaden your horizons.

What Is a Research Report?

A **research report** presents information gathered from reference books, observations, interviews, or other sources. By citing these sources, a research writer lets others check the facts for themselves. A good research report also helps readers form an overall picture of the subject. The elements of an effective research report include

- an overall focus or main idea expressed in a thesis statement.
- information gathered from a variety of sources.
- clear organization and smooth transitions.
- facts and details to support each main point.
- accurate, complete citations identifying sources.

To preview the criteria on which your report may be evaluated, see the Rubric for Self-Assessment on page 161.

Writers in ACTION

Virginia Hamilton grew up in Ohio, where her grandfather settled after escaping slavery. In her novels and nonfiction, she relies on research:

"I use primary sources, which are actual events that are written down by the participants. . . . I work on something that I'm reporting until the very last minute, until they literally yank it out of my hands, because I want to get everything right. So I look at the facts over and over again."

Types of Research Reports

In addition to a traditional research report, the following are some other types of reports you might write.

- **Biographical sketches**, which report high points in the life of a notable person.
- **Reports of scientific experiments**, which present the materials, procedures, and results of experiments.
- **Documented essays**, which use research to support a point or examine a trend.

PREVIEW Student Work IN PROGRESS

Joseph Hochberger, a student at Gotha Middle School in Windermere, Florida, wrote a research report about Benjamin Franklin. In this chapter, you will see how Joseph used featured strategies to choose a topic, to gather information, to elaborate, and to analyze patterns between and within paragraphs.

11.2 Prewriting

Choosing Your Topic

Use the following strategies to choose a research topic that interests you and on which enough information is available:

Strategies for Generating a Topic

1. **Browsing** Scan reference books at the library: a volume from an encyclopedia set, a biographical dictionary, an almanac, an atlas, and so on. You might also surf on the Internet. Jot down each interesting subject that you find. Review your notes, and choose your topic.
2. **Newswatch** Flip through recent magazines or newspapers. Tune in to television or radio broadcasts. List people, places, events, or current issues that you want to investigate. Choose one of these issues as a topic for research.
3. **Self-Interview** Create a chart like the one below, and answer the questions shown. Circle words and draw lines to show connections between items on your list. Choose a topic from among these linked items.

Try it out! Use the interactive Conducting a Self-Interview activity in **Section 11.2,** on-line or on CD-ROM.

Student Work IN PROGRESS

Name: Joseph Hochberger
Gotha Middle School
Windermere, FL

Conducting a Self-Interview

Joseph used a self-interview to identify people, places, and things in which he was interested. He remembered that his science teacher, Mr. Sanchez, had mentioned Benjamin Franklin's experiments with electricity.

People	Places	Things	Events
What interesting people do I know or know about?	What interesting places have I been to or heard about?	What interesting things do I know about?	What interesting events have happened to me or have I heard about?
Jan (Ben Franklin) Michael Jordan Melissa	hospital hockey rink ~~library~~ (Philadelphia) zoo	baseball compact disk hat newspaper (kite)	hockey game homecoming crafts fair (July Fourth parade)

TOPIC BANK

If you're having trouble finding a topic, consider the following possibilities:

1. **Biographical Report** Choose someone who had a major impact on a specific period in American history—for example, the American Revolution, World War II, or the civil rights movement of the 1960's. Write a biographical report explaining his or her decision to become involved in important affairs.
2. **Research Report on a Planet** Choose a planet in our solar system. Research its atmosphere, composition, orbit, and so on. Have any probes landed there? What information have they gathered? Write a report of your findings, and include photographs if possible.

Responding to Fine Art

3. Jot down a few notes about this painting. Review your notes for suggestions about research topics on American life during the nineteenth century. Choose one of these topics for your research paper.

Miners in the Sierras, Charles Christian Nahl, National Museum of American Art, Washington, DC

Responding to Literature

4. Read "The Drummer Boy of Shiloh," a short story by Ray Bradbury. List topics related to the Civil War suggested by the story, such as soldiers' daily lives. Choose one of these topics for your report. You can find "The Drummer Boy of Shiloh" in *Prentice Hall Literature: Timeless Voices, Timeless Themes,* Silver.

Cooperative Writing Opportunity

5. **Teenagers of the Past** With a small group, investigate the life of teenagers in nineteenth-century America. Divide the following tasks: researching life on the frontier using primary sources, such as letters and journals; researching life in the big cities; and creating charts, drawings, and other graphics to illustrate the report. Compile your research in a report and present it to the class.

Narrowing Your Topic

Once you have chosen a topic, you may still need to modify it. Make sure that your topic is narrow enough to cover fully in a short report. One strategy for narrowing a topic is a questioning strategy called "Classical Invention."

Use "Classical Invention" Questions

To help you narrow your topic, answer questions about your topic like the ones shown in the feature below. Simply replace "Benjamin Franklin" with a phrase summarizing your own topic.

Review your answers to the Classical Invention questions. Circle interesting details, and look for links among them. Then, summarize the narrowed topic to which these linked details belong. Use this topic as the focus of your research paper.

Try it out! Use the interactive Classical Invention activity in **Section 11.2,** on-line or on CD-ROM.

Student Work IN PROGRESS

Name: Joseph Hochberger
Gotha Middle School
Windermere, Fl

Using "Classical Invention" to Group Details

Joseph used Classical Invention to narrow his topic: the life of Benjamin Franklin.

General Topic: Benjamin Franklin

- In what general category does your topic belong?
  Inventor, Founding Father
- How is your topic similar to or different from other topics in this category?
  People still know Franklin's sayings, unlike words of other Founding Fathers; Jefferson was also an inventor.
- Into what other topics can your topic be divided?
  Franklin's role in American politics; Franklin's writings; Franklin's inventions
- What causes and effects does your topic involve?
  Franklin helped invent the postal system; Franklin persuaded others to approve the Constitution.

Franklin's contribution to American politics.

Franklin's contribution to American literature.

Narrowed Topic
The variety of Franklin's accomplishments.

Franklin's contribution to science.

Narrowed Topic: Franklin's Contribution to Science

Considering Your Audience and Purpose

The **purpose** of any research report is to present facts on the topic clearly. A report may be written, though, for different groups of readers, or **audiences.** Your audience's background and interest in your topic will determine how much you say about each detail.

For instance, you would explain the most basic facts about pollution to a group of young children. For readers of the local newspaper, you might focus just on the aspects of the topic affecting them directly, such as the results of a recent water test in the area. For a science class, though, you would want to explain the complexities of pollution in detail.

Gathering Details

Use a Variety of Sources

By using several different sources, you can ensure that your information is current, accurate, and balanced. Follow these guidelines for improving accuracy:

- Check to see when printed sources were published to make sure that the information in them is up-to-date.
- If you note discrepancies in the information given by two sources, check the facts in a third source. If three or more sources disagree, mention the disagreement in your paper.
- Whenever possible, cross-check information from the Internet or from an interview by consulting other sources.

Research Tip

For more sources on your topic, check the bibliographies of reference books you use.

Take Notes

Use Note Cards When you find information related to your topic, take detailed notes on index cards.

- Write one note on each card.
- Double-check the spelling of names and technical terms.
- Use quotation marks whenever you copy words exactly.
- On each card, record the title of the book or article and the page number, or the name of the Web site or interviewee.
- Create a source card for each book, article, Web site, or interviewee. For print sources, list the author, title, publisher, and place and date of publication. For Internet sources, list the sponsor, page name, date of last revision, the date you visited it, and the address. For an interview, give the date and the person's name, address, and phone number.

Use Technology You can also make photocopies of source material or print out pages from the Internet. Highlight the information you will use on your copy.

11.3 Drafting

▲ **Critical Viewing** Cite a fact you know about Franklin D. Roosevelt. Then, write a thesis statement for a report that might include this fact. **[Apply]**

Shaping Your Writing

After you have gathered your information, decide how to organize and present it. Drafting your report is the process of bringing your details together and making sense of them.

Choose a Perspective

Review your notes, and choose a perspective for your report. A **perspective** is a point of view on your subject—the "spin" or "take" you offer on your subject. For example, one biographical report might use facts from a person's life to illustrate one or two personal characteristics such as cleverness or bravery. Another report might use those same facts to explain the significance of the person's contribution to a field.

Develop a Thesis Statement

Once you know your perspective, sum up the point of your paper in a sentence, called a **thesis statement**. For example, in a report on Franklin D. Roosevelt, your thesis statement might read: "In fighting for the New Deal, Roosevelt showed the same characteristic he showed in fighting his disability—determination." Include your thesis statement in the introduction to your report.

Make an Outline

Using a Formal Outline For your outline, use Roman numerals (I, II, III) for your most important points. Under each Roman numeral, use capital letters (A, B, C) for the details that support each main point.

Title of Your Report

I. Introduction

II. First main point
   A. Supporting detail #1
   B. Supporting detail #2
   C. Supporting detail #3

III. Second main point . . .

Providing Elaboration

Be Your Own Reader

After you write each paragraph, pause. Pretend you are a typical reader from your selected audience. What statements or details might confuse or surprise such a reader? Add clarifying details, such as definitions and explanations, where needed to help your reader. (For help defining your audience, see page 151.)

Bring Out Your Perspective

If you have done a good job researching your topic, you will have gathered more details than you can use. As you draft, make sure that you include the details that are most relevant to your perspective. Consider the following example:

TOPIC:	California Gold Rush
PERSPECTIVE:	The lives led by miners were often harsh.
APPROPRIATE DETAIL:	facts about miners' housing
UNNECESSARY DETAIL:	facts about routes to California

After you write a paragraph, pause and review the details you have included. Eliminate or revise those that do not contribute to your perspective. Build on those that do.

Student Work IN PROGRESS

Name: Joseph Hochberger
Gotha Middle School
Windermere, FL

Sharpening Perspective

Joseph's perspective in his report on Franklin was that Franklin's talents were diverse. He changed this paragraph to bring out that perspective more. He also added explanations to help readers with little background in his subject.

Writer, community planner, and inventor—but Ben didn't stop there. He became drawn into politics as well. His ~~Franklin's~~ involvement in public service began with his appointments as clerk of the Pennsylvania Legislature in 1736 and as postmaster of Philadelphia in 1737. He served in both these positions for over fifteen years. In 1753, he became Deputy Postmaster General, in charge of all mail for the northern colonies.

Joseph added the first sentence here to tie this paragraph to his perspective.

By adding this phrase, Joseph clarifies the significance of Franklin's new job.

11.4 Revising

Revising Your Overall Structure

Analyze Organization

After you have completed a first draft, analyze the organization of your report to make sure it works well.

REVISION STRATEGY
Matching Your Draft to Your Outline

Mark each paragraph with a Roman numeral and a capital letter showing where the paragraph fits on your outline. For example, if topic I.A. on your outline concerns opinion surveys, mark any paragraph discussing them "I.A." When you have finished labeling each paragraph, review your labels.

- Are all of the paragraphs tagged with the same Roman numeral placed next to each other in the draft?
- Are all of the paragraphs with the same Roman numeral–capital letter combination next to each other?
- Does the sequence of Roman numerals and capital letters in the report match your outline? If not, is the change an improvement? Why or why not?

Consider reordering paragraphs so that those with the same label are next to each other, and so that the order of paragraphs matches your outline.

▼ Critical Viewing
What perspective on the Gold Rush does this poster present?
[Interpret]

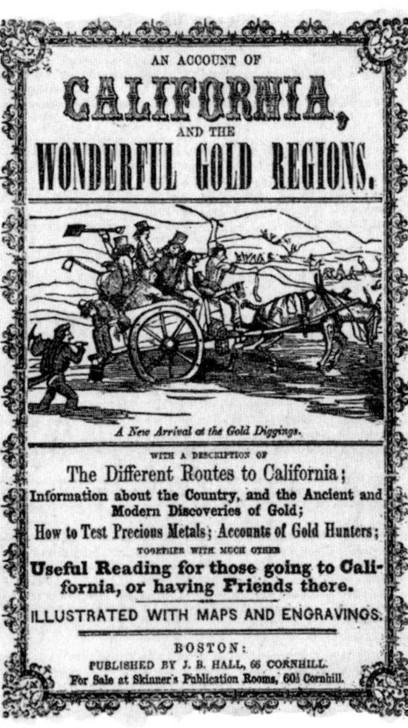

Analyze Perspective

Next, check your draft to make sure it effectively presents your perspective. Use the following strategy:

REVISION STRATEGY
Coding Details for Perspective

To check your perspective, follow these steps:

1. On an index card, write a sentence or phrase summarizing the perspective of your report.
2. Run the card down your draft, holding it under each line in turn.
3. When you find a detail related to your overall perspective, draw a rectangle around it. Circle details that are unrelated to your perspective and that do not provide needed background information.

Review your draft. Consider eliminating circled details. If you find a paragraph without any details connected to your perspective, consider revising it.

Revising Your Paragraphs

Develop Paragraph Blocks

Sometimes you will need more than one paragraph to discuss one of the main points in your report. You may need to create a series, or "block," of paragraphs.

A **paragraph block** is a group of paragraphs concerning a single topic. The topic sentence of the first paragraph gives the topic of the entire block. Subsequent paragraphs are linked back to the first paragraph with transitional phrases and clauses, such as "The problem grew worse when . . . ".

Learn More

To learn more about paragraph blocks, see Chapter 3.

REVISION STRATEGY
Coding Paragraph Blocks

Review your draft. When you find two or more paragraphs in a row discussing different aspects of the same topic, mark them with brackets: [ ]. Then, review the first sentence of each paragraph in the block. Circle first sentences that simply state a new fact without connecting it back to the previous paragraph. Then, to every paragraph with a circled first sentence, add a transition sentence showing its connection to the block.

Student Work IN PROGRESS

Name: Joseph Hochberger
Gotha Middle School
Windermere, FL

Unifying Paragraph Blocks

Joseph found a paragraph block about Franklin's public service. He circled the first sentence of the second paragraph because it did not clearly link the paragraphs in a block. Then, he added a transition sentence.

[His involvement in public service began with his appointments as clerk of the Pennsylvania Legislature in 1736 and as postmaster of Philadelphia in 1737. He served in both these positions for over fifteen years. . . .

Franklin's public service was not limited to the United States. ~~Four years later, in~~ In 1757, ~~Franklin~~ he traveled to England to negotiate between the family of William Penn, the founder of Pennsylvania, and the state government over tax matters. . . .]

To make a paragraph block about Franklin's public service, Joseph added transitions connecting these two paragraphs.

Revising Your Sentences

Use Sentence Structure to Create Emphasis

Using the right sentence structure, you can show connections between ideas. One way to show connections is to combine sentences by rewriting some as phrases, as in this example:

SEPARATE: He dreamed of fame. He asked the queen for funds. This money would make his voyage possible.

COMBINED: *Dreaming of fame,* he asked the queen *to fund his voyage.*

The second example expresses in phrases the ideas supporting the main action. Use the following strategy for combining sentences to show connections between ideas.

REVISION STRATEGY
Coding the Main Action

Circle clusters of short sentences. In each cluster, draw a triangle next to sentences expressing a main action. Rewrite other sentences in the cluster as phrases, and add them to the sentence expressing the main action.

Get instant help! Apply the combining Sentences by Coding the Main Action strategy by using the Essay Builder, accessible from the menu bar, on-line or on CD-ROM.

Student Work IN PROGRESS

Name: Joseph Hochberger
Gotha Middle School
Windermere, FL

Combining Sentences by Coding the Main Action

When Joseph found this cluster of short sentences, he decided to combine them.

Born in Boston, Massachusetts, the tenth son of seventeen children, he ~~Franklin was born in Boston, Massachusetts. He was the tenth son of seventeen children.~~ ▲ ~~He~~ was raised by parents who had immigrated from England. Having attended school for two years and worked for his father in the soap trade, ~~Franklin attended school for only two years. He also worked for his father in the soap trade.~~ ▲ ~~Then,~~ Franklin next became an apprentice in his older brother James's printing shop.

Joseph first coded sentences expressing a main action. Then, he rewrote other supporting sentences as phrases and added them to the sentence expressing the main action. Notice his use of participial phrases.

Grammar in Your Writing

Participial Phrases

To show the relationship between ideas in a sentence, you may need to use participial phrases. A **present participle** is the *-ing* form of a verb. A **past participle** is the past form of a verb, typically ending in *-ed* or *-d*.

Present Participles:	voting	exploring	hiding
Past Participles:	voted	explored	hidden

A **participial phrase** combines a participle with another group of words. It acts as an adjective, answering the question *What kind? Which one? How much?* or *How many?* about another word in the sentence. To avoid confusing your reader, always place a participial phrase near the word it modifies.

participial phrase → word modified

Gliding swiftly, the **canoe** approached the rapids.

In a participial phrase, a present or past participle may be joined with an adverb or adverb phrase modifying (telling more about) the participle. A participial phrase may also include a **complement,** a word or group of words naming the thing that receives the action of the participle.

participle ← adverb

With Modifiers: Gliding **swiftly,** the canoe approached the rapids.

participle ← adverb phrase

The canoe, tossed **by the current,** nearly overturned.

participle → complement

With Complements: Seeing **the danger,** he steered away from the rocks.

participle → complement

He nearly hit a boat crossing **his path.**

Find It in Your Reading Find two participial phrases in a short story you have read. Explain what information each phrase adds to the sentence.

Find It in Your Writing Identify two participial phrases in your research report. If you can't find two examples, challenge yourself to use at least two participial phrases in your report.

To learn more about participial phrases, see Chapter 20.

11.4

Revising Your Word Choice

Check Specialized Words

In doing research, you will learn more about an interesting topic. You may come across new words, and you may also encounter words that look familiar but are used with specialized meanings. For example, in sources about Revolutionary America, the word *mechanic* might mean a manual laborer or small manufacturer, rather than a person who does repairs. Dictionaries identify older or obsolete meanings for words with the label *Archaic*. Make sure you have defined archaic or specialized words in your report.

Writers in ACTION

Virginia Hamilton comments as follows on the importance of revision: "It's like being at the bottom of a lake and rising to the top. You want to make things clearer and clearer, and the way to do that is revise, revise, revise."

REVISION STRATEGY
Highlighting Technical Words

Review your prewriting notes and highlight archaic or specialized words. Check each word in a dictionary and in the source where you found it to make sure you understand its use. Then, reread your report to see whether you have used these terms. Add a definition for each term the first time it appears in your draft.

Peer Review

Analytic Talk

Once you have finished revising your report on your own, you can still benefit from the suggestions of your classmates. Analytic talk allows you to polish specific parts of your writing.

Join a group of four other classmates. Read your entire report to the group, pause briefly, then read it a second time. Listeners should take notes during the second reading. Then, ask your peers to answer the following questions:

- Was the opening clear and interesting?
- Would I continue reading if I read the opening in a magazine?
- Did I ever get lost or confused during the reading? If so, where?
- Was I left hanging at the end? If so, what extra information did I need?

Consider your classmates' comments as you prepare the final revision of your draft.

11.5 Editing and Proofreading

Your report may contain complete and accurate information, but you have not finished work on it until you have proofread it for errors in grammar, spelling, and mechanics. To ensure that readers can check the sources you have used, make sure that you have followed one of the standard forms for citation.

Focusing on Citations

In a research report, you should cite the sources for quotations, facts that are not common knowledge, and ideas that are not your own. One widely used form of citation is the Modern Library Association style for internal citations.

Internal Citations An internal citation appears in parentheses. It includes the author's last name and the page number on which the information appears. The citation directly follows the information from the source cited. If several sentences in a row contain information from the same source, the citation need only appear at the end of the last sentence.

> "The duke of Lancaster in 1888 . . . controlled more than 163,000 acres of British countryside" (Pool 163).

◀ **Critical Viewing** Using the section on Citing Sources and Preparing Manuscript on page 570, explain how this student should cite the information she gains from this interview. **[Apply]**

"Works Cited" List Provide full information about your sources in an alphabetical "Works Cited" list at the end of your report. The following is an example of the correct form:

Pool, Daniel. *What Jane Austen Ate and Charles Dickens Knew: From Fox Hunting to Whist—the Facts of Daily Life in Nineteenth-Century England.* New York: Simon and Schuster, 1993.

For each work cited, follow these guidelines:

- Give the author's last name first. If no author is credited, list the work by its title.
- If there are two or more authors, list the authors in the order in which they are credited in the work. Only the name of the first author is listed last name first.
- If an organization, rather than an individual, is credited with the work, use the name of the organization.
- Use a period after the author's name, after the title of the work, and at the end of the citation. Use a colon between the place of publication and the publisher. Use a comma between the publisher and the year of publication.
- Give the place of publication listed that is closest to you. To avoid confusion, add necessary information. For instance, you would write "Cambridge, MA" to distinguish this city from Cambridge, England.

Grammar in Your Writing

Quotation Marks and Underlining With Titles of Works

Underline (or style in italics) the titles of long written works and the titles of magazines and other periodicals. Also, underline or italicize the titles of movies, television series, and works of music and art.

Sounder (book) | the Pastorale (symphony)
Birth of a Nation (film) | Guernica (painting)

Use quotation marks around the titles of short written works, such as short stories, poems, and newspaper articles. Also, use quotation marks for song titles and Internet sites.

"The Tell-Tale Heart" (short story) | "Dog Bites Man" (newspaper article)
"Ring Out, Wild Bells" (poem) | "Greensleeves" (song)

Find It in Your Writing Review your essay to see whether you have used underlining and quotation marks correctly for the titles of works.

To learn more about the form for titles, see Chapters 26 and 27.

11.6 Publishing and Presenting

Building Your Portfolio

Consider the following ideas for publishing and presenting your report:

1. **Sharing With a Large Audience** Do research to determine which organizations (historical societies, fan clubs, and so on) might be interested in the topic of your report. Submit a copy of your report to such a group for publication in its newsletter or on its Web site.
2. **Panel Discussion** Join with classmates who have written on a similar subject, and organize a panel discussion. Each student should present his or her report and respond to questions and comments from other panel members.

Reflecting on Your Writing

Jot down a few notes about your experience writing a research report. You might begin by answering these questions:

- What was the most interesting thing you learned about your topic? Why?
- Which strategy for prewriting, drafting, revising, or editing might you recommend to a friend? Why?

Internet Tip

To see research reports scored with this rubric, go on-line:
PHSchool.com
Enter Web Code: eck-8001

Rubric for Self-Assessment

Use these criteria to evaluate your research report:

	Score 4	Score 3	Score 2	Score 1
Audience and Purpose	Focuses on a clearly stated thesis, starting from a well-framed question; gives complete citations	Focuses on a clearly stated thesis; gives citations	Focuses mainly on the chosen topic; gives some citations	Presents information without a clear focus; few or no citations
Organization	Presents information in logical order, emphasizing details of central importance	Presents information in logical order	Presents information logically, but organization is poor in places	Presents information in a scattered, disorganized manner
Elaboration	Draws clear conclusions from information gathered from multiple sources	Draws conclusions from information gathered from multiple sources	Explains and interprets some information	Presents information with little or no interpretation or synthesis
Use of Language	Shows overall clarity and fluency; contains few mechanical errors	Shows good sentence variety; contains some errors in spelling, punctuation, or usage	Uses awkward or overly simple sentence structures; contains many mechanical errors	Contains incomplete thoughts and mechanical errors that make the writing confusing

Chapter 12 Response to Literature

Mask Maker, Venice, Joanna Calabro, Courtesy of the artist

▲ **Critical Viewing** Describe the characters that two of these masks suggest to you. **[Interpret]**

Responding to Literature in Everyday Life

Some things you can't do on your own. It takes two to have a conversation or to play a game of catch. Reading, though, is an activity just for one. No one but you can read the words on a page and weave them into a picture in your mind. Yet, the first thing that might occur to you after finishing a book is, "I've got to tell someone else about this!"

By telling others about a book, you turn what you experienced by yourself into something others can also appreciate. Responding to a work in conversation or in writing will also prompt you to understand the work better. Reading may start out as a solitary activity—but a response to literature quickly gets others involved.

What Is a Response to Literature?

A **response to literature** is an essay or other form of writing that discusses what is of value in a book, short story, essay, article, or poem. A response might show why a story is moving, point out the beauties of a poem, or analyze the shortcomings of a play. A response to literature includes

- a strong, interesting focus on some aspect of the work.
- a clear organization.
- a summary of the important features of the work.
- supporting details for each main idea.
- a judgment about the success or value of the work.

To learn the criteria on which your response will be assessed, see the Rubric for Self-Assessment on page 179.

Writers in ACTION

Marilyn Stasio is a reviewer of mystery novels for a newspaper. This is what she said about responding to literature in the course of her critical work:

"Too often people think that the critic is someone who is always criticizing, but that's not what I do at all. What I do is I love the books and I respond to the books. And it's sort of passing on your enthusiasm to the reader."

Types of Responses to Literature

These are some of the responses to literature that you might write:

- **Book reviews** sum up the reviewer's experience of a book, often comparing it with other works, then encourage readers either to read it or to avoid reading it.
- **Letters to an author** let a writer know what a reader found enjoyable or disappointing in a work. It may include suggestions for future work and questions about past work.
- **Comparisons of works** highlight aspects of two or more works by comparing them.

Stacy Osborn, a student in the Gilmer Independent School District in Gilmer, Texas, wrote a response to a short story by Pearl S. Buck. In this chapter, you will see how Stacy applied featured strategies to choose a topic and revise her work.

Prewriting

Choosing Your Topic

Your liveliest responses to literature will probably involve a work to which you have a strong reaction—positive or negative. Use the strategies that follow to choose such a work.

Strategies for Generating a Topic

1. **Reader's Response Journal** If you have recorded your thoughts about your reading in a reader's response journal, look through your journal for works to which you had a strong reaction. Select one of these works as your topic.
2. **Interview Yourself** Ask yourself questions about your favorite kind of reading, your favorite books, the character you would most like to be, and the fictional place you would most like to visit. Write down your answers, and review them. Choose your topic from the works you mention.
3. **Browsing** Browse the literature sections of a library or bookstore. Flip through works you have already read or new short works by familiar authors. Take notes on each, and choose the most interesting one as your topic.

Try it out! Take notes using the interactive Browsing chart in **Section 12.2,** on-line or on CD-ROM.

Student Work IN PROGRESS

Name: Stacy Osborn
Gilmer Independent School District
Gilmer, TX

Browsing

Stacy looked through several anthologies of short stories. She listed features of the stories in a chart and chose "Christmas Day in the Morning" as her subject.

STORY	AUTHOR	SUBJECT	CHARACTERS
"Christmas Day in the Morning"	Pearl S. Buck	How people express love for each other	Rob, his wife, his father
"Charles"	Shirley Jackson	How parents don't see their kids as they really are	Laurie, his parents, his teacher
"The Necklace"	Guy de Maupassant	A couple work for 10 years to replace a cheap necklace	Mathilde, her husband, Mme. Forestier

TOPIC BANK

If you're having trouble finding a topic, consider the following possibilities:

1. **Analyze a Theme** Think of a novel, short story, essay, or poem that sends a message to readers. Write an essay showing how the author uses plot, characters, images, language, and other techniques to convey the message. Then, give your own opinion of the theme.
2. **Essay About an Author** Write about two or more works by the same author. Detail what is similar and what is different about the works. Draw conclusions about the writer's subject matter and style.

Responding to Fine Art

3. Jot down notes on this painting. Who is the woman? What is she doing? What do formal elements of the painting—colors, her pose and position—suggest about her mood? Review your notes, and then list characters from stories and novels of which the painting reminds you. Select a work to write about from your list.

The Girl I Left Behind Me, Eastman Johnson, National Museum of American Art, Washington, D.C.

Responding to Literature

4. Read and take notes on Walt Whitman's poem, "Poets to Come." Think about what he means when he asks poets of the future to "justify" him. Then, read a poem by E. E. Cummings such as "love is a place." Explain whether you think Cummings's experiments with punctuation and line shape "justify" Whitman. You can find both poems in *Prentice Hall Literature: Timeless Voices, Timeless Themes*, Silver.

Cooperative Writing Opportunity

5. **Festival for a Work** With a group of students, choose a poem, short story, or novel. Plan a festival to celebrate it. Divide the following tasks: acting out scenes from the work; inventing games based on the work for other students to play; and designing posters or creating commercials to advertise the work. As part of the day's events, hold a panel discussion about the work.

Focusing Your Response

After you have chosen a work to which to respond, read or review it carefully. Then, use a pentad to focus your topic.

Use a Pentad

Draw a large five-pointed star as a graphic organizer. Label each point as follows:

- **Actors** Who performed the action?
- **Acts** What was done?
- **Scenes** When or where was it done?
- **Agencies** How was it done?
- **Purposes** Why was it done?

Fill in the star with details matching each label. Highlight details that interest you, and sum them up to create a focus.

Student Work IN PROGRESS

Name: Stacy Osborn
Gilmer Independent School District
Gilmer, TX

Using a Pentad

Once Stacy decided on "Christmas Day in the Morning" as her topic, she filled out a pentad and highlighted the points she wanted to cover in her paper.

Actors: Rob in the present; Rob in the past; Rob's wife; Rob's children; Rob's father; Rob's mother

Acts: Rob's children won't share Christmas with him; young Rob discovers his father's love for him and in return milks the cows; old Rob decides to write his wife a love letter.

Purposes: to awaken love by giving love; to create happiness by sharing love

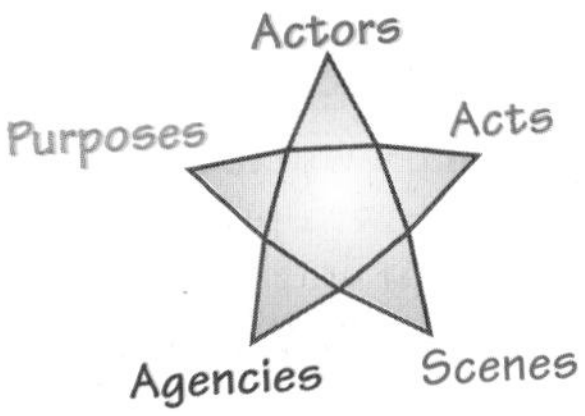

Agencies: love; gifts; memories; Christmas spirit

Scenes: old Rob wakes up early in the morning (present); he remembers his wife's unhappiness about Christmas (recent past); flashback: young Rob in the past (distant past); old Rob on Christmas morning

Focus: The message of the story is that you have to receive love before you can give it. Then, it is up to you to give it in return. Buck uses a flashback to show how love in the past can help in the present.

Considering Your Audience and Purpose

After focusing your topic, think about your audience and your purpose for writing. Use your answers to the following questions to guide you as you gather details and draft:

My Audience

- **Are my readers practiced, older readers?** If so, you need not explain every detail of the work. For instance, you might sum up the pacing and setting of a book as follows: "From desolate moors to high-class hotels, the book rushes headlong from one exotic location to the next."
- **Am I writing for less sophisticated readers?** Spell out each point, with specific references to the work. For instance, you might give these readers a feel for the rhythm of a book by writing: "The heroine of the book must travel to many exotic places in her search for her lost brother. Each chapter is set in a different place, so the reader may feel as if he or she is rushing around the globe."

My Purpose

- **Am I trying to persuade readers?** If your purpose is to persuade readers to read (or to avoid reading) the work, concentrate on examples supporting your evaluation.
- **Am I trying to enhance readers' appreciation of the work?** Concentrate on qualities and patterns in the work that a reader might not otherwise see.

◀ **Critical Viewing** What details about this scene from *Oliver Twist* might you need to spell out for less sophisticated readers? What details might you highlight to enhance a reader's appreciation of the scene? **[Apply]**

12.2

Gathering Details

Before you can write a response to a literary work, you must gather details from the work—examples of what makes the work unique. Use the following strategies to help.

Use Hexagonal Writing

Cut out six triangles of equal size, three each from two different-colored sheets of construction paper. Arrange the triangles and label them, as shown below. Then, fill in each triangle with details from the work for that category. If you need more room, make another hexagon or use note cards labeled with the categories shown.

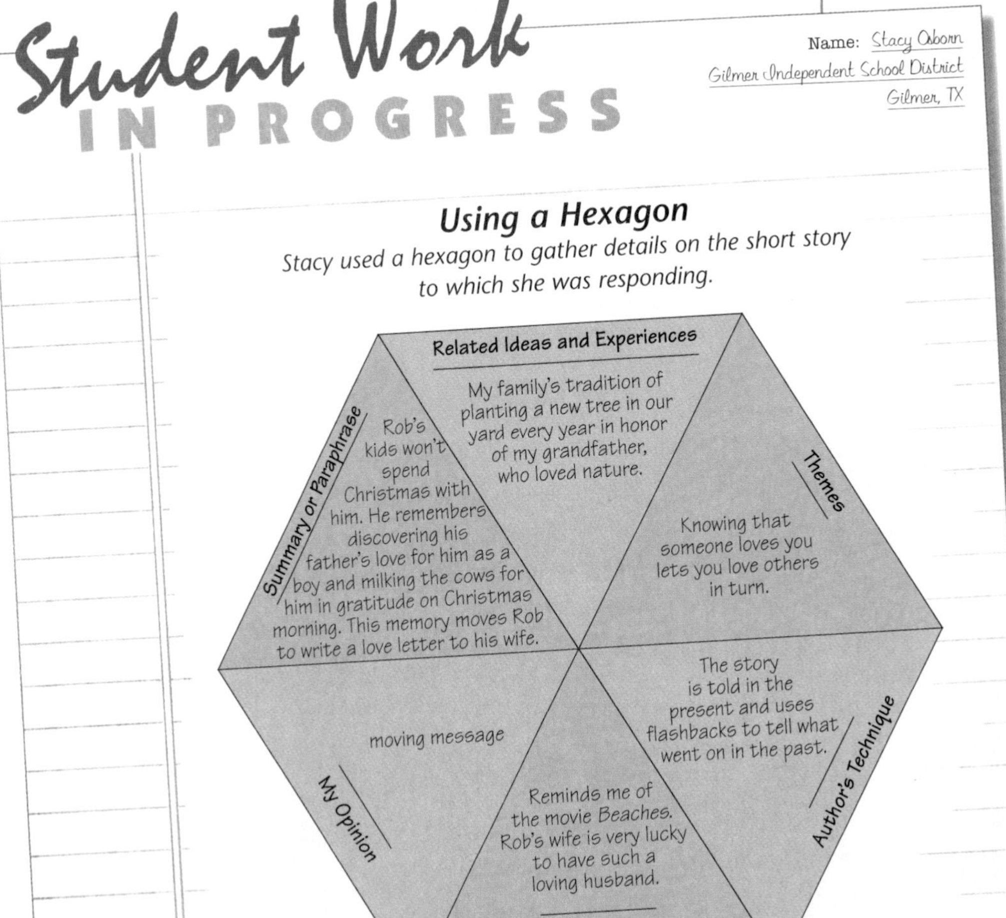

Look for Patterns

As you fill out a "hexagonal" on literature to which you are responding, look for patterns in the details you are gathering. Works of literature use patterns such as repetitions, contrasts, and resemblances to create or convey meaning. Often, writers use patterns to suggest **themes** (lessons or questions about life).

Here are some examples of the way patterns may create themes:

CHARACTERS:	The main characters are brothers. One is a success in business, the other a failure.
THEME:	This contrast may cause readers to ask questions about the nature or value of success. "Success" is a theme of the story.
IMAGES:	A poem uses images of stray kittens and abandoned cars.
THEME:	These images resemble each other in one way: They suggest the idea of neglect or abandonment. "Abandonment" is a theme of the poem.
WORDS:	The poet uses words such as *looping, slothful,* and *sprawling* to describe a river.
THEME:	The sounds of these words, as well as the meanings, suggest slow, lazy speeds. "Ease" or "inactivity" may be themes of the poem.

Finding Patterns To find patterns in the work, go through your notes a few times. Each time, think of different ways to describe the events, characters, images, and ideas you have noted. For instance, you might describe two main characters as "two young men" or "one a failure, one a success." Note when your descriptions fit together in interesting ways.

▼ **Critical Viewing** What theme does this photograph suggest? **[Analyze]**

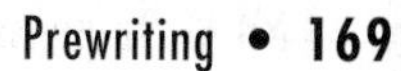

12.3 Drafting

Shaping Your Writing

Once you have gathered details from the work, you must organize them. As you draft, create a center of interest—a focus—to which each detail connects. You should also build to a main point—an insight into the work.

Define and Develop Your Focus

You have already narrowed your topic, but you must still find a focus for your response. A **focus** is a statement of your reaction to a specific aspect of the work.

To define a focus for your response, review your notes. Then, write out your response to the work in a single sentence, explaining which aspect of the work led to your response.

FOCUS: In "The Tell-Tale Heart," Edgar Allan Poe creates a nightmare experience by telling of a murder from the murderer's point of view.

Elaborate on your focus statement as you draft.

Conclude With an Insight

A good response to literature gives insight into a work. An insight might include an evaluation of the work, an interpretation of the theme, or an analysis of how the parts of the piece work together.

To achieve an insight into the work, consider your focus statement. Ask yourself the following questions:

- What details of the work contributed to my reaction? How?
- How do they fit with other details in the work?

For instance, in the case of "The Tell-Tale Heart," your insight might concern Poe's use of the first-person perspective to add to the horror of the tale.

INSIGHT: A first-person perspective makes the tale even more like a nightmare from which you can't wake up.

The narrator "collars" the reader and offers no break in the story until the end.

Because the narrator is the reader's only source of information, the reader feels stuck inside the narrator's delusion.

Providing Elaboration

As you draft your response, consider the different perspectives the work includes. Literary works have complex meanings. A poem doesn't simply say "black" or "white." It might say "either black or white" or "both black and white." As you draft, draw on these varied perspectives.

Day and Night, M. C. Escher © 1998, Cordon Art B. V. -Baarn-The Netherlands. All Rights Reserved

▲ **Critical Viewing** Explain how the artist has made one scene out of two. **[Analyze]**

Turn Your Perspective Upside Down

After you write a paragraph on an important point, look it over. In the margin, jot down the perspective of the paragraph. For instance, you might write, "Dr. Morbid is a selfish, evil villain."

Then, turn your perspective upside down. Look for the negative in the positive or the positive in the negative. You might write, for example, "In a way, Dr. Morbid is enviable, because he does whatever he pleases."

Student Work IN PROGRESS

Name: Stacy Osborn
Gilmer Independent School District
Gilmer, TX

Turning Your Perspective Upside Down

Stacy looked over her concluding paragraph and turned her perspective on the theme of the story upside down.

His memories give Rob the power to turn a depressing Christmas into a happy one. They also show him that it is up to him to keep love alive.

Perspective
Rob is responsible for keeping love alive.

Upside-Down Perspective
Is that fair to Rob? What about his kids? Why aren't they as nice to him as he was to his father?

One question remains, though: What about his own children? They do not show him the kind of love that he showed his father. Buck seems to be saying that it is up to Rob to keep love alive, but that he might not get love back from others. . . .

Stacy realized that the theme of the story was not as simple as she first thought. She added sentences reflecting her new insight.

12.4 Revising

Revising Your Overall Structure

Now that you have finished your first draft, review it to build on its strengths and eliminate its weaknesses. Start by looking at your overall structure—the organization of your main points and support. Then, analyze your paragraphs, sentences, and word choice.

Analyze for Focus

Your focus should be a central organizing force in your response. Check to make sure that you have included a statement of your focus in your introduction. Then, code points related to your focus to determine how your organization can be improved.

REVISION STRATEGY
Coding Points Related to Focus

Jot down your focus statement on an index card. Run the card down your draft, one line at a time. Underline sentences that relate to your focus. When you have finished coding, review your draft. If you find a paragraph with few or no underlined sentences in it, consider eliminating the paragraph or adding details related to your focus.

▼ **Critical Viewing** Why might Edgar Allan Poe have been drawn to write tales of horror? **[Speculate]**

Build to a Point

An effective response does not just have a logical order—it should also have a dramatic order, building to a point. Use the following strategy to help you build to a point:

REVISION STRATEGY
Building to Your Best Point

Read your paper over quickly. Circle the strongest point you made. It could be a statement that sums up your other ideas. It might be your most interesting insight.

Consider moving this point to the end of your paper. If you do move this point to the end, review your draft for places where you can add ideas preparing for this point. For instance, after each of your less important points in a paper on "The Tell-Tale Heart," you might add a sentence such as this: "While this technique is important, it does not fully explain the way Poe increases the terror of his tale." Your best point would, in fact, explain how Poe achieves his results.

Revising Your Paragraphs

Add Support

In a response to a literary work, you should support every point you make with details from the work. Use the following strategy to ensure that you have provided necessary support.

REVISION STRATEGY
Adding Support by Using Points to Illuminate

Follow these steps to "illuminate" your work:

1. Circle each general statement you make about the work.
2. Cut out a few five-pointed stars from construction paper, one for each main point in your draft. Label the points of each star with the following terms: *quotation, character, event, figure of speech,* and *theme.*
3. Glue a star near each circled sentence.
4. Inside each star, check off supporting details for your general point. For instance, if you illustrate a point with two quotations, place two check marks under "quotations."
5. Next, review your stars. If, overall, there are few check marks for a certain kind of support, consider adding details of that kind. If there are no check marks in a star, consider adding more support for the corresponding point.

Student Work IN PROGRESS

Name: Stacy Osborn
Gilmer Independent School District
Gilmer, TX

Using Points to Illuminate

This is an example of how Stacy used the strategy of illuminating .

quotation
character
theme
figure of speech
event

To show that he returns this love, Rob wakes up extra early on Christmas morning and milks the cows all by himself. This is his surprise gift to his father. Once the father realizes what Rob has done, he ~~is very happy.~~

kneels down and gives Rob a big hug. " 'Nobody ever did a nicer thing—' " he tells Rob.

Stacy realized that she needed more details to illustrate the father's reaction. She added a summary of an action and a quotation of dialogue.

Revising Your Sentences

Use Sentence Structure to Link Ideas

Variety in the structure of your sentences can make your writing more interesting to read. In addition, you can show the relationships between ideas by using the right structure.

REVISION STRATEGY
Highlighting Related and Contrasting Points

In one color, highlight pairs of sentences in your draft that make related points. In another color, highlight sentences that make contrasting points. Consider combining these pairs of sentences into compound or complex sentences.

RELATED POINTS:	The three sisters keep talking about a trip they hope to take. They are dreamers.
COMBINED:	The three sisters, who are dreamers, keep talking about a trip they hope to take.
CONTRASTING POINTS:	His triumph is celebrated by the town. His private life, however, is as bad as ever.
COMBINED:	His triumph is celebrated by the town; his private life, however, is as bad as ever.

Grammar and Style Tip

A complex sentence can suggest specific links between ideas: The idea in the independent clause is the focus of the sentence, to which the subordinate clauses contribute.

Student Work IN PROGRESS

Name: Stacy Osborn
Gilmer Independent School District
Gilmer, TX

Highlighting Related and Contrasting Points

After highlighting related points, Stacy decided to combine sentences.

Rob is fifteen years old. He overhears his father tell his mother that he hates to wake Rob for the chores~~. He~~ [, because he] thinks Rob needs his sleep. [When] Rob hears ~~this. He~~ [this, he] realizes that his father loves him.

Grammar in Your Writing
Compound and Complex Sentences

To join two ideas, you can create a compound sentence or a complex sentence.

Compound Sentences

A **compound sentence** is made up of two or more independent clauses. (A clause is a group of words with its own subject and verb. An **independent clause** is a clause that can stand on its own as a sentence.) In a compound sentence, the clauses are either joined with a comma and one of the coordinating conjunctions—*and, but, for, nor, or, so,* or *yet*—or with a semicolon.

Comma and Coordinating Conjunction: [We were sorry for the delay,] **but** [it couldn't be avoided.] (independent clause / independent clause)

Semicolon: [My brother promised to do better]; [we were doubtful.] (independent clause / independent clause)

Complex Sentences

A **complex sentence** consists of one independent clause—called the main clause—and one or more subordinate clauses. A **subordinate clause** has a subject and verb, but it cannot stand on its own as a sentence. Subordinate clauses begin with one of the relative pronouns—*who, whom, whose, which,* or *that*—or with a subordinating conjunction, such as *after, although, as, because, before, if, since, when, where, while, until,* or *unless.* If the subordinate clause comes before the main clause, it is followed by a comma.

In the following examples, the relative pronoun and subordinating conjunction are in boldface.

Relative Pronoun: [I'm the only one] [**who** understands the situation.] (main clause / subordinate clause)

Subordinating Conjunction: [**Unless** we hear otherwise,] [we'll meet the bus at 3:00 P.M.] (subordinate clause / main clause)

Find It in Your Reading Find one compound sentence and one complex sentence in a short story you have read recently. Identify the independent clauses in each.

Find It in Your Writing Find one compound sentence and one complex sentence in your response to literature. Identify the independent clauses in each See whether there are other places where using compound and complex sentences will make your writing smoother or clearer.

To learn more about compound and complex sentences, see Chapter 20.

Revising Your Word Choice

Choose and Reuse Key Terms

To unify a piece of writing about a literary work, you can reuse a phrase that refers to one of the features on which you are focusing. For instance, in a response to Poe's "The Tell-Tale Heart," you might refer to the "claustrophobia" of the tale—the reader's feeling of being stuck in a nightmare. You might use this word whenever you refer to details that add to that feeling. By reusing your word or phrase, you can join the parts of your paper into a unified whole.

REVISION STRATEGY

Coding Key Terms

Circle each of the main points you make in your paper. Review them, and underline any phrase or term you use that could apply to more than one of your points. For example, you might use the term *brotherhood* when discussing a theme or the phrase *surprising metaphors* when describing a poet's style.

Then, mark with a red triangle places in your draft where you discuss ideas related to this term or phrase. Consider reusing the word or phrase in the places you have marked.

Student Work IN PROGRESS

Name: Stacy Osborn
Gilmer Independent School District
Gilmer, TX

Coding Key Terms

Stacy found a key term in Buck's story that she decided to repeat for effect.

▲ In the story "Christmas Day in the Morning," Pearl S. Buck shows the way one person's love can ~~help another person love.~~ awaken another's.

Stirred by the memory of his gift to his father, he realizes that he is able to love his wife so much because he learned long ago that his father loved him. Here, Buck states the central message of her story: "love alone could waken love." Rob then decides to write his wife a letter telling her how much he loves her.

Stacy discovered Buck's memorable statement in one paragraph and underlined it. She realized she could repeat it effectively in her introductory paragraph as well.

Peer Review

You have finished revising on your own, but you can still get extra help polishing your draft. For suggestions, share your writing process—what goals you set and what steps you took toward them—with peers. Use the following strategy.

Conduct a "Process Share"

In a small group, describe what you planned to achieve in your writing and what stage you have reached in the writing process. Then, read your draft to the group. To start a discussion about your draft, the others should ask these questions:

- Do you think you succeeded in doing what you intended?
- What problems have you encountered?
- What changes have you made already? Why did you make them?
- About what aspects of your writing do you have doubts?
- On what aspects of your response do you want suggestions from the group?

As you answer these questions, group members should make suggestions to you about your work. Take notes on what they tell you. Use what you learn in preparing the final version of your writing.

◀ **Critical Viewing** Explain how well prepared this writer appears for her peer review session. **[Evaluate]**

12.5 Editing and Proofreading

Whenever you write, proofread carefully to catch errors in spelling, punctuation, or grammar. In a response to literature, pay close attention to the indenting, capitalization, and punctuation of quotations you use to support your points.

Focusing on Quotations

Long quotations from a literary work should be indented in your writing. Shorter quotations are treated exactly like the quotations in the dialogue of a story. Be sure that, when you quote, you copy the words exactly as they appear in the work.

Grammar in Your Writing

Punctuating and Formatting Quotations

Following are two ways to present quotations from a literary work:

Long quotations Introduce the quotation with a colon; indent the entire quotation on the left.

The writer uses several unusual similes to describe Terry's feelings:

> When the concert began, Terry felt as excited as a puppy in a roomful of kittens. She couldn't wait for her turn. As she walked onto the stage, her knees felt like rubber bands. "If I can only get to the piano," she said to herself, "I'll be calm as a robot."

Brief quotations Use quotation marks and commas to separate the quotation from the rest of a sentence. Use single quotation marks for a quotation within another quotation:

> Terry's excitement is clear when she gets offstage and says to her brother, "Did you hear me? I made three mistakes, but no one noticed. The emcee told me, 'Good work, kid.'"

Find It in Your Reading Find an example of a quotation in a novel you have read, and note how it is punctuated.

Find It in Your Writing Read over your response to literature, and check each quotation to be sure that it is set off or punctuated correctly.

To learn more about punctuating quotations, see Chapter 26.

12.6 Publishing and Presenting

Building Your Portfolio

Consider the following ideas for publishing and presenting your response to literature.

1. **"Good Reading for Teens" Booklet** Working with other students, assemble your responses to literature into a book-review booklet for your school or public library. Include your ratings of the works.
2. **Electronic Recommendations** With classmates, create a literary list or page on a Web site on the school server. Post your responses to literature, and invite visitors to share their own opinions and reactions.

Reflecting on Your Writing

Jot down some notes on your experience of writing a response to literature. Begin by answering the following questions:

- Did writing about a work of literature help you to understand it more completely or in a deeper way? Did your feelings about the work change as you thought and wrote about it?
- What advice would you give another student about writing a response to literature? Did you encounter problems that could have been avoided?

Internet Tip

To see responses to literature scored with this rubric, go on-line: PHSchool.com
Enter Web Code: eck-8001

Rubric for Self-Assessment

Evaluate your response to literature using the following criteria:

	Score 4	Score 3	Score 2	Score 1
Audience and Purpose	Presents sufficient background on the work(s); presents the writer's reactions forcefully	Presents background on the work(s); presents the writer's reactions clearly	Presents some background on the work(s); presents the writer's reactions at points	Presents little or no background on the work(s); presents few of the writer's reactions
Organization	Presents points in logical order, smoothly connecting them to the overall focus	Presents points in logical order and connects many to the overall focus	Organizes points poorly in places; connects some points to an overall focus	Presents information in a scattered, disorganized manner
Elaboration	Supports reactions and evaluations with elaborated reasons and well-chosen examples	Supports reactions and evaluations with specific reasons and examples	Supports some reactions and evaluations with reasons and examples	Offers little support for reactions and evaluations
Use of Language	Shows overall clarity and fluency; uses precise, evaluative words; makes few mechanical errors	Shows good sentence variety; uses some precise evaluative terms; makes some mechanical errors	Uses awkward or overly simple sentence structures and vague evaluative terms; makes many mechanical errors	Presents incomplete thoughts; makes mechanical errors that create confusion

Chapter 13 Writing for Assessment

Girl Writing, 1908, Pierre Bonnard, Barnes Foundation, Merion, Pennsylvania

▲ **Critical Viewing** This girl might be studying for a test. Compare her study habits with your own. **[Compare and Contrast]**

Assessment in Everyday Life

You make assessments every day. They range from the informal—"That's a great jacket!" or "Learning to inline skate was fun but grueling."—to the formal, such as writing an evaluation of a poem for your English class.

In school, some testing situations are called "writing for assessment." To do well on these tests, you must call on all the writing techniques you've learned in the past. You also must learn some special tips and practice certain skills that will help you succeed in testing situations. This chapter will prepare you for writing for assessment.

What Is Writing for Assessment?

When you give a written answer on a test to present your ideas or show what you have learned, you are producing **writing for assessment.** Although the length of your written response may vary from test to test or from question to question, most successful writing for assessment contains

- responses that match the question or questions asked.
- main points that are supported by various types of details.
- a clear and logical organization of details.
- correct grammar, spelling, and punctuation.

To learn the criteria on which your essay may be evaluated, see the Rubric for Self-Assessment on page 189.

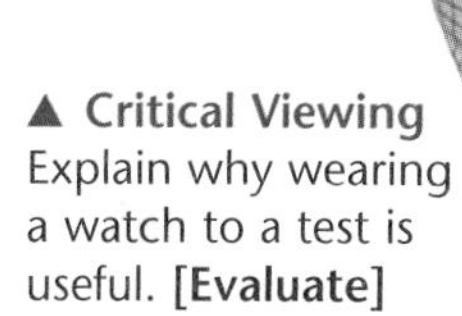

▲ **Critical Viewing** Explain why wearing a watch to a test is useful. **[Evaluate]**

Types of Writing for Assessment

A writing prompt on a test may call for a full-length essay or for a short response of ten to fifteen lines. Prompts may call for writing of the following kinds:

- **Persuasive writing** requires you to support an opinion on an issue, using persuasive language.
- **Expository writing** requires you to give information in a clear and well-organized fashion. It includes:
  - **Comparison-and-contrast writing,** requiring you to compare in an organized form the similarities and differences between two subjects.
  - **Cause-and-effect writing,** requiring you to explain a process or series of events.

In this chapter, you'll follow the work of Paul Keller, a student at Roosevelt Middle School in Oceanside, California, as he responds to a writing prompt on an essay test. You will see how Paul used featured strategies to prewrite and draft his essay.

13.1 Prewriting

Choosing Your Topic

Finding a topic is not a problem when you're writing for assessment. Someone else, a teacher, has already chosen the topic for you. In some cases, though, you may choose your topic from among two or three different options.

If you do have a choice, carefully consider the topic alternatives, the types of writing required, and the target audiences. Use the following strategies to help you decide on a topic:

Strategies for Choosing an Assessment Topic

- **Scan all the topic choices.** Eliminate questions for which your knowledge is limited or incomplete. Then, from the remaining choices, choose the topic you find most interesting.
- **Examine the purpose and the type of writing specified.** A prompt will always specify a purpose for and type of writing. It may ask you, for instance, to identify, examine, analyze, or evaluate a certain topic. Make sure you are comfortable with the purpose for writing specified for the question you choose.
- **Examine the format required.** Sometimes, a question tells what form the answer should take. For example, a question may ask you to write a letter. Consider the format with which you are most comfortable as you decide which question to answer.
- **Mentally gather details.** Choose to answer the question for which you can immediately think of at least five related facts, arguments, or other details.

TOPIC BANK

Following are some sample essay-test questions. If you plan to practice writing for assessment, choose one of these, or ask your teacher to provide you with one.

1. **Effects of a Historical Event** In an essay, examine how the Great Depression affected the day-to-day life of most Americans.
2. **Comparison of Presidents** Evaluate the presidencies of Abraham Lincoln and John F. Kennedy. Then, support your ideas in an essay about who was the "greater" president.
3. **Analysis of Insect Societies** Choose a social insect, and analyze the workings of its society, including the different roles of the insects, their means of obtaining food, the care they give their young, and the type of home they use.

Narrowing Your Topic

Before you start writing, narrow your topic by clarifying what the question is asking, what the main point of your response will be, and which details will help you make your case. Use the following strategy to help you narrow your topic:

Analyze the Prompt

1. **Identify the question.** Copy the essay question. Underline the specific subject it concerns and what it asks you to do—for instance, *explain.*
2. **Circle the format.** Circle the format the response is to take, if it is specified in the question.
3. **Box the audience.** If an audience is specified, draw a box around the phrase that identifies it. Decide what effect the audience should have on your choice of details and words.
4. **Write a thesis statement.** Below the essay question, jot down your thesis statement—the main point you plan to make in your response.

Student Work IN PROGRESS

Name: Paul Keller
Roosevelt Middle School
Oceanside, CA

Narrowing a Topic

Paul copied down the essay question he was to answer. Then, he made the following notations to be sure that his topic was narrow and focused.

Assignment: Assume the role of a colonist living in America in 1776. Write a letter to King George explaining what problems you are experiencing. Use detailed, historical examples to support your point of view. Propose at least one solution to these problems, and convince King George that your solutions are viable.

Thesis: Colonists want to settle western lands. If they do, they will help England.

I need to follow letter format.

I need to write in a respectful tone, since I'm writing to a king.

I need to explain a problem and propose a solution in a persuasive way.

13.2 Drafting

Shaping Your Writing

One of your most important goals in writing for assessment is to organize your ideas in a clear, logical way. Your final score on a writing test depends to a large degree on how well you have organized your writing. Keep in mind, though, that your time is limited, so choose a clear, simple organization.

Organize Details in Order of Importance

When you want to persuade someone or to emphasize certain key points, organize your ideas according to **Nestorian order.** When you choose this method of organization:

- Label or number your main ideas, from most important to least important.
- Then, create an outline. Save your most important point for the end, so you can conclude with a "bang." Lead off the body of your essay with your second-most important point. Then, present your remaining points, except your most important one, in decreasing order of importance. End with your most convincing point.

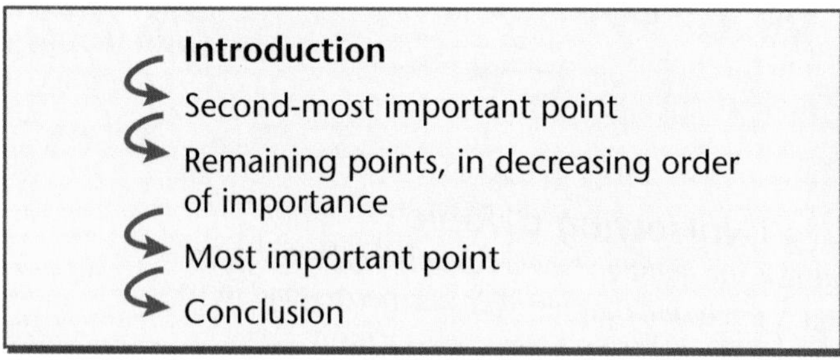

Organize Details in Chronological Order

If you are writing a summary, an explanation, or a narrative, you'll probably organize your details in **chronological order** (the order in which events happen). Make a timeline like the one below to help you organize your ideas.

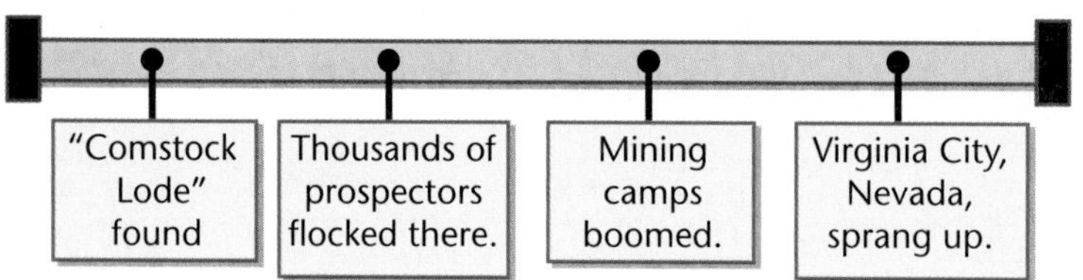

Try it out! Use the interactive Timeline in **Section 13.2,** on-line or on CD-ROM.

Providing Elaboration

Give Details

Once you've organized your ideas, look in your notes for places where you can add explanation or support. Next to each main idea on your outline, add details you can use to support the idea. As you draft, draw on your notes. Follow these guidelines for incorporating details in your writing:

- **Define.** Provide definitions to show that you fully understand your subject.
- **Explain.** Give reasons for your statements. Reasons may be scientific or historical, or they may be drawn from personal experience.
- **Support.** Cite statistics, expert testimony, and examples from your life to make your arguments convincing.
- **Illustrate.** Give examples from history, science, your own experience, or everyday life to illustrate your points.

Student Work IN PROGRESS

Name: Paul Keller
Roosevelt Middle School
Oceanside, CA

Giving Details

As he drafted, Paul included several types of details to make his writing effective and convincing.

Sire, my name is Lieutenant Colonel Paul Keller of the 23rd Infantry Brigade, Boston, Massachusetts. I feel very honored and privileged to wake up and salute the British flag. But, Your Majesty, I write to you to protest a grave injustice. For did I not fight against the French and did we not win? As part of their surrender, they had to give the land west of the Appalachians to England. Now, as I write, British troops stand constant vigil over the land for which so many of us died. I plead with you, let us settle the land west of the Appalachians, for the greater glory of England!

As required by the prompt, Paul assumes the identity of a colonist.

Paul explains the exact historical situation he is addressing.

In ringing tones, he presents a summary of the support he will provide for his argument.

13.3 Revising

When writing for assessment, always make time, even if it is only a few minutes, to revise your work.

Revising Your Overall Structure

One way to show evaluators that your writing is well-organized is to include a strong introduction and conclusion.

REVISION STRATEGY
Checking Your Introduction and Conclusion

Reread the writing prompt to make sure that you have interpreted it correctly. Then, read your introduction. Ask yourself the following questions as you revise:

- Does my introduction accurately reflect the instructions in the writing prompt?
- Does it clearly state what I will explain, argue, summarize, or narrate in the rest of my paragraphs?

Now, read your conclusion, and ask yourself the following questions as you revise:

- Does my conclusion accurately restate what I have explained, summarized, narrated, or argued in the essay?
- Does it leave the reader with a final thought on the subject or with a call to action?

Revising Your Paragraphs

Paragraphs are the basic blocks from which a good essay is built. Check to be sure that they are effective and unified.

REVISION STRATEGY
Checking for Unity

Identify the main idea in each paragraph. Then, study the details the paragraph includes. Does each sentence support, illustrate, or add to the paragraph's topic or main idea? If not, neatly cross out the sentence. If necessary, replace the crossed-out sentence with one that effectively supports the main idea.

Revising Your Sentences

Teachers will evaluate your writing for assessment to see how well your sentences are constructed.

REVISION STRATEGY
Eliminating Fragments and Run-Ons

Read through your sentences, and check to be sure that each expresses a complete thought. If not, you have a fragment that should be rewritten to make it a full sentence. Next, reread to find sentences that have more than one subject. Check each of them to be sure that the sentence is correctly punctuated and is not a run-on sentence.

Revising Your Word Choice

Choose Precise and Vivid Words

A good writer works hard to select words that convey ideas vividly and precisely. To get a good score on a writing test, make sure that you choose words that say exactly what you mean. If you are describing a person, place, or thing, use words that will help readers picture the subject in their minds. If you are writing to persuade, use words with strong emotional associations that will help convince your readers.

▼ **Critical Viewing** Write a sentence using precise, vivid words to describe how this boy feels. **[Apply]**

REVISION STRATEGY
Replacing Flat Word Choices

As you revise your writing for assessment, look for places to improve your word choices. In a descriptive passage, look for places where you can substitute a more vivid word or phrase. In a persuasive passage, look for places where you can substitute a word that conveys a strong favorable or unfavorable impression. The sentences below illustrate how much more effective a sentence that uses precise, vivid words is than one that does not.

FLAT: I pulled in the fish, and it landed in our boat.

VIVID: I reeled in a huge, rainbow trout, and it slapped into the bottom of our little rowboat.

13.4 Editing and Proofreading

Before turning in your writing for assessment, check it carefully to be sure that you have eliminated all errors in grammar, spelling, and punctuation.

Focusing on Punctuation

Check the punctuation of sentences within your essay to be sure that your punctuation of compound sentences is correct.

Grammar in Your Writing

Avoiding Comma Splices

One of the most common sentence errors students make involves joining two clauses with just a comma. This error is called a **comma splice.** Look for comma splices in your writing, and use the following techniques to correct them.

INCORRECT

Comma Splice:	Responsible teenagers deserve to have the right to drive, we ask you to help us keep this right.

CORRECT

Comma With Conjunction:	Responsible teenagers deserve to have the right to drive, and we ask you to help us keep this right.
Semicolon:	Responsible teenagers deserve to have the right to drive; we ask you to help us keep this right.
Two Sentences:	Responsible teenagers deserve to have the right to drive. We ask you to help us keep this right.

To learn more about avoiding comma splices, see Chapter 21.

13.5 Publishing and Presenting

Building Your Portfolio

Consider these possibilities for sharing your work:

1. **Group Discussion** Share your thoughts about the test—the choices offered, the difficulties encountered—in a group. Then, exchange drafts, and comment on the choices others made in responding on the test.
2. **Create a Review Folder** Create a folder for old tests, and place a copy of your writing for assessment in it. When studying for future tests, leaf through your review folder for reminders about strategies that did or did not work for you.

Reflecting on Your Writing

Take a few moments to think about writing for assessment. Then, answer the following questions, and save your responses in your portfolio.

- Were you satisfied with your choice of a question to answer? Why or why not?
- Which stage of the writing process did you find most useful as you wrote for assessment? Why?

Internet Tip

To see essays scored with this rubric, go on-line:
PHSchool.com
Enter Web Code:
eck-8001

Rubric for Self-Assessment

Evaluate your writing for assessment essay using these criteria:

	Score 4	Score 3	Score 2	Score 1
Audience and Purpose	Uses word choices and supporting details appropriate to the specified audience; clearly addresses writing prompt	Mostly uses word choices and supporting details appropriate to the specified audience; adequately addresses prompt	Uses some inappropriate word choices and details; addresses writing prompt	Uses inappropriate word choices and details; does not address writing prompt
Organization	Presents a clear, consistent organizational strategy	Presents a clear organizational strategy with few inconsistencies	Presents an inconsistent organizational strategy	Shows a lack of organizational strategy
Elaboration	Adequately supports the thesis; elaborates on each idea; links all details to the thesis	Supports the thesis; elaborates on most ideas; links most information to the thesis	Partially supports the thesis; does not elaborate on some ideas	Provides no thesis; does not elaborate on ideas
Use of Language	Uses excellent sentence variety and vocabulary; includes very few mechanical errors	Uses adequate sentence variety and vocabulary; includes few mechanical errors	Uses repetitive sentence structure and vocabulary; includes some mechanical errors	Demonstrates poor use of language; includes many mechanical errors

PART 2

Grammar, Usage, and Mechanics

Snoopy-Early Sun Display on Earth, 1970, Alma Woodsey Thomas, National Museum of Art, Washington, D.C.

Chapter 14

Nouns and Pronouns

▲ **Critical Viewing** Power lines such as these keep communications moving. Use two or three nouns in a sentence to describe who this worker is. **[Infer]**

Words are the building blocks of communication. You assemble words to deliver your ideas to other people. Communication technology—including computers—has grown rapidly over the last five decades. Because words are the tools of communication, it makes sense to study them in detail.

The English language has eight kinds of words, or parts of speech: nouns, pronouns, verbs, adjectives, adverbs, prepositions, conjunctions, and interjections. This chapter will help you learn more about two important parts of speech: nouns and pronouns.

Diagnostic Test

Directions: Write all answers on a separate sheet of paper.

Skill Check A. List the nouns from the following sentences. Label each one *person, place,* or *thing.*

1. Communication is the way we connect with one another.
2. People have communicated in one form or another since the beginning of human history.
3. Writing and speaking are two methods of communication.
4. Communication can also be accomplished by other means.
5. We can also communicate how we feel or what we need through body language and gestures.
6. Another type of communication that is growing rapidly is electronic communication.
7. This includes such things as computers, radio, and television.
8. Many people around the world use electronic communication several times every day.
9. The technology of electronic communication keeps growing and is becoming faster and easier to use in today's world.
10. These developments are a big part of everyone's life and are used in both business and education.

Skill Check B. Copy the following phrases, and underline the nouns. Label each noun *common* or *proper.* If the noun is collective or compound, label it so.

11. a family of computers
12. in the United States or Canada
13. to call a trouble-shooter for help
14. a team of specialists
15. Alexander Graham Bell and other inventors

Skill Check C. Identify the pronouns in the following sentences, and label each pronoun *personal, demonstrative, relative, interrogative,* or *indefinite.*

16. Who took her class on computer technology?
17. Someone told me about it, but that was only yesterday.
18. Did she teach her class on the computers of today?
19. These are some good questions about computers: How did they begin, and what will they be like in the future?
20. I can't believe the many improvements that have been made to computers since the first ones were introduced.
21. The first computer was invented by Herman Hollerith; he invented it in the 1890's.
22. My teacher also described how companies began building calculators, which were the first forms of computers.
23. Did your teacher tell you what year they built these calculators?
24. Does anyone know if it was in the 1930's?
25. We have much to learn about the growth of technology in communication. I need to take another class!

Section 14.1

Nouns

Nouns are naming words. Nouns help people identify what they are talking or thinking about.

KEY CONCEPT A **noun** is the name of a person, place, thing, or idea. ■

Study the list of nouns in the chart. (You may be surprised that some of these are, in fact, nouns.)

People	
farmer	Alexander Graham Bell
Bostonians	pilot
Places	
Chicago	waiting room
theater	Madison Square Garden
Things	
Living and Nonliving Things That You Can See	
flowers	ballpoint pen
goldfish	modem
elephant	poem
Ideas and Things That You Cannot Usually See	
success	revolution
happiness	fairness
anger	health

Theme: Communication

In this section, you will learn how nouns are classified. The examples and exercises are about the ways in which we communicate.

Cross-Curricular Connection: Science and Social Studies

Exercise 1 **Identifying Nouns** Identify the nouns in each of the following sentences. Explain why each word you have identified functions as a noun.

1. A *medium* is defined as a means of communication, and comes from the Latin word *medius,* meaning "the middle" or "between."
2. *Media* is plural, describing all the various forms of communication.
3. The media provide a way for messages to travel over distance and time.
4. A computer, for instance, is a medium for sending messages between communicators.
5. Radios, books, and telephones are media used by almost everyone.

▼ Critical Viewing This man is able to communicate while biking in the woods. Explain how he does this, using nouns for things you can and cannot see in your sentences. **[Describe]**

Recognizing Collective Nouns

Certain nouns name groups of people or things. For example, a jury is a group of people; a herd is a group of animals. These nouns are called *collective nouns.*

KEY CONCEPT A **collective noun** is a noun that names a group of individual people or things. ■

Following are some examples of collective nouns:

EXAMPLES: team, class, committee, crowd, group, audience

Exercise 2 Recognizing Collective Nouns On your paper, list the nouns in the following sentences. Underline the five that are collective nouns.

1. It was common for a group to use drums, signals, or lanterns to send messages.
2. These messages could only be seen or heard by a crowd a short distance away.
3. During World War I, messages were tied to the legs of pigeons and sent to distant troops.
4. Flags or lights were used by a team to send a message over hilltops or between ships at sea.
5. These codes were called *semaphore systems* by their audience.

More Practice

Grammar Exercise Workbook
- pp. 1–4

On-line Exercise Bank
- Section 14.1

Go on-line: PHSchool.com *Enter Web Code:* eck-8002

Get instant feedback! Exercises 1 and 2 are available on-line or on CD-ROM.

GRAMMAR IN LITERATURE

from E-Mail From Bill Gates

John Seabrook

The nouns in this excerpt are highlighted in blue italics. The noun in red is a collective noun.

At the *moment*, the best *way* to communicate with another *person* on the *information highway* is to exchange electronic *mail*: to write a *message* on a *computer* and send it through the *telephone lines* into someone else's *computer*.

14.1

Recognizing Compound Nouns

You have probably used the words *soft* and *drink* separately many times. When both words are used together, however, they form a single noun that has a special meaning, as in "She had a soft drink with her pizza."

KEY CONCEPT A **compound noun** is a noun made up of two or more words. ■

Compound nouns are usually written in one of three ways:

TYPES OF COMPOUND NOUNS		
Separate Words	Hyphenated Words	Combined Words
hard drive chief justice Empire State Building	cure-all cha-cha mother-in-law	congresswoman network classroom

Check a dictionary for the spelling of unfamiliar compound nouns. If a word is not listed, write it as two separate words.

Exercise 3 **Recognizing Compound Nouns** The following paragraph has a total of ten compound nouns. Copy the paragraph onto your paper, and underline each compound noun.

EXAMPLE: A special mail service was established in the United States in 1789.

ANSWER: A special <u>mail service</u> was established in the <u>United States</u> in 1789.

The U.S. Postal Service was established by the government. The position of postmaster general was created to supervise the mail service. The first postmaster general was Benjamin Franklin. The pony express was started by the United States Post Office. The riders carried mail on horseback and were known for their prompt delivery. Mail was also carried on stagecoaches. Today, the United States Postal Service is self-supporting and is exploring many new technologies.

▼ **Critical Viewing** The first postmaster general of the United States was Benjamin Franklin. Tell what else you know about him, using compound nouns in your sentences. **[Support]**

Using Common and Proper Nouns

All nouns can be divided into two large groups: *common nouns* and *proper nouns.*

KEY CONCEPT A **common noun** names any one of a class of people, places, or things. A **proper noun** names a specific person, place, or thing. ■

Common nouns are not capitalized. Proper nouns are always capitalized.

Common Nouns	Proper Nouns
inventor	Alexander Graham Bell
village	Tarrytown
story	"Rikki-tikki-tavi"

Adding proper nouns will help make your writing more informative. Instead of writing "The telephone was invented in the 1800's," you might write, "The telephone was invented by Alexander Graham Bell in the 1800's."

Exercise 4 **Identifying Common and Proper Nouns** Copy the following nouns. Place a *C* after each common noun and a *P* after each proper noun. Write a proper noun that gives an example of each common noun. Then, write a common noun that gives an example of a class to which each proper noun belongs.

1. government
2. pony express
3. postmaster general
4. United States
5. city
6. president
7. postal service
8. Benjamin Franklin
9. century
10. history

More Practice

Grammar Exercise Workbook
- pp. 5–6

On-line Exercise Bank
- Section 14.1

Go on-line: PHSchool.com
Enter Web Code: eck-8002

Exercise 5 **Using Common and Proper Nouns** Copy the following paragraph. Replace each underlined common noun (and its article) with one of the proper nouns supplied. You will use one of the proper nouns twice. Make other minor changes as needed.

Samuel F. B. Morse
Morse Code
New York
United States

The telegraph was the first electronic medium. It sent and received electrical signals over long-distance wires. One of the first inventors of the telegraph was a man. He was an artist and inventor who lived in a country. In 1837, the man demonstrated the system in a city/state. The code later evolved from his invention.

If you're not sure whether or not a noun is proper and should be capitalized, always check in a dictionary.

14.1

Hands-on Grammar

Collecting Compound Nouns Hallway

In this exercise, you will collect and display compound nouns that are formed in different ways. Follow the directions given and look at the illustration.

1. Take a piece of 5-1/4" x 6-1/2" paper and fold it in half the long way. Make a fold about 2" from the end so the paper will stand up.
2. Cut three doors in one half of your paper. Make each door approximately 1-1/4" wide and deep. On the first door, write *Separate Words.* On the second door, write *Hyphenated Words*; on the third, *Combined Words.*
3. Cut three strips of paper, 1" wide x 4" long. Tape a strip of paper inside each of the three doors. You can fold them up like steps so that you can close the doors.
4. Write appropriate compound nouns on the strips of paper behind each door. For example, for *Separate Words*, you can use *hard drive, chief justice, high school;* for *Hyphenated Words*, use *mother-in-law, maid-of-honor;* and for *Combined Words*, use *network, classroom, football.*
5. Keep this hallway in your notebook and add compound nouns to the list when you come across them in your reading and writing. If you are unsure how to form the compound noun, look it up in a dictionary.

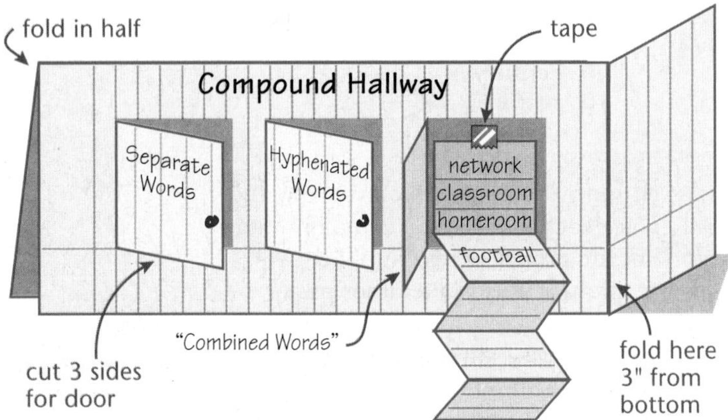

Find It in Your Reading As you read your assignments in your textbooks, look for and jot down compound nouns. Then, put them behind the appropriate door in your hallway.

Find It in Your Writing Look through some essays in your portfolio for examples of compound nouns. Make sure that you have spelled them correctly. Add them to your lists.

Section 14.1

Section Review

GRAMMAR EXERCISES 6–12

Exercise 6 **Identifying Nouns** Identify the nouns in each of the following sentences. Explain why each word that you identified functions as a noun.

1. Alexander Graham Bell invented the telephone.
2. His invention was patented in 1876.
3. This invention was able to transmit a voice over wires.
4. Before the telephone, people could only transmit clicks, using the telegraph.
5. Bell then founded the Bell Telephone Company.

Exercise 7 **Classifying Nouns** Write the *collective, compound,* or *proper* noun in each of the following sentences. Label each type of noun.

1. In 1895, a system was built that enabled a group to send and receive signals through the air.
2. This system of sending electrical signals was called *radio* by its audience.
3. A crowd in New York heard the first broadcast in 1906.
4. Philo T. Farnsworth was the first American inventor to use television technology.
5. The first regularly scheduled program was broadcast on July 1, 1941, in New York City.
6. Eventually, department stores began to carry these new appliances.
7. Thanks to teams of experts, radio technology improved rapidly.
8. Today, radio stations offer communities many choices.
9. How would Americans follow football without radio and television?
10. In the United States, about one of every 250 Americans had a telephone by the year 1894.

Exercise 8 **Supplying Nouns** In the following sentences, fill in the missing word with the kind of noun requested.

1. (Proper noun) invented the (common noun).
2. A television transmission is called a (compound noun).
3. Because we have (compound noun), we are able to watch more than 60 channels.
4. Before the (common noun), people had to listen to the radio for news.
5. My favorite baseball (collective noun) is the (proper noun).

Exercise 9 **Writing Sentences With Nouns** Use each of the following kinds of nouns in a sentence.

1. common noun that names a place
2. proper noun that names a person
3. collective noun
4. hyphenated compound noun
5. noun that names an idea

Exercise 10 **Find It in Your Reading** Examine a newspaper or magazine article to find examples of common and proper nouns.

Exercise 11 **Find It in Your Writing** Review a piece of your own writing to find at least two examples of collective and compound nouns.

Exercise 12 **Writing Application** Write ten sentences of your own to describe your use of a type of technology. Include at least ten common nouns and four proper nouns in your description.

Section 14.2

Pronouns

Pronouns are words that take the place of nouns. They are generally used when it would not make sense to repeat a noun over and over again. Imagine, for example, that you are writing about Aunt Jenny. If you were using only nouns, you might write the following sentence:

WITH NOUNS: Aunt Jenny was late because *Aunt Jenny* had waited for *Aunt Jenny's* computer technician.

WITH PRONOUNS: Aunt Jenny was late because *she* had waited for *her* computer technician.

KEY CONCEPT A **pronoun** is a word that takes the place of a noun or of a group of words acting as a noun.

Sometimes a pronoun takes the place of a noun in the same sentence.

EXAMPLE: My father opened *his* files first.

A pronoun can also take the place of a noun used in an earlier sentence.

EXAMPLE: My father opened his e-mail first. *He* couldn't wait any longer.

A pronoun may take the place of an entire group of words.

EXAMPLE: Trying to make the team is hard work. *It* takes hours of practice every day.

Theme: Computers

In this section, you will learn about pronouns. The examples and exercises are about the history and uses of computers.

Cross-Curricular Connection: Science and Social Studies

▼ **Critical Viewing** What pronouns would you use to take the place of nouns in describing this photograph? **[Classify]**

Recognizing Antecedents of Pronouns

A pronoun is closely related to the noun it replaces. The noun that the pronoun replaces has a special name. It is called the *antecedent.*

KEY CONCEPT An **antecedent** is the noun (or group of words acting as a noun) for which a pronoun stands. ■

The Latin prefix *ante-* means "before," and most antecedents do come before the pronouns that take their place. In the following examples, *father* and *Trying to make the team* are the antecedents of the pronouns *his* and *It.*

EXAMPLES: My *father* opened *his* mail first. He couldn't wait any longer.
Trying to make the team is hard work. *It* takes hours of practice every day.

Sometimes an antecedent will come after the pronoun.

EXAMPLE: Although *he* was known as an expert software developer, *Darryl* enjoyed selling computers.

Occasionally, a pronoun will have no definite antecedent.

EXAMPLES: *Who* will represent the class?
Everything was lost in the flood.

In these examples, the pronouns *who* and *everything* do not stand for any specific person or thing.

Get instant feedback! Exercise 13 is available on-line or on CD-ROM.

Exercise 13 **Recognizing Antecedents** In each of the numbered items below, a pronoun is underlined. Write the antecedent for each pronoun on your paper.

EXAMPLE: People use <u>their</u> computers for all kinds of work.
ANSWER: People

1. The earliest computers were used to calculate numbers. <u>They</u> were used in the 1890's to total the U.S. Census.
2. International Business Machines Company (IBM) was founded in 1924. The electromechanical calculator was <u>its</u> invention.
3. The first general-purpose computer in America was called the Electrical Numerical Integrator and Computer (ENIAC). <u>It</u> was completed in 1945.
4. One of <u>its</u> inventors was John P. Eckert. He and John W. Mauchly later built the first computer for commercial use.
5. The explosion of word-processing technology occurred in the 1970's. <u>It</u> gave us the ability to compose documents on computers.

More Practice

Grammar Exercise Workbook
- pp. 8–10

On-line Exercise Bank
- Section 14.2

Go on-line: PHSchool.com
Enter Web Code: eck-8002

14.2

Using Personal Pronouns

The pronouns used most often are *personal pronouns.*

KEY CONCEPT **Personal pronouns** refer to (1) the person speaking, (2) the person spoken to, or (3) the person, place, or thing spoken about. ■

PERSONAL PRONOUNS	
I, me, my, mine	we, us, our, ours
you, your, yours	you, your, yours
he, him, his she, her, hers it, its	they, them, their, theirs

First-person pronouns, such as *I, my, we,* and *our,* are used by the person or people speaking to refer to himself, herself, or themselves.

EXAMPLE: *I* waited for *my* computer to boot up.

Second-person pronouns, such as *you* and *your,* are used to speak directly to another person or to other people.

EXAMPLE: Sheila, *you* left *your* computer on.

Third-person pronouns have many forms. There are separate masculine pronouns *(he, him, his)* and feminine pronouns *(she, her, hers)* for people and neuter pronouns *(it, its)* for things. Third-person pronouns refer to someone or something that may not even be present.

EXAMPLE: I haven't seen my grandfather in a year. *He* will arrive from Florida tomorrow.

Exercise 14 **Supplying Personal Pronouns** Copy the sentences below, filling the blanks with an appropriate pronoun. Then, identify each pronoun's antecedent. If a pronoun has no antecedent, write *none.*

1. Most computer users have accessed the Internet through ___?___ service providers.
2. Karen, ___?___ service provider is one of many.
3. Mark got ___?___ service through AmeriServe; ___?___ also provides Internet access.
4. ___?___ used Local Serve Network at one time. ___?___ was another Internet provider.
5. Jan just installed a Local Area Network (LAN) on ___?___ computer system.

More Practice

Grammar Exercise Workbook
- pp. 7–8

On-line Exercise Bank
- Section 14.2

Go on-line:
PHSchool.com
Enter Web Code:
eck-8002

Using Demonstrative Pronouns

Demonstrative pronouns are pointers.

KEY CONCEPT A **demonstrative pronoun** points out a specific person, place, or thing. ■

There are four demonstrative pronouns:

DEMONSTRATIVE PRONOUNS			
Singular		Plural	
this	that	these	those

A demonstrative pronoun can come before or after its antecedent.

EXAMPLES: *This* is the book I chose.
Those are my new friends.
Of all my stamps, *these* are the most valuable.
We stopped in Bad Neustadt and Salz. *These* are the towns where our ancestors lived.

Exercise 15 Recognizing Demonstrative Pronouns For the numbered items below, write each demonstrative pronoun, and give its antecedent.

EXAMPLE: That is not the network I would have chosen.
ANSWER: That (network)

1. Our home computer has a large memory. This helps it operate faster.
2. Today's computers have developed rapidly since the 1970's. These represent the latest technology.
3. We can use computers for graphic design. That is some people's favorite use of the computer.
4. One can also send electronic mail; most people call this *e-mail.*
5. My mom made her airline reservations on our computer. That is something my grandmother could never do.

▼ Critical Viewing Use two demonstrative pronouns in a sentence to describe what the man in the photograph is doing. **[Infer]**

14.2

Using Relative Pronouns

Relative pronouns are connecting words.

KEY CONCEPT A **relative pronoun** begins a subordinate clause and connects it to another idea in the same sentence. ■

There are five relative pronouns:

RELATIVE PRONOUNS				
that	which	who	whom	whose

The following chart gives examples of relative pronouns connecting subordinate clauses to independent clauses. (See Section 20.2 for more information about relative pronouns and clauses.)

Independent Clauses	Subordinate Clauses
Here is the book	that Betsy lost.
Dino bought our old house,	which needs many repairs.
She is a singer	who has an unusual range.
Is this the man	whom you saw earlier today?
She is the one	whose house has a fire alarm.

Exercise 16 **Supplying Relative Pronouns** On your paper, write the appropriate relative pronoun for each sentence below.

EXAMPLE: Anyone __?__ can type can use a computer.
ANSWER: who

1. Communication technology is one thing __?__ is continually changing.
2. It has influenced everyone __?__ needs to communicate with someone else.
3. All societies have had people __?__ tried to improve communication.
4. Writing, __?__ was one of the first forms of communication technology, paved the way for many other developments.
5. The last century saw many people __?__ lives changed after the invention of radio and television.

More Practice

Grammar Exercise Workbook
- pp. 9–10

On-line Exercise Bank
- Section 14.2

Go on-line:
PHSchool.com
Enter Web Code:
eck-8002

Get instant feedback! Exercises 16 and 17 available on-line or on CD-ROM.

Using Interrogative Pronouns

Some relative pronouns can also be used as *interrogative pronouns.*

KEY CONCEPT An **interrogative pronoun** is used to begin a question. ■

INTERROGATIVE PRONOUNS				
what	which	who	whom	whose

GRAMMAR IN LITERATURE

from E-Mail From Bill Gates

John Seabrook

In this excerpt from a letter to Bill Gates, John Seabrook has used two relative pronouns (blue italics). He has also used one interrogative pronoun (red italics).

Dear Bill,

I am the guy *who* is writing the article about you for the New Yorker. It occurs to me that we ought to be able to do some of the work through e-mail. *Which* raises this fascinating question—*What* kind of understanding of another person can e-mail give you? . . .

Exercise 17 Recognizing Interrogative Pronouns Write the interrogative pronoun in each of the following sentences.

1. What did the first computer look like?
2. Do you know which of these software programs you use most often?
3. He asked, "Who is the computer expert here?"
4. To whom did you speak about your computer?
5. Who knows the best kind of computer for word processing?
6. Who can help me purchase a computer?
7. One computer is making a strange sound. Whose is it?
8. What happened? Which one is making the noise?
9. Of these keys, which one will make it stop?
10. What did I do wrong?

14.2

Using Indefinite Pronouns

You should learn to recognize one other kind of pronoun—the *indefinite pronoun.*

KEY CONCEPT **Indefinite pronouns** refer to people, places, or things, often without specifying which ones. ■

Notice that a few indefinite pronouns can be either singular or plural, depending upon their use in the sentence.

INDEFINITE PRONOUNS			
Singular		Plural	Singular or Plural
another	much	both	all
anybody	neither	few	any
anyone	nobody	many	more
anything	no one	others	most
each	nothing	several	none
either	one		some
everybody	other		
everyone	somebody		
everything	someone		
little	something		

WITHOUT ANTECEDENTS: *Anyone* can learn to operate a computer.

WITH ANTECEDENTS: *All* of the students learned to operate a computer.

Get instant feedback! Exercise 18 is available on-line or on CD-ROM.

Exercise 18 **Recognizing Indefinite Pronouns** Write the indefinite pronoun(s) in the sentences below.

EXAMPLE: Only a few of my relatives have ever used a computer.

ANSWER: few

1. Everyone agrees that new technologies provide new opportunities.
2. Many do their banking, shopping, and research at home on their computers.
3. Some believe this is a much more convenient way to conduct their business.
4. Almost everyone uses a credit card made available through technology.
5. Others go to the grocery store, where technology—a scanner—will tally their purchases.

More Practice

Grammar Exercise Workbook
- pp. 11–12

On-line Exercise Bank
- Section 14.2

Go on-line: PHSchool.com
Enter Web Code: eck-8002

Section 14.2 **Section Review**

GRAMMAR EXERCISES 19–25

Exercise 19 Recognizing Antecedents On your paper, write the antecedent for each underlined pronoun.

1. Electronic communication is continually expanding. We use it daily.
2. Humans have a complex system of language. It is sometimes confusing.
3. We use language every day because it conveys our ideas and emotions.
4. Individuals as well as entire cultures have their own unique languages.
5. The Latin language, for instance, is no longer spoken, but it is still written.

Exercise 20 Identifying Personal Pronouns Identify the personal pronoun(s) in each of the following sentences.

1. Not only do languages have a spoken form, they also have a written form.
2. Our teacher told us that the oldest written languages are more than 5,000 years old.
3. She also said that they began in the form of drawings.
4. The earliest pictures, she told us, were found in France.
5. I know the drawings represented the lives of people and what was happening to them at that time.

Exercise 21 Recognizing Personal, Demonstrative, Relative, Indefinite, and Interrogative Pronouns Write the personal, demonstrative, relative, indefinite, and interrogative pronouns in the following sentences. Label each type.

1. Those paintings in France are more than 30,000 years old.
2. These are the symbols representing words.
3. The person to whom you are speaking may be a good listener.
4. He or she is the one who is on the other side of this conversation.
5. There were two people. To which one were you speaking?

Exercise 22 Supplying Indefinite Pronouns On your paper, write an appropriate indefinite pronoun to fill in each blank.

1. Were it not for __?__ discovering electricity, much of today's communication might never have taken place.
2. __?__ of the most revolutionary devices was the telegraph.
3. Before 1861, __?__ expected to send signals of any kind across the country.
4. After 1861, __?__ saw telegraph lines constructed along railway lines.
5. Not __?__ thinks about the telegraph anymore, but at one time it seemed like a miracle to __?__.

Exercise 23 Find It in Your Reading Reread a favorite short story or poem. Identify at least five personal or indefinite pronouns.

Exercise 24 Find It in Your Writing Look through your portfolio. Find an example of a demonstrative, relative, or interrogative pronoun.

Exercise 25 Writing Application Write a dialogue in which two people discuss their friends. Use pronouns in the conversation, and underline each one.

Chapter 15 Verbs

▲ **Critical Viewing** This illustration shows a group of newly freed slaves, along with Union soldiers, during the Civil War. What verbs would you use to describe the action in this image? **[Analyze]**

Verbs are a necessary part of every sentence—they indicate whether events are taking place in the present, past, or future. Verbs do more than just tell time, however. Some verbs express action. Actions can be dramatic, or they can be subtle. Other verbs provide a link between two parts of a sentence. Still others simply point out that something exists.

This chapter will describe the two main kinds of verbs—*action verbs* and *linking verbs*—and will show you how these verbs can be used with another kind of verb—*helping verbs.*

Diagnostic Test

Directions: Write all answers on a separate sheet of paper.

Skill Check A. Write the verb or verb phrase that appears in each sentence below, and label it *transitive* or *intransitive.*

1. In 1861, the Northern states (the Union) and the Southern states (the Confederacy) prepared themselves for a civil war.
2. This "War for Southern Independence" lasted more than four years.
3. The Civil War left devastating effects on America.
4. The war took more than 600,000 lives.
5. The war eliminated the possibility of secession from the Union by the Southern states.

Skill Check B. Write the following sentences. Underline the linking verb in each, and draw a double-headed arrow connecting the words linked by the verb.

6. Slavery was a major issue leading to the Civil War.
7. Slavery had been illegal in the North.
8. However, in the South, slave labor was an important part of the economy.
9. Slavery in newly acquired western lands also became an issue between the North and South.
10. It would be a bloody four-year war.

Skill Check C. Write the verb(s) or verb phrase(s) from each sentence below, and label each one *action* or *linking.*

11. Each side—North and South—grew increasingly hostile.
12. Disagreement over the various issues grew into full-fledged war.
13. To the South, the election of Abraham Lincoln in 1860 seemed a threat.
14. To many in the South, President-elect Lincoln appeared unsympathetic to their interests.
15. As war seemed likely, both the North and the South looked for ways to win.

Skill Check D. Write the complete verb phrase in each sentence below, and underline the helping verbs within each phrase.

16. Before 1862, the Civil War might have been considered only a series of minor skirmishes.
17. However, battles were becoming bloodier and more frequent.
18. By the height of the war, military actions had been occurring almost daily.
19. For instance, on October 3 and 4 of 1862, the South was fighting in Corinth, Mississippi.
20. The next day, a thirty-minute battle was fought at La Vergen, Tennessee.

Section 15.1

Action Verbs

The following verbs—*see, plan, run, eat, shout, tell,* and *sit*—are used frequently and have one thing in common: They all express *action.*

KEY CONCEPT An **action verb** tells what action someone or something is performing. ■

In the sentence "My father *waited* at the station for the train," the verb *waited* tells what the father did. In the sentence "The swans *float* gracefully on the water," the verb *float* tells what swans do. The performers of the action *(father, swans)* are the subjects of the verbs. You may think of action as something you can see someone or something *do.* Some verbs, such as *hear* and *hope,* express mental actions—actions that cannot be seen.

Theme: The Civil War

In this section, you will learn about action verbs and the difference between transitive and intransitive action verbs. The examples and exercises are about the United States Civil War.

Cross-Curricular Connection: Social Studies

Exercise 1 **Identifying Action Verbs** Identify the action verb in each of the following sentences.

EXAMPLE: Most people consider slavery the chief cause of the Civil War.

ANSWER: consider

1. We study the Civil War in history class.
2. Many call it the War Between the States.
3. Indeed, the war split our nation apart.
4. Some people thought the issues unresolvable.
5. The main issues concerned slavery and the economy.
6. The Southern states used slaves to support their economy.
7. Most Northerners believed slavery to be immoral.
8. Few Northerners, however, strongly opposed slavery.
9. Most of them just disagreed with it.
10. The North and South debated the slavery issue before the war.

More Practice

Grammar Exercise Workbook
- pp. 13–14

On-line Exercise Bank
- Section 15.1

Go on-line: PHSchool.com
Enter Web Code: eck-8002

Get instant feedback! Exercises 1, 2, and 3 are available on-line or on CD-ROM.

Exercise 2 **Writing Sentences Using Action Verbs** Write a sentence for each of the following action verbs.

1. examine
2. sprint
3. exploded
4. regretted
5. involve
6. listened
7. convinced
8. charged
9. argue
10. divided

Using Transitive Verbs

Some action verbs are *transitive.*

KEY CONCEPTS An action verb is **transitive** if the receiver of the action is named in the sentence. The receiver of the action is called the **object** of the verb. ■

EXAMPLES: Sandy opened the window with great difficulty.

The truck suddenly hit the pedestrian.

In the first example, *window* receives the action of the verb *opened. Opened* is transitive because the object of the verb—*window*—tells what Sandy opened. In the second example, *hit* is transitive because the object of the verb—*pedestrian*—tells whom the truck hit.

Exercise 3 **Recognizing Transitive Action Verbs** Copy the following sentences. Underline each transitive action verb, and draw an arrow from the verb to its object.

EXAMPLE: The North and the South fought a war.

1. Differing opinions drove the North and South apart.
2. Southerners used slaves to work their extensive cotton plantations.
3. The North developed an industrialized economy that was not dependent on slavery.
4. The South imported most manufactured goods.
5. The South, therefore, opposed high tariffs.
6. The North demanded high tariffs to protect its products from competition.
7. The election of Abraham Lincoln angered the South.
8. Southerners rejected Lincoln's position on slavery.
9. The North supported Lincoln in his fight to end slavery.
10. Such differences finally ignited the Civil War.

More Practice

Grammar Exercise Workbook
- pp. 15–16

On-line Exercise Bank
- Section 15.1

Go on-line:
PHSchool.com
Enter Web Code:
eck-8002

▶ **Critical Viewing**
This painting shows escaping enslaved Africans receiving help from abolitionists. Write a brief caption for the painting, using transitive verbs in your sentences. **[Speculate]**

15.1

Using Intransitive Verbs

Some action verbs are *intransitive*.

KEY CONCEPT An action verb is **intransitive** if no receiver of the action is named in the sentence. An intransitive verb does not have an object. ■

EXAMPLES: The war began.
The bus raced through the traffic light.

Exercise 4 **Recognizing Intransitive Action Verbs** On your paper, write the intransitive action verb in each sentence below. Be prepared to explain why the verb is intransitive.

EXAMPLE: Political disagreements mounted between the North and the South.

ANSWER: mounted

1. The North and South grew further apart.
2. The North fought continually for a central government.
3. Northerners believed in government help for citizens.
4. The North's trading and financial interests benefited from a strong central government.
5. A strong central government would also interfere with slavery.
6. Many people hoped for a country built on compromise.
7. Neither the North nor the South dominated in the Senate.
8. The Senate grew with the addition of Alabama in 1819.
9. Other territories struggled over the question of being "free" or "slave."
10. The North and South prepared for war.

More Practice

Grammar Exercise Workbook
- pp. 15–16

On-line Exercise Bank
- Section 15.1

Go on-line:
PHSchool.com
Enter Web Code:
eck-8002

ADVERTISEMENT.

Twenty Pounds Reward.

RUN away laſt Night, WILLIAM BURNS, aged about 22 Years, about 5 Feet 11 Inches high, of a fair Complexion, ſmooth Face and ſhort black Hair: he is but ſlenderly made, and looks pale and weakly from Sickneſs. He ſays, he has ſerved ſome Time to a Barber; is apt to drink, and is talkative. He took with him, when he went away, a white cloth Coat, a pair of Leather Breeches very well made and almoſt new, three pair of fine Thread Stockings, marked L V F with a ſilver Shaving-Box, ſilver Table-Spoon, a ſmall Rifle-Gun, and a green Livery-Coat with Vellum Button-Holes and faced with white.

WHOEVER takes up the ſaid *Burns*, and will deliver him to Capt. *Fuſer*, in *Charleſtown*, ſhall have TWENTY POUNDS, *South-Carolina* Currency Reward; and if taken above fifty Miles from *Charleſtown*, all reaſonable Charges will be allowed.

New-Barracks, near *Charleſtown*, Nov

▶ **Critical Viewing** This "advertisement" offers a reward for the return of a runaway slave. Write your own advertisement, offering a reward for helping the slave to escape. Use sentences with intransitive verbs. **[Infer]**

Section 15.1 Section Review

GRAMMAR EXERCISES 5–11

Exercise 5 **Identifying Action Verbs** On your paper, write the action verb in each sentence below.

1. On July 1, 1863, Union and Confederate armies stumbled onto each other near Gettysburg, Pennsylvania.
2. The forces quickly began a fierce battle.
3. Union troops held a position on Cemetery Hill for two days.
4. Dramatic action occurred on the third day of battle.
5. General Pickett of the Confederate Army charged the Union forces.

Exercise 6 **Recognizing Transitive Action Verbs** Rewrite the following sentences. Underline each transitive verb, and draw an arrow from the verb to its object.

1. During the Civil War, armies used the railroads for the first time in a large conflict.
2. Railroads quickly transported thousands of soldiers and tons of supplies.
3. The North had almost twice as many railroad lines as the South.
4. The telegraph also brought many advantages to the combatants.
5. Generals could coordinate military movements on the battle fronts.

Exercise 7 **Recognizing Intransitive Action Verbs** Write the intransitive action verb used in each sentence below. Be prepared to explain why the verb is intransitive.

1. In the Civil War, almost all exchanges of prisoners stopped in 1864.
2. People argued in the North and South about the treatment of prisoners.
3. Union prisoners suffered in Confederate camps such as the one at Andersonville.
4. Confederates suffered in Union camps such as Camp Douglas.
5. Enormous death rates resulted from ill treatment, sanitation problems, and malnutrition.

Exercise 8 **Revising Sentences With Transitive Verbs** Revise the following sentences by adding an object to each sentence, making the intransitive verbs transitive.

1. The soldier fired.
2. Both armies suffered.
3. The officer shouted.
4. The cannonball destroyed.
5. After the war, people rebuilt.

Exercise 9 **Find It in Your Reading** Write down the verbs that are used in these lines from Ray Bradbury's "The Drummer Boy of Shiloh." Then, label each one *transitive* or *intransitive.*

> . . . He swallowed. He wiped his eyes. He cleared his throat. He settled himself.

Exercise 10 **Find It in Your Writing** Choose a paper from your portfolio, and identify the action verbs. If you find many forms of the verb *be (am, is, are, was, were)*, try to revise by using action verbs.

Exercise 11 **Writing Application** Write a paragraph about what it might feel like to be a soldier on the first day of battle. Include at least three transitive verbs and three intransitive verbs.

Linking Verbs

Some widely used verbs do not show action. These are called *linking verbs.*

KEY CONCEPT A **linking verb** is a verb that connects a subject with a word that describes or identifies it. ■

EXAMPLES: He is a general for the North.
The winners were Tony and I.
He looks tired from all the fighting.

Recognizing Forms of *Be*

The verb *be* is the most commonly used linking verb.

THE FORMS OF *BE*		
am	can be	have been
are	could be	has been
is	may be	had been
was	might be	could have been
were	must be	may have been
am being	shall be	might have been
are being	should be	must have been
is being	will be	shall have been
was being	would be	should have been
were being		will have been
		would have been

Exercise 12 Recognizing Forms of *Be* as Linking Verbs Copy each of the following sentences onto your paper. Underline the form of *be*, and draw a double-headed arrow connecting the words that are linked by the verb.

EXAMPLE: The Civil War was a long campaign.

ANSWER: The Civil War was a long campaign.

1. Many events were responsible for the Civil War.
2. The Missouri Compromise was not enough to prevent slavery.
3. It was a solution to keep balance in the Senate.
4. Later, the Compromise of 1850 was an agreement making California a free state.
5. The other states were "slave" or "free" by choice.

Theme: The Civil War

In this section, you will learn about linking verbs and the difference between linking verbs and action verbs. The examples and exercises are about the United States Civil War.

Cross-Curricular Connection: Social Studies

More Practice

Grammar Exercise Workbook
- pp. 17–18

On-line Exercise Bank
- Section 15.2

Go on-line:
PHSchool.com
Enter Web Code:
eck-8002

Using Other Linking Verbs

In addition to the verb *be*, a number of other verbs can be used as linking verbs.

OTHER LINKING VERBS					
appear	feel	look	seem	sound	taste
become	grow	remain	smell	stay	turn

These verbs often set up the same relationship between words as the linking verb *be* does. The words that follow the verbs identify or describe the words that precede the verbs.

EXAMPLES: He *became* a general in the Northern army.
Everything *smells* damp and musty.
He *looks* very dirty from all the fighting.

Exercise 13 **Identifying Other Linking Verbs** Copy each of the following sentences onto your paper. Underline the linking verb in each. Then, draw a double-headed arrow connecting the words that are linked by the verb.

1. At the outset, both sides felt confident of a victory.
2. However, their goals remained different.
3. The Confederacy stayed focused on its goal of independence.
4. The goal of the North looked impossible.
5. The North appeared stronger at the beginning.

Exercise 14 **Supplying the Correct Form of Linking Verbs** On a separate sheet of paper, supply an appropriate linking verb for each of the following sentences.

1. Northerners __?__ hopeful of getting Southerners to submit by weakening their ability to fight.
2. The South __?__ very determined, however.
3. Lincoln __?__ unrelenting in pursuing his goal of keeping the Union together.
4. Winfield Scott __?__ a prominent figure in Lincoln's plan.
5. Scott's plan for winning the war __?__ foolproof.
6. After several early Union defeats, however, the war __?__ bloody and drawn out.
7. The Union plan __?__ to seize the Confederate capital, Richmond.
8. The South's leaders __?__ that fighting a defensive battle __?__ enough to win.
9. Instituting a draft meant that Union armies __?__ larger.
10. Many believed that the North's advantage in resources __?__ enough to defeat the South.

More Practice

Grammar Exercise Workbook
- pp. 17–18

On-line Exercise Bank
- Section 15.2

Go on-line: PHSchool.com
Enter Web Code: eck-8002

Get instant feedback! Exercises 12, 13, and 14 are available on-line or on CD-ROM.

15.2

Distinguishing Between Action Verbs and Linking Verbs

Most of the twelve verbs in the chart on page 215 can be used as either linking verbs or action verbs.

LINKING: General Lee felt confident.
ACTION: The doctor felt my pulse.
LINKING: The meal tasted cold to the soldiers.
ACTION: The chef tasted the cake.

To see whether a verb is a linking verb or an action verb, substitute *am*, *is*, or *are* for the verb. If the sentence still makes sense and if the new verb links a word before it to a word after it, then the original verb is a linking verb.

EXAMPLE: The soldiers *look* tired.
SUBSTITUTION: The soldiers *are* tired. (LV)

▲ **Critical Viewing** Write several sentences describing what you infer from this photograph about Harriet Tubman's personality and character. Be sure to use at least one action verb and one linking verb in your sentences. **[Infer]**

GRAMMAR IN LITERATURE

from Harriet Tubman: Conductor on the Underground Railroad

Ann Petry

In this excerpt, the linking verb in blue italics is one that often acts as an action verb.

. . . For a while, as they walked, they seemed to carry in them a measure of contentment; some of the serenity and the cleanliness of that big warm kitchen lingered on inside them. But as they walked farther and farther away from the warmth and the light, the cold and the darkness entered into them. They *fell* silent, sullen, suspicious.

Exercise 15 **Distinguishing Between Action Verbs and Linking Verbs** On your paper, write the verb from each of the following sentences. After each action verb, write *AV*, and after each linking verb, write *LV*.

1. The drafting of civilians during wartime became a serious issue.
2. In 1863, the draft became effective in New York City.
3. The laboring class grew fearful of being drafted.
4. They turned against police, firemen, and local militia.
5. New York City looked to the federal army for control.

More Practice

Grammar Exercise Workbook
- pp. 19–20

On-line Exercise Bank
- Section 15.2

Go on-line: PHSchool.com
Enter Web Code: eck-8002

Section 15.2 Section Review

GRAMMAR EXERCISES 16–22

Exercise 16 **Recognizing Forms of *Be* as Linking Verbs** Copy the sentences below, then underline the form of *be* in each. Draw a double-headed arrow connecting the words linked by the verb.

1. Antietam was the most devastating one-day battle of the Civil War.
2. A victory for the South could have been the turning point of the war.
3. Antietam would be a one-day battle.
4. Neither of the armies would be victorious in this battle.
5. However, Antietam would be a major success for the Union.

Exercise 17 **Identifying Other Linking Verbs** Copy the sentences below, then underline the linking verb in each. Draw a double-headed arrow connecting the words linked by the verb.

1. Lee grew apprehensive about invading the North.
2. The battle at Antietam appeared to change Union policy.
3. Lincoln remained consistent in his dream of an undivided Union.
4. After Antietam, Lincoln's views seemed changed.
5. In Lincoln's mind, the abolition of slavery became crucial.

Exercise 18 **Distinguishing Between Action Verbs and Linking Verbs** Write the verb from each sentence below. Label each action verb *AV*, and each linking verb *LV*.

1. Nearly every American became involved in the Civil War in some way.
2. Women's roles grew in the workplace.
3. Business looked to women to fill jobs in factories and hospitals.
4. Many Southern women remained dutiful and courageous.
5. Southern women stayed on their family farms and tended them.

Exercise 19 **Writing Sentences Using Action Verbs and Linking Verbs** Write two sentences for each word below. In the first sentence, use the verb as an action verb; in the second sentence, use it as a linking verb.

1. feel
2. taste
3. look
4. appear
5. sound
6. become
7. grow
8. smell
9. turn
10. remain

Exercise 20 **Find It in Your Reading** In this excerpt from *Harriet Tubman: Conductor on the Underground Railroad*, identify the two linking verbs.

> There were eleven in this party, including one of her brothers and his wife. It was the largest group that she had ever conducted.

Exercise 21 **Find It in Your Writing** Review a draft of a paper you are currently working on, and identify the linking verbs. To make your writing more lively, try to replace some of the linking verbs with action verbs.

Exercise 22 **Writing Application** Write an account of an event from which you have learned something important. It might be a historical event, the results of a science experiment, or an event from your life. Underline the verb(s) in each sentence, and label them *AV* or *LV*.

Section 15.3 Helping Verbs

The following verbs—*be, do, have, will,* and *can*—are also used often and have one thing in common: They all *help other verbs* to create verb phrases.

KEY CONCEPT Helping verbs are placed before other verbs to form verb phrases. ■

In the following examples, the helping verbs are italicized. Notice how they help to change the meaning of *opened.*

EXAMPLES: *has* opened
will have opened
could have been opened
is being opened

Forms of the verb *be* are often used as helping verbs.

SOME FORMS OF *BE* USED AS HELPING VERBS	
Helping Verbs	**Verbs**
is	opening
was being	trained
should be	written
had been	sent
might have been	played

Some other verbs can also be used as helping verbs.

OTHER HELPING VERBS			
do	have	shall	can
does	has	should	could
did	had	will	may
		would	might
			must

Many different verb phrases can be formed using one or more of these helping verbs. The chart below shows just a few.

VERB PHRASES	
Helping Verbs	**Verbs**
does	find
had	gone
should	see
will have	talked
might have	told

Theme: The History of Human Flight

In this section, you will learn about helping verbs and how they are used in verb phrases. The examples and exercises are about the history of flight by humans.

Cross-Curricular Connection: Social Studies

Exercise 23 **Identifying Helping Verbs** For each sentence below, identify the helping verb(s) and the main verb.

EXAMPLE: More people should have been encouraged to study flight.

ANSWER: should have been (helping verbs)
encouraged (main verb)

1. During the eighteenth century, few people had applied themselves to the study of flight.
2. Flapping-wing machines had been studied by Leonardo da Vinci during the fifteenth century.
3. Three important aviation devices were being invented in Europe.
4. These early inventions might have been an inspiration to Leonardo.
5. By 1809, Sir George Cayley had begun to develop the concept of the modern airplane.

Sometimes the words in a verb phrase are separated by other words, such as *not* or *certainly*. The parts of the verb phrase in certain questions are also usually separated. In the following examples, the parts of each verb phrase are italicized.

WORDS SEPARATED: She *could* certainly *have been reached* by phone earlier.
This *has* not *happened* before.
Did you ever *expect* to see such a heavy machine floating in the air?

Exercise 24 **Recognizing Verb Phrases** On your paper, write the complete verb phrase from each sentence below.

EXAMPLE: Patty did not leave the airport until after four.

ANSWER: did leave

1. The airplane, like many other life-changing inventions throughout history, was not immediately recognized for its potential.
2. Prior to World War I, the airplane had occasionally been presented at county fairs.
3. Daredevil pilots would often draw large crowds and a few investors.
4. The United States War Department had quickly expressed interest in the heavier-than-air craft.
5. The Wright brothers did not demonstrate their airplane until 1908.

More Practice

Grammar Exercise Workbook
• pp. 21–22
On-line Exercise Bank
• Section 15.3
Go on-line:
PHSchool.com
Enter Web Code:
eck-8002

Get instant feedback! Exercises 23 and 24 are available on-line or on CD-ROM.

Grammar and Style Tip

Some words within verb phrases may not be verbs themselves. They may be adverbs that describe the main verb.

Hands-on Grammar

Helping-Verb Ring Toss

To help you understand the way helping verbs function in sentences, create a helping-verb ring toss game, and play it with your classmates. Cut the center out of about ten paper plates to use as rings. Around the rim of each ring, write a different helping verb. See the examples below.

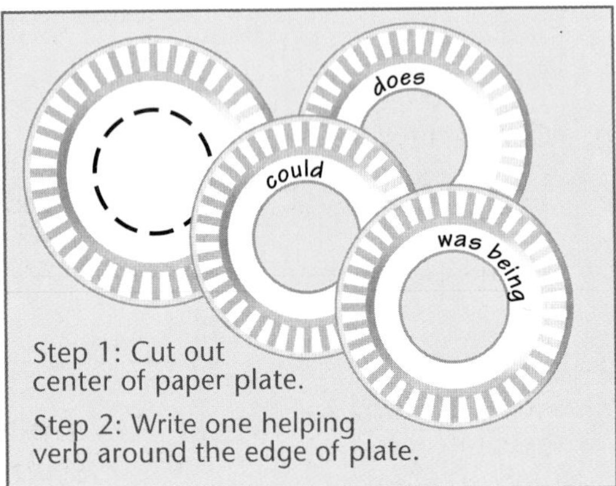

Step 1: Cut out center of paper plate.

Step 2: Write one helping verb around the edge of plate.

Follow these steps to create the stakes onto which the rings will be tossed: (1) Cut out five cardboard T's. The stem of each T should be 1" wide by 7" long; the top of each T should be 1" wide by 5" long. In the center of the top, cut a 1" slot, as shown below. Turn the T upside down, so that the top is now on the bottom. (2) Cut out five more pieces, approximately 1" wide by 5" long. Each of these pieces, when inserted in the slot of each of the five T's, creates a base. On each stake, write a verb in the present tense that is not a helping verb.

1" slit
7"
Walk
1"
5"
5"
1"

Take turns tossing different rings onto different stakes. Once a player succeeds in getting a ring onto a stake, the other team must write a sentence, using both the helping verb on the plate and the verb on the stake correctly. Award points for correct sentences. Your teacher can judge whether a sentence is correct. Continue playing until both sides have had an opportunity to write sentences using each helping verb and each verb on a stake.

Find It in Your Reading In your language arts and social studies textbooks, find five to ten sentences that use helping verbs. For each of the sentences, identify the helping verb(s) and the main verb.

Find It in Your Writing Review your writing portfolio to find ten sentences that include helping verbs. For each sentence, identify the helping verbs and the main verb.

Section 15.3

Section Review

GRAMMAR EXERCISES 25–30

Exercise 25 Identifying Helping Verbs For each of the following sentences, identify the helping verb(s) and the main verb.

1. The year 1913 has been called the "glorious year of flying."
2. Airplanes would be flown with acrobatic maneuverability.
3. Long-distance flights had been made from France to Egypt.
4. A plane might fly across the Mediterranean Sea without any stops.
5. Commercial aviation would begin in January of 1914.
6. This accomplishment might have been credited to the pioneering of the Wright brothers.
7. Commercial aviation would develop slowly during the 1920's and 1930's.
8. In the 1920's, the air-cooled engine had been perfected.
9. This invention would soon influence the airline industry.
10. After World War II, the airline industry would become prosperous.

Exercise 26 Identifying Verb Phrases Write the complete verb phrase from each sentence below, and label its helping and main verbs.

1. Commercial aviation was being used as early as 1914.
2. The first passenger line was being operated between St. Petersburg, Florida, and Tampa, Florida.
3. Improvements in airplane technology were encouraged by World War I.
4. Many pilots had been hired to accommodate the rapid growth of the airlines.
5. Pilots were put through extensive training and were given rigorous written examinations.

Exercise 27 Writing Sentences With Verb Phrases Use the following verb phrases in original sentences.

1. had long been using
2. did not recognize
3. would soon create
4. should be opened
5. have not been tested
6. might have been lost
7. must not disobey
8. can run
9. is climbing
10. could not be heard

Exercise 28 Find It in Your Reading On your paper, write the verb phrases that appear in the following lines from Mark Twain's "Cub Pilot on the Mississippi." Underline the helping verbs.

> . . . An hour later Henry entered the pilothouse, unaware of what had been going on. He was a thoroughly inoffensive boy, and I was sorry to see him come, for I knew Brown would have no pity on him.

Exercise 29 Find It in Your Writing Look over the draft of one of your recent papers, and identify five sentences using verb phrases. On a separate sheet of paper, revise each verb or verb phrase to express your thoughts more precisely.

Exercise 30 Writing Application Write a brief narrative telling what happened on a trip you took in an airplane, a train, a boat, a bus, or a car. Choose verbs that make the event clear. Then, underline each of your verb phrases.

Chapter 16

Adjectives and Adverbs

The stately U.S. Supreme Court building stands majestically in Washington, D.C.

▲ Critical Viewing Write three additional adjectives to describe this famous courthouse. **[Analyze]**

Sometimes a noun cannot communicate all that you want to express. For example, what if you wanted to describe your local courthouse? What words would you use—*large, gray, marble, imposing?* These descriptive words are called adjectives, and they add information about the noun *courthouse.*

Adverbs also help to clarify the meaning of a sentence. They make the meaning of verbs, adjectives, or other adverbs more precise.

There are many uses for adjectives and adverbs. This chapter will cover some of the most common of these uses.

Diagnostic Test

Directions: Write all answers on a separate sheet of paper.

Skill Check A. Write the underlined adjective on your paper, and then label each one *adjective, proper adjective, noun used as an adjective,* or *compound adjective.* Next to each adjective, write the noun it modifies.

1. The Supreme Court is an important American institution.
2. Article III of the United States Constitution sets definite provisions for the establishment of the Supreme Court.
3. The United States Supreme Court is composed of a Chief Justice and eight associate justices.
4. The nine-member bench has been constant in size since 1869.
5. The bench began with six justices in 1789.

Skill Check B. On your paper, write the article that will correctly complete each of the following sentences.

6. (definite) United States government is controlled by a written constitution with rules that guide government leaders.
7. (definite) judicial system makes sure those rules are interpreted and followed correctly.
8. The courts are (indefinite) part of the judicial system used to interpret the laws.
9. Cases generally reach the Supreme Court either from (indefinite) lower federal court or from a state supreme court.
10. The Supreme Court usually takes cases from (indefinite) appeal of a lower court.

Skill Check C. Write each underlined word, and label it *possessive adjective, demonstrative adjective, interrogative adjective,* or *indefinite adjective.* Then, write the noun each adjective modifies. If the word is not used as an adjective, write *pronoun.*

11. When can the defendant appeal this court case to a higher court?
12. Whose court case needs to be appealed?
13. We count on our courts to interpret the law.
14. How many court cases are like that?
15. Few court cases are involved with these proceedings.

Skill Check D. Write the adverbs in each sentence. After each adverb, write the verb, adjective, or adverb it modifies.

16. The sessions of the Supreme Court open in October of each year and almost always adjourn toward the end of June.
17. The Supreme Court rarely ever calls a special session outside that time period.
18. Only four special sessions were called in the last century.
19. A session normally lasts approximately 38 weeks.
20. Justices too often find themselves working between sessions.

Section 16.1

Adjectives

Adjectives add description and other kinds of information to two other parts of speech.

KEY CONCEPT An **adjective** is used to describe a noun or a pronoun. ■

Here are some examples of adjectives used with nouns: *serious* judges, *sleek* jets, *violet* eyes, *tall, majestic* oaks.

Adjectives With Nouns and Pronouns To *modify* means to "change slightly." Adjectives are modifiers because they slightly change the meaning of nouns and pronouns. Adjectives modify meaning by adding information that answers one of four questions: *What kind? Which one? How many?* or *How much?* In the following chart, notice how adjectives answer these questions.

What Kind?	
brick house	*white* paper
Which One?	
that judge	*each* answer
How Many?	
one daffodil	*several* roses
How Much?	
no time	*enough* raisins

An adjective usually comes before the noun it modifies, as do all the adjectives in the chart. Sometimes, however, adjectives come after the nouns they modify.

EXAMPLE: The legal system, *serious* and *complex*, fascinated her.

Predicate adjectives and adjectives that modify pronouns usually come after linking verbs. Sometimes, however, adjectives may come before pronouns.

EXAMPLE: The judge seemed *kind* and *understanding*.
She was *quiet* and *thoughtful*.
Tall and *elegant*, she walked into the room.

Theme: Justice System

In this section, you will learn how adjectives modify the meaning of nouns and pronouns. The examples and exercises in this section are about courts and the American justice system.

Cross-Curricular Connection: Social Studies

▼ **Critical Viewing** Compare the Capitol building with the Supreme Court building on page 222. Use four adjectives in your comparison. **[Compare and Contrast]**

GRAMMAR IN LITERATURE

from *Brown vs. Board of Education*

Walter Dean Myers

In this passage, the adjectives segregated, 1896, *and* legal *(first appearance) come before the nouns they modify.* Separate, equal, *and* legal *(second appearance) are predicate adjectives—they follow a linking verb and describe the subject.*

The states with *segregated* schools relied upon the ruling of the Supreme Court in the *1896 Plessy* vs. *Ferguson* case for *legal* justification: Facilities that were "*separate* but *equal*" were *legal*.

Exercise 1 Recognizing Adjectives and the Words They Modify Copy the following sentences onto your paper. Draw an arrow from each underlined adjective to the noun or pronoun it modifies.

EXAMPLE: Originally, legal aid was financed almost exclusively by private donations.

1. Providing legal counsel for poor people is called legal aid.
2. It is available in civil and criminal cases.
3. The government assumes responsibility for the legal aid of criminal defendants.
4. In some jurisdictions, the judge appoints private lawyers to represent poor people.
5. In 1963, the U.S. Supreme Court declared that every poor defendant charged with a felony is entitled to free counsel as a matter of constitutional right.
6. As a result, the number of public defenders multiplied, as did governmental budgets for legal aid.
7. In 1965, civil legal aid to poor people increased substantially.
8. Free counsel for poor people in civil cases does not yet exist, although some see a slight tendency in that direction.
9. Certain civil cases have been found to be a constitutional right in some state supreme courts.
10. Different types of legal aid in civil cases exist in other countries.

More Practice

Grammar Exercise Workbook
- pp. 16–18

On-line Exercise Bank
- Section 16.1

Go on-line:
PHSchool.com
Enter Web Code:
eck-8002

Get instant feedback! Exercise 1 is available on-line or on CD-ROM.

16.1

Articles

Three commonly used adjectives are called *articles—the, a,* and *an.* These three words are adjectives because they come before nouns and answer the question *Which one?* Because of the way it modifies nouns, *the* is called the *definite* article.

KEY CONCEPT *The,* the **definite article,** refers to a specific person, place, or thing.

EXAMPLES: *the* court *the* attorney *the* broken law

The other two articles, *a* and *an,* are not as specific as *the.*

KEY CONCEPT *A* and *an,* the **indefinite articles,** refer to any one of a class of people, places, or things. ■

EXAMPLES: *a* court *an* attorney *a* broken law

▼ **Critical Viewing** Identify three objects in the picture—one that can be introduced by *the,* one by *a,* and one by *an.* **[Identify]**

A is used before consonant sounds. *An* is used before vowel sounds. Notice that you choose between *a* and *an* according to *sound.* The letter *h,* a consonant, may sound like either a consonant or a vowel. *O* and *u* are vowels, but they may sometimes sound like consonants.

EXAMPLES:
a hero
an honor
a university
an understanding
a one-act play
an open door

Exercise 2 **Distinguishing Between Definite and Indefinite Articles** On your paper, write the article that will correctly complete each of the following sentences. The word in parentheses tells you *what kind* of article.

1. The right to legal representation is (definite) basis of our legal tradition.
2. (indefinite) honest lawyer does not profit from (definite) outcome of a case if it is contrary to the client's interests.
3. (Indefinite) lawyer's primary responsibility toward (indefinite) client may conflict with certain ethical principles.
4. (definite) majority of lawyers believe the conflict must be resolved in favor of the client in most cases.
5. In (indefinite) criminal case, for example, a lawyer may have to choose between losing (definite) case or knowingly allowing the client to commit perjury in testifying.

More Practice

Grammar Exercise Workbook
- pp. 16–18

On-line Exercise Bank
- Section 16.1

Go on-line:
PHSchool.com
Enter Web Code:
eck-8002

Nouns Used as Adjectives

Nouns are sometimes used as adjectives. When a noun is used as an adjective, it comes before another noun and answers the question *What kind?* or *Which one?*

NOUNS: court, morning
ADJECTIVES: a court date, a morning appointment

Exercise 3 **Identifying Nouns Used as Adjectives** Each of the following sentences contains one noun used as an adjective. Write the modifying noun on your paper, and next to it write the noun it modifies.

EXAMPLE: The states, not Congress, make state laws.
ANSWER: state (laws)

1. Congress makes public laws.
2. Congress is made up of two government houses, the House of Representatives and the Senate.
3. When the President of the United States signs a bill, it becomes not just state law, but the law of the land.
4. Congress is also responsible for determining whether public policies are being administered according to the law.
5. Both houses of Congress are concerned with protecting citizen rights.
6. House members and senators are expected to represent the people in their districts and states.
7. Although the two houses of Congress meet separately, they sometimes meet in joint sessions.
8. Often, business begins after a roll call of all members.
9. House members must have been citizens of the United States for at least seven years before running for office.
10. Sometimes, government business in Congress may be broadcast to the public on radio or television.

Proper Adjectives Some proper adjectives are simply proper nouns used as adjectives. Others are adjectives made from proper nouns.

KEY CONCEPTS A **proper adjective** is (1) a proper noun used as an adjective or (2) an adjective formed from a proper noun.

When a proper noun is used as an adjective, its form does not change.

Proper Nouns	Used as Proper Adjectives
Arizona	*Arizona* desert (*What kind* of desert?)
Tuesday	*Tuesday* morning (*Which* morning?)
Churchill	*Churchill* memorial (*Which* memorial?)

Proper Nouns	Proper Adjectives Formed From Proper Nouns
Elizabeth	*Elizabethan* literature (*What kind* of literature?)
Boston	*Bostonian* architecture (*What* kind of architecture?)

Exercise 4 **Recognizing Proper Adjectives** Find the proper adjective(s) in each sentence, and write them on your paper. Next to each proper adjective, write the noun it modifies.

EXAMPLE: The United States senators serve in the upper house of the Congress.

ANSWER: United States (senators)

1. United States citizens elect senators every six years.
2. Until the 1900's, however, Senate seats were filled by members elected by individual state legislatures.
3. Then, an Oregon initiative began direct election of senators by the citizens of the state.
4. In 1911, a Kansas senator offered a resolution proposing a constitutional amendment for the election of all senators by the people.
5. The oath taken by each senator to uphold the Constitution dates back to the Civil War era.
6. The Senate floor leaders are elected by the members of their party.
7. Party leaders in the Senate often meet with House party leaders.
8. The United States Constitution gives the Senate certain unique powers.
9. For example, the Senate has the power to accept or reject the President's appointments of Supreme Court justices.
10. However, both Senate and House approval are needed to send a bill to the President for signing.

More Practice

Grammar Exercise Workbook
- pp. 16–18

On-line Exercise Bank
- Section 16.1

Go on-line: PHSchool.com
Enter Web Code: eck-8002

Get instant feedback! Exercises 4 and 5 are available on-line or on CD-ROM.

Exercise 5 Revising Sentences With Proper Adjectives

Revise each sentence, replacing the underlined phrase with a proper adjective.

EXAMPLE: Our court system is based on the common law <u>of England</u>.

ANSWER: Our court system is based on English common law.

1. Law <u>in Asia</u> developed differently from our own.
2. Between 403 B.C. and 221 B.C., legalists <u>in China</u> believed that every aspect of life should be ruled by a set of strict and impersonal laws.
3. The beginnings of our legal system came from laws <u>of ancient Greece.</u>
4. Democracy <u>in Athens</u> included a jury system to decide court cases.
5. Later, in courts <u>of ancient Rome</u>, juries composed of senators and knights ruled on crimes such as corruption, treason, and poisoning.
6. Most legal systems <u>of Europe</u> grew out of the laws of these ancient cultures.
7. Both the court system <u>of America</u> and the court system <u>of Britain</u> share the same historic roots.
8. In the sixteenth and seventeenth centuries, it was determined that the monarch <u>of England</u> would be subject to the law, and the courts would be independent of the monarch.
9. Now, many countries <u>in North America, South America, Asia, Africa, and Europe</u> have independent court systems.
10. Some other legal systems are tied to a national religion; for example, law <u>in Iran</u> is based on the beliefs <u>of Islam</u>.

▼ **Critical Viewing** Lawyers in England wear white wigs such as this. What proper adjective would you use to describe a lawyer from England? **[Connect]**

◀ Critical Viewing Here is one compound adjective and noun pairing to describe the Capitol building: *backbreaking steps.* Can you name three others? **[Analyze]**

Compound Adjectives

Just as there are compound nouns, there are also *compound adjectives.* A compound adjective is made up of more than one word.

Most compound adjectives are written as hyphenated words. Sometimes, however, they are written as combined words. If you are uncertain about which way to write a compound adjective, consult a dictionary for the correct spelling.

HYPHENATED: one-sided opinion
so-called expert

COMBINED: heartbreaking news
nearsighted witness

Exercise 6 Recognizing Compound Adjectives Find the compound adjective in each sentence and write it on your paper. Next to the compound adjective, write the noun it modifies.

EXAMPLE: A member of Congress should be well qualified for his or her job.

ANSWER: well qualified (member)

1. The House of Representatives is the larger governmental body in our two-chambered Congress.
2. Members of the House of Representatives serve two-year terms, and the entire membership stands for reelection every second year.
3. Population-based seats in the House are used to assure fair representation for all citizens.
4. The day-to-day activities of the House of Representatives can be seen on cable television.
5. You may notice outspoken representatives arguing about some issues.

Grammar and Style Tip

Sometimes two or more adjectives of equal importance are used to describe a noun. These should be separated with commas. A compound adjective, however, is not written with commas and may sometimes require a hyphen.

Pronouns Used as Adjectives

Pronouns, like nouns, can sometimes be used as adjectives.

KEY CONCEPT A pronoun is used as an adjective if it modifies a noun. ■

Four kinds of pronouns are sometimes used as adjectives. They are *personal, demonstrative, interrogative,* and *indefinite* pronouns.

Possessive Adjectives The following personal pronouns are often called *possessive adjectives: my, your, his, her, its, our,* and *their.* Because they have antecedents, they are considered to be pronouns. They are also adjectives, because they answer the question *Which one?*

EXAMPLE: The President is preparing *his* state-of-the-union message.

This example shows that *his* is an adjective modifying the noun *message. His* is also a pronoun because it has an antecedent, *President.*

Exercise 7 **Identifying Possessive Adjectives** On your paper, make three columns as shown in the example. Write the underlined word in the first column. Then, find the noun it modifies and its antecedent, and put them in the second and third columns.

EXAMPLE: The President exerts a unifying influence through <u>his</u> position as head of state.

ANSWER:

Possessive Adjective	Noun Modified	Antecedent
his	position	President

1. The President of the United States performs <u>his</u> many duties as head of state, head of government, and Commander in Chief of the armed forces.
2. Presidential candidates are nominated by <u>their</u> political parties.
3. The President is officially elected only after the Electoral College announces <u>its</u> vote tally.
4. We as a nation count on <u>our</u> President to uphold the Constitution.
5. As First Lady, the President's wife also has a responsibility to <u>her</u> country.

More Practice

Grammar Exercise Workbook
- pp. 19–20

On-line Exercise Bank
- Section 16.1

Go on-line: PHSchool.com
Enter Web Code: eck-8002

Get instant feedback! Exercises 6 and 7 are available on-line or on CD-ROM.

Demonstrative Adjectives The four demonstrative pronouns—*this, that, these,* and *those*—can be used as demonstrative adjectives.

PRONOUN: I saw *this*.
ADJECTIVE: I'll vote on *this* issue.

PRONOUN: I want *those*.
ADJECTIVE: Count *those* ballots.

Exercise 8 **Recognizing Demonstrative Adjectives** Find the word *this, that, these,* or *those* in each of the sentences below and copy it. If it is used as a pronoun, write *pronoun* after it. If it is used as an adjective, write the noun it modifies.

EXAMPLE: That is the United States President.
ANSWER: That (pronoun)

1. Chief Executive: This is the one title of the President.
2. This office has powers as well as limitations.
3. These are the cabinet members appointed by the President.
4. The Senate now must approve those judgeships recommended by the President.
5. The President appointed that ambassador.

More Practice

Grammar Exercise Workbook
- pp. 19–20

On-line Exercise Bank
- Section 16.1

Go on-line: PHSchool.com
Enter Web Code: eck-8002

Get instant feedback! Exercises 8, 9, and 10 are available on-line or on CD-ROM.

GRAMMAR IN LITERATURE

from Brown vs. Board of Education

Walter Dean Myers

In this passage, the demonstrative adjective these *modifies the nouns* men *and* women.

It was Thurgood Marshall and a battery of N.A.A.C.P. attorneys who began to challenge segregation throughout the country. *These* men and women were warriors in the cause of freedom for African Americans, taking their battles into courtrooms across the country.

Interrogative Adjectives Three interrogative pronouns—*which, what,* and *whose*—can be used as *interrogative adjectives.*

PRONOUN: *What* did he want?
ADJECTIVE: *What* sentence did he give?

PRONOUN: *Whose* is that?
ADJECTIVE: *Whose* courtroom is that?

Exercise 9 **Recognizing Interrogative Adjectives** Find the word *which, what,* or *whose* in each of the sentences below and copy it. If it is used as a pronoun, write *pronoun* after it. If it is used as an adjective, write the noun it modifies.

EXAMPLE: What verdict is the jury going to reach?
ANSWER: What (verdict)

1. What would cause the impeachment of a judge?
2. Which law states that a judge must have good behavior?
3. Whose salary cannot be reduced while he or she holds office?
4. What are the powers of the Supreme Court justices?
5. Which court has the authority to hear a case without its being heard elsewhere first?

Indefinite Adjectives A number of indefinite pronouns—*both, few, many, each, most,* and *all,* among others—can also be used as *indefinite adjectives.*

PRONOUN: I bought one of *each.*
ADJECTIVE: *Each* judge writes an opinion.

PRONOUN: I don't want *any.*
ADJECTIVES: I don't want *any* help.

Exercise 10 **Recognizing Indefinite Adjectives** Write the indefinite pronoun or adjective in each of the sentences below onto your paper. If it is used as a pronoun, write *pronoun* after it. If it is used as an adjective, write the noun it modifies.

EXAMPLE: Few cases are thrown out of court.
ANSWER: Few (cases)

1. Each Supreme Court justice may serve for life.
2. All Supreme Court justices are appointed by the President.
3. Very few judicial questions are not resolved.
4. Many are the basis of new laws.
5. The Supreme Court acts as both referee and overseer.

Spelling Tip

The interrogative pronoun *whose* is one word. The word *who's* is a contraction formed from the two words *who* and *is.*

Hands-on Grammar

Demonstrative, Interrogative, and Indefinite Adjectives Pop-up

1. Fold a piece of 6-1/2" X 8-1/2" paper so that it has a pocket as shown.
2. On the left side of the fold, list all the demonstrative, interrogative, and indefinite pronouns, such as *this, that, these, those, each, few, what,* and *whose.*
3. On the right side of the fold, complete the sentence, and making sure that the verb agrees in number with the pronoun: *This is the best. Those are the best.*
4. Now, make a list of nouns in the pocket, so that when you open the paper fully, you get a complete sentence in which adjective, noun, and verb all agree in number.
5. When you open the paper, the pronouns become adjectives.

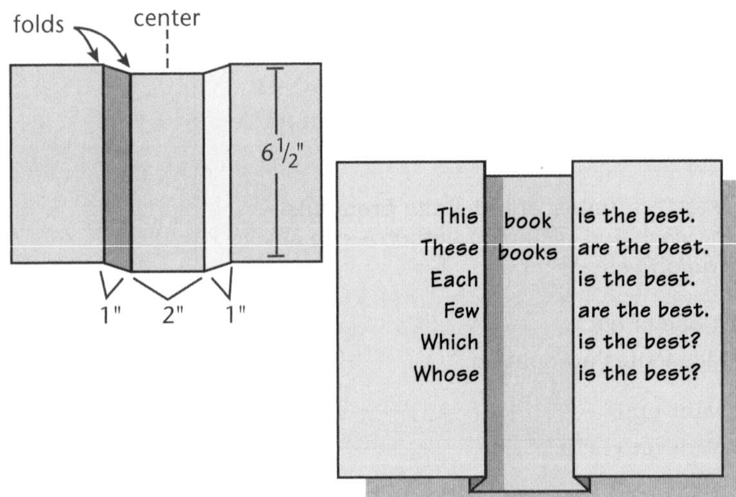

Find It in Your Reading In a short story or in a textbook, pick out examples of demonstrative, interrogative, and indefinite adjectives. Rewrite the examples, using the adjectives as pronouns.

Find It in Your Writing Look through your portfolio to find examples of demonstrative, interrogative, and indefinite adjectives. Make sure that they agree in number with the nouns they modify and with the verbs.

Section 16.1 Section Review

GRAMMAR EXERCISES 11–16

Exercise 11 **Recognizing and Classifying Adjectives and the Words They Modify** Copy each sentence onto your paper. Draw an arrow pointing from each underlined adjective to the noun it modifies. Indicate whether each underlined word is (a) an *adjective,* (b) a *proper adjective,* (c) a *compound adjective,* (d) a *possessive adjective,* or (e) a *noun used as an adjective.*

1. A court is a government agency.
2. It makes decisions in legal disputes.
3. The disputes are often serious.
4. Courts also provide much-needed protection from illegal actions.
5. Sometimes courts resolve disputes of great political and social significance.
6. Our court system is based on English common law.
7. Defense attorneys offer legal advice.
8. American, Canadian, and English governments abide by common law.
9. In 1848, David Dudley Field worked on the New York code of civil procedure.
10. His work influenced the development of our modern judicial system.

Exercise 12 **Using Definite and Indefinite Articles** On your paper, write the article or articles that correctly complete each of the following sentences.

1. A dispute before a court may be called (indefinite) action.
2. (Indefinite) civil case involves possible violation of (indefinite) person's rights.
3. (Indefinite) broken contract suit is (indefinite) example of a civil case.
4. (Indefinite) criminal case involves alleged violations of (definite) public laws.
5. Crimes are seen as (indefinite) threat to (definite) whole society.

Exercise 13 **Revising Sentences With Demonstrative, Interrogative, and Indefinite Adjectives and Pronouns** Identify whether each underlined word in the following sentences is being used as a *pronoun* or an *adjective.*

1. The Supreme Court made that decision.
2. Whose case was in court today?
3. The defendant denied he took those.
4. All felt he was guilty.
5. Any defendant can waive the right to a jury trial.
6. What did the jury decide in the case?
7. That is a lie, the plaintiff argued.
8. Which juror was the foreperson?
9. Is either eligible for jury service?
10. The judge will use these facts to decide.

Exercise 14 **Find It in Your Reading** In this passage from "Brown *vs.* Board of Education," find a proper adjective and two nouns used as adjectives

> At Howard there was a law professor, Charles Hamilton Houston, who would affect the lives of many African-American lawyers and who would influence the legal aspects of the civil rights movement.

Exercise 15 **Find It in Your Writing** Look in your portfolio for a paragraph that describes something or someone. Circle the adjectives you used.

Exercise 16 **Writing Application** Imagine that you are a court reporter covering a civil or criminal trial. Write a brief description of events or people that you notice in the courtroom.

Section 16.2

Adverbs

Adverbs modify three different parts of speech.

KEY CONCEPT An **adverb** modifies a verb, an adjective, or another adverb. ■

To recognize adverbs, you need to know how they modify each of these three parts of speech.

Theme: Life in the Wetlands

In this section, you will learn how adverbs modify the meaning of verbs, adjectives, and other adverbs. The examples and exercises in this section are about plant and animal life in wetlands.

Cross-Curricular Connection: Science

Adverbs Modifying Verbs

An adverb modifying a verb will answer one of four questions about the verb: *Where? When? In what way?* or *To what extent?*

ADVERBS MODIFYING VERBS

Where?	
drove *down* is *here*	stay *nearby* jump *away*
When?	
report *later* will leave *soon*	come *tomorrow* appeared *suddenly*
In What Way?	
cautiously approached smiled *happily*	walk *quietly* tell *unwillingly*
To What Extent?	
nearly won *hardly* counted	had *almost* left *scarcely* escaped

Exercise 17 Recognizing How Adverbs Modify Verbs Write the underlined adverb and the verb it modifies on your paper. Then, identify the question the adverb answers about the verb.

EXAMPLE: Animals in the wetlands interact somewhat.
ANSWER: somewhat (interact; *To what extent?*)

1. Wetlands primarily are caused by water saturating an area.
2. Often, these wetlands result from ground water coming to the surface.
3. Ground water moves slowly through the soil and accumulates near the surface.
4. The water table will then rise.
5. If the water table in an area reaches the surface, wetlands develop there.

More Practice

Grammar Exercise Workbook
- pp. 21–23

On-line Exercise Bank
- Section 16.2

Go on-line: PHSchool.com *Enter Web Code:* eck-8002

Exercise 18 Revising Sentences by Adding Adverbs

Rewrite each sentence below, adding an adverb that answers the question in parentheses.

EXAMPLE: Wetland vegetation (to what extent?) includes woody plants, such as trees.

ANSWER: Wetland vegetation mostly includes woody plants, such as trees.

1. Wetlands (to what extent?) form in places where water is trapped.
2. Wetlands (to what extent?) look mossy, grassy, shrubby, or wooded.
3. In a marshy wetland, tall grassy plants sway (in what way?) above the water.
4. Cypress trees grow (in what way?) in swampy areas of the South.
5. Because rain falls (when?) in these areas, plant life thrives.
6. Swamps (to what extent?) have a distinct odor of decay.
7. Tannic acid, derived from decaying vegetation, (in what way?) changes the color of the swamp water.
8. The water (where?) becomes dark brown or tea-colored.
9. Wetlands along Florida's coasts are (to what extent) dominated by mangrove forests.
10. The thick roots of mangrove trees anchor them (in what way?) against tropical winds and storms.

▼ **Critical Viewing** Use adverbs in sentences to describe how the wind is blowing, how the grasses are swaying, and how the clouds are moving in the Everglades National Park in Florida. **[Analyze]**

Adverbs Modifying Adjectives

When an adverb modifies an adjective, it answers the question *To what extent*?

ADVERBS MODIFYING ADJECTIVES		
almost right	*not* sad	*unusually* rich

Exercise 19 **Recognizing Adverbs That Modify Adjectives** On your paper, write the adverb from each sentence. After each adverb, write the adjective it modifies.

EXAMPLE: Marshes can be very peaceful.
ANSWER: very (peaceful)

1. A marsh is somewhat similar to a swamp.
2. A marsh has meadow plants and mostly grassy vegetation.
3. Marshes are usually treeless and shrubless.
4. They tend to have mostly soft-stemmed plants.
5. In a marsh, plants are surrounded by nearly still water.
6. Cattails, rushes, arrowheads, and pickerel weed grow with partly submerged stems and leaves.
7. Waterlilies root in the bottom of a marsh, and their rather wide leaves float on the water's surface.
8. Tiny duckweed, water lettuce, and water hyacinth sprout in the relatively open waters of southern marshes and swamps.
9. Completely submerged aquatic plants, such as pondweeds and waterweeds, grow in the deepwater marshes.
10. Pondweeds and waterweeds can grow near the shore of shallow ponds, which can be quite marshlike.

Exercise 20 **Revising Sentences With Adverbs** On your paper, write each sentence given below and add at least one adverb to modify the adjective or the verb.

1. Quicksand is a deep mass of fine sand.
2. It forms on stream bottoms and along seacoasts.
3. Thick layers of quicksand are dangerous.
4. The sand loses its firmness.
5. It cannot support heavy weight.
6. Unwary people and animals can be trapped.
7. If you fall into quicksand, it is important that you stay calm.
8. Do not try to swim with your arms and legs.
9. Fall on your back with your arms stretched out.
10. Then, roll off the sand to firm ground.

More Practice

Grammar Exercise Workbook
- pp. 21–23

On-line Exercise Bank
- Section 16.2

Go on-line: PHSchool.com
Enter Web Code: eck-8002

Get instant feedback! Exercises 19, 20, 21, and 22 are available on-line or on CD-ROM.

Adverbs Modifying Other Adverbs

When adverbs modify other adverbs, they again answer the question *To what extent?*

ADVERBS MODIFYING ADVERBS	
traveled *less* slowly	move *very* cautiously
lost *too* easily	lived *almost* happily

Exercise 21 **Recognizing Adverbs That Modify Other Adverbs** In each sentence, find an adverb that modifies another adverb by answering the question *To what extent?* Write this adverb, followed by the adverb it modifies.

1. Wetland animal life is rather highly diverse and includes many aquatic insects.
2. Some aquatic insects spend only their very early stages of life in the water.
3. Other aquatic insects are nearly permanently bound to the water.
4. The anhinga, or snakebird, is most often seen spearing its fish as it dives beneath the open-water areas of marshes.
5. Muskrats quite voluntarily frequent cattail marshes, where they feed on the roots of cattail plants.
6. Large groups of muskrats can almost completely clear an entire area of cattails.
7. Many species of amphibians most certainly live in wetlands.
8. Alligators are quite often found in Florida swamp areas during the dry season.
9. Many of the animals that inhabit swamps almost always live in marshes, too.
10. The raccoon and beaver are hardly ever seen in dry areas of the forest.

Exercise 22 **Writing Sentences With Adverbs That Modify Other Adverbs** Write sentences using the following adverbs.

1. unusually slowly
2. most often
3. quite easily
4. very quickly
5. hardly ever

▼ **Critical Viewing** Use at least four adverbs in sentences describing how this alligator moves, looks, or feeds. **[Infer]**

Adverb or Adjective?

Some words can be either adverbs or adjectives. An adverb always modifies a verb, an adjective, or another adverb. An adjective modifies a noun or a pronoun.

ADVERB MODIFYING VERB: He drove *fast.*
ADJECTIVE MODIFYING NOUN: He is a *fast* driver.

ADVERB MODIFYING ADJECTIVE: She is *much* happier now.
ADJECTIVE MODIFYING NOUN: I ate too *much* food.

Although many adverbs end in *-ly*, not all words ending in *-ly* are adverbs. Some adjectives are formed by adding *-ly* to nouns.

Nouns	Adjectives With *-ly* Endings
a beautiful *home*	a *homely* animal
an *elder* in the church	an *elderly* man
his true *love*	*lovely* flowers

▼ **Critical Viewing** These great blue herons live in a marshland. Use adjectives and adverbs to write a brief description of the advantages for these birds of living in a marshland. **[Speculate]**

GRAMMAR IN LITERATURE

from Saving the Wetlands

Barbara A. Lewis

The adverb highlighted in blue italics describes how *he was carried. It modifies the verb* carried.

Then he carried him *upside-down* for a quarter of a mile—all the way to his house. He knew that skunks can't spray when held by the tail.

Exercise 23 **Distinguishing Between Adverbs and Adjectives** On your paper, indicate whether the underlined word in each of the following sentences is an adverb or an adjective.

EXAMPLE: Some might consider a salt marsh ugly.
ANSWER: adjective

1. Many lively animals inhabit Florida's Everglades.
2. Some species of snakes live only in the Everglades.
3. The Florida panther is not the only endangered animal living there.
4. Naturalists hope they have not begun too late to save the Florida panther.
5. It is a truly beautiful animal.
6. Suzette was a late arrival to our touring group.
7. The animal I enjoyed most was the flamingo.
8. The best time to view many swamp animals is early in the morning.
9. Most swamp birds have long, thin legs.
10. The herons flew straight to their homes in the wetland marsh.

More Practice

Grammar Exercise Workbook
- pp. 21–23

On-line Exercise Bank
- Section 16.2

Go on-line:
PHSchool.com
Enter Web Code:
eck-8002

Get instant feedback! Exercise 23 is available on-line or on CD-ROM.

◀ **Critical Viewing** Imagine that you are walking down this nature trail in the Big Cypress Swamp in Florida. Briefly describe what you might see and hear. Use adjectives and adverbs in your sentences. **[Infer]**

Section 16.2 **Section Review**

GRAMMAR EXERCISES 24–30

Exercise 24 **Recognizing Adverbs and the Words They Modify** On your paper, write the adverbs in the sentences below. Then, identify the question each answers and the word each modifies.

1. This marsh is mostly filled with plants.
2. Many snails make their homes there.
3. The waterlily is very commonly found in the wetlands.
4. It is characterized by large, nearly circular leaves.
5. Its wide, floating leaves are normally known as lily pads.
6. Its rather bright flowers can be white, yellow, pink, scarlet, blue, or purple.
7. The pleasantly fragrant flowers attract insects.
8. Clams, shrimp, and worms jointly created a burrow system in this swamp.
9. The small creatures often hide within these muddy tunnels.
10. Fishermen nearly always search for these areas.

Exercise 25 **Distinguishing Between Adverbs and Adjectives** On your paper, label the underlined word in each sentence *adverb* or *adjective*.

1. Raccoons take nightly trips for food.
2. They can move very fast.
3. They are not the only night prowlers.
4. Raccoons come out in the daytime only if they are not feeling well.
5. The raccoon came too late to find food.

Exercise 26 **Revising With Adverbs** On your paper, revise the following paragraph by adding adverbs.

The eastern diamondback rattlesnake is the largest poisonous snake in the United States. Eastern diamondbacks can grow as long as eight feet, with the average length being two to six feet. Like other rattlesnakes, they make a buzzing sound with the rattles on their tails when they feel threatened. They live in the southeastern United States and eat rabbits, rodents, and birds.

Exercise 27 **Revising Sentences by Adding Adverbs** Add an adverb to modify the underlined word. Identify the part of speech of the underlined word.

1. Coral snakes are beautiful.
2. Coral snakes are also poisonous.
3. They live in the southern United States.
4. They can be identified by their bands of color.
5. If you see one, move cautiously.

Exercise 28 **Find It in Your Reading** Identify two adverbs in this sentence from "Saving the Wetlands." Tell what words they modify.

> I finally came clean, but we had to throw my sneakers away.

Exercise 29 **Find It in Your Writing** Look through your portfolio for sentences that describe how someone did something. Circle any adverbs you used.

Exercise 30 **Writing Application** Imagine that you have put together a photo essay from your visit to a swamp. Write captions for several photos, making sure to include adverbs.

Chapter 16 Chapter Review

GRAMMAR EXERCISES 31–34

Exercise 31 **Recognizing Adjectives and the Words They Modify** Each of the following sentences contains at least one underlined adjective. Write the adjectives on your paper, and label each one *adjective, proper adjective, compound adjective, noun used as adjective, definite article* or *indefinite article.*

1. The American bittern is a typical bird of the wetlands.
2. Many bitterns have brownish bodies with dark, longitudinal stripes.
3. The stripes help them blend in with the tall grasses in their habitats.
4. They feed on small aquatic animals.
5. The American bittern builds its small nest on the ground.
6. A well-known Floridian attraction is the marshland areas of the Everglades.
7. This became the home region of the Seminole Indians.
8. Its mangrove swamps are fascinating to explore.
9. Visitors can often spot alligator nests.
10. The American government is trying to protect endangered animals there.
11. Gallinules are birds that have cone-shaped bills.
12. They live in weed-filled Florida marshes and swamps.
13. One common gallinule is sooty-colored with a red, shieldlike forehead.
14. The more colorful purple gallinule is quite attractive.
15. Their widespread toes permit them to walk on lily pads or aquatic plants.

Exercise 32 **Recognizing Demonstrative, Interrogative, and Indefinite Adjectives** Label each underlined word in the following sentences *pronoun* or *adjective.*

1. Is that a green tree frog?
2. What place does it call home?
3. That one lives in a swamp in Georgia.
4. Those feet allow the tree frog to cling to tree trunks.
5. This coloration helps him blend into the background.
6. Which are its favorite foods?
7. Insects like these are what he eats.
8. What is that threadlike green stuff?
9. Few people in our group had ever seen it before.
10. Did you see which tree had Spanish moss on it?

Exercise 33 **Writing Sentences With Demonstrative, Interrogative, and Indefinite Adjectives** Use each of the words below in a sentence.

1. which (pronoun)
2. what (adjective)
3. each (pronoun)
4. few (adjective)
5. this (pronoun)
6. that (adjective)
7. his (adjective)
8 any (adjective)
9. whose (pronoun)
10. those (pronoun)

Exercise 34 **Identifying Adverbs and the Words They Modify** In each of the following sentences, identify the adverb and the word it modifies. Also, identify the part of speech of the modified word.

1. The red-winged blackbird commonly inhabits wetland marshes.
2. It generally flies in the marshes and upland fields of North America.
3. The male red-winged blackbird clearly bears flashing-red shoulder patches.
4. Many blackbirds nest sociably in colonies.

Chapter 17 Prepositions

▲ **Critical Viewing** What prepositions can you use to tell the location of the high jumper in relation to the bar? **[Analyze]**

Prepositions show how some words in your sentences relate to others. They can make important differences in your ideas. For instance, in writing about track-and-field events, it might be important to identify the distance *between* two competitors, the leaders *in* a race, the runner who sprinted first *across* the finish line. As you see, prepositions help to identify location.

In this chapter, you will learn to recognize prepositions and to use them effectively in your sentences.

Diagnostic Test

Directions: Write all answers on a separate sheet of paper.

Skill Check A. Identify the prepositions in the following sentences.

1. You can think about a sport as an athletic game or a test of skill.
2. Sports can be a source of diversion for those who play or observe them.
3. Sports have existed for various purposes since the times of the ancient Egyptians and Greeks.
4. The ancient Egyptians swam, raced, wrestled, and played games with sticks and round objects.
5. At first, the ancient Greeks held athletic contests in honor of the gods or in thanksgiving to them.

Skill Check B. Identify the compound preposition in each sentence.

6. The games provided entertainment, in addition to having religious significance.
7. According to historians, the games were a vital part of ancient Greek civilization.
8. Eventually, professional athletes played in place of volunteer citizens.
9. Because of the importance of the games, winners were treated as heroes.
10. Warring city-states sometimes called a truce due to the games.

Skill Check C. Write the prepositional phrase(s) you find in each sentence below. Circle the object of each preposition.

11. In Rome, games took place at the beginning of each year.
12. At first, the public treasury provided funds for the events.
13. Corrupt politicians later tried winning the support of the people by lavishly spending excessive amounts of money on the games.
14. These politicians held games on the slightest pretext so that they could compete for the favor of the public.
15. Over time, athletic events lost their original religious meaning and purpose among the people.

Skill Check D. Write *prep* if the underlined word in each sentence below is used as a preposition. Write *adv* if it is used as an adverb.

16. We have learned a lot <u>about</u> the games.
17. They were celebrated <u>over</u> the summer every four years.
18. Each city-state brought <u>along</u> its best athletes.
19. The athletes walked <u>about</u>, waiting to be called.
20. Some stood in lines <u>along</u> the edge of the arena.

Recognizing Prepositions

Prepositions are words such as *against, among, at, beyond, during, of,* and *on.*

KEY CONCEPT A **preposition** relates the noun or pronoun following it to another word in the sentence. ■

The chart below lists fifty of the most commonly used prepositions.

FREQUENTLY USED PREPOSITIONS				
about	behind	during	off	to
above	below	except	on	toward
across	beneath	for	onto	under
after	beside	from	opposite	underneath
against	besides	in	out	until
along	between	inside	outside	up
among	beyond	into	over	upon
around	but	like	past	with
at	by	near	since	within
before	down	of	through	without

Theme: Sports

In this chapter, you will learn about prepositions and prepositional phrases. The examples and exercises are about sports.

Cross-Curricular Connection: Physical Education

Exercise 1 **Recognizing and Revising Prepositions** Write the preposition in each of the following sentences. Then, revise the sentence, using a different preposition.

EXAMPLE: The boys played basketball at noon.
ANSWER: at—The boys played basketball <u>before</u> noon.

1. Basketball is a game played between two opposing five-person teams.
2. The basketball court features a large circle at the center.
3. A basketball hoop is suspended above each end.
4. Each player has a position to play in the game.
5. The center often stands beneath the basket to catch rebounds.
6. There are also two guards, who are leaders within the team, as well as two forwards.
7. In the beginning, a jump ball gets the game started.
8. Shooting the ball into the hoop can give a team either one, two, or three points.
9. A team must also defend its basket from its opponents' attacks.
10. The team that has the most points by the end wins.

More Practice

Grammar Exercise Workbook
- pp. 39–40

On-line Exercise Bank
- Chapter 17

Go on-line: PHSchool.com
Enter Web Code: eck-8002

KEY CONCEPT Prepositions consisting of two or three words are called *compound prepositions.* ■

Some compound prepositions are listed in this chart.

COMPOUND PREPOSITIONS		
according to	by means of	instead of
ahead of	in addition to	in view of
apart from	in back of	next to
aside from	in front of	on account of
as of	in place of	on top of
because of	in spite of	out of

The choice of preposition affects the way the other words in a sentence relate to each other. In the following example, read the sentence, using each preposition in turn. Notice how each preposition changes the relationship between *played* and *gym.*

EXAMPLE: The girls played {near / opposite / in back of} the gym.

▼ **Critical Viewing** How many different prepositions can you use to describe the positions of the players in relation to one another and in relation to the ball? **[Analyze]**

Exercise 2 **Recognizing Compound Prepositions** Identify the compound preposition in each of the following sentences.

EXAMPLE: In spite of its limited popularity in the United States, soccer is one of the most popular sports in the world.

ANSWER: in spite of

1. According to archaeologists, kicking games were played in many ancient societies.
2. However, the modern game of soccer was developed in England in the nineteenth century, in addition to other kicking games developed there.
3. In 1863, out of the many different varieties of kicking games, the London Football Association recognized two: rugby football and association football ("soccer" in the United States).
4. In rugby football, the athlete controls the ball by means of handling and carrying; however, association football forbids the use of hands.
5. Later, because of the rules established by the London Football Association, soccer became widely popular among people of the working classes.

17

Recognizing Prepositional Phrases

A preposition must always be followed by a noun or a pronoun. The group of words beginning with the preposition and ending with the noun or pronoun is called a *prepositional phrase.* The noun or pronoun that follows the preposition is called the *object of the preposition.* Notice that when identifying the object of a preposition, you do not include any modifiers of the noun or pronoun.

EXAMPLES:

PREP OBJ of PREP
with us

PREP OBJ of PREP
according to the new coach

PREP OBJ of PREP
inside the large, modern stadium

Exercise 3 **Recognizing Prepositional Phrases** Write the prepositional phrase or phrases in each sentence, and underline the object of each preposition.

EXAMPLE: Professional football players were recognized for the first time in 1885.

ANSWER: for the first time; in 1885

1. The Football Association Cup, a soccer tournament, was first organized in 1871.
2. The tournament, which is still played today, finishes at Wembley Stadium in London with the annual Cup Final.
3. After its organization, soccer spread rapidly through England.
4. Around 1888, regular league play was begun in many areas of the country.
5. In 1872, the first international game took place at Glasgow between all-star teams from England and Scotland.
6. About the end of the nineteenth century, soccer spread across the globe.
7. British sailors, traders, and workers carried the game with them around the world.
8. In Europe, Germans, Austrians, and Italians quickly took to the sport.
9. In South America, Brazilians, Argentines, and Uruguayans adapted to it quickly and enjoyed the challenges that came with the game.
10. Finally, the first World Championship, now known as the World Cup, was organized in 1930, and it is now wildly popular all around the world.

Grammar and Style Tip

The object of a preposition may be more than one word, such as a compound proper noun *(in the Grand Canyon)* or two objects linked by a conjunction *(between the defenders and the goal).*

Distinguishing Between Prepositions and Adverbs

Some words can be either prepositions or adverbs, depending on how they are used in a sentence. To be a *preposition*, a word must have an object and be part of a prepositional phrase. An *adverb* modifies a verb and has no object.

PREPOSITION: The ball flew *past* third base.
ADVERB: The umpire ran *past* quickly.

PREPOSITION: They sat *inside* the dugout.
ADVERB: Please come *inside* soon.

▲ **Critical Viewing** Where might the ball have gone? Use one or more prepositions in your answer. Then, see if you can use the same word as an adverb. **[Speculate]**

Exercise 4 **Distinguishing Between Prepositions and Adverbs** In each of the following pairs of sentences, one sentence contains a word used as a preposition, and the other contains the same word used as an adverb. Find the words that appear in both sentences. If the word acts as a preposition, write *preposition* on your paper. If the word acts as an adverb, write *adverb.*

EXAMPLE: Umpires stand along the baselines. We waited for the hot dog vendor to come along.
ANSWER: along the baselines (preposition)
along (adverb)

1. In modern baseball, an umpire stands behind home plate. A single strikeout can cause one team to win a game or to fall behind.
2. At a night game, the lights are turned on. The pitcher stands on the mound.
3. The players warm up before the game. They've practiced the skills many times before.
4. Through popular legend, Abner Doubleday invented baseball. However, those doubting the claim find it quite easy to see through.
5. Most scholars believe that a variety of similar games over time eventually gave rise to baseball. They believe these games carried over from other cultures.
6. By April, the season has begun. By November, it has gone by.
7. Eager fans are in line for tickets. All want to get in on time.
8. The pitcher threw the ball across the plate. The catcher ran across to the pitcher.
9. The ball was pitched low and outside. Nevertheless, the batter hit it outside the park.
10. Fans don't like to sit around waiting for hits. They like to see players running around the bases.

More Practice

Grammar Exercise Workbook
• pp. 41–42
On-line Exercise Bank
• Chapter 17
Go on-line:
PHSchool.com
Enter Web Code:
eck-8002

GRAMMAR IN LITERATURE

from Raymond's Run
Toni Cade Bambara

In the following passage from "Raymond's Run," the prepositional phrases appear in blue. The prepositions are underlined.

. . . I'm the fastest thing *on two feet.*

There is no track meet that I don't win the first place medal. I used to win the twenty-yard dash when I was a little kid *in kindergarten.* Nowadays, it's the fifty-yard dash. And tomorrow I'm subject to run the quarter-meter relay all *by myself* and come in first, second, and third. The big kids call me Mercury cause I'm the swiftest thing *in the neighborhood.*

Exercise 5 **Writing Sentences With Prepositional Phrases and Adverbs** Using the following prepositional phrases, write ten sentences about running or a runner. Then, write five more sentences, using words 11–15 as adverbs.

1. in first place
2. behind the others
3. for a long time
4. with ease
5. beyond belief
6. after a while
7. in spite of the distance
8. past the others
9. against the competition
10. of endurance
11. around
12. in
13. outside
14. along
15. across

▼ **Critical Viewing** What will happen when this relay runner hands off her baton? Answer using at least one prepositional phrase. **[Analyze]**

Hands-on Grammar

Bridge and Tunnel Preposition Practice

With a partner, build and use a bridge and tunnel to help you practice your prepositions and prepositional phrases.

Begin with two sheets of paper. One sheet will be your base. Fold another sheet in half the short way, and roll it into a cylinder with the edges overlapping about two inches. Tape the edges together; then, tape down the cylinder the long way in the middle of your base sheet. Using a ruler as a guide, draw a two-lane road entering and leaving the "tunnel." Next, cut out a strip that is 8 1/2" long and 1 1/2" wide. Draw a two-lane road down the middle of the strip. Position the "bridge" horizontally on your base, over the tunnel, and tape it to the edges of the paper. Finally, from another piece of paper, cut out two small, simple cars, one for you and one for your partner. (See illustration.)

Now, with your partner, take turns "driving" your cars. See how many prepositional phrases you can use to describe where each car is and where it is going in relation to the bridge, the tunnel, and the other car. You should be able to think of at least fifteen prepositions.

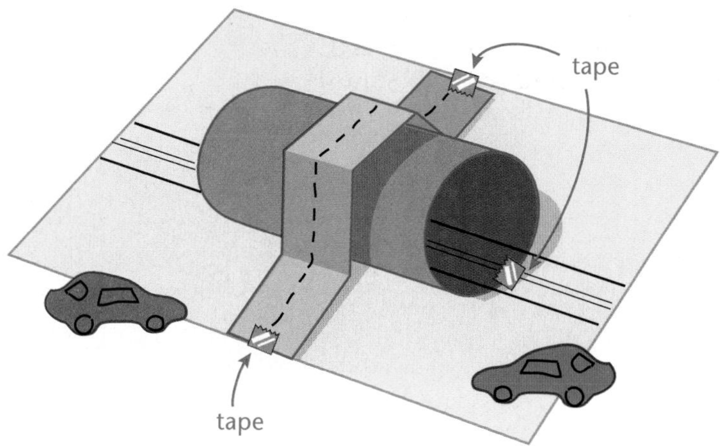

Find It in Your Reading Read several paragraphs of a sports article. See how many prepositional phrases you can identify. Can you find any adverbs that are commonly used as prepositions?

Find It in Your Writing Review a piece of your writing, and identify the prepositonal phrases. See if you can find places where you can add a prepositional phrase to expand or clarify information.

Chapter 18

Conjunctions and Interjections

The Vietnam Veterans Memorial in Washington, D.C., honors soldiers who fought in the Vietnam War.

Conjunctions and interjections play special roles in sentences. Conjunctions connect ideas, and interjections help to clarify a writer's feelings.

Whatever you write, you will undoubtedly use conjunctions. In an essay about famous landmarks, for instance, you would need conjunctions to add one fact or detail to another or to clarify relationships among your ideas. You will use conjunctions both in your formal writing and in your informal writing.

Interjections, on the other hand, are usually single-word additions to sentences that express a writer's personal feelings. Most often, you will use interjections in your informal writing.

▲ **Critical Viewing** What are some elements that link the soldiers in this picture? What are some words that link ideas in sentences? **[Connect]**

Diagnostic Test

Directions: Write all answers on a separate sheet of paper.

Skill Check A. Copy the following sentences, and circle the coordinating conjunction in each. Then, underline the words or groups of words connected by the conjunction.

1. The Arlington National Cemetery is a historic burial place, and it is reserved for soldiers.
2. There are more than 240,000 graves, yet there is room for more.
3. The land previously belonged to Robert E. Lee and his family.
4. During the Civil War, the Union army took over the property, so the residents had to leave.
5. Many recipients of the Medal of Honor or the Distinguished Flying Cross are buried there.

Skill Check B. Copy the following sentences, and circle both parts of the correlative conjunction in each. Then, underline the two words or the two groups of words connected by the conjunction.

6. Both soldiers and war heroes are buried in Arlington.
7. Not only men are buried there, but also many brave women.
8. Many graves are of soldiers who died in either the Vietnam War or the Civil War.
9. Neither the cemetery nor its inspiring memorials existed before the Civil War.
10. People buried in the cemetery today must either have died in war or spent twenty years in the military.

Skill Check C. Copy the following sentences, and circle the subordinating conjunction in each. Then, underline the dependent idea following the conjunction.

11. Wherever important events have occurred, there are landmarks.
12. Monuments and other landmarks are constructed so that important people and events can be remembered.
13. Many are built after the people themselves have died.
14. Some landmarks were constructed because they mark an important historic spot.
15. Whenever people visit, they are reminded of the person or event.
16. Even though many landmarks are old, they remain popular.
17. As long as important events occur, landmarks will be built.
18. If you want to see monuments honoring American heroes, you should visit Washington, D.C.
19. Although the landmarks are crowded, they are worth visiting.
20. Because many landmarks are free, your visit will not be costly.

Skill Check D. List the interjections in the following sentences.

21. Wow! This park is amazing!
22. Yeah, but I am sure that it gets cold here in the winter.
23. Oh, I would hate to be stuck outside in the cold.
24. Ouch! I knew this bench would be freezing cold!
25. I, uh, would much rather be at home in my warm house.

Section 18.1

Conjunctions

Conjunctions act like the cement between bricks. Words such as *and, as,* and *when* connect individual words or groups of words. They are the "cement" of sentences.

KEY CONCEPT A **conjunction** connects words or groups of words. ■

Conjunctions fall into three groups: *coordinating conjunctions, correlative conjunctions,* and *subordinating conjunctions.*

Theme: U.S. Landmarks

In this section, you will learn how conjunctions link words and ideas. The examples and exercises are about historic landmarks in the United States.

Cross-Curricular Connection: Social Studies

Coordinating Conjunctions

KEY CONCEPT **Coordinating conjunctions** connect words of the same kind, such as two or more nouns or verbs. They can also connect larger groups of words, such as prepositional phrases or even entire sentences. ■

COORDINATING CONJUNCTIONS			
and	for	or	yet
but	nor	so	

In the following examples, the coordinating conjunctions are circled. The words they connect are italicized.

CONNECTING NOUNS:	My *cousin* (and) his *wife* left yesterday for a trip to Washington, D.C.
CONNECTING VERBS:	They *printed* out directions (but) *forgot* to bring them.
CONNECTING PREPOSITIONAL PHRASES:	Put the luggage *on the doorstep* (or) *in the garage.*
CONNECTING TWO SENTENCES:	*Our family wanted to go to the White House,* (but) *we decided to go to the Capitol first.*

▶ **Critical Viewing** What thoughts come to mind when you view this photograph of Mount Rushmore? Link two thoughts with *and* and two others with *but.* **[Analyze]**

Exercise 1 **Recognizing Coordinating Conjunctions** Copy the following sentences onto your paper, and circle the coordinating conjunction in each. Then, underline the words or groups of words connected by the conjunction.

EXAMPLE: South Dakota is an exciting (and) interesting vacation spot.

1. Are you going to visit Mount Rushmore or the Black Hills?
2. At Mount Rushmore, the faces of Washington, Jefferson, Lincoln, and Roosevelt are carved out of a mountain.
3. Gutzon Borglum and his workers carved the monument.
4. Visitors hike near the monument but cannot climb on it.
5. The mountain is rugged, yet the carved faces look smooth.
6. Borglum began work in 1927 and finished in 1939.
7. His original plan called for the sculptures to be formed from the waist up, but that would have been very costly.
8. The stone was hard, so only the faces were sculpted.
9. The project was expensive but clearly worth it.
10. The sculpture was carved into Mt. Rushmore 152 meters, or approximately 500 feet, above the valley floor.

More Practice

Grammar Exercise Workbook
- pp. 43–46

On-line Exercise Bank
- Section 18.1

Go on-line:
PHSchool.com
Enter Web Code:
eck-8002

Get instant feedback! Exercise 1 is available on-line or on CD-ROM.

Correlative Conjunctions

KEY CONCEPT **Correlative conjunctions** connect the same kinds of words or groups of words as do coordinating conjunctions, but correlative conjunctions are used in pairs. ■

CORRELATIVE CONJUNCTIONS		
both . . . and	neither . . . nor	whether . . . or
either . . . or	not only . . . but also	

CONNECTING NOUNS: We have seen both the *Hoover Dam* and the *Grand Canyon Dam.*

CONNECTING PRONOUNS: Either *you* or *I* will be the leader on the trail.

CONNECTING VERBS: The sick hiker would neither *eat* nor *drink.*

CONNECTING PREPOSITIONAL PHRASES: We hiked slowly, whether *in a large group* or *by ourselves.*

CONNECTING TWO SENTENCES: Not only *are the Sierra Mountains rugged,* but *they are* also *beautiful.*

Exercise 2 **Recognizing Correlative Conjunctions** Copy the following sentences onto your paper, and circle the correlative conjunction in each. Then, underline the two words or groups of words connected by the conjunction.

EXAMPLE: The attack on Pearl Harbor was (not only) unexpected (but also) devastating.

1. Pearl Harbor is both majestic and awe inspiring.
2. Visitors can see either the Pearl Harbor monument or the memorial to the USS *Arizona*, a ship that was partly sunk.
3. The Japanese air attack shocked the United States not only because it was a surprise attack but also because it was the first attack on American soil.
4. Before the attack, the United States had been uncertain about whether to join the war or to let European countries fight by themselves.
5. Neither the Japanese nor the Germans believed the United States would recover from the attack.

More Practice

Grammar Exercise Workbook
- pp. 43–46

On-line Exercise Bank
- Section 18.1

Go on-line:
PHSchool.com
Enter Web Code:
eck-8002

Get instant feedback! Exercises 2, 3, and 4 are available on-line or on CD-ROM.

Subordinating Conjunctions

KEY CONCEPT **Subordinating conjunctions** connect two ideas by making one idea dependent on the other. ■

FREQUENTLY USED SUBORDINATING CONJUNCTIONS			
after	as though	since	until
although	because	so that	when
as	before	than	whenever
as if	even though	though	where
as long as	if	till	wherever
as soon as	in order that	unless	while

You will find that the subordinating conjunction always comes before the dependent idea. The subordinating conjunction connects the dependent idea to the main idea.

EXAMPLES: I did the planning (after) *he made reservations.*
(When) *he phoned this morning,* he was unable to reach the senator.

The examples show that the main idea can come at the beginning or at the end of the sentence. Notice the important difference in punctuating the two examples. When the dependent idea comes first, it must be separated from the main idea with a comma.

Exercise 3 **Recognizing Subordinating Conjunctions** Copy the following sentences onto your paper, and circle the subordinating conjunction in each. Then, underline the dependent idea following the conjunction.

EXAMPLE: (Because) we were in Washington, we decided to visit the Washington Monument.

1. Although George Washington was much admired, the government would not finance a memorial honoring him.
2. When no action was taken, a group of citizens formed the Washington National Monument Society in 1833.
3. The monument was not dedicated until 1885 even though it had been started almost fifty years earlier.
4. The monument includes two different colors of bricks since there was a shortage of the original brick.
5. Because the base is a 55-foot square, the monument is ten times taller than it is wide.

The Washington Monument stands 555 feet high.

▲ **Critical Viewing** In a sentence, explain how or why this monument is a good symbol for George Washington. Try to use a subordinating conjunction in your sentence. **[Interpret]**

Exercise 4 **Writing Sentences With Subordinating Conjunctions** Write a sentence using each of the following subordinating conjunctions.

1. after
2. while
3. as long as
4. because
5. until

GRAMMAR IN LITERATURE

from Travels with Charley

John Steinbeck

The author uses coordinating, correlative, and subordinating conjunctions to link ideas in the passage: And *is a coordinating conjunction,* not . . . but *is a correlative conjunction, and* because *is a subordinating conjunction.*

. . . The grieving sky turned the little water to a dangerous metal *and* then the wind got up—*not* the gusty, rabbity wind of the seacoasts I know *but* a great bursting sweep of wind with nothing to inhibit it for a thousand miles in any direction. *Because* it was a wind strange to me, . . . it set up mysterious responses in me.

18.1

Hands-on Grammar

Conjunction Chains

In this exercise, you will illustrate how conjunctions are the links that hold sentences together.

1. Cut ten strips of paper approximately 1/2" x 6 1/2" long. Cut five strips of paper 1/2" x 4 1/2" long.
2. On each of the ten longer strips of paper, write one of the following sentences:
   We went to the zoo.
   We saw the gorillas.
   We wanted to see the lions.
   They were hiding.
   Should we go to the beach?
   Should we go to the mountains?
   We want to go surfing.
   We should go to the beach.
   Mom doesn't want to surf.
   Dad does.
3. On each of the five shorter strips of paper, write the coordinating conjunctions *and, or, but, so,* and *yet.*
4. Combine each pair of sentences with a coordinating conjunction by forming the longer strips of paper into circles and joining them with the conjunction to form a paper chain.

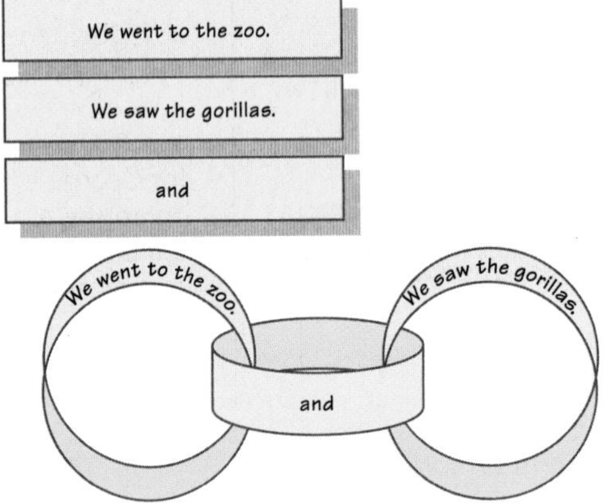

Find It in Your Reading In your textbook or in a story you are reading, find sentences that can be joined together with a conjunction. Alternatively, find sentences that are already joined together and use them to create a chain.

Find It in Your Writing Look through your writing portfolio for sentences that can be combined. Rewrite the sentences, joining them with a coordinating conjunction.

Section 18.1 Section Review

GRAMMAR EXERCISES 5–9

Exercise 5 **Recognizing Conjunctions** Copy the following sentences onto your paper. Then, circle each conjunction and label it *coordinating, correlative,* or *subordinating*. Underline the words or groups of words connected by the conjunction.

1. The Lincoln Memorial is constructed of marble, granite, and limestone.
2. Even though construction was begun in 1914, it was not completed until 1922.
3. The architect Henry Bacon wanted the memorial to reflect the greatness of Lincoln's life, so he followed the style of classical Greek architecture.
4. The building itself is impressive, but the Lincoln statue inside is the memorial's highlight.
5. Gettysburg, Pennsylvania, contains both a Civil War memorial and a historic site dedicated to President Eisenhower.
6. Visiting Gettysburg, you can tour either a battlefield or a cemetery.
7. Not only was the Battle of Gettysburg a fierce confrontation, but it was also a major turning point in the Civil War.
8. The Statue of Liberty greets travelers as soon as they enter New York Harbor.
9. Since the statue's dedication in 1886, it has been a symbol of freedom to all.
10. Learn about the statue's symbolism so that you can fully appreciate it.

Exercise 6 **Combining Sentences With Conjunctions** Combine each of the following pairs of sentences with a coordinating, correlative, or subordinating conjunction.

1. Henry Bacon, the architect, wanted the Lincoln Memorial to reflect the greatness of Lincoln's life. He followed the style of classical Greek architecture.
2. The building itself is impressive. The Lincoln statue inside is the monument's highlight.
3. You might visit St. Louis, Missouri. You will see the city's famous Gateway Arch.
4. It has become a symbol for St. Louis. It dramatizes that St. Louis is the "Gateway to the West."
5. The Alamo is a great tourist attraction in San Antonio. The River Walk is also a great tourist attraction there.

Exercise 7 **Find It in Your Reading** Identify the conjunctions in this passage from *Travels With Charley:*

> I waited for him to ask something or to say something so we could go on, but he didn't. And as the silence continued, it became more and more impossible to think of something to say.

Exercise 8 **Find It in Your Writing** Look through examples of your own writing to find conjunctions. Challenge yourself to use conjunctions to combine ideas and sentences.

Exercise 9 **Writing Application** Imagine that you are leading a tour of a famous monument. Write a description of the monument, linking ideas with different types of conjunctions.

Section 18.2

Interjections

The *interjection* is the part of speech that is used the least. Its only use is to express feelings or emotions.

KEY CONCEPT An **interjection** expresses feeling or emotion and functions independently from the rest of a sentence. ■

An interjection has no grammatical relationship to any other word in a sentence. It is, therefore, set off from the rest of the sentence with a comma or an exclamation mark.

Interjections can express different feelings or emotions:

JOY:	*Wow!* I can't believe the size of this statue.
SURPRISE:	*Oh,* I didn't expect to hear from you.
PAIN:	*Ouch!* That hurts.
IMPATIENCE:	*Tsk!* How long do they expect me to wait?
HESITATION:	I, *uh,* think we should leave now.

Some other common interjections include *ah, alas, gee, golly, hah, help, hey, hooray, no way, oh my, oh no, oh, oops, psst, so, ugh, uh-oh, well, whew, whoa,* and *yeah.*

The statue of Abraham Lincoln dominates the Lincoln Memorial.

Theme: U.S. Landmarks

In this section, you will learn how interjections add emotions and feelings to your writing. The examples and exercises are about additional historic landmarks in the United States.

Cross-Curricular Connection: Social Studies

◀ **Critical Viewing** What emotions do you feel when you see this statue? What are some words you might use to express those emotions? **[Connect]**

Grammar and Style Tip

Use interjections to express feelings in your informal writing, but don't use them in formal writing except as part of a quotation or other special reference.

The Alamo still reminds Texans of their war to win independence from Mexico.

▲ **Critical Viewing** What emotions do you think some Texans feel when they see the Alamo? Can you express those emotions in additional sentences for Exercise 10? **[Connect]**

Exercise 10 **Supplying Interjections** Rewrite each of the following sentences using an appropriate interjection in place of the feeling shown in parentheses.

EXAMPLE: (sadness) I missed the tour of the Alamo.
ANSWER: Gee, I missed the tour of the Alamo.

1. (surprise) The Alamo is neat.
2. (impatience) Can we go inside now?
3. (impatience) How long do we have to wait for the tour to begin?
4. (fear) I heard the Alamo was haunted.
5. I (uncertainty) think maybe we should leave.
6. (anger) It's not haunted.
7. (amazement) I can't believe you guys were so scared.
8. (fear) I hear something.
9. (pain) Something poked me in the arm.
10. (impatience) Please watch where you are going!

More Practice

Grammar Exercise Workbook
- pp. 47–48

On-line Exercise Bank
- Section 18.2

Go on-line: PHSchool.com
Enter Web Code: eck-8002

Section 18.2 **Section Review**

GRAMMAR EXERCISES 11–17

Exercise 11 Identifying Interjections On your paper, list the interjections in the following sentences.

1. Wow, the Oregon Trail sure is long!
2. Man, I can't believe we decided to follow it on mountain bikes.
3. Oh, no! This trip is going to take us months.
4. Ouch! My feet hurt!
5. Stop! I can't go any farther.

Exercise 12 Supplying Interjections Rewrite each of the following sentences using an appropriate interjection in place of the feeling shown in parentheses.

1. (amazement) Devil's Tower sure is tall.
2. (amazement) I can't believe it was formed by lava.
3. (pain) I bet it would hurt to fall from up there.
4. (uncertainty) I don't think I want to find out.
5. (impatience) Let's get hiking.
6. (surprise) Did you know this was a landmark for Native Americans?
7. I (uncertainty) think they believed it was formed by the claws of a giant bear.
8. (amazement) It would have to have been a very large bear!
9. (disappointment) We can't climb that.
10. (agreement) You're right. Let's go.

Exercise 13 Supplying Interjections Rewrite the following dialogue. Replace the words in parentheses with appropriate interjections.

JOE: (sadness) Custer's battlefield sure is a sad place.

TOM: (amazement) A lot of people died there.

JOE: (wonder) Is it true that you can sometimes still find slugs from bullets?

TOM: (excitement) I think I see one!

JOE: (disappointment) It's only a rock.

Exercise 14 Writing Sentences With Interjections Use each of the following interjections in a sentence.

1. Oops!
2. Uh-oh!
3. Oh, no!
4. Tsk!
5. uh

Exercise 15 Find It in Your Reading Identify the interjection in this dialogue from *Travels With Charley*. What other interjections might be used in a dialogue such as this?

LOCAL MAN: "New York, huh?"

ME: "Yep."

LOCAL MAN: "I was there in nineteen thirty-eight—or was it thirty-nine . . .?"

ALICE: "It was thirty-six . . . ."

Exercise 16 Find It in Your Writing Revise a piece of dialogue from your own writing by adding interjections to show the speakers' emotions.

Exercise 17 Writing Application Write a brief letter to a friend describing an interesting landmark you have visited. Use at least two interjections in your letter.

Chapter 18

Chapter Review

GRAMMAR EXERCISES 18–20

Exercise 18 **Recognizing Conjunctions** Copy the following sentences, and circle the conjunction in each. Label each conjunction *coordinating, correlative*, or *subordinating*, and underline the words or groups of words being connected.

1. Yellowstone Park was formed when volcanoes exploded and violent earthquakes shook the land.
2. Neither Yosemite nor Yellowstone Park was visited by explorers before 1800.
3. Not only do many tourists visit these parks today, but tourists also visited them in the 1850's.
4. It is difficult to visit the park unless you go during the summer.
5. Whenever you visit a park, you should be prepared for weather changes.
6. In 1959, an earthquake with a magnitude of 7.5 or more on the Richter scale caused major damage.
7. In August 1988, fires broke out in Yellowstone, so emergency efforts were begun to protect park landmarks.
8. The fire was a catastrophe for many officials and rangers.
9. Firefighters tried to control the fires, but they finally had to rely on snow to extinguish the blaze.
10. The firefighters worked valiantly, yet 35 percent of the park burned.
11. Luckily, there were very few casualties among birds or forest animals.
12. The fire disturbed them, but they were more upset by firefighters' helicopters.
13. Tourists enjoyed observing both natural wonders and abundant wildlife.
14. Rock climbers often visit Yosemite to climb either El Capitán or Half Dome.
15. While you are sightseeing in the park, be sure to take your camera.

Exercise 19 **Classifying Conjunctions** Identify the conjunctions you find in the following paragraph. Then, label each one *coordinating* or *correlative*.

(1) Thousands of California residents and tourists travel across the Golden Gate Bridge every day. (2) They are traveling south toward San Francisco or north toward Marin County. (3) Not only is the bridge dramatically beautiful, but it is also a technological wonder. (4) The bridge has been rocked by several earthquakes, but it has not been damaged. (5) Both painters and ironworkers provide constant maintenance. (6) The workers must fear neither heights nor wind. (7) Although most bridges are painted either gray or silver, the Golden Gate is a bright orange color. (8) Its architect felt that orange fit better with the bridge's surroundings and design. (9) Whether you are visiting San Francisco or traveling nearby, you should go to the Golden Gate Bridge. (10) The view is magnificent, so you will enjoy the side trip.

Exercise 20 **Revising With Conjunctions** Rewrite the following paragraph, adding conjunctions to connect and relate ideas clearly. Underline the conjunctions you use.

You visit St. Louis, Missouri. You must see the city's famous Gateway Arch. It is a stainless-steel structure. It glistens in the light. It stands more than 600 feet high. It forms a graceful curve, arching above the ground. The Gateway Arch was completed in 1965. It has become a part of St. Louis history. The arch is dramatic. The arch is symbolic. It shows that St. Louis is the "Gateway to the West."

Chapter 19

Basic Sentence Parts

The Coming and Going of the Pony Express, Frederic Remington

The western frontier of the United States during the 1800's is sometimes referred to as the Wild West. The Wild West and the cowhands who lived there are an exciting part of history. To learn and share information about the Wild West, you need more than just words. You must put words together in patterns that express ideas.

By assembling the eight parts of speech in various patterns, you can express your ideas and communicate them to others. Patterns of words that communicate ideas are called **sentences**. All sentences must have certain basic parts. In this chapter, you will learn about the basic parts of a sentence and how you can use them to express your thoughts clearly.

▲ **Critical Viewing** Write several sentences describing this scene. Be sure to use basic sentence parts correctly. **[Speculate]**

Diagnostic Test

Directions: Write all answers on a separate sheet of paper.

Skill Check A. Copy the following sentences onto your paper. Draw a vertical line between the complete subject and the complete predicate. Underline each subject once and each verb twice.

1. We hear stories about cowboys and life in the old West.
2. Pecos Bill is a legendary cowboy of the Southwest.
3. Ingenuity was one of his characteristics.
4. This legendary cowboy was born in Texas in the 1830's.
5. Stories of his early escapades entertain readers.

Skill Check B. In the sentences below, label each compound subject and compound verb.

6. Strength, courage, and humor also characterized Pecos Bill.
7. According to legend, roping and branding were his inventions.
8. He teethed on a bowie knife and played with bears.
9. Young Bill became lost and was raised by coyotes.
10. Paul Bunyan and other fictional heroes were the models for this character.

Skill Check C. Identify the subject in each sentence below.

11. Have you heard the legend of Pecos Bill?
12. Listen carefully!
13. There are many exaggerations in the legend.
14. Long ago in the West lived this hero of American folklore.
15. Are the myths about Pecos Bill true?

Skill Check D. Copy the following sentences, underlining each direct object once and each indirect object twice. Circle each object of a preposition. (Not every sentence has all three.)

16. William Cody showed his fans and audiences an entertaining perspective of the "Wild West."
17. The name "Buffalo Bill" gave Cody a character for his shows.
18. Wild West shows brought entertainment to crowds across the country.
19. However, they gave their audience incorrect ideas about what life was like in the West.
20. William Cody also founded the town of Cody, Wyoming.

Skill Check E. Copy the following sentences, labeling each *predicate noun, predicate pronoun,* and *predicate adjective.*

21. Pecos Bill and Paul Bunyan are only two of the numerous legends of the Wild West.
22. My favorite legendary heroes are those two.
23. Cowboys were part of the foundation of the Wild West.
24. The stories about these characters are always humorous.
25. The settlement of the West was exciting and entertaining.

Section 19.1

The Basic Sentence

A sentence is a group of words that expresses a complete thought. A sentence has two basic parts—a subject and a verb.

KEY CONCEPT A **complete sentence** has a subject and a verb and expresses a complete thought. ■

KEY CONCEPT The **subject** of a sentence is the word or group of words that answers the question *Who?* or *What?* before the verb. ■

EXAMPLES: Cowboys herd cattle for a living.

Our ranch was in Texas.

In the first example, the noun *Cowboys* is the subject that tells us *who* herd cattle. The noun *ranch* in the second example is the subject that tells *what* was in Texas.

Not all subjects are this easy to find. (See Section 19.4 for more information about finding subjects in sentences.)

KEY CONCEPT The **verb** in a sentence tells *what the subject does, what is done to the subject,* or *what the condition of the subject is.* ■

EXAMPLES: Bobby gave an unforgettable show.

Their prize horse was stolen.

She has been blue all day.

Gave is the verb in the first example. It tells what the subject, *Bobby,* did. In the second example, *was stolen* tells what was done to the subject *horse. Has been* in the third example is a linking verb. It tells something about the condition of the subject by linking *she* to the word *blue.*

Theme: The Western Frontier

In this section, you will learn about the two basic elements of a sentence. The examples and exercises are about life on the western frontier of the United States during the 1800's.

Cross-Curricular Connection: Social Studies

Exercise 1 **Recognizing Subjects and Verbs** Copy each of the following sentences onto your paper. Underline each subject once and each verb twice.

EXAMPLE: Sometimes, cowboys searched for their cattle for hours.

1. Cowboys are described as "mounted herders" in the United States.
2. The term simply describes these cowboys on a horse.
3. They have many responsibilities to their herds of cattle.
4. The cattle must be kept together in a group.
5. The herd may be driven to the pasture for grazing.
6. While on a drive, the cattle must be protected from rustlers, or thieves.
7. Other herds might mix with the cattle.
8. All cattle are branded by the cattle owner's unique symbol.
9. The brand distinguishes one herd from another.
10. In the United States, people admire these heroes of the West.

More Practice

Grammar Exercise Workbook
- pp. 49–50

On-line Exercise Bank
- Section 19.1

Go on-line: PHSchool.com
Enter Web Code: eck-8002

Get instant feedback! Exercise 1 is available on-line or on CD-ROM.

KEY CONCEPT A group of words expresses a **complete thought** if it can stand by itself and still make sense. ■

Making sure that your words express complete thoughts is especially important when you write. *Incomplete thoughts* will leave readers with questions in their minds. Consider the group of words in the following example:

INCOMPLETE THOUGHT: The man in the cowboy hat.

"What about the man in the cowboy hat?" a reader might ask. Standing by itself, this group of words makes no sense. An important element is missing—the verb. Using *man* as a subject, you can turn this incomplete thought into a sentence by adding any number of different verbs.

▶ **Critical Viewing** Write a brief monologue in which the man pictured below is talking to his horse. Be sure that your sentences express complete thoughts. **[Speculate]**

Partners, Charles M. Russell

COMPLETE THOUGHTS
The man (S) in the cowboy hat rides (V) gracefully.
The man (S) in the cowboy hat left (V).
The man (S) in the cowboy hat is riding (V) a horse.

▼ **Critical Viewing** Use complete sentences to describe the skills being exhibited by the cowboy pictured below. **[Analyze]**

Notice that each of the examples in the chart has all of the ingredients necessary for a sentence: Each has a *subject* and a *verb*, and each expresses a *complete thought.*

Sometimes, an incomplete thought may be a group of words with no word in it that can be used as a subject.

INCOMPLETE THOUGHT: Near the stream by the roadside.

This incomplete thought is merely two prepositional phrases. Both a subject and a verb are needed.

COMPLETE: Wild irises (S) are growing (V) near the stream by the roadside.

In grammar, incomplete thoughts are often called *fragments.*

Exercise 2 **Revising to Create Complete Sentences** Five of the following items are sentences. The rest are incomplete thoughts. If a group of words is a sentence, write *sentence.* If a group of words expresses an incomplete thought, add words to make it a sentence. Underline the subject once and the verb twice in each new sentence.

EXAMPLE: The cowboy's attire.
ANSWER: The cowboy's attire serves practical purposes.

1. Cowboys dress according to their environment.
2. The hats on their heads.
3. Wore a handkerchief.
4. Cowboys wear leather chaps to protect their legs.
5. Protect them from grass and brush.
6. Boots are worn to keep their feet in the stirrups.
7. The saddle on the horse.
8. The lasso is coiled around the saddle horn.
9. Sometimes, cowboys must use a lasso or lariat on their cattle.
10. They use the lasso in order to.

More Practice

Grammar Exercise Workbook
- pp. 49–50

On-line Exercise Bank
- Section 19.1

Go on-line: PHSchool.com *Enter Web Code:* eck-8002

Section 19.1 Section Review

GRAMMAR EXERCISES 3–7

Exercise 3 **Recognizing Subjects and Verbs** Copy each of the following sentences. Underline each subject once and each verb or verb phrase twice.

1. After the Civil War, cowboys often drove their cattle to the nearest railroad.
2. Then, the cattle were shipped to the East in response to a demand for beef.
3. The cowboy performed his job from sunup to sundown.
4. The cattle drive may have earned him about one dollar each day.
5. The cook was a very important member of the drive.
6. He prepared three meals a day for many hungry cowboys.
7. The meals might have included beans, biscuits, coffee, beef stew, and sometimes a sweet dessert.
8. In his spare time, the cook served as a doctor, dentist, barber, and mediator.
9. Eventually, the need for cattle drives diminished.
10. However, cowboys remained in the public eye through competition in rodeos.
11. Rodeos began in the mid-nineteenth century on cattle drives.
12. They started as informal competitions between cowhands.
13. The cowhands displayed their roping skills and horsemanship.
14. The first formal rodeo was held in Cheyenne, Wyoming, in 1872.
15. Americans have continued to be fascinated with the lives of cowboys.

Exercise 4 **Revising to Create Complete Sentences** Five of the following items are sentences. The rest are incomplete thoughts. If a group of words is a sentence, write *sentence*. If a group of words expresses an incomplete thought, add words to make it a sentence.

1. The western United States during the 1800's had many colorful characters.
2. During the second half of the nineteenth century.
3. We read about many of the men and women of the West.
4. Calamity Jane was among them.
5. She was an American frontierswoman who grew up in the West.
6. A sharpshooter and horsewoman.
7. Always created contention.
8. Calamity Jane said that she was equal to any man.
9. Wore men's clothing.
10. A scout in the United States Cavalry.

Exercise 5 **Find It in Your Reading** Identify the two subjects and the two verbs in these lines from the poem "The Closing of the Rodeo" by William Jay Smith. Underline the subject of each sentence once and the verb twice.

The lariat snaps; the cowboy rolls
His pack . . .

Exercise 6 **Find It in Your Writing** Review a paragraph from a piece of your writing to make sure that every sentence expresses a complete thought. Underline the subject of each sentence once and the verb twice.

Exercise 7 **Writing Application** Write a brief narrative of an event that might have occurred in the frontier West. Write at least five complete sentences. In each sentence, underline each subject once and each verb twice.

Section 19.2 Complete Subjects and Predicates

Every sentence is built around its two essential elements, the subject and the verb. The subject and verb together support the many details that a sentence may include to express a complete thought.

DIFFERENT SENTENCES BUILT AROUND THE SAME SUBJECT AND VERB	
Cowboys	ride.
Many cowboys	ride daily.
Many cowboys in our town	ride daily at the ranch.

Notice the line that divides the parts of each sentence. The words to the left of the line include the subject *cowboys* and any other words that add details to it. In each sentence, the words to the left of the line make up the *complete subject.* (In this case, the subject *cowboys* is often called, in contrast, the *simple subject.*)

KEY CONCEPT The **complete subject** of a sentence consists of the subject and any words related to it. ■

As you can see in the examples above, a complete subject may be just one word—the subject itself—or it may be several words.

In the preceding examples, the words to the right of the line include the verb *ride* and any words that add details to it. This part of the sentence is called the *complete predicate.* (The verb itself, a word such as *ride* or a phrase such as *has ridden*, is often called the *simple predicate.*)

KEY CONCEPT The **complete predicate** of a sentence consists of the verb and any words related to it. ■

As you can see in the examples, a complete predicate may be just one word—a verb—or it may be several words.

Theme: The Western Frontier

In this section, you will learn about complete subjects and complete predicates. The examples and exercises are about life on the western frontier of the United States during the 1800's.

Cross-Curricular Connection: Social Studies

▼ **Critical Viewing** Use complete subjects and complete predicates in sentences comparing this mode of transportation with traveling by automobile. **[Compare and Contrast]**

GRAMMAR IN LITERATURE

from The Closing of the Rodeo

William Jay Smith

In the following excerpt, the complete subjects are shown in red and the complete predicates in blue.

Plumes of smoke from the factory sway
In the setting sun. The curtain falls,
A train in the darkness pulls away.

Exercise 8 **Recognizing Complete Subjects and Predicates** Copy each of the following sentences onto your paper. Underline the subject once and the verb twice. Then, draw a vertical line between the complete subject and the complete predicate, as shown in the example.

EXAMPLE: Some famous outlaws | played a big part in the Wild West.

1. Jesse James was an American outlaw.
2. He was known throughout the country for bank and train robberies.
3. The young man joined a band of pro-Confederate raiders at the age of fifteen.
4. The group was led by William Clarke Quantrill.
5. Jesse James later organized his own group of robbers.
6. The members of the group included his older brother, Frank, and Robert Younger.
7. One infamous bank robbery occurred at the First National Bank of Northfield in Minnesota.
8. The clerk would not open the safe.
9. The gang shot him before they escaped.
10. Jesse, along with his brother Frank, was able to avoid capture.

More Practice

Grammar Exercise Workbook
- pp. 51–52

On-line Exercise Bank
- Section 19.2

Go on-line: PHSchool.com
Enter Web Code: eck-8002

Get instant feedback! Exercise 8 is available on-line or on CD-ROM.

Hands-on Grammar

Sentence-Part Grab Bag

Create a sentence-part grab bag to help you understand the way subjects and predicates function. Create two sets of index cards. On the first set, write the part of a sentence that tells the person, place, or thing that does the action, including all the adjectives, adverbs, phrases, and clauses that rename or describe the noun.

EXAMPLE: Movies about cowboys and the Old West

On the second set of cards, write actions or conditions.

EXAMPLE: are fun to watch.

Create eight to ten cards for each set. Try to use a wide variety of nouns, verbs, and modifiers. Then, take two envelopes, and label one "Complete Subjects" and the other "Complete Predicates."

Place each set of cards in its labeled envelope. Working with a partner, randomly select complete subjects and complete predicates and put them together to create different sentences. Chances are, some of your sentences will be very humorous. Next, try selecting just one card—a complete predicate or a complete subject. Write it on your paper along with an original subject or predicate to complete the sentence. Another activity to try is blindly selecting a sentence part from one envelope or the other and trying to identify whether it is a complete subject or a complete predicate. Then, use it in an original complete sentence.

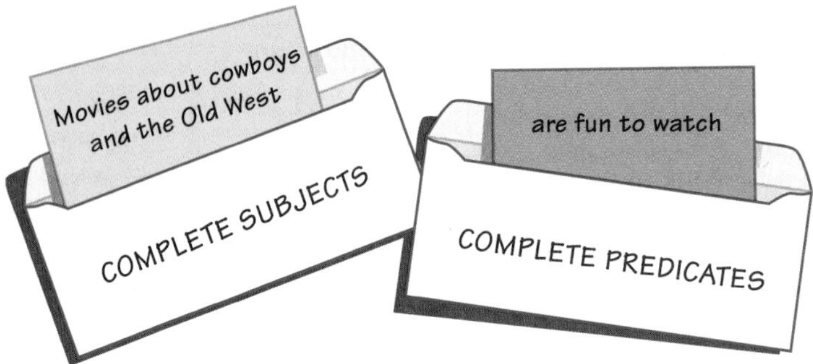

Find It in Your Reading Choose several sentences from your social studies or language arts textbooks to add to your grab bag. You may have to reorder some words to get all the words of the complete predicate on one card.

Find It in Your Writing Review your writing portfolio for appropriate sentences to add to your grab bag. Choose several sentences and write their complete subjects and complete predicates on index cards. If necessary, reorder the words to get all the words of the complete predicate on one card. Add the sentences to their appropriate envelopes.

Section 19.2 Section Review

GRAMMAR EXERCISES 9–13

Exercise 9 **Recognizing Complete Subjects and Predicates** Make two columns labeled *Complete Subject* and *Complete Predicate*. Write each complete subject in the first column and each complete predicate in the second column.

1. Jesse James was living with his family in Saint Joseph, Missouri, in 1882.
2. The outlaw was using the name Thomas Howard at that time.
3. Governor Thomas Crittenden issued a reward of $10,000 for the capture of Jesse and his brother Frank.
4. They were wanted dead or alive.
5. A member of James's own gang wanted the reward money.
6. He shot Jesse James from behind.
7. Jesse was mortally wounded and died later that day, on April 3, 1882.
8. After his brother's death, the American public treated Frank like a hero.
9. Juries acquitted him twice.
10. The James brothers have gained worldwide notoriety for both real and legendary actions.
11. Billy the Kid was another well-known outlaw of the West.
12. He was born in New York City in 1859.
13. His given name was William H. Bonney.
14. He moved to Silver City, New Mexico, in 1873 after his father's death.
15. He soon became known for robbery and murder.

Exercise 10 **Writing Sentences by Combining Complete Subjects and Predicates** Write a complete sentence for each item below by following the directions in parentheses.

1. In the old western movie, a rancher (Add a complete predicate.)
2. herded the cattle to a town on the line. (Add a complete subject.)
3. stampeded during a lightning storm and many were lost. (Add a complete subject.)
4. Once in town, the cowboys (Add a complete predicate.)
5. The town's sheriff (Add a complete predicate.)
6. led to holding pens near the railroad station. (Add a complete subject.)
7. Next, the cattle herd (Add a complete predicate.)
8. After the train left, the cowboys (Add a complete predicate.)
9. were relieved that the cowboys had finally left. (Add a complete subject.)
10. Back at the ranch, the rancher and his wife (Add a complete predicate.)

Exercise 11 **Find It in Your Reading** Reread the excerpt from "The Closing of the Rodeo" on page 271. In the excerpt, the complete subjects are red and the complete predicates are blue. Identify each simple subject and simple verb.

Exercise 12 **Find It in Your Writing** Choose a paragraph from your writing. Identify the complete subject and complete predicate in each sentence. Revise any sentences that do not have a complete subject or a complete predicate.

Exercise 13 **Writing Application** Write a short essay telling why you would or would not have wanted to live during the days of the frontier West. Choose five sentences, and underline the complete subject once and the complete predicate twice.

Compound Subjects and Compound Verbs

Many sentences have a single subject and a single verb. Some sentences, however, have more than one subject. Others have more than one verb.

Theme: Musical Instruments

In this section, you will learn how to recognize and form compound subjects and compound verbs. The examples and exercises are about musical instruments.

Cross-Curricular Connection: Music

Recognizing Compound Subjects

A sentence with more than one subject is said to have a *compound subject.*

KEY CONCEPT A **compound subject** is two or more subjects that have the same verb and are joined by a conjunction such as *and* or *or.* ■

The parts of the compound subjects in the following examples are underlined once. Each verb is underlined twice.

EXAMPLES: Ted and Louise are both musicians.
My sister or she will represent our music club.
Pianos, flutes, and saxophones are sold at that store.

Exercise 14 **Recognizing Compound Subjects** Identify the subjects that make up each compound subject in the following sentences.

EXAMPLE: Sound and time are two important components of music.
ANSWER: Sound, time

1. Music or rhythm plays a role in all societies throughout the world.
2. Many styles or types of music exist in different societies.
3. Feelings and ideas are both expressed in music.
4. Geographical region and historical era will influence the type of music in a society.
5. Each culture or society has its own unique style of music.
6. Western cultures and people define music as an art form.
7. Classical and popular are two of the principal forms of music in western culture.
8. Jazz, rap, rhythm and blues, and rock are some of the forms of popular music.
9. Opera, ballet, and motion pictures use many music styles.
10. Singing and banging tools or rocks together may have created the earliest music forms.

More Practice

Grammar Exercise Workbook
- pp. 53–54

On-line Exercise Bank
- Section 19.3

Go on-line: PHSchool.com *Enter Web Code:* eck-8002

Recognizing Compound Verbs

A sentence with two or more verbs is said to have a *compound verb.*

KEY CONCEPT A **compound verb** is two or more verbs that have the same subject and are joined by a conjunction such as *and* or *or.* ■

EXAMPLES: He reads music and plays the piano.
The composition will succeed or fail within a year.
She composes, plays, and often directs her own pieces.

Sometimes, a sentence will have both a compound subject and a compound verb.

EXAMPLE: Jane and Sharon both sing and dance.

Get instant feedback! Exercises 14 and 15 are available on-line or on CD-ROM.

Exercise 15 **Recognizing Compound Verbs** Identify the verbs that make up each compound verb in the following sentences.

EXAMPLE: Musical instruments provide and expand musical sound.

ANSWER: provide, expand

1. Instruments are played and enjoyed around the world.
2. Different instruments are played in various ways and make distinctive sounds.
3. Stringed instruments may be plucked or strummed.
4. Musicians blow into or strike other instruments.
5. While listening to instruments, people often clap, stamp, whistle, hum, and sing, simply for fun.

More Practice

Grammar Exercise Workbook
- pp. 53–54

On-line Exercise Bank
- Section 19.3

Go on-line:
PHSchool.com
Enter Web Code:
eck-8002

◀ **Critical Viewing** Use compound subjects and compound verbs in sentences describing your favorite muscial instrument. **[Compare]**

GRAMMAR IN LITERATURE

from The White Umbrella

Gish Jen

The compound verb in the following excerpt is highlighted in blue italics.

Huddling at the end of Miss Crosman's nine-foot leatherette couch, Mona and I watched Eugenie play. She *was* a grade ahead of me and, according to school rumor, *had* a boyfriend in high school.

Exercise 16 **Combining Sentences With Compound Subjects and Compound Verbs** Combine each pair of sentences below by using compound subjects or compound verbs.

EXAMPLE: Violins are stringed instruments.
Cellos are stringed instruments.

ANSWER: Violins and cellos are stringed instruments.

1. Sarah is going to the next music recital.
   Sarah is performing in the next music recital.
2. She is singing with the choir.
   She is also dancing in a solo performance.
3. First Rhonda will play.
   After Rhonda, Emily will perform.
4. We will arrive early at the recital.
   We will be sure to find good seats.
5. The students prefer singing to dance.
   Their teacher prefers singing, too.
6. Rap music is the music of choice for many students.
   Rock music is also preferred by the students.
7. Sarah has a large collection of compact discs.
   Emily has many compact discs in her collection.
8. Serena enjoys buying new music on compact discs.
   She enjoys selling her oldest compact discs.
9. Jazz is a type of music with which the girls aren't familiar.
   Blues is another style of music that they have never heard.
10. They don't realize that jazz and blues have inspired modern musicians.
    They don't realize that jazz and blues have been played by modern musicians.

More Practice

Grammar Exercise Workbook
- pp. 53–54

On-line Exercise Bank
- Section 19.3

Go on-line:
PHSchool.com
Enter Web Code:
eck-8002

Section 19.3 **Section Review**

GRAMMAR EXERCISES 17–21

Exercise 17 **Recognizing Compound Subjects and Compound Verbs** Identify the compound subject or compound verb in each sentence. If there are none, write *none.*

1. Beethoven, Bach, Mozart, and Haydn were all famous composers.
2. They coordinated and synthesized music in a very special way.
3. Many musicians admire Bach's music.
4. In the 1800's, there was an interest in and revival of Bach's music.
5. Felix Mendelssohn arranged and performed one of Bach's compositions.
6. Other composers and musicians may have been greater.
7. His expressiveness and touch inspire listeners everywhere.
8. String quartets, chamber music, songs, an opera, and nine symphonies were among Beethoven's compositions.
9. Mozart and Haydn influenced the musical compositions of Beethoven.
10. His forceful style and dreamy melodies have made Beethoven's music timeless.

Exercise 18 **Revising to Combine Sentences With Compound Subjects and Verbs** Combine each pair of sentences below by using compound subjects, compound verbs, or both.

1. The history of Western music has been influenced by Johann Sebastian Bach. The development of Western music has been influenced by Johann Sebastian Bach.
2. Musicians consider him one of the most talented composers of all time. Other admirers also consider him one of the most talented composers ever.
3. Bach was a self-taught musician. Bach followed in the musical traditions of his family.
4. In seven generations of his family, fifty-three members studied music. They also became prominent musicians.
5. Bach composed during the 1700's. During the 1700's, Bach conducted.
6. He combined different rhythmic patterns in one composition. He expanded rhymic patterns in the same composition.
7. Bach composed 295 cantatas. Bach also produced the cantatas.
8. Casual listeners still play many of these pieces today. Many music critics greatly enjoy them, too.
9. Bach's music was forgotten and neglected for 80 years after his death. His musical theories were also forgotten and neglected.
10. Bach's style was unique. His method was one-of-a-kind.

Exercise 19 **Find It in Your Reading** In the excerpt from "The White Umbrella" on page 276, identify the compound subject.

Exercise 20 **Find It in Your Writing** Look through your writing portfolio. In your writing, find at least one example of a compound subject and one example of a compound verb. If you cannot find any, add at least one.

Exercise 21 **Writing Application** Write a description of a musical instrument that you play or enjoy hearing. Include at least one sentence with a compound subject and one sentence with a compound verb.

Section 19.4

Hard-to-Find Subjects

In the first three sections of this chapter, each subject that you were asked to find appeared somewhere early in the sentence—with the verb following immediately or soon after. This pattern—a subject followed by a verb—is the pattern most often used in English.

SUBJECT-VERB WORD ORDER:

S V
The song raced up the charts.

Yesterday morning after breakfast,
S V
Uncle George left on a concert tour.

Delayed by bad weather and traffic,
S V
he finally arrived.

In several kinds of sentences, however, the subject and verb do not follow normal word order. In some sentences, the subject may seem to be missing entirely. In others, the subject may follow the verb or come between the parts of a verb phrase. This section will give you practice in recognizing sentences that do not follow normal word order. It will also help you find the subjects in these sentences.

Theme: Musical Instruments

In this section, you will learn how to recognize sentences that do not follow normal word order. The examples and exercises are about musical instruments.

Cross-Curricular Connection: Music

Finding the Subject in Orders and Directions

Some sentences give orders or directions. In most of these sentences, the subject does not appear before the verb.

KEY CONCEPT In sentences that give orders or directions, the subject is understood to be *you*. ■

On the left side of the following chart are three examples of sentences that give orders or directions. The verbs are underlined twice. On the right side, the same sentences appear with the understood subjects shown in parentheses.

Order or Direction	With Understood *You* Added
Drive carefully!	(You) Drive carefully!
After waiting a moment, sing the song again.	After waiting a moment, (you) sing the song again
Lucy, leave the room.	Lucy, (you) leave the room.

Exercise 22 **Recognizing Subjects That Give Orders or Directions** Write the subject of each of the following sentences. (Three of the sentences give orders or directions. The other two are ordinary sentences in normal word order.)

EXAMPLE: David, listen!
ANSWER: (you)

1. Popular music is produced for a broad audience.
2. Learn about jazz, country-and-western music, soul music, and rock music.
3. After listening to various artists, choose your favorite music.
4. A person's musical tastes may change over time.
5. David, try listening to some operatic music.

More Practice

Grammar Exercise Workbook
- pp. 55–56

On-line Exercise Bank
- Section 19.4

Go on-line:
PHSchool.com
Enter Web Code:
eck-8002

Finding the Subject in Questions

A sentence that is not in normal word order is usually in *inverted word order.* The subject in such a sentence comes after its verb. This order is seen most often in questions.

KEY CONCEPT In questions, the subject often follows the verb. ■

Many questions begin with a verb or a helping verb. Others begin with such questioning words as *what, which, whose, who, when, why, where,* and *how.* In the following examples, notice that the subject sometimes comes between the parts of a verb phrase.

VERB FIRST: Are the songs very long?
HELPING VERB FIRST: Have you opened your compact disc?
QUESTIONING WORD FIRST: Where are the compact discs?
When will they begin the concert?

If you have trouble finding the subject in a question, you can use a trick: Simply reword the question as a statement. The subject will then appear before the verb.

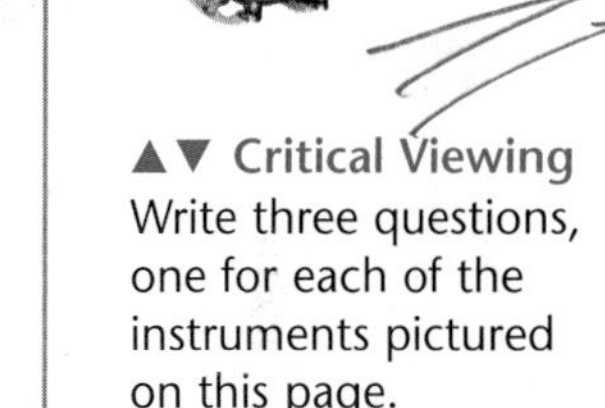

▲▼ **Critical Viewing** Write three questions, one for each of the instruments pictured on this page. **[Analyze]**

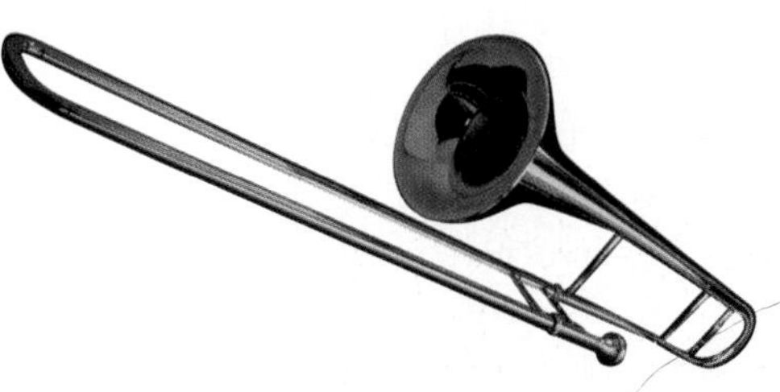

Question	Reworded as Statement
Are the songs very long?	The songs are very long.
Have you opened your compact disc?	You have opened your compact disc.
Where are the compact discs?	The compact discs are where.
When will they begin the play?	They will begin the play when.

Many questions use inverted word order, but some do not.

EXAMPLES: Which songs were selected by the band?
Who has taken my compact disc player?

Exercise 23 **Finding the Subject in Questions** Write the subject of each sentence below.

EXAMPLE: Which type of popular music do you like best?
ANSWER: you

1. Is melody important in popular music?
2. Have you listened to any jazz music?
3. Where are those country music stars performing?
4. When will the tickets for their concert go on sale?
5. Which groups are most popular today?

More Practice

Grammar Exercise Workbook
- pp. 55–56

On-line Exercise Bank
- Section 19.4

Go on-line:
PHSchool.com
Enter Web Code:
eck-8002

◀ **Critical Viewing** Imagine that you want to join this music group. Write several questions you would ask before joining. **[Analyze]**

Finding the Subject in Sentences Beginning With *There* or *Here*

Sentences beginning with *there* or *here* are usually in inverted word order.

KEY CONCEPT *There* or *here* is never the subject of a sentence. ■

There can be used in two ways at the beginning of sentences. First, it can be used to start the sentence.

SENTENCE STARTER: There are (V) two musicians (S) from Tennessee in the office.

There can also be used as an adverb at the beginning of sentences, as can the word *here*. As adverbs, these two words point out *where* and modify the verbs.

ADVERBS: There goes (V) the rock star (S).

Here are (V) the invitations (S) to the party.

Be alert to sentences beginning with *there* and *here*. They are probably in inverted word order. If you cannot find the subject, reword the sentence in normal word order. If *there* is just a sentence starter, it can be dropped from the sentence.

Sentence Beginning With *There* or *Here*	Reworded With Subject Before Verb
There is a mistake on your paper.	A mistake is on your paper.
Here comes the star of the show.	The star of the show comes here.

Exercise 24 **Finding the Subject in Sentences Beginning With *There* or *Here*** Write the subject of each sentence below.

1. There were many pioneers of rock-and-roll music, including Elvis Presley, Chuck Berry, and Bill Haley.
2. Here are some memorable songs from the rock-and-roll period.
3. There were many singing groups in the early 1960's.
4. There, in the cabinet, are some old records by the Beatles.
5. There was an expansion of the music in the late 1960's.

Grammar and Style Tip

Try to use sentences with inverted word order, including some beginning with *here* or *there*, in your own writing. Such sentences add variety to your writing, making it more pleasing to read.

Get instant feedback! Exercises 23 and 24 are available on-line or on CD-ROM.

More Practice

Grammar Exercise Workbook
- pp. 57–58

On-line Exercise Bank
- Section 19.4

Go on-line: PHSchool.com *Enter Web Code:* eck-8002

Finding the Subject in Sentences Inverted for Emphasis

Sometimes a subject is intentionally put after its verb to draw attention to the subject.

KEY CONCEPT In some sentences, the subject follows the verb in order to receive greater emphasis. ■

In the following example, notice how the order of the words builds suspense by leading up to the subject.

EXAMPLE: In the midst of the crowd outside the theater stood (V) Buddy Holly (S).

Sentences such as this one can be reworded in normal word order to make it easier to find the subject.

Inverted Word Order	Reworded With Subject Before Verb
In the midst of the crowd outside the theater stood Buddy Holly.	Buddy Holly stood in the midst of the crowd outside the theater.

Exercise 25 **Finding the Subject in Inverted Sentences** Write the subject of each sentence below.

EXAMPLE: With the increased popularity of the guitar came the growth of country-and-western music.

ANSWER: growth

1. Important in this history of music is the development of rock-and-roll.
2. Combined with rock-and-roll were the elements of country-and-western music.
3. Out of this combination came country singers such as Johnny Cash, Waylon Jennings, and Dolly Parton.
4. Now known as the home of country music is Nashville, Tennessee.
5. High on the weekly sales charts sit country-and-western albums.

More Practice

Grammar Exercise Workbook
- pp. 57–58

On-line Exercise Bank
- Section 19.4

Go on-line: PHSchool.com
Enter Web Code: eck-8002

Get instant feedback! Exercise 25 is available on-line or on CD-ROM.

Section 19.4

Section Review

GRAMMAR EXERCISES 26–31

Exercise 26 **Recognizing Subjects That Give Orders and Directions** Write the subject of each of the following sentences. (Some sentences give orders or directions; others are in normal word order.)

1. Zachary, come here!
2. Listen to this music from the 1970's.
3. Disco, punk rock, reggae, and funk were introduced during this time.
4. These styles were less individualized than previous styles.
5. After comparing these styles, watch this music video.

Exercise 27 **Finding the Subject in Questions** Write the subject in each sentence below.

1. Which compact disc did you buy?
2. Are the compact discs very expensive?
3. Have you bought the latest single yet?
4. Where can we find the compact discs?
5. Which artist sold the most records?
6. When was *Thriller*, by Michael Jackson, released?
7. Are you sure of that date?
8. Who recorded the most albums during the 1980's?
9. Have you heard of Bruce Springsteen or the artist formerly known as Prince?
10. Did you watch the Grammy Awards?

Exercise 28 **Revising Sentences by Reversing the Order of Subjects and Verbs** Some of the sentences that follow are in normal word order; others are not. Rewrite each sentence, reversing the subject-verb order. When you have finished, underline the subject of each sentence.

1. There have been many changes in popular music over time.
2. Los Angeles, Nashville, and New York City are among the cities associated with popular music.
3. The musicians work and write their songs here.
4. In Los Angeles and New York are many sophisticated recording studios.
5. Many would-be country music stars live in the city of Nashville.
6. Among the hot spots for country music is the Grand Ole Opry.
7. Here can be seen the biggest names in country music.
8. Country legend Dolly Parton stood in the midst of the crowd outside the theater.
9. High above the audience on the stage were the enormous speakers.
10. In concert halls all over the world sit fans of popular music.

Exercise 29 **Find It in Your Reading** Look through newspaper articles for sentences with hard-to-find subjects. Write down examples of the following: a sentence giving an order, a sentence asking a question, a sentence beginning with *there* or *here*, and a sentence whose subject-verb order is changed for emphasis.

Exercise 30 **Find It in Your Writing** Look through your writing portfolio. Find two questions and two sentences beginning with *here* or *there*. Identify the subject in each sentence.

Exercise 31 **Writing Application** Write a description of a concert you have attended or a music video you have seen. Include one sentence beginning with *here* or *there*, one that asks a question, and one sentence inverted for emphasis.

Section 19.5

Complements

Often, a subject and verb alone can express a complete thought. For example, "Birds fly" can stand by itself as a sentence, even though it contains only a subject and a verb. In other sentences, however, the thought begun by a subject and its verb must be completed with other words. For example, the sentences "Toni bought," "The eyewitness told," "Our mechanic is," and "Richard feels" all contain a subject and verb, but none expresses a complete thought. All these ideas need *complements.*

KEY CONCEPT A **complement** is a word or group of words that completes the meaning of a subject and verb. ■

Complements are usually nouns, pronouns, or adjectives. They are located right after or very close to the verb. In the chart that follows, the subjects are underlined once and the verbs twice, and the complements are boxed.

DIFFERENT KINDS OF COMPLEMENTS
Toni bought [cars].
The eyewitness told [us] the [story].
Our mechanic is a [poet].
Richard feels [sad].

This section will describe three types of complements: *direct objects, indirect objects,* and *subject complements.*

Theme: Automobiles

In this section, you will learn about complements, such as direct objects, indirect objects, and subject complements. The examples and exercises are about the history of the automobile.

Cross-Curricular Connection: Social Studies

◀ **Critical Viewing** Add complements to the following subject-verb pairs to complete the thoughts about this photograph:
1. mechanic worked
2. engine needed
3. he said
[Interpret]

Recognizing Direct Objects

Direct objects are complements that are used after action verbs.

KEY CONCEPT A **direct object** is a noun or pronoun that receives the action of a transitive verb. ■

A direct object can be found by asking *Whom?* or *What?* after an action verb.

EXAMPLE: The message reached the lawyer (DO).
Reached *whom? Answer:* lawyer

Direct objects, like subjects and verbs, can be compound.

EXAMPLE: Mother invited Uncle Bill (DO) and Aunt Clara (DO).
Invited *whom? Answer:* Uncle Bill, Aunt Clara

GRAMMAR IN LITERATURE

from An American Childhood

Annie Dillard

The direct objects in the following excerpt are highlighted in blue italics.

It was a swift spirit; it was an awareness. It made *noise.* It had two joined *parts,* a head and a tail, like a Chinese dragon. It found the *door, wall,* and *headboard;* and it swiped *them,* charging them with its luminous glance.

Exercise 32 **Recognizing Direct Objects** Copy each sentence below, and underline each direct object. (Some of the sentences have compound direct objects.)

1. In the fourteenth century, Martini, an Italian painter, designed a human-propelled carriage on four wheels.
2. However, the Greeks used wheels and carts as far back as the eighth century B.C.
3. Henry Ford introduced his first automobile as the "Quadricycle."
4. The name *automobile* gained acceptance in 1897.
5. Some of the first powered cars employed windmills and clockwork motors.

Get instant feedback! Exercise 32 is available on-line or on CD-ROM.

More Practice

Grammar Exercise Workbook
- pp. 59–60

On-line Exercise Bank
- Section 19.5

Go on-line: PHSchool.com
Enter Web Code: eck-8002

19.5

Distinguishing Between Direct Objects, Adverbs, and Objects of Prepositions

Not all action verbs have direct objects. Be careful not to confuse a direct object with an adverb or with the object of a preposition.

KEY CONCEPT A direct object is never an adverb or the noun or pronoun at the end of a prepositional phrase. ■

Compare the following examples. Notice that the action verb *drove* has a direct object only in the first sentence.

EXAMPLES: Joanne drove her car. (DO: car)
Joanne drove quickly.
Joanne drove through the town.

Each example shows a very common sentence type. The first consists of a subject, a verb, and a direct object. The noun *car* is the direct object of the verb *drove.* The second example consists of a subject, a verb, and an adverb. Nothing answers the question *What?*, so there is no direct object. *Quickly* modifies the verb. The third example consists of a subject, a verb, and a prepositional phrase. Again, no noun or pronoun answers the question *What?* The prepositional phrase tells *where* Joanne drove.

Notice also that a single sentence can contain more than one of these three.

EXAMPLE: Joanne drove her car quickly through the town. (DO: car; ADV: quickly; PREP PHRASE: through the town)

Exercise 33 **Distinguishing Between Direct Objects, Adverbs, and Objects of Prepositions** Copy each of the following sentences onto your paper. Underline each direct object. Circle any adverbs or prepositional phrases. (Not every sentence has all three.)

EXAMPLE: The first steam-driven automobile moved (slowly) (at two miles per hour.)

1. A British inventor built a steam automobile in 1801.
2. This automobile moved rather quickly at twelve miles per hour.
3. People complained immediately about the automobiles' noise.
4. The speed limit restricted drivers to four miles per hour.
5. Many countries developed automobiles during this time.

More Practice

Grammar Exercise Workbook
- pp. 61–62

On-line Exercise Bank
- Section 19.5

Go on-line:
PHSchool.com
Enter Web Code:
eck-8002

Finding Direct Objects in Questions

A direct object in a sentence in normal word order is located after the verb. In questions, which are often in inverted order, the position of a direct object in the sentence may change.

KEY CONCEPT A direct object in a question is sometimes near the beginning of the sentence, before the verb. ■

In the chart below, compare the positions of the direct objects in the sentences. The sentences in the first column are questions. In the second column, the questions have been reworded as statements in normal word order.

Questions	Normal Word Order
DO Whom did you ask for help?	DO You did ask whom for help.
DO What does he want from us?	DO He does want what from us.
DO Which car does he want from the dealership?	DO He does want which car from the dealership.

If you have trouble finding the direct object in a question, rephrase the sentence in normal word order, as shown in the examples.

Exercise 34 **Finding Direct Objects in Questions** Copy each of the following sentences onto your paper, and underline each direct object. (Note that in two of the sentences, the direct objects follow the verbs.)

EXAMPLE: What have you heard about the early electric-powered vehicle?

1. Which articles did she read about this experimental vehicle?
2. What disadvantages did the electric automobile have?
3. What does he know about the size and reliability of its batteries?
4. Whom did you see in the automobile museum?
5. When did manufacturers begin production of the electric automobile?

Get instant feedback! Exercises 33 and 34 are available on-line or on CD-ROM.

More Practice

Grammar Exercise Workbook
- pp. 63–64

On-line Exercise Bank
- Section 19.5

Go on-line: PHSchool.com
Enter Web Code: eck-8002

Recognizing Indirect Objects

Sentences with a direct object may also contain another kind of complement, called an *indirect object.* A sentence cannot have an indirect object unless it has a direct object.

KEY CONCEPT An **indirect object** is a noun or pronoun that comes after an action verb and before a direct object. It names the person or thing to which something is given or for which something is done. ■

An indirect object answers the questions *To or for whom?* or *To or for what?* after an action verb. To find an indirect object, find the direct object first. Then, ask the appropriate question.

EXAMPLE: I told them the story. (IO: them; DO: story)
Told *to whom? Answer:* them

Keep in mind the following pattern: Subject + Verb + Indirect Object + Direct Object. An indirect object will almost always come between the verb and the direct object in a sentence.

Like a subject, verb, or direct object, an indirect object can be compound.

EXAMPLE: Dave gave each car and truck a new color. (IO: car; IO: truck; DO: color)
Gave *to what? Answer:* car, truck

Get instant feedback! Exercises 35 and 36 are available on-line or on CD-ROM.

Exercise 35 **Recognizing Indirect Objects** Copy the sentences below, and underline the simple or compound indirect objects.

1. In 1912, twenty companies offered customers electric cars.
2. The internal-combustion engine gave the electric cars new competition.
3. Engineers had given automobile makers plans for internal-combustion automobiles.
4. Owners showed neighbors and friends their automobile.
5. However, the automobile often taught the driver and passengers humility.
6. Automobile engines often gave owners and drivers problems.
7. Ever-dependable horses would then give the car and stranded passengers a tow.
8. The ability of a horse to pull gave the automobile and its engine a new name for its power: "horsepower"!
9. However, cars driven by steam gave Americans a dependable method of travel.
10. Stanley Steamers gave drivers the thrill of quick, noisy travel.

More Practice

Grammar Exercise Workbook
- pp. 65–66

On-line Exercise Bank
- Section 19.5

Go on-line: PHSchool.com
Enter Web Code: eck-8002

Distinguishing Between Indirect Objects and Objects of Prepositions

Do not confuse an indirect object with the object of a preposition.

KEY CONCEPT An indirect object never follows the preposition *to* or *for* in a sentence. ■

Compare the following examples:

EXAMPLES: Father bought him (IO) a car (DO).

Father bought a car (DO) for him.

In the first example, *him* is an indirect object. It comes after the verb and before the direct object. In the second, *him* is the object of the preposition *for* and follows the direct object.

Exercise 36 Distinguishing Between Indirect Objects and Objects of Prepositions Copy each sentence below. Underline each indirect object. Circle each object of a preposition.

EXAMPLE: Automobiles brought people other problems.

1. The automobile brought danger for drivers.
2. Accidents caused town officials great concern.
3. Towns quickly set low speed limits for motorists.
4. They soon gave speeders fines.
5. All motorists have a responsibility to their passengers and other drivers.

More Practice

Grammar Exercise Workbook
- pp. 67–68

On-line Exercise Bank
- Section 19.5

Go on-line:
PHSchool.com
Enter Web Code:
eck-8002

◀ **Critical Viewing** Compare and contrast the automobile pictured here with one you know well. When you have finished, go back and identify any complements you have used. **[Compare and Contrast]**

Using Subject Complements

Both direct objects and indirect objects are complements used with action verbs. Linking verbs, however, have a different kind of complement, called a *subject complement.*

KEY CONCEPT A **subject complement** is a noun, a pronoun, or an adjective that follows a linking verb and tells something about the subject. ■

Predicate Nouns and Pronouns

Both nouns and pronouns are sometimes used as subject complements after linking verbs.

KEY CONCEPT A **predicate noun** or **predicate pronoun** follows a linking verb and renames or identifies the subject of the sentence. ■

It is easy to recognize *predicate nouns* and *predicate pronouns.* The linking verb acts much like an equal sign between the subject and the noun or pronoun that follows the verb. Both the subject and the predicate noun or pronoun refer to the same person or thing.

PREDICATE NOUNS AND PRONOUNS

Examples	Relationships
Ronnie will be the captain (PN) of our team.	The predicate noun *captain* renames the subject *Ronnie.*
Ford's first car was the Model A (PN).	The predicate noun *Model A* identifies the subject *car.*
The two winners are they (PRED PRON).	The predicate pronoun *they* identifies the subject *winners.*

Learn More

The verbs in these examples are all forms of the linking verb *be.* See Chapter 15, Verbs, for a complete list of the forms of *be* and other linking verbs.

Exercise 37 Recognizing Predicate Nouns and Pronouns
Identify the predicate noun or predicate pronoun in each sentence below.

EXAMPLE: The automobile is an American institution.
ANSWER: institution

1. Europe was the home of some early automobiles.
2. Americans quickly became fans of the automobile.
3. Hartford and Cleveland were the cities in which the American auto industry began.
4. The first successful American car was the Duryea brothers' invention.
5. Many car models were poor designs.
6. Henry Ford was the man who had financial backing for his invention.
7. He was the inventor of the Model A.
8. Ford was also the inventor of the Model T, his most popular automobile.
9. He was the creator of the world's first auto assembly line.
10. The assembly line was a method of constructing cars on a conveyor belt.

More Practice

Grammar Exercise Workbook
- pp. 69–70

On-line Exercise Bank
- Section 19.5

Go on-line:
PHSchool.com
Enter Web Code:
eck-8002

Get instant feedback! Exercise 37 is available on-line or on CD-ROM.

Predicate Adjectives

A linking verb can also be followed by a *predicate adjective.*

KEY CONCEPT A **predicate adjective** follows a linking verb and describes the subject of the sentence. ■

A predicate adjective is considered part of the complete predicate of a sentence because it comes after a linking verb. In spite of this, a predicate adjective does not modify the words in the predicate. Instead, it describes the noun or pronoun that serves as the subject of the linking verb.

PREDICATE ADJECTIVES

Examples	Relationship of Words
The flight to Houston was swift (PA).	The predicate adjective *swift* describes the subject *flight.*
The saleswoman seems very sensitive (PA) to the needs of her customers.	The predicate adjective *sensitive* describes subject *saleswoman.*

Exercise 38 **Recognizing Predicate Adjectives** Write the predicate adjective in each sentence below.

EXAMPLE: The Model T was popular with early drivers.
ANSWER: popular

1. The assembly line was extremely efficient, constructing one car in 93 minutes.
2. However, assembly line work was unpleasant.
3. Workers grew tired of the daily monotony and pressure of production quotas.
4. A monthly labor turnover of 40 to 60 percent was inescapable.
5. Ford's plan for doubling the daily wage was smart.

More Practice

Grammar Exercise Workbook
- pp. 69–72

On-line Exercise Bank
- Section 19.5

Go on-line: PHSchool.com
Enter Web Code: eck-8002

Get instant feedback! Exercises 38 and 39 are available on-line or on CD-ROM.

Compound Subject Complements

Like other sentence parts, subject complements can be compound.

KEY CONCEPT A **compound subject complement** consists of two or more predicate nouns, pronouns, or adjectives. ■

EXAMPLES: My two best friends are Phil (PN) and Mark (PN).

The highway seems slick (PA) and icy (PA).

Exercise 39 **Recognizing Compound Subject Complements** Copy the following sentences onto your paper, and underline the parts of each compound subject complement. If a compound subject complement is made up of predicate adjectives, draw arrows pointing from each adjective to the subject.

EXAMPLE: In America, the automobile became a fixture as well as a necessity in everyday life.

1. The Museum of Automobile History in Syracuse, New York, is exciting and interesting to people of all ages.
2. Information on thousands of cars is available and accessible to all visitors.
3. The display of collector's items is sleek and huge.
4. The museum has become both a historic site and a showroom for classic cars.
5. It will be a popular attraction and tourist site for years to come.

Section 19.5

Section Review

GRAMMAR EXERCISES 40–45

Exercise 40 **Distinguishing Between Direct Objects, Adverbs, and Objects of Prepositions** Copy each of the following sentences onto your paper. Underline each direct object. Circle any adverbs or prepositional phrases. (Not every sentence has all three.)

1. More automobiles created more traffic and traffic jams.
2. Soon, drivers needed traffic lights for safety.
3. The automobile has created conveniences for drivers.
4. Banks and restaurants provide service quickly to drive-through customers.
5. What effects has the automobile had on your life?

Exercise 41 **Distinguishing Between Indirect Objects and Objects of Prepositions** Copy the sentences below onto your paper, and underline each indirect object or compound indirect object. Circle each object of a preposition. (Not every sentence has both.)

1. Connecticut gave drivers the first license plates for their vehicles.
2. The state also provided a leather strap for the license plate.
3. The state assigned each driver and vehicle an identification number.
4. In 1903, Massachusetts offered each owner state-made license plates.
5. States soon required a license for each driver.

Exercise 42 **Revision Practice: Sentence Combining** Combine sentences in the following paragraph by using compound complements.

License plates are now more attractive than in the past. They are also more personal. The buyer of that personalized license plate is she. The owner is she, too. Such plates are common now. They are inexpensive to purchase. In today's busy world, cars are an essential means of transportation. They are a popular means of transportation. Fortunately, they have also become safer. Cars have also become more efficient. Cars have become a hobby for many. They are a pastime for others. Some old cars are restored for car shows. Other old cars are stripped for their parts. One winner at the car show was that couple. Another winner was that woman. The Model T was the oldest car. It was also the most well preserved.

Exercise 43 **Find It in Your Reading** Reread the excerpt from *An American Childhood* on page 285. Identify two predicate nouns.

Exercise 44 **Find It in Your Writing** Look through your writing portfolio. Find a piece of writing that contains two direct objects, two indirect objects, one predicate noun, and one predicate adjective. Copy the appropriate sentences onto another piece of paper and identify each complement.

Exercise 45 **Writing Application** Write an advertisement for your dream car. Underline all the complements in your sentences. Include at least one example of each of the following: direct object, indirect object, predicate noun, predicate adjective.

Chapter 20

Phrases and Clauses

▲ **Critical Viewing** What are the different parts, or features, that make up this landscape? **[Analyze]**

The formation of a culture occurs at the beginning of its history. Everything, even small things, that happens has an influence on what that culture will become. Sentences, like cultures, are made up of little things. What a sentence is, or what a sentence means, depends on its parts. In this chapter, you will learn the sentence parts—phrases and clauses—and their different variations.

Diagnostic Test

Directions: Write all answers on a separate sheet of paper.

Skill Check A. Label each underlined phrase below an *adjective phrase* or an *adverb phrase.*

1. A huge silver deposit was discovered during the year 1546.
2. The soldiers thought the mountains of New Mexico looked like the mountains in Mexico where the silver had been discovered.
3. This led them to expand their exploration into New Mexico.
4. A merchant decided to sponsor an expedition to New Mexico.
5. He was personally interested in the area.

Skill Check B. Identify appositives, appositive phrases, participles, and participial phrases in the following sentences. Label each item you identify.

6. Gaspar Castano de Sosa, a lieutenant-governor from Spain, thought that exploring New Mexico would win him riches.
7. The people of the area, the Native Americans, told him legends of wealth in the unexplored areas.
8. De Sosa, the governor, threw a silver cup into the ore sample.
9. The sample showed the desired results, a high silver content.
10. Thus, he was able to convince many people that the desired destination, New Mexico, was indeed a worthy goal.

Skill Check C. Identify gerunds, gerund phrases, and infinitives in the following sentences. Label each item you identify.

11. In 1590, 170 people left from Almaden to seek their fortunes.
12. Searching for wealth proved fruitless in the New Mexico desert.
13. Two months later, soldiers set out to arrest de Sosa.
14. The soldiers returned him to New Spain to be thrown into prison.
15. However, de Sosa's traveling was important because his was the first expedition to New Mexico to be supported by a private party.

Skill Check D. Label each underlined word below *gerund, verb,* or *participle.* If it is a participle, tell whether it is *present* or *past.* Then, label each sentence *simple, complex, compound,* or *compound-complex.*

16. Establishing San Gabriel, Juan de Onate led a group to New Mexico at the end of the sixteenth century.
17. When they arrived, the Native Americans shared their homes with the settlers, and they helped them to find urgently needed food.
18. At this time, the Spanish were planning to build a town next to the Indian pueblo, but Onate ordered them to build San Gabriel next to the west bank of the Rio Grande.
19. While Onate was settling the area, he claimed that his purpose was establishing peace with the Indians.
20. However, it seems that becoming rich was his desire; in addition to his packing the ordinary supplies, Onate had also brought mining tools.

Section 20.1

Phrases

Sentences are built with more than just a subject and a predicate. *Phrases* of all kinds play an important role by adding information to a sentence.

KEY CONCEPT A **phrase** is a group of words that functions in a sentence as a single part of speech. Phrases do not contain a subject and verb. ■

There are several kinds of phrases: *prepositional, appositive, participial, gerund,* and *infinitive.* They get their names from the word that begins the phrase or from the most important word in it. You are probably most familiar with the prepositional phrase.

Theme: New Mexico

In this section, you will learn about phrases. The examples and exercises are about New Mexico.

Cross-Curricular Connection: Social Studies

Using Prepositional Phrases

A *prepositional phrase* begins with a preposition and ends with a noun or pronoun called the *object of the preposition.*

EXAMPLES: under (PREP) the window (OBJ) near (PREP) them (OBJ) at (PREP) the store (OBJ)

Prepositional phrases may also have compound objects.

EXAMPLE: near (PREP) the flowers (OBJ) and the trees (OBJ)

In a sentence, a prepositional phrase can act as an adjective and modify a noun or pronoun. It can also act as an adverb and modify a verb, an adjective, or an adverb.

Exercise 1 **Identifying Prepositional Phrases** Identify the prepositional phrase(s) in each of the following sentences.

1. Colorado lies to the north of New Mexico.
2. The southern border of this beautiful state is Mexico.
3. By the sixteenth century, Spanish explorers had arrived in Mexico.
4. They heard grand tales about rich treasures in the land to the north of Mexico.
5. They called this land "new" Mexico. They did not find gold when they arrived, but the name has remained with the land ever since.

Exercise 2 **Writing With Prepositional Phrases** Write a description of the photograph on page 430. Use at least five prepositional phrases. Circle each one.

Using Prepositional Phrases That Act as Adjectives

A prepositional phrase that acts as an adjective is called an *adjective phrase.*

KEY CONCEPT An **adjective phrase** is a prepositional phrase that modifies a noun or pronoun by telling *what kind* or *which one.* ■

The following chart compares adjective phrases to one-word adjectives. Notice that an adjective phrase usually follows its noun or pronoun.

Adjectives	Adjective Phrases
The *New Mexican* climate is warm.	The climate *of New Mexico* is warm.
The *blue-eyed* acrobat slipped and fell.	The acrobat *with the blue eyes* slipped and fell.

The adjective phrases answer the same questions as the one-word adjectives. *Which* climate is warm? The climate *of New Mexico* is warm. *Which one* of the acrobats slipped and fell? The acrobat *with the blue eyes* did.

Exercise 3 **Identifying Adjective Phrases** Copy the following sentences onto your paper. Underline each adjective phrase, and draw an arrow pointing from it to the word it modifies.

1. Scientists believe that the first humans in this area were the Sandia People.
2. Caves in the central mountains were their homes.
3. Bones and fossils of these people are 25,000 years old.
4. Ruins around this area can still be seen today.
5. Now, the Native Americans from the area are the Pueblo, the Navajo, and the Apache Indians.

Exercise 4 **Writing With Adjective Phrases** Write a series of sentences in which you use each of the following nouns as part of an adjective phrase or in which you use an adjective phrase to describe the noun.

1. desert
2. Santa Fe
3. weavings
4. attractions
5. mountains

More Practice

Grammar Exercise Workbook
- pp. 73–74

On-line Exercise Bank
- Section 20.1

Go on-line: PHSchool.com
Enter Web Code: eck-8002

Get instant feedback! Exercises 1, 2, 3, and 4 are available on-line or on CD-ROM.

20.1

Using Prepositional Phrases as Adverbs

Prepositional phrases can also be used as adverbs.

KEY CONCEPT An **adverb phrase** is a prepositional phrase that modifies a verb, an adjective, or an adverb. Adverb phrases point out *where, when, in what way*, or *to what extent*. ■

The examples in the following chart show that adverb phrases serve the same function as one-word adverbs.

Adverb	Adverb Phrases
The bus left *late.*	The bus left *after a two-hour delay.*
Put the package *there.*	Put the package *in the closet.*

In the first pair of examples, both *late* and *after a two-hour delay* answer the question *Left when?* In the second pair, *there* and *in the closet* answer the question *Put where?*

Like one-word adverbs, adverb phrases can modify verbs, adjectives, or adverbs. Unlike adjective phrases, adverb phrases do not always appear close to the words they modify. They can appear in almost any position in a sentence.

Exercise 5 **Identifying Adverb Phrases** Copy the following sentences onto your paper. Underline each adverb phrase, and draw an arrow pointing from it to the word it modifies.

1. Cabeza de Vaca escaped from a shipwreck in 1528.
2. He and his men then walked through the Mexican desert.
3. They journeyed for eight years.
4. During their journey, they covered about 10,000 miles.
5. Eventually, they traveled to an area that would later be known to the Spaniards as New Mexico.

Exercise 6 **Writing With Adverb Phrases** Rewrite each item below as a complete sentence by adding an adjective phrase.

1. The tourists journeyed . . .
2. At Taos ski resort, expert skiers plunge . . .
3. The heat subsided . . .
4. The sun rose . . .
5. The desert extended . . .

More Practice

Grammar Exercise Workbook
- pp. 73–74

On-line Exercise Bank
- Section 20.1

Go on-line:
PHSchool.com
Enter Web Code:
eck-8002

Get instant feedback! Exercises 5 and 6 are available on-line or on CD-ROM.

Using Appositives in Phrases

Appositives, like adjective phrases, give information about nouns or pronouns.

KEY CONCEPT An **appositive** is a noun or pronoun placed after another noun or pronoun to identify, rename, or explain the preceding word. ■

Appositives are very useful in writing because they give additional information without using many words.

EXAMPLES: The poet *Robert Frost* is much admired.

This antique car, a *Studebaker,* is worth thousands of dollars.

The conquistador *Francisco de Coronado* led a group of 1,100 people looking for gold.

An appositive with its own modifiers creates an *appositive phrase.*

KEY CONCEPT An **appositive phrase** is a noun or pronoun with modifiers. It is placed next to a noun or pronoun and adds information or details. ■

The modifiers in the phrase can be adjectives or adjective phrases.

EXAMPLES: San Juan de los Caballeros, *the Spanish capital of the New Mexico territory,* was moved to a new site in 1610.

The painting, *a mural in many bright colors,* highlights the entrance.

Appositives and appositive phrases can also be compound.

EXAMPLES: Volunteers, *boys* or *girls,* are wanted.

These poems, "The Sea Gypsy" and "Before the Squall," are about a love for the sea.

Grammar and Style Tip

Appositives provide an excellent way to combine certain types of sentences. Look at the following pair of sentences: "This antique car is a Studebaker. It is worth thousands of dollars." These sentences can be combined using an appositive, as in the example.

Exercise 7 **Identifying Appositives and Appositive Phrases** Copy the following sentences onto your paper. Underline each appositive or appositive phrase, and draw an arrow pointing from it to the noun or pronoun it renames.

1. The capital, Santa Fe, was the place from which the Spaniards ran their territorial government.
2. El Palacio, the Palace of the Governors, was the building where government business was carried out.
3. Pope, a Native American leader, led a revolt against the Spanish in 1680.
4. This revolt drove their enemies, the Spanish, out of the area.
5. Twelve years later, the Spanish general Diego de Vargas returned to conquer the area for the Spaniards again.

▼ **Critical Viewing** What can you learn about New Mexico from this photograph alone? **[Connect]**

Exercise 8 **Combining Sentences With Appositives and Appositive Phrases** Combine each pair of sentences below by using an appositive or appositive phrase.

EXAMPLE: New Mexico is a popular tourist destination. The state is known for its beauty.

ANSWER: New Mexico, a popular tourist destination, is known for its beauty.

1. After Mexico won its independence in 1821, the New Mexico Territory was open to settlement by Americans. The territory consisted of present-day Arizona, New Mexico, Nevada, and Utah.
2. When trade began with the United States, the Santa Fe Trail became popular. It was a route from Santa Fe to Missouri.
3. In 1846, the United States declared war on Mexico, and the capture of northern Mexico became one of its first objectives. The area is now known as New Mexico.
4. A United States officer entered and captured Santa Fe. His name was General Stephen Watts Kearny.
5. Today, New Mexico has a diverse population. It is a state filled with rich cultural traditions.

Using Verbals and Verbal Phrases

Verbals are verb forms that are used as another part of speech. There are three kinds of verbals: *participles, gerunds,* and *infinitives.* Participles are used as adjectives, gerunds as nouns, and infinitives as nouns, adjectives, or adverbs.

Verbals have two important characteristics of verbs: (1) They can be followed by a complement, and (2) they can be modified by adverbs and adverb phrases. A verbal with a complement or a modifier is called a *verbal phrase.*

Participles

Many of the adjectives you use are actually *participles.*

KEY CONCEPT A **participle** is a form of a verb that acts as an adjective. ■

There are two kinds of participles: *present participles* and *past participles.* Present participles end in *-ing.*

PRESENT PARTICIPLES: going, playing, growing, telling, reading

Past participles usually end in *-ed,* although those formed from irregular verbs will have different endings, such as *-t* or *-en.* (See Section 22.1 for a list of irregular verb endings.)

PAST PARTICIPLES: marked, jumped, moved, hurt, chosen

Present Participles	Past Participles
A *growing* baby sleeps much of the day.	The *conquered* territory was under Spanish control.
Many people in New Mexico live in *farming* communities.	*Troubled,* she asked for advice.

More Practice

Grammar Exercise Workbook
- pp. 75–80

On-line Exercise Bank
- Section 20.1

Go on-line: PHSchool.com *Enter Web Code:* eck-8002

Get instant feedback! Exercises 7, 8, and 9 are available on-line or on CD-ROM.

Exercise 9 **Identifying Present and Past Participles** Write the participle from each sentence below, and label it *past* or *present.*

1. New Mexico's tiring distances made it difficult to commute.
2. Until 1847, there was only one completed schoolhouse.
3. Only a selected few were given education at this time.
4. The sons of the educated wealthy were sent east to school.
5. In 1847, a Catholic bishop, John B. Lamy, started a free school where his students were taught in English.

Participle or Verb?

Sometimes, verb phrases (verbs with helping verbs) are confused with participles. In the chart, however, note that a verb phrase always begins with a helping verb. A participle used as an adjective stands by itself and modifies a noun or pronoun.

Verb Phrases	Participles
The car *was racing* around the curve.	The *racing* car crashed into the wall.
Cabeza de Vaca and his group *may have walked* through New Mexico.	The *walked* trail may have gone through New Mexico.

Exercise 10 **Distinguishing Between Verbs and Participles** Label each underlined word a *verb* or a *participle.* If the word is a participle, also write the word it modifies.

EXAMPLE: Preaching missionaries taught religion and also set up schools.

ANSWER: participle (missionaries)

1. By 1856, the government was taking steps to create a public-school system.
2. Progressing, the legislature passed the first public-school law in 1860.
3. This encouraged other districts that were building schools in other parts of the territory.
4. The University of New Mexico was built for the increasing population of Albuquerque in 1889.
5. Established schools became more numerous in some areas by the early 1900's.
6. Also rising in popularity were cattle ranches.
7. These, however, declined when sheep were brought in.
8. Homesteaders needed fenced land to farm.
9. Consequently, ranchers would run into newly built fences where they used to graze their cattle.
10. With competition that was coming from two directions, many cattle owners were giving up cattle ranching.

More Practice

Grammar Exercise Workbook
- pp. 75–80

On-line Exercise Bank
- Section 20.1

Go on-line: PHSchool.com
Enter Web Code: eck-8002

Get instant feedback! Exercise 10 is available on-line or on CD-ROM.

Participial Phrases

A participle can be expanded into a phrase by adding one or more modifiers or complements to it.

KEY CONCEPT A **participial phrase** is a present or past participle that is modified by an adverb or adverb phrase or that has a complement. The entire phrase acts as an adjective in a sentence. ■

The following examples show a few of the ways that participles can be expanded into phrases.

EXAMPLES: The diner, *chewing rapidly,* called for a waiter.

The waiter, *eating his lunch,* did not respond.

The first participial phrase is formed by adding the adverb *rapidly,* the second by adding the direct object *lunch.*

In these examples, notice that each participial phrase appears right after the noun it modifies. Both sentences could be reworded to move the phrases before the modified words.

EXAMPLES: *Chewing rapidly,* the diner called for a waiter.

Eating his lunch, the waiter did not respond.

GRAMMAR IN LITERATURE

from A Horseman in the Sky

Ambrose Bierce

Notice how the writer has used participles in this passage. The present participles are red, and the past participle is blue.

. . . the left hand, holding the bridle rein, was invisible. In silhouette against the sky the profile of the horse was cut with the sharpness of a cameo; it looked across the heights of air to the confronting cliffs beyond. The face of the rider, turned slightly away, showed only an outline of temple and beard. . . .

Exercise 11 **Recognizing Participial Phrases** Copy the following sentences. Underline each participial phrase and draw an arrow pointing from it to the word or words it modifies.

1. Discovered in the northwest, petroleum reserves helped to boost the economy of New Mexico.
2. More oil reserves, hiding in the southeast, were also found in the 1920's.
3. Twenty years later, the federal government, looking for a sparsely populated area, went to New Mexico.
4. They decided that the desert, acting as a testing site, was to be used to explode atomic bombs during World War II.
5. Los Alamos, established as the headquarters, became busy with atomic energy research.

Exercise 12 **Combining Sentences Using Participial Phrases** Combine each pair of sentences below into a single sentence containing a participial phrase.

EXAMPLE: A new dam was completed in 1916. It made large-scale irrigation farming possible.

ANSWER: A new dam, making large-scale irrigation farming possible, was completed in 1916.

1. The first atomic bomb was tested in 1945. It was exploded on the White Sands Proving Grounds.
2. The production of atomic weapons began at Sandia Base of Albuquerque. It gave rise to many other industries.
3. Oil reserves were found on the Navajo and Jicarilla reservations. The reserves increased New Mexico's wealth.
4. These resources are now owned by the Navajo and the Jicarilla. They generate income for Native Americans there.
5. The money has been used for areas such as education. It has improved living conditions.

More Practice

Grammar Exercise Workbook
- pp. 77–82

On-line Exercise Bank
- Section 20.1

Go on-line: PHSchool.com
Enter Web Code: eck-8002

Get instant feedback! Exercises 11, 12, 13, and 14 are available on-line or on CD-ROM.

▼ **Critical Viewing** Write two sentences to describe this picture, and include a participial phrase in each one. **[Describe]**

Gerunds

Like present participles, *gerunds* end in *-ing.* While present participles are used as adjectives, gerunds are used as nouns. Like other nouns, gerunds can be used as subjects, direct objects, predicate nouns, and objects of prepositions.

KEY CONCEPT A **gerund** is a form of verb that acts as a noun. ■

USE OF GERUNDS IN SENTENCES	
Subject	*Remodeling* the building's style was a good idea.
Direct Object	Michael enjoys *painting.*
Predicate Noun	His favorite sport is *fishing.*
Object of a Preposition	Lucille never gets tired of *singing.*

Exercise 13 **Identifying Gerunds** Write the gerund(s) from the sentences below, and label each one *subject, direct object, predicate noun,* or *object of a preposition.*

EXAMPLE: Touring New Mexico's beautiful sites is recommended.

ANSWER: Touring (subject)

1. Tourists in New Mexico may enjoy horseback riding at a dude ranch.
2. Hiking and camping are year-round activities in New Mexico.
3. Visitors may also find excitement in visiting the ancient ruins of the Native Americans who have lived here for thousands of years.
4. Native American dancing and festivals draw many visitors to New Mexico.
5. Above all, touring New Mexico is a pleasant vacation.

Exercise 14 **Writing With Gerunds** Write a series of sentences using each of the following gerunds.

1. weaving
2. skiing
3. traveling
4. ballooning
5. golfing

Gerund Phrases

A gerund can also be part of a phrase.

KEY CONCEPT A **gerund phrase** is a gerund with modifiers or a complement, all acting together as a noun. ■

The chart shows how gerunds are expanded.

GERUND PHRASES	
Gerund With Adjectives	*The loud, shrill howling* continued all morning.
Gerund With Direct Object	*Using trees as lumber* is an important part of the New Mexican economy.
Gerund With Prepositional Phrase	He helped the police by *telling about his experience.*
Gerund With Adverb and Prepositional Phrase	Pueblo tribe members astound spectators by *dancing skillfully on stage.*

Exercise 15 **Identifying Gerund Phrases** Write the gerund phrase(s) in the sentences below. Label each one *subject, direct object, predicate noun,* or *object of a preposition.*

EXAMPLE: One skill of the Pueblo people in New Mexico is making jewelry.
ANSWER: making jewelry (predicate noun)

1. Setting turquoise stones in silver is a common jewelry-making practice.
2. The Pueblo also earn their money by shaping pottery.
3. The next step after baking a piece of pottery is painting it.
4. Some Pueblo groups teach pottery making to tourists.
5. The San Ildefonso Pueblo is famous for its black-on-black pottery making.
6. Camping and fishing on the Isleta Reservation are popular tourist activities.
7. Not all Pueblo people are interested in attracting tourists.
8. During some of the ceremonial dances, video recording is not allowed.
9. Another way of making a living is by raising livestock.
10. Government reports consider farming a major source of employment in the area.

More Practice

Grammar Exercise Workbook
- pp. 81–82

On-line Exercise Bank
- Section 20.1

Go on-line: PHSchool.com
Enter Web Code: eck-8002

Get instant feedback! Exercise 15 is available on-line or on CD-ROM.

Infinitives

Infinitives can be used as three different parts of speech: nouns, adjectives, and adverbs.

KEY CONCEPT An **infinitive** is the form of a verb that comes after the word *to* and acts as a noun, an adjective, or an adverb. ■

As a noun, an infinitive can be used as a subject, direct object, predicate noun, object of a preposition, or appositive, as shown in the chart below.

INFINITIVES USED AS NOUNS	
Subject	*To whistle* is difficult for some people.
Direct Object	As soon as she gets home, she hopes *to write.*
Predicate Noun	His dream has always been *to travel.*
Object of a Preposition	The Spaniards had no choice except *to leave.*
Appositive	Her decision, *to listen,* was a wise one.

Infinitives can also be used as adjectives and adverbs. In the chart below, infinitives answer the same questions as adjectives and adverbs.

INFINITIVES USED AS ADJECTIVES AND ADVERBS	
Adjective	In New Mexico, the first radio station *to succeed* was KOB in Albuquerque. (Which kind of station?) The person *to contact* is the dean. (Which person?)
Adverb	This is easy *to do.* (Easy in what manner?) Ready *to please,* the guides at Carlsbad Caverns work hard to provide enjoyable tours. (Ready in what manner?)

Grammar and Style Tip

Prepositional phrases beginning with the word *to* are often confused with infinitives. If the word immediately following *to* is a verb, then the phrase is an infinitive; otherwise, *to* begins a prepositional phrase.

Exercise 16 **Identifying Infinitives** List the infinitives in the following sentences.

EXAMPLE: The Taos were said to be the first apartment-house builders.

ANSWER: to be

1. Tall homes, some five stories high, were built to accommodate the ancient Taos population.
2. When the Europeans arrived, they thought the houses were fascinating to look at.
3. To use these same houses today is not uncommon.
4. The Navajo tribe had homes to sleep in called hogans.
5. Navajo hogans, in contrast to the homes of the Taos, were built to have only one room.

Exercise 17 **Writing Sentences With Infinitives** Use the infinitives below to write ten sentences. Label each use of an infinitive a *noun*, an *adjective*, or an *adverb*.

1. to sing
2. to drive
3. to give
4. to walk
5. to tell
6. to contribute
7. to act
8. to be
9. to sleep
10. to dream

More Practice

Grammar Exercise Workbook
- pp. 83–84

On-line Exercise Bank
- Section 20.1

Go on-line: PHSchool.com *Enter Web Code:* eck-8002

▼ Critical Viewing The homes in which the Taos lived, called pueblos, are pictured here. How would you describe them? What infinitives might you use in your description? **[Describe]**

Infinitive Phrases

Infinitives, like gerunds and participles, can be combined with other words to form phrases.

KEY CONCEPT An **infinitive phrase** is an infinitive with modifiers or a complement, all acting together as a single part of speech. ■

The following chart shows how infinitives can be expanded.

INFINITIVE PHRASES	
Infinitive With Adverb	It will be important *to listen carefully.*
Infinitive With Prepositional Phrase	*To ski in New Mexico,* you must travel high into the mountains.
Infinitive With Direct Object	In 1912, the United States Legislature decided *to admit New Mexico* to the Union.
Infinitive With Indirect and Direct Objects	I need *to give you my new telephone number.*

▼ Critical Viewing Judging by this photograph, what can you conclude about a miner's work? **[Analyze]**

Exercise 18 **Identifying Infinitive Phrases** List the infinitive phrases in the following sentences.

EXAMPLE: It is an advantage for a state to have rich mineral resources.

ANSWER: to have rich mineral resources

1. New Mexico has petroleum, potash, copper, and natural gas—to name a few.
2. During the spring of 1950, a man bent down to pick up a yellow rock.
3. This rock turned out to be high-grade uranium ore.
4. New Mexico now claims to have 72 percent of the country's uranium reserves.
5. Uranium is a radioactive element that is used to create nuclear energy.

Hands-on Grammar

Fill in the Blanks With Phrases

To demonstrate how adjective and adverb phrases affect the overall meaning of a sentence, complete the following activity with a small group.

Brainstorm for a list of sentences in which you leave a blank for an adjective phrase or an adverb phrase. (See the examples below.) Write these sentences with magic markers on construction paper.

Then, come up with different adverb phrases and adjective phrases you can use to complete each sentence. Have a group member record each phrase that is suggested.

When you have finished, try piecing some of the sentences together to form a paragraph. Share your paragraph with the class.

We left ________.

We left at three in the morning.

We left after a three-hour delay.

We left before anyone else.

The singer ________ was the first to perform.

The singer with the terrible voice was the first to perform.

The singer with the bright blue suit was the first to perform.

Find It in Your Reading Take some of your sentences from a short story or piece of nonfiction you have just read.

Find It in Your Writing Try this process with a piece of your own writing. Cut out small pieces of paper, and place them over the adjective and adverb phrases. Experiment with other adjective and adverb phrases. See if any of the replacements convey your intended meaning better than the original phrase.

Section 20.1 Section Review

GRAMMAR EXERCISES 19–25

Exercise 19 **Identifying Verbs and Participles** Label each underlined word a *verb* or a *participle*. If it is a participle, write the word it modifies.

1. When the Spaniards arrived in New Mexico, the Pueblo population numbered between 40,000 and 50,000.
2. Many had adopted a farming lifestyle.
3. Domesticated animals included dogs and turkeys.
4. The arriving Spaniards gave the name "Pueblos," meaning "Townsmen," to the people of this area because most of them lived in organized cities.
5. Almost all of their well-built villages were eventually destroyed.

Exercise 20 **Identifying Gerunds and Gerund Phrases** Write the gerund or gerund phrase from each sentence below.

1. Living in the desert posed a problem for some early settlers.
2. Spanish power was destroyed because of internal bickering.
3. The organizing of a revolt by Native Americans was undertaken by a man named Pope.
4. The planning took about five years.
5. Most of the five years were spent uniting the various Pueblo peoples.

Exercise 21 **Identifying Infinitives and Infinitive Phrases** Write the infinitive or infinitive phrase from each sentence.

1. Pope's revolt included plans to launch a surprise attack on the Spaniards.
2. He thought the weakly guarded settlement would be easy to conquer.
3. Pope wanted to return the Native Americans to their former way of life.
4. He wanted to completely expel the Spaniards from the region.
5. Even though many supported Pope, this idea was not to be popular among all of the Pueblo people.

Exercise 22 **Classifying All Types of Phrases** Identify the adverb phrases, adjective phrases, appositives, participles, gerunds, and infinitives in the following:

Our visit to New Mexico was great. Watching the sun rise over the desert is one of the greatest memories I have from any vacation. Taos, a small town in the mountains, was my favorite place to visit. The skiing there is fantastic, and the town is filled with great restaurants and interesting shops.

Exercise 23 **Find It in Your Reading** Identify the prepositional phrases and participial phrases in this passage from a story by Ambrose Bierce.

> So Carter Druse, bowing reverently to his father, who returned the salute with a stately courtesy that masked a breaking heart, left the home of his childhood to go soldiering.

Exercise 24 **Find It in Your Writing** Look through your portfolio. Find two examples of each type of phrase you've learned about in this section.

Exercise 25 **Writing Application** Write a short paper about New Mexico. Include sentences that contain prepositional phrases, participial phrases, and appositive phrases. Circle and label each example.

Section 20.2

Clauses

This section explains the second important sentence element, the *clause.*

KEY CONCEPT A **clause** is a group of words with its own subject and verb. ■

There are two basic types of clauses, which have an important difference between them. The first type is called an *independent clause.*

KEY CONCEPT An **independent clause** has a subject and a verb and can stand by itself as a complete sentence. ■

The length of a clause has little to do with whether it can stand alone. Each of the following examples can stand alone because it expresses a complete thought.

INDEPENDENT CLAUSES:	The reporter shouted. Jerusalem is a relatively small city in area. The Dome of the Rock, a Jerusalem landmark, is a holy site.

The second type of clause is called a *subordinate clause.* Like an independent clause, it contains both a subject and a verb. A subordinate clause, however, is not a sentence.

KEY CONCEPT A **subordinate clause** has a subject and a verb but cannot stand by itself as a sentence. It is only part of a sentence. ■

A subordinate clause does not express a complete thought, even though it contains a subject and a verb.

SUBORDINATE CLAUSES:	when the phone (S) rang (V) whom I (S) often admired (V) since the country (S) was divided (V)

Each of these clauses has a subject and a verb, but each lacks something. Examine, for example, the first clause: *when the phone rang. When the phone rang,* what happened? More information is needed to complete the thought.

Theme: Jerusalem

In this section, you will learn about clauses. The examples and exercises are about Jerusalem.

Cross-Curricular Connection: Social Studies

More Practice

Grammar Exercise Workbook
- pp. 85–86

On-line Exercise Bank
- Section 20.2

Go on-line: PHSchool.com *Enter Web Code:* eck-8002

KEY CONCEPT Subordinate clauses begin with subordinating conjunctions or relative pronouns. ■

Why does a subordinate clause not express a complete thought? The answer can often be found in the first word of the clause. Some subordinate clauses begin with subordinating conjunctions, such as *if, since, when, although, because,* and *while.* Others begin with relative pronouns, such as *who, which,* or *that.* These words are clues that the clause may not be able to stand alone. Compare, for example, the independent clauses and the subordinate clauses in the following chart. Notice how the addition of subordinating words changes the meaning of the independent clauses.

COMPARING TWO KINDS OF CLAUSES

Independent	Subordinate
He (S) arrived (V) this morning	*if* he (S) arrived (V) this morning
The mosque (S) has (V) a golden dome.	*since* the mosque (S) has (V) a dome

In order to make sense, a subordinate clause usually must be combined with an independent clause. In the following examples, the subordinate clauses are italicized.

EXAMPLES: *Since he arrived this morning,* he has been working at top speed.
I will call the manager of the hotel tomorrow *if the room is not clean.*

Exercise 26 Identifying Subordinate and Independent Clauses Copy each of the following sentences. Underline the main clause twice. Underline the subordinate clause once.

1. Even though it is not large, Jerusalem has many museums and holy sites.
2. Since the city was politically divided in 1948, various religions have claimed ownership of the holy sites.
3. When the city was divided, Jerusalem became known as East and West Jerusalem.
4. East Jerusalem has most of the tourist attractions and museums because it is centered around the walled Old City.
5. Because Jerusalem has three Sabbaths, a large portion of West Jerusalem closes down on Friday, Saturday, and Sunday.

▼ **Critical Viewing** Use the subordinate clause *Because the buildings are close together* in a sentence about this picture. **[Describe]**

20.2

Using Adjective Clauses

Some subordinate clauses act as adjectives.

KEY CONCEPT An **adjective clause** is a subordinate clause that modifies a noun or pronoun. ■

Adjective clauses, like one-word adjectives or adjective phrases, answer the questions *What kind?* or *Which one?*

The possessive form of the word *who* is *whose*. The word *who's* is a contraction of *who is*.

Recognizing Adjective Clauses

Most adjective clauses begin with one of the five relative pronouns: *that, which, who, whom,* or *whose*. Sometimes, an adjective clause will begin with an adverb such as *when* or *where*.

In the following chart, the adjective clauses are italicized. The arrow in each sentence points to the word in the independent clause that the adjective clause modifies.

ADJECTIVE CLAUSES
They visited the memorial *that remembers Holocaust victims.*
That British stamp, *which depicts Queen Victoria,* will be sold at auction.
The man *who opened the door* is my brother-in-law.
Marcia is the student *whom we chose to represent us in the debate.*
The museum *whose artifacts include the Dead Sea Scrolls* is located in West Jerusalem.

Get instant feedback! Exercises 27 and 28 are available on-line or on CD-ROM.

Exercise 27 **Identifying Adjective Clauses** Copy the following sentences onto your paper, and underline each adjective clause. Then, identify the word each clause modifies.

1. East Jerusalem covers an area that is almost twice as large as West Jerusalem.
2. East Jerusalem includes the Old City, which lies on the site of ancient Jerusalem.
3. West Jerusalem has modern factories that produce chemicals, clothing, leather goods, and machinery.
4. In ancient times, the temple, which was the heart of the city, stood on a hill in eastern Jerusalem.
5. In the time since the temples were destroyed, other buildings have been constructed on the site.

More Practice

Grammar Exercise Workbook
- pp. 85–88

On-line Exercise Bank
- Section 20.2

Go on-line:
PHSchool.com
Enter Web Code:
eck-8002

Combining Sentences With Adjective Clauses

Two sentences can be combined into one sentence by changing one of them into an adjective clause. Such a combination is useful when the information in both sentences is closely related. Notice how the two sentences in the following example are changed into one sentence. The new sentence consists of an independent clause and an adjective clause.

TWO SENTENCES: My history teacher has written books on John Adams, Thomas Jefferson, and Benjamin Franklin. My teacher is considered by many scholars to be an expert on the American Revolution.

SENTENCE WITH ADJECTIVE CLAUSE: My history teacher, *who is considered by many scholars to be an expert on the American Revolution,* has written books on John Adams, Thomas Jefferson, and Benjamin Franklin.

▼ **Critical Viewing** Describe the scene shown here in a single sentence that contains an adjective clause. **[Describe]**

Exercise 28 **Combining Sentences Using Adjective Clauses** Change the second sentence in each of the following pairs into an adjective clause. Then, make the adjective clause part of the first sentence. You may have to add commas before and after some of the adjective clauses.

EXAMPLE: Israel is a small country in southwestern Asia. Israel is made up of the Coastal Plain, the Judeo-Galilean Highlands, the Rift Valley, and the Negev Desert.

ANSWER: Israel, which is made up of the Coastal Plain, the Judeo-Galilean Highlands, the Rift Valley, and the Negev Desert, is a small country in southwestern Asia.

1. Most Israelis live in the Coastal Plain.
   The Coastal Plain is a strip of fertile land along the Mediterranean Sea.
2. The Dead Sea is in the Rift Valley.
   The Rift Valley is a narrow strip of land in eastern Israel.
3. The West Bank is in the Judeo-Galilean Highlands.
   Several mountain ranges run through the Judeo-Galilean Highlands.
4. Parts of the Negev Desert are being irrigated to grow crops.
   The Negev Desert is the driest part of Israel.
5. The River Jordan empties into the Dead Sea.
   The River Jordan flows through the Rift Valley.

Using Adverb Clauses

Some subordinate clauses act as adverbs.

KEY CONCEPT An **adverb clause** is a subordinate clause that modifies a verb, an adjective, or an adverb. ■

Adverb clauses can answer any of the following questions about the words they modify: *Where? When? In what manner? To what extent? Under what condition?* or *Why?*

Recognizing Adverb Clauses

Adverb clauses begin with subordinating conjunctions.

SUBORDINATING CONJUNCTIONS				
after	because	in order that	though	whenever
although	before	since	unless	where
as	even though	so that	until	wherever
as if	if	than	when	while
as long as				

In the following example, the adverb clause is italicized. The arrow points to the word that the clause modifies.

EXAMPLE: Jerusalem is interesting *because it is home to several diverse religions.*

When an adverb clause begins a sentence, a comma is used.

EXAMPLE: *When she reached the station,* Marie phoned.

Exercise 29 **Identifying Adverb Clauses** Copy the sentences below onto your paper, and underline each adverb clause.

1. Because most of the region is desert, climate dictates where people live in the Middle East.
2. Unless there is enough rain, farming is not possible.
3. Wherever there have been floods, fertile soil is left behind.
4. Ancient Egyptians built irrigation systems so that they could grow crops in the desert.
5. As population grows in the Middle East, the demands for water will become greater.

Exercise 30 **Combining Sentences With Adverb Clauses** Combine each pair of sentences by changing one of them into an adverb clause. Choose an appropriate subordinating conjunction from the chart on the previous page. Compare your sentences to a classmate's, and discuss how the choice of the subordinating conjunction affects the meaning of the sentence.

1. Jerusalem is a great vacation destination. It is filled with interesting historical sites.
2. Traveling through the desert in Israel can be tiring for visitors. Temperatures often exceed 100 degrees.
3. We went to Israel. We experienced jet lag on our first day there.
4. Israel won its independence in 1948. The people celebrated.
5. Tel Aviv is the largest city in Israel. Many more tourists visit Jerusalem.

More Practice

Grammar Exercise Workbook
- pp. 89–92

On-line Exercise Bank
- Section 20.2

Go on-line:
PHSchool.com
Enter Web Code:
eck-8002

Get instant feedback! Exercises 29, 30, and 31 are available on-line or on CD-ROM.

Elliptical Adverb Clauses

In certain adverb clauses, words are left out. These clauses are said to be *elliptical.*

KEY CONCEPT In an *elliptical adverb clause,* the verb or the subject and verb are understood rather than stated. ■

Many elliptical adverb clauses are introduced by one of two subordinating conjunctions: *as* or *than.* In the following examples, the understood words have been added in parentheses. The first elliptical adverb clause is missing a verb; the second is missing a subject and a verb.

EXAMPLES: My brother can eat as much *as I* (*can eat*).
I liked this book more *than* (*I liked*) that one.

Exercise 31 **Recognizing Elliptical Adverb Clauses** For each of the following sentences, write the elliptical clause. Next to it, write out the full adverb clause, adding the understood words.

1. The Dead Sea in Israel has a lower elevation than Death Valley in California.
2. I enjoyed Jerusalem more than Tel Aviv.
3. Israel's population is larger than Ireland's.
4. Israel's history is as interesting as ours.
5. I have spent more time in Israel than in Lebanon.

20.2

Classifying Sentences by Structure

There are four basic sentence structures: *simple, compound, complex,* and *compound-complex.*

The Simple Sentence

KEY CONCEPT A **simple sentence** consists of a single independent clause. ■

A simple sentence can be short or long. It must contain a subject and a verb. It may also contain complements, modifiers, and phrases. Some simple sentences contain various compounds—a compound subject, a compound verb, or both. Other parts of the sentence may also be compound. A simple sentence, however, does not contain any subordinate clauses.

The following examples show a few of the many possible variations of a simple sentence. The subjects have been underlined once and the verbs twice.

ONE SUBJECT AND VERB: The siren sounded.

COMPOUND SUBJECT: Cats and dogs ran down the street.

COMPOUND VERB: My sister acts and sings in the play.

COMPOUND SUBJECT AND VERB: Art and archaeology reflect and explain Jerusalem's history.

WITH PHRASES AND COMPLEMENTS: A written history dating back to 600 B.C. was found in a cave near Jerusalem.

Exercise 32 **Recognizing Simple Sentences** Copy each of these simple sentences onto your paper, and underline the subject once and the verb twice. (Some of the subjects and verbs may be compound.)

1. The Dome of the Rock was completed around 692.
2. The dome surrounds a huge rock.
3. The dome is a holy site for Muslims.
4. The walls and ceiling of this shrine are decorated in Islamic style.
5. Jews and Christians also have holy places in Jerusalem.

Exercise 33 **Identifying Simple Sentences in Real-World Writing** Read through an article in a newsmagazine to identify ten simple sentences. Notice whether these sentences appear together or are mixed in with other types of sentences.

Grammar and Style Tip

Following a series of longer sentences with a brief simple sentence is a good way to reinforce or emphasize a key point in your writing.

▼ **Critical Viewing** Write a simple sentence describing the outside of the Dome of the Rock (shown here). **[Describe]**

The Compound Sentence

Independent clauses are the key elements in a *compound sentence.*

KEY CONCEPT A **compound sentence** consists of two or more independent clauses. ■

The independent clauses in most compound sentences are joined by a comma and one of the coordinating conjunctions (*and, but, for, nor, or, so, yet*). Sometimes a semicolon (;) is used to join independent clauses in a compound sentence. Like simple sentences, compound sentences contain no subordinate clauses.

EXAMPLE: The population of Israel is approximately 4,700,000, but only 8 percent of the people live in rural areas.

Exercise 34 **Recognizing Compound Sentences** Copy the following compound sentences. Underline the subject once and the verb twice in each independent clause.

EXAMPLE: Israel is a democratic republic, and it has a parliament-cabinet form of government.

ANSWER: Israel is a democratic republic, and it has a parliament-cabinet form of government.

1. The prime minister is the head of the government, but the people also elect a president.
2. The president is elected to a five-year term, yet most of his or her duties are ceremonial.
3. The Knesset is the name of the parliament, and it is made up of 120 elected members.
4. Eighteen-year-olds can vote in Israel, but they must also serve in the armed forces.
5. Israeli men and women serve in the armed forces; men serve for three years, and women serve for two years.

Exercise 35 **Combining Simple Sentences to Form Compound Sentences** Go through a magazine article or a piece of your own writing to find five pairs of simple sentences that are related in meaning. Then, combine each pair of sentences into a compound sentence by adding a coordinating conjunction or a semicolon.

More Practice

Grammar Exercise Workbook
- pp. 93–94

On-line Exercise Bank
- Section 20.2

Go on-line: PHSchool.com
Enter Web Code: eck-8002

Get instant feedback! Exercises 32, 33, 34, and 35 are available on-line or on CD-ROM.

20.2

The Complex Sentence

A sentence with an adjective or adverb clause is called a *complex sentence.*

KEY CONCEPT A **complex sentence** consists of one independent clause and one or more subordinate clauses. ■

The independent clause in a complex sentence is often called the *main clause* to distinguish it from the subordinate clause or clauses. The main clause and each subordinate clause have their own subjects and verbs. Those in the independent clause are called the *subject of the sentence* and the *main verb.*

EXAMPLES: When the fog lifted, we continued our trip. (subordinate clause: When the fog lifted; main clause: we continued our trip)

The person who will speak last is my sister. (main clause: The person … is my sister; subordinate clause: who will speak last)

In the first example, *we* is the subject of the sentence, and *continued* is the main verb. In the second example, *person* is the subject of the sentence, and *is* is the main verb.

Exercise 36 Identifying the Parts of Complex Sentences

Copy each of the following complex sentences onto your paper. In each clause, underline the subject once and the verb twice. Then, put parentheses around each subordinate clause.

EXAMPLE: Four thousand years ago, the land where the Temple Mount now lies was in the hands of the Jebusites.

ANSWER: Four thousand years ago, the land (where the Temple Mount now lies) was in the hands of the Jebusites.

1. Because the city was on a hill surrounded by canyons and caverns, its location was very safe.
2. However, David discovered, when he came to conquer the city with his army, that the Jebusites got their drinking water from a spring outside the city walls.
3. The water entered the city from tunnels that were built under the city.
4. David's nephew, Joab, was able to unlock the city gates at night when he swam through the tunnel.
5. Because David's army entered the city unexpectedly, the Jebusites were conquered.

▼ **Critical Viewing** Judging by this picture, would you be interested in visiting Temple Mount? Why or why not? **[Connect]**

The Compound-Complex Sentence

A *compound-complex sentence*, as the name indicates, contains the elements of both a compound sentence and a complex sentence.

KEY CONCEPT A **compound-complex sentence** consists of two or more independent clauses and one or more subordinate clauses. ■

EXAMPLE: As he was leaving for school, Larry remembered to take his lunch, but he forgot the report that he had finished the night before.
(subordinate clause: As he was leaving for school; independent clause: Larry remembered to take his lunch; independent clause: he forgot the report; subordinate clause: that he had finished the night before)

Exercise 37 **Identifying the Parts of Compound-Complex Sentences** Copy each of the following compound-complex sentences onto your paper. In each clause, underline the subject once and the verb twice. Then, put parentheses around each subordinate clause.

EXAMPLE: The Israel Museum, which is found in West Jerusalem, has artifacts dating back to prehistoric man, and it keeps them on display for visitors.

ANSWER: The Israel Museum, (which is found in West Jerusalem), has artifacts dating back to prehistoric man, and it keeps them on display for visitors.

1. Tools and weapons that date back to before 500 B.C. show great skill, and they serve as evidence that their makers were very talented.
2. Because Israelites picked up many customs from the Egyptians, idols and extravagant jewelry are also on display; these artifacts date back to the time of Moses.
3. When we visited the museum, we also marveled at documents containing historical accounts written thousands of years ago; the accounts are recorded on clay and stone.
4. Because they have been preserved well over time, many ancient scrolls can be read by those who know Hebrew; included on these scrolls is the oldest spelling of "Jerusalem."
5. These writings have been determined to be as old as 2,600 years; because they are so old, they must be carefully protected behind glass.

More Practice

Grammar Exercise Workbook
- pp. 93–94

On-line Exercise Bank
- Section 20.2

Go on-line: PHSchool.com
Enter Web Code: eck-8002

Get instant feedback! Exercises 36 and 37 are available on-line or on CD-ROM.

GRAMMAR IN LITERATURE

from Hamadi

Naomi Shihab Nye

In the following passage, the writer has used complex sentences. The subjects are underlined once, the verbs are underlined twice, and the subordinate clauses are in parentheses.

Sometimes Susan felt polite with them, (sorting attendance cards during her free period,) (listening to them gab about fingernail polish and television.) And other times she felt (she could run out of the building yelling.) That's when she daydreamed about Saleh Hamadi, (who had nothing to do with any of it.)

Exercise 38 **Writing Different Types of Sentences** Write a brief composition about a tourist destination that you find especially interesting. Vary the types of sentences that you use. Make sure that your paper includes at least two examples of each of the four sentence structures.

Exercise 39 **Revising to Improve Sentence Variety** Revise the following passage, combining simple sentences into compound, complex, and compound-complex sentences to improve variety.

The Shrine of the Book is part of the Israel Museum. It was designed and built to hold the Dead Sea Scrolls. The Dead Sea Scrolls were discovered in 1947. The Shrine of the Book has been considered one of the finest examples of modern architecture. The building has enjoyed this reputation throughout its brief history. The humidity, temperature, and light are controlled in the museum. This is done to preserve the Dead Sea Scrolls. The scrolls are believed to be ancient religious texts. However, only fragments of each exist. The restoration of the fragments is a slow and painstaking process.

Section **20.2** Section Review

GRAMMAR EXERCISES 40–45

Exercise 40 **Identifying Types of Clauses** Copy the paragraph below. Circle each independent clause. Underline the subject and the verb. Put two lines under each subordinate clause, and identify it as an adjective clause or an adverb clause.

Although Israel is 260 miles long, in places it is no more than twelve miles wide. Even though it is small, Israel has several different kinds of geological features. A coastal plain that lines the western side of Israel and borders the Mediterranean Sea has the country's richest farmland. East of the border between Egypt and Israel lies a range of rough hills, which are separated from the southern hills by a fertile plain. A deep, narrow valley that borders the west side of Jordan lies to the east of this range.

Exercise 41 **Combining Sentences With Adverb and Adjective Clauses** Combine each pair of sentences below by using an adjective or adverb clause.

1. The ancient Hebrews migrated into the Fertile Crescent. The Fertile Crescent supports agriculture.
2. The kingdom of Israel dates from about 1025 B.C. It started in Canaan.
3. Israel flourished under David and Solomon. They were its two greatest kings.
4. King David was a skilled general. He unified Israel.
5. Solomon was David's son. He was noted for his wisdom.

Exercise 42 **Identifying Sentence Structure** Label the following sentences *simple, complex, compound,* or *compound-complex.*

1. The area that is known as the Middle East stands at the crossroads of three continents.
2. Since ancient times, it has connected major trade routes, over land and sea.
3. Caravans from India and China brought goods to the busy markets.
4. Over thousands of years, migrating peoples spread the ideas, inventions, and achievements of many civilizations.
5. Some of these ideas we use today, and others have been lost.

Exercise 43 **Find It in Your Reading** Read this passage from "Hamadi" by Naomi Nye. Identify the subject, verb, and types of phrases.

She would picture the golden Sphinx sitting quietly in the desert with sand blowing around its face, never changing its expression.

Exercise 44 **Find It in Your Writing** Look through your writing portfolio to find examples of simple, compound, complex, and compound-complex sentences. Combine two pairs of simple sentences into compound, complex, or compound-complex sentences.

Exercise 45 **Writing Application** (1) Write a complex sentence that contains an adjective clause. (2) Write a compound-complex sentence that contains an adverb clause. (3) Make three simple sentences out of sentence 2. (4) Write a compound sentence connected by the conjunction *yet.* (5) Write a compound-complex sentence containing an elliptical adverb clause and the conjunction *but.*

Chapter 21

Effective Sentences

▲ **Critical Viewing** How is a train like a sentence? **[Connect]**

Just as a train is one of the basic forms of transportation, a sentence is a basic unit of communication. We use sentences every day—to ask questions, make statements, express emotions, or share information. Trains must be assembled correctly in order to provide transportation. In the same way, words must be put together correctly in sentences to provide effective and clear communication.

In this chapter, you will learn about how sentences can function in different ways. You will learn how to vary sentence styles and how to combine ideas into a more efficient sentence. You will also learn how to avoid some of the problems that writers encounter when they are writing sentences.

Diagnostic Test

Directions: Write all answers on a separate sheet of paper.

Skill Check A. Indicate whether each of the following sentences is *declarative, interrogative, imperative,* or *exclamatory.* After each answer, write the appropriate end mark for that sentence.

1. In the late nineteenth century, trains run by steam power were challenged by electric locomotives
2. Why don't we use very many electric trains today
3. Imagine the high cost of overhead wire and power substations
4. Wow That would surely be expensive
5. In addition, electric trains lack the flexibility of diesel trains

Skill Check B. Combine each pair of sentences below as indicated in parentheses.

6. Electric trains are still used today. Diesel trains are still used today. (Combine the subjects.)
7. The electric locomotive has a few drawbacks. Many of the advantages of the diesel locomotive are also found in the electric locomotive. (Use the conjunction *however.*)
8. Electric trains are clean. Electric motors do not pollute the environment. (Use the conjunction *because.*)
9. Electric train operations can be profitable. They are usually profitable only in areas with large, dense populations. (Use the conjunction *but.*)
10. Large, dense populations are found in many cities. Tokyo, New York, New Delhi, and Paris are a few of them. (Use a semicolon.)

Skill Check C. On your paper, write *F* if the numbered item below is a fragment, *RO* if it is a run-on, *MM* if it has a misplaced modifier, or *DN* if it contains a double negative.

11. The invention of the diesel locomotive.
12. Which caused great increases in operating efficiency.
13. Rudolf Diesel was a German mechanical engineer, he invented the diesel engine in the 1890's.
14. People rode trains from New York to Chicago with diesel engines.
15. By the mid-1930's, the Union Pacific Railroad didn't use no steam power for its new, streamlined passenger trains.

Skill Check D. For each of the following sentences, choose the correct word or phrase from the choices in parentheses.

16. During World War II, most railroads (didn't use no, didn't use) steam- or electric-powered trains.
17. Diesel power was used (further, farther) as time went on.
18. The reason railroads converted to diesel from steam engines was (because, that) the diesel was more efficient.
19. While railroads (in, into) the United States were switching to diesel trains, a similar trend was occurring worldwide.
20. By 1957, all American trains, (except, accept) for a few, were diesel-powered.

The Four Functions of a Sentence

Sentences can be classified according to what they do. The four types of sentences in English are *declarative, interrogative, imperative,* and *exclamatory.*

Declarative sentences are the most common type. They are used to state, or "declare," facts.

KEY CONCEPT A **declarative sentence** states an idea and ends with a period. ■

DECLARATIVE: A great network of railways crisscrosses the vast Indian subcontinent.
The trains are fast and efficient.

Interrogative means "asking." An *interrogative sentence* is a question.

KEY CONCEPT An **interrogative sentence** asks a question and ends with a question mark. ■

INTERROGATIVE: Whose ticket is this?
Which countries in Europe and Asia have high-speed trains?

The word *imperative* comes from the Latin word for commanding. *Imperative sentences* are commands.

KEY CONCEPT An **imperative sentence** gives an order or a direction and ends with either a period or an exclamation mark. ■

Most imperative sentences start with a verb. In this type of sentence, the subject is understood to be *you.*

IMPERATIVE: Follow the directions carefully to get to the correct platform.
Wait for me!

Notice the punctuation at the end of these examples. In the first sentence, the period suggests that a mild command is being given, in an ordinary tone of voice. The exclamation mark at the end of the second sentence suggests a strong command, one given in a loud voice.

To exclaim means to "shout out." Exclamatory sentences are used to "shout out" emotions such as happiness, fear, delight, and anger.

Theme: Railroads

In this section, you will learn how to recognize and use four types of sentences. The examples and exercises are about railroads.

Cross-Curricular Connection: Social Studies

▲ **Critical Viewing** Some people consider steam trains part of our romantic past. What sort of emotion does this picture bring out in you? **[Relate]**

KEY CONCEPT An **exclamatory sentence** conveys strong emotion and ends with an exclamation mark. ■

EXCLAMATORY: She's not telling the truth!
What an outrage that is!

Exercise 1 **Identifying the Four Types of Sentences** On your paper, identify each of the following sentences as *declarative, interrogative, imperative,* or *exclamatory.* After each answer, write the appropriate end mark for that sentence.

EXAMPLE: A vehicle that runs on rails and is self-propelled is called a train
ANSWER: declarative (.)

1. A locomotive can use several forms of energy
2. Steam, electricity, and diesel power are a few forms of energy used to run a train
3. What was the first form of energy used to run a train
4. The first steam locomotive was built in 1804
5. What does a train do
6. A train pulls railroad cars carrying a variety of different things
7. That's what a train does
8. Ride one when you get a chance
9. I can't *believe* how much trains have changed
10. Hey Our train is *really* late

More Practice

Grammar Exercise Workbook
- pp. 97–98

On-line Exercise Bank
- Section 21.1

Go on-line: PHSchool.com *Enter Web Code:* eck-8002

Get instant feedback! Exercise 1 is available on-line or on CD-ROM.

Section 21.1

Section Review

GRAMMAR EXERCISES 2–7

Exercise 2 **Identifying the Four Types of Sentences** Read the following sentences, and identify each one as *declarative, interrogative, imperative,* or *exclamatory.*

1. The steam locomotive was first developed in 1804 in England.
2. What was the first steam locomotive like?
3. Picture a steam engine mounted on a wheeled vehicle on rails.
4. How neat!
5. How well did it work?
6. It could haul about twenty-five tons, but it was too heavy for the wooden track.
7. How long was it until there was a steam train designed to carry people?
8. The Stockton and Darlington Railway opened in 1825.
9. That was quick!
10. Look up more information on-line.

Exercise 3 **Punctuating the Four Types of Sentences** Copy the sentences below onto your paper. Add the appropriate end mark, and identify the type of sentence.

1. Tell me about English trains
2. How did English locomotives play a role in early American railroad history
3. The American railways imported more than 100 English locomotives
4. Wow
5. Realize that the United States could not have made its own trains
6. *The Stourbridge Lion* was one of the first trains to be imported
7. When did the U.S. start building trains
8. In 1830, the first locomotive was built for sale in the United States
9. What were American trains like
10. Henry Campbell designed an eight-wheeled engine

Exercise 4 **Writing the Four Types of Sentences** Write one sentence for each of the numbered directions below.

1. Write a declarative sentence about a method of travel.
2. Write an exclamatory sentence about bad weather.
3. Write an imperative sentence reminding a friend to do something.
4. Write a declarative sentence about a favorite movie or TV show.
5. Write an interrogative sentence about weekend plans.

Exercise 5 **Find It in Your Reading** Have a closer look at a book you are reading. Identify and write down two examples of each of the four sentence types. If you can't find all four types, give an explanation of why you think the writer has used only the types you found.

Exercise 6 **Find It in Your Writing** Look through your portfolio for a piece of writing containing examples of all four types of sentences. If you can't find examples of each, revise your writing to vary the sentence types.

Exercise 7 **Writing Application** Think of something that happened to you yesterday. Then, write four sentences about what happened, one of each type. Label and punctuate each one correctly.

Section 21.2 Combining Sentences

Writing should include sentences of varying lengths and complexity so that the ideas flow. One way to achieve sentence variety is by combining sentences. Look at the examples below.

EXAMPLE: We went to the railroad yard.
We saw trains.

COMBINED: We went to the railroad yard and saw trains.
We saw trains at the railroad yard.
When we went to the railroad yard, we saw trains.

Theme: Railroads

In this section, you will learn several methods for combining sentences. The examples and exercises tell more about railroads.

Cross-Curricular Connection: Social Studies

Combining Sentence Parts

KEY CONCEPT Sentences can be combined by using a compound subject, a compound verb, or a compound object. ■

EXAMPLE: Joe enjoyed seeing the trains.
Martha enjoyed seeing the trains.

COMPOUND SUBJECT: Joe and Martha enjoyed seeing the trains.

EXAMPLE: Mike bought a whistle. Mike blew on the whistle.

COMPOUND VERB: Mike bought a whistle and blew on it.

EXAMPLE: Brandon examined the steam train.
Brandon examined the diesel.

COMPOUND OBJECT: Brandon examined the steam train and the diesel.

▼ **Critical Viewing** In what ways is this train similar to or different from the one in the photograph on page 324? Use at least one compound subject or compound verb in your response. **[Compare and Contrast]**

Exercise 8 **Combining Sentences Using Compound Subjects, Verbs, or Objects** Combine each pair of sentences below in the most logical way, identifying each combination as *compound subject, compound verb,* or *compound object.*

EXAMPLE: Railroads appeared in the early nineteenth century.
Railroads played a major role in the Industrial Revolution.

ANSWER: Railroads appeared in the early nineteenth century and played a major role in the Industrial Revolution. (compound verb)

1. Early in the twentieth century, railroads were challenged by new modes of transportation. Railroads started to decline due to losses in employment and traffic.
2. Finished products were transported by trains for much of the century. People were transported by trains for much of the century.
3. Trains were the principal method of transporting materials. Trains were the principal method of transporting mail.
4. The locomotives were awesome, powerful machines. They were capable of pulling many loaded freight cars.
5. Thousands of people ride trains from their homes to work. Thousands travel by train just for the fun of it.

More Practice

Grammar Exercise Workbook
• pp. 99–100
On-line Exercise Bank
• Section 21.2
Go on-line:
PHSchool.com
Enter Web Code:
eck-8002

Get instant feedback! Exercises 8 and 9 are available on-line or on CD-ROM.

Joining Clauses

KEY CONCEPT Sentences can be combined by joining two independent clauses to create a compound sentence. ■

Use a compound sentence when combining ideas that are related but independent. Compound sentences are created by joining two independent clauses with a comma and a coordinating conjunction, such as *and, but, nor, for, so, or,* and *yet.* You can combine two sentences with a semicolon if they are closely related.

EXAMPLE: John Henry was an actual person.
His deeds were the subject of tall tales.

COMPOUND SENTENCE: John Henry was an actual person, but his heroic deeds were the subject of tall tales.

EXAMPLE: John Henry had a contest with a steam engine.
He beat the steam engine.

COMPOUND SENTENCE: John Henry had a contest with a steam engine; he beat the steam engine.

Spelling Tip

Sometimes, compound nouns are written as two words, such as *pen pal.* However, the compound noun *railroad* is written as one word.

Exercise 9 **Combining Independent Clauses to Make Compound Sentences** Combine the following sentences, using the connector indicated in parentheses.

EXAMPLE: A railroad is a form of land transportation. The rails provide a track for cars pulled by engines. (semicolon)

ANSWER: A railroad is a form of land transportation; the rails provide a track for cars pulled by engines.

1. During the seventeenth century, horse-drawn wagons were used in European mines. Between 1797 and 1813, Richard Trevithick adapted steam locomotives for use in the mines. (comma with *but*)
2. In 1825, George Stephenson built the twenty-mile Stockton and Darlington Railway. It was the first public railway to be powered by a steam locomotive. (semicolon)
3. Railroads first appeared in England. Railroads had the most dramatic growth in the United States. (comma with *yet*)
4. More than 3,000 miles of railroad were built in the eastern states by 1840. This figure is 40 percent greater than the railroad mileage in Europe. (semicolon)
5. By the end of the Civil War, the railroad in the United States was more than 30,000 miles long. It had replaced steamboats in commercial transportation. (comma with *and*)

KEY CONCEPT Two sentences can be combined by changing one of them into a subordinate clause. ■

Use a compound sentence when you are combining sentences to show the relationship between ideas. A subordinating conjunction will help readers understand the relationship. Common subordinating conjunctions are *after, although, because, before, if, since, unless,* and *when.*

EXAMPLE: George Stephenson was a coal mine engineer. He built his first locomotive in 1814.

COMBINED WITH A SUBORDINATE CLAUSE: George Stephenson was a coal mine engineer before he built his first locomotive in 1814.

EXAMPLE: The railroads decided on a standard gauge. Tracks were different widths all over the country.

COMBINED WITH A SUBORDINATE CLAUSE: Because tracks were different widths all over the country, the railroads decided on a standard gauge.

Journal Tip

Does the history of railroads interest you? If so, jot down in your journal some facts from this section; then, review them to find a topic for an expository essay or a research report.

Learn More

To find out more about subordinating conjunctions, see Chapter 18.

Exercise 10 **Combining Sentences With Subordinating Conjunctions** Rewrite the following sentence pairs, using the subordinating conjunction indicated in parentheses.

1. George Stephenson and his son Robert worked together as engineers. They made major contributions to the first English locomotives and railroads. (when)
2. George Stephenson was a builder of engines used in coal mines. He built his first locomotive. (before)
3. The Stockton and Darlington Railway was planned. George Stephenson was hired as the company's engineer. (when)
4. He convinced the owners of Stockton and Darlington Railway to use steam power. He built the line's first locomotive. (as)
5. Stephenson transferred to the Liverpool and Manchester Railway. He and his son Robert built the *Rocket.* (after)

Exercise 11 **Combining Sentences by Forming Subordinate Clauses** Combine each of the following pairs of sentences with a subordinating conjunction. Underline the subordinating conjunction.

1. The first railroads appeared in the United States during the late 1820's. The British invented the steam locomotive.
2. The Delaware and Hudson Canal and Railroad Company purchased a British-built locomotive in 1829. They found it to be too heavy for the track in the United States.
3. The South Carolina Railroad began passenger service with the *Best Friend of Charleston.* It became the first railroad in the nation to use steam power.
4. The *Best Friend of Charleston* had pulled a passenger train over the six miles of completed lines. The locomotive exploded.
5. The engine's fireman had tied down the safety valve of the boiler. The noise bothered him.

▼ **Critical Viewing** Is this a steam train or a diesel? How can you tell? Include a sentence with a subordinate clause in your response. **[Analyze]**

KEY CONCEPT Two sentences can be combined by changing one of them into a phrase. ■

When you are combining a pair of sentences in which one simply adds detail, change one of the sentences into a phrase.

EXAMPLE: The Pennsylvania Railroad Museum is interesting. It is in Strasberg.
COMBINED: The Pennsylvania Railroad Museum in Strasberg is interesting.

EXAMPLE: The Pennsylvania Railroad Museum is interesting. It is the home of the *John Bull* replica.
COMBINED: The Pennsylvania Railroad Museum, home of the *John Bull* replica, is interesting.

Exercise 12 **Combining Sentences Using Phrases** Rewrite the following sentence pairs, combining them by changing one into a phrase.

EXAMPLE: Many trains have been invented over the years. English and American engineers invented them.
ANSWER: Many trains have been invented over the years by English and American engineers.

1. The *Rocket* was an early English locomotive. George and Robert Stephenson built it.
2. The *Rocket* won a competition sponsored by the Liverpool and Manchester Railway in 1829. The competition was called the Rainhill Trials.
3. The *Rocket* completed the trials. It had an average speed of fifteen mph.
4. George went on to become engineer of the Birmingham and London Railway. George was Robert's son.
5. George also built several famous bridges. He built them in addition to engineering trains.
6. The *John Bull* was a locomotive built in England. Robert Stephenson and Company built it.
7. The *John Bull* was exported to the Camden and Amboy Railroad. It was exported in 1831.
8. The *John Bull* was acquired by the Smithsonian. The Smithsonian acquired it in 1884.
9. In 1981, the *John Bull* was driven on the Old Georgetown Branch railroad tracks. It was its 150th anniversary.
10. Compare the *John Bull* with a modern-day diesel train. The *John Bull* was quite small.

More Practice

Grammar Exercise Workbook
- pp. 99–100

On-line Exercise Bank
- Section 21.2

Go on-line:
PHSchool.com
Enter Web Code:
eck-8002

Get instant feedback! Exercises 10, 11, and 12 are available on-line or on CD-ROM.

21.2

Hands-on Grammar

Sentence Combining Twosome

With a classmate, form a twosome to practice combining sentences. First, cut out thirteen small rectangles, and print one of these conjunctions on each of them: *and, but, yet, after, although, because, before, if, since, unless, until, when,* and *while.* Put them in an envelope. Then, cut eleven strips of paper, 6" x 3/4", and on each, print one of these sentences:

THE TRAIN PULLED INTO THE STATION
AUNT LUCY HAD FORGOTTEN THE TICKETS
ALICE WAS WATCHING THE LUGGAGE
THE WHISTLE BLEW
THE PASSENGERS MOVED TOWARD THE TRAIN
DAD BROUGHT THE TICKETS
ALICE AND JASON SAW THEIR FRIEND MICHAEL
IT WAS ALMOST NOON
THE CONDUCTOR CALLED, "ALL ABOARD"
THE TRAIN WAS READY TO DEPART
MICHAEL JOINED ALICE AND JASON

To begin, one person chooses a sentence strip. The other person then pulls a conjunction randomly from the envelope. Now, the first person uses the conjunction to combine the sentence logically with another sentence strip. Lay out the combined sentence on a desk or table. (See examples.)

Continue taking turns, combining the sentences in as many different ways as you can. Try to use each of the conjunctions in the envelope and each sentence strip at least twice.

Find It in Your Reading Look through a story or essay for several examples of sentences that have been combined using conjunctions. Notice how the writer varied the position of the conjunctions.

Find It in Your Writing See if you can smooth a piece of your writing and add interest to it by combining some of the sentences.

Section 21.2 **Section Review**

GRAMMAR EXERCISES 13–18

Exercise 13 **Combining Sentences**
Combine each pair of sentences below in the way that makes the most sense. Identify each combination as *compound subject, compound verb,* or *compound object.*

1. The Japanese and French built high-speed trains. The British built a high-speed train.
2. The Japanese had built their famous "bullet" train by 1964. The Japanese began to operate their famous "bullet" train by 1964.
3. The famous train was called the *Shinkansen.* The *Shinkansen* ran from Tokyo to Nagoya.
4. The French completed their train in 1981. They called it the *Train à Grande Vitesse (TGV).*
5. The *TGV* uses dedicated track. *Shinkansen* uses dedicated track.

Exercise 14 **Combining Clauses**
Rewrite each sentence pair below with a comma and a coordinating conjunction, a semicolon, or a subordinating conjunction.

1. Oregon and California joined the United States. Interest in a transcontinental railroad increased.
2. The transcontinental railroad became a reality on May 10, 1869. The tracks of the Union Pacific met those of the Central Pacific at Promontory, Utah.
3. The Central Pacific built eastward from Sacramento, California. The Union Pacific built westward from Omaha, Nebraska.
4. The two railroads hired about 25,000 laborers. They built the railroads.
5. The Union Pacific laid 1,086 miles of track. The Central Pacific laid only 689 miles of track.

Exercise 15 **Combining Sentences Using Phrases** Combine each sentence pair below by changing one sentence into a phrase.

1. George Westinghouse was an American. George Westinghouse was an inventor and an industrialist.
2. He invented a brake for trains. The brake was called an air brake.
3. George Westinghouse obtained patents. He obtained approximately 400 patents in his lifetime.
4. In 1865, he patented a device. The device helped return derailed freight cars to tracks.
5. He founded the Westinghouse Air Brake Company. He founded the company in 1869.

Exercise 16 **Find It in Your Reading** Read the following sentence from Adrien Stoutenburg's retelling of the tall tale "Hammerman." Identify the ideas that have been combined and state each idea as a separate sentence.

Down South, and in the North, too, people still talk about John Henry and how he beat the steam engine at the Big Bend Tunnel.

Exercise 17 **Find It in Your Writing** Look through your portfolio for a paragraph that contains several short sentences. Combine two of the short sentences to form one longer sentence.

Exercise 18 **Writing Application**
Write five sentences about your hobbies. Combine ideas, using one of the ways suggested in this section.

Section 21.3

Varying Sentences

Vary your sentences to create a rhythm, to achieve an effect, or to emphasize the connections between ideas. There are several ways you can create variety in your sentences.

Theme: Model Railroads

In this section, you will learn ways to vary sentence length, word order, and sentence beginnings. The examples and exercises are about model railroads.

Cross-Curricular Connection: Social Studies

Varying Sentence Length

You have already learned that you can combine several short, choppy sentences to create a longer, more fluid sentence. However, too many long sentences in a row is as uninteresting as too many short sentences. When you want to emphasize a point or surprise a reader, insert a short, direct sentence to interrupt the flow of long sentences.

EXAMPLE: In the 1830's, model railroading was not a hobby. However, during that decade the first true miniature railroad was built. Mathias Baldwin crafted a small model of a locomotive, several passenger cars, and an area of track. His creation was not for entertainment; it was a model for a locomotive he was planning to build. *That first model served its purpose well.*

Some sentences in the example contain only one idea and can't be broken down. It may be possible, however, to state the idea in a shorter sentence. Other sentences contain two or more ideas and might be shortened by breaking down the ideas.

Exercise 19 **Revising to Create Shorter Sentences** Revise the paragraph below to create shorter, more direct sentences.

Years ago, when most of today's model railroaders were still growing up, the toy world offered a number of fantastic electric train sets that included engines with real steam and whistles that blew, train stations with people waiting for trains, and even trees and houses for landscaping. The train sets were often purchased as Christmas gifts for children and were brought out of the closet and set up only during the holiday season each year. Although these train sets were generally sold and used as toys for children who had spent the year looking longingly through shop windows, adults seemed to enjoy them as much or more. The children would have to wait for hours while their fathers and mothers played engineer. These sets fascinated the would-be modeler, hinting at how much more could be accomplished with some imagination and a little more money.

Varying Sentence Beginnings

Another way to create sentence variety is to avoid starting each sentence in the same way. You can start sentences with different parts of speech.

START WITH A NOUN:	*A model boxcar* is not hard to build.
START WITH AN ADVERB:	Surprisingly, a model boxcar is not hard to build.
START WITH AN INFINITIVE:	*To build* a model boxcar is not hard.
START WITH A PREPOSITIONAL PHRASE:	*For the model railroading enthusiast*, a model boxcar is not hard to build.

Exercise 20 Revising to Vary Sentence Beginnings

Rewrite the following sentences, revising them to begin with the part of speech indicated in parentheses.

EXAMPLE: When miniature trains were first built, they were only design models. (adverb)

ANSWER: Originally, miniature trains were built to serve as design models.

1. Model trains were carefully detailed to resemble what the manufacturer planned to build. (participle)
2. Constructed carefully, the models were made of hand-tooled metal and hand-crafted wood. (noun)
3. Many models were made with a combination of both metal and wood. (prepositional phrase)
4. The more elaborate models were powered by miniature steam engines. (noun)
5. Train sets, carefully made to withstand heavy usage, lasted for years. (adverb)
6. Today's model railroader's hobby did not get underway until the mid 1930's, when motors and electrical systems became readily available. (adverb)
7. Just as model railroading began to be a popular new hobby, World War II interrupted it. (participle)
8. After the war, the numbers of hobbyists of model railroads again increased at an amazing rate until the competition from television began. (noun)
9. When the novelty of television wore off, people began to return to model railroading. (noun)
10. In recent years, the hobby has seen an impressive growth. (adverb)

More Practice

Grammar Exercise Workbook
- pp. 101–104

On-line Exercise Bank
- Section 21.3

Go on-line: PHSchool.com *Enter Web Code:* eck-8002

KEY CONCEPT You can also vary sentence beginnings by reversing the traditional subject-verb order.

EXAMPLES:

S V ADV
The bus is here.

ADV V S
Here is the bus.

S V PREP PHRASE
The ship sailed into the bay.

PREP PHRASE V S
Into the bay sailed the ship.

▲ **Critical Viewing** Describe the attention to detail needed to build a model locomotive like this one. Use inverted word order in your response. **[Infer]**

Exercise 21 **Revising Word Order** Revise these sentences by inverting the subject-verb order. Make any other changes necessary to retain the meaning of the sentence.

EXAMPLE: Arriving every month at the hobby shop are new model railroad kits.

ANSWER: Every month, new model railroad kits arrive at the hobby shop.

1. There is a great variety of trains and accessories available at all prices.
2. The cost of a simple train set is between $35 and $60.
3. Landscape features made at home cost less than the ready-made versions.
4. Here are some elaborate locomotives and cars built from expensive kits.
5. The costs of tools and other supplies are added to the price of the kits.

More Practice

Grammar Exercise Workbook
- pp. 101–104

On-line Exercise Bank
- Section 21.3

Go on-line:
PHSchool.com
Enter Web Code:
eck-8002

Section 21.3 Section Review

GRAMMAR EXERCISES 22–27

Exercise 22 **Revising to Create Simpler Sentences** Revise the sentences below to be simpler and more direct.

1. Railroading modelers build locomotives with a lot of details using tools that are specially made for model building.
2. One of the most difficult parts of model building is applying the tiny decals that come with the kits and create an accurate model of a train.
3. Tweezers and a magnifying glass are helpful tools in model building, as well as a dish of water for soaking the decals until they are wet enough.
4. The quality of detail is more important than the quantity; however, it is necessary that the model have more detail than is usually expected to be considered "super detailed."
5. The term "scratch built" means that the builder has made all of the pieces of the layout by hand instead of using "store-bought" pieces, which are considered good enough for amateurs.

Exercise 23 **Revising to Vary Sentence Beginnings** Revise the following sentences to begin with the parts of speech indicated in parentheses.

1. Most model railroading costs come at the beginning of the hobby, when one is just getting started. (participle)
2. To begin, one usually needs a model train set containing the basics. (adverb)
3. A locomotive, some cars, several pieces of railroad track, and a relatively simple power pack are enough to get a beginning modeler started. (noun)
4. It is wise to take a good look at what is available before buying a train set. (prepositional phrase)
5. A hobby shop usually carries a selection of model railroad sets. (adverb)

Exercise 24 **Inverting Sentences** Invert the following sentences by reversing the subject-verb order.

1. There are three ways to power full-size locomotives.
2. Most model trains run on electricity.
3. The important aspect of full-size locomotives to the modeler is the way the trains look.
4. Most types of steam engines have been given names.
5. Diesel engines are classified with letters and numerals.

Exercise 25 **Find It in Your Reading** Notice the use of long and short sentences in this passage from *Baseball* by Lionel G. García.

> We loved to play baseball. We would take the old mesquite stick and the old ball across the street to the parochial school grounds to play a game. Father Zavala enjoyed watching us.

Exercise 26 **Find It in Your Writing** Find examples of long sentences in compositions in your portfolio. Rewrite them, forming shorter, more direct sentences.

Exercise 27 **Writing Application** Write a paragraph about model building. Use both short and long sentences in your paragraph. Vary sentence beginnings.

Section 21.4

Avoiding Sentence Problems

Being able to recognize the parts of sentences can help you avoid certain errors in your writing.

Avoiding Sentence Fragments

Some groups of words, even though they have a capital letter at the beginning and a period at the end, are not complete sentences. They are *fragments.*

KEY CONCEPT A **fragment** is a group of words that does not express a complete thought. A fragment is only *part of a sentence.* ■

A complete sentence always has a subject and a verb. A fragment does not. A fragment can be a group of words with no subject; a group of words that includes a possible subject but no verb; or a group of words with a possible subject and only part of a possible verb. It can even be a subordinate clause standing alone. See the examples in the first chart.

FRAGMENTS
In the early evening.
Felt happy and relaxed.
The sign in the corridor.
The train coming around the bend.
When she first smiled.

In this chart, you see the fragments turned into complete sentences.

COMPLETE SENTENCES
The flight arrived *in the early evening.*
I *felt happy and relaxed.*
The sign in the corridor is surprising.
The train was *coming around the bend.*
When she first smiled, the whole world seemed to light up.

Each of the preceding examples needed one or more new parts. The first needed both a subject and a verb. The second needed only a subject. The third became complete when a verb and an adjective were added. The fourth became complete when a helping verb was added. The final example needed a complete independent clause to go with the subordinate clause.

Theme: Transportation

In this section, you will learn about sentence fragments and run-ons, misplaced modifiers, and many common usage problems. The examples and exercises are about transportation.

Cross-Curricular Connection: Social Studies

Speaking and Listening Tip

One trick to telling whether a group of words expresses a complete thought is to read the words aloud. With a partner or alone, practice reading aloud each italicized fragment in the chart on the left; then, read the complete sentence. Can you hear the difference?

Exercise 28 **Recognizing Sentence Fragments** On your paper, write *F* for each numbered item below that is a fragment, and *S* for each one that is a sentence.

EXAMPLE: From place to place.
ANSWER: F

1. Transportation is the movement of persons and goods.
2. From one location to another.
3. From ancient times to the twentieth century.
4. Humans have tried to make their transportation facilities more efficient.
5. We want to move people and products with the least amount of time, effort, and cost.
6. Improvements in transportation have helped make.
7. Possible the progress toward better living.
8. Modern systems of manufacturing and commerce are possible because of transportation.
9. There are many types of vehicles for transportation.
10. Cars, trains, buses, airplanes, bicycles, and ships.

Avoiding Phrase Fragments

A phrase by itself is a fragment. It cannot stand alone because it does not have a subject and a verb.

KEY CONCEPT A phrase should not be capitalized and punctuated as though it were a sentence. ■

A *phrase fragment* can be corrected by adding it to a nearby sentence. The example below shows a prepositional phrase following a complete sentence.

FRAGMENT:	The explorers left for the Arctic. *On the morning of March 4.*
ADDED TO NEARBY SENTENCE:	The explorers left for the Arctic *on the morning of March 4.*

You can correct other fragments simply by attaching them to the beginning of a sentence. The participal phrase fragment in the next example can easily be corrected in this manner.

FRAGMENT:	*Arriving at the airport.* The prince and princess were greeted by cheers.
ADDED TO NEARBY SENTENCE:	*Arriving at the airport,* the prince and princess were greeted by cheers.

You may not be able to correct a phrase fragment by adding it to a nearby sentence. You might have to correct the fragment by adding to the phrase whatever is needed to make it a complete sentence, usually a subject and a verb.

More Practice

Grammar Exercise Workbook
- pp. 105–108

On-line Exercise Bank
- Section 21.4

Go on-line:
PHSchool.com
Enter Web Code:
eck-8002

Get instant feedback! Exercise 28 is available on-line or on CD-ROM.

Technology Tip

If you notice that the grammar checker on your word-processing program indicates a problem that is not immediately obvious to you, check to be sure that you have typed a complete sentence and not a fragment.

CHANGING PHRASE FRAGMENTS INTO SENTENCES	
Phrase Fragment	**Complete Sentence**
Near the old creek.	The treasure (S) was found (V) *near the old creek.*
Touching his hand.	*Touching his hand,* she (S) asked (V) for her father's advice.
To type well.	Sam (S) learned (V) *to type well.*

There are, of course, many ways to add words to phrase fragments in order to make them into sentences. If your teacher points out a phrase fragment in your writing, first try adding it to a nearby sentence. If that does not work, then add the necessary words to turn the fragment into a sentence.

More Practice

Grammar Exercise Workbook
- pp. 105–108

On-line Exercise Bank
- Section 21.4

Go on-line: PHSchool.com
Enter Web Code: eck-8002

Exercise 29 Changing Phrase Fragments Into Sentences

Use each of the following phrase fragments in a sentence. You may use the phrase at the beginning, at the end, or in any other position in the sentence. Check to see that each of your sentences contains a subject and a verb.

EXAMPLE: In the morning after breakfast.
ANSWER: In the morning after breakfast, we left on our trip.

1. Leaving early to catch the plane.
2. Stopped the car on the way.
3. Making it there late.
4. Pulling in quickly.
5. Running to catch the plane.
6. Traveling by plane.
7. Watching out the window.
8. Thinking of the friends she would see.
9. After she arrived.
10. Greeting her friends.

▼ **Critical Viewing** Identify several features of this plane that make it different from other types of planes. In your response, use at least one complete sentence containing a phrase. **[Distinguish]**

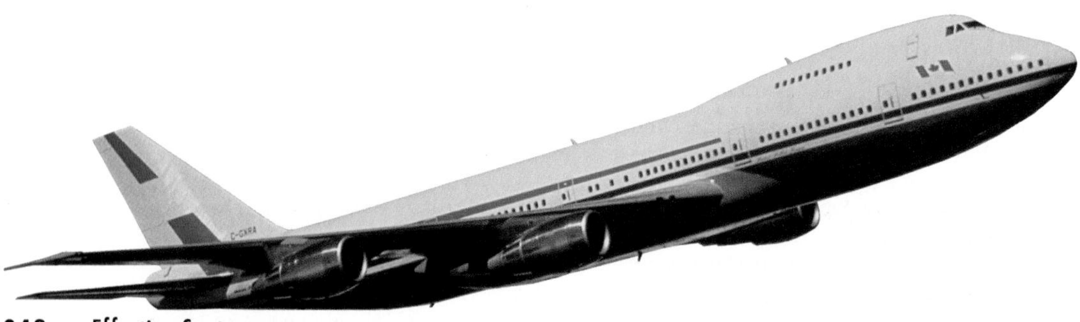

Avoiding Clause Fragments

All clauses have subjects and verbs, but some cannot stand alone as sentences.

KEY CONCEPT A subordinate clause should not be capitalized and punctuated as though it were a sentence. ■

Like phrase fragments, *clause fragments* can usually be corrected in either of two ways: by attaching the fragment to a nearby sentence or by adding whatever words are needed to make the fragment into a sentence.

FRAGMENT: The class enjoyed the poem. *That I recited to them as part of my oral report.*

ADDED TO NEARBY SENTENCE: The class enjoyed the poem *that I recited to them as part of my oral report.*

FRAGMENT: I'll play the game. *If you play it, too.*

ADDED TO NEARBY SENTENCE: I'll play the game *if you play it, too.*

To change a clause fragment into a sentence by using the second method, you must add an independent clause.

CHANGING CLAUSE FRAGMENTS INTO SENTENCES	
Clause Fragment	**Complete Sentence**
That you described.	I found the necklace *that you described.* The necklace *that you described* has been found.
When he knocked.	I opened the door *when he knocked.* *When he knocked,* I opened the door.

Exercise 30 **Changing Clause Fragments Into Sentences**

Add a clause to each fragment below to create a complete sentence.

EXAMPLE: That she wanted to use.

ANSWER: I lent her the suitcase that she wanted to use.

1. Where she had planned.
2. That she got there on time.
3. That she rode.
4. When she left.
5. As long as we go together.

Grammar and Style Tip

Although you should avoid fragments in formal writing, you may find them useful when writing dialogue. However, to keep the sense of your dialogue clear, take care not to overuse fragments.

Learn More

See Chapter 20 for more information about subordinate clauses and the words that begin them.

Avoiding Run-ons

A fragment is an incomplete sentence. A *run-on,* on the other hand, is an overcrowded sentence—one that has too much information.

KEY CONCEPT A **run-on** is two or more complete sentences that are not properly joined or separated. ■

Recognizing Two Kinds of Run-ons

There are two kinds of run-ons. One kind consists of two sentences run together without any punctuation between them. The other kind consists of two or more sentences separated only by a comma.

RUN-ONS	
With No Punctuation	**With Only a Comma**
I use our library often the reference section is my favorite part.	The Florida Keys are a chain of small islands, they are located off the southern tip of Florida.

Exercise 31 **Recognizing Run-ons** On your paper, write *S* if an item below is a sentence and *RO* if an item is a run-on.

EXAMPLE: Transportation has made its greatest improvements in the last two centuries it has changed the economic life of the entire world.

ANSWER: RO

1. In the 1760's, James Watt perfected the steam engine it provided power for many factories in England.
2. From there, inventors tried to apply the steam engine to navigation.
3. In 1775, Jacques Perier built an early steamboat.
4. The steamer *Savannah* crossed the Atlantic in 1819.
5. By the middle of the nineteenth century, steam navigation was replacing the sailing vessel many new ships were built of iron rather than wood.

More Practice

Grammar Exercise Workbook
- pp. 109–110

On-line Exercise Bank
- Section 21.4

Go on-line: PHSchool.com
Enter Web Code: eck-8002

Get instant feedback! Exercise 31 is available on-line or on CD-ROM.

Correcting Run-ons

Run-ons usually result from haste. Check your sentences carefully to see where one sentence ends and the next begins.

KEY CONCEPT Use an end mark to separate a run-on into two sentences. ■

Properly used, an end mark splits a run-on into two shorter but complete sentences. Which end mark you use depends upon the function of the sentence.

RUN-ON: In his search for a northeast passage to the Orient, Marco Polo finally reached northern China he made the name Cathay famous on his return to Italy.

CORRECTED SENTENCES: In his search for a northeast passage to the Orient, Marco Polo finally reached northern China. He made the name Cathay famous on his return to Italy.

RUN-ON: Have you heard of James Cook, he sailed his ship the *Endeavour* to the East Indies in 1768.

CORRECTED SENTENCES: Have you heard of James Cook? He sailed his ship the *Endeavour* to the East Indies in 1768.

KEY CONCEPT Form a compound sentence by using a comma and a coordinating conjunction to join two or more independent clauses. ■

The five coordinating conjunctions used most often are *and, but, or, for,* and *nor.*

RUN-ON: My mother and father go shopping on Saturdays, I stay home and clean.

CORRECTED SENTENCE: My mother and father go shopping on Saturdays, and I stay home and clean.

RUN-ON: I want to go to the circus, I haven't any money.

CORRECTED SENTENCE: I want to go to the circus, but I haven't any money.

KEY CONCEPT Form a compound sentence by using a semicolon to join two closely related independent clauses. ■

RUN-ON: The first train to the city leaves at 6:05 A.M., the express doesn't leave until an hour later.

CORRECTED SENTENCE: The first train to the city leaves at 6:05 A.M.; the express doesn't leave until an hour later.

Grammar and Style Tip

When referring to the specific name of a ship or a train, be sure to capitalize and underline it. If you are using a word-processing program, use italics instead of underlining.

▲ **Critical Viewing** How has this kind of transportation affected life in cities over the past century? Give reasons for your answer. **[Support]**

Exercise 32 **Correcting Run-ons** Rewrite each of the following run-ons, using any of the three methods described in this section. Use each method at least once.

EXAMPLE: Forms of transportation have been around for a long time primitive humans trained animals to carry small loads.

ANSWER: Forms of transportation have been around for a long time. Primitive humans trained animals to carry small loads.

1. Originally, humans domesticated animals for transportation the first animals to be used this way were camels, goats, and oxen.
2. Another important event was the invention of the wheel, later crude carts and wagons were invented.
3. The trails used by pack animals could not be used by wheeled vehicles, soon early roads were being built.
4. On the new roads, travelers could move at speeds of six miles per hour, the rate was not significantly increased until the nineteenth century.
5. Transportation was aided by other inventions as well the horse collar, coaches with springs, and new methods of road construction are just a few of these inventions.

More Practice

Grammar Exercise Workbook
- pp. 111–112

On-line Exercise Bank
- Section 21.4

Go on-line: PHSchool.com
Enter Web Code: eck-8002

Correcting Misplaced Modifiers

A phrase or clause that acts as a modifier should be placed close to the word it modifies. Otherwise, the meaning of the sentence may be unclear. Paying close attention to the placement of modifiers will help you to avoid confusion, and sometimes unintended humor, in your writing.

KEY CONCEPT A modifier should be placed as close as possible to the word it modifies. ■

Misplaced Modifiers

When a modifier is placed too far away from the word it modifies, it is called a *misplaced modifier*. Because they are misplaced, such phrases and clauses modify the wrong word in a sentence.

MISPLACED MODIFIER: We rented a house in the mountains *with a view*.

The misplaced modifier is the phrase *with a view*. In this sentence, it sounds as though the mountains have a view. The sentence needs to be reworded to put the modifier closer to *house*.

CORRECTED SENTENCE: In the mountains, we rented a house *with a view*.

The following example is a somewhat different type of misplaced modifier.

MISPLACED MODIFIER: *Sailing into the harbor*, the Statue of Liberty was awe inspiring.

In this sentence, *Sailing into the harbor* should modify a person or a ship. Instead, it incorrectly modifies *Statue of Liberty*, making it seem as though it is the statue doing the sailing. The sentence not only needs to be reworded, but the person or ship sailing into the harbor needs to be added.

CORRECTED SENTENCE: *Sailing into the harbor*, Elizabeth found the Statue of Liberty awe inspiring.

ALTERNATE: *Sailing into the harbor*, our ship provided an awe-inspiring view of the Statue of Liberty.

Spelling Tip

Compound adjectives such as *awe inspiring* are not hyphenated if they follow the noun they modify. However, if they come before the noun, they should be hyphenated: *the awe-inspiring Statue of Liberty.*

Exercise 33 **Recognizing Misplaced Modifiers** On your paper, copy the sentences below, and underline the misplaced modifier in each one. Then, write the word that is being modified.

EXAMPLE: Transportation began early in human history over water.

ANSWER: Transportation began early in human history <u>over water</u>. (transportation)

1. Floating down the river, the trees looked lovely.
2. Dugout canoes were used by people that were made out of hollowed logs.
3. The Egyptians built with bundles of papyrus rushes crude watercrafts.
4. The earliest recorded voyage took place about 3200 B.C. by sea.
5. Ships were later built by the Phoenicians with a single sail.
6. Before the Europeans, the ships of the Phoenicians were the first to sail around Africa.
7. When sailing at night, the constellations kept the sailors on course.
8. When weather kept them from seeing the stars, magnetized needles were used by Chinese to navigate.
9. Around A.D. 835, strong ships were made by the Vikings that were silent, swift, and light.
10. Ships built in England, France, Portugal, and Spain were a vast improvement with three masts over earlier craft.

More Practice

Grammar Exercise Workbook
- pp. 113–114

On-line Exercise Bank
- Section 21.4

Go on-line: PHSchool.com
Enter Web Code: eck-8002

▶ **Critical Viewing** Imagine a trip across the ocean on a ship like this! How many people do you think this ship would hold? **[Speculate]**

Revising Sentences With Misplaced Modifiers

Among the most common misplaced modifiers are prepositional phrases, participial phrases, and adjective clauses. All are corrected in the same way—by placing the modifier as close as possible to the word it modifies.

First, consider a misplaced prepositional phrase. This error usually occurs in a sentence with two or more prepositional phrases in a row.

MISPLACED: Ships called dhows were sailed by ancient Arabs *with triangular sails.*

In this example, the misplaced modifier (and second prepositional phrase) should be moved closer to *dhows*.

CORRECTED: Ships called dhows *with triangular sails* were sailed by ancient Arabs.

Participial phrases are sometimes used at the beginning of sentences. When a participial phrase is used in this position, it must be followed immediately by a word that it can logically modify.

MISPLACED: *Flying over the mountains*, an electrical storm endangered our safety.

What is flying over the mountains? The sentence needs to be rewritten to insert a logical word, such as *airplane*, next to the modifier.

CORRECTED: *Flying over the mountains*, our airplane was endangered by an electrical storm.

A misplaced adjective clause should also be moved closer to the word it modifies. In the following sentence, the clause is so far away from *ring* that it seems to modify *months* or *searching*. The sentence needs to be rearranged.

MISPLACED: I found the ring after several months of searching *that my grandmother gave me.*

CORRECTED: After several months of searching, I found the ring *that my grandmother gave me.*

Internet Tip

To learn about the history of sailing ships, go to the Age of Exploration Time Line of The Mariners' Museum at this site: **http://www.mariner.org/age/menu.html**

Exercise 34 Revising to Correct Misplaced Modifiers

Revise the following sentences to eliminate the misplaced modifiers. In each new sentence, underline the modifier that was misplaced in the original. Then, draw an arrow pointing from the modifier to the word it modifies.

EXAMPLE: A submarine is basically a frame designed to withstand deep ocean pressures and move easily in water with an air space.

ANSWER: A submarine is basically a frame with an air space designed to withstand deep ocean pressures and move easily in water.

1. Submarines were used in the two world wars with sharply pointed bows and long, slender hulls.
2. These early submarines could remain underwater only a few hours at a time with immature designs.
3. During the majority of their time at sea, at the water's surface the submarines had to function.
4. In contrast, nuclear submarines were designed for lengthy underwater operation with bluntly rounded bows and tapering sterns.
5. Surface frames for stability are widest above the waterline.
6. Underwater frames increase strength and reduce surface area and friction drag with more circular cross sections.
7. The submarine framework is called a hull with a double steel shell.
8. Ballast tanks are opened and flooded when the vessel submerges with seawater.
9. For surfacing, ballast tanks are refilled after they force out the seawater with compressed air.
10. When the desired depth is reached, trim tanks keep the craft stable by adjusting the water level within the tanks in the vessel.

Exercise 35 Revising a Paragraph to Correct Misplaced Modifiers

Revise the following paragraph, correcting the misplaced modifiers.

Ship size continued to increase in the eighteenth century with new technology. Growing trade markets also contributed to increasing ship size around the world. The ships were found difficult to control by sailors with their greater size. Working with new technology, a steering wheel for ships was developed by ship designers. A smoother operation of the rudder resulted from this new arrangement with less effort.

More Practice

Grammar Exercise Workbook
- pp. 115–118

On-line Exercise Bank
- Section 21.4

Go on-line: PHSchool.com
Enter Web Code: eck-8002

Get instant feedback! Exercises 34, 35, and 36 are available on-line or on CD-ROM.

Solving Special Problems

Many mistakes involve words and expressions considered wrong by today's standards, or words that are confused because they are spelled almost alike. In the following pages, note those problems that might occur in your speaking or writing.

Avoiding Double Negatives

Some people use *double negatives*—two negative words—when only one is required.

KEY CONCEPT Do not use sentences with double negatives. ■

Notice in the following chart that double negatives can be corrected in either of two ways.

Double Negatives	Corrected Sentences
Silas did*n't* invite *nobody.*	Silas did*n't* invite anybody. Silas invited *nobody.*
I have*n't* *no* time now.	I have*n't* any time now. I have *no* time now.
She *never* told us *nothing* about her party.	She *never* told us anything about her party. She told us *nothing* about her party.

Exercise 36 **Revising to Correct Double Negatives** Correct each sentence below in two ways.

EXAMPLE: There isn't no invention that has had a greater effect on the twentieth century than the airplane.

CORRECT: There isn't any invention that has had a greater effect on the twentieth century than the airplane.
There is no invention that has had a greater effect on the twentieth century than the airplane.

1. A powered aircraft wasn't invented by nobody before the Wright *Flyer I.*
2. There wasn't no one who could fly it.
3. It couldn't never "fly by itself" because it had to be constantly controlled by the pilot.
4. Inventors didn't think no aircraft should be unstable.
5. They didn't know no reason the design could not be improved.

Speaking and Listening Tip

If you find that using double negatives is a habit, try practicing the correct usage aloud. Together with a classmate, take turns reading the examples and exercises on this page to accustom yourselves to using negatives correctly.

Solving Common Usage Problems

Listed below are expressions that you should avoid or words that are often confused.

(1) accept, except *Accept*, a verb, means "to agree to." *Except*, a preposition, means "other than."

VERB: She willingly *accepted* a ride on the bus.
PREPOSITION: Everyone *except* him will be at the party.

(2) advice, advise *Advice*, a noun, means "an opinion." *Advise*, a verb, means "to give an opinion to."

NOUN: My mother gave me *advice* on how to dress.
VERB: My mother *advised* me to wear a skirt.

(3) affect, effect *Affect*, a verb, means "to influence" or "to cause a change in." *Effect*, usually a noun, means "result."

VERB: The cold weather *affected* the car's engine.
NOUN: What is the *effect* of global warming?

(4) at Do not use *at* after *where*.

INCORRECT: Do you know *where* we're *at?*
CORRECT: Do you know *where* we are?

(5) because Do not use *because* after *the reason*. Eliminate one or the other.

INCORRECT: *The reason* I am late is *because* I got lost.
CORRECT: *The reason* I am late is *that* I got lost.

Exercise 37 **Avoiding Common Usage Problems** For each of the following sentences, choose the correct form from the choices in parentheses and write it on your paper.

EXAMPLE: Don't (accept, except) a ride in a car with a stranger.
ANSWER: accept

1. The reason humans use automobiles is (because, that) they can transport people and small cargoes quickly.
2. An automobile can quickly take you from where (you are, you are at) to where you want to go.
3. The parts of cars and trucks are basically the same (except, accept) for the body.
4. One word of (advice, advise) is to always wear a seat belt when riding in any kind of vehicle.

More Practice

Grammar Exercise Workbook
- pp. 119–120

On-line Exercise Bank
- Section 21.4

Go on-line:
PHSchool.com
Enter Web Code:
eck-8002

Get instant feedback! Exercise 37 is available on-line or on CD-ROM.

5. If he had not been wearing a seat belt, the accident would have had a serious (affect, effect) on him.

(6) beside, besides These two prepositions have different meanings and cannot be interchanged. *Beside* means "at the side of" or "close to." *Besides* means "in addition to."

EXAMPLES: We stood *beside* the house until the car arrived.
No one *besides* us was there.

(7) different from, different than *Different from* is generally preferred over *different than.*

EXAMPLE: The trip across country was *different from* what I had hoped.

(8) farther, further *Farther* is used to refer to distance. *Further* means "additional" or "to a greater degree or extent."

EXAMPLES: A mile is *farther* than a kilometer.
When he began raising his voice, I listened no *further.*

(9) in, into *In* refers to position. *Into* suggests motion.

POSITION: The truck is *in* the garage.
MOTION: Put the ruler *into* the top drawer.

(10) kind of, sort of Do not use *kind of* or *sort of* to mean "rather" or "somewhat."

INCORRECT: My new sweater feels *kind of* itchy.
CORRECT: My new sweater feels somewhat itchy.

GRAMMAR IN LITERATURE

from The Story-Teller

Saki

The words in blue italics demonstrate the correct use of words that sometimes cause usage problems.

An aunt belonging *to* the children occupied one corner seat, and the . . . seat on the opposite side was occupied by a bachelor *who* was a stranger to *their* party, but the small girls and the small boy emphatically occupied the compartment.

(11) like *Like*, a preposition, means "similar to" or "in the same way as." It should be followed by an object. Do not use *like* before a subject and a verb. Use *as* or *that* instead.

	Obj
PREPOSITION:	The rubbing alcohol felt *like* ice on my feverish skin.

	S V
INCORRECT:	This neighborhood doesn't look *like* I remember.
CORRECT:	This neighborhood doesn't look *as* I remember.

(12) that, which, who *That* and *which* refer to things. *Who* should be used to refer only to people.

THINGS: The car *that* I raced won first prize.
PEOPLE: The dancer *who* performed is my brother.

(13) their, there, they're Do not confuse the spelling of these three words. *Their*, a possessive adjective, always modifies a noun. *There* is usually used either as a sentence starter or as an adverb. *They're* is a contraction for *they are*.

POSSESSIVE ADJECTIVE: The teams won all of *their* games.
SENTENCE STARTER: *There* is a new record set each year.
ADVERB: Drive the truck over *there*.
CONTRACTION: *They're* trying to set new track records.

(14) to, too, two Do not confuse the spelling of these words. *To*, a preposition, begins a prepositional phrase or an infinitive. *Too* is an adverb and modifies adjectives and other adverbs. *Two* is a number.

PREPOSITION:	*to* the vehicle	*to* Maine
INFINITIVE:	*to* eat	*to* see
ADVERB:	*too* lonely	*too* slowly
NUMBER:	*two* buttons	*two* buses

(15) when, where, why Do not use *when, where,* or *why* directly after a linking verb such as *is*. Reword the sentence.

INCORRECT: In the evening *is when* I drive to work.
CORRECT: I drive to work in the evening.

INCORRECT: The gym *is where* our wrestling team practices.
CORRECT: Our wrestling team practices in the gym.

INCORRECT: To see Yellowstone National Park *is why* we came to Wyoming.
CORRECT: We came to Wyoming to see Yellowstone National Park.

Grammar and Style Tip

Using *there is* or *there are* as a sentence starter is grammatically correct. However, if you can revise a sentence to eliminate those words, you will make it more direct.

Example: There is a new record set each year.

Revised: A new record is set each year.

Exercise 38 **Avoiding Common Usage Problems** For each of the following sentences, choose the correct form from the choices in parentheses and write it on your paper.

EXAMPLE: Passengers usually stand (beside, besides) a bus stop sign to wait for a ride.
ANSWER: beside

1. The bus is the most common form of public transportation (into, in) the United States and throughout the world.
2. (Beside, Besides) the fact that it is relatively inexpensive to purchase and operate, a bus can also be used on existing roads and highways.
3. The bus is (kind of, somewhat) similar to a large passenger van; it is equipped with seats for passengers.
4. (Farther, Further), a bus is usually operated on a regular schedule along a fixed route.
5. A bus system is not too different (from, than) any other transit system.
6. When we traveled from Michigan to California, it was the (farthest, furthest) I'd ever gone on a bus.
7. (They're, There are) almost no words to describe the beauty of the Rocky Mountains.
8. We passed through some spectacular deserts, (to, too).
9. It was interesting and fun, just (like, as) a vacation should be.
10. The bus trip was much different (from, than) the train trip we took the next year.

More Practice

Grammar Exercise Workbook
- pp. 119–120

On-line Exercise Bank
- Section 21.4

Go on-line:
PHSchool.com
Enter Web Code:
eck-8002

▼ Critical Viewing How does traveling by bus compare to traveling by train? Include at least two of the usage topics in your response. **[Compare and Contrast]**

Exercise 39 Revising to Correct Common Usage Problems

Revise each of the following sentences, correcting the problems in usage. If a sentence contains no error, write *correct.*

EXAMPLE: The bicycle, to, is a common form of transportation.

ANSWER: The bicycle, too, is a common form of transportation.

1. A two-wheeled vehicle who is propelled by its rider is called a bicycle.
2. There the most energy-efficient form of transportation.
3. The bicycle is used throughout the world to travel.
4. In developing countries such as China, the bicycle has been the common form of local transportation for years.
5. In developing countries is where the bike is the common form of transportation, it is normal to see 300 or more bikes on the road.
6. We rode on the boardwalk on a tandem bicycle, which is a bicycle built for too.
7. The children were too short to get on they're bicycles by themselves.
8. Noon is the time when we were supposed to meet.
9. Bicycling is the reason why I came with this group to Iowa.
10. Take a picture of us over their!

More Practice

Grammar Exercise Workbook
- pp. 119–120

On-line Exercise Bank
- Section 21.4

Go on-line:
PHSchool.com
Enter Web Code:
eck-8002

▼ Critical Viewing Describe how someone might feel zooming down a hill on a bicycle. Use at least two of the usage topics in your response. **[Infer]**

Section 21.4 **Section Review**

GRAMMAR EXERCISES 40–46

Exercise 40 **Changing Fragments Into Sentences** Correct the fragments below by adding words to form sentences.

1. Most American bicycles.
2. Riding his bike.
3. When I went car shopping.
4. To get to the top.
5. Which are useful for pedaling.
6. That you admired.
7. Exerting all his effort.
8. Up the hill.
9. That he just bought.
10. Finally arriving.

Exercise 41 **Revising to Correct Run-ons and Misplaced Modifiers** Identify each sentence below as a run-on *(RO)* or misplaced modifier *(MM)*. Then, revise the sentences to eliminate the run-on or misplaced modifier.

1. A self-propelled vehicle is considered a motorcycle with two wheels.
2. Motorcycles have become lighter and faster they are usually specialized.
3. Four-stroke engines generally power large street bikes with two cylinders.
4. Off-road motorbikes typically have two-stroke engines, four-stroke engines are regaining popularity though.
5. Motorcycles are designed to be ridden on streets as well as off the road that meet federal requirements.

Exercise 42 **Revising to Eliminate Double Negatives** Revise the sentences below, correcting the double negatives.

1. Some sailors don't call no vessel a boat unless it can be carried on a ship.
2. Tug boats and ferryboats aren't small enough to be carried by no ships, but they are still considered boats.
3. Sailboats without no sails will move only short distances.
4. Hardly no small boats are propelled by oars or a motor.
5. A boat can't transport nobody without no water to float on.

Exercise 43 **Revising to Eliminate Usage Problems** Revise the sentences below, eliminating problems in usage.

1. Roller-skating is a sport who involves moving on special shoes.
2. The first roller skates were as ice skates with the wheels in one row.
3. The affect of roller-skating on the knees is under investigation.
4. Other people beside children, enjoy roller-skating.
5. Roller skates are different than ice skates.

Exercise 44 **Find It in Your Reading** In your reading, you have no doubt seen sentence fragments. Explain why writers might choose to use sentence fragments.

Exercise 45 **Find It in Your Writing** Look through your portfolio to see whether you have used fragments, run-ons, or misplaced modifiers. Rewrite the incorrect sentences.

Exercise 46 **Writing Application** Write a description of a trip you have taken. Use a variety of sentences to describe the kind of transportation you used. Write at least five sentences, avoiding common usage errors.

Chapter

22 Using Verbs

Over the years, rules have been established that reflect the way most educated Americans use their language. The rules in this and the following chapters are those of standard English. Learning and following these rules will help you convey ideas more clearly when you are writing or speaking.

Verb usage is an area that causes many communication problems. Because verbs have many forms and uses, you may find yourself occasionally making mistakes with them. This chapter will help you learn their various forms and will guide you in using them correctly in your speaking and writing. The themes of this chapter—education, statistics, and exploration—all reflect the importance of clear and precise communication.

▲ **Critical Viewing** Write three sentences describing actions of people who might have used this old map. Use past-tense verbs in your sentences. **[Connect]**

Diagnostic Test

Directions: Write all answers on a separate sheet of paper. (The sentences that follow are not intended to maintain a consistent verb tense. Read each sentence as though it were standing alone.)

Skill Check A. Identify the principal part used to form each italicized verb or verb phrase below as *present, present participle, past,* or *past participle.* Label each verb *regular* or *irregular.*

1. My mother *teaches* at a middle school for boys.
2. She *has worked* there for nine years.
3. Ten years ago, she *sold* cars at a local dealership.
4. She *has helped* me so much.
5. We *are becoming* very close friends.

Skill Check B. Write the present participle, the past, and the past participle of the following verbs.

6. tutor
7. shut
8. find
9. lose
10. do

Skill Check C. Copy each of the following sentences onto your paper, supplying the form of the verb indicated in parentheses.

11. My math teacher (teach—past progressive) a lesson on fractions.
12. He (call—past perfect) on me to explain my answer.
13. I (speak—past) in a very shaky voice.
14. My classmates (notice—past perfect progressive) my fear.
15. I (shout—future) at them at lunch later today.

Skill Check D. Indicate whether the verb in each sentence below is in the *active* or *passive* voice.

16. My teacher gave me a good grade.
17. My sister was given a bad grade.
18. She was reprimanded by our parents.
19. Recently, I had helped her prepare for the big test.
20. By next year, we will have been challenged for a full ten months by new math standards.

Skill Check E. In the sentences below, write the correct verb from the choices in parentheses.

21. My math score (ain't, isn't) the highest in my class.
22. I think I should (have, of) studied more for the test.
23. When I got the test back, I realized that my tutor hadn't (learned, taught) me much at all about fractions.
24. I hope my teacher will (leave, let) me take it again.
25. I have no idea why I (done, did) so badly on the test.

Section 22.1

The Principal Parts of Verbs

Verbs take different forms in order to indicate time. The form of the verb *talk* in the sentence "She *talks* about her plans" expresses action in the present. In "She *talked* about her plans," the verb shows that the action occurred in the past. These forms of verbs are known as *tenses.* To use the various tenses of verbs correctly, you must know how to form the *principal parts* of a verb.

KEY CONCEPT A verb has four principal parts: *present, present participle, past,* and *past participle.* ■

Following are the four principal parts of the verb *talk:*

PRINCIPAL PARTS OF *TALK*			
Present	Present Participle	Past	Past Participle
talk	(am) talking	talked	(have) talked

Notice in the chart the first principal part, the present. This is the form of the verb that you would find listed in a dictionary. Notice also the second and fourth principal parts and the words before them in parentheses. When these two principal parts are used as verbs in sentences, helping verbs are always used with them. Common helping verbs include *has, have, had, am, is, are, was,* and *were.*

A principal part together with its helping verbs is called a *verb phrase.*

Each of the following four sentences uses one of the principal parts of the verb *talk.*

EXAMPLES: I sometimes *talk* too much in class. (present)
We *were talking* to the guidance counselor about courses for next year. (present participle)
They *talked* together for hours. (past)
He *has talked* about becoming a teacher for a long time. (past participle)

By looking at the third and fourth principal parts of a verb, you can learn whether the verb is *regular* or *irregular.*

Theme: Teachers

In this section, you will learn about principal parts of verbs. The examples and exercises are about teachers and schools.

Cross-Curricular Connection: Social Studies

Using Regular Verbs

Most verbs in English are *regular*, which means that the formation of the past and past participle follows a predictable pattern.

KEY CONCEPT The past and past participle of a regular verb are formed by adding *-ed* or *-d* to the present form. ■

The past and past participle of such regular verbs as *lift* and *contain*, which do not end in *e*, are formed by adding *-ed* to the present form. With regular verbs that end in *e*, such as *save* and *change*, you simply add *-d* to the present form.

Sometimes you will have to double the final consonant before adding *-ed* (or *-ing*, to form the present participle).

PRINCIPAL PARTS OF REGULAR VERBS

Present	Present Participle	Past	Past Participle
lift	(am) lifting	lifted	(have) lifted
contain	(am) containing	contained	(have) contained
save	(am) saving	saved	(have) saved
change	(am) changing	changed	(have) changed

Exercise 1 **Recognizing the Principal Parts of Regular Verbs** The verb or verb phrase in each of the following sentences is underlined. Identify the principal part used to form each verb.

EXAMPLE: Frank was grading papers when he heard the news.

ANSWER: present participle

1. Teachers have helped students for thousands of years.
2. In ancient Greece, Socrates worked with small groups of students.
3. He was opening their minds to new ideas.
4. In the Middle Ages, students learned from priests and other church officials.
5. Only wealthy children would have attended those schools.
6. Most other children received lessons at home.
7. Today, students usually attend formal schools.
8. Recently, our society has noted many advances in science and technology.
9. These advances are creating new opportunities for learning.
10. We will need well-prepared teachers to help children understand the world of the future.

More Practice

Grammar Exercise Workbook
- pp. 121–122

On-line Exercise Bank
- Section 22.1

Go on-line: PHSchool.com *Enter Web Code:* eck-8002

Get instant feedback! Exercise 1 is available on-line or on CD-ROM.

Exercise 2 **Using the Principal Parts of Regular Verbs**
Copy each of the following sentences onto your paper, writing the correct form of the word given in parentheses.

EXAMPLE: The student has (ask) for more help from his teacher.

ANSWER: The student has asked for more help from his teacher.

1. My friends and I are (study—present participle) the history of education in the United States.
2. Young people have (attend—past participle) schools since the early days of United States history.
3. Even in colonial times, people (create—past) laws about schools.
4. In 1647, a law in the colony of Massachusetts (order—past) towns with fifty or more families to establish a school for their children.
5. In the 1700's, secondary schools, called "academies," were (open—past participle).
6. Some of these schools were (offer—present participle) classes in bookkeeping and navigation.
7. Girls were (allow—past participle) to attend some academies.
8. The state of Georgia (establish—past) a charter for the first state university.
9. In 1874, the Michigan Supreme Court (rule—past) that taxes could be (collect—past participle) to support public schools.
10. Recent laws (assure—present) that education will be available to all citizens.

◀ **Critical Viewing** Write a sentence about this teacher, using the present participle form of a verb. Write a sentence about the students, using the past form of a verb. **[Connect]**

Memorizing Irregular Verbs

While most verbs in the English language are regular, many of the most commonly used English verbs are *irregular,* which means that the formation of the past and past participle does not follow a predictable pattern. Irregular verbs can pose some special problems for writers and speakers.

KEY CONCEPT With an irregular verb, the past and past participle are *not* formed by adding *-ed* or *-d* to the present form. ■

The third and fourth principal parts of irregular verbs are formed in many different ways. You will need to memorize these principal parts. With some irregular verbs, the past and past participles are spelled the same, as shown in the chart below. With some other irregular verbs, the present, past, and past participle forms are all the same word, as shown in the chart at the top of page 364.

SOME IRREGULAR VERBS WITH THE SAME PAST AND PAST PARTICIPLE

Present	Present Participle	Past	Past Participle
bring	(am) bringing	brought	(have) brought
build	(am) building	built	(have) built
buy	(am) buying	bought	(have) bought
catch	(am) catching	caught	(have) caught
fight	(am) fighting	fought	(have) fought
find	(am) finding	found	(have) found
get	(am) getting	got	(have) got *or* (have) gotten
hold	(am) holding	held	(have) held
lay	(am) laying	laid	(have) laid
lead	(am) leading	led	(have) led
lose	(am) losing	lost	(have) lost
pay	(am) paying	paid	(have) paid
say	(am) saying	said	(have) said
sit	(am) sitting	sat	(have) sat
spin	(am) spinning	spun	(have) spun
stick	(am) sticking	stuck	(have) stuck
swing	(am) swinging	swung	(have) swung
teach	(am) teaching	taught	(have) taught

SOME IRREGULAR VERBS WITH THE SAME PRESENT, PAST, AND PAST PARTICIPLE			
Present	Present Participle	Past	Past Participle
bid	(am) bidding	bid	(have) bid
burst	(am) bursting	burst	(have) burst
cost	(am) costing	cost	(have) cost
hurt	(am) hurting	hurt	(have) hurt
put	(am) putting	put	(have) put
set	(am) setting	set	(have) set

Exercise 3 **Supplying Irregular Verbs** Use the verbs in the chart above to complete the following sentences. You may use some verbs more than once.

1. The student __?__ into the room.
2. He hurried to his desk and __?__ down his books.
3. "I must tell you something before I __?__," he said.
4. "On-line the other day, my father __?__ on tickets to the playoffs, and he got them!"
5. "Playoff tickets usually __?__ a lot, but these __?__ practically nothing."

▲ **Critical Viewing** Use the past or past participle forms of *get* and *put* in a sentence about this picture. **[Connect]**

GRAMMAR IN LITERATURE

from The Ninny

Translated by Robert Payne

Regular verbs are printed in red italics and irregular verbs in blue italics in this passage.

"Then around New Year's Day you *broke* a cup and saucer. *Subtract* two rubles. The cup *cost* more than that—it was an heirloom, but we won't *bother* about that. We're the ones who *pay.* Another matter. Due to your carelessness Kolya *climbed* a tree and *tore* his coat. . . . You ought to have *kept* your eyes open. So we *dock* off five more."

SOME IRREGULAR VERBS THAT CHANGE IN OTHER WAYS			
Present	Present Participle	Past	Past Participle
arise	(am) arising	arose	(have) arisen
be	(am) being	was	(have) been
begin	(am) beginning	began	(have) begun
blow	(am) blowing	blew	(have) blown
break	(am) breaking	broke	(have) broken
choose	(am) choosing	chose	(have) chosen
come	(am) coming	came	(have) come
do	(am) doing	did	(have) done
draw	(am) drawing	drew	(have) drawn
drink	(am) drinking	drank	(have) drunk
drive	(am) driving	drove	(have) driven
eat	(am) eating	ate	(have) eaten
fall	(am) falling	fell	(have) fallen
fly	(am) flying	flew	(have) flown
freeze	(am) freezing	froze	(have) frozen
give	(am) giving	gave	(have) given
go	(am) going	went	(have) gone
grow	(am) growing	grew	(have) grown
know	(am) knowing	knew	(have) known
lie	(am) lying	lay	(have) lain
ride	(am) riding	rode	(have) ridden
ring	(am) ringing	rang	(have) rung
rise	(am) rising	rose	(have) risen
run	(am) running	ran	(have) run
see	(am) seeing	saw	(have) seen
shake	(am) shaking	shook	(have) shaken
sing	(am) singing	sang	(have) sung
sink	(am) sinking	sank	(have) sunk
speak	(am) speaking	spoke	(have) spoken
spring	(am) springing	sprang	(have) sprung
swear	(am) swearing	swore	(have) sworn
swim	(am) swimming	swam	(have) swum
take	(am) taking	took	(have) taken
tear	(am) tearing	tore	(have) torn
throw	(am) throwing	threw	(have) thrown
wear	(am) wearing	wore	(have) worn
write	(am) writing	wrote	(have) written

Check a dictionary whenever you are in doubt about the correct form of an irregular verb.

Internet Tip

You can use the present participle to find information on the Internet. For example, to find information about choral groups or songs, you can type "singing" on the search engine.

Exercise 4 Completing the Principal Parts of Irregular Verbs Without looking back at the charts, write the missing principal parts for the following irregular verbs on your paper.

EXAMPLE:	Present	Present Participle	Past	Past Participle
	?	writing	?	?
ANSWER:	write		wrote	written

	Present	Present Participle	Past	Past Participle
1.	?	seeing	?	?
2.	let	?	?	?
3.	?	?	?	gone
4.	?	?	spun	?
5.	?	sleeping	?	?
6.	eat	?	?	?
7.	creep	?	?	?
8.	?	?	?	spoken
9.	?	?	got	?
10.	?	teaching	?	?

Exercise 5 Identify the Principal Parts of Irregular Verbs For each of the following sentences, identify the irregular verb(s) and the principal part(s) used.

EXAMPLE: After the principal had shaken my hand, he spoke to me.

ANSWER: shaken (past participle); spoke (past)

1. A new student teacher came to our class today.
2. She stood up after the bell rang.
3. She put her name at the top of the chalkboard.
4. She was shaking with nervousness.
5. She spoke to us in a very soft voice.
6. She told us a little bit about herself.
7. She had worn a bright yellow dress to class.
8. After a few minutes, she grew less nervous.
9. We quickly saw that she knew a lot about algebra.
10. She was teaching a small group of students.
11. They were sitting in a circle around her.
12. They all fought to answer her questions first.
13. They said that she had done a great job.
14. I have made a decision.
15. I will choose to be in her group tomorrow.

More Practice

Grammar Exercise Workbook
- pp. 121–124

On-line Exercise Bank
- Section 22.1

Go on-line: PHSchool.com
Enter Web Code: eck-8002

Get instant feedback! Exercises 4, 5, and 6 are available on-line or on CD-ROM.

Exercise 6 **Using the Past and Past Participle of Irregular Verbs** For each sentence below, choose the correct verb from the choices in parentheses, and write it on your paper.

EXAMPLE: We (freezed, froze) the leftovers.
ANSWER: froze

1. For the final project, our science teacher had (gave, given) us a choice of topics.
2. My group (choosed, chose) to build a robot cow.
3. Unfortunately, our teacher had (set, setted) a one-week time limit for finishing the project.
4. Completing the project on time (become, became) our goal.
5. We (sticked, stuck) to a strict plan.
6. The project had (drove, driven) us to work hard.
7. Whenever a problem (arose, arised), we worked diligently to fix it.
8. We even (spoke, spoken) to science students in other schools via the Internet.
9. The robot cow was a success, and we (got, gotten) *A*'s.
10. More important, our classmates (payed, paid) us many compliments.

▼ **Critical Viewing** Write a sentence about this teacher, using the past form of *hold.* Write a sentence about the children, using the past form of *stand.* **[Connect]**

Exercise 7 **Supplying the Correct Principal Part of Irregular Verbs** Copy the following sentences onto your paper, writing the correct past or past participle form of the verb given in parentheses.

EXAMPLE: The substitute had (draw—past participle) up a lesson plan.
ANSWER: The substitute had drawn up a lesson plan.

1. The world has (see—past participle) many great teachers.
2. Perhaps one of the most remarkable (be—past) Anne Mansfield Sullivan.
3. Sullivan (find—past) great joy in teaching the blind.
4. In 1887, she had (begin—past participle) teaching Helen Keller, a young girl who was deaf and blind.
5. Slowly, Sullivan (teach—past) Keller to read the Braille writing system.
6. By age ten, Keller (know—past) how to write using a special typewriter.
7. She had also (speak—past participle) her first words.
8. Keller eventually (go—past) to Radcliffe College.
9. She (write—past) many books about her experiences.
10. Keller's book *The Story of My Life* has (lead—past participle) many people to admire her.

▲ **Critical Viewing** Name two irregular verbs you might use in sentences about this photograph of Helen Keller. **[Analyze]**

Exercise 8 **Revising Sentences With Incorrect Principal Parts of Irregular Verbs** Where necessary, revise each sentence below to use the correct principal part of an irregular verb. If a sentence is correct, write *correct.*

EXAMPLE: Angel has spoke to his guidance counselor.
ANSWER: Angel has spoken to his guidance counselor.

1. Education has saw many changes over the years.
2. Good teachers have rose to meet new challenges.
3. Skilled teachers have become invaluable.
4. I am sure that you known many good teachers.
5. These teachers have came from all backgrounds.
6. The profession has drawn people with many different talents.
7. Early on, they chosen to use their skills to enrich young people.
8. Over the years, they have gave their best to help their students.
9. Many grateful students have wrote about the help and encouragement of their teachers.
10. In recent years, many teachers began to receive recognition for what they had did.

Section 22.1 Section Review

GRAMMAR EXERCISES 9–14

Exercise 9 **Identifying Regular and Irregular Verbs** Label the following verbs *regular* or *irregular.*

1. bring
2. impress
3. cut
4. lose
5. deliver
6. stick
7. cover
8. remove
9. shake
10. say

Exercise 10 **Recognizing the Principal Parts of Verbs** On your paper, write the verb or verb phrase in each of the following sentences. Then, identify the principal part used to form the verb.

1. Maria Montessori was an Italian educator and physician.
2. In 1907, she introduced a new method for the education of young children.
3. Her method encourages self-reliance in children.
4. The Montessori method has become popular throughout the world.
5. Today, thousands of children are attending Montessori schools.

Exercise 11 **Supplying the Correct Principal Part** Copy the following sentences onto your paper. Supply the correct principal part. If there is no helping verb in the sentence, do not add one.

1. Before writing was (develop), teachers (present) their lessons orally.
2. The invention of writing (lead) to new methods of teaching.
3. In ancient Egyptian schools, students (spend) hours writing the same passages over and over again.
4. They were (give) arithmetic lessons by copying business records.
5. Most of their teachers (be) priests, and classes were (hold) in the temples.
6. In ancient Greece, all children (receive) physical and military training.
7. Only a few children were also (teach) how to read and write.
8. The ancient Hebrews (offer) an education to boys of all economic groups.
9. Hebrew girls (spend) their time learning at home.
10. The Roman system was (pattern) after the one used in ancient Greece.
11. However, the Romans (permit) girls to attend classes.
12. Roman students (speak) both Greek and Latin in class.
13. Roman teachers were (instruct) older boys in engineering and law.
14. These students also (read) and (write) poems.
15. We are (begin) a study of the history of education in our social studies class.

Exercise 12 **Find It in Your Reading** Find two irregular verbs and one regular verb in the following passage from "The Ninny." Which principal part is used?

> I gave her the eleven rubles. With trembling fingers she took them and slipped them into her pocket.

Exercise 13 **Find It in Your Writing** Look through your writing portfolio for examples of sentences that contain regular and irregular verbs. Identify the principal parts of each verb you find.

Exercise 14 **Writing Application** Write a description of your favorite elementary-school teacher. Identify the four principal parts of any verbs you use.

Section 22.2

The Six Tenses of Verbs

In English, verbs have six *tenses*—the *present*, the *past*, the *future*, the *present perfect*, the *past perfect*, and the *future perfect*.

KEY CONCEPT A **tense** is a form of a verb that shows time of action or state of being. ■

Every tense has both *basic* forms and *progressive* forms.

Theme: Statistics

In this section, you will learn about the six tenses of verbs in their basic and progressive forms. The examples and exercises are about collecting data and using statistics.

Cross-Curricular Connection: Mathematics

Identifying the Basic Forms of the Six Tenses

The following chart shows the *basic* forms of the six tenses, using the verb *speak* as an example. As you can see in the third column, the six basic forms make use of just three of the principal parts: the present, the past, and the past participle.

BASIC FORMS OF THE SIX TENSES OF *SPEAK*

Tense	Basic Form	Principal Part Used
Present	I speak	Present
Past	I spoke	Past
Future	I will speak	Present
Present Perfect	I have spoken	Past Participle
Past Perfect	I had spoken	Past Participle
Future Perfect	I will have spoken	Past Participle

Exercise 15 **Identifying the Basic Forms of Verbs** Identify the tense of the underlined verb in each sentence below.

EXAMPLE: We have collected data on recycling savings.
ANSWER: present perfect

1. Statistics is a branch of mathematics.
2. It deals with the study of numerical data.
3. Many people have studied statistics for work or fun.
4. Batting averages and scoring averages represent statistics.
5. People have compiled statistics for thousands of years.
6. Ancient Egyptians kept records of their livestock and crops.
7. Ancient Hebrews took a census after they left Egypt.
8. Later, the Romans conducted a census of their own.
9. People will gather statistics for many years to come.
10. By the next century, people will have benefited from statistics for nearly four thousand years.

More Practice

Grammar Exercise Workbook
- pp. 125–126

On-line Exercise Bank
- Section 22.2

Go on-line: PHSchool.com
Enter Web Code: eck-8002

Get instant feedback! Exercise 15 is available on-line or on CD-ROM.

Conjugating the Basic Forms of Verbs

A helpful way to become familiar with all the forms of a verb is by *conjugating* it.

KEY CONCEPT A **conjugation** is a list of the singular and plural forms of a verb in a particular tense. ■

Each tense in a conjugation has six forms that correspond to the first-, second-, and third-person forms of the personal pronouns. (See Chapter 14 for a review of personal pronouns.)

To conjugate any verb, begin by listing its principal parts.

PRINCIPAL PARTS OF *GO*			
Present	Present Participle	Past	Past Participle
go	going	went	gone

The following chart shows the conjugation of all the basic forms of *go* in all six tenses.

CONJUGATION OF THE BASIC FORMS OF *GO*		
	Singular	Plural
Present	I go you go he, she, it goes	we go you go they go
Past	I went you went he, she, it went	we went you went they went
Future	I will go you will go he, she, it will go	we will go you will go they will go
Present Perfect	I have gone you have gone he, she, it has gone	we have gone you have gone they have gone
Past Perfect	I had gone you had gone he, she, it had gone	we had gone you had gone they had gone
Future Perfect	I will have gone you will have gone he, she, it will have gone	we will have gone you will have gone they will have gone

Exercise 16 **Conjugating the Basic Forms of Verbs** The following sentences are written in the present tense. Rewrite each sentence in each of the other five tenses. Refer to the chart on the previous page if you need help.

1. I collect.
2. You split.
3. They teach.
4. We give.
5. It remains.

An important verb to know how to conjugate is the verb *be*. It is both the most common and the most irregular verb in English. You will use the basic forms of *be* when you conjugate the progressive forms of verbs later in this section.

PRINCIPAL PARTS OF *BE*			
Present	Present Participle	Past	Past Participle
be	being	was	been

CONJUGATION OF THE BASIC FORMS OF *BE*		
	Singular	Plural
Present	I am you are he, she, it is	we are you are they are
Past	I was you were he, she, it was	we were you were they were
Future	I will be you will be he, she, it will be	we will be you will be they will be
Present Perfect	I have been you have been he, she, it has been	we have been you have been they have been
Past Perfect	I had been you had been he, she, it had been	we had been you had been they had been
Future Perfect	I will have been you will have been he, she, it will have been	we will have been you will have been they will have been

Exercise 17 **Supplying the Correct Tense** On your paper, write the basic form of the verb indicated in parentheses.

EXAMPLE: Selena (calculate—past) the average score in her head.

ANSWER: Selena calculated the average score in her head.

1. Over the years, people (collect—present perfect) statistics to study a wide range of subjects.
2. A sociologist routinely (apply—present) statistics to study how people live and work together.
3. Demographics (be—present) the study of population patterns and movement.
4. Researchers (study—present perfect) such factors as age, income, and education among different groups of people.
5. Demographics, as a field of study, (begin—past) many centuries ago.
6. Before the telephone was invented, researchers (conduct—past perfect) most polls in person.
7. Today, researchers routinely (collect—present) data by using the telephone.
8. Some researchers also (take—present perfect) advantage of e-mail to collect data.
9. In the future, it is likely that researchers (develop—future) even more sophisticated ways to gather information about people.
10. By the year 2040, an infant born in 1990 (live—future perfect) for fifty years.

▼ **Critical Viewing** What finding have the students made from their survey? Write two sentences using verbs in present perfect or past perfect tense. **[Speculate]**

22.2

Recognizing the Progressive Forms of Verbs

The charts on pages 371 and 372 showed the six tenses of *go* and *be* in their basic forms. Each of these tenses also has a *progressive* form. All six of the progressive forms of a verb are made using just one principal part: the present participle. This is the principal part that ends in *-ing*.

The chart below shows the progressive form for all six tenses of the verb *analyze*.

PROGRESSIVE FORMS OF THE SIX TENSES OF *ANALYZE*

Tense	Progressive Form	Principal Part Used
Present	I am analyzing	Present Participle
Past	I was analyzing	
Future	I will be analyzing	
Present Perfect	I have been analyzing	
Past Perfect	I had been analyzing	
Future Perfect	I will have been analyzing	

Exercise 18 **Identifying the Tense of Progressive Forms of Verbs** Study the preceding chart, which shows the progressive form for the six tenses of a verb. Then, identify the tense of each of the following verb phrases.

EXAMPLE: was counting
ANSWER: past progressive

1. am measuring
2. was comparing
3. have been checking
4. will be demanding
5. had been noticing
6. were outlining
7. are verifying
8. have been joining
9. will be ordering
10. were requesting
11. will have been digging
12. had been migrating
13. will be entering
14. were exiting
15. had been handling
16. has been delaying
17. will be renting
18. will have been questioning
19. had been rating
20. have been changing

Conjugating Progressive Forms

Conjugating the progressive forms of any verb is easy if you know how to conjugate the basic forms of the verb *be.*

KEY CONCEPT To conjugate the progressive forms of a verb, add the present participle of the verb to a conjugation of the basic forms of *be.* ■

A complete conjugation of the basic forms of *be* is shown on page 372. Compare that conjugation with the following conjugation of the progressive forms of *go.* To form the progressive forms of a verb, you must know the basic forms of *be.*

CONJUGATION OF THE PROGRESSIVE FORMS OF *GO*

	Singular	Plural
Present Progressive	I am going you are going he, she, it is going	we are going you are going they are going
Past Progressive	I was going you were going he, she, it was going	we were going you were going they were going
Future Progressive	I will be going you will be going he, she, it will be going	we will be going you will be going they will be going
Present Perfect Progressive	I have been going you have been going he, she, it has been going	we have been going you have been going they have been going
Past Perfect Progressive	I had been going you had been going he, she, it had been going	we had been going you had been going they had been going
Future Perfect Progressive	I will have been going you will have been going he, she, it will have been going	we will have been going you will have been going they will have been going

Exercise 19 **Supplying the Correct Tense** Copy each of the following sentences onto your paper, supplying the progressive form of the verb as directed in parentheses.

EXAMPLE: He (study—past perfect progressive) the birthrate of Canadians.

ANSWER: He had been studying the birthrate of Canadians.

1. Many scholars (study—present progressive) the effect of modern inventions on people's lifestyles.
2. The impact of technology on people's lives (intrigue—present perfect progressive) social scientists for many years.
3. People (live—present progressive) today in a way that is very different from the way their parents and grandparents once lived.
4. Until about sixty years ago, many families (function—past perfect progressive) without refrigerators and telephones.
5. Without the convenience of refrigerators, most people (shop—past progressive) for only small quantities of food.
6. Other changes (affect—present perfect progressive) people's spending patterns and lifestyles.
7. Before credit cards became popular, few people (buy—past perfect progressive) things with borrowed money.
8. Today, the average American (borrow—present progressive) more money than ever before.
9. It is likely that most Americans (use—future progressive) even more credit in the future.
10. By the year 2020, people probably (spend—future perfect progressive) their money using advanced electronic methods for many years.

More Practice

Grammar Exercise Workbook
- pp. 127–128

On-line Exercise Bank
- Section 22.2

Go on-line:
PHSchool.com
Enter Web Code:
eck-8002

Get instant feedback! Exercises 19 and 20 are available on-line or on CD-ROM.

Identifying Active and Passive Voice

Just as verbs change tense to show time, they may also change form to show whether or not the subject of the verb is performing an action.

KEY CONCEPT **Voice** is a verb form that shows whether or not the subject is performing the action. ■

In English, most verbs have two *voices—active,* to show that the subject is performing an action, and *passive,* to show that the subject is having an action performed upon it.

KEY CONCEPT A verb is in the **active voice** when its subject performs the action. ■

ACTIVE VOICE: Sharon (S) *is conducting* (V) a survey (DO).

Bob (S) *responded* (V) to the questionnaire.

In each example, the subject performs the action. Sharon did the conducting; Bob did the responding. Notice also that an active verb may or may not have a direct object.

KEY CONCEPT A verb is in the **passive voice** when its subject does not perform the action. ■

PASSIVE VOICE: The survey (S) *is being conducted* (V) by Sharon.

Bob (S) *was asked* (V) to respond.

In each example, the subject is the receiver rather than the performer of the action. In the first sentence, the performer is Sharon. *Sharon*, however, is the object of the preposition *by* and is no longer the subject. In the second sentence, the performer of the action is not named. The sentence does not tell who asked Bob to respond.

Exercise 20 **Distinguishing Between Active and Passive Voice** On your paper, write the verb or verb phrase from each sentence below, and label its voice *active* or *passive*.

EXAMPLE: Those flowers were sent without a card.
ANSWER: were sent (passive)

1. The researchers conducted the poll.
2. The poll was conducted by volunteers.
3. Volunteers used the phone to conduct interviews.
4. Random people were selected for the poll by volunteers.
5. Some people were visited by pollsters.
6. The poll was designed by a famous scholar from Holland.
7. The statistics were collected by the researcher.
8. A philanthropist supplied the funding for the research.
9. The conclusion was supported by his data.
10. The conclusion will be issued by a publisher in Ohio.

Forming the Tenses of Passive Verbs

A passive verb always has two parts:

KEY CONCEPT A **passive verb** is always a verb phrase made from a form of *be* plus a past participle. ■

Here is a short conjugation of the passive forms of the verb *report* with the pronoun *it:*

CONJUGATION OF THE PASSIVE FORMS OF *REPORT*	
Tense	**Passive Form**
Present	it is reported
Past	it was reported
Future	it will be reported
Present Perfect	it has been reported
Past Perfect	it had been reported
Future Perfect	it will have been reported

Exercise 21 **Conjugating Verbs in the Passive Voice** Using the chart above as your model, conjugate the following two verbs in the passive voice. Use the pronoun in parentheses.

1. demonstrate (it)
2. restore (they)

Using Active and Passive Voices

Each of the two voices has its proper use in English.

KEY CONCEPT Use the active voice whenever possible. ■

Sentences with active verbs are less wordy and more forceful than those with passive verbs. Compare, for example, the following sentences. Notice the different number of words each sentence needs to report the same information.

ACTIVE: Students *conducted* a taste test.
PASSIVE: A taste test *was conducted* by students.

Although you should aim to use the active voice in most of your writing, there will be times when you will need to use the passive voice.

KEY CONCEPT Use the passive voice to emphasize the receiver of an action rather than the performer of the action. ■

In the following example, the receiver of the action is the subject *candidate.*

EMPHASIS ON RECEIVER: The candidate *was supported* by the voters.

The passive voice should also be used when there is no performer of the action.

KEY CONCEPT Use the passive voice to point out the receiver of an action when the performer is unknown or unimportant and is not named in the sentence. ■

PERFORMER UNKNOWN: The secret research *was ordered* sometime last year.

PERFORMER UNIMPORTANT: The crime scene *was* quickly *closed* while the police searched for clues.

Exercise 22 **Revising Sentences to Use the Active Voice** Revise the following sentences, changing the verb from the passive voice to the active voice whenever possible. If you choose to leave a sentence in the passive voice, explain why.

EXAMPLE: This old watch was found by me in my grandmother's bureau.

ANSWER: I found this old watch in my grandmother's bureau.

1. Research on people's habits has often been conducted by scientists.
2. A study on television-viewing habits was initiated by a team of researchers from the local university.
3. Two hundred people were selected to participate in the study.
4. By the time the study began, dozens of questions had been prepared by the team.
5. These questions were answered by participants.
6. The number of hours of television each participant watched daily was recorded by researchers.
7. The participants have been visited by field workers on a weekly basis since the beginning of the research.
8. The data have been carefully examined to determine trends.
9. All findings will soon be published by the university.
10. The findings will certainly be valued by television executives.

More Practice

Grammar Exercise Workbook
- pp. 129–132

On-line Exercise Bank
- Section 22.2

Go on-line:
PHSchool.com
Enter Web Code:
eck-8002

Hands-on Grammar

Turning to Active Verbs

You should use active voice verbs in most of your sentences. Use the passive voice only when you want to emphasize the receiver of an action or when you are not naming the performer. In those two cases, passive voice verbs are proper. To practice revising sentences from passive to active voice, try the following activity.

Take several index cards and cut out an opening in each to create a box with two arms, as in the model below. In the box on one side of the card, write a verb phrase consisting of *was* or *were* and a past participle form of a verb. Examples: *was given, were selected, was taught, were found.* Flip the card over and write a subject and the past form of the verb. Examples: *Sandra gave, they selected, Henry taught, I found.*

Tape the edges of the wings of a card onto a piece of paper. In the opening, write an article or a possessive adjective and a noun. On the paper to the right of the card, write an article and a direct object. You should now be able to see a sentence such as *My brother was given a tangerine.* Now, fold the card over on its wings and you will see *Sandra gave my brother a tangerine.* The new active voice sentence is more direct and provides more information than the passive voice sentence. (An active voice sentence is also shorter; to include the performer of the action, *Sandra,* in your passive voice sentence, you would have needed to add *by Sandra* at the end of the passive sentence.) Note that if you did not know the performer of the action, your sentence would stay in passive voice.

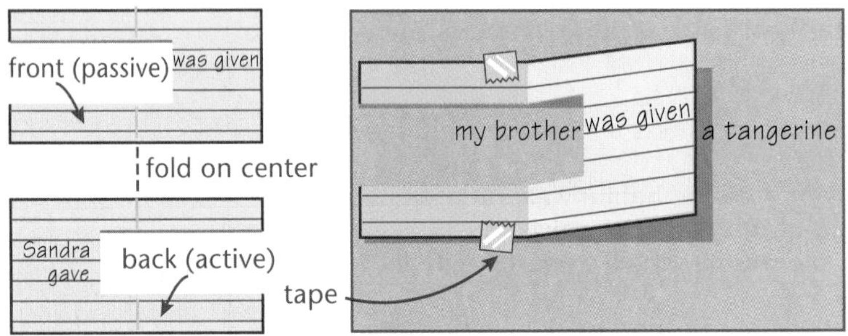

Find It in Your Reading Select a paragraph from a story in your literature book that contains sentences with both active and passive voice verbs. Discuss with a partner why the writer chose each voice.

Find It in Your Writing Use this activity to determine whether some of the sentences in your own compositions should be changed from passive to active voice. If you discover some passive voice sentences, consider whether to revise them to be in active voice.

Section Review

GRAMMAR EXERCISES 23–29

Exercise 23 **Identifying the Tense and Form of Verbs** Write the tense and form of the underlined verbs.

1. The arithmetic mean has been used frequently in statistics.
2. You probably know it by another name.
3. People often call it the average.
4. What was your average score in math?
5. Your teacher will determine your average score at the end of the semester.
6. You are working to improve your grade.
7. People routinely have been determining averages in sports.
8. Until recently, statisticians had computed averages with pencil and paper.
9. People had been doing that for years.
10. Baseball fans will be compiling batting averages as long as baseball is played.

Exercise 24 **Forming Progressive Tenses of Verbs** Write the tense indicated for each verb below.

1. present perfect progressive of *decide*
2. future progressive of *permit*
3. past perfect progressive of *tear*
4. present progressive of *determine*
5. past progressive of *break*.

Exercise 25 **Revising to Eliminate Problems With Verb Forms** Revise the following sentences by writing the correct form of the underlined verb.

(1) Electronics experts have develop calculators for many industries. (2) You may have saw an electrician carrying a calculator to measure code requirements. (3) Another calculator has be build for real estate agents to figure mortgage rates. (4) Carpet installers are now determine room size with an electronic tape measure. (5) Undoubtedly, plans for new calculators be draw up in the future.

Exercise 26 **Revising Sentences to Use the Active Voice** Revise the following sentences, changing the verb from the passive voice to the active voice whenever possible. If you choose to leave a sentence in the passive voice, explain why.

1. Opinion polls are relied on by politicians.
2. Around election time, many surveys are conducted by pollsters.
3. These polls are used by politicians to determine how voters feel about issues.
4. Opinion polls have been transformed into vital political tools by analysts.
5. The results of polls are often published in newspapers.

Exercise 27 **Find It in Your Reading** Identify the basic and progressive forms of the verbs used in this passage from "Flowers for Algernon" by Daniel Keyes.

> . . . They're all pretending that Algernon's behavior is not . . . significant for me. But it's hard to hide the fact that some of the other animals who were used in this experiment are showing strange behavior.

Exercise 28 **Find It in Your Writing** Look through your writing portfolio for sentences that contain active and passive verbs. Rewrite the sentences with passive verbs, changing them to active verbs.

Exercise 29 **Writing Application** Write several questions for an opinion poll to gauge your classmates' radio-listening habits. Use both basic and progressive verb forms in your questions.

Section 22.3

Troublesome Verbs

The following verbs cause problems for many speakers and writers. Some of the problems involve using the principal parts of certain verbs. Other problems involve learning to distinguish between the meanings of certain confusing pairs of verbs. As you read through the following list, note those verbs that have caused you difficulty in the past and concentrate on them. Use the exercises to test your understanding. When you are writing and revising your compositions, refer to this section to check your work.

Theme: Explorers of the Americas

In this section, you will learn about twelve verbs that often cause problems for speakers and writers. The examples and exercises are about explorers of North and South America.

Cross-Curricular Connection: Social Studies

(1) *ain't* *Ain't* is not considered correct English. Avoid using it in speaking and in writing.

INCORRECT: He *ain't* the first person to explore this island.
CORRECT: He *isn't* the first person to explore this island.

(2) *did, done* Remember that *done* is a past participle and can be used as a verb only with a helping verb such as *have* or *has.* Instead of using *done* without a helping verb, use *did.* Otherwise, you can add the helping verb before *done.*

INCORRECT: I already *done* my history project.
CORRECT: I already *did* my history project.
I *have* already *done* my history project.

(3) *dragged, drug* *Drag* is a regular verb. Its principal parts are *drag, dragging, dragged,* and *dragged. Drug* is never correct as the past or past participle of *drag.*

INCORRECT: The sailor *drug* the heavy box up the gangplank. You *should have drug* the sack of potatoes below deck.
CORRECT: The sailor *dragged* the heavy box up the gangplank. You *should have dragged* the sack of potatoes below deck.

▲ Critical Viewing Find direct objects in this picture to go with each of these verbs: *set, raised, laid.* **[Analyze]**

(4) *gone, went* *Gone* is the past participle of *go* and can be used as a verb only with a helping verb such as *have* or *has. Went* is the past of *go* and is never used with a helping verb.

INCORRECT: Jean and Frank *gone* to the museum.
We *should have went* along with them.
CORRECT: Jean and Frank *have gone* to the museum.
Jean and Frank *went* to the museum.
We *should have gone* along with them.

(5) *have, of* In conversation, the words *have* and *of* often sound very similar. Be careful not to write *of* when you really mean the helping verb *have* or its contraction *'ve.*

INCORRECT: Columbus should *of* continued until he reached India.

CORRECT: Columbus should *have* continued until he reached India.
Columbus *should've* continued until he reached India.

(6) *lay, lie* These verbs are troublesome to many people because they look and sound almost alike and have similar meanings. The first step in learning to distinguish between *lay* and *lie* is to become thoroughly familiar with their principal parts. Memorize the principal parts of both verbs.

PRINCIPAL PARTS:	lay	laying	laid	laid
	lie	lying	lay	lain

The next step is to compare the meaning and use of the two verbs. *Lay* usually means "to put (something) down" or "to place (something)." This verb is almost always followed by a direct object.

EXAMPLES: The captain *lays* his map (DO) and glasses (DO) on the desk.

The workers *will be laying* new flooring (DO) in the ship's galley tomorrow.

Lie usually means "to rest in a reclining position." It also can mean "to be situated." This verb is used to show the position of a person, place, or thing. *Lie* is never followed by a direct object.

EXAMPLES: The sailors must *lie* down in narrow bunks.
Pieces of the shattered ship *are lying* in the water.

Pay special attention to one particular area of confusion between *lay* and *lie. Lay* is the present tense of *lay. Lay* is also the past tense of *lie.* The past tense of *lay* is *laid.*

PRESENT TENSE OF LAY: I *lay* the treasure map on the dining room table.

PAST TENSE OF LIE: The sailor *lay* down on his narrow bunk.

PAST TENSE OF LAY: The sailors *laid* their uniforms on their bunks.

◀ **Critical Viewing** Would you *rise* or *raise* the flag above this ship? Would the flag *rise* up or *raise* up when pulled? **[Connect]**

(7) *learn, teach* *Learn* means "to receive knowledge." *Teach* means "to give knowledge." Do not use *learn* in place of *teach.*

INCORRECT: Dan *learned* me how to use a compass.

CORRECT: Dan *taught* me how to use a compass.

(8) *leave, let* *Leave* means "to allow to remain." *Let* means "to permit." Do not reverse the meanings.

INCORRECT: *Leave* me think in peace!
Let the poor dog alone!

CORRECT: *Let* me think in peace!
Leave the poor dog alone!

(9) *raise, rise* *Raise* has several common meanings: "to lift (something) upward," to build (something)," "to grow (something)," "to increase (something)." The verb is usually followed by a direct object.

EXAMPLES: *Raise* the anchor (DO) so we can cast off.
The captain *raised* $3,000 (DO) to finance the voyage.

Rise, on the other hand, is not usually followed by a direct object. This verb means "to get up," "to go up," or "to be increased."

EXAMPLES: The sailors must *rise* before five in the morning.
The waves *rose* and fell, rocking the ship.

(10) *saw, seen* *Seen* is a past participle and can be used as a verb only with a helping verb such as *have* or *has.* Instead of using *seen* without a helping verb, use *saw.* Otherwise, you can add the helping verb before *seen.*

INCORRECT: I *seen* that exhibit on sixteenth-century ships when it was in town last year.

CORRECT: I *saw* that exhibit on sixteenth-century ships when it was in town last year.

(11) *says, said* A common mistake in reporting what someone said is to use *says* (present tense) rather than *said* (past tense).

INCORRECT: The captain turned ghostly white, and then he *says,* "I need to sit down."

CORRECT: The captain turned ghostly white, and then he *said,* "I need to sit down."

(12) *set, sit* The first step in learning to distinguish between *set* and *sit* is to become thoroughly familiar with their principal parts.

PRINCIPAL PARTS:	set	setting	set	set
	sit	sitting	sat	sat

To avoid confusing these two verbs, understand the difference in their meanings. *Set* commonly means "to put (something) in a certain place or position." It is usually followed by a direct object.

EXAMPLES: He *set* (not *sat)* the cup (DO) on the coaster.

They *are setting* the sails (DO) into proper position.

We have *set* the spice plants (DO) safely in the cargo bay.

Sit usually means "to be seated" or "to rest." It is usually not followed by a direct object.

EXAMPLES: The house where the famous explorer was born *sits* (not *sets)* atop that hill.
The mutineers *have been sitting* in a tiny cell for six months.
Mona *sat* on the captain's chair.
The parrot *has sat* on the perch since it learned to speak last year.

Exercise 30 Avoiding Problems With Troublesome Verbs

For each of the following sentences, choose the word in parentheses that supplies the correct verb and write it on your paper.

EXAMPLE: They (did, done) what they wanted to do.
ANSWER: did

1. It (ain't, isn't) often that a person changes our understanding of the world.
2. Christopher Columbus (done, did) just that.
3. Columbus (says, said) to the king and queen of Spain, "I believe the world is round."
4. He begged them to (let, leave) him lead an expedition to find a westward route to Asia.
5. Sailing from Palos, Spain, he (gone, went) west.
6. Before sailing, Columbus's crew (drug, dragged) supplies onto their three ships.
7. They (set, sat) these supplies in the ships' cargo decks.
8. After more than two months at sea, the sailors' hopes (raised, rose) when the lookout (saw, seen) land.
9. Columbus and his crew landed on an island that (lay, laid) in the Caribbean Sea.
10. Although Columbus was thousands of miles away from Asia, where he should (of, have) been, his voyage (learned, taught) other Europeans much about the Western Hemisphere.

Exercise 31 Revising Usage of Troublesome Verbs

Rewrite the paragraph below, correcting errors in verb usage.

(1) History books have learned us many facts about Sir Francis Drake. (2) Much of Drake's fame lays in his having sailed around the world. (3) What he done was amazing. (4) In 1577, sailing from England, Drake had went around the world. (5) After traveling through the Straits of Magellan, which laid off the southern tip of South America, he traveled up the western coast of South America. (6) During that leg of his journey, he seen the Pacific Ocean. (7) When Magellan saw that body of water, he says that it was pacific, or peaceful, so he gave the ocean that name. (8) Drake eventually reached the area near what is now San Francisco and sat his anchor in the water there. (9) Drake raised up early one morning and began sailing even farther west. (10) By the time Drake finally reached England again in 1580, he had drug his crew on an epic voyage for almost three years.

More Practice

Grammar Exercise Workbook
- pp. 133–134

On-line Exercise Bank
- Section 22.3

Go on-line:
PHSchool.com
Enter Web Code:
eck-8002

Get instant feedback! Exercises 30 and 31 are available on-line or on CD-ROM.

Section 22.3 **Section Review**

GRAMMAR EXERCISES 32–37

Exercise 32 **Recognizing Verbs That Use Direct Objects** Write each verb below on your paper. Write *yes* next to each verb that is usually followed by a direct object and *no* next to each one that is *not* usually followed by a direct object.

1. raised
2. laid
3. sat
4. rose
5. lain
6. set
7. lay (past tense)
8. sits
9. lay (present tense)
10. raises

Exercise 33 **Revising to Eliminate Verb Usage Errors** Revise the sentences below, correcting verb usage errors. Write *correct* if the sentence contains no errors.

1. She done a project on explorers.
2. Her interests laid in John Cabot.
3. He was raised in Italy in the mid-1400's.
4. In school, he was learned about mapmaking.
5. In the 1480's, he had went to England to live.
6. Cabot seen reports about Christopher Columbus.
7. He wished he could of sailed along with Columbus.
8. Cabot asked several kings to leave him have a ship.
9. He believed a route to the Indies lay north of where Columbus had sailed.
10. He met with the king of Portugal and says, "I plan to find that route."

Exercise 34 **Supplying Correct Verb Forms** Choose the correct verb in parentheses, and write it on your paper.

1. Cabot (sat, set) his idea before the kings of Portugal and Spain.
2. He (said, says), "I know I can find the Indies and make you rich."
3. Neither king would help him (raise, rise) the funds for the voyage.
4. Somewhat depressed, Cabot (dragged, drug) himself to the king of England.
5. Henry VII said, "(Let, Leave) me think about your plan."
6. Henry (saw, seen) the positive side of Cabot's plan.
7. A few months later, Cabot's English ship (lay, laid) just off the coast of Canada.
8. He became the first European to (sit, set) foot in that part of the world.
9. Although he never reached the Indies, Cabot (did, done) what he said.
10. The wealth of England (raised, rose) as a result of his discoveries.

Exercise 35 **Find It in Your Reading** Look through newspapers and magazines to find sentences in which the troublesome verbs in this section are used correctly.

Exercise 36 **Find It in Your Writing** Look through your writing portfolio. Find examples of sentences in which you have used some of the troublesome verbs in this section. Make certain that you used them correctly.

Exercise 37 **Writing Application** Imagine that you are leading an expedition to an uncharted island in the middle of the Pacific Ocean. Write an entry in your captain's log, describing part of your journey. Try to use some of the troublesome verbs described in this section in your journal entry.

Chapter 23 Using Pronouns

▲ **Critical Viewing** Using the personal pronouns *he, him,* and *his*, describe the stickball action in this photograph. **[Analyze]**

Some pronouns change form according to how they are used. For example, in the sentence "I hit the ball," the pronoun *I* is a subject. However, in "The ball hit me," *I* changes to *me* to show that the pronoun is now a direct object. In "The ball was hit by my stick," the possessive form *my* is used to show ownership. The relation between a pronoun's form and its use is known as its *case*.

This chapter will show you how to use pronouns correctly by making sure that their case fits the way you use them in your sentences.

Diagnostic Test

Directions: Write all answers on a separate sheet of paper.

Skill Check A. Write *nominative*, *objective*, or *possessive* to identify the case of the underlined personal pronoun in each sentence.

1. Many of our children's games are based on rules and routines that are as old as organized society.
2. Some of them have been adapted from ancient ceremonies.
3. Today, we may play games that originated in folk customs.
4. The running, jumping, throwing, and tagging of outdoor games provide us with a form of exercise.
5. Children invent their own versions of such old favorites as hopscotch and hide-and-seek.

Skill Check B. Identify the nominative pronoun(s) in each sentence. Then, tell how each pronoun is used in the sentence.

6. I read that the game of marbles originated long ago.
7. It is played all over the world in many different forms.
8. In one version, a player will shoot a marble, called a shooter, at other marbles in a circle marked on the ground; he or she will win any marbles that are driven out of the circle.
9. It is she who won the most marble games.
10. However, it was he who won the marble tournament.

Skill Check C. Write an objective pronoun to complete each sentence. Then, tell how each pronoun is used in the sentence.

11. Jacks requires special equipment—a small rubber ball and ten or twelve jacks—without __?__ you cannot play the game.
12. After snatching up jacks and catching a bouncing ball, a player must keep __?__ all in his hand in order to win.
13. Jessica and I played jacks at recess. I let __?__ go first.
14. I threw __?__ the ball so that she could begin.
15. The ball fell out of my hand when I fumbled __?__.

Skill Check D. Choose the correct word in parentheses.

16. My friend Josh brought (his, his') ball so we could play stickball.
17. The stick we used for a bat was (ours, our's).
18. (It's, Its) weight and balance are perfect for big hits.
19. (It's, Its) a great game if you have a big group of players.
20. Stella said that pitcher is a favorite position of (her's, hers).

Skill Check E. Use *who* and *whom* correctly to complete each of the following sentences.

21. __?__ wants to play jacks?
22. Josh was the one __?__ she had defeated earlier.
23. Emily was the one __?__ asked to play next.
24. By __?__ was she taught the game?
25. Emily thanked Susan, from __?__ she had learned to play.

Recognizing Cases of Personal Pronouns

In Chapter 14, you learned that personal pronouns can be arranged in three groups: first person, second person, and third person. Pronouns can also be grouped by their *cases*.

KEY CONCEPT English has three cases: *nominative, objective,* and *possessive.* ■

The chart below shows the personal pronouns grouped according to the three cases.

THE THREE CASES OF PERSONAL PRONOUNS	
Nominative Case	Use in a Sentence
I, we you he, she, it, they	subject of a verb predicate pronoun
Objective Case	Use in a Sentence
me, us you him, her, it, them	direct object indirect object object of a preposition
Possessive Case	Use in a Sentence
my, mine, our, ours your, yours his, her, hers, its, their, theirs	to show ownership

Exercise 1 **Identifying Case** Identify the case of each underlined personal pronoun below.

EXAMPLE: Melvin left the marbles for us.
ANSWER: objective

1. John, Ashley, and I played marbles on the playground.
2. We took turns trying to hit our opponents' marbles.
3. John hit my marble on the first try.
4. I gave him my marble because he hit it.
5. Ashley hit her own marble by accident.
6. She didn't win any of our marbles during that round.
7. We decided to play longer so that we could have an extra turn.
8. Everyone wanted to play with us.
9. I let some friends use my marbles.
10. I hope they don't lose them.

Theme: Street and Stoop Games

In this chapter, you will learn about the different cases of pronouns and how to use them correctly in sentences. The examples and exercises are about games you play outdoors.

Cross-Curricular Connection: Physical Education

More Practice

Grammar Exercise Workbook
- pp. 135–138

On-line Exercise Bank
- Chapter 23

Go on-line:
PHSchool.com
Enter Web Code:
eck-8002

The Nominative Case

Personal pronouns in the nominative case have two uses:

KEY CONCEPT Use the nominative case (1) for the subject of a verb and (2) for a predicate pronoun. ■

Note that predicate pronouns follow linking verbs. Pronouns that follow linking verbs should normally be in the nominative case.

SUBJECTS: *She* hopes to be on our team.
With excitement, *they* prepared for the game.

PREDICATE PRONOUNS: It was (LV) *I* who suggested a picnic.
The best players are (LV) *she* and Mark.

People seldom forget to use the nominative case for a pronoun that is used by itself as a subject. Problems sometimes arise, however, when the pronoun is part of a compound subject.

INCORRECT: John and *me* played jacks.

To make sure you are using the correct case of the pronoun in a compound subject, use just the pronoun with the verb in the sentence. *Me played* is obviously wrong, so the nominative case *I* should be used instead.

CORRECT: John and *I* played jacks.

Exercise 2 **Supplying Pronouns in the Nominative Case** Complete each sentence, using a nominative pronoun. Identify how the pronoun is used in the sentence.

EXAMPLE: Gordon and __?__ played hopscotch.
ANSWER: she (subject)

1. Yesterday, my little sister Jessica and __?__ played hopscotch on the sidewalk.
2. It was __?__ who drew the hopscotch board with chalk.
3. __?__ collected rocks to mark our places on the hopscotch board.
4. __?__ kept getting stuck on number six.
5. It was __?__ who finally won the game.

▼ **Critical Viewing** Using the nominative case pronouns *she* and *it,* tell one possible outcome of this game. **[Speculate]**

The Objective Case

Personal pronouns in the objective case have three uses:

KEY CONCEPT Use the objective case (1) for a direct object, (2) for an indirect object, and (3) for the object of a preposition. ■

DIRECT OBJECT: Frank's comment on the game upset *me.*

INDIRECT OBJECT: Tell *her* the good news.

OBJECT OF PREPOSITION: The players swarmed around *me.*

As with the nominative case, people seldom forget to use the objective case for a pronoun that is used by itself as a direct object, indirect object, or object of a preposition. Problems may arise, however, when the pronoun is part of a compound object.

INCORRECT: The players swarmed around Lucy and *I.*

To make sure you are using the correct case of the pronoun in a compound object, use just the pronoun with the rest of the sentence. *The players swarmed around I* is obviously wrong, so the objective case *me* should be used instead.

CORRECT: The players swarmed around Lucy and *me.*

Learn More

For a review of direct and indirect objects and objects of prepositions, you can turn to Chapter 17.

Exercise 3 **Supplying Pronouns in the Objective Case** Complete each sentence below, using an objective pronoun. Then, tell how each pronoun is used in the sentence.

EXAMPLE: His grandmother's old jump rope gave __?__ a clue about her childhood.

ANSWER: him (indirect object)

1. Skipping rope is a good form of exercise. Some athletes use __?__ in their training.
2. My sister loves to jump rope. It gives __?__ a chance to exercise and have fun.
3. My mother gave my friends and __?__ a long jump rope to use for our game.
4. I taught __?__ a rhyme to sing while we jumped.
5. It was hard for some of __?__ to jump and sing at the same time.

More Practice

Grammar Exercise Workbook
- pp. 137–138

On-line Exercise Bank
- Chapter 23

Go on-line: PHSchool.com
Enter Web Code: eck-8002

The Possessive Case

Personal pronouns in the possessive case show ownership of one sort or another.

KEY CONCEPT Use the possessive case of personal pronouns before nouns to show possession. In addition, certain personal pronouns may also be used by themselves to indicate possession. ■

BEFORE NOUNS: The team won *its* game.
Chris held *my* baseball glove.

BY THEMSELVES: Is this marble *yours* or *mine*?
Hers was the best score.

Personal pronouns in the possessive case are never written with an apostrophe. Keep this in mind, especially with possessive pronouns that end in *s*.

INCORRECT: These seats are *our's*, not *their's*.

CORRECT: These seats are *ours*, not *theirs*.

When the pronoun *it* is followed by an apostrophe and an *s*, it becomes a contraction of *it is*. The possessive pronoun *its* does not have an apostrophe.

CONTRACTION: *It's* going to rain.

POSSESSIVE PRONOUN: The team loved *its* uniforms.

Keep in mind the two homonyms of the word *their*: *Their* is used to show possession. *There* normally refers to a place. *They're* is a contraction of *they are*.

Exercise 4 **Using Pronouns in the Possessive Case** Choose the correct word from the pair in parentheses to complete each sentence.

EXAMPLE: Fortunately, the lost ball was not (our's, ours).
ANSWER: ours

1. Jake and I love playing box ball with our friends after school. Yesterday, it was (his, his') turn to host the game.
2. Jake's family has a great concrete surface in (their, theirs) backyard on which we can play.
3. (Its, It's) surface is very smooth.
4. The chalk we used to draw the box for the game is (my, mine).
5. The ball we played with is (our's, ours).

More Practice

Grammar Exercise Workbook
- pp. 139–140

On-line Exercise Bank
- Chapter 23

Go on-line: PHSchool.com
Enter Web Code: eck-8002

Get instant feedback! Exercises 3 and 4 are available on-line or on CD-ROM.

GRAMMAR IN LITERATURE

from Baseball

Lionel G. García

Notice how the author has used pronouns in all three cases in this passage.

My uncle Adolfo, who had pitched for the Yankees and the Cardinals in the majors, had given *us* the ball several years before. Once when *he* returned for a visit, *he* saw *us* playing from across the street and walked over to ask *us* what *we* were doing.

▼ **Critical Viewing** Use *it* and *its* in a sentence describing the distinctive features of a baseball. **[Analyze]**

Exercise 5 **Revising to Correct the Case of Personal Pronouns** Some of the underlined pronouns in the following sentences are incorrect. On your paper, revise each sentence that contains an error. If the pronoun is used correctly, write *correct.*

EXAMPLE: We played HORSE with Jeremy and he.
ANSWER: We played HORSE with Jeremy and him.

1. HORSE is a game that is often played by my friend and I on the basketball court.
2. Jesse, Tara, and me like to play the game.
3. It's rules are not difficult.
4. A player who misses a difficult shot that someone else has already made is given a letter in the word *HORSE*. After a player has five misses, he or she is eliminated.
5. Them and me try to get each other out by setting up shots that are difficult to make.
6. Tara gave Jesse and I an "H" when we couldn't make over-the-shoulder shots.
7. It was her who spelled HORSE first and had to sit out.
8. Jesse and I both had "H-O-R-S."
9. He shot over his head and made it.
10. When I missed the shot and got an "E," the winner was him.

More Practice

Grammar Exercise Workbook
- pp. 135–140

On-line Exercise Bank
- Chapter 23

Go on-line: PHSchool.com *Enter Web Code:* eck-8002

Get instant feedback! Exercise 5 is available on-line or on CD-ROM.

Cases of *Who* and *Whom* The pronouns *who* and *whom* are often confused. *Who* is a nominative case pronoun, and *whom* is an objective case pronoun. *Who* and *whom* have two common uses in sentences: They can be used in questions or to begin subordinate clauses in complex sentences.

Learn More

To learn more about subordinate clauses, turn to Chapter 20.

KEY CONCEPTS Use *who* for the subject of a verb. Use *whom* (1) for the direct object of a verb and (2) for the object of a preposition. ■

You will often find *who* used as the subject of a question.

SUBJECT IN A QUESTION:	*Who* hit the most home runs?

Who may also be used as the subject of a subordinate clause in a complex sentence.

SUBJECT IN A SUBORDINATE CLAUSE:	I admire the player *who* hit the most home runs.

In the example above, *who* is part of an adjective clause—*who hit the most home runs.* Within the clause itself, *who* is the subject of the verb *hit.*

The following examples show *whom* used in questions.

DIRECT OBJECT:	*Whom* did he see at the game?
OBJECT OF PREPOSITION:	From *whom* is she getting the new softball?

Questions that include *whom* will generally be in inverted word order. If you reword the first example in normal word order, you will see that *whom* is the direct object of the verb *did see: He did see whom at the game.* In the second example, it is easy to see that *whom* is the object of the preposition *from.* Again, rewording may help: *She is getting the new softball from whom.*

Rewording is also useful when *whom* is part of a subordinate clause. A subordinate clause that should begin with *whom* will always be in inverted word order. To check whether you have used the correct case of the pronoun, isolate the clause and put it into normal word order.

INVERTED ORDER:	I know the person *whom* he met at the game.
REWORDED ORDER:	He met *whom* at the game.
INVERTED ORDER:	Janet thanked her aunt, from *whom* she had received a ball.
REWORDED ORDER:	She had received a ball from *whom.*

◀ **Critical Viewing** Using *who* and *whom*, ask two questions about what is happening in this photograph. **[Question]**

Exercise 6 **Using *Who* and *Whom* in Questions** For each of the following sentences, choose the correct pronoun from the pair given in parentheses.

EXAMPLE: (Who, Whom) did you invite to play stickball?
ANSWER: Whom

1. We are going to play stickball in the street. (Who, Whom) would like to play first base?
2. The best pitcher would be (who, whom)?
3. (Who, Whom) would you like to be catcher?
4. (Who, Whom) were you thinking about as shortstop?
5. Of those remaining, (who, whom) will be playing outfield?
6. (Who, Whom) is setting up the batting order?
7. The stick and the ball are being brought by (who, whom)?
8. Our parents asked, "With (who, whom) are you playing?"
9. (Who, Whom) made the first out?
10. The first run was scored by (who, whom)?

Grammar and Style Tip

One way to know when to use *who* or *whom* is to substitute the pronoun *him*. If the sentence is correct using *him*, you can safely use *whom*; if not, use *who*.

Exercise 7 **Revising to Correct *Who* and *Whom* in Subordinate Clauses** Revise the sentences below in which *who* or *whom* is used incorrectly. Then, indicate how *who* or *whom* is used in each sentence.

EXAMPLE: Let's decide whom will start the game.
ANSWER: Let's decide who will start the game. (subject)

1. To play Kick the Can, the group must make a decision about whom will be counting.
2. Everyone else must hide from the person who is counting.
3. It was Tom who we caught hiding behind the car.
4. Tara was the one from whom he was running.
5. We know whom will count next time.
6. The boy who was hiding behind the tree kicked the can.
7. Who did he chase?
8. I wasn't the one to whom he called out.
9. Is Helen the one whom was chosen to be the counter?
10. Now we've lost track of whom goes next.

More Practice

Grammar Exercise Workbook
- pp. 140–141

On-line Exercise Bank
- Chapter 23

Go on-line:
PHSchool.com
Enter Web Code:
eck-8002

Hands-on Grammar

Nominative Case Pronouns Two-Way Reader

Make a two-way reader to help you practice using pronouns in the nominative case correctly. Cut a sheet of 6 1/2" x 8 1/2" paper to make a strip that is 6 1/2" x 5". Fold in each side edge 1 3/4", leaving a space of about 1 1/2" wide in the middle. Next, use a ruler to draw eight lines across the paper at 3/4" intervals and a vertical line along each folded edge. Then, open the folds, finish drawing the lines on the inside from crease to crease, and refold the edges. On the lines down the middle section, print eight of the following pronouns: *I, he, it, they, he and she, he and I, you, she, we, you and I, we,* and *they.*

Next, on the outside of the left fold, write a question on each line that might be answered by the pronoun facing it in the middle. Examples: *Who is the boss? I. Who were my friends?* Then, cut the lines as far as the fold on each side, creating a double "fringe." Inside the fold on the left, write each answer so that the pronoun becomes a predicate pronoun; on the right, write the answer so that the pronoun is the subject. Examples: *The boss is I am the boss. My friends were* he and she *were my friends.* The illustration below shows the you part of a reader.

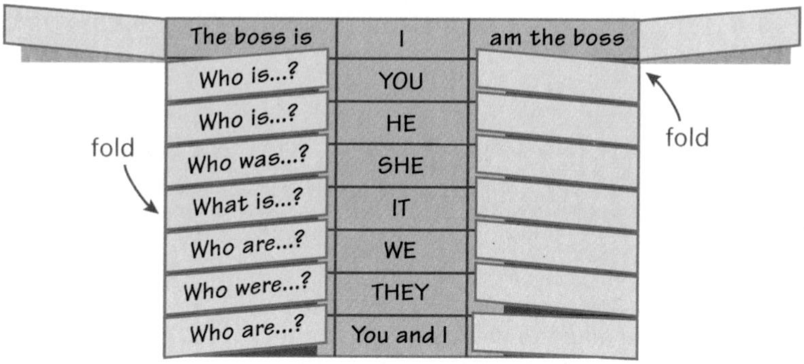

Finally, with a partner, practice answering the questions on the other person's two-way reader. Check under each piece of "fringe" to see if you are correct. Practice reading aloud in order to accustom yourselves to hearing the correct usage of nominative pronouns, especially when they are compound subjects or predicate nouns.

Find It in Your Reading Read a biographical sketch in your literature book or a magazine. Note the number of pronouns in the three cases.

Find It in Your Writing Review a piece of your autobiographical writing, and check to see that you have used all personal pronouns correctly. Correct those that are in the wrong case.

Chapter 24

Making Words Agree

A B-17 bomber with a fighter escort flies in formation during a World War II mission.

Subjects and verbs work together in sentences. For example, you would never say, *"I are going* to write a report about World War II," or *"Am you going* to class today?" You would hear that something is wrong with these sentences. The problem is that the subjects and verbs do not *agree*.

In most of the sentences you speak and write, you automatically make subjects and verbs agree. In some sentences, however, the mind can be tricked into making the verb agree with a word that is not the subject of the sentence. In such a case, check to find the real subject and make sure it agrees with its verb.

Pronouns, too, must agree with the words they replace, their *antecedents*. This chapter will explain the importance of agreement and will give you practice making the parts of sentences work together.

▲ Critical Viewing Think of two sentences about this picture—one that describes what all of the planes are doing and one that describes what only one of the planes is doing. How do your verbs change when the number of the subject changes? **[Analyze]**

Diagnostic Test

Directions: Write all answers on a separate sheet of paper.

Skill Check A. Choose the verb in parentheses that agrees with the subject of each sentence.

1. World War II (was, were) a conflict that took place from 1939 to 1945.
2. The leader of Allied forces during World War II (was, were) Dwight Eisenhower.
3. My classmates (tells, tell) me that Eisenhower led troops in both Africa and Europe.
4. Either Germany or Italy (was, were) the main Axis power.
5. Spain and Portugal (was, were) neutral during World War II.
6. Not until later in the war (was, were) the Axis powers joined by Japan.
7. Japan and its allies (was, were) hoping to gain control of the Pacific region.
8. On Memorial Day, veterans of World War II (is, are) honored.
9. A Memorial Day parade in many towns (features, feature) veterans who fought in wars throughout the twentieth century.
10. (Where's, Where are) the beautiful floats we came to see?
11. Most of the children in town (looks, look) forward to the Memorial Day parade.
12. Each of the veterans (is, are) asked to participate.
13. Neither my neighbor nor her children (wants, want) to miss the parade.
14. Neither rain showers nor cool weather (halts, halt) the parade.
15. Marching in the parade (is, are) bands from all over the state.

Skill Check B. Choose the correct pronoun in each sentence.

16. My grandfather was sent along with (his, their) unit to fight in Europe during World War II.
17. Each person at home wrote to (his or her, their) relatives overseas.
18. Almost every woman whose husband was fighting overseas had (her, their) own deep worries about (his, their) survival.
19. Grandmother and other women worked at a munitions factory to support (her, their) families.
20. Everyone in the family tried to do (his or her, their) part to help the troops who were fighting overseas.
21. If a person had a special skill (you, he or she) used it.
22. Mother and her sister spent (her, their) free time knitting socks for soldiers.
23. Many did (his or her, their) part by collecting old pots and pans for scrap metal.
24. All who could tried (his or her, their) best to help.
25. Each of the women my grandmother knew seemed to contribute (her, his or her, their) time in a selfless way.

Section 24.1

Subject and Verb Agreement

Subject and verb agreement has one main rule:

KEY CONCEPT A verb must agree with its subject in number. ■

In grammar, the concept of *number* is simple. The number of a word can be either *singular* or *plural.* A singular word indicates *one.* A plural word indicates *more than one.* Only nouns, pronouns, and verbs have number.

Recognizing the Number of Nouns and Pronouns

The difference between the singular and plural forms of most nouns and pronouns is easy to recognize. Compare the singular and plural forms of the nouns below:

NOUNS	
Singular	**Plural**
soldier	soldiers
bus	buses
child	children
goose	geese

Most nouns are made plural by adding *-s* or *-es* to the singular form (soldier*s*, bus*es*). Some nouns become plural in other ways (child*ren*, g*ee*se).

Section 14.2 and Chapter 23 list the singular and plural forms of the various kinds of pronouns. For example, *I, he, she, it, this,* and *anyone* are singular; *we, they, these,* and *both* are plural; and *you, who,* and *some* can be either singular or plural.

Being able to recognize the number of nouns and pronouns will help you to determine whether a subject is singular or plural.

Theme: World War II

In this section, you will learn to make verbs agree in number with their subjects. The examples and exercises are about events that occurred during World War II.

Cross-Curricular Connection: Social Studies

▲ Critical Viewing Identify some items in the picture that are singular and some that are plural. **[Identify]**

Exercise 1 **Recognizing the Number of Nouns and Pronouns** On your paper, label each of the following words *singular* or *plural.*

EXAMPLE: mice (plural)

1. war
2. we
3. armies
4. nation
5. they
6. he
7. it
8. us
9. men
10. these

Recognizing the Number of Verbs

As shown in the conjugations in Section 22.2, verbs have many forms to indicate tense. Few of these forms cause problems in agreement because most of them can be used with either singular or plural subjects (I *go*, we *go;* he *ran*, they *ran*). Problems involving the number of verbs usually occur only with third-person forms in the present tense and with forms of *be.*

The following chart shows all the basic forms of two different verbs—*send* and *go*—in the present tense.

SINGULAR AND PLURAL VERBS IN THE PRESENT TENSE		
Singular		Plural
First and Second Person	**Third Person**	**First, Second, and Third Person**
(I, you) send (I, you) go	(he, she, it) sends (he, she, it) goes	(we, you, they) send (we, you, they) go

Notice that the verb form changes only in the third-person singular column, where an *-s* or *-es* is added to the verb. Unlike nouns, which usually become *plural* when *-s* or *-es* is added, verbs with *-s* or *-es* added to them are singular.

The helping verb *be* may also indicate whether a verb is singular or plural. The following chart shows only those forms of the verb *be* that are always singular.

FORMS OF THE HELPING VERB *BE* THAT ARE ALWAYS SINGULAR			
am	is	was	has been

Get instant feedback! Exercises 1 and 2 are available on-line or on CD-ROM.

Exercise 2 **Recognizing the Number of Verbs** For each of the following items, choose the verb in parentheses that agrees in number with the pronoun. After each answer, write whether the verb is singular or plural.

EXAMPLE: he (begin, begins)
ANSWER: begins (singular)

1. she (leads, lead)
2. we (retreats, retreat)
3. they (was, were)
4. I (is, am)
5. it (flies, fly)

More Practice

Grammar Exercise Workbook
- pp. 143–144

On-line Exercise Bank
- Section 24.1

Go on-line: PHSchool.com
Enter Web Code: eck-8002

Making Verbs Agree With Singular and Plural Subjects

To check subject-verb agreement, determine the number of the subject. Then, make sure the verb has the same number.

KEY CONCEPT A singular subject must have a singular verb. A plural subject must have a plural verb. ■

In the following examples, the subjects are underlined once and the verbs are underlined twice.

SINGULAR SUBJECT AND VERB: Larry always volunteers to fight in the front line.

PLURAL SUBJECT AND VERB: Those soldiers never arrive on time. According to the announcements, both planes are preparing to land.

KEY CONCEPT A prepositional phrase that comes between a subject and its verb does *not* affect subject-verb agreement. ■

In the following examples, the subject is *poster,* and the word *planes* is the object of the preposition *of.* Because *poster* is singular, the plural verb *fill* does not agree with it.

INCORRECT: The poster of combat planes fill the wall.

CORRECT: The poster of combat planes fills the wall.

Exercise 3 **Making Verbs Agree With Singular and Plural Subjects** For each of the following sentences, choose the correct verb in parentheses, and write it on your paper.

EXAMPLE: The books on the shelf (is, are) about World War II.

ANSWER: are

1. At conferences, historians (discusses, discuss) how World War II began.
2. The causes and effects of World War II (is, are) the focus of our social studies class.
3. When children in elementary school (learns, learn) about war, the subject may frighten them.
4. The date, September 1, 1939, (marks, mark) the start of World War II.
5. Once Germany (invades, invade) Poland on that date, several European countries (declares, declare) war on Germany.

More Practice

Grammar Exercise Workbook
- pp. 145–148

On-line Exercise Bank
- Section 24.1

Go on-line: PHSchool.com *Enter Web Code:* eck-8002

Get instant feedback! Exercises 3 and 4 are available on-line or on CD-ROM.

Making Verbs Agree With Compound Subjects

A compound subject is two or more subjects that are joined by a conjunction, usually *and*, *or*, or *nor*.

KEY CONCEPT A compound subject joined by *and* is usually plural and must have a plural verb. Exceptions occur when the parts of the compound subject equal one thing or when the word *each* or *every* is used before the compound subject. ■

EXAMPLES: The soldier and the sergeant are ready for combat.
Franks and beans is a popular army dish.
Every soldier and sergeant is ready for combat.

KEY CONCEPT Two or more singular subjects joined by *or* or *nor* must have a singular verb. ■

EXAMPLE: Either Alice *or* Mike is going to help us study.

In the example, *or* joins two singular subjects. Although two names make up the compound subject, the subject does not take a plural verb. Either Alice or Mike will help us study, not both of them.

Exercise 4 Making Verbs Agree With Compound Subjects

On your paper, write the correct verb from each pair in parentheses.

EXAMPLE: Every plane and tank (has, have) been inspected.
ANSWER: has

1. During World War II, Europe and the Pacific (was, were) the two main theaters of war.
2. Any soldier or civilian who (was, were) involved in the war often faced a life-threatening situation.
3. Either Belgium or Holland (was, were) chosen by the Germans for an early attack.
4. Because their grandparents fought in World War II, Carl and Robert (has, have) conducted interviews with them.
5. Each girl and boy in my class (agrees, agree) that civilians in Europe suffered terribly during World War II.

A memorial to the brave Marines who raised the flag on Iwo Jima.

▲ **Critical Viewing** Based on the picture, complete two sentences that begin: *All of the Marines . . .* and *Each of the Marines . . .* Which sentence needs a singular verb, and which needs a plural verb? **[Analyze]**

One situation that sometimes causes confusion involves a compound subject in which a singular subject and a plural subject are joined by *or* or *nor*. In that situation, the verb agrees in number with the subject that is closer to it.

KEY CONCEPT When singular and plural subjects are joined by *or* or *nor*, the verb must agree with the subject closer to the verb. ■

SINGULAR SUBJECT CLOSER:	Neither the students nor their teacher has seen the World War II film.
PLURAL SUBJECT CLOSER:	Neither the teacher nor the students have seen the World War II film.

Exercise 5 **Recognizing Subjects and Verbs That Agree** For each of the following sentences, choose the correct verb in parentheses, and write it on your paper.

1. Either D-Day or the Battle of Stalingrad (was, were) a key to Germany's military downfall.
2. Marines and paratroopers from the United States (was, were) landing in France on D-Day in 1944.
3. Neither Emily nor her sisters (knows, know) much about the Battle of Stalingrad in 1942.
4. Emily, her sister, and her father (was, were) looking for books on World War II at the library.
5. They read that fish and chips (was, were) a favorite of many American soldiers based in England during the war.

Exercise 6 **Revising for Subject-Verb Agreement** On your paper, revise the paragraph below so that each verb agrees with its subject. Some sentences may be correct.

We students and our teacher is reading about Nazi Germany this term. Either Emily or Sharon have been assigned to do a report on Adolf Hitler. They learned that neither Great Britain nor its allies were willing to stop Hitler from taking over Austria and Czechoslovakia in 1938. Hitler and Benito Mussolini in Italy was hoping to take over all of Europe. Every act and order of the two dictators were designed to further that goal. The Nazi army and air force was set to attack Poland on September 1, 1939. Either Great Britain or France were planning to declare war on Germany should the attack take place. Neither Hitler nor his generals was concerned. The generals and Hitler were certain that Germany would be victorious. Within months, Great Britain and France was facing their own attacks by German forces.

Checking for Problems With Subject-Verb Agreement

Agreement in Inverted Sentences

In most sentences, the subject comes before the verb. Sometimes, however, this order is inverted, or turned around.

KEY CONCEPT When a subject comes after the verb, the subject and verb still must agree with each other in number. ■

In the following example, the plural verb *were* agrees with the plural subject *soldiers*. The singular noun *shore* is the object of a preposition.

EXAMPLE: Waiting along the shore were many nervous soldiers.

Sentences beginning with *there* or *here* are nearly always in inverted word order. Many questions are in inverted word order, such as, "Where's the newspaper?" Also, note that the contractions *there's* and *here's* contain the singular verb *is*: *there is, here is*. Do not use these contractions with plural subjects.

EXAMPLES: There were many soldiers waiting along the shore.
Here's the relief unit that we were promised.
Where are the relief units you promised me?
Here are the relief units I promised you.

▼ **Critical Viewing** Think of three question about this memorial. What is the subject and verb in each question? Do they agree with each other in number? **[Analyze]**

USS *Arizona* Memorial at Pearl Harbor in Hawaii

Exercise 7 **Checking Agreement in Sentences with Inverted Word Order** Write the subject of each sentence below. Then, choose the correct verb in parentheses, and write it next to the subject.

EXAMPLE: There (is, are) the enemy troops.
ANSWER: troops (are)

1. It is December 7, 1941, and there (is, are) a surprise attack on Pearl Harbor, Hawaii.
2. Beyond the horizon (looms, loom) 350 Japanese airplanes.
3. Docked at Pearl Harbor (is, are) the U.S. Pacific fleet.
4. Many Americans ask themselves, "Why (is, are) Japan attacking the United States?"
5. Today, there (is, are) various memorials commemorating the bombing of Pearl Harbor.

More Practice

Grammar Exercise Workbook
- pp. 149–150

On-line Exercise Bank
- Section 24.1

Go on-line:
PHSchool.com
Enter Web Code:
eck-8002

Agreement With Indefinite Pronouns

When used as subjects, indefinite pronouns can also cause problems.

KEY CONCEPT Either a singular verb or a plural verb can agree with an indefinite pronoun, depending on the pronoun's form and meaning. ■

Look again at the list of indefinite pronouns in Section 14.2. Some of the pronouns are always singular. Included here are those ending in *-one* (*anyone, everyone, someone*), those ending in *-body* (*anybody, everybody, somebody*), and those that imply one (*each, either, every*). Other indefinite pronouns are always plural: *both, few, many, others,* and *several.* A few can be either singular or plural: *all, any, more, most, none, some.*

ALWAYS SINGULAR:	One of the submarines is equipped with radar. Everybody on the submarine was frightened by thoughts of attack. Neither of the strategies seems workable.
ALWAYS PLURAL:	Many of the soldiers are fighting on the war's front lines. Others are working to supply them with food and ammunition. Several contribute by working as code breakers.
EITHER SINGULAR OR PLURAL:	Most of the war has been fought. Most of the battles have been fought.

Exercise 8 **Checking Agreement With Indefinite Pronouns** For each of the following sentences, choose the correct verb in parentheses, and write it on your paper.

EXAMPLE: All of the flags on the battleship (was, were) waving in the wind.

ANSWER: were

1. Many of the ships that crossed the Atlantic Ocean during World War II (was, were) filled with supplies.
2. Most of the vessels (was, were) carrying vital supplies from the United States to Great Britain.
3. Everyone (hopes, hope) that the ships get to their destinations safely.
4. Several (is, are) sunk by German submarines, called U-boats.
5. Some (reaches, reach) Britain to deliver their cargoes.

Section 24.1

Section Review

GRAMMAR EXERCISES 9–14

Exercise 9 **Choosing the Verb That Agrees With Its Subject** For each sentence below, choose the correct verb in parentheses, and write it on your paper. After each answer, write whether the subject and verb are singular or plural.

1. During World War II, U.S. troops in the Pacific (is, are) locked in battle with Japanese troops.
2. There (is, are) new strategies developed by U.S. leaders, such as *island hopping.*
3. An island or group of islands controlled by the Japanese (is, are) selected for attack.
4. Only key islands (is, are) captured to be used as steppingstones for U.S. troops to "hop" to the next island.
5. Over a period of two years, either island hopping or other strategies (is, are) used by the United States to gain control of the Pacific.

Exercise 10 **Revising Verbs to Agree With Compound Subjects** Revise the sentences below so that each verb agrees with its subject. If a sentence is correct, write *correct.*

1. Sam and his brothers has always wondered why Nazi Germany carried out the Holocaust.
2. Neither his mother nor his father have been able to explain the tragic events.
3. Perhaps callousness or fear are to blame, they suggested.
4. Sam read a story in which a mother and her child was executed by Nazi troops.
5. Neither the story nor a movie that Sam later saw adequately describes the horrors suffered by concentration camp victims.

Exercise 11 **Revising to Eliminate Special Problems in Agreement** Revise the sentences below so that each verb agrees with its subject. If a sentence is correct, write *correct.*

1. Many who come to Amsterdam visits the Anne Frank House.
2. There are visitors to the house who do not know about the Franks' life there.
3. Invading Nazis were hunting down Jews in Holland, and most was forced to leave their homes.
4. Nearly every one of the captured Jews were sent to a concentration camp.
5. Everyone visiting the museum learn that Anne Frank's family was forced to leave their home to go into hiding.

Exercise 12 **Find It in Your Reading** Find one singular indefinite pronoun and one plural indefinite pronoun in this excerpt from *The Diary of Anne Frank.* List each pronoun and the verb it takes.

> *Everyone is listening, hardly breathing.* MR. FRANK *starts quietly down the steps to the door.* DUSSEL *and* PETER *follow him. The others stand rigid, waiting, terrified.*

Exercise 13 **Find It in Your Writing** Choose a piece of writing from your portfolio. Copy five of the sentences. Circle the subjects and verbs, and label them *singular* or *plural.* Rewrite any sentences in which the subject and verb do not agree.

Exercise 14 **Writing Application** Write a paragraph about a book, television program, or film that deals with a war. Include several sentences with compound subjects joined by *or* or *nor.*

Section 24.2

Agreement Between Pronouns and Antecedents

Making Personal Pronouns and Antecedents Agree

An antecedent is the word or group of words for which a pronoun stands. Sometimes, a pronoun's antecedent is a single noun. At other times, the antecedent is a group of words acting as a noun or even another pronoun.

Personal pronouns should agree with their antecedents in two ways—person and number.

KEY CONCEPT A personal pronoun must agree with its antecedent in both person and number. ■

Person indicates whether a pronoun refers to the person speaking (first person), the person spoken to (second person), or the person, place, or thing spoken about (third person). *Number* indicates whether a pronoun is singular or plural.

EXAMPLE: *Lisa* presented *her* report on careers in firefighting to the class yesterday.

In the example, the pronoun *her* is third person and singular. It agrees with its antecedent *Lisa*, which is also third person and singular.

Exercise 15 Making Pronouns and Antecedents Agree

Rewrite each of the following sentences, filling in the blank with an appropriate pronoun. Draw an arrow from the pronoun to its antecedent.

EXAMPLE: Sometimes, a fire seems to have a life of __?__ own.

ANSWER: Sometimes, a fire seems to have a life of its own.

1. The students are going on __?__ first trip to the fire station.
2. Julia and Sara brought __?__ notebooks on the trip.
3. Sam remembered to bring __?__ lunch money.
4. The class listened as the firefighters explained how __?__ use special equipment to put out fires.
5. Each piece of equipment has __?__ own special function.

Theme: Dangerous Occupations

In this section, you will learn how to make pronouns agree with their antecedents in number and person. The examples and exercises are about jobs that can be dangerous.

Cross-Curricular Connection: Social Studies

▼ Critical Viewing Think of a sentence about this picture that includes the words *firefighters, fire, it,* and *them.* What is the number and person of each pronoun and antecedent? **[Analyze; Identify]**

Avoiding Shifts in Person A common error in agreement occurs when a personal pronoun does not have the same person as its antecedent. This error usually involves the careless use of *you* with a noun in the third person.

INCORRECT: *Alexander* is practicing climbing, a skill *you* need to master if *you* want to be a firefighter.

CORRECT: *Alexander* is practicing climbing, a skill *he* needs to master if *he* wants to be a firefighter.

▲ **Critical Viewing** If you shift the subject of a sentence about this picture from *fire-fighter* to *firefighters,* how does that affect a pronoun that stands for the subject later in the sentence? **[Infer]**

KEY CONCEPT Use a singular personal pronoun to refer to two or more singular antecedents joined by *or* or *nor.* ■

Two or more singular antecedents joined by *or* or *nor* must have a singular pronoun, just as they must have a singular verb. When a compound antecedent is joined by *and*, a plural personal pronoun is used.

EXAMPLES: Either *Bob* or *Jim* is bringing *his* camera to the fire station.
Andrea and *Jane* brought *their* helmets.

Exercise 16 Revising to Avoid Shifts in Person and Number Revise each sentence below to correct an error in pronoun-antecedent agreement. Underline the pronoun that you have substituted and its antecedent.

EXAMPLE: Bill wants to know where you can go to study to become a police officer.

ANSWER: Bill wants to know where he can go to study to become a police officer.

1. A police officer is highly trained to perform their duties.
2. Neither Caroline nor Jessica has decided whether they will become a police officer.
3. Both Andrew and Matthew think that he can become law enforcement officials.
4. Jim found out that to become a police officer you must be eighteen.
5. Each police agency has their own age and education requirements.

More Practice

Grammar Exercise Workbook
- pp. 151–152

On-line Exercise Bank
- Section 24.2

Go on-line:
PHSchool.com
Enter Web Code:
eck-8002

Making Personal Pronouns and Indefinite Pronouns Agree

Indefinite pronouns (listed in Section 14.2) are words such as *each, everyone, neither,* and *one.* Pay special attention to the number of a personal pronoun when the antecedent is a singular indefinite pronoun.

KEY CONCEPT Generally, use a singular personal pronoun when its antecedent is a singular indefinite pronoun. ■

In making a personal pronoun agree with an indefinite pronoun, ignore the object of any prepositional phrase that might fall between them. In the two incorrect examples below, the pronoun *their* mistakenly agrees with *EMTs* and *instruments* rather than the singular indefinite pronouns *neither* and *each.*

INCORRECT: *Neither* of the EMTs has completed *their* training.
Put each of the instruments in *their* place.

CORRECT: *Neither* of the EMTs has completed *her* training.
Put each of the instruments in *its* place.

You may use one of three methods to make pronouns agree when you don't know the gender of the antecedent. Traditionally, the masculine pronouns *he* and *his* have been used to stand for both males and females. Now, using *he or she* and *him or her* is preferred. If those seem awkward, you may rewrite the sentence.

EXAMPLES: Each of the crew members checked *his* equipment.
Each of the crew members checked *his or her* equipment.
All of the crew members checked *their* equipment.

Exercise 17 Making Personal Pronouns and Indefinite Pronouns Agree For each of the following sentences, select the correct pronoun in parentheses, and write it on your paper.

EXAMPLE: Each of the students has (his or her, their) own first-aid kit.

ANSWER: his or her

1. All of us can give some of (our, their) time to volunteering.
2. One of my friends volunteers (his, their) time to work on the ambulance squad.
3. Each squad has openings on (their, its) night shift.
4. Every emergency medical technician (EMT) needs to use (his or her, their) skills to save lives.
5. Only one of the EMTs had (his or her, their) driver's license.

▲ **Critical Viewing** Identify an antecedent in the picture to agree with each of these pronouns: *his, her, its,* and *their.* **[Identify]**

Exercise 18 Revising for Agreement Between Pronouns and Antecedents Rewrite the sentences below that contain errors in pronoun-antecedent agreement. If a sentence contains no errror, write *correct.*

EXAMPLE: Neither of the girls told their parents of their desire to be an astronaut.

ANSWER: Neither of the girls told her parents of her desire to be an astronaut.

1. Max is learning skills that you need to be an astronaut.
2. Some of my friends wrote to NASA in his spare time to find out how to become an astronaut.
3. Many astronauts began their careers in the military.
4. Either civilians or military personnel may begin his or her training while in college.
5. Every astronaut spends most of their time on the ground.
6. The space shuttle offers their crew the latest technology.
7. Before a shuttle mission, an astronaut will practice at least one of his or her maneuvers underwater.
8. Either Pam or Sally wants to spend their life flying in space.
9. One of Pam's parents is reluctant to give their support to the decision.
10. Few fathers and mothers would willingly allow his or her daughters to fly into space.

Hands-on Grammar

Pronoun Memory Game

To practice identifying which personal pronouns agree with which indefinite pronouns, create a pronoun memory game. Write each of the following *indefinite* pronouns on its own index card: *each, all,* and *both.* Make two additional sets of indefinite pronoun cards. Then, create three cards with the pronoun pair *his or her.* Create three cards that say *their.* Finally, create three cards that say *its* and *their* on the same card. Turn all the cards face down.

As you would in the game Memory, alternate with other players in turning over two cards to show the words listed. If you turn over an indefinite pronoun and a personal pronoun that agree in number, you can keep the pair. Cards with indefinite pronouns that can be singular or plural count as agreeing only with cards that show both *its* and *their.* (If you allow them to agree with cards that have only singular or only plural pronouns, you will run out of matches before you run out of cards.) Use the chart on page 206 to check that you and the other players are correctly identifying the number of each indefinite pronoun.

their	both	all
each	his or her	its their

Find It in Your Reading In your reading, find examples of sentences that contain indefinite pronouns used as subjects. Write the sentences on your paper, and indicate whether the pronouns are singular or plural.

Find It in Your Writing Write sentences using the pairs matched during the game. (Choose from among all the pairs, not just the ones you matched.) Ask your teacher to check that you are correctly using indefinite and personal pronouns that agree.

Section 24.2 **Section Review**

GRAMMAR EXERCISES 19–24

Exercise 19 **Supplying Pronouns That Agree With Antecedents** Rewrite each of the following sentences, filling in the blank with an appropriate pronoun.

1. Wilderness firefighters spend __?__ time fighting forest fires.
2. Each of these firefighters must be aware of the dangers __?__ faces.
3. All learn the importance of working closely with __?__ team members.
4. John told __?__ parents that he is planning to study firefighting.
5. John's parents responded to __?__ son's statement by wishing him luck.
6. Rachel said that in __?__ opinion, smoke jumping is very dangerous.
7. Smoke jumpers perform __?__ duties by parachuting near a forest fire.
8. Despite the dangers, Rachel says that smoke jumping is __?__ chosen career.
9. Neither John nor Rachel feels uncertain about __?__ career choice.
10. Both plan to enter __?__ careers after receiving __?__ college diplomas.

Exercise 20 **Revising to Eliminate Shifts in Person and Number** Rewrite the sentences below, correcting any errors in pronoun-antecedent agreement.

1. Henry wants to study biology because that is a subject you need to know to become a paramedic.
2. An ambulance is equipped with all of the supplies their staff needs.
3. Sometimes ambulances are stationed near an area where it might be needed.
4. In some crowded cities, a paramedic drives a specially equipped motorcycle to reach their destination quickly.
5. For accidents that occur at sea, a paramedic uses marine ambulances to rush their equipment to the scene.

Exercise 21 **Revising to Eliminate Problems in Pronoun-Antecedent Agreement** Rewrite the paragraph below, correcting problems in pronoun-antecedent agreement.

(1) Sarah, one of my friends, is considering police work as their profession. (2) She and her sister have submitted her applications for the police academy. (3) Either hopes they will join a SWAT team in the future. (4) The girls know so much about police work because her uncle is a police officer. (5) Sarah has been working out in the gym because you have to pass a physical test to get into the police academy.

Exercise 22 **Find It in Your Reading** Identify the antecedents for *they'll* and *them* in this excerpt from *The Diary of Anne Frank*.

> ". . . he'll make a bargain with the Green Police . . . if they'll let him off, he'll tell them where some Jews are hiding!"

Exercise 23 **Find It in Your Writing** Choose a piece of writing from your portfolio that contains personal or indefinite pronouns. Underline the pronouns and antecedents, and correct any mistakes in person or number.

Exercise 24 **Writing Application** Write a paragraph about people who have difficult jobs. Try to include at least two personal and two indefinite pronouns in your writing. Make sure the pronouns agree with their antecedents.

Chapter 25

Using Modifiers

▲ **Critical Viewing** Use adjectives and adverbs to compare the two ships in this photograph. **[Describe]**

Shipwrecks and other disasters are major events that leave their mark on the people who experience them. When people speak about such events, they may use descriptive words, such as *horrible* and *violently*, to convey their emotions. These words are adjectives and adverbs.

Adjectives and **adverbs** can be used to compare two or more people, places, or things that share the same basic qualities. These two parts of speech have different forms, or degrees, depending on the kind of comparison that is being made.

The first section in this chapter will explain how the three degrees are formed and will show you how the different degrees should be used. The second section will discuss troublesome adjectives and adverbs, as well as provide practice in using them correctly.

Diagnostic Test

Directions: Write all answers on a separate sheet of paper.

Skill Check A. Write the comparative and superlative degrees of the following modifiers. If the degrees can be formed in two ways, write the *-er* and *-est* forms.

1. eager
2. happily
3. sharp
4. delicious
5. well
6. quietly
7. priceless
8. strong
9. famous
10. bad

Skill Check B. Choose the word or phrase in parentheses that correctly completes each sentence.

11. Shipwrecks used to be a (more common, most common) occurrence.
12. Of the two ships, that one is the (more, most) seaworthy.
13. The captain is the (more, most) experienced of the two.
14. Modern-day wrecks can be (worse, more worse) than those of previous eras because modern ships can carry more passengers.
15. That ship's cargo is the (heaviest, most heaviest) it has ever carried.

Skill Check C. Rewrite each of the following sentences, correcting the illogical comparisons by making them balanced or by adding *other* or *else*.

16. This ship's hull is larger than that ship.
17. The ship weathered more hurricanes than any ship.
18. That storm was worse than any storm.
19. The captain was more scared than anyone when the ship went down.
20. The shipping company's loss was worse than the other shipping company.

Skill Check D. Choose the word or phrase in parentheses that correctly completes each sentence.

21. The ship foundered (bad, badly) in the rough seas.
22. After the helmsman was injured, (only the captain could, the captain could only) steer them to safety.
23. The ship (just needed, needed just) one large wave to push it over the shoal.
24. The crew had (fewer, less) fear of sinking than of facing the captain's wrath.
25. After they had weathered the storm, the captain praised the crew for performing so (good, well).

Section 25.1

Comparisons Using Adjectives and Adverbs

Like verbs, adjectives and adverbs can be either *regular* or *irregular*. Two rules govern *regular* modifiers. The first covers adjectives and adverbs of one or two syllables. The second concerns adjectives and adverbs of three or more syllables.

Using Modifiers of One or Two Syllables

KEY CONCEPT Use *-er* or *more* to form the comparative degree and *-est* or *most* to form the superlative degree of most one- and two-syllable modifiers. ■

The most common way to form these degrees is by adding *-er* or *-est*.

COMPARATIVE AND SUPERLATIVE DEGREES FORMED WITH *-ER* AND *-EST*		
Positive	Comparative	Superlative
deep	deeper	deepest
hard	harder	hardest
salty	saltier	saltiest
slimy	slimier	slimiest

More and *most* can also be used to form the comparative and superlative degrees of most one- and two-syllable modifiers. They should not be used, however, when their use would sound awkward, as in "The water is *more deep* in the ocean." Notice in the following chart that two of the modifiers from the preceding chart, *salty* and *slimy*, can use *more* and *most* to form the comparative and superlative degrees. *More* and *most* are used with most adverbs ending in *-ly* and with one- and two-syllable modifiers that would sound awkward with *-er* and *-est*. If you are in doubt about which form to use, consult a dictionary.

COMPARATIVE AND SUPERLATIVE DEGREES FORMED WITH *MORE* AND *MOST*		
Positive	Comparative	Superlative
salty	more salty	most salty
slimy	more slimy	most slimy
quickly	more quickly	most quickly
often	more often	most often

Theme: Sailing Ships

In this section, you will learn how the comparative and superlative degrees of adjectives and adverbs are formed. The examples and exercises are about sailing ships and shipwrecks.

Cross-Curricular Connection: Social Studies

Spelling Tip

Words that end in *y* exchange the *y* for an *i* when the endings for the comparative and superlative degrees are added.

Exercise 1 **Forming the Comparative and Superlative Degrees of One- and Two-Syllable Modifiers** On your paper, write the comparative and superlative degrees of the following modifiers. If the degrees can be formed in two ways, write the *-er* and *-est* forms.

1. high
2. friendly
3. fully
4. low
5. steep
6. painful
7. early
8. small
9. brisk
10. near

More Practice

Grammar Exercise Workbook
- pp. 86–89

On-line Exercise Bank
- Section 25.1

Go on-line: PHSchool.com
Enter Web Code: eck-8002

Get instant feedback! Exercises 1 and 2 are available on-line or on CD-ROM.

Using Modifiers of Three or More Syllables

KEY CONCEPT Use *more* and *most* to form the comparative and superlative degrees of all modifiers of three or more syllables. ■

DEGREES OF MODIFIERS WITH THREE OR MORE SYLLABLES		
Positive	**Comparative**	**Superlative**
gracefully poisonous flexible	more gracefully more poisonous more flexible	most gracefully most poisonous most flexible

Less and *least,* which mean the opposite of *more* and *most,* can be used to form the comparative and superlative degrees of any of the modifiers in the chart. *Less* and *least* can also be used with modifiers of one or two syllables.

EXAMPLES:

gracefully	less gracefully	least gracefully
poisonous	less poisonous	least poisonous

Exercise 2 **Forming the Comparative and Superlative Degrees of Modifiers With Three or More Syllables** Write the comparative and superlative degrees of the following modifiers. Use *more* and *most* and then *less* and *least* for each.

EXAMPLE: carefully

ANSWER:

more carefully	most carefully
less carefully	least carefully

1. rapidly
2. powerful
3. suddenly
4. eagerly
5. acceptable

Exercise 3 **Forming the Comparative and Superlative Degrees of Regular Modifiers** Write the comparative and superlative degrees of the following modifiers. Use *more* and *most* and then *less* and *least* when necessary.

1. fully
2. difficult
3. slippery
4. playful
5. favorable

Memorizing Irregular Adjectives and Adverbs

The comparative and superlative degrees of a few adjectives and adverbs are *irregular* in form. The only way to learn them is to memorize them.

KEY CONCEPT Memorize the comparative and superlative forms of certain irregular adjectives and adverbs. ■

The chart below lists the most common irregular modifiers.

DEGREES OF IRREGULAR ADJECTIVES AND ADVERBS

Positive	Comparative	Superlative
bad	worse	worst
badly	worse	worst
far (distance)	farther	farthest
far (extent)	further	furthest
good	better	best
well	better	best
many	more	most
much	more	most

Exercise 4 **Recognizing the Degree of Irregular Modifiers** Identify the degree of the underlined word in each sentence.

EXAMPLE: The <u>worst</u> shipwrecks are described in this book.
ANSWER: superlative

1. For <u>many</u> thousands of years, people have feared shipwrecks.
2. Sailors did their <u>best</u> to avoid these costly disasters.
3. The <u>farther</u> from shore a ship traveled, the less chance it had to receive aid.
4. <u>Better</u> charts and navigation methods allowed captains to steer clear of trouble spots.
5. The <u>best</u> advances came with the invention of new technology, such as radio waves and satellites.

GRAMMAR IN LITERATURE

from The Wreck of the Hesperus

Henry Wadsworth Longfellow

The poet has used the comparative degree of cold *to describe how the wind blew.*

Colder and *colder* blew the wind,
A gale from the Northeast,
The snow fell hissing in the brine,
And the billows frothed like yeast.

Exercise 5 **Supplying the Comparative and Superlative Degrees of Irregular Modifiers** Copy each sentence below, supplying the form of the modifier indicated in parentheses.

EXAMPLE: People on shore did their (good—superlative) to rescue the crew of the sinking ship.
ANSWER: best

1. Shipwrecks often occur during the (bad—superlative) weather conditions.
2. They may happen (far—comparative) out to sea than a person could possibly swim.
3. (Many—superlative) crew members could not reach land.
4. Surf boats are one of the (good—superlative) methods for rescuing crew members.
5. The boats are (much—comparative) useful for retrieving cargo that would otherwise sink with the ship.
6. In a mild storm, surf boats can reach the ship, but in (bad—comparative) weather, even these boats will overturn.
7. Helicopters work (well—comparative) in calmer weather.
8. Rescue teams developed a new method to overcome the (bad—superlative) weather conditions.
9. It seemed a (good—comparative) idea to shoot a rope out of a cannon in the direction of the ship; the crew would then secure the rope to the ship's mast.
10. The rescue team then used pulleys to bring people to shore before (far—comparative) damage could be done to the ship.

More Practice

Grammar Exercise Workbook
- pp. 86–89

On-line Exercise Bank
- Section 25.1

Go on-line: PHSchool.com
Enter Web Code: eck-8002

Get instant feedback! Exercises 3, 4, and 5 are available on-line or on CD-ROM.

25.1

Using Comparative and Superlative Degrees

Keep two rules in mind when you use the comparative and superlative degrees:

KEY CONCEPTS Use the **comparative degree** to compare *two* people, places, or things. Use the **superlative degree** to compare *three or more* people, places, or things. ■

Usually, you do not need to mention specific numbers when you are making a comparison. The other words in the sentence should help make it clear whether you are comparing two items or three or more items.

EXAMPLES: The captain felt *better* once all the crew was safely on shore.
The rescue team completed the practice session in their *best* time.

Pay particular attention to the modifiers you use when you are comparing just two items. Do not make the mistake of using the superlative degree.

INCORRECT: Of their two practice runs, that one was *best*.
CORRECT: Of their two practice runs, that one was *better*.

INCORRECT: They were the *fastest* of the two teams competing.
CORRECT: They were the *faster* of the two teams competing.

Do not make *double comparisons*. You should never use both *-er* and *more* to form the comparative degree or both *-est* and *most* to form the superlative degree. Also, be sure not to use *-er* or *more* and *most* with an irregular modifier.

INCORRECT: That ship sank the *most fastest*.
CORRECT: That ship sank the *fastest*.

INCORRECT: The disaster was *more worse* than the sinking last summer.
CORRECT: The disaster was *worse* than the sinking last summer.

More Practice

Grammar Exercise Workbook
- pp. 86–89

On-line Exercise Bank
- Section 25.1

Go on-line:
PHSchool.com
Enter Web Code:
eck-8002

Exercise 6 Revising Sentences to Correct Errors in Degree
On your paper, rewrite the following sentences to correct errors in the degree of modifiers. If a sentence contains no errors, write *correct.*

1. Originally, lifesaving services were run by private organizations that tried to help the sinking ships most closest to shore.
2. American shipping magnates knew that their crew and cargo could be saved if help could get to them sooner.
3. Some critics claimed that of the crew and cargo, the magnates would miss the cargo the most.
4. By the late 1840's, Congress agreed to fund the construction of lifesaving stations to guard the worse areas of the shoreline.
5. Which of these two stations is closest to the ship in distress?

▼ Critical Viewing
Compare this sixteenth-century ship to one you might take a cruise on today. Make logical comparisons in your sentences. **[Compare and Contrast]**

Making Logical Comparisons

In most situations, you will have no problems forming the degrees of modifiers and using them correctly in sentences. Sometimes, however, you may find that the way you have phrased a sentence makes your comparison unclear. You will then need to think about the words you have chosen, and revise your sentence, making sure that your comparison is logical.

Balanced Comparisons Most comparisons make a statement or ask a question about the way in which basically similar things are either alike or different.

EXAMPLE: Is Chesapeake Bay deeper than Puget Sound?

Because the sentence compares depth to depth, the comparison is *balanced.* Problems can occur, however, when a sentence compares basically dissimilar things. For example, it would be illogical to compare the *depth* of one bay to the *shape* of another bay. Depth and shape are not basically similar things and cannot be compared meaningfully.

KEY CONCEPT Make sure that your sentences compare only similar items. ■

An unbalanced comparison is usually the result of carelessness. The writer generally has simply left something out. Read the following incorrect sentences carefully.

INCORRECT: This ship's sail is bigger than that ship.

The number of shipwrecks off the east coast is larger than the west coast.

In the first sentence, a sail is mistakenly compared to an entire ship. In the second sentence, events are compared to a place. Both sentences can easily be corrected to make the comparisons balanced.

CORRECT: This ship's sail is bigger than that ship's sail.

The number of shipwrecks off the east coast is larger than the number off the west coast.

▲ **Critical Viewing** In sentences using balanced comparisons, compare the small boat to the sailing ship. **[Compare and Contrast]**

Exercise 7 **Revising Sentences to Make Balanced Comparisons** Revise each of the following sentences, making the illogical comparisons more balanced.

EXAMPLE: This ship's hull is longer than that ship.
ANSWER: This ship's hull is longer than that ship's hull.

1. That crew is more experienced than the other ship.
2. The gusts of wind at the center of the storm are stronger than the edge.
3. Ships with larger sails are more likely to capsize than smaller sails.
4. A ship with a smaller sail than that ship could weather the storm better.
5. The distance of that ship to the barrier reef is greater than the other ship.

***Other* and *Else* in Comparisons** Another common error in writing comparisons is to compare something with itself.

KEY CONCEPT When comparing one of a group with the rest of the group, make sure your sentence contains the word *other* or *else*. ■

Adding *other* or *else* in such situations helps make the comparison clear. For example, because the United States is itself a country, it cannot logically be compared to *all* countries. It must be compared to all *other* countries.

Problem Sentences	Corrected Sentences
A salvor is someone who returns an abandoned or sunken ship to shore before anyone.	A salvor is someone who returns an abandoned or sunken ship to shore before anyone else.
U.S. laws may allow a salvor to collect a larger reward than any country's laws do.	U.S. laws may allow a salvor to collect a larger reward than any other country's laws do.

Exercise 8 **Revising Sentences to Make Logical Comparisons** Rewrite each of the following sentences, adding *other* or *else* to make the comparisons more logical.

EXAMPLE: Because there are no limits on salvage rewards in the United States, a salvor could conceivably earn more money in U.S. waters than anywhere.

ANSWER: Because there are no limits on salvage rewards in the United States, a salvor could conceivably earn more money in U.S. waters than anywhere else.

1. That salvor has rescued more ships than anyone.
2. The salvor is given cash more often than any type of payment.
3. The salvor's job may be more dangerous than any job on the high seas.
4. The master of the salvage ship receives a larger payment than anyone on board.
5. The amount of salvage retrieved from the British cruiser the *Edinburgh* was larger than any amount of salvage.

More Practice

Grammar Exercise Workbook
- pp. 86–89

On-line Exercise Bank
- Section 25.1

Go on-line: PHSchool.com
Enter Web Code: eck-8002

Get instant feedback! Exercises 7 and 8 are available on-line or on CD-ROM.

25.1

Hands-on Grammar

Comparison Balance

In this exercise, you will learn how to form balanced comparisons using the comparison balance as a guide.

Cut two triangles of equal size out of lightweight cardboard and make slots in them as shown in the first illustration. Fit the triangles together so that they stand up, and tape them together. Cut a balance beam out of cardboard, and put it in the slot at the top of the standing triangle. You can use a paper clip to hold your comparative in the center of the balance. You now need some sentences to balance. Cut some strips of paper and fold one edge over so that the paper will hang on your balance beam.

cut slits – halfway down

balance beam

paper clip

In the third illustration, you will see that the sample sentence used is *This ship's sail is bigger than that ship.* You should notice that the sentence is *not* balanced. The slip of paper that says *that ship's sail* would balance the sentence if hung on the beam. Use the sentence *This dog's coat is shinier than that dog*, and *This dog's coat is shinier than that dog's coat.* Which is the balanced sentence? Work with a partner to correct other sentences.

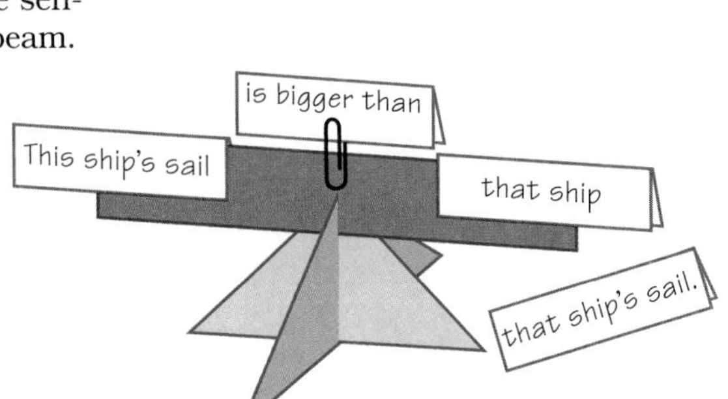

Find It in Your Reading In a short story or in a textbook, pick out examples of comparative sentences. Put them on strips of paper, and hang them on your balance.

Find It in Your Writing Look through your portfolio to find examples of comparatives. Make sure that they are balanced. If they are not, rewrite them correctly.

Section Review

GRAMMAR EXERCISES 9–15

Exercise 9 **Forming the Comparative and Superlative Degrees** Write the comparative and superlative of each modifier below.

1. faintly
2. sympathetic
3. firm
4. wryly
5. badly
6. pale
7. physically
8. many
9. fabulous
10. good

Exercise 10 **Revising Sentences to Correct Errors in Degree** Rewrite the sentences below, correcting the errors in modifiers.

1. More people who discover shipwrecks are professional treasure hunters.
2. Their searches are most likely to be successful if they consult old records than if they search randomly.
3. The treasure of the *Nuestra Señora de Atocha* is one of the most largest treasures ever recovered.
4. The *Titanic* is probably the more famous shipwreck today.
5. This is the most valuable of the two bells found on that ship.

Exercise 11 **Revising Sentences to Make Logical Comparisons** Rewrite each of the following sentences. Correct the illogical comparisons by balancing them or by adding *other* or *else.*

1. The professional reputation of underwater archaeologists is more respected than treasure hunters.
2. However, until the 1960's, underwater archaeologists were more apt to be shunned than any archaeologists.
3. Before then, exploration of shipwrecks was considered a field more appropriate for adventurers than for anyone.
4. The explorations of archaeologists were more systematic than adventurers.
5. Bob Ballard, head of the American part of the *Titanic* excavation team, is probably more famous than anyone in the business of underwater archaeology.

Exercise 12 **Writing Logical Comparisons** On your paper, write a sentence that makes the comparison specified in each of the following items.

1. Compare a sail boat to a speed boat.
2. Compare one city with all the rest.
3. Compare winter with other seasons.
4. Compare a sail boat to all other boats.
5. Compare a blizzard with a thunderstorm.

Exercise 13 **Find It in Your Reading** Write the adjective from these lines from "The Wreck of the Hesperus," and identify its degree.

For I can weather the roughest gale,
That ever wind did blow.

Exercise 14 **Find It in Your Writing** Look through your writing portfolio. Find two adjectives in the comparative degree and two in the superlative degree. Check to make sure that your comparisons are clear and logical.

Exercise 15 **Writing Application** Imagine that you are caught at sea during a fierce storm. Write a brief narrative describing your experience. Use at least two comparative degrees and two superlative degrees of adjectives.

Section 25.2

Troublesome Modifiers

Certain commonly used adjectives and adverbs can cause problems, both in speaking and in writing. As you read through the following list, make a note of those words that have puzzled you in the past, and use the exercises to test your understanding. When you are writing and revising a composition, refer to this section to check your work.

(1) *bad, badly* *Bad* is an adjective; *badly* is an adverb. Use *bad* after linking verbs, such as *appear, feel, look,* and *sound.* Use *badly* after action verbs, such as *act, behave, do,* and *perform.*

INCORRECT: She felt (LV) *badly* all winter long.

CORRECT: She felt (LV) *bad* all winter long.

INCORRECT: She coughed (AV) *bad* because of her cold.

CORRECT: She coughed (AV) *badly* because of her cold.

(2) *fewer, less* The adjective *fewer* answers the question *How many?* Use it to modify things that can be counted. The adjective *less* answers the question *How much?* Use it to modify amounts that cannot be counted.

HOW MANY: *fewer* snowmen, *fewer* green leaves, *fewer* warm nights

HOW MUCH: *less* snow, *less* foliage, *less* heat

(3) *good, well* *Good* is an adjective. *Well* can be either an adjective or an adverb. Most mistakes in the use of these modifiers occur when *good* is placed after an action verb. Use the adverb *well* instead.

INCORRECT: Caroline makes (AV) snow forts *good.*

CORRECT: Caroline makes (AV) snow forts *well.*

As adjectives, these words have slightly different meanings. *Well* is usually used to refer to a person's health.

Theme: Winter

In this section, you will learn how to use troublesome modifiers correctly. The examples and exercises are about winter and winter activities.

Cross-Curricular Connection: Humanities

▼ **Critical Viewing** Use *good* in one sentence about this picture. Use *well* in another sentence about the picture. **[Apply]**

EXAMPLES: John feels *good* after playing outside in the snow.
The snowfall this year is especially *good*.
Selena wasn't *well* enough to play outside in the snow.

(4) *just* As an adverb, *just* often means "no more than." When *just* has this meaning, make sure it is placed immediately before the word it logically modifies.

INCORRECT: Tim *just* wanted one last ride on his sled.

CORRECT: Tim wanted *just* one last ride on his sled.

(5) *only* The position of *only* in a sentence sometimes affects the entire meaning of the sentence. Consider the meaning of the following sentences:

EXAMPLES: *Only* expert skiers go down that slope. (Nobody else goes down that slope.)
Expert skiers *only* go down that slope. (They do nothing else on that slope.)
Expert skiers go down *only* that slope. (They don't go down any other slopes.)

Problems can occur when *only* is placed in a sentence in such a way that it makes the meaning imprecise.

IMPRECISE: *Only* wear warm clothes in the winter.
BETTER: Wear warm clothes *only* in the winter.

Grammar and Style Tip

Deciding where to put these modifiers can be tricky. Try to keep the modifier close to the word it is modifying.

GRAMMAR IN LITERATURE

from The Centaur

May Swenson

In the first stanza of this poem, the modifier only *is in blue italics. It modifies the word* one.

The summer that I was ten—
Can it be there was *only* one
summer that I was ten? . . .

Exercise 16 **Revising Sentences With Troublesome Adjectives and Adverbs** On your paper, rewrite the following sentences that contain errors in the use of modifiers. Write *correct* if a sentence contains no errors.

EXAMPLE: Carla's winter jacket from last year no longer fits good.

ANSWER: Carla's winter jacket from last year no longer fits well.

1. Winter visits only one hemisphere, northern or southern, at a time.
2. The hemisphere that is farther from the sun receives fewer sunlight, so it is colder and darker.
3. In December, January, February, and March, the Northern Hemisphere is farther from the sun, which thus cannot warm it good.
4. Therefore, winter comes to just the Northern Hemisphere then.
5. The term *winter* is used just to indicate one climatic season.
6. Winter only comes once a year in each hemisphere.
7. Some people react bad to the shorter days and weaker sunlight of winter.
8. Because areas near the equator are nearly always the same distance from the sun, they have less cold days than anywhere else.
9. If you time your travel plans good, you can arrange to be in summer all year round.
10. Of course, some people would consider year-round summer to be a bad idea.

More Practice

Grammar Exercise Workbook
- p. 90

On-line Exercise Bank
- Section 25.2

Go on-line:
PHSchool.com
Enter Web Code:
eck-8002

Exercise 17 **Writing Sentences With Troublesome Adjectives and Adverbs** Write sentences demonstrating the proper use of the modifiers listed below.

1. bad, badly
2. good, well
3. just
4. *only* modifying *go*
5. *only* modifying *seven*

▶ **Critical Viewing** Is this what winter looks like where you live? Use the comparative or superlative degree of the troublesome modifiers *bad* and *good* correctly in the sentences of your response. **[Compare and Contrast]**

Section 25.2 Section Review

GRAMMAR EXERCISES 18–24

Exercise 18 **Using Troublesome Adjectives and Adverbs Correctly** For each of the following words, choose the correct modifier in parentheses.

1. verb—play (bad, badly)
2. verb—shovels (good, well)
3. noun—(fewer, less) darkness
4. noun—(good, well) snowman
5. verb—feels (bad, badly)
6. noun—(fewer, less) sleds
7. verb—skis (bad, badly)
8. noun—(bad, badly) fall
9. noun—(good, well) home
10. noun—(fewer, less) snowballs

Exercise 19 **Revising Sentences With Troublesome Modifiers** Rewrite the sentences below that contain errors in the use of modifiers. Write *correct* if a sentence contains no errors.

1. During the winter, there are less hours of daylight than in the summer.
2. The drop in temperature affects some animals bad.
3. Many animals only can live in warm temperatures.
4. Coldblooded animals cannot perform good in the cold.
5. It is not only coldblooded animals that experience difficulties in the cold weather.

Exercise 20 **Revising a Paragraph With Troublesome Modifiers** Rewrite the following paragraph, correcting all errors caused by troublesome modifiers.

Rose performs good in all winter sports. There isn't any game or athletic feat she does not do good. Her brother, Jorge, on the other hand, is very bad at sports. Snowshoeing only is the winter sport he likes. He just needs his snowshoes and a set of poles to be happy all afternoon. Rose has time for fewer sports this season. It is hard for her to just concentrate on one activity. She only competes in skating; the other sports are for fun. At her last competition, she had a bad fall, but she got right up again. Overall, she did very good, earning a bronze medal.

Exercise 21 **Writing Sentences With Troublesome Modifiers** Use each of the following modifiers correctly in a sentence.

1. fewer
2. less
3. just
4. only
5. badly

Exercise 22 **Find It in Your Reading** Look for an article on a seasonal sport in a newspaper or magazine. Find examples of at least three of the following modifiers: *good, well, bad, badly, fewer,* and *less.* Explain why the form used is the correct one in each case.

Exercise 23 **Find It in Your Writing** Look through your writing portfolio to find examples of at least three of the troublesome modifiers discussed in this section. Check to make sure that you have used each modifier correctly.

Exercise 24 **Writing Application** Write a short essay about your favorite aspect of winter. Include four of the following modifiers: *bad, badly, fewer, less, good, well, just,* and *only.*

Chapter 26

Punctuation

▲ **Critical Viewing** How would you describe this photograph of a coyote pup? Write a three-sentence description. Then, review the punctuation marks you used. **[Analyze]**

Punctuation marks act as signals to readers. They tell readers when to pause or stop, when to read with a questioning tone, and when to read with excitement. Punctuation marks also connect ideas or set ideas apart. **Punctuation** is a commonly accepted set of symbols used to convey specific directions to the reader. This chapter will help you become more familiar with punctuation marks and the rules for using them.

Diagnostic Test

Directions: Write all answers on a separate sheet of paper.

Skill Check A. Write the end marks that belong in the following sentences.

1. What factors are responsible for the temperature of a desert
2. I read that latitude and longitude determine temperature
3. Wow some deserts are *so* hot
4. Weren't you surprised to learn that the base elevation of the Great Basin Desert is as high as many mountains
5. The Sonoran Desert has a low base elevation, and it is the warmest desert in the United States

Skill Check B. Copy the following sentences, adding commas, colons, and semicolons where needed.

6. The Mojave Desert has the lowest elevation but its latitude is relatively high.
7. The Sonoran Desert is south of the Mojave but the Mojave has lower average temperatures.
8. The elevation of the Great Basin Desert is almost 5000 feet at its lowest point.
9. Generally high temperatures and a lack of water make desert air drier this affects our perception of the actual temperature.
10. Arizona's heat is drier than the moist heat of some other areas Florida Georgia and Washington D.C.

Skill Check C. Copy the following sentences, adding quotation marks, commas, end punctuation, and underlining where needed. If the sentence needs no added punctuation, write *correct.*

11. Wasn't there a television program about the Mojave Desert asked Anne.
12. Yes answered Martha It was called Death Valley Days.
13. Anne remembered that the program was hosted by former President Ronald Reagan.
14. I think said Martha the space shuttle landed in the desert
15. Anne asked Wasn't there a movie called Death Valley that was filmed in Death Valley

Skill Check D. Copy the following sentences, adding hyphens and apostrophes where needed.

16. Desert animals survival is related to special behavior and physical features.
17. By midmorning, most desert animals have found shelter from the heat.
18. In southwestern deserts, coyotes dig their own dens or enlarge smaller animals dens.
19. The coyotes sense of smell is excellent.
20. The coyote senses its prey and then stalks it for 20 to 30 minutes before pouncing.

Section 26.1

End Marks

End marks signal the end or conclusion of a sentence, word, or phrase. There are three end marks: the period (.), the question mark (?), and the exclamation mark (!).

Theme: Deserts

In this section, you will learn about the proper use of periods, question marks, and exclamation marks. The examples and exercises are about deserts.

Cross-Curricular Connection: Geography

Using Periods

The period is the most frequently used of all the end marks.

KEY CONCEPT Use a period to end a declarative sentence, a mild imperative, or an indirect question. ■

A *declarative sentence* is a statement of fact or opinion. An *imperative sentence* is a direction or command. An *indirect question* restates a question in a declarative sentence.

STATEMENT OF FACT:	Death Valley is the lowest point in the Western Hemisphere.
STATEMENT OF OPINION:	This is a beautiful park.
DIRECTION:	Turn left at the next intersection.
COMMAND:	Come here.
INDIRECT QUESTION:	Jackie asked what time it was.

KEY CONCEPT Use a period to end most abbreviations. ■

INITIALS:	L. J. Fergusson			
TITLES:	Mr.	Mrs.	Dr.	Gen.
PLACE NAMES:	St.	Mt.	Calif.	Mass.

When a sentence ends with an abbreviation that makes use of a period, it is not necessary to put a second period at the end.

Get instant feedback! Exercises 1 and 2 are available on-line or on CD-ROM.

Exercise 1 **Supplying Periods to Sentences** Copy each of the sentences below, adding periods as needed. If the sentence is correct, write *correct.*

1. A V Humboldt helped to develop geography as a science.
2. Today, one wonders how geographers categorize deserts
3. He asked how deserts form.
4. Some develop in regions of persistent high atmospheric pressure
5. Some form behind large mountain ranges.
6. During their cross-country drive, Mr and Mrs Lynch stopped in St Louis, Mo, as they drove west.
7. They also drove through the Mojave Desert in California.
8. The Lynches found the desert beautiful.
9. They wondered how it would be to live there year round.
10. Next year, they plan on visiting Death Valley, Calif

More Practice

Grammar Exercise Workbook
- pp. 163–164

On-line Exercise Bank
- Section 26.1

Go on-line:
PHSchool.com
Enter Web Code:
eck-8002

Using Question Marks

KEY CONCEPT Use a question mark to end an interrogative sentence—a direct question. ■

INTERROGATIVE SENTENCES: Where are you staying in the desert?
Was there a valid reason for her absence?

Do not confuse an interrogative sentence, which is a direct question, with an indirect question. An indirect question requires no answer and should end with a period.

Sometimes a single word or phrase is used to ask a question. Use a question mark to end an incomplete question in which the rest of the question is understood.

EXAMPLE: Of course, I will meet you. When?

A question that shows surprise is sometimes phrased as a declarative sentence. Use a question mark to indicate that the sentence is a question.

KEY CONCEPT Use a question mark to end a statement that is intended as a question. ■

EXAMPLES: There is no electricity?
You invited him for dinner?

▲ **Critical Viewing** Write three to five questions you would like answered about the cactus in this photograph. Be sure to use question marks correctly. **[Analyze]**

Exercise 2 **Supplying Question Marks and Periods** Each of the following sentences is either a direct question, an indirect question, or a statement intended as a question. Copy each sentence onto your paper, adding the correct end mark.

EXAMPLE: How are deserts formed
ANSWER: How are deserts formed?

1. I just had to ask why deserts are hot and dry
2. Don't deserts form in areas of high atmospheric pressure
3. Deserts are formed because of large-scale climatic patterns
4. Why might deserts form behind mountain ranges
5. Mountain ranges create a rain shadow effect Where did you learn that

More Practice

Grammar Exercise Workbook
- pp. 163–164

On-line Exercise Bank
- Section 26.1

Go on-line: PHSchool.com
Enter Web Code: eck-8002

26.1

Using Exclamation Marks

KEY CONCEPT Use an exclamation mark to end an exclamatory sentence—a statement showing strong emotion. ■

EXAMPLES: I finally understand the problem!
That was a terrifying experience!

The exclamation mark may also be used to end an urgent imperative sentence.

KEY CONCEPT Use an exclamation mark after an imperative sentence if the command is urgent and forceful. ■

EXAMPLE: Run for your life!

In addition, an exclamation mark often follows an interjection.

KEY CONCEPT Use an exclamation mark after an interjection expressing strong emotion. ■

EXAMPLE: Oh! You've ruined the surprise!

Note About *Using Exclamation Marks*: Exclamation marks should not be used too often. Overusing them makes writing too emotional and less effective.

Exercise 3 Supplying Exclamation Marks to Sentences
Copy the items below, adding exclamation marks as needed. Then, label each item an *exclamatory sentence*, an *imperative sentence*, or an *interjection*.

EXAMPLE: I am *hot*
ANSWER: I am *hot!* (exclamatory sentence)

1. I *hate* being lost in a desert
2. I want water
3. Yippee It's going to rain.
4. Oh, no It's a flash flood
5. Get to high ground
6. Hurry The water is rising quickly
7. That was close
8. What a frightening sight that is
9. Whew Let's go home
10. I can't wait to tell my friends

More Practice

Grammar Exercise Workbook
- pp. 163–164

On-line Exercise Bank
- Section 26.1

Go on-line:
PHSchool.com
Enter Web Code:
eck-8002

Section 26.1 Section Review

GRAMMAR EXERCISES 4–10

Exercise 4 **Supplying Periods and Question Marks** Copy each of the sentences below, adding the correct punctuation mark.

1. What does a desert look like
2. Isn't a desert mostly a barren area of rock, soil, and sand
3. Luella asked if the nights were cool
4. Is it true that we can get lost in the desert
5. You will take your camera

Exercise 5 **Revising Sentences Using the Exclamation Mark** Copy each of the following items, adding exclamation marks as needed. Label each an *exclamatory sentence*, an *imperative sentence*, or an *interjection.*

1. The desert is beautiful
2. Man Is it hot
3. What You didn't bring water
4. I have got to find water
5. Wow See all that blowing sand

Exercise 6 **Supplying End Marks** Copy the following items, adding the correct end marks.

1. How would you describe a desert
2. Hot *Very* hot
3. Are you sure of your answer
4. Were you aware that not all regions defined as deserts are in warm climates
5. Imagine Deserts can be found in some regions of the North and South poles
6. They are called deserts because moisture freezes and plant life cannot grow
7. I must ask whether you would like to learn more about these frozen deserts
8. Well, use library resources to answer all your questions
9. Good luck
10. Tom wondered where he could find books

Exercise 7 **Proofreading for End Marks in a Paragraph** Copy the following paragraph on a separate sheet of paper, revising end marks where necessary. (Some sentences are correct as is.)

The Sahara is the largest desert in the world. Wow It's even larger than the United States? Did you know that not all of the Sahara is dry wasteland. There are lush oases scattered throughout the region? Are these areas inhabited! You bet.

Exercise 8 **Find It in Your Reading** Find a magazine or encyclopedia article on desert life. Locate sentences ending with a period, with a question mark, or with an exclamation point. Find three examples of each. Explain why the author uses each.

Exercise 9 **Find It in Your Writing** Look through your portfolio, and find examples of sentences ending with a period, a question mark, and an exclamation point. Explain why you used each mark.

Exercise 10 **Writing Application** Write a brief paragraph about a landform or landmark that has impressed you. Include a variety of sentence types and use end marks correctly. Then, label each sentence *declarative*, *imperative*, *indirect*, *interrogative*, or *exclamatory*.

Section 26.2

Commas

A *comma* (,) in a sentence signals the reader to pause briefly. Often, writers either neglect commas or overuse them. If you use a comma only when you have a specific rule in mind, your writing will be smoother and clearer.

Theme: Deserts

In this section, you will learn the many uses of commas. The examples and exercises are about deserts.

Cross-Curricular Connection: Geography

Using Commas With Compound Sentences

A compound sentence consists of two or more independent clauses that are joined by a coordinating conjunction, such as *and, but, for, nor, or, so,* or *yet.*

KEY CONCEPT Use a comma before the conjunction to separate two independent clauses in a compound sentence. ■

COMPOUND SENTENCES:	The Thar Desert has little rain or vegetation, and the herders must collect the leaves from the tops of trees for their flocks.

Use a comma before a conjunction only when there are complete sentences on both sides of the conjunction. If the conjunction joins single words, phrases, or subordinate clauses, do not use a comma.

SINGLE WORDS:	Heat and sand are common desert features.
PHRASES:	Deserts are found north and south of the equator.
SUBORDINATE CLAUSES:	They have decided that you should study more and that you should watch less television.

Get instant feedback! Exercises 11 and 12 are available on-line or on CD-ROM.

Exercise 11 **Revising Compound Sentences Using Commas** Rewrite the sentences below, inserting commas where they are needed. If no comma is needed, write *correct.*

EXAMPLE:	Clouds appeared but there was no rain.
ANSWER:	Clouds appeared, but there was no rain.

1. The Thar Desert spans India and Pakistan and it is one of the world's harshest areas.
2. However, a rich desert culture and colorful people can be found in the Thar.
3. You can take a bus tour or you can join a camel safari.
4. You'll have a great time visiting the villages and exploring the markets.
5. You won't be disappointed nor will you ever forget your visit.

More Practice

Grammar Exercise Workbook
- pp. 165–166

On-line Exercise Bank
- Section 26.2

Go on-line: PHSchool.com *Enter Web Code:* eck-8002

Using Commas Between Items in a Series

A series consists of three or more similar items.

KEY CONCEPT Use commas to separate three or more words, phrases, or clauses in a series. ■

Notice that the number of commas used is one fewer than the number of items in the series.

SERIES OF WORDS: The desert animals included *camels*, *toads*, *gerbils*, and *insects*.

SERIES OF PHRASES: The treasure map directed them *over the dunes*, *into the oasis*, and *past the palm tree*.

SERIES OF CLAUSES: The house was rather quiet *before she arrived*, *before her luggage was piled up in the hall*, and *before her three poodles took over*.

▲ **Critical Viewing** Write a description of the rabbit in this photograph. Include at least one sentence using items in a series separated correctly with commas. **[Classify]**

When each item is joined to the next by a conjunction, no commas are necessary.

EXAMPLE: For this journey, you will need two camels *and* a guide *and* a canteen.

A second exception to the rule concerns words that are considered to be one item.

EXAMPLE: Every table in the diner was set with *a knife and fork*, *a cup and saucer*, and *salt and pepper*.

Exercise 12 **Proofreading for Commas to Separate Items in a Series** Copy each of the following sentences onto your paper, adding commas as needed.

1. The surface of a desert may be covered with sand gravel or polished stones.
2. An oasis is a place where ground water pools plant growth flourishes and animals begin to feed.
3. The location of deserts is determined by ocean currents the location of mountains and prevailing wind patterns.
4. Most deserts are located near and between the Tropic of Cancer the equator and the Tropic of Capricorn.
5. The Gobi and the Takla Makan and the Kyzyl Kum are some Asian deserts.

More Practice

Grammar Exercise Workbook
- pp. 165–166

On-line Exercise Bank
- Section 26.2

Go on-line:
PHSchool.com
Enter Web Code:
eck-8002

Using Commas Between Adjectives

Sometimes, two or more adjectives are placed before the noun they describe. Use the following rule to determine whether to use a comma between them.

▲ Critical Viewing What adjectives come to mind when you look at this camel? Write a sentence using adjectives of equal rank separated by commas. **[Analyze]**

KEY CONCEPT Use commas to separate adjectives of *equal* rank. ■

If the word *and* can be placed between the adjectives without changing the meaning of the sentence, the adjectives are of equal rank. If the order of the adjectives can be changed, then they are of equal rank.

EXAMPLES: She left *detailed, precise* instructions for the substitute.
A *smooth, round* stone was cupped in her hand.

KEY CONCEPT *Do not* use commas to separate adjectives that must stay in a specific order. ■

In the following examples, you can see that either adding *and* or changing the order of the adjectives would result in a sentence that makes no sense.

EXAMPLES: *Three brief* hours will be enough to reach the mountains.
An *experienced desert* guide led us into the Sahara.

Note About *Commas With Adjectives:* Never use a comma to separate the last adjective in a series from the noun it modifies.

INCORRECT: A large, gentle-looking, camel sat by the road.
CORRECT: A large, gentle-looking camel sat by the road.

Exercise 13 **Supplying Commas Between Adjectives** Copy the following sentences onto your paper, adding commas between the underlined adjectives as needed.

1. The long dry stretches of sand were mesmerizing.
2. Two small goats were grazing.
3. A large threatening vulture circled overhead.
4. The white fluffy clouds were an illusion.
5. The few hard rocks we found were cracked.

More Practice

Grammar Exercise Workbook
- pp. 165–166

On-line Exercise Bank
- Section 26.2

Go on-line: PHSchool.com
Enter Web Code: eck-8002

Using Commas After Introductory Material

Commas are often used to set off information at the beginning of a sentence.

KEY CONCEPT Use a comma after most introductory words, phrases, or clauses. ■

KINDS OF INTRODUCTORY MATERIAL	
Introductory Words	*No,* we don't need any. *Hey,* give me your camera quickly before the kangaroo rat moves. *Smiling,* the flight attendant greeted the passengers.
Introductory Phrases	*Storing water in their roots,* succulent desert plants survive dry periods. *Protected by thorns,* other plants keep their water supply from animals. *To conserve water,* some plants drop their leaves.
Introductory Adverb Clauses	*When the wind blows constantly,* rocks are eroded into unusual shapes. *Although the alarm had gone off,* the police arrived too late.

Exercise 14 Using Commas After Introductory Material

For the sentences below, write the introductory word or words, the comma, and the word following the comma.

EXAMPLE: Shocked you see a huge spider with long, hairy legs.
ANSWER: Shocked, you

1. Fearsome looking the desert tarantula is three inches long.
2. Shrinking back you might think it will jump and bite you.
3. However they can jump only a few inches.
4. For the most part they are harmless creatures.
5. Even if you are bitten the venom is not fatal.
6. When attacked the tarantula will raise its front legs.
7. Looking for a meal desert tarantulas often feed on lizards.
8. Although desert tarantulas are large the largest tarantulas live in South America.
9. Known as bird eaters they often have ten-inch leg spans.
10. The largest spiders in the world they are known to attack small birds.

More Practice

Grammar Exercise Workbook
- pp. 167–168

On-line Exercise Bank
- Section 26.2

Go on-line:
PHSchool.com
Enter Web Code:
eck-8002

Get instant feedback! Exercises 13 and 14 are available on-line or on CD-ROM.

Using Commas With Parenthetical Expressions

A *parenthetical expression* is a word or phrase that is not essential to the meaning of the sentence.

KEY CONCEPT Use commas to set off parenthetical expressions. ■

A parenthetical expression in the middle of a sentence needs two commas. A parenthetical expression at the end of a sentence needs only one.

KINDS OF PARENTHETICAL EXPRESSIONS	
Names of People Being Addressed	Listen carefully, *Bob and Lucinda,* while I explain. That's a logical conclusion, *Pete.*
Certain Adverbs	The other sand dune, *therefore,* is several meters higher. Roberta will not be able to go with us, *however.*
Common Expressions	The sand, *I think,* is scarce on Peruvian deserts. They believe in her ability, *of course.*
Contrasting Expressions	These dunes, *not those,* resemble crescents. The decision should be mine, *not yours.*

Get instant feedback! Exercises 15 and 16 are available on-line or on CD-ROM.

Exercise 15 **Proofreading Sentences for Commas With Parenthetical Expressions** Copy the following sentences on a separate sheet of paper, adding commas as needed to set off the parenthetical expressions.

1. The position of Earth's deserts is explainable not accidental.
2. Without a doubt Jason Earth's tilt on its axis contributes to the desert climates.
3. Different areas of Earth as we know are angled toward the sun at specific times each year.
4. The same areas of course do not receive as much sunlight at other times.
5. This tilt of Earth therefore causes the four seasons.

More Practice

Grammar Exercise Workbook
- pp. 167–168

On-line Exercise Bank
- Section 26.2

Go on-line: PHSchool.com *Enter Web Code:* eck-8002

Using Commas With Nonessential Expressions

To determine when a phrase or clause should be set off with commas, decide whether the phrase or clause is *essential* or *nonessential* to the meaning of the sentence.

KEY CONCEPT Use commas to set off nonessential expressions. ■

Appositives and Appositive Phrases

ESSENTIAL: The 1943 movie *Sahara* takes place in North Africa.

NONESSENTIAL: *Sahara*, a 1943 movie, takes place in North Africa.

Participial Phrases

ESSENTIAL: The man *waiting in the van* is our guide.

NONESSENTIAL: Pat, *waiting in the van*, asked us to hurry.

Adjective Clauses

ESSENTIAL: We need someone *who can lead us to the oasis.*

NONESSENTIAL: We cheered enthusiastically for Darius, *who could lead us to the oasis.*

▼ Critical Viewing Compare and contrast this ostrich with the bird pictured on page 443. As you revise, make sure you have used commas correctly. **[Compare and Contrast]**

Exercise 16 Using Commas With Nonessential Expressions Read each of the sentences below carefully to determine whether the underlined expression is essential or not essential. If the material is essential, write *E*. If the material is not essential, copy the sentence onto your paper, adding any commas that are needed.

EXAMPLE: The Joshua tree <u>a desert plant</u> has thin leaves to slow water loss.

ANSWER: The Joshua tree, a desert plant, has thin leaves to slow water loss.

1. The baboon <u>eating the baobab fruit</u> belongs to the zoo.
2. Desert insects <u>dormant for most of the year</u> appear when rain causes flowers to bloom.
3. Ostriches are large African birds <u>that lay eggs with very hard shells.</u>
4. The roadrunner <u>racing by our car</u> could fly if it had to.
5. The desert tortoise <u>a reptile</u> stores fluid in sacs under its shell.

More Practice

Grammar Exercise Workbook
- pp. 169–170

On-line Exercise Bank
- Section 26.2

Go on-line: PHSchool.com *Enter Web Code:* eck-8002

26.2

Using Commas With Dates and Geographical Names

Dates usually have several parts, including months, days, and years. Commas prevent such dates from being unclear.

KEY CONCEPT When a date is made up of two or more parts, use a comma after each item except in the case of a month followed by a day. ■

EXAMPLES: Saturday, July 20, is their anniversary.
January 1, 1945, was the beginning of an exciting year.
September 7, 1999, was my first day of school.

When dates contain only months and years, commas are unnecessary.

EXAMPLE: It wasn't until July 1999 that records were kept for that part of the Sahara.

Geographical names may also consist of more than one part. Again, commas help prevent confusion.

KEY CONCEPT When a geographical name is made up of two or more parts, use a comma after each item. ■

EXAMPLES: Amos moved from Tripoli, Libya, to Fez, Morocco.
Many antiquities were stolen from Cairo, Egypt, and shipped to Paris, France.

Exercise 17 **Using Commas With Dates or Geographical Names** Copy each of the following sentences onto your paper, adding commas where they are needed. Write *correct* if no commas are needed.

EXAMPLE: They began their cruise on the Nile near Alexandria Egypt in June.
ANSWER: They began their cruise on the Nile near Alexandria, Egypt, in June.

1. There was no reason to go to New Delhi India in June.
2. We were in India in August 1999; the monsoon affected our journey.
3. However by January 6 2000 we'd left for home.
4. Amman Jordan is the capital of that mostly arid country.
5. You'll find Eilat Israel bordering Aqaba Jordan at the southern tip of the Negev Desert.

More Practice

Grammar Exercise Workbook
• pp. 171–172

On-line Exercise Bank
• Section 26.2
Go on-line: PHSchool.com
Enter Web Code: eck-8002

Get instant feedback! Exercise 17 is available on-line or on CD-ROM.

Other Uses of the Comma

The following rules govern the use of commas in addresses, letter salutations and closings, numbers, and quotations. A final rule concerns using commas to avoid misunderstandings.

KEY CONCEPT Use a comma after each item in an address made up of two or more parts. ■

As you can see in the following example, commas are placed after the name, street, and city. No comma separates the state from the ZIP Code.

EXAMPLE: Write to Maxwell Hunnicutt, 54 Monmouth Avenue, Dallas, Texas 75243.

Fewer commas are needed when an address is stacked, such as in a letter or on an envelope.

EXAMPLE: Maxwell Hunnicutt
54 Monmouth Avenue
Dallas, Texas 75243

KEY CONCEPT Use a comma after the salutation in a personal letter and after the closing in all letters. ■

SALUTATIONS: Dear Bill, Dear Aunt Harriet and Uncle Bill,
CLOSINGS: Sincerely, Best wishes, Yours truly,

KEY CONCEPT With numbers of more than three digits, insert a comma before every third digit, counting from the right. ■

EXAMPLES: 1,750 feet
3,608,787 square miles

Note About *Commas With Numbers*: Do not use commas with ZIP Codes, telephone numbers, page numbers, or serial numbers.

ZIP CODE: Niagara Falls, New York 14301
TELEPHONE NUMBER: (212) 555-2473
PAGE NUMBER: on page 1022
SERIAL NUMBER: 059 94 6106

▼ **Critical Viewing** How do you think this bird is able to perch on this spiny cactus? How do you suppose it survives in the desert? Write answers to these questions. Be sure to use commas correctly. **[Speculate]**

KEY CONCEPT Use commas to set off a direct quotation from the rest of a sentence. ■

As you read the following examples, notice that the correct location of the commas depends upon the "he said/she said" part of the sentence. (See Section 27.4 for more information about the punctuation used with quotations.)

EXAMPLES: Bret said, "Hold the door open."
"I can't," Lorna replied, "because my arms are full of books."

KEY CONCEPT Use a comma to prevent a sentence from being misunderstood. ■

Without commas, the following sentences are confusing. The addition of commas clarifies the meaning.

UNCLEAR: Beyond the mountains were clearly visible.
CLEAR: Beyond, the mountains were clearly visible.
UNCLEAR: After watching Zack asked to join the game.
CLEAR: After watching, Zack asked to join the game.

Exercise 18 **Proofreading for Commas in Other Situations** Copy each item below onto your paper, adding commas as needed.

1. Kayla said "Two kinds of camels live in the desert."
2. Nearby the one-humped dromedary waited patiently.
3. Most camels used for caravans are dromedaries or one-humped camels.
4. Often called "the ships of the desert" camels have flat feet that are well suited for walking on sand.
5. "Camels store food in their humps and in parts of their stomachs" he said "so they can go a long time without food or drink."
6. The area of Mongolia where many camels live the harsh Gobi is 604800 square miles.
7. Protecting themselves from the unfriendly desert people wear clothes that cover them completely.
8. "Our heads are never left uncovered in the sun" said the desert nomad.
9. To find out more write the Camel Cruise Corporation 1035 Camelback Way New Found City Hawaii 99900.
10. "We went on a camel cruise last year" she told us excitedly.

More Practice

Grammar Exercise Workbook
- pp. 169–170

On-line Exercise Bank
- Section 26.2

Go on-line:
PHSchool.com
Enter Web Code:
eck-8002

Get instant feedback! Exercise 18 is available on-line or on CD-ROM.

Section 26.2

Section Review

GRAMMAR EXERCISES 19–24

Exercise 19 **Using Commas to Separate Basic Elements in a Sentence** Write the following sentences on your paper, adding commas where needed. If no commas are needed, write *correct.*

1. Scientists are determined to help desert people prevail so they have made careful studies of the desert environment.
2. Their work has not been limited to plants and animals.
3. The situation remains urgent yet it takes time to understand the effects of soil depletion.
4. China limited the size of sheep herds and protected oases from overuse.
5. The land was rejuvenated and vegetation animals and people thrived.

Exercise 20 **Using Commas With Series and Introductory Elements** Write the sentences below on your paper, inserting commas where needed.

1. In the United States deserts were restored to health through the careful management of grazing lands.
2. Areas were fenced off plowed clear or burned off so new grass could grow.
3. Now struggling crops will have a better chance to grow.
4. Although the trees provide shade other benefits are also seen.
5. First of all the root system of the trees will help the desert soil hold moisture.

Exercise 21 **Using Commas With Added Elements** Write the sentences that follow on your paper, using commas as needed to set off parenthetical expressions. If no commas are needed, write *correct.*

1. The Nile River which flows through Egypt is a source of irrigation water.
2. The Nile flood waters covering the fields left important nutrients.
3. When the flood waters subsided the ground was useless however.
4. The farmers needed a system that would trap the waters for later use.
5. "The solution" Russell said "was to build canals to hold the water."

Exercise 22 **Find It in Your Reading** Read this excerpt from *The World Almanac* about Egypt. On your paper, rewrite the sentences, adding commas where necessary.

The Aswan High Dam completed in 1971 provides irrigation for more than a million acres of land. Artesian wells drilled in the Western Desert reclaimed 43000 acres from 1960–1966.

Exercise 23 **Find It in Your Writing** Look through your portfolio for at least one example of each of the following uses of commas:

- compound sentences
- commas between items in a series
- nonessential expressions

Exercise 24 **Writing Application** Write a short letter to a friend describing an imaginary trip across the desert. Include the following elements:

- address, date, and greeting
- one sentence with a series of four items
- one sentence with two equal adjectives and a contrasting expression
- one sentence with an introductory phrase

Section 26.3

Semicolons and Colons

The *semicolon* looks like a period above a comma (;). It joins related independent clauses and takes the place of a comma or a period.

Using Semicolons

KEY CONCEPT Use a semicolon to join related independent clauses that are not already joined by the conjunctions *and, or, nor, for, but, so,* or *yet.* ■

TWO INDEPENDENT CLAUSES:	The fire began with a tossed match. Jamestown was burned in 1676.
CLAUSES WITH SEMICOLONS:	The fire began with a tossed match; in that one moment in 1676, all of Jamestown began to burn. Marianne's report was about Christopher Newport; Dave's was about General George McClellan.

Note that when a sentence contains three or more related independent clauses, they may still be separated with semicolons.

EXAMPLE: The birds vanished; the sky grew dark; the little pond was still.

KEY CONCEPT Use a semicolon to join independent clauses separated by either a conjunctive adverb or a transitional expression. ■

CONJUNCTIVE ADVERBS:	also, besides, furthermore, however, indeed, instead, moreover, nevertheless, otherwise, then, therefore, thus
TRANSITIONAL EXPRESSIONS:	as a result, at this time, consequently, first, for instance, in fact, on the other hand, second, that is
EXAMPLE:	We were very impressed with the child's knowledge of history; *indeed*, she was remarkably well informed about the first English settlement.

Remember to place a comma after the conjunctive adverb or transitional expression. The comma sets off the conjunctive adverb or transitional expression, which acts as an introductory expression to the second clause.

Theme: Virginia

In this section, you will learn about using semicolons to join clauses and to avoid confusion, as well as the special uses of colons. The examples and exercises are about historic Virginia.

Cross-Curricular Connection: Social Studies

GRAMMAR IN LITERATURE

from The Man Without a Country

Edward Everett Hale

In this excerpt, the author has used semicolons (in blue) to join a series of independent clauses

. . . He says, "Take us home; take us to our own country; take us to our own house; take us to our own children and our own women."

More Practice

Grammar Exercise Workbook
- pp. 173–174

On-line Exercise Bank
- Section 26.3

Go on-line: PHSchool.com *Enter Web Code:* eck-8002

KEY CONCEPT Consider the use of a semicolon to avoid confusion when independent clauses or items in a series already contain commas. ■

EXAMPLE: Three important dates in Jamestown history are April 30, 1607; September 10, 1607; and January 7, 1608.

Exercise 25 **Revising Sentences Using Semicolons to Join Independent Clauses and to Avoid Confusion** Rewrite each sentence below, replacing commas with semicolons where necessary.

1. English investors supported the Jamestown settlement, therefore, Virginia became a popular destination.
2. The desire to acquire land inspired the colonists, indeed, many Virginians joined in the westward expansion.
3. It was not an easy voyage, the immigrants traveled on small ships for many months.
4. The cities of Williamsburg, Virginia, New Bern, North Carolina, Charleston, South Carolina, and Savannah, Georgia, became centers of commerce.
5. In Williamsburg, particularly, there were wig makers, who provided wigs for successful men and women, saddlers, who made saddles and other horse equipment, and cabinet makers, who produced fine furniture.

▼ **Critical Viewing** Describe the picture below in a sentence that includes two independent clauses joined by a semicolon. **[Analyze]**

Using Colons

The *colon* looks like one period placed above another (:). This mark directs attention to the information that follows it.

KEY CONCEPT Use a colon before a list of items following an independent clause. ■

EXAMPLE: You can visit these historic places in Virginia: the Jamestown Archaeological Laboratory, Jamestown Festival Park, and James Fort.

KEY CONCEPT A colon is used to indicate time with numerals, to end salutations in business letters, and to signal important ideas. ■

The following examples show special uses of the colon.

NUMERALS GIVING THE TIME:	3:04 P.M. 5:00 A.M.
SALUTATIONS IN BUSINESS LETTERS:	Dear Ms. Langly:
LABELS:	Notice: Shop is closed for repairs.

Exercise 26 **Revising Sentences Using Colons** Rewrite each item below, inserting the missing colon.

EXAMPLE: The settler wanted three things a horse, a saddle, and boots.
ANSWER: The settler wanted three things: a horse, a saddle, and boots.

1. Settlers in Virginia during the early eighteenth century included German settlers of many religious backgrounds Amish, Lutherans, and Mennonites.
2. Caution Deer Crossing
3. We saw several deer in the woods two bucks, five does, and three fawns.
4. Dear Mr. Connolly
5. Notice Classes Canceled
6. Gentlemen This is to inform you of a change in schedule.
7. The meeting will be held today at 200 P.M., not 330 P.M.
8. The meeting will cover these topics schedule, budget, guidelines, and goals.
9. Does your flight arrive at 830 or 900?
10. Help Wanted Full- or Part-Time

More Practice

Grammar Exercise Workbook
- pp. 175–176

On-line Exercise Bank
- Section 26.3

Go on-line: PHSchool.com
Enter Web Code: eck-8002

Get instant feedback! Exercise 26 is available on-line or on CD-ROM.

Section 26.3 **Section Review**

GRAMMAR EXERCISES 27–32

Exercise 27 **Using Semicolons in Independent Clauses** Some of the sentences below need semicolons to join related independent clauses. On your paper, write the word before the semicolon, the semicolon, and the word that follows.

1. Many educated people in Virginia knew slavery was wrong they believed that the custom should be abolished.
2. In the late eighteenth century, James Monroe offered plans to free the slaves however, few were actually returned to their homeland.
3. Abolitionist John Brown took control of Harper's Ferry in 1859 his planned revolt failed without the support of the slaves.
4. Brown was captured by Robert E. Lee consequently, he was tried for treason.
5. There was talk of Virginia's seceding nevertheless, it stayed with the Union until later.

Exercise 28 **Using Colons** Some of the items below should have colons. On your paper, write the word before the colon, the colon, and the word that follows, if applicable. If no colon is needed, write *correct.*

1. Dear President Lincoln
2. During Reconstruction, several forms of travel were available rail, boat, and wagon.
3. General Billy Malone helped provide these things for Virginia funding of public education, abolishment of the poll tax, and establishment of a college for African American teachers.
4. The polls in Richmond will be open from 8:00 A.M. to 9:00 P.M.
5. Please Note No campaigning is allowed near the polls.

Exercise 29 **Revising With Semicolons and Colons** Rewrite the letter below, supplying semicolons and colons where necessary.

Dear Madam

I've learned that you provide assistance to new residents. Therefore, I am asking for your help in obtaining these things part-time computer work, in which I am skilled an apartment near town and information about your adult school, where I might take a car-maintenance course.

Sincerely,
Louise Casella

Exercise 30 **Find It in Your Reading** Read the labels of at least three common household products. On your paper, explain the use of colons and semicolons on the labels.

Exercise 31 **Find It in Your Writing** Review your writing portfolio. Find examples of sentences that could be combined by using colons or semicolons. On your paper, write the new sentences, and explain how the colons or semicolons are used correctly.

Exercise 32 **Writing Application** Write a paragraph about a historic time that interests you. Include at least three of the following in your sentences:

1. colon to introduce a series of items
2. semicolon to avoid confusion
3. semicolon before a conjunctive adverb
4. transitional expression
5. semicolon before items in a series that already contain commas

Section 26.4

Quotation Marks and Underlining

There are many reasons for using quotation marks. Sometimes, you may want to show that you are repeating the exact words spoken by a person or printed in a book. At other times, you may want your characters to reveal themselves in their own words or to show action through dialogue.

Theme: Virginia

In this section, you will learn various uses for quotation marks and underlining. The examples and exercises are about historic Virginia.

Cross-Curricular Connection: Social Studies

Using Direct and Indirect Quotations

There are two types of quotations: *direct* and *indirect.* A direct quotation requires the use of special punctuation.

KEY CONCEPT A **direct quotation** represents a person's exact speech or thoughts and is enclosed in quotation marks (" "). ■

EXAMPLES: Kate said, "Williamsburg had the first theater."
"What play was presented?" Dorothy wondered.

KEY CONCEPT An **indirect quotation** reports the general meaning of what a person said or thought and does not require quotation marks. ■

EXAMPLES: Margo said that she would do it for me.
Don wondered why she hadn't called him.

Exercise 33 **Distinguishing Between Direct and Indirect Quotations** If a sentence below contains a direct quotation, write *D* on your paper. If it contains an indirect quotation, write *I.* (Notice that quotation marks have been intentionally omitted.)

EXAMPLE: Governor Alexander Spotswood negotiated with the Indians, said Ruby.

ANSWER: D

1. Cheryl said *Assaragoa* means 'long knife' in Iroquois.
2. Peter said that Governor Spotswood made a good treaty with the Iroquois.
3. Many of the immigrants who benefited from that treaty were German Karen added.
4. The teacher said that two leaders of German immigration were Joist Hite and Jacob Stover.
5. Many Germans said Cheryl moved westward to farm.

More Practice

Grammar Exercise Workbook
- pp. 177–178

On-line Exercise Bank
- Section 26.4

Go on-line: PHSchool.com
Enter Web Code: eck-8002

Get instant feedback! Exercise 33 is available on-line or on CD-ROM.

Using Direct Quotations With Introductory, Concluding, and Interrupting Expressions

A writer will generally identify a speaker by using words such as *he asked* or *she said* with a quotation. These expressions can introduce, conclude, or interrupt a quotation.

KEY CONCEPT When an introductory expression precedes a direct quotation, place a comma after the introductory expression and write the quotation as a full sentence. ■

EXAMPLES: The guide explained, "All historical buildings should be treated with respect."
Barney asked, "Is it difficult to identify artifacts?"

KEY CONCEPT When a concluding expression follows a direct quotation, write the quotation as a full sentence ending with a comma, question mark, or exclamation mark inside the quotation mark. Then, write the concluding expression. ■

EXAMPLES: "That depends on several factors," the guide replied.
"Could you show us one of the houses?" interrupted Barney.
"Please!" everyone chorused.

Notice also that the concluding expressions do not begin with capitals.

▲ **Critical Viewing** Write several lines of dialogue between the two figures in this photograph. As you revise, check to make sure you have used quotation marks correctly. **[Analyze]**

KEY CONCEPT When the direct quotation of one sentence is interrupted, end the first part of the direct quotation with a comma and a quotation mark. Place a comma after the interrupting expression, and then use a new set of quotation marks to enclose the rest of the quotation. ■

EXAMPLES: "This," the trainer said, "is Carter's Grove Plantation, a mid-eighteenth-century mansion."
"What would we have done," asked Corrina, "if we had lived there?"

KEY CONCEPT When two sentences in a direct quotation are separated by an interrupting expression, end the first quoted sentence with a comma, question mark, or exclamation mark and a quotation mark. Place a period after the interrupter, and then write the second quoted sentence as a full quotation. ■

EXAMPLES: "That would be exciting," the guide explained. "Plantation owners were very rich."
"Did you see those rooms?" asked Mark. "I can't imagine having such a large house."

Exercise 34 **Using Direct Quotations With Introductory, Concluding, and Interrupting Expressions** Copy each of the following sentences onto your paper, making the necessary corrections.

EXAMPLE: Elena said we will need at least two hours to see the museum.
ANSWER: Elena said, "We will need at least two hours to see the museum."

1. Mark said the College of William and Mary was built in Williamsburg
2. Yes Garth agreed and do you know what was taught there
3. I do know one subject Jenny added they taught religion
4. Didn't they teach science, literature, and philosophy also asked Mark
5. Of course Garth assured him William and Mary had many fine professors
6. One of their science professors was William Barton Rogers Jenny said he founded the Massachusetts Institute of Technology
7. The college was however noted Jenny slow to educate women
8. What exactly do you mean by that Mark asked
9. She's talking about the educational needs of women Garth explained women weren't admitted to the college until 1918
10. Although Jenny said a few women did attend some classes as early as the 1830's

More Practice

Grammar Exercise Workbook
- pp. 177–178

On-line Exercise Bank
- Section 26.4

Go on-line: PHSchool.com
Enter Web Code: eck-8002

▶ **Critical Viewing** Use direct quotations with interrupting expressions in a dialogue between two or more of the figures in this photograph. **[Analyze]**

Using Quotation Marks With Other Punctuation Marks

Sometimes, it may be hard to decide whether to place another punctuation mark inside or outside a quotation mark. You have seen that a comma or period used with a direct quotation goes inside the final quotation mark. In some cases, however, an end mark comes after the quotation mark. The following rules can help you choose the correct placement.

KEY CONCEPT Always place a comma or a period inside the final quotation mark. ■

EXAMPLES: "This area needs attention," Mrs. Finch said. She added, "It looks like a junkyard."

KEY CONCEPT Place a question mark or an exclamation mark inside the final quotation mark if the end mark is part of the quotation. Do not use an additional end mark. ■

EXAMPLES: Joseph asked, "Didn't I already clear that rubble?" Salvatore, his brother, protested loudly, "I helped rebuild three buildings last summer!"

INCORRECT: Rodney asked, "Will you stop arguing?".

CORRECT: Rodney asked, "Will you stop arguing?"

KEY CONCEPT Place a question mark or exclamation mark outside the final quotation mark if the end mark is part of the entire sentence, not part of the quotation. ■

EXAMPLES: Did anyone say, "You have been negligent"? Mary said, "I'm not responsible"!

Exercise 35 Using End Marks With Direct Quotations Decide whether the missing end mark in each sentence below should be placed inside or outside the quotation marks. Copy the sentences, and include the necessary end mark.

1. Does anyone remember hearing the guide say, "Now I'll tell you the name of the first religious order in Virginia"
2. I can't believe he just shouted out, "There was no real education system in Virginia until 1870"
3. Cathy asked, "What constitutes a real education system"
4. Did he say, "The lawn of the University of Virginia was *planted* by Thomas Jefferson"
5. No, he said, "The lawn of the University of Virginia was *planned* by Thomas Jefferson"

Grammar and Style Tip

Ellipsis marks (. . .) can be used to indicate that words have been omitted. They can be used at the beginning, middle, or end of a quotation. A period or other end mark is added to the ellipsis marks at the end of a sentence. For example: ". . . and then we visited Colonial Williamsburg," continued Sarah. "We drove from Washington, D.C., to . . . Colonial Williamsburg," Sarah added. Sarah said, "After the plane landed, we were on our way. . . ."

More Practice

Grammar Exercise Workbook
- pp. 179–180

On-line Exercise Bank
- Section 26.4

Go on-line: PHSchool.com
Enter Web Code: eck-8002

Using Quotation Marks for Dialogue

Dialogue is a direct conversation between two or more people.

KEY CONCEPT When writing dialogue, begin a new paragraph with each change of speaker. ■

EXAMPLE:

"Will you be going with us on the family trip this summer?" Noreen asked her cousin.

Gwen hesitated before answering. "I'm afraid so. My parents think I enjoy the experience."

"You fooled me, too," Noreen replied. "Maybe the trip will be better this year."

"Well, at least it can't be any worse," sighed Gwen. "On the last trip, we waited in line at three different historic homes in one day!"

Notice that each sentence is punctuated according to the rules discussed earlier in this section. When writing dialogue, you also need to remember to indent whenever a new speaker talks.

Exercise 36 **Revising Using Quotation Marks and Paragraph Indentations With Dialogue** The following selection is a dialogue. However, it is missing some punctuation marks and paragraph indentations. Decide where quotation marks, other punctuation marks, and indentations are needed. Then, copy the dialogue onto your paper, making the necessary changes.

Thomas Jefferson, commented Ray was eleven years younger than Washington. Also said Mary he was somewhat more artistic and liberal in his politics. Yes, and like Washington he was buried near his home, Ray said. Mary wondered Was that a common tradition in Virginia I don't know said Ray but I will try to find the answer

More Practice

Grammar Exercise Workbook
- pp. 179–180

On-line Exercise Bank
- Section 26.4

Go on-line:
PHSchool.com
Enter Web Code:
eck-8002

◀ **Critical Viewing** Write a three-line dialogue between Thomas Jefferson and you about what he is wearing in this picture. Punctuate carefully. **[Describe]**

Using Underlining, Italics, and Quotation Marks

Underlining, italics, and quotation marks help make titles and other special words and names stand out in your writing.

KEY CONCEPT Underline or italicize the titles of long written works and the titles of publications that are published as a single work. ■

WRITTEN WORKS THAT ARE UNDERLINED	
Title of a Book	The Adventures of Tom Sawyer
Title of a Play	A Raisin in the Sun
Title of a Long Poem	Paradise Lost
Title of a Magazine	The William and Mary Quarterly
Title of a Newspaper	The New York Times

KEY CONCEPT Underline or italicize the titles of movies, television and radio series, long works of music, and art. ■

ARTISTIC WORKS THAT ARE UNDERLINED	
Title of a Movie	Notting Hill
Title of a Television Series	Friends
Title of a Long Work of Music	Surprise Symphony
Title of a Compact Disc	Elton John's Greatest Hits
Title of a Painting	Christina's World
Title of a Sculpture	The Thinker

KEY CONCEPT Underline or italicize the names of individual air, sea, space, and land craft. ■

AIR: the Kitty Hawk SPACE: Gemini 5
SEA: the Titanic LAND: the Tom Thumb

KEY CONCEPT Underline or italicize words, letters, or numbers used as names for themselves. ■

EXAMPLE: The word maybe is not part of her vocabulary.

Technology Tip

Underlining is used only in handwritten and typed work. In work done on a word processor and in printed materials, italics take the place of underlining.

Exercise 37 **Underlining Titles, Names, and Words** Each of the following sentences contains a title, name, or word that needs underlining. Write the items that require underlining on your paper, and underline them.

EXAMPLE: The Lusitania sank in 1915 off the coast of Ireland.

ANSWER: Lusitania

1. William Shakespeare wrote The Tempest, a play about a shipwreck off the coast of Virginia.
2. Sue frequently leaves the u out of Iroquois.
3. John Smith of early Jamestown wrote Generall Historie of Virginia, New England, and the Summer Isles.
4. The spelling of the words generall and historie is correct for that era.
5. Also, Virginia was sometimes spelled without the third i.
6. My favorite book is Gone With the Wind.
7. Have you ever seen Touched by an Angel on television?
8. The pilgrims sailed across the Atlantic in the Mayflower.
9. The number seven is considered lucky by many.
10. I often add a second c in necessary.

More Practice

Grammar Exercise Workbook
- pp. 181–182

On-line Exercise Bank
- Section 26.4

Go on-line: PHSchool.com
Enter Web Code: eck-8002

Get instant feedback! Exercises 37 and 38 are available on-line or on CD-ROM.

When to Use Quotation Marks

In general, quotation marks are used for short works and works that are part of a longer work.

KEY CONCEPT Use quotation marks to enclose the titles of short written works. ■

The following chart contains examples of titles that should be enclosed in quotation marks.

WRITTEN WORKS THAT TAKE QUOTATION MARKS	
Title of a Short Story	"The Gift of the Magi"
Chapter From a Book	"The Test Is in the Tasting" from *No-Work Garden Book*
Title of a Short Poem	"Lucy"
Title of an Article	"How to Build a Birdhouse"

KEY CONCEPT Use quotation marks around the titles of episodes in a series, songs, and parts of a long musical composition. ■

KEY CONCEPT Use quotation marks around the title of a work that is mentioned as part of a collection. ■

The title of the play *Uncle Vanya* normally is underlined or italicized. In the following example, however, the title is placed in quotation marks because it is cited as part of a larger work.

EXAMPLE: "Uncle Vanya" in *Eight Great Comedies*

▲ **Critical Viewing** Write the titles of your favorite novel, short story, and song. Use quotation marks and underlining as needed. **[Apply]**

Exercise 38 **Using Quotation Marks With Titles** Each of the following sentences contains a title that needs quotation marks. Some of the sentences also contain titles that need underlining. Copy the titles onto your paper, either enclosing them in quotation marks or underlining them.

EXAMPLE: My favorite song is Getting to Know You from The King and I.

ANSWER: "Getting to Know You"; The King and I

1. John Brown's Body is a short poem written about the abolitionist leader.
2. Pygmalion, by George Bernard Shaw, can be found in the collection Masterpieces of Drama.
3. Michael Drayton, England's poet laureate in 1606, wrote Ode to the Virginian Voyage, a long poem.
4. I read about Virginia in The Virginia Magazine of History and Biography.
5. In 1903, a train wreck in Danville inspired the folk song The Wreck of the Old '97.
6. My favorite Greek myth is Perseus, which can be found in the collection Classic Greek Myths and Legends.
7. We found a great article entitled Discovering Virginia's Heritage in Travel Virginia magazine.
8. My favorite short poem is Mending Wall by Robert Frost.
9. For homework, we were assigned to read Chapter 13, The Southern Colonies, in our history book.
10. Have you ever heard the song Whatever Became of Delilah?

More Practice

Grammar Exercise Workbook
- pp. 181–182

On-line Exercise Bank
- Section 26.4

Go on-line: PHSchool.com
Enter Web Code: eck-8002

Section 26.4

Section Review

GRAMMAR EXERCISES 39–44

Exercise 39 **Revising Sentences Using Quotation Marks** Write the following sentences on your paper, capitalizing correctly and placing commas and quotation marks in the proper places. If the quotation is indirect, write *I* on your paper.

1. Buck told us, on April 9, 1865, General Lee surrendered at Appomattox.
2. The time after the war during which the South was recovering is called the Reconstruction Buck recalled.
3. Sally sighed some in Congress were determined to treat the South like a conquest.
4. Sally asked when it was that Virginia was able to return to the Union.
5. It was I believe Robert said in 1870 before Virginia was back in Congress.

Exercise 40 **Supplying Punctuation and Capitalization for Quotations** Copy these sentences onto your paper. Insert quotation marks, end marks, and capitalization as needed.

1. Have you ever visited Colonial Williamsburg asked Keesha
2. Not since I was in second grade I answered
3. Keesha said that she'd been there during spring vacation
4. So much history she exclaimed it's called the largest living museum in the world
5. She went on we were able to experience firsthand how people in colonial times lived

Exercise 41 **Using Underlining and Quotation Marks With Titles** Write the titles from the following sentences, using underlining or quotation marks.

1. The first ships to arrive in Virginia were the Susan Constant, the Goodspeed, and the Discovery.
2. Pocahontas is a movie about a Powhatan woman who married a settler, John Rolfe.
3. I read about Virginia history in David Goldfield's American Journey.
4. Shenandoah is a song about the Shenandoah River valley in Virginia.
5. The first newspaper in Williamsburg was the Gazette, started in 1736.

Exercise 42 **Find It in Your Reading** Copy the following paragraph onto a separate sheet of paper. Then, insert the proper underlining and quotation marks.

Carla reported The Drummer Boy of Shiloh by Ray Bradbury tells the story of a boy on the eve of his first Civil War battle. Sean asked if it was exciting to read. Dion exclaimed It is better than the movie The Red Badge of Courage.

Exercise 43 **Find It in Your Writing** Look through your writing portfolio for a piece of writing that uses quotation marks. Check to make sure you have used quotation marks correctly. Then, challenge yourself to add six more sentences using quotation marks in dialogue, titles, special words, or names.

Exercise 44 **Writing Application** Write ten sentences of dialogue between two students and their teacher about a history lesson. Use question marks and other punctuation marks to show the questions and answers that these three characters share.

Section 26.5 Hyphens and Apostrophes

The *hyphen* is used to combine numbers and word parts, to join certain compound words, and to show that a word has been broken between syllables at the end of a line.

Using Hyphens

KEY CONCEPT Use a hyphen when writing out two-word numbers from twenty-one through ninety-nine. ■

EXAMPLES: There were *thirty-four* people panning for gold.

KEY CONCEPT Use a hyphen when writing fractions that are used as adjectives. ■

EXAMPLE: A *four-fifths* majority wanted to head west.

Notice, however, that a fraction used as a noun, rather than as an adjective, does not need a hyphen.

EXAMPLE: *Two thirds* of the ore had been placed in the cart.

KEY CONCEPT Use a hyphen after a prefix that is followed by a proper noun or adjective. ■

The following prefixes are often used before proper nouns: *ante-*, *anti-*, *mid-*, *post-*, *pre-*, *pro-*, and *un-*.

EXAMPLE: Many settlers moved west in the *post-Revolutionary* years.

KEY CONCEPT Use a hyphen in words with the prefixes *all-*, *ex-*, and *self-* and with the suffix *-elect.* ■

EXAMPLES: all-powerful
self-determined
ex-leader
governor-elect

KEY CONCEPT Use a hyphen to connect two or more nouns that are used as one word, unless the dictionary gives a different spelling. ■

EXAMPLES: lady-in-waiting, great-grandfather, cave-in, secretary-treasurer

Theme: The Yukon

In this section, you will learn several purposes for hyphens and apostrophes. The examples and exercises are about the Yukon and the gold rush in the Klondike.

Cross-Curricular Connection: Social Studies

▼ **Critical Viewing** Use *pre-* or *post-* as a prefix in a description of this picture. **[Apply]**

KEY CONCEPT Use a hyphen to connect a compound modifier that comes before a noun. ■

EXAMPLE: Cass was a *big-hearted* miner.

No hyphen is necessary when a compound modifier follows the noun it describes.

BEFORE: The settlers moved in an *east-to-west* direction.
AFTER: They moved in the direction *east to west.*
BEFORE: They traveled in *well-equipped* wagons.
AFTER: They traveled in wagons that were *well equipped.*

However, if a dictionary spells a word with a hyphen, the word must always be hyphenated, even when it follows a noun.

EXAMPLES: This *poor-spirited* man will never find gold.
This man is *poor-spirited.*

KEY CONCEPT Do *not* use a hyphen with a compound modifier that includes a word ending in *-ly* or in a compound proper adjective. ■

INCORRECT: clearly-written
CORRECT: clearly written
INCORRECT: West-Indian music
CORRECT: West Indian music

Exercise 45 **Proofreading for Hyphens in Numbers, Word Parts, and Compound Words** Rewrite the sentences below, adding hyphens where needed. If an item does not require a hyphen, write *correct.*

EXAMPLE: Freshly fallen snow covered the area.
ANSWER: correct

1. Sir John Franklin was the first nonnative to see any part of the Yukon Territory.
2. This part of Canada was not a clearly mapped region.
3. Franklin was a self confident man.
4. He first reached the Yukon from the Arctic side, a once in a lifetime accomplishment.
5. In 1841, Robert Campbell explored the Yukon, thirty four years after The Hudson Bay Company navigated the area.

Plurals of compound nouns that are written with hyphens are frequently formed by making the first word plural:

lady-in-waiting
ladies-in-waiting

mother-in-law
mothers-in-law

jack-of-all-trades
jacks-of-all-trades

More Practice

Grammar Exercise Workbook
- pp. 183–184

On-line Exercise Bank
- Section 26.5

Go on-line:
PHSchool.com
Enter Web Code:
eck-8002

Rules for Dividing Words at the End of a Line

Avoid dividing words at the end of a line whenever possible. If a word must be divided, divide it between syllables.

EXAMPLE: You must not feel that your contribution was insignificant.

KEY CONCEPT Do *not* divide one-syllable words even if they seem long or sound like words with two syllables. ■

INCORRECT:	sch-ool	bru-ised	thro-ugh
CORRECT:	school	bruised	through

KEY CONCEPT Do *not* divide a word so that a single letter stands alone. ■

INCORRECT:	a-mid	ver-y	o-kay
CORRECT:	amid	very	okay

Avoid placing *-ed* at the beginning of a new line.

INCORRECT: halt-ed
CORRECT: halted

KEY CONCEPT Divide a hyphenated word or phrase only after the hyphen. ■

INCORRECT: During the gold rush, many prospec-
tor-friendly towns popped up.

CORRECT: During the gold rush, many prospector-
friendly towns popped up.

Exercise 46 **Using Hyphens to Divide Words** Decide whether you can hyphenate each of the following words. If you can divide the word, write it with a hyphen at each point that it can be divided. If it cannot be divided, write the whole word. If you are not sure how a word should be divided, check a dictionary.

1. counter
2. empty-handed
3. engage
4. snowfall
5. tent
6. regroup
7. overrun
8. farther
9. digging
10. queen

Technology Tip

Many word-processing programs include the option of automatically dividing words as you type them.

Get instant feedback! Exercises 45 and 46 are available on-line or on CD-ROM.

More Practice

Grammar Exercise Workbook
- pp. 183–184

On-line Exercise Bank
- Section 26.5

Go on-line:
PHSchool.com
Enter Web Code:
eck-8002

26.5

Using Apostrophes With Possessive Nouns

Apostrophes are used with nouns to show ownership or possession.

KEY CONCEPT Add an apostrophe and *-s* to show the possessive case of most singular nouns. ■

EXAMPLE: The role *of the parent* becomes the *parent's* role.

Even when a singular noun already ends in *-s*, you can usually add an apostrophe and *-s* to show possession.

EXAMPLE: The color *of an iris* becomes an *iris's* color.

In classical or ancient names that end in *-s*, such as Odysseus or Democritus, it is common practice to leave the final *-s* off for ease of pronunciation.

EXAMPLE: *Odysseus'* voyages were dangerous.

KEY CONCEPT Add just an apostrophe to show the possessive case of plural nouns ending in *-s* or *-es*. ■

EXAMPLES: The mother of the *bears* becomes the *bears'* mother.
The belief of the *multitudes* becomes the *multitudes'* belief.

◀ **Critical Viewing** Use possessive nouns in three sentences about the moose in this photograph. Be sure to place apostrophes correctly. **[Apply]**

Exercise 47 **Supplying Apostrophes to Plural Possessive Nouns** Write the possessive case of the plural nouns in the sentences below, adding apostrophes as needed.

1. The gold seekers need for money led them to the Yukon.
2. At that time, many countries economies were suffering.
3. The prospectors haste to reach the Yukon began in 1896.
4. It was many travelers belief that they could find gold.
5. Fifteen hundred adventurers dreams were lost.
6. The prospectors preferred method of travel was by dog sled.
7. The dogs lives were not altogether unpleasant, although they worked hard.
8. The dog teams task was to pull heavily loaded sleds through the snow.
9. The sleds loads were often hundreds of pounds.
10. The dogs and the prospectors comfort was less important than hauling enough supplies to survive in the cold.

More Practice

Grammar Exercise Workbook
- pp. 185–186

On-line Exercise Bank
- Section 26.5

Go on-line:
PHSchool.com
Enter Web Code:
eck-8002

Get instant feedback! Exercises 47 and 48 are available on-line or on CD-ROM.

KEY CONCEPT Add an apostrophe and *-s* to show the possessive case of plural nouns that do not end in *-s* or *-es.* ■

EXAMPLE: The trek *of the men* becomes the *men's* trek.

KEY CONCEPT Add an apostrophe and *-s* (or just an apostrophe if the word is a plural ending in *-s)* to the last word of a compound noun to form the possessive. ■

EXAMPLES: the *Girl Scouts'* cookie sale
my *sister-in-law's* car

Exercise 48 **Using Apostrophes to Form the Possessives of Nouns** Copy each underlined noun below onto your paper, putting it into the possessive form by adding an apostrophe and *-s* as needed.

EXAMPLE: The region museums of the gold rush have been a great success.
ANSWER: region's

1. Many prospectors would seek a guide assistance.
2. Explorers depended on the native peoples knowledge.
3. Settlers lives were eased by friendships with the Chinook people.
4. The Hudson Bay traders ingenuity led them to create a common language with the Chinook.
5. The Chinooks home was along the Columbia River.

26.5

Using Apostrophes With Pronouns

Both indefinite and personal pronouns can show possession.

KEY CONCEPT Use an apostrophe and *-s* with indefinite pronouns to show possession. ■

EXAMPLES: another's preference
nobody else's business

KEY CONCEPT Do not use an apostrophe with possessive personal pronouns. ■

None of the following personal pronouns needs an apostrophe to show possession: *my, mine, your, yours, his, her, hers, its, our, ours, their,* and *theirs.*

Some of these pronouns act as adjectives.

EXAMPLES: The spider caught a fly in *its* web.
Our house is for sale.

Others act as subjects, objects, and subject complements.

EXAMPLES: *Mine* is the yellow crayon.
Someone broke *yours.*
The red one is *his.*

Exercise 49 **Proofreading for Apostrophes With Pronouns** The following sentences contain possessive pronouns. If a possessive is written incorrectly, rewrite it to make it correct. If all pronouns in a sentence are used correctly, write *correct.*

EXAMPLE: In the new claim, the lake was <u>his</u> and the island was <u>their's</u>.
ANSWER: theirs

1. Once prospectors reached the Klondike, they had only to find open land and stake their claims.
2. If a prospector took anothers claim, it was called "claim jumping."
3. Imagine the disappointment of surviving the trip to the Klondike only to lose what was yours' to claim jumping!
4. Finally, the Miners' Association was formed to protect everyones legal claims.
5. The association had its first building in Discovery, the tent city on the Pine Creek.

More Practice

Grammar Exercise Workbook
- pp. 185–186

On-line Exercise Bank
- Section 26.5

Go on-line:
PHSchool.com
Enter Web Code:
eck-8002

Get instant feedback! Exercises 49 and 50 are available on-line or on CD-ROM.

Using Apostrophes With Contractions

Contractions are shortened forms of words or phrases.

KEY CONCEPT Use an apostrophe in a contraction to indicate the position of the missing letter or letters. ■

COMMON CONTRACTIONS WITH VERBS		
Verb + *not*	are not (aren't) is not (isn't) was not (wasn't) were not (weren't) cannot (can't)	could not (couldn't) did not (didn't) do not (don't) should not (shouldn't) would not (wouldn't)
Pronoun + the Verb *will*	I will (I'll) you are (you'll) he will (he'll) she will (she'll)	we will (we'll) they will (they'll) who will (who'll)
Pronoun or Noun + the Verb *be*	I am (I'm) you are (you're) he is (he's) she is (she's) it is (it's)	we are (we're) they are (they're) who is (who's) where is (where's) Lee is (Lee's)
Pronoun or Noun + the Verb *would*	I would (I'd) you would (you'd) he would (he'd) she would (she'd)	we would (we'd) they would (they'd) who would (who'd) Nancy would (Nancy'd)

An apostrophe is also used to form contractions of years.

EXAMPLE: the 2001 yearbook (the *'01* yearbook)

Exercise 50 **Using Contractions in Informal Writing** On your paper, write the contractions possible in each sentence below.

EXAMPLE: Where is the new history book?
ANSWER: Where's

1. Yukon life was not without heartache.
2. The majority of prospectors did not find their fortune.
3. Often, a gold seeker's family would not hear of his fate.
4. After the gold rush ended, a woman could move to the Yukon if she thought she would find work.
5. One German prospector sent for his wife— "If she will make the voyage," he said.

More Practice

Grammar Exercise Workbook
- pp. 187–188

On-line Exercise Bank
- Section 26.5

Go on-line:
PHSchool.com
Enter Web Code:
eck-8002

26.5

Hands-on Grammar

Contractions-Fold

To review which letters are dropped and where apostrophes belong in common contractions, try this contractions-fold activity. Start by cutting out fifteen strips of paper. Each strip should be 1" wide and 3 1/4" long. On each strip, print one of the following words exactly as they appear below. Write each word in capital letters and as large as possible on the strip.

ISNOT	IHAVE	IWOULD
ARENOT	SHEWILL	YOUWOULD
DIDNOT	WEHAVE	HEWOULD
WERENOT	YOUARE	WEWOULD
CANNOT	YOUWILL	THEYWOULD

COULDNOT

Place the completed strips of paper into an envelope or some other receptacle from which they can be chosen at random. Working alone or with a group, select strips of paper from the envelope. Look at the word you selected and decide the proper form of its contraction. Fold the strip of paper in such a way as to cover up the letters to be replaced by an apostrophe. To do this, fold the paper once in the middle of the letters you want to cover and again next to the first letter to the right of where the apostrophe should be placed.

After you have correctly folded the strip of paper to show the proper form of the contraction, use it in a sentence.

Find It in Your Reading Review several nonfiction articles from your literature textbook or from newspapers and magazines. Note the types of contractions used and their frequency. Then, analyze how formal each nonfiction article is, and determine whether there is a correlation between how formal the writing is and how many contractions are used.

Find It in Your Writing Review your writing portfolio, and select a piece of writing in which you have used contractions. Make sure you have used contractions correctly in the piece. If not, revise your writing.

Section 26.5

Section Review

GRAMMAR EXERCISES 51–56

Exercise 51 **Supplying Hyphens in Numbers, Word Parts, and Compound Words** On your paper, write the hyphenated word, compound word, or number that needs a hyphen in the sentences below. If no hyphen is needed, write *correct.*

1. Strong bonds were formed between the adventurers during the two year rush to the Yukon.
2. The native peoples were open to newly formed friendships.
3. Each person in an exploration party had three much needed items.
4. It was an unheard of occurrence to leave civilization without a compass.
5. Equally important was a fairly high quality magnifying glass.

Exercise 52 **Indicating Where Hyphens Divide Words and Compound Words at the End of a Line** Copy each word or phrase below, drawing a vertical line at each point where it could be divided. (Not every item can be divided.) If you are unsure of a word, use a dictionary.

1. constructive
2. Europe
3. all-powerful
4. to-and-fro
5. Yukon
6. strummed
7. tomorrow
8. above
9. turkey
10. compass

Exercise 53 **Supplying Apostrophes With Plural and Singular Nouns to Form Possessives of Words Ending in *-s* or *-es*** Each of the following sentences needs at least one apostrophe to form the possessive case. Write the word or words with the apostrophe.

1. During the gold rush, the Yukon Rivers largest settlement was Dawson.
2. In 1899, the inhabitants homes were tents and quickly built cabins.
3. Dawsons population was an astonishing 25,000 people.
4. The womens lives were difficult, as were the mens.
5. The people of Dawson always depended on one anothers kindness.

Exercise 54 **Find It in Your Reading** Find a textbook or encyclopedia article about the Yukon Territory. Find examples of apostrophes used with possessive nouns and pronouns and hyphens used to divide words. Write down at least one example of each.

Exercise 55 **Find It in Your Writing** Choose a paragraph of writing from your portfolio. Imagine that you have been asked to narrow the right-hand margin of your paper; therefore, you have to decide whether to hyphenate the words at the end of each line or to write the complete word on the next line. If you can divide the word, write the part of the word that would appear at the end of the first line on your paper. If you cannot divide the word, write the complete word.

Exercise 56 **Writing Application** Write a brief narrative about an exciting adventure you or someone you know has experienced. Include at least three of the following in your narrative:

1. hyphenated number
2. apostrophe to show possession
3. apostrophe to form a contraction
4. contraction of *he is* or *she is*
5. hyphen at the end of a line

Chapter 27

Capitalization

▲ **Critical Viewing** What features of this picture would be named by words that begin with capital letters? Why? **[Speculate]**

If you were to travel across the country, you would pass many geographical locations and landmarks. You might start a journal to keep track of the interesting sites you visit along the way. When you write about your adventures, you will need to capitalize the names of towns, rivers, landmarks, and buildings, among other things. *Capital letters* may signal the beginning of a sentence, an important word within a sentence, or a proper noun.

A sentence written without capitals is confusing: *mr. bailey traveled with the band from youngstown to visit the birthplace of john philip sousa.* With the addition of capitals, the same sentence is easier to read: *Mr. Bailey traveled with the band from Youngstown to visit the birthplace of John Philip Sousa.*

The meaning of a sentence is clearer when words are capitalized correctly.

Diagnostic Test

Directions: Write all answers on a separate sheet of paper.

Skill Check A. Copy the following sentences onto your paper, adding the missing capitals.

1. i have never been to West Virginia, but i would like to go there.
2. "where is West Virginia," asked Charlotte, "in relation to Ohio?"
3. ohio and Virginia are two states that border West Virginia.
4. what beautiful foliage in the fall!
5. "driving through the mountains is fun to do," said Hector.

Skill Check B. On your paper, write each name, geographical place, or other proper noun that you find in the following sentences, adding the missing capitals.

6. rebecca told me that white sulphur springs boasts a house made of 30 tons of coal.
7. When the o'connel family went to west virginia, they visited the beckley exhibition coal mine in beckley.
8. When samuel drives to valley falls, west virginia, he is going to take route 79 from charleston.
9. We drove down a winding road to get to stonewall jackson lake.
10. tomorrow, we will visit the seneca caverns in sendleton county.

Skill Check C. Complete each of the following sentences by supplying a proper adjective that is correctly capitalized.

11. The Statue of Liberty is an __?__ symbol.
12. If you mentioned the Eiffel Tower, anyone would know that you were referring to a __?__ structure.
13. The Leaning Tower of Pisa represents __?__ architecture.
14. The __?__ pyramids are one of the Wonders of the World.
15. Tortillas are a staple item in __?__ cuisine.

Skill Check D. On your paper, write each title or family name that you find in the following sentences, adding all the capitals that are missing.

16. president Jimmy Carter was given a 10-foot-tall peanut in 1977.
17. Yesterday, aunt Jane said that it was made in Evanston, Illinois.
18. My other aunt, professor Deirdre Thomas, told me that the peanut sits in Plains, Georgia, now.
19. Come meet uncle Rodney, a retired navy captain who now lives in Plains, Georgia.
20. He met the president when carter was home for a visit.

Skill Check E. Write each title of the works of art and courses correctly, adding all the capitals that are missing.

21. I am taking biology 201 next semester.
22. In english, we read <u>bearstone</u> and <u>the pearl</u>.
23. I took art 160 so that I could learn about Van Gogh.
24. When Jack was in a humanities class, he had to study selections from <u>swan lake</u> and <u>the nutcracker</u>.
25. The spanish 201 class is reading <u>don quixote de la mancha</u>.

Using Capitals for First Words

Capital letters are used for the first words in all sentences and in many quotations. They are also used for the word *I*, whatever its position in a sentence.

Theme: Tourist Attractions

In this chapter, you will learn the many instances in which you must use capital letters. The examples and exercises are about quaint and unusual tourist attractions.

Cross-Curricular Connection: Social Studies

Sentences

One of the most common uses of a capital is to signal the beginning of a sentence.

KEY CONCEPT Capitalize the first word in declarative, interrogative, imperative, and exclamatory sentences. ■

DECLARATIVE: Strong gusts of wind made it dangerous to drive on the bridge.

INTERROGATIVE: Who found the clue leading to the suspect's arrest?

IMPERATIVE: Think carefully before you decide.

EXCLAMATORY: What an amazing coincidence this is!

Sometimes only part of a sentence is written out. The rest of the sentence is understood. In these cases, a capital is still needed for the first word.

EXAMPLES: When? Why not? Certainly!

Exercise 1 **Using Capitals to Begin Sentences** Copy the following sentences onto your paper, adding the missing capitals.

EXAMPLE: great! when do we leave?

ANSWER: Great! When do we leave?

1. tomorrow, we will begin our road trip across the country.
2. bring your camera.
3. will you be ready to make many stops along the way?
4. that roadside scene is amazing!
5. how big do you think that lake is?

▼ **Critical Viewing** Describe this famous American landmark, making sure to use capitalization correctly. **[Describe]**

Quotations

A capital letter also signals the first word in a quotation.

KEY CONCEPT Capitalize the first word in a quotation if the quotation is a complete sentence. ■

In each of the following examples, the first word of the quotation is capitalized because it begins a complete sentence.

EXAMPLES: Several people shouted, "Stop the bus!"
"She really wants to skip that monument," Arlene confided.

When a quotation consists of one complete sentence in two parts, only one capital is needed.

EXAMPLE: "How much longer," asked Brian, "until we reach the next attraction?"

If a quotation contains more than one sentence, capitalize the first word of each sentence.

EXAMPLE: "Please distribute these maps to everyone," said the director. "They show the location of each exhibit."

More Practice

Grammar Exercise Workbook
- pp. 189–190

On-line Exercise Bank
- Chapter 27

Go on-line:
PHSchool.com
Enter Web Code:
eck-8002

Exercise 2 **Using Capitals for Quotations** Copy each of the following sentences onto your paper, adding the missing capitals.

EXAMPLE: "isn't this an incredible place?" he asked.
ANSWER: "Isn't this an incredible place?" he asked.

1. Charles said, "my little brothers like the cows the best."
2. "there is no way that a mosquito that big can be real!" exclaimed Roberta.
3. "if you will look to your right," directed the tour guide, "you will see the jackalope."
4. "do not pet the mastodon," said their mother. "its coat is made of polyester and fiberglass."
5. "if we can't stop here," whined the twins, "can we go sightseeing in the next town?"

▼ **Critical Viewing** What words would be capitalized in a sentence describing this scene? **[Analyze]**

Capitalizing the Word *I*

The pronoun *I* is always written as a capital.

KEY CONCEPT Capitalize the word *I* wherever it appears in a sentence. ■

EXAMPLE: I worked for two years as a clerk before I received the promotion.

Exercise 3 **Capitalizing the Pronoun *I*** Copy the following sentences onto your paper, adding the missing capitals.

EXAMPLE: she and i were the last to arrive.
ANSWER: She and I were the last to arrive.

1. While traveling through Ohio, i stopped in the quaint town of Dresden.
2. i saw the World's Largest Basket there.
3. When i arrived in Wilmot, i stopped at the World's Largest Cuckoo Clock.
4. Because i was there when the clock struck the hour, i got to see the animated figures come to life.
5. i was amazed that a clock could be twenty-three feet tall.

Using Capitals for Proper Nouns

A proper noun is capitalized because it names a specific person, place, or thing.

KEY CONCEPT Capitalize all proper nouns. ■

EXAMPLES: Joe Smyth Joshua Tree National Monument
the Tappan Zee Bridge the Eiffel Tower

KEY CONCEPT Capitalize each part of a person's full name. ■

EXAMPLES: Michelle T. Como P. A. Sullivan

When a last name has two parts and the first part is *Mc, O',* or *St.*, the second part of the last name must also be capitalized.

EXAMPLES: McMurphy O'Connor St. John

For two-part last names that do not begin with *Mc, O',* or *St.*, the capitalization varies. Check a reliable source, such as a biographical dictionary, for the correct spelling.

Exercise 4 **Using Capitals for Names of People** On your paper, write each name that you find in the following sentences, adding the missing capitals.

EXAMPLE: Her best friend was andrea mcmahon.
ANSWER: Andrea McMahon

1. martin maurer got the idea to build the Big Duck after seeing a coffee shop shaped like a pot in California.
2. george reeve, w. collins, and s. collins built the duck to be used as a roadside stand to sell ducks and eggs.
3. In 1991, christie brinkley narrated the history of the Big Duck.
4. Martha's friend, kathleen o'rourke, came from Ireland to see this attraction.
5. d. st. john told his friend bill that he had never seen anything so funny.

More Practice

Grammar Exercise Workbook
- pp. 191–194

On-line Exercise Bank
- Chapter 27

Go on-line: PHSchool.com
Enter Web Code: eck-8002

GRAMMAR IN LITERATURE

from The Man Without a Country

Edward Everett Hale

In Edward Everett Hale's "The Man Without a Country," the narrator tells of a letter he once read. Titles, names of people, and names of places are capitalized.

Sir:

You will receive from Lieutenant Neale the person of Philip Nolan, late a lieutenant in the United States Army.

This person on his trial by court-martial expressed, with an oath, the wish that he might "never hear of the United States again."

▼ **Critical Viewing** Where do you think this tall ship might be going? What ocean or sea might it be sailing on? How would you capitalize the names of countries and bodies of water? **[Speculate]**

KEY CONCEPT Capitalize geographical names. ■

Any place listed on a map should be capitalized.

GEOGRAPHICAL NAMES	
Streets	First Avenue, Spencer Road
Towns and Cities	Plainfield, Los Angeles, Tokyo
Counties	Orange County, Wayne County
States and Provinces	Oklahoma, Manitoba
Nations	France, Ecuador, Saudi Arabia
Continents	South America, Africa, Asia
Valleys and Deserts	Death Valley, Mojave Desert
Mountains	Rocky Mountains, Mount Rushmore
Sections of a Country	New England, Southwest
Islands	Pitcairn Island, Long Island
Scenic Spots	Everglades, Yosemite National Park
Rivers and Falls	Colorado River, Rainbow Falls
Lakes and Bays	Lake Superior, Saginaw Bay
Seas and Oceans	Dead Sea, Indian Ocean

Compass points, such as north, southwest, or east, are considered proper nouns only when they name specific geographical locations. In those cases, they are capitalized. When they simply refer to directions, they are not.

EXAMPLES: We spent our vacation in the Southeast.
Our boat headed north on the river.

◄ **Critical Viewing** Using capitals correctly in a sentence, give the possible geographic location of this picture. **[Infer]**

Exercise 5 **Using Capitals for Geographical Places** On your paper, write each geographical place name that you find in the following sentences, adding all the missing capitals.

EXAMPLE: They had seen niagara falls in 1997.
ANSWER: Niagara Falls

1. From east to west on the north american continent, there are many roadside sites, especially in the midwest.
2. If you've ever been to moose jaw, saskatchewan, canada, you have probably seen Mac, the World's Largest Moose.
3. If you stop in jackson on your way to yellowstone national park, you will see the World's Biggest Ball of Barbed Wire.
4. There is a lighthouse in hannibal, missouri, near the mississippi river.
5. The World's Largest Kaleidoscope can be found in mt. tremper, new york, in the heart of the catskill mountains.
6. white lake is the former home port of the *Ellenwood*, a lumber schooner.
7. In 1901, after the *Ellenwood* sank in lake michigan, its nameplate drifted east across lake michigan to white lake.
8. The *Ellenwood* is now pictured on the top of the World's Largest Weather Vane in montague, michigan.
9. Several cities in minnesota are home to famous "World's Largest" attractions, such as a dog dish and an ear of corn.
10. Balls of twine in mountain springs, texas; cawker city, kansas; and darwin, minnesota, are among the world's largest.

More Practice

Grammar Exercise Workbook
- pp. 191–194

On-line Exercise Bank
- Chapter 27

Go on-line:
PHSchool.com
Enter Web Code:
eck-8002

Get instant feedback! Exercise 5 is available on-line or on CD-ROM.

KEY CONCEPT Capitalize the names of specific events and periods of time. ■

The following chart gives examples of events and times that are capitalized.

SPECIFIC EVENTS AND TIMES	
Historical Periods	Golden Age, Renaissance
Historical Events	Boxer Rebellion, World War I
Documents	Bill of Rights, Homestead Act
Days	Friday, Sunday
Months	March, June
Holidays	Memorial Day, New Year's Day
Religious Days	Easter, Pentecost, Muharram
Special Events	Orange Bowl, State Fair of Texas

Even though the names of seasons represent specific times of the year, they are not capitalized.

EXAMPLES: Last winter was the coldest in a decade.
We can't wait for summer.

KEY CONCEPT Capitalize the names of various organizations, government bodies, political parties, and nationalities, as well as the languages spoken by different groups. ■

The following chart shows examples of each of these categories.

SPECIFIC GROUPS	
Clubs	Lincoln School Camera Club, Philadelphia Pioneer Track Club
Organizations	International Red Cross, Girl Scouts
Institutions	Georgia Institute of Technology, Tenakill School, Beth Israel Hospital
Government Bodies	Congress of the United States, Supreme Court, Los Angeles City Council
Political Parties	Republican Party, Democratic Party
Nationalities	Algerian, Japanese, Mexican, American
Languages Spoken by Different Groups	English, Portuguese, Arabic, Norwegian

◀ **Critical Viewing** What is the name of this ship? How would you capitalize it and why? **[Analyze]**

KEY CONCEPT Capitalize references to religions, deities, and religious scriptures. ■

The following chart presents a list of five of the world's major religions. Listed next to each are the words that each religion uses to refer to important religious figures and holy writings. Be sure to capitalize these in your writing. Note that the name of each religion is also capitalized.

RELIGIOUS REFERENCES	
Christianity	God, Lord, Father, Son, Holy Ghost, Bible, books of the Bible (such as Genesis, Exodus, Matthew, Mark)
Judaism	God, Lord, Father, Prophets, Torah, Talmud, Midrash
Islam	Allah, Prophet, Muhammad, Koran
Hinduism	Brahma, Bhagavad-Gita, Vedas
Buddhism	Buddha, Mahayana, Hinayana

KEY CONCEPT Capitalize the names of other special places and items. ■

This final rule applies to proper nouns such as monuments, memorials, buildings, celestial bodies, awards, names of specific vehicles, and trademarks.

The following chart shows specific examples of these other kinds of proper nouns.

OTHER SPECIAL PLACES AND ITEMS	
Monuments	Eiffel Tower, Statue of Liberty
Memorials	Tomb of the Unknown Soldier
Buildings	Museum of Natural History
Celestial Bodies (except the moon and the sun)	Spiral Galaxy, Jupiter, Orion, Earth
Awards	Pulitzer Prize, Nobel Peace Prize
Air, Sea, Space, and Land Craft	*Air Force One, Lusitania, Apollo 12,* Ford Model A
Trademarks	Krispy Crackers, Seemore Electronics

Exercise 6 **Using Capitals for Other Proper Nouns** On your paper, write all the proper nouns that do not have capitals in the following sentences.

1. While traveling through Utah last may, Naira and her friends discovered many fascinating places.
2. In Salt Lake City, they gathered at the state capitol building, where the utah legislature was in session.
3. They saw statues of the "Father of Television" Philo Farnsworth and the mormon leader Brigham Young.
4. Because they were downtown on sunday, they stopped to hear a catholic mass given in spanish.
5. In the afternoon, they spent two hours at Salt Lake's living traditions festival.
6. In cedar city, they saw the old sorrel house monument.
7. They decided to pass through Myton, the home of the grave of Sidney, the three-legged dog.
8. If they hadn't been driving a new yuma 4 × 4, they would not have reached the grave of Old Ephraim, "The Last Grizzly Bear in Utah."
9. The skull of the bear, however, was on display at the library of utah state university.
10. Naira and her friends wished they could have gone to Strasburg, Iowa, to see the 56-foot-tall golden spike.

More Practice

Grammar Exercise Workbook
- pp. 191–196

On-line Exercise Bank
- Chapter 27

Go on-line: PHSchool.com
Enter Web Code: eck-8002

Get instant feedback! Exercises 6 and 7 are available on-line or on CD-ROM.

Using Capitals for Proper Adjectives

KEY CONCEPT Capitalize proper adjectives. ■

In the following examples, notice that both proper nouns and proper adjectives are capitalized. Common nouns that are modified by proper adjectives, however, are not capitalized.

PROPER NOUNS:	World War I	Canada
PROPER ADJECTIVES:	a World War I battle a Canadian flag	

A trademark, the name of a company's product, is considered a proper noun. If you use only part of the trademark, or brand name, to describe a common noun, the brand name becomes a proper adjective. In this case, capitalize only the proper adjective.

PROPER NOUN:	Healthy Grains
PROPER ADJECTIVE:	Healthy Grains cereal

Grammar and Style Tip

The names of some countries and states must be modified to be used as proper adjectives. For example, something from Kenya is Kenyan, someone from Texas is Texan, a chair from Spain is a Spanish chair, and a building in France is a French building.

Exercise 7 **Using Capitals for Proper Adjectives** Complete each of the following sentences by supplying a proper adjective that is correctly capitalized.

EXAMPLE: Her most treasured possession was an antique __?__ sofa.

ANSWER: Victorian

1. Although Moorhead, Minnesota, is far from the home of the Vikings, you can find an exact replica of a __?__ ship there.
2. In honor of the settlers from Norway, who came to Illinois in 1835, there is a __?__ Settlers State Memorial.
3. At Florida Splendid China theme park, you can see replicas of the Great Wall of China and __?__ temples.
4. From San Diego to San Francisco, one can enjoy the beautiful __?__ scenery.
5. Holland, Michigan, has much in common with its European counterpart, including thousands of tulips, windmills, and __?__ wooden shoes.

▲ **Critical Viewing** Where might this windmill be located? If it is in the Netherlands, what proper adjective would you use to describe it? **[Speculate]**

Using Capitals for Titles of People

Several rules govern the use of capitals for titles of people.

Social and Professional Titles Social and professional titles may be written before a person's name or may be used when speaking directly to another person.

KEY CONCEPT Capitalize a person's title when it is followed by the person's name or when used in direct address. ■

The following chart gives examples of some of these titles.

TITLES OF PEOPLE	
Social	Mister, Madam or Madame, Miss, Sir
Business	Doctor, Professor, Superintendent
Religious	Reverend, Father, Rabbi, Bishop, Sister
Military	Private, Ensign, Captain, General, Admiral, Colonel
Government	President, Secretary of State, Ambassador, Senator, Representative, Governor, Mayor

KEY CONCEPT Capitalize the titles of certain high government officials even when the titles are not followed by a person's name or used in direct address. ■

WITH A PERSON'S NAME:	Queen Victoria ruled England.
WITHOUT A PERSON'S NAME:	The President greeted the Queen.

The titles of other government officials may also be capitalized when there is no name given, but only when they refer to the specific person who has that title.

SPECIFIC REFERENCE:	The Mayor will speak with you now.
GENERAL REFERENCE:	The mayor of a large city works hard.

▲ **Critical Viewing** Who might have traveled through this landscape to Echo Cliffs, Arizona? Write two sentences describing these travelers. Capitalize titles in your sentences. **[Speculate]**

Exercise 8 **Using Capitals for Social and Professional Titles** If the title in each of these sentences is correctly capitalized, write *correct*. If it is not, rewrite the title correctly.

1. It is likely that the state of Washington is named after president George Washington.
2. A shoe of mr. Robert Wadlow is found in a collection of giant shoes in Seattle, Washington.
3. Will you please take a picture of me, Sir?
4. The president was seated in the Oval Office.
5. Because the Professor was teaching a class about chickens, the class visited the world's largest egg.
6. At the Whitman Massacre Site Interpretive Center, there are depictions of doctor Marcus Whitman and his wife.
7. If you want to visit with the Pastor of the Evangelisch Lutherisch Kirche, you will have to wait for the service.
8. Excuse me, Miss, there is room for only forty-six people in that little church.
9. When we visit uncle Fred, we always see interesting tourist attractions.
10. Josh wondered if the mayor had made a statement about the gigantic concrete troll in Fremont, Washington.

KEY CONCEPT Capitalize titles showing family relationships when the title is used with the person's name or as the person's name. ■

WITH A NAME:	We invited Aunt Rebecca to the party.
AS A NAME:	Watch out, Uncle Tom, or you'll slip. Is Grandmother going?

Exercise 9 **Using Capitals for Family Titles** Complete each of the following sentences by filling in the blank with a family title or a title with a name.

EXAMPLE: Please, __?__, take us to see the ball of twine.
ANSWER: Please, Grandfather, take us to see the ball of twine.

1. Meredith will visit __?__ in Minneapolis.
2. __?__ Paul catches big fish, but they are nothing compared to the plastic 28-foot codfish in Madison, Minnesota.
3. Will __?__ come with us to see the walleye?
4. When my __?__ took me to the mall in Bloomington, we saw Snoopy.
5. __?__ Sophia explained that the dog dish in front of Snoopy is the largest in the world.

KEY CONCEPT Capitalize the first word and all the other important words in the titles of books, periodicals, poems, stories, plays, song titles, movies, and works of art. ■

Notice the use of underlining and quotation marks in the following examples. Also, notice that no matter how short, verbs—such as *Is* in the poem title—are always capitalized.

BOOK: The Red Pony
PERIODICAL: National Geographic
POEM: "It Is a Beauteous Evening"
SHORT STORY: "The Gold Bug"
PAINTING: A Girl With a Watering Can

Get instant feedback! Exercises 8, 9, and 10 are available on-line or on CD-ROM.

Exercise 10 Rewrite the titles below, adding the missing capitals.

EXAMPLE: the family in the garden at argenteuil
ANSWER: The Family in the Garden at Argenteuil

1. starry night (painting)
2. "america the beautiful" (song)
3. tarean the golden lion (movie)
4. "o captain, my captain!" (poem)
5. a wrinkle in time (book)

More Practice

Grammar Exercise Workbook
- pp. 197–198

On-line Exercise Bank
- Chapter 27

Go on-line:
PHSchool.com
Enter Web Code:
eck-8002

KEY CONCEPT Capitalize titles of school courses when the courses are language courses or when the courses are followed by a number. ■

EXAMPLE: My schedule includes Latin, English, and Science 101.

Although languages are always capitalized, other school subjects should not be capitalized when discussed in a general manner.

EXAMPLE: This semester I will study typing, algebra, and Spanish.

Exercise 11 **Using Capitals for Titles of Things** For each of the following, choose the correctly written course title from the choices in parentheses, and write it on your paper.

1. If you want to go to Mexico, you should take a (Spanish, spanish) class.
2. Carlos took (English, english), (Italian, italian), (Biology 200, biology 200), and (Literature, literature) during his first semester.
3. The students had to decide between (Physical Science, physical science) and (English, english).
4. There was not enough time in Martha's schedule to take (Agriculture 204, agriculture 204)
5. Paul and Connie were happy to have (Accounting, accounting) together.

More Practice

Grammar Exercise Workbook
- pp. 199–200

On-line Exercise Bank
- Chapter 27

Go on-line: PHSchool.com
Enter Web Code: eck-8002

Get instant feedback! Exercises 11 and 12 are available on-line or on CD-ROM.

KEY CONCEPT Capitalize the first word and all nouns and pronouns in letter salutations, as well as the first word in letter closings. ■

SALUTATIONS:	Dear Mr. Perkins:	Dear Aunt Maude,
CLOSINGS:	Sincerely yours,	Yours truly,

Spelling Tip

To recall the correct spelling of *sincerely*, remember that the adjective *sincere* becomes an adverb by adding *-ly*.

Exercise 12 **Using Capitals for Letter Salutations and Closings** Rewrite each of the following letter parts, adding the missing capitals.

1. to whom it may concern,
2. thank you,
3. my beloved brothers and sisters,
4. dear uncle dave,
5. with love,

Hands-on Grammar

Proper Noun Package

Classify proper nouns into categories so that you will be able to remember to capitalize them.

Fold a piece of 6 1/2" x 8 1/2" paper in half the short way. Crease it. Open it back up, and fold each end down to the crease to form pockets, as shown in the illustration. Cut four 3/4" slots in each pocket. These will hold your proper noun lists. Then, cut eight strips of paper 1 3/4" wide x 3 1/4" long. On the top of each list, put a category of proper noun, such as *desert, river, title, event, island, mountain, day, country, state.*

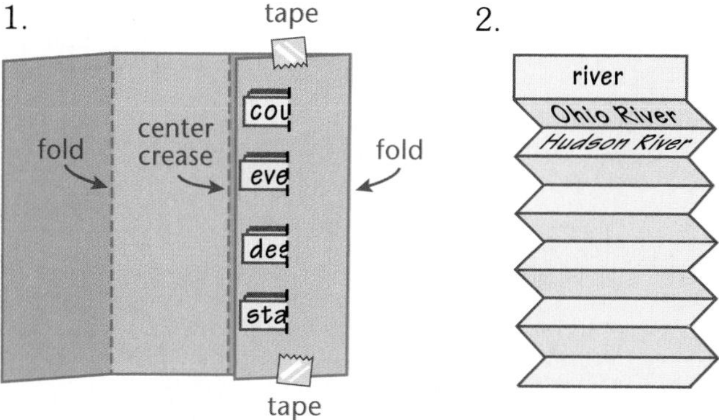

List the following proper nouns on the appropriate strip of paper: *Memorial Day, New Year's Day, Long Island, Orcas Island, Mount Rainier, Rocky Mountains, Utah, Maine, Arizona, Rose Bowl, New York State Fair, Mojave Desert, Gobi Desert, Ohio River, Hudson River, Algeria, Spain, Uncle John, Aunt Joan, Queen Anne, Admiral Nelson.* Then, for each strip, make approximately 1/2" folds back and forth like an accordion or a fan, and slip it into a slot in the pocket of the package. You can fold this package in half and keep it in your notebook or desk. Add proper nouns to your lists from your daily reading.

Find It in Your Reading In your reading, find sentences with capitalized proper nouns and titles. Copy each of these words onto the appropriate list in your package. Make additional lists with other categories, if necessary.

Find It in Your Writing Look through samples of your own writing to find sentences in which you have used both proper and common nouns to see whether you have capitalized the proper nouns.

PART 3

Academic and Workplace Skills

Emblems, Roger De La Fresnaye, The Phillips Collection, Washington, DC

Chapter

28 Speaking, Listening, Viewing, and Representing

▲ **Critical Viewing** What type of presentation do you think this student is giving? Why? **[Analyze]**

In today's world, more and more information is being presented through visual media, such as television, radio, and Internet Web sites. To be an effective communicator in today's media-rich age, it is essential not only to be a strong writer but also to be a strong speaker, listener, viewer, and presenter. In this chapter, you will learn strategies for developing all of these skills.

Section 28.1

Speaking and Listening Skills

If you speak well, you can communicate your ideas clearly. If you listen well, you can remember and understand more of what you hear. Speaking and listening require that you actively engage in thinking about how you want to express yourself and how you process what you hear.

Using Informal Speaking Skills

Every day, you practice informal speaking in the classroom, with your friends, and at home with your family. By making a conscious effort to build your informal speaking skills, you will become a more effective participant in class discussions and improve your ability to give directions.

Take Part in Class Discussions Practice and preparation are keys to improving your classroom participation.

1. Do the required homework and reading so that you are well prepared.
2. Plan the points you want to make, and review homework before the discussion begins.
3. Volunteer to contribute your ideas.
4. Listen to the discussion carefully, and make sure that your points are relevant to the discussion.
5. Ask questions about what you do not understand or would like to know more about.

Give Directions Being able to give clear and accurate directions that people can follow easily is a valuable skill.

1. Think through directions carefully before you speak.
2. Speak slowly so that your listeners can follow.
3. Choose your words carefully, being as specific as you can. Give only one step of the directions in each sentence.
4. Give the most important details, but do not confuse your listener with unnecessary information.

Speaking and Listening Tip

A great way to build confidence for participating in class discussions is to practice your group discussion skills with friends. Hold informal group discussions about subjects you are studying in school. Make sure that everyone in the group participates.

Exercise 1 **Improving Class Participation Skills** Set a goal for how many times per week you will participate in each of your classes, and record your contributions for one week.

Exercise 2 **Writing Directions** Write directions from one location in school to another. Read your directions aloud to a classmate, and have that person evaluate them.

28.1

Using Formal Speaking Skills

As a student—and later, when you enter the work force—you will be called on to deliver formal speeches in front of audiences. By understanding the different types of speeches and learning strategies for preparing and delivering a speech, you can build the confidence and the skills necessary to succeed in these situations.

Recognize the Different Types of Speeches There are numerous different topics and occasions for speeches. However, virtually all speeches can be classified into one of the following categories: *explanatory, persuasive,* or *entertaining.*

- An **explanatory** speech provides information about or explanations of an idea, an object, or an event. A speech you deliver in school about information you have gathered about a historical event is an example of an explanatory speech.
- A **persuasive** speech is one in which the speaker attempts to persuade the audience to agree with a point of view or to take some course of action. Most political speeches are examples of persuasive speeches.
- An **entertaining** speech is given to amuse the audience. Speeches given at weddings and parties are most often entertaining speeches.

KEY CONCEPT Choose the kind of speech you will give by considering both the purpose of the speech and your audience. Use appropriate language when presenting your speech. ■

Exercise 3 **Listing Kinds of Speeches** Give two topic examples for each speech described above. Then, identify appropriate audiences for each.

Prepare Your Speech Thorough preparation is the key to delivering a successful speech. Follow these steps to help you choose a topic, gather information, and rehearse.

Choose Your Topic Sometimes, a topic is assigned to you—either in school or at work. When it is up to you to choose a topic, consider the kind of speech you will be giving as well as your audience, and search for a topic that will interest them. For example, if you are delivering an entertaining speech to friends at a party, think of topics that will amuse them.

Technology Tip

One of the best ways to build your speaking skills is to see and hear models of good speeches. Consult with your teacher or librarian to find examples of each type of speech on videotape, audiotape, or on the Internet.

Gather Information If your topic is an area in which you are not an expert, you will want to gather information by conducting research in the library or on the Internet.

Outline Main Points and Supporting Details Organize your information into an outline like the one to the right. Group your details under subtopics or main points. Arrange the subtopics in a logical order.

Prepare Note Cards Print the information in your outline on small index cards to which you can refer as you deliver your speech.

- Make note cards that contain your opening and closing statements.
- Create at least one note card for each subtopic. Underline the subtopic, and list the key details beneath it.
- Number your note cards to help you keep them in order.

Practice Your Speech Before you deliver your speech, rehearse, either on your own or with a family member or classmate. Don't try to memorize what you will say. Instead, use your note cards to guide you in presenting your key points. Use body language and the tone and volume of your voice to emphasize key points.

SAMPLE OUTLINE

Making a Terrarium

A. Selection of basic ingredients
 1. Use a fish tank or bowl
 2. Find good soil, sand, and gravel
 3. Choose plants

B. Preparation of soil
 1. Line bottom with layer of gravel
 2. Place equal amounts of sand and soil on gravel

C. Rooting of plants
 1. Dig holes and press roots into holes
 2. Add stones and bark
 3. Place near window for sunlight

Deliver Your Speech When it is time to deliver your speech, use the following strategies:

1. Review your note cards to refresh your memory before you start.
2. Do not read to your audience. Use your note cards to help you focus on your key points, but do not read from the cards word for word.
3. Speak slowly, pronouncing each of your words clearly.
4. Make eye contact with members of the audience.
5. Use *verbal* techniques, such as altering the tone and loudness of your voice, to emphasize key points.
6. Use *nonverbal* techniques, such as your movements, posture, facial expressions, and gestures, to reinforce your ideas and to maintain the attention of your audience.

Exercise 4 **Preparing and Presenting a Speech** Prepare a short speech on a current issue about which you feel strongly or on a topic of special interest to you. Follow the steps presented in this section to plan and deliver your speech.

Evaluate a Speech Evaluating the speeches of others can help you improve your own speaking skills.

KEY CONCEPT When you evaluate a speech, critically examine the effectiveness of the content and the delivery. ■

Following is a checklist that will help guide you in evaluating a speech:

CHECKLIST FOR EVALUATING A SPEECH

- Did the speech achieve its purpose? For example, did it explain thoroughly, persuade convincingly, or entertain effectively?
- Did the speaker elaborate his or her main ideas and support each with facts or appropriate details?
- Did the speaker introduce the topic clearly, develop it well, and conclude it effectively?
- Did the speaker's facial expressions, gestures, and movements reinforce the spoken message?
- Did the speaker give complete answers to audience questions?

Exercise 5 **Evaluating a Speech** Using the checklist, write an evaluation for a speech given in class. Consider the content and credibility of the information presented, as well as the speaker's delivery. Then, give a copy of your evaluation to the person who gave the speech.

Listening Effectively

When you think about listening, you probably think of it as something you do naturally—not as a skill that you have to practice and develop. However, there is a major difference between simply hearing what is being said and effectively listening to what is being said. To be an effective listener, you have to get involved with what you are hearing and use strategies to make sure that you understand what is being said.

▲ **Critical Viewing** What details in this photograph suggest that these students are listening effectively to one another? **[Analyze]**

KEY CONCEPT The keys to effective listening include setting a purpose for listening, eliminating distractions, asking questions, and taking good notes. ■

Determine Your Purpose for Listening When you determine your purpose for listening, you identify what you want to take away from what you are hearing. Your purpose will affect how you listen and how you respond to what is said. Following are possible purposes for listening:

- **To Gain Information** Listen for main ideas and major details.
- **To Solve Problems** Listen and ask questions to clarify problems so that a solution can be found.
- **To Enjoy and Appreciate** Listen for artistic elements, such as rhyme, imagery, and descriptive language.

Eliminate Barriers Prepare to listen by putting away all distracting material (books, magazines, homework). Block out all distracting noises, inside and outside the classroom, so that you can concentrate on the speaker and his or her message.

Summarize Main Ideas and Supporting Details Summarizing a speaker's message forces you to listen attentively and to make decisions about what is important. Use the suggestions below to summarize a speaker's message:

- Write down in your own words only main ideas and supporting details—the information you want to remember.
- Underline main ideas to make them easy to locate when you want to refer to them.
- Write notes in short phrases, not complete sentences.

Exercise 6 **Becoming an Active Listener** For one week, practice active listening techniques in one of your classes. Track your progress in your notebook.

Listening Critically

In addition to listening effectively in order to comprehend what is said, it is important to critically evaluate the points a speaker is making.

KEY CONCEPT Become a critical listener by learning to distinguish fact from opinion, recognize persuasive language, and interpret a speaker's use of both verbal and nonverbal techniques. ■

Recognize Facts and Opinions A **fact** is something that can be verified as true. An **opinion** is something that cannot be proved to be true. Speakers must support opinions with facts before the opinions can be accepted as valid. Listen for opinions unsupported by evidence.

Analyze Persuasive Language Pay close attention to the words a speaker chooses. The **denotation** of a word is its literal or exact meaning. The **connotation** is its suggested or implied meaning. Speakers may choose words with negative connotations to present someone or something unfavorably. Positive connotations present someone or something favorably.

NEUTRAL: He *walked* through the crowd.

NEGATIVE CONNOTATION: He *stumbled* through the crowd.

POSITIVE CONNOTATION: He *paraded* through the crowd.

Interpret the Speaker's Message To interpret the speaker's message, be aware of verbal and nonverbal gestures.

- **Verbal Signals** Notice how a speaker chooses to emphasize or elaborate some points over others. Pay attention to when the speaker raises or lowers, or slows down or speeds up, his or her voice.
- **Nonverbal Signals** Notice a speaker's movements, such as arm waving, head nodding, or moving closer to or farther away from the audience.

Paying careful attention to verbal and nonverbal signals can enhance your comprehension of a speaker's message and reveal the speaker's attitudes and emotions about a subject.

Technology Tip

Apply all of these strategies when you are watching political speeches and debates on television.

Exercise 7 **Listening Critically** Listen to a speech in school or on television. Record examples of fact and opinion statements, denotation and connotation, and verbal and nonverbal signals.

Evaluate Your Listening One way to improve your listening skills is to evaluate them, deciding which listening skills work for you and which skills need improvement.

KEY CONCEPT Improve your listening skills through self-evaluation and comparison and contrast. ■

Monitor Your Understanding You can test your understanding of the speaker's message by restating parts of it to the speaker. If your restatement is accurate, you know you have listened well. If it is inaccurate, ask questions to improve it.

Compare and Contrast Interpretations Write your interpretation of a speaker's message, and then compare and contrast it with another student's interpretation. Use a Venn diagram to list the points on which you agree and disagree. Resolve these points of disagreement through discussion.

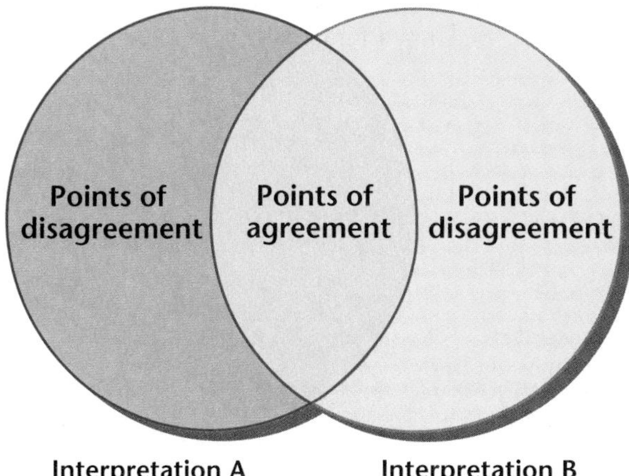

Technology Tip

Practice your listening skills with audio books at your school or public library.

Exercise 8 **Evaluating Your Listening Skills** Work with another classmate to complete the following activities.

1. Have your classmate read a paper or present a speech to you. Have him or her pause periodically so that you can restate the information. Afterward, exchange roles.
2. With your classmate, listen to a speech in class, then write your interpretations of the speaker's message. Afterward, compare and contrast what you have written..
3. Write an evaluation of your listening skills. Identify the areas in which you excelled and those in which you need improvement.

Section 28.2

Viewing and Representing Skills

Interpreting Maps and Graphs

Textbooks and other written works use an assortment of maps and graphs to convey information.

KEY CONCEPT Interpret maps and graphs to become a more informed reader. ■

Maps

Maps can do more than simply guide you to a destination. Maps can also show you historical information, indicate the borders and sizes of countries, or provide vital statistics of population or agriculture. To interpret a map: **(1)** Determine the type and purpose of the map. **(2)** Examine the map's distance scale and any symbols. **(3)** Relate the map's information to any accompanying written information.

CHOOSING SIDES IN THE CIVIL WAR

Graphs

Graphs provide a visual comparison of several pieces of related information. Different kinds of graphs are used to show different kinds of information.

Pie Graph A **pie graph** shows the relationship of parts to a whole. The graph is a circle that stands for 100 percent of something. Each part stands for a certain portion, or percentage, of the whole. This pie graph shows France's Gross Domestic Product, the total output of all goods and services produced in one year. To interpret the pie graph: **(1)** Look at the numbers that go with the individual parts. **(2)** Match the individual parts with the key. **(3)** Use the numbers and parts to make comparisons.

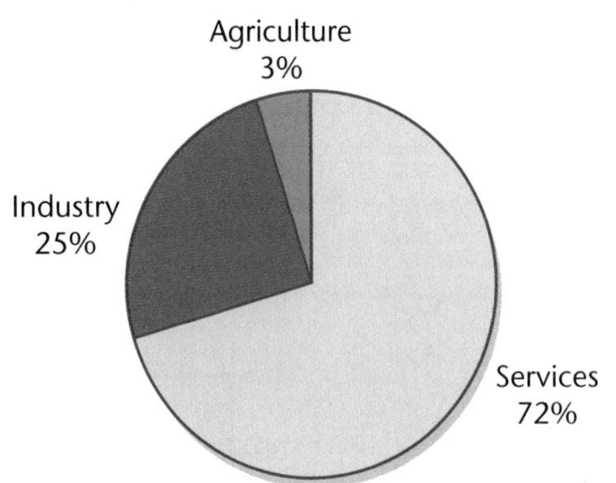

Bar Graph A **bar graph** compares and contrasts amounts. In a bar graph, you read the heights or lengths of bars to see the numbers they represent. To interpret a bar graph: **(1)** Look at the heights or lengths of the bars. **(2)** Match the subject that goes with the bar to the number the bar reaches. **(3)** Compare and contrast the heights or lengths of bars.

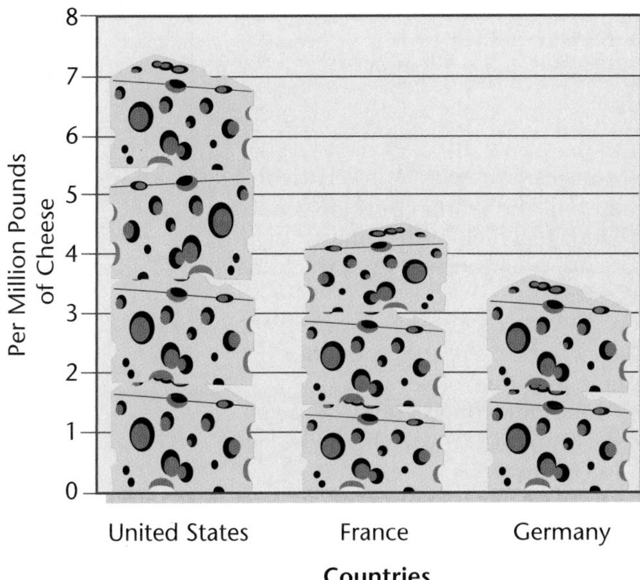

Data from *World Book Encyclopedia*

Line Graph A **line graph** shows changes over a specific period of time. It features a line that connects points. The points, which may appear as actual dots, represent numbers or amounts of something. To interpret a line graph: **(1)** Look across the horizontal and vertical lines to determine what information is shown. **(2)** Compare and contrast points. **(3)** Identify patterns of change.

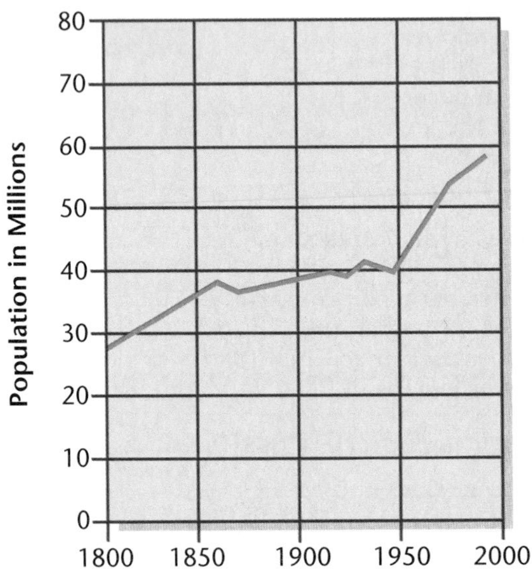

Exercise 9 **Interpreting Maps and Graphs** Answer the following questions about the map and the graphs in this section.

1. Use the Civil War map to identify which state split in two in 1861, leading to the formation of another state that was admitted to the Union in 1863.
2. Use the pie graph to determine the combined percentage of France's industry and agriculture. What is the difference between this percentage and that of services?
3. Use the bar graph to determine how much cheese is produced in the United States. How much more cheese is produced in France than in Germany?
4. Use the line graph to determine the increase in France's population from 1850 to 1950, and from 1950 to 2000. What is the difference between the two?

Viewing Information Media Critically

Since the media distribute large amounts of information, it is important to learn how to view this information critically. As a critical viewer, you will learn to evaluate the information for content, quality, and importance.

KEY CONCEPT Become a critical viewer by learning to identify and evaluate different types of visual media and images. ■

Recognize Kinds of Information Media Knowing the characteristics of various kinds of media will help you to identify them during your viewing. The following chart describes several forms of information media.

TYPES OF INFORMATION MEDIA

Television News Program	Television Newsmagazine
• Covers current news events • Gives information objectively	• Covers a variety of topics • Entertains and informs
Documentary	**Commercial**
• Focuses on one topic of social interest • Sometimes expresses controversial opinions	• Presents products, people, or ideas • Persuades people to buy or take action

Research Tip

Many television news organizations have Web sites with in-depth coverage of current events.

Exercise 10 Identifying Types of Information Media Identify each of the four types of information media in your viewing. For each type, describe the topics covered, and then write down your impressions of the way the topics were presented.

Evaluate Persuasive Techniques The media sometimes use persuasive techniques to present information in a particular way. Knowledge of these techniques will help you to evaluate the credibility of information presented through the media.

Facts and opinions are important to separate when watching the media. A *fact* is a statement that can be proved to be true. An *opinion* is a viewpoint that cannot be proved to be true.

Bias is a tendency to think in a certain way. As you watch, consider whether the information is being presented in a one-sided way, or whether it takes into account all viewpoints.

Loaded language and images are emotional words and visuals used to persuade you to think a certain way.

Evaluate Information From the Media Combine your knowledge of persuasive techniques with the following strategies to increase your understanding of the messages conveyed through the media:

- Be aware of the kind of program you are watching. What is its purpose? What are its limitations?
- Sort out facts from opinions. Make sure that any opinions presented are solidly backed up with facts.
- Be aware of any loaded language or images that may cause you to react in a certain way.
- Listen for bias, and note any points of view not discussed. If you detect bias, try to gather information on other points of view that have not been presented before deciding with which point of view you agree.
- Check surprising or questionable information in other sources.
- View the complete program before reaching a conclusion. Then, develop your own views on the issues, people, and information presented.

Learn More

For more information about methods of persuasion, see Chapter 7.

Exercise 11 Evaluating Information From the Media
Watch a news or other informative program, including the commercials. In an essay, identify the kind of program you watched and describe the topics it covered. Also, identify what each commercial was selling and the slogans and images that were used to impress viewers. Then, evaluate the information on each topic in the program and in the commercials, using the viewing strategies on this page. Write a summary of your evaluation.

Interpreting Fine Art

Paintings, drawings, sculptures, and photographs are all examples of fine art. When you view fine art, you have to use different standards for evaluation than when you view the media. Instead of looking for persuasive techniques, you look for artistic ones, such as shape, line, and color. Learning how to view fine art will help you to see and experience the vision of the artist.

KEY CONCEPT Enrich your enjoyment and understanding of fine art by interpreting the elements that create the work. ■

INTERPRETING ELEMENTS OF VISUAL ART

- What kind of artwork are you viewing?
- What is the subject or central focus of the piece?
- What mood, theme, or message does the work convey?
- What colors and shapes are present in the artwork?
- What feelings does the art evoke?

Exercise 12 **Interpreting Fine Art** Interpret the painting below—*Zinnias* by John Hollis Kaufmann—by asking the questions from the chart above. Write your answers in your notebook, along with any other observations you might care to make.

Zinnias, 1937, John Hollis Kaufmann, Private Collection

In addition to learning how to interpret the visual information that you encounter, it is important to develop the ability to use visuals to present your own ideas. For example, you can use visual aids when delivering a speech, or you can create a report that consists entirely of multimedia elements.

▲ Critical Viewing What types of visual aids could you create with a pen and a piece of paper, as this girl is doing? For what types would you have to use a computer? **[Analyze]**

Creating Visual Aids

When you have technical data or important information to present, consider putting that information into a visual form that is easy to comprehend. Visual aids can also help you to organize research for a paper or to study for a test.

KEY CONCEPT To make complex information easier to understand, create a visual aid in which to organize it. ■

Use these strategies to construct your own visual aids:

Use Text Descriptions When you read a textbook or another informational text, you may notice that information is organized with headings and subheadings to indicate various sections. To help you understand all this information, create a graphic organizer, such as a concept map, to display the information visually. For text with many descriptions, you may want to create a drawing to clarify these details.

Learn More

You can find several different types of graphic organizers in the chapters on writing.

Look at Text Structure The organization or structure of a text can help you create graphic organizers. First, identify the text structure. Is it comparison-and-contrast, cause-and-effect, main-idea-and-details, or chronological order? For comparison and contrast, a Venn diagram or a comparison chart can show similarities and differences. A flowchart can help you understand cause-and-effect relationships. An outline is a good way to organize main ideas with supporting details. One way to visualize chronological order is with a timeline.

Identify Your Purpose Consider which part of the text you would like to understand better. Then, decide which type of graphic organizer will help you to communicate this information effectively. For instance, perhaps you would like to show the contrast between two characters in a story or chart the outcomes of their actions. You may also want to make an outline of a persuasive essay so that you can understand the author's main points.

Following are descriptions of various types of visual aids:

Charts, Graphs, and Tables To present columns of numbers or survey statistics, create a chart, graph, or table. A *chart* can be any shape or color and contain any type of information. A *graph*, such as a bar or line graph, is a good way to show changes that take place over time. *Tables* enable you to present scientific and mathematical information clearly and logically.

Diagrams and Illustrations Diagrams and illustrations are line drawings that indicate the features of something.

Maps To explain directions to your house or present geographical information about one or more regions, put that information into map form. Maps can show almost any type of information—from mountain ranges to airplane flight patterns to important monuments and landmarks. The map below shows important landmarks in Paris.

PARIS LANDMARKS

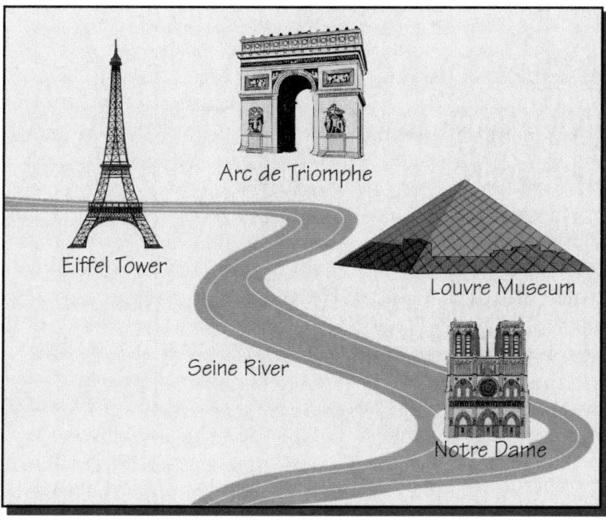

Exercise 13 **Creating Visual Aids** Complete the following:

1. Create one visual aid to illustrate a portion of a chapter from one of your textbooks. Write your reasons why this particular visual aid best represents the information.
2. Take a poll on any topic in your class, and arrange the information into a pie graph or a bar graph. Clearly label your graph, and include titles and a key, if necessary.

Technology Tip

Use a computer to make charts, graphs, and tables. Look in the computer manual or use the Help function to find out how you can draw diagrams and illustrations on the screen.

Using Formatting Features

Using basic formatting features, found on most word processors, can enhance any written work. Following are some tips for creating effective visual enhancements to your text:

- **Capital Letters** Use capital letters in heads to call out important ideas and topics.
- **Boldface or Italics** Boldface or italics can direct the reader's eyes or give special emphasis to key concepts or ideas.
- **Numbered or Bulleted Lists** When you have steps to be followed in sequence, use a numbered list. Items that can be presented in any order can go in a bulleted list.
- **Graphics and Color** Use graphics and color to attract a reader's attention and to reinforce your message.

EXPERIENCED, DEPENDABLE BABYSITTERS WILL CARE FOR YOUR CHILDREN

- Excellent references
- Formal babysitter training
- Neat, clean, and careful
- Love children
- Available after school and weekends

Call or e-mail
Rhonda, Jackie, or Melanie
to set up an appointment
phone: 210-555-5182
e-mail: www.babysit.place

Exercise 14 **Using Formatting to Create a Flyer** Use the tips on formatting and design to create a flyer that promotes a student-run business. When your flyer is complete, ask a classmate to evaluate your use of formatting features.

Technology Tip

Find out how to use these formatting techniques on your computer. Experiment with other formatting options, such as page borders and shading, different fonts (type styles), and special effects on type, such as outlines and shadows.

Working With Multimedia

In a multimedia presentation, the presenter gives an oral report and then uses media selections to illustrate main points. With careful planning and creativity, this kind of presentation can be informative and memorable.

KEY CONCEPT Multimedia presentations supply information through a variety of media, including text, slides, videos, music, maps, charts, and artwork. ■

Prepare and Give a Multimedia Presentation The first step in preparing a multimedia presentation is to consider the topic, the audience, and the equipment available to you. Then, follow these suggestions to create your presentation:

- Create an outline of your report, and then decide which parts to illustrate using media.
- Choose a medium that is suited to your topic. For example, if you were discussing the plays of William Shakespeare, you might use video to show scenes from the plays, music from his time period, and charts to show the order in which the plays were written.
- Evenly space the media you use within your presentation. Do not present all the media at the beginning or at the end, or their effectiveness will be diminished.
- Check to ensure that the media you've selected will be able to be seen and/or heard by everyone. Images that are too small cannot be seen by everyone, and music that is too loud will overwhelm your presentation.
- Before the presentation, check your equipment—slide projectors, overhead projectors, microphones, cassette players—to be sure that they are in working order.
- Rehearse with the equipment before the day of the presentation.
- Always have a backup plan in case anything goes wrong with the equipment.

Research Tip

Your school or public library may have slides, videos, and audiocassettes that you can use in your multimedia presentation.

Exercise 15 **Preparing a Multimedia Presentation** Read through some writings in your portfolio. Select one piece to prepare as a multimedia presentation. Choose appropriate forms of media to illustrate your writing. Then, outline a plan showing how you will use the media, and the order in which it will be presented. Rehearse your presentation, and then present it to your classmates.

Creating a Video

Telling a story or reporting on a topic by using images, sound, and dialogue is a powerful way to communicate. A film allows your viewers to see the particular subject matter, event, or story through your eyes. A film can be informative, humorous, or dramatic.

KEY CONCEPT Create a film to communicate information, to entertain, or to do both. ■

Organization is the most essential component in making a film. Follow these basic steps:

Basic Steps

1. Write out the story or message in the form of a shooting script. A *shooting script* contains lines to be spoken, or dialogue among the characters. It also contains directions about camera angles and descriptions of settings, costumes or wardrobe, and props.
2. Create an outline of the scenes, places, and shots you want to cover. Use your outline while shooting.
3. Select locations for shooting, and get permission to use them.
4. Cast people to play the various roles, and rehearse.
5. Film the scenes. Edit the film.

Tips for Filming

- Hold the camera steady.
- Use the following filming techniques for effect:

  Pan: Move the camera to the left or right.

  Zoom: Adjust from a distant to a close shot while filming.

  Fade: Increase or reduce the intensity of a picture.

  Cut: Move directly from one shot to another.
- When in doubt, shoot more. It is easier to cut scenes than to have to reassemble the cast to refilm.
- Keep scenes simple and short.

Exercise 16 **Creating a Film** Create a three-minute film on a topic in which you are interested. Write out a script to follow while you are filming, and use your outline to ensure that you do not leave anything out. Select the location and actors for your film. Then, shoot and edit your work. Present the finished product to your classmates.

▼ **Critical Viewing** What type of video do you think these students are shooting? Why? **[Analyze]**

Performing and Interpreting

We have all experienced the thrill of watching a live performance in a theater or an auditorium. Actors, singers, musicians, and dancers are all performing artists.

KEY CONCEPT Performers use a variety of techniques to convey the meaning of a text. ■

Perform a Scene or Monologue Whether you are planning a performance or an original piece, the following steps can help to make your performance a success:

1. Write the text of the scene or monologue in a notebook, and highlight its most important words and ideas.
2. Read the text aloud several times, experimenting with the tone and pitch of your voice.
3. Consider selecting props, music, costumes, and settings to help express the meaning and mood of the text.
4. Rehearse, using gestures and other body language to express yourself.
5. Keep your performance simple and direct to ensure that it will have clarity and power.

Research Tip

You can learn more about how plays were performed in Shakespeare's time by doing research on the Globe Theater.

Exercise 17 **Performing a Scene From a Play** Select a scene from a play to interpret and perform, either alone or with others. Copy it, and highlight important ideas. Decide what you want to communicate, and take performance notes on setting, mood, costumes, and props. Rehearse, and then perform the scene for your class.

Reflecting on Your Speaking, Listening, Viewing, and Representing Skills

Review all the different strategies and suggestions discussed in this chapter. Write a journal entry discussing these experiences. Begin your inquiry by asking yourself these questions:

- What are my strengths and weaknesses as a speaker and as a listener? Which skills need improvement?
- What viewing experiences gave me the most information?
- What representing experiences did I find the most enjoyable?

Chapter 29 Vocabulary and Spelling

▲ **Critical Viewing** In what ways might taking notes as you read help you to increase your vocabulary and improve your spelling? **[Deduce]**

As your vocabulary and spelling improve, your pleasure in reading and writing will grow as well. You will be pleasantly surprised to see your reading comprehension become deeper as you become more knowledgeable about the meaning of a whole variety of words.

Adding to your vocabulary gives you new resources for your writing and, therefore, more ways to express yourself. Improving your spelling will help readers to form a good impression of your work and will allow them to focus on *what* you are writing, instead of being distracted by errors. Finally, as you work on both vocabulary and spelling skills, your standardized test-taking skills will improve. There are several techniques that can help you to develop your skills, and the reward is well worth the effort.

Section 29.1 Developing Vocabulary

Developing Your Vocabulary Through Listening

Conversation

Your vocabulary development began on the day you were born! Everyone is born with the ability to learn language. As a baby and a toddler, you soaked up words and grammar at an amazing rate. You used your listening skills to increase your vocabulary and to learn how to pronounce new words.

Now you can read and write, but one of your most important skills in language learning is still your listening skill. Throughout your life, you can (and should) learn and use new words in conversation. Whenever you talk with teachers, people from different places, and people whose interests and ideas are different from yours, listen for unfamiliar words. You can find out the meanings of the words by asking, listening for clues, and looking up the words in a dictionary.

Works Read Aloud

Listening to works of literature read aloud is another good way to build your vocabulary. Numerous books are available on audiocassette or CD, and most libraries have them. When you listen to a recorded book, you hear how unfamiliar words are pronounced, and how they are used in context. If you have a copy of the book, you may try reading along with the recording so that you can both see and hear new words.

Speaking and Listening Tip

Together with a partner, take turns reading a literary work aloud. Note words that are unfamiliar, and try to guess their meanings from the context in which they are used. Keep a list of the words, and check their meanings in a dictionary later.

Wide Reading

The more you read, the more new words you will encounter. When you see those words over and over again in different contexts, they will become familiar to you and part of your own vocabulary. Each time you read a word in a different context, you will increase your understanding of the word's meaning and usage. Read from a broad range of sources—books, magazines, newspapers, Internet articles—in order to encounter the widest variety of words.

Using Context

When you come across an unfamiliar word, you may not always need to use a dictionary. You might be able to figure out the meaning of the word by using clues from the author.

Recognize Context Clues

If you look carefully at the sentence or paragraph that contains the unfamiliar word, you can sometimes figure out the word's meaning.

KEY CONCEPT The **context** of a word means the group of words that surround it. ■

USING CONTEXT CLUES

1. Read the sentence, leaving out the unfamiliar word.
2. Find clues in the sentence to figure out the word's meaning.
3. Read the sentence again, substituting your possible meaning for the unfamiliar word.
4. Check your possible meaning by looking up the unfamiliar word in the dictionary. Write the word and its definition in your vocabulary notebook.

Figurative Language Figurative language is not meant to be taken literally. Many types of figurative language use words in unfamiliar ways. For example, you might read or hear the sentence, "This assignment is a piece of cake." The assignment does not literally have anything to do with making or eating cake; the comment is interpreted to mean that the assignment is easy.

Idioms An idiom is an expression used by people of a particular region or background. Sometimes, you will be unfamiliar with idioms used by people who are not from your area. When you recognize an unusual expression as an idiom, compare it to expressions that you use in similar instances.

Exercise 1 **Using Context Clues** Use context clues from the selection below to define the underlined words below.

In 1972, Michel Siffre entered a <u>subterranean</u> cave to experiment with living underground and alone. The cave was silent and seemed like a suitable <u>retreat</u>, away from society. Initially, Michel spent time reading, but after a week of the same thing, the activity became <u>tedious</u>. Soon, his condition began to <u>deteriorate</u>, and now, weak and gloomy, he sat <u>passively</u>, not moving for hours. He finally realized humans need companionship.

More Practice

Academic and Workplace Skills Activity Book
• pp. 19–20

Use Context Clues in All of Your Reading In any reading, whether it is fiction or nonfiction, you can often figure out the meaning of a word from its context.

Use Possible Sentences One good method for helping you to increase your vocabulary and your understanding of words in context is the possible-sentences strategy. Use it to experiment with unfamiliar words.

STEPS FOR USING POSSIBLE SENTENCES

1. Find an unfamiliar word in your reading, and try to figure out its meaning.
2. Write a sentence for the unfamiliar word in your vocabulary notebook.
3. Check the actual meaning of the word in a dictionary.
4. Evaluate your sentence to see whether you have used the word correctly.
5. Revise your sentence to make it correct.

Internet Tip

In an on-line encyclopedia, find a short entry on a subject of interest to you. Find three unfamiliar words, look them up in a dictionary, and add them to your notebook.

Exercise 2 **Using the Possible-Sentences Strategy With Words in Context** Choose a book about a subject that interests you, such as music, geography, computers, or gardening. Find five words that are unfamiliar to you. Use the possible-sentences strategy to define the words. Enter the words and their correct meanings in your vocabulary notebook.

Exercise 3 **Writing Possible Sentences to Learn New Words** Use the possible-sentences strategy to define the following words.

1. phonetic
2. renown
3. tangible
4. reverie
5. configuration

29.1

Studying Meanings in the Content Areas

Use a Notebook and a Glossary

When you are reading in your school subjects, you can often use context clues to help you figure out the meaning of unfamiliar words. However, you should make a practice of recording and studying words that are related to the content area. Keep a section of your notebook for each subject area, and list new words and their meanings. Use the glossary at the back of your textbook to find the specific definitions of unfamiliar words.

▲ **Critical Viewing** How will writing the definitions of various landforms help this geography student to increase her vocabulary? **[Infer]**

Social Studies In your social studies classes, you will discover new words that deal with historical events, government, political activities, and physical features of an area. Use the categories that apply to your subject to group words according to what they name or describe. Look for words that name or describe related features or situations.

Science Unfamiliar words in science often have Latin origins. Categorize science words by their prefixes, suffixes, or roots. For example, you could group *ultrasonic* with *ultraviolet* because both begin with *ultra-*. Once you learn that *ultra-* means "beyond the range of," you will more easily remember the meaning of each word.

Current Events By listening to the news or reading a newspaper, you increase the chances that you will encounter the words you learn in science and social studies. The more you see and hear a word used, the better you will understand its meaning. Use current-events topics to reinforce your vocabulary building.

Exercise 4 **Studying Words in the Content Areas** With a partner, look over a chapter in your science or social studies book, and list any unfamiliar words and their definitions. You might want to write them on index cards so that you can group the words in various ways. When you have the words defined and logically grouped, record them in your notebook.

Research Tip

Choose five unfamiliar words from any textbook. Check their definitions in the book's glossary, then use a thesaurus to find a synonym for each word.

Section 29.2

Studying Words Systematically

Keeping a Vocabulary Notebook

There are a variety of methods for studying and reviewing new words. Use the method that works best for you.

KEY CONCEPT Along with a dictionary, keep a notebook available to list new words. ■

Divide the page of your notebook into three sections: List (1) the word, (2) a bridge word or hint to help you remember the meaning, and (3) its dictionary definition.

SAMPLE VOCABULARY

Word	Bridge Word	Definition
tempestuous	"tempest"—violent storm	violent
amendment	to mend	a change for the better

Exercise 5 **Setting Up a Vocabulary Notebook** Focus on a textbook that you are using in one of your classes or on a story or poem you are reading in English. As you read, list any unfamiliar words. Afterwards, look up the words in a dictionary and record their meanings in your notebook.

More Practice
Academic and Workplace Skills Activity Book
• p. 22

Studying New Words

Use Your Notebook Practice learning the meanings by covering the definition and looking only at the word and the bridge word. Then, uncover the definition, and read it. Finally, write a new sentence using the word.

Write Sentences With Vocabulary Words When you write sentences using vocabulary words, reinforce the meaning of the word by using the word's definition in the sentence.

EXAMPLE: The crowd *dispersed* quickly, *scattering in all directions* when the performance ended.

Review New Words With Flashcards You can practice your vocabulary using a set of flashcards. Make a card for each word in your vocabulary notebook. On the front, write the word you want to remember. On the back, write the definition and the subject to which it relates. You can test yourself or ask others to test you.

Use a Tape Recorder Record a vocabulary word. First, pronounce the word carefully. Then, after a pause, record its definition. To review, play the tape. During the pause, recall the word's definition. Listen to the recorded definition to check yourself and to reinforce the word's meaning.

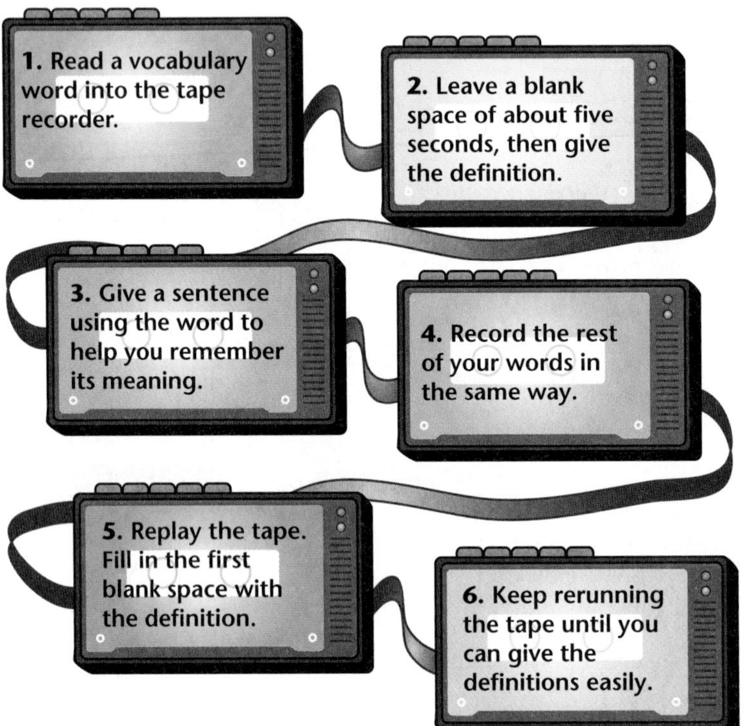

Research Tip

Find a book about outdoor sports—mountain climbing, hiking, skiing, kayaking, and so on. Find five unfamiliar words, and guess their meanings using context clues. Check their meanings in a dictionary.

Exercise 6 Making Flashcards or Tapes Make a set of flashcards or tapes to study the following words. Add words from your own reading or from assigned vocabulary lists.

1. context
2. elongate
3. periscope
4. anxiously
5. predisposed

Using a Dictionary

A dictionary provides more than just the definitions of a word. Look in a dictionary when you want to find out a word's pronunciation, its origins, or its uses as different parts of speech and in various expressions. Note that reading the origins of a word can help you make associations with other words that share the origin. Words in a dictionary are listed in alphabetical order. Whenever you are unsure of the meaning of a word you encounter in your reading, look it up. Record the words you look up in your vocabulary notebook.

Using Other Reference Aids

Thesaurus A thesaurus lists a word's synonyms (words with similar meanings) and, sometimes, its antonyms (words with opposite meanings). Words in some thesauruses are listed alphabetically. In others, words are arranged by categories according to an alphabetical index.

Synonym Finder Many word-processing programs have a synonym finder or thesaurus in their menus. If you are drafting on-line, highlight a word for which you want to find a synonym, and use the synonym finder or thesaurus to check alternative words.

▲ Critical Viewing What kinds of words would you expect to see defined in the glossary of a math book? **[Relate]**

Glossary A glossary is a list of terms and definitions specific to a field of study. Each of your textbooks will likely have a glossary that lists the words you need to know in that subject area. Check the book's table of contents to find out where the glossary appears.

Software Like most references, dictionaries and thesauruses are available in electronic form. Some can be purchased on CD-ROM and loaded onto your hard drive, while many others are available on the Internet. Search "on-line dictionary" or "on-line thesaurus."

Exercise 7 Using Vocabulary Reference Aids Look up each of the following words in the references indicated. Compare and contrast the information found in both sources.

1. deciduous (science textbook glossary, dictionary)
2. topography (social studies textbook glossary, dictionary)
3. constitutes (dictionary, thesaurus)
4. carnivorous (science textbook glossary, on-line dictionary)
5. steadfast (dictionary, synonym finder)

More Practice

Academic and Workplace Skills Activity Book
• p. 22

Section 29.3

Studying Word Parts and Origins

Using Roots

Learning the roots of words, their most fundamental part, will help you learn the meanings of entire groups of words. For example, if you know that the root *-script-* means "write," you have a key to the meaning of the following words: *script, manuscript, transcript, prescription, proscription,* and *postscript.*

KEY CONCEPT A **root** is the base of a word. ■

Knowing the roots of words is fundamental to developing your vocabulary. Roots have come into the English language from many sources, such as Latin and Greek (noted as L. and Gr.) or Anglo-Saxon (noted as A.S.). In the first column below, other versions of the same root are in parentheses.

SOME COMMON ROOTS		
Root and Origin	Meaning	Example
-cap- (-capt-) [L.]	to take, seize	*cap*tivate (to take hold of)
-dic- (-dict-) [L.]	to say in words	pre*dict* (to say before)
-dyna- [Gr.]	to be strong	*dyna*sty (a state of strength)
-nym- [Gr.]	to name	anto*nym* (to name as an opposite)
-pon- (-pos-) [L.]	to put, place	com*pose* (to put together)
-spec- (-spect-) [L.]	to see	*spect*ator (one who sees)
-vert- (-vers-) [L.]	to turn	in*vert* (to turn upside down)
-vid- (-vis-) [L.]	to see	*vis*ible (able to be seen)

Exercise 8 **Using Roots to Define Words** Match the words below with their definitions in the second column.

1. prospect	a. to change places
2. inversion	b. a false name
3. transpose	c. operated by the strength of water
4. pseudonym	d. a turning upside down
5. hydrodynamic	f. future outlook

Using Prefixes

KEY CONCEPT A **prefix** is one or more syllables joined to the beginning of a word to change its meaning or form a new word. ■

TEN COMMON PREFIXES		
Prefix and Origin	Meaning	Example
ad- [L.]	to, toward	*ad*here (to stick to)
dis- [L.]	away, apart	*dis*grace (to lose favor)
ex- [L.]	from, out	*ex*port (to send out)
mis- [A.S.]	wrong	*mis*lead (to lead in a wrong direction)
mono- [Gr.]	one, alone	*mono*rail (a single rail)
post- [L.]	after	*post*war (after the war)
re- [L.]	back, again	*re*view (to view again)
sub- [L.]	beneath, under	*sub*merge (to place under water)
syn- [Gr.]	with, together	*syn*onym (to name together)
un- [A.S.]	not	*un*known (unable to be determined)

Challenge

With two or three of your classmates, see how many more words you can list, using the roots and prefixes on these two pages. Have a dictionary nearby to check word meanings, if necessary. Make copies of the lists for each group member to keep as a reference.

As you combine prefixes with words or roots, you will see that some of them change their spellings. The root remains the same.

EXAMPLES: *ad-* → *ac-* (*ac*cept), *ap-* (*ap*ply), *as-* (*as*sume)
sub- → *suc-* (*suc*ceed), *suf-* (*suf*fix), *sup-*(*sup*port)

Exercise 9 **Using Prefixes to Form New Words** On a piece of paper, use prefixes from the chart above to create new words from the ones below. In your notebook, write the definition next to each word. Use a dictionary to check your answers.

1. syllable
2. arm
3. marine
4. place
5. read
6. thesis
7. venture
8. script
9. change
10. reliable

29.3

Using Suffixes

KEY CONCEPT A **suffix** is a letter, syllable, or group of syllables added to the end of a word to change its meaning or function or to form a new word. ■

TEN COMMON SUFFIXES		
Suffix and Origin	Meaning and Example	Part of Speech
-able (-ible) [L.]	capable of being: comfort*able*	adjective
-ance (-ence) [L.]	the act of: confid*ence*	noun
-cy (-acy) [Gr.]	quality of: hesitan*cy*	noun
-ful [A.S.]	full of: joy*ful*	adjective
-ist [Gr.]	a person skilled in: pian*ist*	noun
-ity [L.]	state of being: char*ity*	noun
-less [A.S.]	without, lacking: humor*less*	adjective
-ly [Gr.]	in a certain way: firm*ly*, love*ly*	adverb or adjective
-ment [L.]	result of being: amaze*ment*	noun
-tion (-ion, -sion) [L.]	state of being: act*ion*, ten*sion*,	noun

Exercise 10 **Using Suffixes to Change Words From One Part of Speech to Another** Use the suffixes from the chart above to change the following words. Then, write a brief definition of the word you create, and include the word's new part of speech.

Original Word	New Word	Definition	Part of Speech
1. perform	?	?	?
2. regret	?	?	?
3. social	?	?	?
4. invent	?	?	?
5. timid	?	?	?

More Practice

Academic and Workplace Skills Activity Book

• pp. 23–25

Examining Word Origins

English is considered part of the Indo-European family of languages. Within that family, its closest relatives are other Germanic languages, such as Dutch and German. Not only is English the most widely spoken language in the Western world, it is also the most global in the number of languages from which it has borrowed. More than seventy percent of words we call English have been borrowed from other languages.

Understand Historical Influences

If English had developed in isolation, it would have fewer borrowed words. No language develops in complete isolation, however. Battles, travels, new inventions and technologies—each of these events or circumstances contributes to the growth and change of a language. In the chart below, you will see examples of new words that came into English as a result of specific historic events. What the chart does not show is the great impact of these events on the structure of English.

THE GROWTH OF ENGLISH

Events	New Words
790—Danish invasions begin	law, bylaw, window, steak, knives, happy
1066—Norman Conquest	govern, reign, court, honor, glory, army, war, battle, officer
1500's—Renaissance	describe, perfect, adventure, language, equal, color, machine

Internet Tip

To find Internet sites about how other languages influenced the development of English, type "origins of English" in the query field of your search engine.

Exercise 11 **Analyzing Word Origins** Look up each of the following words in a print or electronic dictionary. Write the word on a separate sheet of paper. Then, write the language from which it comes.

1. mosquito
2. mansion
3. pork
4. squash
5. oral
6. terrestrial
7. zero
8. bungalow
9. schooner
10. balcony

Section 29.4

Improving Your Spelling

Starting a Personal Spelling List

The ability to write effectively has always been recognized as a valuable skill. One of the first steps in improving your writing is to improve your spelling. Doing so will allow people to read your work without being distracted by errors.

KEY CONCEPT Select the words you want for your personal spelling list, enter them in your notebook, and study them regularly. ■

Record Frequently Misspelled Words Set aside a special section of your notebook to list words that you frequently misspell. Look through your corrected tests, essays, and homework to find your personal problem words. Include with each word its spelling and pronunciation, a definition, and either a sentence or a memory aid.

Frequently Misspelled Words

Word	Pronounciation	Definition	Sentence/ Memory Aid
accept	ək sept′	to receive willingly	She accepts two C's.
schedule	ske′ jool	a list of times	It's a school schedule.

Technology Tip

Do an on-line search to find more "commonly misspelled words."

Exercise 12 Adding to Your Personal Spelling List

Correct the misspelled word in each sentence below. Check your answers in a dictionary. Add any difficult words to your list.

1. Sarah loves to do experiments in the science labratory.
2. Nate accidently spilled his glass of lemonade.
3. The detective received an anonymus tip.
4. How many books did you borrow from the libary?
5. The camel is well-adapted to dessert life.
6. Every Febuary we celebrate the birthdays of presidents George Washington and Abraham Lincoln.
7. A tropical climate is very diffrent from a temperate one.
8. One book I like to recommend is *A Seperate Peace*.
9. Our best athaletes were selected for an all-star team.
10. Lily saved her allowence for a special occasion.

More Practice

Academic and Workplace Skills Activity Book
• pp. 26–30

Studying Spelling Words

Study spelling words regularly. It helps to divide your list into small groups of five or ten words. Then, study each group for a week. As you become accustomed to the method, test yourself on larger groups of words. Include words you have already mastered and those you are in the process of learning.

KEY CONCEPT Review your spelling words each week, several times a week. ■

STEPS FOR REVIEWING PROBLEM WORDS

1. *Look* at each word carefully to notice the arrangement or pattern of the letters. Try to see the word in your mind.
2. *Pronounce* each syllable of the word to yourself.
3. *Write* the word, and check its spelling in the dictionary.
4. *Review* your list until you can write each word correctly.

Exercise 13 **Spelling Difficult Words** Write *correct* if an underlined word below is spelled correctly. If it is not, correct it. Check a dictionary. Enter misspelled words on your list.

1. Molly Pitcher was a courragous figure of the Revolution.
2. Grandma served warm apple pie for dessert.
3. Jason wrote the address on the outside of the envelope.
4. Check the calender to see when our vacation begins.
5. Dale, an expert gymnast, excels on the parallel bars.
6. The libary has a section of rare books.
7. I taught a rat to run through a maze in the labratory.
8. Those who criticize have obviously not tried it.
9. To suceed, one must keep trying.
10. We bought a used car that had low milage.

Exercise 14 **Identifying Commonly Misspelled Words** Look through your writing portfolio and tests that have been returned to you. Find words you have misspelled, and record them in your notebook. Study them. Then, have a partner test you on the words.

▶ **Critical Viewing** The strength of this gymnast's performance is in his good form. How does good spelling add strength to your writing? **[Relate]**

Applying Spelling Rules

In addition to studying words that give you particular trouble, study rules that apply to groups of words.

Rules for *ie* and *ei*

Observing the basic rules for *ie* and *ei* words will help you. You will need to memorize certain exceptions to these rules.

KEY CONCEPTS Remember the rule: *i* before *e* except after *c* and when sounded as *ay* as in *neighbor* and *weigh*.

- When a word has a long *e* sound, use *ie*.
- When a word has a long *a* sound, use *ei*.
- When a word has a long *e* sound preceded by the letter *c*, use *ei*. ■

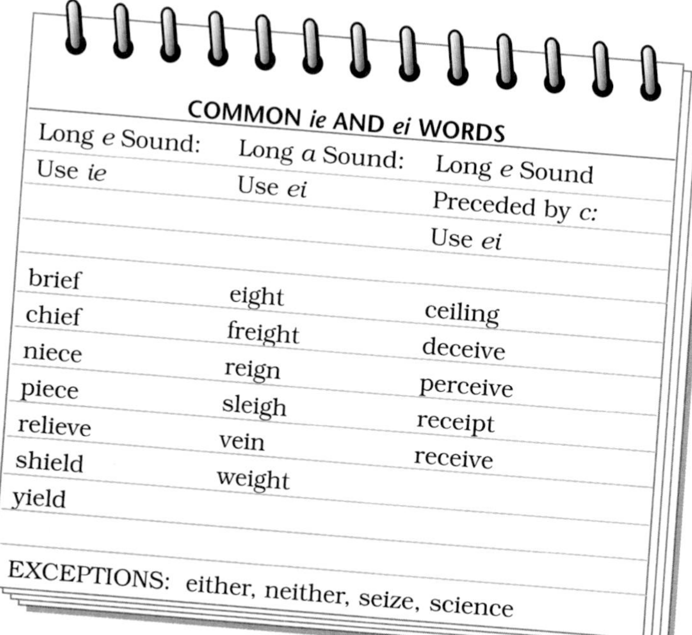

COMMON *ie* AND *ei* WORDS

Long *e* Sound: Use *ie*	Long *a* Sound: Use *ei*	Long *e* Sound Preceded by *c*: Use *ei*
brief	eight	ceiling
chief	freight	deceive
niece	reign	perceive
piece	sleigh	receipt
relieve	vein	receive
shield	weight	
yield		

EXCEPTIONS: either, neither, seize, science

Technology Tip

Many word-processing programs have automatic spelling checkers that alert a writer immediately if a word is misspelled. Check to see whether your program has that function, and be sure to use it whenever you write.

Exercise 15 **Spelling *ie* and *ei* Words** Fill in the blanks below with either *ie* or *ei*. Check the spellings in a dictionary. Add difficult words to your personal spelling list.

1. The c _ _ ling in the room was powder blue.
2. We noticed the farmer in his f _ _ ld plowing the soil.
3. A p _ _ ce of watermelon can be very refreshing.
4. Tom is giving a nutrition report in our hyg _ _ ne class.
5. How many cars were on that fr _ _ ght train?

More Practice

Academic and Workplace Skills Activity Book
- pp. 26–30

Adding Suffixes

Recall that a suffix is one or more syllables added to the end of a word.

KEY CONCEPT Adding a suffix often involves a spelling change in the word. ■

When adding suffixes to some words, it is necessary to change the spelling. The following summarizes the major kinds of spelling changes that can take place when a suffix is added.

▲ **Critical Viewing** If the *e* in *judge* is dropped in *judgment,* how might this exception to a rule apply to *acknowledge*? **[Connect]**

Spelling changes in words ending in *y*: Use the following rules for spelling changes for words ending in *y*, paying careful attention to the rule's exceptions:

1. When adding a suffix to words ending in *y* preceded by a consonant, change *y* to *i*. Most suffixes beginning with *i* are the exception to the rule:

   ply + -able = pliable　　happy + -ness = happiness
   defy + -ing = defying　　cry + -ing = crying

2. For words ending in *y* preceded by a vowel, make no change when adding most suffixes. A few short words are the exceptions:

   annoy + -ance = annoyance　　enjoy + -ment = enjoyment
   day + -ly = daily　　pay + -ed = paid

Spelling changes in words ending in *e*: Use the following rules for spelling changes for words ending in *e*, paying careful attention to the rule's exceptions:

1. Drop the *e* when adding a suffix beginning with a vowel. The exceptions to the rule are (1) words ending in *ce* or *ge* with suffixes beginning with *a* or *o*, (2) words ending in *ee*, and (3) a few special words:

   move + -able = movable　　drive + -ing = driving
   trace + -able = traceable　　courage + -ous = courageous
   see + -ing = seeing　　agree + -able = agreeable
   dye + -ing = dyeing　　be + -ing = being

2. Make no change when adding a suffix beginning with a consonant.
   peace + -ful = peaceful　　brave + -ly = bravely

   A few special words are the exceptions:
   argue + -ment = argument　　judge + -ment = judgment

Doubling the final consonant before suffixes: Use the following rules for cases in which a final consonant may or may not change, paying careful attention to the rule's exceptions:

1. For words ending in a consonant + vowel + consonant in a stressed syllable, double the final consonant when adding a suffix beginning with a vowel. The exceptions to the rules are (1) words ending in *x* or *w* and (2) words in which the stress changes after the suffix is added:

   mud´ + -y = mud´ dy — submit´ + -ed = submit´ ted
   mix + -ing = mixing — row + -ing = rowing
   refer´ + -ence = ref´ erence — confer´ + -ence = con´ ference

2. For words ending in a consonant + vowel + consonant in an unstressed syllable, make no change when adding a suffix beginning with a vowel. There are no major exceptions to this rule.

▲ Critical Viewing Use words ending in *-ing* and *-ence* to describe the activity in this scene. **[Analyze]**

Exercise 16 Making New Words With Suffixes Make new words by combining root words and suffixes. Check the spellings in a dictionary, and add difficult words to your list.

1. value + -able
2. grow + -ing
3. imagine + -ary
4. hope + -ful
5. rely + -able
6. scarce + -ly
7. revere + -ence
8. busy + -ness
9. beauty + -ful
10. pay + -ment

Adding Prefixes

When a prefix is added to a word, the spelling of the root word remains the same.

EXAMPLES: re- + cover = recover
un- + necessary = unnecessary
dis- + satisfied = dissatisfied

Exercise 17 Using Prefixes Combine the prefixes and root words below to make new words.

1. in- + complete
2. mis- + read
3. dis- + solve
4. un- + usual
5. re- + fill
6. dis- + appear
7. un- + fortunate
8. in- + visible
9. dis- + appoint
10. un- + noticed

Using Memory Aids

In English, many spelling rules do not apply, mainly because so many of our words come from different languages. Some words must be memorized. Try making up sentences to help you remember the correct spelling of difficult words.

KEY CONCEPT Use memory aids to help remember difficult spelling words. ■

You can associate the troublesome part of a word with a word you know or find a short word within a longer word.

EXAMPLES: The lib*rar*y has *rare* books.
A *rat* is in the labo*rat*ory.

Exercise 18 **Making Memory Aids** Make up a memory aid for each of the following words.

1. accidentally
2. believe
3. amateur
4. clothes
5. attendance

Understanding the Influence of Other Languages and Cultures

Because more than 70 percent of English words are borrowed from other languages, it is very difficult to make a set of rules for spelling and pronunciation. For this reason, English uses a wide variety of letters to spell certain "silent letters." When you are writing, use a dictionary to confirm the spelling of any word about which you are unsure.

KEY CONCEPT Because other languages contribute to the spelling and pronunciation of words in English, different letters may be used in different words to spell the same sound. ■

EXAMPLES:	puff	phone	giraffe
	cough	fuel	jump

Exercise 19 **Choose the Correct Spelling** Select the correct word in each group below. Check your answers in a dictionary. Enter problem words on your personal list.

1. skuash	squash	skwash
2. filosophy	philosofy	philosophy
3. enouff	enouph	enough
4. forin	foreign	phoreign
5. sizzers	scissors	sissers

More Practice
Academic and Workplace Skills Activity Book
• pp. 26–30

Section 29.5

Using Basic Spelling Rules

Forming Plurals

The plural form of a noun indicates "more than one." The plural forms can be either regular or irregular.

KEY CONCEPT The plural of regular nouns is formed by adding *-s* or *-es*. Most nouns have regular plural forms. ■

The spelling of some regular nouns changes in the plural form. The chart below lists some examples of words that change slightly.

FORMING REGULAR PLURALS

Word Ending	Rule	Examples
-s, -ss, -x, -z, -zz, -sh, -ch	Add *-es*.	circus, circuses dress, dresses tax, taxes wish, wishes bench, benches buzz, buzzes
-o preceded by a consonant	Add *-es*.	echo, echoes EXCEPTIONS: piano, pianos (and other musical terms)
-o preceded by a vowel	Add *-s*.	patio, patios
-y preceded by a consonant	Change *y* to *i* and add *-es*.	city, cities enemy, enemies
-y preceded by a vowel	Add *-s*.	key, keys
-ff	Add *-s*.	staff, staffs cuff, cuffs
-fe	Change *f* to *v* and add *-es*.	wife, wives knife, knives
-f	Add *-s*. OR Change *f* to *v* and add *-es*.	proof, proofs leaf, leaves wolf, wolves

Learn More

To learn more about making verbs and pronouns agree with plural nouns, turn to Chapter 24.

KEY CONCEPT Use a dictionary to look up the correct spelling of irregular plurals. Memorize them. ■

IRREGULAR PLURALS		
Singular Forms	**Ways of Forming Plurals**	**Plural Forms**
ox	Add *-en.*	oxen
child	Add *-ren.*	children
tooth, mouse, woman	Change one or more letters.	teeth, mice, women
radius, focus, alumnus	Change *-us* to *-i.*	radii, foci, alumni
alumna	Change *-a* to *-ae.*	alumnae
crisis, emphasis	Change *-is* to *-es.*	crises, emphases
medium, datum, curriculum	Change *-um* to *-a.*	media, data, curricula
phenomenon, criterion	Change *-on* to *-a.*	phenomena, criteria
deer, sheep	plural form same as singular	deer, sheep
	plural form only	scissors, slacks

Most one-word compound nouns have regular plural forms. If one part of the compound noun is irregular, the plural form will also be irregular.

EXAMPLES: armchair, armchairs (regular)
snowman, snowmen (irregular)

For most compound nouns written with hyphens or as separate words, form the plural by making the modified word plural. The modified word is the word being described.

EXAMPLES: mother-in-law, mothers-in-law
field mouse, field mice

Exercise 20 **Writing Plurals** Write the plural form for each of the following words. Use a dictionary if necessary. Add any difficult words to your personal spelling list.

1. veto	3. ax	5. thief	7. crisis	9. activity
2. house	4. tariff	6. turkey	8. wolf	10. crash

More Practice

Academic and Workplace Skills Activity Book
• pp. 26–30

29.5

Spelling Homophones

KEY CONCEPT **Homophones** are words that sound the same but have different meanings and may have different spellings. ■

Learn the homophones below, and be careful to spell and use them correctly in your writing.

EXAMPLES:

their: a possessive pronoun that means "belonging to them"
they're: a contraction for *they are*
there: a place word or sentence starter, as in "There are five cookies"

threw: past tense of the verb *throw,* meaning "to cause to fly through the air"
through: a preposition that means "in one side and out the other"

who's: a contraction for *who is*
whose: a possessive pronoun that means "that or those belonging to whom"

to: begins a prepositional phrase or an infinitive
too: also
two: a number

▲ **Critical Viewing** *The boat was on sale.* If you were to rewrite this sentence, changing *on* to *in full,* what else would change? **[Apply]**

Exercise 21 **Spelling Homophones** Select the correct word from each pair in parentheses below. Check your answers in a dictionary.

1. Are you going to (their, they're) party?
2. I would like a (pear, pair) of blue shoes.
3. The ball flew (threw, through) the window.
4. I have (to, two, too) sisters who like (to, two, too) help our mother.
5. (Who's, Whose) going to clean up the mess?

Exercise 22 **Writing Sentences With Homophones** Write a sentence for each lettered word in each numbered pair below. Check a dictionary to make sure that you are spelling and using each word correctly.

1. (a) sew (b) so
2. (a) bare (b) bear
3. (a) sail (b) sale
4. (a) night (b) knight
5. (a) sum (b) some

More Practice

Academic and Workplace Skills Activity Book
• pp. 31–32

Proofreading and Using References

Proofread all your written work to make sure that you have eliminated all spelling errors. If you are unsure whether you have spelled a word correctly, double-check it in a reference.

KEY CONCEPT Use dictionaries, electronic spell-checkers, and glossaries to check spellings. ■

Exercise 23 **Proofreading Sentences** Copy and proofread the following sentences. Correct any words that are written incorrectly. Use a dictionary, spell-checker, or glossary to confirm the spelling of any words about which you are unsure. If a sentence contains no errors, write *correct.*

1. Nate accidently spilled his glass of milk.
2. Our teacher was absent, so we had a substatute.
3. I wonder wheather Jennifer will win the race.
4. What foriegn languages can you speak?
5. The captain of the ship wore a blue uniform.

Exercise 24 **Proofreading a Paragraph** Copy and proofread the following paragraph. Correct any words that are written incorrectly. Check the spelling of any words about which you are unsure.

For Joanna's fiffteenth brithday, she hoped to have a skating party. All of her freinds had there own skates. Sum of them had taken lesons with a perfesional skater. Jennifer was very exsited. Her mother had asksed her friends to meat at the rink. She beleived that everone new where the rink was. By five o'clock nowon was there. She desided to call her best friend, Martha. Martha ansered the fone on the second ring. "Hi, Joanna!" Martha said, "I can't weight for you're party tomorrow." Joanna realised that she had come to her own party a hole day early!

Reflecting on Your Vocabulary and Spelling Skills

Think about what you have learned by answering the following questions:

- Which of these techniques do you find most effective for studying spelling words?
- Which do you find most helpful for studying vocabulary words?
- What do these techniques have in common? How are they different?

Chapter 30 Reading Skills

▲ **Critical Viewing** What details in this photograph make reading look like an appealing and enjoyable experience? **[Analyze]**

Reading in Everyday Life

Knowing how to read well is important to success in school and in life. Being a good reader means more than simply finding and remembering facts in books. It also means applying critical thinking skills to what you read. This chapter will help you to improve your skills in reading all kinds of books.

Section 30.1 Reading Methods and Tools

Many books—particularly textbooks—have a number of features that provide important information related to the main content of the book. Learning to use these features effectively will help you to improve your understanding of the content.

Using Sections in Textbooks

Most textbooks have a number of special sections located at the front and back of the book. Learn what these sections are and how to use them so that you take full advantage of the material in your textbooks.

KEY CONCEPT Use the special sections of your textbook to become familiar with its contents. ■

Table of Contents The table of contents is at the front of your textbook. It lists the units, chapters, and sections of the book, as well as the pages where each one begins.

Table of Contents

UNIT ONE: MATTER: BUILDING BLOCKS of the UNIVERSE..2

CHAPTER 1 Exploring Physical Science........................4

1–1 Science—Not Just for Scientists...........6

1–2 The Scientific Method—A Way of Problem Solving...........................11

1–3 The Metric System...........................20

1–4 Tools of Measurement.......................26

1–5 Safety in the Science Laboratory..........31

Chapter Introduction and Summary A chapter introduction tells you the main ideas of the chapter. The chapter summary, appearing at the end of the chapter, reviews the main points and other important information.

Glossary The glossary, located at the back of the book, is a list of terms with definitions. Generally, the glossary includes specialized terms that are used within the textbook. These terms are listed alphabetically.

Appendix The appendix is also found at the back of the textbook. It contains useful additional or supplementary material. Some materials that may be found in an appendix include charts, maps, formulas, timelines, essays, and biographical or historical information.

Index This is the final section of the textbook. The index lists alphabetically all the subjects covered in the book and tells on which pages the information can be found.

Using Features of Textbooks

In addition to using the special sections of your textbooks, you should use the textbook's special features to help you read and study the material.

KEY CONCEPT Use the special features of your textbook to aid your reading and studying. ■

Titles, Headings, and Subheadings Most titles, headings, and subheadings are printed in large, heavy type and give you an idea of what the material is about. They also divide the material into sections so you can learn it more easily.

Questions and Exercises Located at the end of the chapter, questions and exercises help you to retain the information you have read.

Pictures and Captions Pictures can make a confusing idea clearer. A caption next to a picture provides information describing the picture.

Exercise 1 **Examining the Sections of a Textbook** Look at one of your textbooks, and follow the directions given below.

1. Read the table of contents. How many units and chapters does the textbook contain?
2. Does your textbook have a glossary? If so, write the definitions of three unusual words.
3. If there is an appendix, tell what information it contains.
4. Pick one subject covered in the textbook. Then, list all the information covered on this topic by using the index.
5. Pick one chapter in the book. Read the introduction, and list the main points that will be made in the chapter.

More Practice

Academic and Workplace Skills Activity Book

• p. 35

Exercise 2 **Examining the Features of a Textbook** Look at one of your textbooks, and answer the following questions.

1. How many headings and subheadings does the first chapter contain? Describe their sizes and colors.
2. How does the size of the headings help you figure out the relationships between topics?
3. Is there a chapter introduction or a chapter summary? What information can be learned from these?
4. Does the chapter have questions and exercises? What can you learn from these?
5. Find three pictures in the textbook that have captions. Describe how the captions explain the pictures. What information in the text does each picture help to explain?

Using Reading Strategies

Three strategies you can use to increase your understanding of the material you read are varying your reading style, learning Question-Answer Relationships, and using the SQ4R method.

KEY CONCEPT Use reading strategies to help you get a better understanding of the material you read. ■

Varying Your Reading Style The three reading styles are *skimming, scanning,* and *close reading*—each used for different purposes. Choose the reading style that best suits your purpose.

Skimming a text means looking it over quickly to get a general idea of its contents. When you skim, look for highlighted or bold type, headings, and topic sentences.

Scanning involves looking the text over to find specific information. When you scan, look for words related to your topic or purpose for reading.

Close reading is reading the material carefully to understand and remember its ideas, to find relationships between the ideas, and to draw conclusions about what you read.

Use Question-Answer Relationships (QARs) There are four general types of questions that you should learn how to answer properly. By getting into the habit of asking and answering these four types of questions, you will also improve your reading skills.

FOUR QUESTION-ANSWER RELATIONSHIPS

RIGHT THERE
The answer is right there in the text, usually in one or two sentences. To answer this question, scan the text to locate specific information.

THINK AND SEARCH
The answer is in the text, but you need to think about the question's answer and then search the text for the evidence to support it.

AUTHOR AND YOU
The answer is not just in the text. To answer this question, think about what the author has said, what you already know, and how these fit together.

ON YOUR OWN
The answer is, for the most part, not in the text. To answer this question, you need to draw from your own experiences. You can, however, revise or expand your answer based on your reading.

Use the SQ4R Method Once you have identified and examined the special sections and features of your textbooks, you can use this knowledge to help you study better. In the SQ4R method described below, you Survey, Question, Read, Record, Recite, and Review. Use this method to help you focus on your reading and to assist you in recalling information.

THE SIX STAGES OF SQ4R

Survey	Look over the material you are going to read for these features: chapter titles, headings, subheadings, introduction, summary, and questions or exercises.
Question	Ask questions about what information might be covered under each heading. Ask the questions *Who? What? When? Where?* and *Why?*
Read	Search for the answers to the questions you asked in the previous step.
Record	Take notes to remember the information better. List the main ideas and major details.
Recite	Aloud or silently, recall the questions and their related answers.
Review	Review the material on a regular basis, using some or all of the steps above.

Technology Tip

If you are reading an article on-line, you can use the software's search feature to find key words in the text.

Exercise 3 **Writing QAR Questions and Using Reading Styles to Answer Them** Using the QAR method described on page 721, write and answer the four general types of questions for your next reading assignment. Use the various reading styles: *Scan* the text to answer the Right There question. *Skim* the text to answer the Think and Search question, and *closely read* the text to prepare your answer for the Author and You question.

More Practice

Academic and Workplace Skills Activity Book
- p. 36

Exercise 4 **Using the SQ4R Method** Use the SQ4R method to study a chapter or section of a textbook. Then, write a brief summary describing how the SQ4R method helped you to learn and remember the information.

Using Graphic Organizers

A graphic organizer is used to summarize information and to show relationships among ideas or details. Because the information is organized in a chart or diagram, the graphic organizer gives a quick snapshot of the subject. Before you make a graphic organizer, think about the subject. How are its parts related? Choose a format that will show those relationships.

KEY CONCEPT Use graphic organizers to help you understand the relationships among the ideas in a text. ■

Technology Tip

Some computer applications will create graphic organizers for you.

Timeline A timeline shows when events occurred. This graphic organizer is a good way to perceive the time between events and the order in which they occurred. Start your timeline by writing the beginning event in the box at the top. The final event is written at the bottom. The horizontal lines are for the events that have occurred between the initial and the final events. On the left, write the events. On the right, record the dates or times when the events took place. In the box at the top, give the unit of time you are using (years, days, minutes).

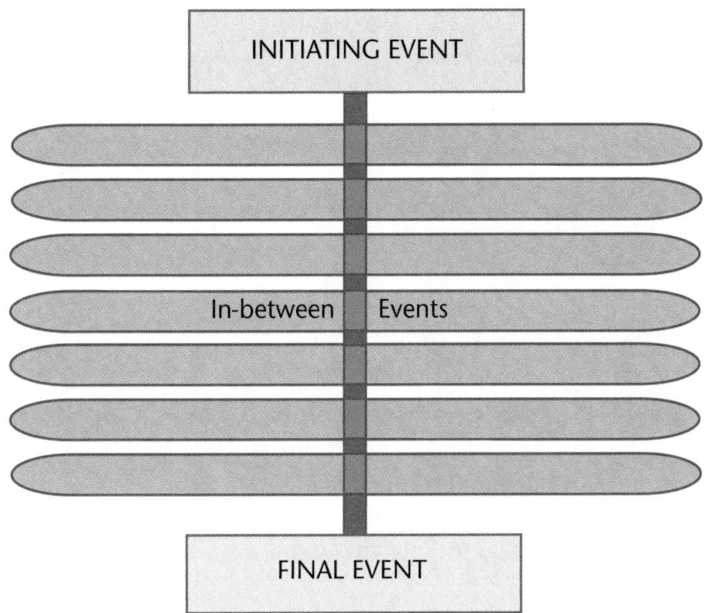

Herringbone Organizer

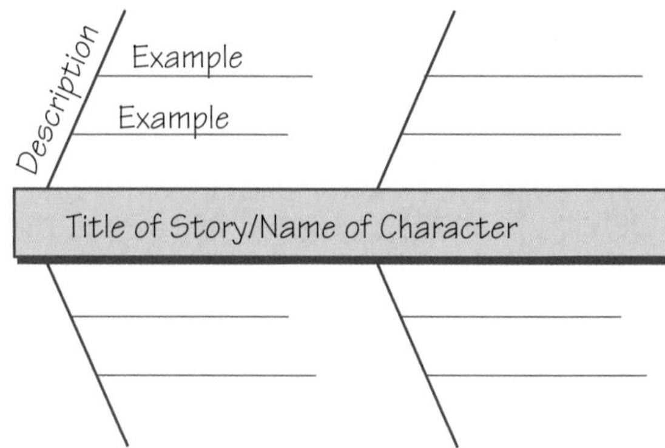

Use a herringbone organizer to organize details around a central idea, such as character development, or to show the multiple causes of a complex event. If you were going to track development, you could use the herringbone this way: Write the name of the character on the center line. Next, on the top left diagonal spine, write a statement that describes a quality of the character. Then, in the attached horizontal lines, record examples of actions or feelings that demonstrate this quality. Continue the process by examining another quality of the character.

Question-and-Answer Chart Use this graphic organizer to help you identify important ideas in your reading by asking questions such as: *Who* is the main character in the piece? *What* is the relationship between two events? *When* and *where* does an action take place? *Why* did a character do or say that? To make your question-and-answer chart, write the subject you want to learn more about in the center. Then, in the surrounding boxes, write the answers to your questions.

QUESTION-AND-ANSWER CHART

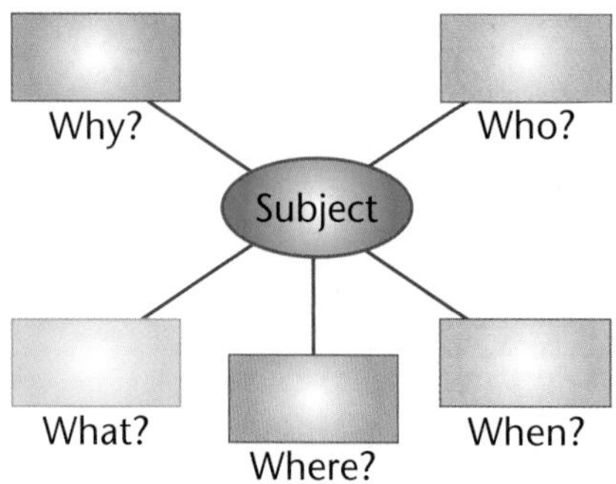

Exercise 5 **Using Graphic Organizers** Read a chapter from one of your textbooks or a work of fiction. Then, use a timeline, a herringbone graphic organizer, or a question-and-answer chart to present ideas from the text. Explain why you chose that particular graphic organizer and why it was best suited for presenting the material.

Section 30.2

Reading Nonfiction Critically

When you read nonfiction critically, you examine and question the ideas the author presents in the text. You learn to distinguish between fact and opinion, to identify the author's purpose, and to recognize when language is being used to distort your understanding of the text.

Comprehending Nonfiction

The first step in reading a text critically is to gain a general understanding of the material. To do so, you need to find and interpret key information, determine the author's purpose, and consider the relationship of the material to the topic you're studying.

KEY CONCEPT Comprehending nonfiction involves understanding the author's purpose as well as the information presented in the writing. ■

These strategies will help you comprehend nonfiction works:

Identify Main Points and Details The main points are the most important ideas in the work. Details are the facts and examples the author uses to support each point.

Interpret What You Read Use the main ideas and major details to help you paraphrase, or state in your own words, the information in the text. Restating the information will help you to remember how ideas relate to one another.

Identify the Author's Purpose in Writing Once you have a general idea of the content of the text, the next step is to determine the author's purpose. You can do this by examining the writer's choice of words and details (how things are said, and what is described). As you continue to read, look for additional clues that support this purpose.

Respond to What You Have Read Think about your own feelings about the topic. Consider how the information relates to the subject you are studying. Consider how you might apply this new knowledge to your life.

Exercise 6 **Comprehending Nonfiction** Use the strategies mentioned above to read a chapter from one of your textbooks. What main points and major details did you find? What was the author's purpose? What points helped you identify it? What is the significance of the information you read?

More Practice

Academic and Workplace Skills Activity Book

• pp. 37–39

30.2

Distinguishing Fact From Opinion

When you read critically, you should learn to separate fact statements from opinion statements.

Fact Statements A statement of fact can be verified or proved to be true by consulting a written source—such as an atlas, an encyclopedia, an almanac, or other reference book—a human authority, or by personally observing something directly.

STATEMENTS OF FACT: Earth revolves around the sun approximately every 365 days. (true)
Earth is the center of the solar system. (false)

The first fact statement is *true* because it can be verified by consulting a written authority, such as an encyclopedia or science textbook. The second fact statement is *false* because these same sources tell us that the sun, and not Earth, is the center of the solar system.

Opinion Statements An opinion statement expresses a person's feelings, judgments, or predictions about a given situation. An opinion statement cannot be proved to be true. It can, however, be a valid statement if it is supported by evidence, such as related facts or an authority.

SUPPORTED OPINION: According to scientists at the university, an excessive amount of sunlight can lead to skin cancer. (valid)

UNSUPPORTED OPINION: The sun is bad for you. (invalid)

The first opinion statement is *valid* because it is based on related facts given by an authority. The second opinion statement, however, is *invalid* because it contains no facts and is not given by an authority.

Learn More

To learn more about distinguishing fact from opinion, see Chapter 7.

Exercise 7 Evaluating Fact and Opinion Statements

Identify each statement below as *fact* or *opinion*. If the statement is a fact, tell whether it is *true* or *false*. If the statement is an opinion, tell whether it is *valid* or *invalid*. Consult a reference book if necessary.

1. John Steinbeck wrote *Romeo and Juliet*.
2. Donna has been training hard all year. She will win first place in the track competition.
3. There are nine planets in the solar system.
4. Broccoli tastes terrible.
5. Because his plays and poetry form a respected part of English literature, William Shakespeare is a great author.

More Practice

Academic and Workplace Skills Activity Book
• pp. 40–42

Identifying the Author's Purpose

A crucial step in becoming a critical reader is determining the author's purpose—why he or she is writing. As you read, remember to look for clues that help you identify the author's purpose. When you think you know the author's purpose, confirm your conclusion by linking it to details in the text.

▲Critical Viewing Assuming each of five authors writes for a different purpose, how might they write about this Civil War scene? **[Speculate]**

KEY CONCEPT Learn to identify the author's purpose by using clues found in the text. ■

The list below describes common purposes of authors. Use these definitions as clues to help you identify the author's purpose in your reading.

- **To inform**—a series of factual statements
- **To instruct**—a step-by-step explanation of an idea or a process
- **To offer an opinion**—presentation of a topic with a certain point of view
- **To sell**—persuasive techniques designed to sell a product
- **To entertain**—narration of an event in a humorous way, often used to lighten a serious topic

Exercise 8 **Determining the Author's Purpose** Read each of the following sentences, and determine the author's purpose. Explain your answer.

1. This booklet will tell you, in three easy steps, how to properly bait a hook for freshwater fishing.
2. The American Civil War ended on April 9, 1865, at Appomattox.
3. I think everyone should go to college, and here are my reasons.
4. If you are looking for the very best prices on the Web, shop at **iluvadiscount.com.**
5. My brother's dream is to be a rock star, but the only instrument he can play is the triangle.

Applying Forms of Reasoning

Once you have learned how to evaluate the material you read, you are ready to draw your own conclusions about the work. Learn to apply forms of reasoning—logical ways of thinking—to get the fullest meaning from your reading.

KEY CONCEPT Examine the details of the material you read to help you make inferences and generalizations. ■

Make Inferences In your reading, you won't always find the author's main ideas stated directly. Sometimes, the main ideas are implied, or stated indirectly. When you make inferences, you put details together to figure out what they mean. Use an inference map like the one below to help you organize details and make inferences that will lead you to conclusions.

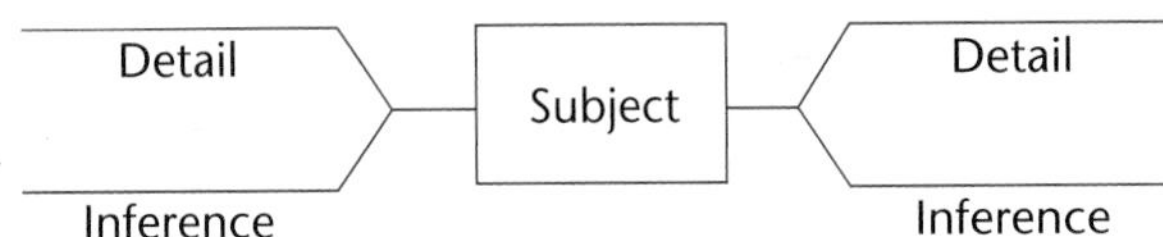

Make Generalizations A generalization is a statement based on facts or examples. A generalization is *valid* when it is based on a large number of examples. A generalization is *invalid* when it is based on too few examples. Use the following questions to make a valid generalization.

- What facts are provided to justify the generalization?
- Will the generalization hold true in all or most cases? Are there exceptions to the generalization?
- Are enough cases given to make the generalization valid?

Exercise 9 **Evaluating Inferences and Generalizations** One way to learn how to make good inferences and generalizations is by learning to identify them. Read the following sentences. Identify each as an *inference* or a *generalization*. Then, explain whether each conclusion is *valid* or *invalid*.

1. Dan plays the piano well; he will become a concert pianist.
2. My father's car got stuck in the snow last winter, so no one should drive during snowy weather.
3. Since the governor was elected, the state population has dramatically declined. Therefore, he should not be re-elected.
4. Studies conducted over the last five years tell us that seatbelts save lives, so all drivers should wear them.
5. Susan has studied a great deal about the Middle Ages; she must know everything about castles.

More Practice

Academic and Workplace Skills Activity Book
• pp. 40–42

Analyzing Text

When you analyze text, you examine how language is used to express thoughts and feelings, and you examine the text's structure to aid your comprehension of the material.

KEY CONCEPT Identify and understand the purposes of the different uses of language and text structure. ■

Examine an Author's Language

Authors sometimes use language in ways that can suggest how you should feel about a particular subject or issue. *Denotation, connotation,* and *jargon* are three ways that authors use language to affect your opinions and ideas about what you are reading.

Denotation and Connotation When words are used in a *denotative* way, they describe a situation in a neutral tone. Words used in a *connotative* way are value-laden. Connotations imply a particular point of view in a positive or negative tone.

Jargon *Jargon* is the use of words with specialized meanings intended for a particular trade or profession. Jargon is meant to have very precise meaning, but it often hides rather than reveals meaning. The opposite of jargon is *direct language.*

Exercise 10 **Analyzing Uses of Language** Identify the pairs of sentences below for the use of *denotation/connotation* or *jargon/direct language.*

1. The girl wore a pink and yellow dress.
   The young girl was dressed in shades of rose and lemon.
2. In preschool, children interface with their peer group.
   In preschool, children play with their classmates.
3. The senator's petty questioning dragged on interminably.
   The senator's interrogation lasted for two hours.
4. The candy has a cloying, sickly sweet taste.
   The candy is too sweet.
5. Declining sales had a negative impact on our financial depository.
   Lower sales caused us to lose money.

Exercise 11 **Identifying Uses of Language** Look through magazines and newspapers. Find three examples of words with positive connotations, three examples of words with negative connotations, and three examples of jargon.

Speaking and Listening Tip

Explore the effects of words with positive and negative connotations. Join with two or three of your classmates, and take turns reading the examples you found for Exercise 11. As you read and listen, be aware of the feelings the words convey.

Identify Text Structure Authors arrange their writing so that they can communicate their ideas in a clear and effective way. Learn to recognize how an author structures the text so that you can understand the relationships among ideas and locate information more easily.

KEY CONCEPT Learn how an author structures his or her text to understand ideas and locate information more easily. ■

Cause and Effect A *cause* is the reason that something happens. An *effect* is the outcome. Together, they form an *event.* A cause-and-effect structure shows a series of events. Also, note that most effects in turn act as a cause for something else, thereby continuing the series of events. Some word clues identifying cause and effect are listed in the following illustration.

CAUSE + EFFECT = EVENT

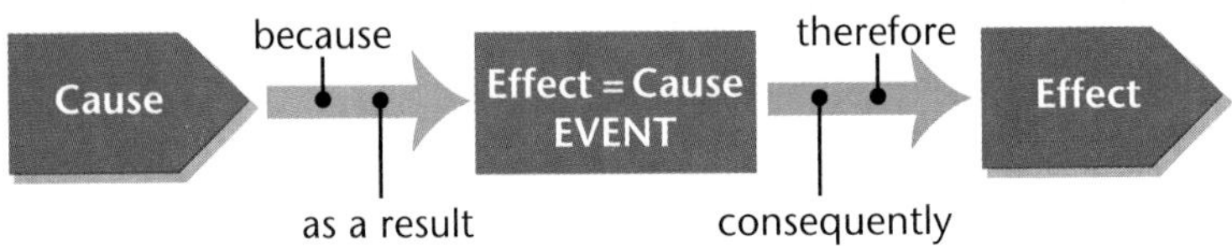

Comparison and Contrast An author uses this text structure to describe similarities and differences between two or more items, either feature by feature or subject by subject. The following words often signal a comparison: *like, similarly, both, in the same way.* The words *but, yet, in spite of, on the other hand, although, nevertheless, in contrast, whereas,* and *unlike* often signal a contrast.

Chronological Order An author uses chronological order when he or she wants to show the arrangement of events in the order in which they occurred during a period of time. Words such as *next, then, later,* and *soon* show the order of events as well as the passing of time.

Exercise 12 **Analyzing Text Structure** Go back to the cause-and-effect professional or student model in Chapter 9, and identify a cause and effect in the essay. Show the details that support your answer. Turn to the comparison-and-contrast professional or student model in Chapter 8, and tell which two items or features are being contrasted. Name two of their similarities and two of their differences.

More Practice

Academic and Workplace Skills Activity Book
- pp. 43–46

Section 30.3

Reading Literary Writings

Fiction, drama, poetry, and tales from the oral tradition are all types of literary writing. While reading literary writing, you use your mind, your emotions, and your imagination. You can also use the following strategies to increase your understanding and appreciation of literary writing.

Reading Fiction

Short stories are brief works of fiction, whereas novels are longer fictional works.

Determine the Point of View The point of view is the vantage point from which the author or narrator tells a story. Three commonly used points of view are omniscient third person, limited third person, and first person.

- In *omniscient third-person point of view,* the narrator has complete knowledge of all the characters and tells what they feel and think.
- In *limited third-person point of view,* the narrator has knowledge of the thoughts and feelings of only one character, and everything is viewed from this character's vantage point.
- In *first-person point of view,* the narrator is a character in the story, referring to himself or herself with the first-person pronoun *I.*

Envision the Action and Setting As you read, allow yourself to create mental pictures of the action, setting, and characters. Look for these kinds of words:

- Action words
- Adverbs—words that tell how an action is performed
- Sensory words—words that tell how things look, feel, taste, smell, and sound

Identify the Conflict Most plots—what happens in a story—develop from conflict, the struggle between opposing forces. There are two kinds of conflict: internal and external. An *internal conflict* is a mental struggle within a character. An *external conflict* is a struggle between the character and an outside force.

Exercise 13 **Reading Fiction** Read a short story or the first chapter of a novel. Then, list experiences or qualities you share with the main character. Make a prediction about what might happen. Find at least two action words, and describe the action taking place.

▼ **Critical Viewing** Explain the kind of conflict depicted in this photograph, and give one action word, one adverb, and one sensory word that you might use to describe the conflict. **[Analyze]**

Reading Drama

Drama is a story designed to be performed on the stage. It is told mostly through what the actors say and do. Stage directions in the script contain instructions about how actors should move and how they should speak their lines. Sometimes, these stage directions contain information about the sets, costumes, lighting, and sound effects. Use the following strategies to increase your understanding of drama:

Read the Cast of Characters Before the play begins, there is usually a list of the characters that take part in the action. Reading this list can tell you the various relationships among the characters. It may also give a brief description of the characters to help you imagine who they are.

Use Stage Directions to Envision the Play As you read, use your imagination to mentally "stage" what is happening in the play.

- Use the stage directions to picture in your mind what the characters look like and how they behave.
- To get more involved in the play, imagine conversations among the characters. You may find it helpful to read these conversations aloud or with a friend.
- If the play does not take place in the present, don't forget to consider what you already know about the time in history when it took place.

Predict After you have read the first act or scene of the play, try to predict, or figure out, what characters will do or which events will happen in the next act or scene. Look for clues in what the characters say or do to help you make your prediction.

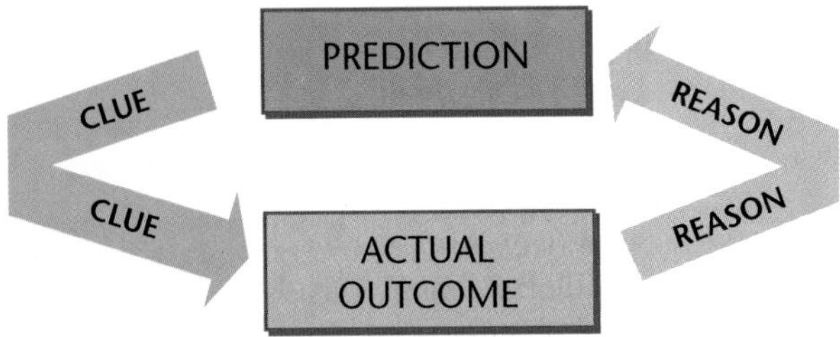

Question A good way to learn more about characters and events is to ask questions. By asking questions, you can also find new relationships between the characters and events within the work. As you continue to read, search the story for the answers to your questions.

Technology Tip

Try looking up famous characters from literature on the Internet. You may find descriptions that help you get involved in the story.

QUESTIONING TO LEARN MORE ABOUT DRAMA

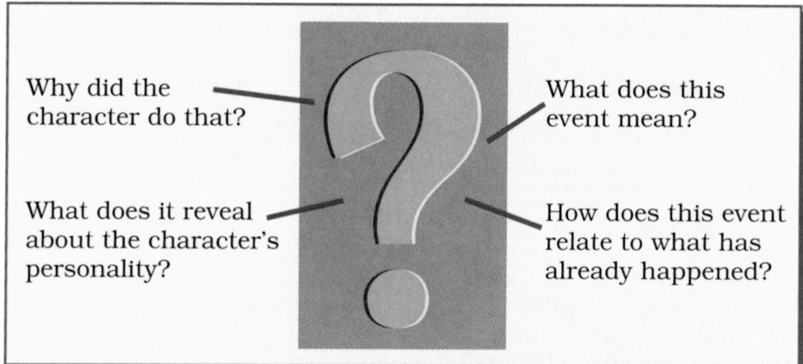

Summarize Dramas are usually broken into parts called acts. Acts are broken into scenes. At the end of an act or a scene, repeat to yourself what has happened to that point.

Exercise 14 **Reading Drama** Read the beginning of a play—a first act or scene. As you read, answer these questions:

1. What do you learn about the characters and setting from reading the cast list and opening stage directions?
2. How do stage directions contribute to your understanding of a mood, an action, or a character?
3. What do you predict will happen in the play? Pick a character, and tell what you think will happen to him or her.

More Practice
Academic and Workplace Skills Activity Book
- pp. 47–48

Reading Poetry

In poetry, the language does more than describe events and characters. It evokes a mood and creates its own reality with sounds, rhythms, and multiple meanings. Poets treat words with reverence. Give every word in the poem the attention it deserves. Here are some strategies to use:

Read Lines According to Punctuation Because lines of poetry are usually short, a single thought or image may continue for several lines. Therefore, instead of pausing in your reading at the end of each line, be aware of the punctuation, and pause only where a comma or an end mark signals a pause.

- Pause slightly for commas and a bit longer for semicolons or dashes.
- Make the longest stops for end marks, such as periods, exclamation marks, and question marks.
- Don't stop at the ends of lines if there is no punctuation.

Identify the Speaker The poet is not always the speaker in the poem. The speaker is the voice that "says" the words. Listen for clues about who the speaker is.

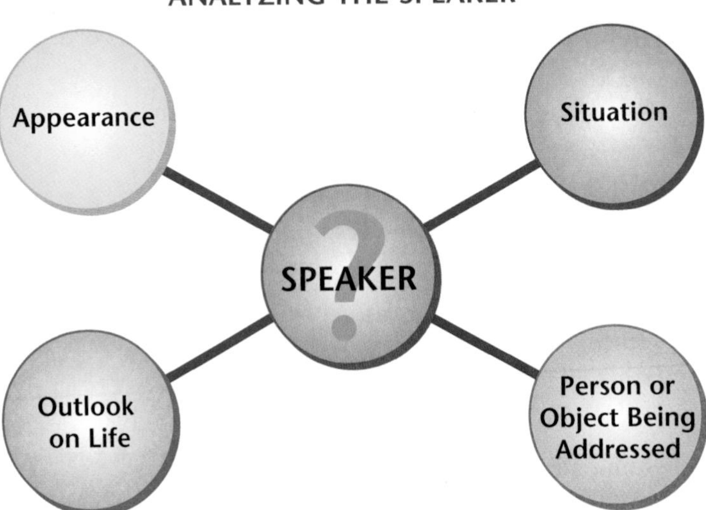

Paraphrase the Lines When reading poetry, pause every stanza or every few lines to paraphrase—or restate in your own words—the poet's ideas. By putting the poet's ideas in your own words, you'll not only be able to understand the poem better, but you'll remember it better, too.

Understand Figurative Language Language that is used to make you see and feel things in a new way is called *figurative language.* Listed below are three types of figurative language:

- **Simile** uses the words *like* or *as* to compare apparently unlike things: *The eagle dives like a thunderbolt.*
- **Metaphor** compares apparently unlike things by describing one item as though it were another without using *like* or *as: Life is a broken-winged bird that cannot fly.*
- **Personification** gives human qualities to nonhuman objects: *Sorrow knocked at my door, but I was afraid to answer.*

Exercise 15 Reading Poetry Read a one- or two-page poem. Number the lines that require pauses at the ends of them. Identify the speaker in the poem, if possible. Give two or three images from the poem, and name the senses to which they appeal. Paraphrase one complete thought in the poem.

More Practice

Academic and Workplace Skills Activity Book
• pp. 49–50

Reading Tales From the Oral Tradition

Folk tales, legends, and myths were originally told orally. They sometimes contain a lot of repetition, which made them easier to remember. To better understand one of these stories, a reader needs to know about the culture or the region from which the story came.

Understand the Culture When you read a folk tale, it helps to know something about the setting of the story and its origins. When was it told and written down? Where did its tellers live? Were they farmers, nomads, or city dwellers? What were their beliefs and social customs?

Recognize the Storyteller's Purpose Some of the reasons folk tales were told include providing entertainment, teaching a lesson, transmitting beliefs, or explaining natural occurrences, such as the rising of the sun or the mystery of birth.

Know What to Expect In folk tales, myths, and legends, there are often special elements you should look for, such as strong moral messages, supernatural events, magic transformations, and animals acting like people.

Learn More

To learn about other ways of responding to literature, see Chapter 12.

Exercise 16 **Reading Myths, Legends, and Folk Tales** Choose a myth, legend, or folk tale from your textbook, and answer the following questions:

1. What three things can you tell about the culture from which your folk tale, myth, or legend comes?
2. What is the storyteller's purpose in writing this tale?
3. What special elements did you find?

▶ **Critical Viewing** In what ways are stories that children tell around a campfire similar to many legends and folk tales? **[Relate]**

Section 30.4

Reading From Varied Sources

Obviously, much of the reading you do involves materials other than textbooks and literary works. You can read from a wide selection of magazines, newspapers, Web pages, advertisements, anthologies, and various manuals and handbooks. What you read depends on why you are reading. Select material that is best suited to your purpose for reading.

Reading Forms and Applications Filling out forms and applications is probably one of the most practical purposes for reading. You should read these carefully so that you understand the information that is being requested. Doing so will help you to fill out forms accurately, which leads to quicker results than if the form must be resubmitted with revised information.

Reading Newspapers Newspapers keep you informed about what is going on in your community and the world. There are many different kinds of newspapers available to you, depending on what your interest is. Local newspapers focus on events that affect a town, city, county, or region. National newspapers cover events and issues that affect the entire country. There are financial newspapers, foreign language newspapers, and newspapers for many different organizations. You can choose the newspaper that will give the most thorough coverage of the type of events that interest you. Except for sections that are intended to offer a viewpoint, such as the editorial page, newspapers should report the news objectively, without adding opinions or viewpoints.

Reading Magazines Magazines exist for almost every interest. When you want to read about something specific, you can usually find the information in a magazine. Some magazines deal with current events, but many magazines are focused on attracting a specific audience with specific interests. You can find magazines on fashion, movies, music, gardening, travel, science, computers, art, and architecture, among many other topics. Unlike newspapers, magazines usually offer an opinion or point of view on the topic they present. Even magazines that cover current events or celebrities set a tone or show an attitude toward the subjects they cover.

Reading Anthologies Perhaps you like to read a particular type of literature, or literature of a certain time period. If so, you might select an anthology, which is a collection of varied works, usually by many different authors. If you want to focus on the work of a single author, look for a collection of that author's writings, often entitled *The Collected Works of . . . .*

Reading Electronic Texts

Articles and information that you can read on Web pages cover a wide range of topics. The information may be objective, or it may present one person's point of view on a topic. Because Web pages comes from such a wide variety of sources, it is very important that you evaluate the authority and the background of the source before using or accepting any of the information presented. Some electronic texts are provided by retailers—companies that want to sell you something—and should be viewed as advertisements rather than as informational texts.

Reading Manuals Whether you are installing a new computer game or putting together a bicycle, you will be more successful if you read the directions. Many new products come with an owner's manual, which has detailed directions and important information that will help you put together and use a product correctly. It is important to read the owner's manual for necessary safety instructions, as well.

▲ **Critical Viewing** What might this student do to judge whether the information he has found on-line is valid? **[Apply]**

Reflecting on Your Reading

After a week of practicing your reading skills, write a paragraph about your progress. Use the following questions to get you started:

- Which sections of my textbooks do I use on a regular basis?
- How does varying my reading style help me to find information and to study?
- Which reading strategies do I find most useful?
- How am I, in general, a more careful and reflective reader?

Chapter 31

Study, Reference, and Test-Taking Skills

▲ **Critical Viewing** What study skills do you think the students in this photograph are using? Explain. **[Analyze]**

You can build a solid foundation for learning by becoming better at studying, researching, and taking tests. In this chapter, you will learn the best ways to use your study time. You will also learn how to find information more quickly in the library and on the Internet and how to use a variety of reference sources. In addition, you will learn strategies to help improve your performance on tests.

Section 31.1 Basic Study Skills

Developing a Study Plan

Create an effective study plan by establishing a study area that works well for you and scheduling regular periods of time for studying.

Find a Suitable Study Area You may not realize it, but the place where you choose to study has a major impact on how well you study. Find a study area that is

- free of distractions.
- comfortable.
- well-lit.
- organized.
- equipped with all the necessary supplies, such as pencils, paper, erasers, a stapler and staples, index cards, a dictionary, and a ruler.

Create a Study Schedule It is also important to schedule set time periods in which to study. Create a study schedule that fits your personal needs. Vary the amount of time you spend on each subject, depending on upcoming tests and long-term projects. Set aside extra time for those subjects that give you the most problems.

SAMPLE STUDY SCHEDULE

	4:30–5:00	5:00–5:30	5:30–6:00	7:00–7:30	7:30–8:00	8:00–8:30
Mon	daily assignments		review for ss test Weds	work on science report	study for math test	
Tues	daily assignments		work on science report	study for ss test		
Wed	daily assignments		finish science report		review for Lit test Fri	

Research Tip

In the library and on the Internet, you can find books and articles that offer additional suggestions for improving your study habits.

Exercise 1 **Planning Your Study Schedule** Create your own study schedule, using the sample above as a model. Follow your schedule for one week, and then evaluate it. Did it help you complete your work on time? Did you follow it every day? Revise the schedule based on your evaluation. Keep a copy of your revised schedule in your notebook, and try to follow it.

31.1

Keeping an Assignment Book

Instead of trusting your memory to recall homework assignments and long-term projects, write them down in an assignment book that makes the due dates clear.

KEY CONCEPT Use an assignment book to record homework and long-term projects and their due dates. ■

One simple way to set up your assignment book is to make five columns on each page. Put the date in the first column. In the second column, list your school subjects. In the third, provide details about your assignments. In the fourth column, list the dates when your assignments are due. In the fifth, check off assignments as they are completed. The sample page below lists two overnight homework assignments and a long-term science project. Notice how the long-term project is divided into a series of steps.

Date	Subject	Assignment	Due	Completed
11/19	English	Read pages 126-136	11/20	✓
11/19	Math	Study for test on decimals	11/20	
11/20	Science	Report on fruit flies	11/30	
		—Research	(11/23)	
		—Drafting	(11/25)	
		—Revising	(11/27)	
		—Final draft	(11/30)	

▼ Critical Viewing What can you conclude about this student's study habits, based on this photograph? **[Evaluate]**

Exercise 2 **Setting Up an Assignment Book** In the back of your notebook or in a separate notebook, set up an assignment book. Date each page, and record your assignments using the sample above as a model. Use your assignment book for two weeks. Then, decide whether you need to revise it. For example, you might need to provide more room for writing assignments, or use colored pencils to code the due dates of tests or reports.

Taking Notes

Taking notes is one of the best ways to remember what you have learned. Organize your notebook by school subject. Then, take notes on what you hear in class and what you read in textbooks. Remember that notes should cover the most important information. You don't have to write down everything.

Use a Modified Outline A modified outline can help you take notes or organize ideas for writing assignments. List main ideas along the margin, indent to show major details, and indent further to show supporting details.

Many Parts of Human Eye — Main idea
1. Iris — Major details
    Colored part
    Filters light — Supporting details
2. Pupil
    Black spot
    Hole opens wider or closes as more or less light comes in
3. Cornea and Lens
    Help focus light
    Project upside-down image on retina
4. Retina
    Like movie screen
    Nerves transmit image to brain, which interprets it

Use Summaries Summaries are an excellent tool to help you review your notes or the chapters you have read. Create a summary by stating in your own words the main ideas and major details of what you have learned.

Exercise 3 **Writing a Paragraph From a Modified Outline** Using the modified outline above, create a paragraph based on the details in it. Examine your paragraph, and ask yourself whether it covers most of the important information.

Exercise 4 **Taking Notes in Outline Form** Create a modified outline based on a chapter in your science textbook.

Exercise 5 **Creating a Summary** Write a summary of a chapter or section of your social studies book.

Learn More

For more information on creating models and taking notes, see Chapter 11, Research.

Section 31.2

Reference Skills

Today, more information is available to people than ever before. Because there is so much information, however, it is essential to develop strong research skills.

Using the Library

Even though there is now a wealth of information available on the Internet, the library is still the best place to begin a research project. To use libraries effectively, it is important to learn the main features of a library and to understand how libraries organize their resources.

Understanding How Resources Are Organized When searching for library resources, be aware that libraries use word-by-word alphabetizing.

- *A, an,* and *the* at the beginning of an entry are not used in alphabetizing. *The Enemy* would be alphabetized under *E.*
- Abbreviations and numbers are read as if they were spelled out. *Dr.* is treated as *Doctor* and *100* as *one hundred.*
- All *Mc* and *Mac* words are alphabetized as if they were *Mac.*

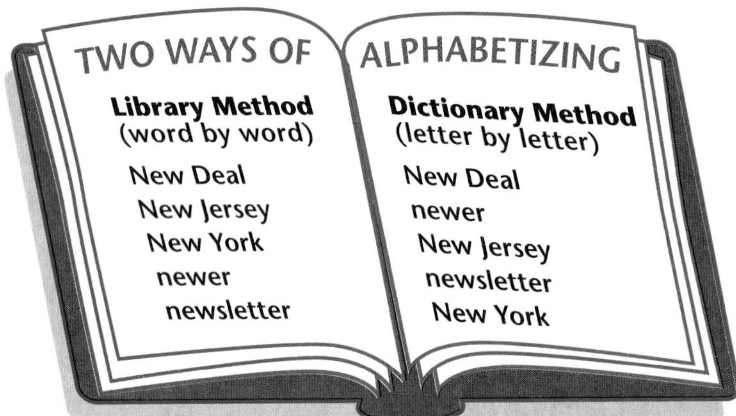

Using the Library Catalog The above methods are used for alphabetizing the resources listed in the library catalog. The library catalog is the starting place for finding most resources in a library. The catalog can be in one of three forms:

Card Catalog This system lists books on index cards, with a separate *author card* and *title card* for each book. If the book is nonfiction, it also has a subject card. Author cards are alphabetized by last names, and title cards, by the title's first word. Look at the sample on the next page.

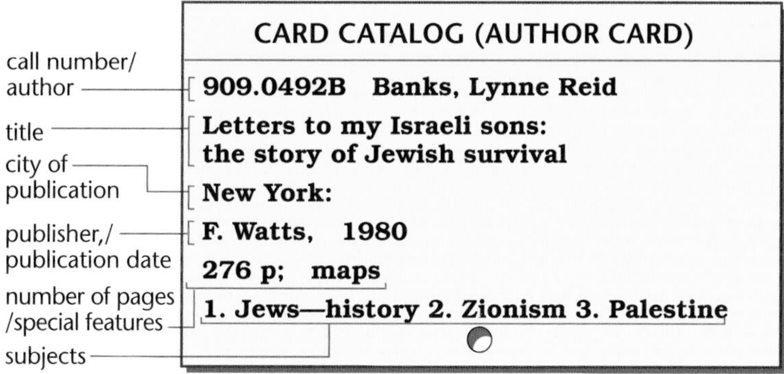

Printed Catalog This catalog lists books in printed booklets, with each book listed alphabetically by author, by title, and—if nonfiction—by subject.

PRINTED CATALOG (TITLE LISTING)

title		author	
LETTERS TO MY ISRAELI SONS: THE STORY OF JEWISH SURVIVAL		Lynne Reid Banks	
city of publication		publisher	publication date
New York:		F. Watts,	1980.
number of pages/illustrations		size of book	
276p.	maps	25cm.	
subject		call number	
Jews; Zionism; Palestine		909.0492 B	

Electronic Catalog This catalog lists books in a CD-ROM or on-line database. Using a library computer, you can find a book's catalog entry by typing in its title, key words in the title, the author's name, or, for nonfiction, a related subject.

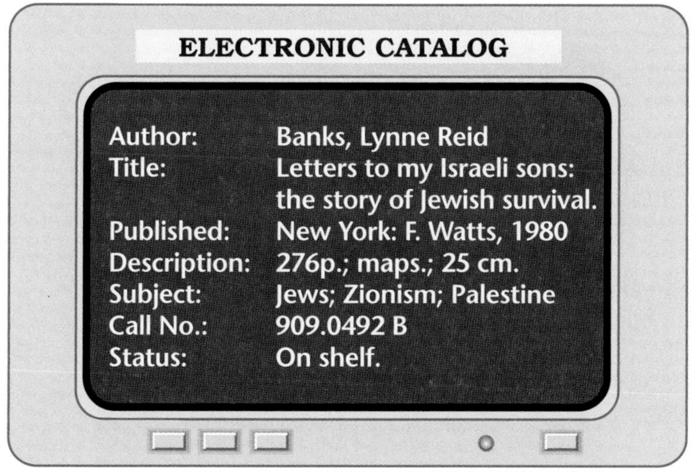

Technology Tip

Some library catalogs can be accessed remotely from home computers. Ask your librarian whether this feature is available.

Exercise 6 **Using the Library Catalog** Visit your school or local library, and find the answers to the following questions:

1. What kind of catalog does the library use—card, printed, or electronic? Where is it located?
2. Who wrote *Silent Spring*? Is it fiction or nonfiction?
3. What are the titles, subjects, and call numbers of two books your library carries by author Diane Ackerman?
4. What are the titles, authors, and call numbers of three books about snakes published since 1985?
5. What are the titles, authors, and call numbers of two books about rock climbing that are more than 100 pages long?

Finding the Book You Want Usually, a library divides and shelves books according to whether they are *fiction* (stories and novels) or *nonfiction* (factual information). Nonfiction also includes two smaller groups that are often shelved separately: *biographies* and *reference books.*

KEY CONCEPT Fiction and nonfiction books are shelved separately in the library, with each following a different method of organization. ■

Fiction Books If you know the author's last name, you can go to the fiction section and look for your book by author. If you do not know the author, look up the book under its title in the library catalog. If there are two or more books by a particular author on the shelf, they will be alphabetized by title.

Nonfiction Books Nonfiction books are arranged according to a *call number*, a combination of a number and one or more letters. It is found on the upper left corner of a catalog card and on the spine (side) of the book. Books are arranged in number-letter order on the shelves—for example, 541.1, 541.2, 541.21A, 541.21C, 541.3. To find a nonfiction book, look it up in the library catalog, find its call number, and then follow number-letter order to locate it on the shelves.

Most school and public libraries use the **Dewey Decimal System** to classify books. In this system, all knowledge is divided into ten main classes, numbered from 000 to 999 (see the chart at the top of the next page). The first digit indicates the general subject of the book. The other digits represent subgroupings of the general subject. To help you find books using the Dewey Decimal System, note that

- libraries display call numbers on each stack of shelves. For example, if you wanted a book with the call number 974.2T, you would go to the shelves labeled "972–979."
- you can find more books on a subject by looking at books with the same call number.

Understanding the main classes of the Dewey Decimal System will also help you find books more quickly.

Main Classes of the Dewey Decimal System

000-099	General Works
100-199	Philosophy
200-299	Religion
300-399	Social Sciences
400-499	Languages
500-599	Pure Sciences
600-699	Technology
700-799	The Arts
800-899	Literature
900-999	History

Finding Special Materials In addition to the fiction and nonfiction sections, libraries usually have other sections that contain specialized books, such as the following:

Biographies Many libraries have a section for biographies. The call number is usually *B* or 92, followed by the first few letters of the subject of the book. For example, *Kit Carson: Trail Blazer and Scout*, by Shannon Garst, would be labeled *B* for biography and *Car* for Carson.

Reference Books Reference works may also be shelved in a special section. Books in the reference section are often labeled *R* or *REF.* A call number follows the abbreviation. If a book you look up in the library catalog has *REF* before its call number, go first to the library's reference section. Then, use the call number to find the book.

Young Adult Books Some libraries also have a section for young adult books. These are books written for teenagers.

Technology Tip

Print the search results from an electronic catalog to search efficiently for several sources in one trip to the shelves.

Exercise 7 **Locating Fiction Books** Arrange the following fiction books in library-shelf order:

1. *Mystery at Crane's Landing* by Marcella Thum
2. *The Martian Chronicles* by Ray Bradbury
3. *Sea Glass* by Laurence Yep
4. *Something Wicked This Way Comes* by Ray Bradbury
5. *Summer of the Swans* by Betsy Byars

Exercise 8 **Locating Nonfiction Books** Arrange the following call numbers in library-shelf order. Then, identify the general subject area of each book.

1. 150.1 G
2. 629 M
3. 301.42 A
4. 301.415 F
5. 629 B

31.2

Using Periodicals and Periodical Indexes

Periodicals are printed materials, such as newspapers and magazines, that are published on a regular basis.

KEY CONCEPT Use magazines, journals, and newspapers to find concise, current information. Use periodical indexes to find articles in periodicals. ■

Periodical Indexes When you are researching a topic, use periodical indexes to locate articles on that topic. Use the subject index to find *citations*, or listings that tell you when and where articles were published on your topic. Some periodical indexes also include *abstracts*, or brief summaries of articles.

Some periodical indexes cover articles from many printed sources; others cover articles from only one source. The periodical index that you will probably use the most is the *Readers' Guide to Periodical Literature.* It lists, by subject, articles that have appeared in most magazines within a specific time frame.

ENTRY FROM THE *READERS' GUIDE*

Main subject heading — **Solar radiation**

Cross-references —
See also
Solar flares
Solar wind
Sunspots
Ultraviolet rays

Title of article — The inconstant solar constant [Solar Max data] R. C. Willson and others. il

Magazine title — *Sky Telesc* 67:501-3 Je '84

Author of article — Liquid droplets on high [water in cirus clouds: research by Kenneth Sassen and Kuo-Nan Liou] C. Simon. *Sci News* 125:406 Je 30 '84

Volume: page numbers and date — Radiation satellite designed for shuttle [Earth Radiation on climate] C. Covault. il *Aviat Week Space Technol* 121:41-3+ S 17 '84

Solar irradiance observations [solar constant; Spacelab data] D. Crommelynck and V. Domingo. bibl f il *Science* 225:180-1 Jl 13 '84

Illustrated — il

Subheading — **Physiological effects**
See also
Seasonal affect disorder
Suntan

Technology Tip

Most periodical indexes are now available electronically, either on CD-ROM or on the Internet. Use the keyword search feature to access citations of articles on your topic. You will find that some electronic indexes include complete articles on some topics.

Exercise 9 **Using the *Readers' Guide*** Use a recent volume of the *Readers' Guide* to locate two articles on earthquakes. For each article, note the periodical, the title of the article, its author, volume, date, and page number(s).

Finding Periodicals Once you've used a periodical index to identify appropriate articles, enlist the help of your librarian to locate the articles. Often, past editions of magazines are stored by a library on a database, on microfilm, or on CD-ROMs. Your librarian can show you how to use these resources.

Using Vertical Files In addition to information stored on shelves, on CD-ROMs, and on microfilm, many libraries have vertical files—file cabinets with large drawers where they store pamphlets on a wide variety of topics. For example, your library might have pamphlets about your local government. Such pamphlets can be a valuable research aid. Ask your librarian about the type of information stored in your library's vertical files.

Internet Tip

Today, most magazines have Web sites. Utilize these Web sites to help you find the articles you've identified in periodical indexes.

Using Dictionaries

A *dictionary* is a collection of words and their meanings. A dictionary explains how words are spelled, how they are pronounced, and how they are used in a sentence. Dictionaries also provide information about a word's history, or *etymology*.

KEY CONCEPT Dictionaries contain a great deal of useful information about words. ■

Using Your Dictionary to Check Spelling The English language can have many spellings for one sound.

KEY CONCEPT Become familiar with the different spelling patterns of sounds in English words. ■

You can usually find the word you want if you guess at the first few letters. *Webster's New World Dictionary* (student edition) has charts like the one below that can help you locate words with tricky sounds.

WORD FINDER CHART

If the sound is like the...	try also the spelling...	as in the words...
a in fat	ai, au	plaid, draught
a in lane	ai, ao, au, ay, ea, ei, eigh, et, ey	rain, gaol, gauge, ray, break, rein, weigh, sachet, they
a in care	ai, ay, e, eu, ei	air, prayer, there, wear, their
a in father	au, e, ea	gaunt, sergeant, hearth
a in ago	e, i, o, u	agent, sanity, comply, focus
ch in chin	tch, ti, tu	catch, question, nature
e in get	a, ae, ai, ay	any, aesthete, said, says

Finding Words Quickly in a Dictionary

Finding Words Quickly in a Dictionary Use the three-step process to help you find words quickly in a dictionary.

1. Step One: Take a Four-Section Approach Mentally divide the dictionary into four sections:

ABCD EFGHIJKL MNOPQR STUVWXYZ

These sections seem unequal, but there are as many English words that start with A–D as with S–Z. Here is how to use this approach: If you are looking for the word *catastrophic*, you know it will be in the first quarter of the dictionary. Similarly, the word *noxious* will be near the middle.

2. Step Two: Use the Guide Words At the top of each page are *guide words*. The guide word on the left tells the first word on the page. The guide word on the right tells the last word on the page. Look for the pair of guide words that come before and after your word.

3. Step Three: Follow Letter-by-Letter Alphabetical Order To locate your word on the page, remember that the entries are in *strict alphabetical order*. This rule holds true even if the entry has more than one word. (For example, *okra* comes before *Olaf*, *Olaf* before *olden*, and *olden* before *old hand*.)

Technology Tip

When using an electronic dictionary, you can find a word by typing in its first few letters. Doing so will take you to a list of words with similar beginnings from which you can choose the word for which you are looking.

Exercise 10 **Alphabetizing Words** List the following words in the order you would find them in a dictionary.

1. ripen
2. riptide
3. ripple
4. Rip Van Winkle
5. ripe

Exercise 11 **Finding Words Quickly** Use the three steps listed above to find these words quickly. Identify the dictionary section and the guide words for the page on which you find each word.

1. tomahawk
2. impassive
3. paradox
4. ripe
5. shilling

Understanding Dictionary Entries

Understanding Dictionary Entries The words that make up a dictionary are called *entry words*. An entry word, with all of the information about it, is called a *main entry*. Entry words include not only single words but also compound words (two or more words acting as one, such as *national bank*), abbreviations (*nat.*), prefixes (*re-*), suffixes (*-ent*), and the names of significant persons and places (*Nigeria*).

Look at the sample main entry on the next page.

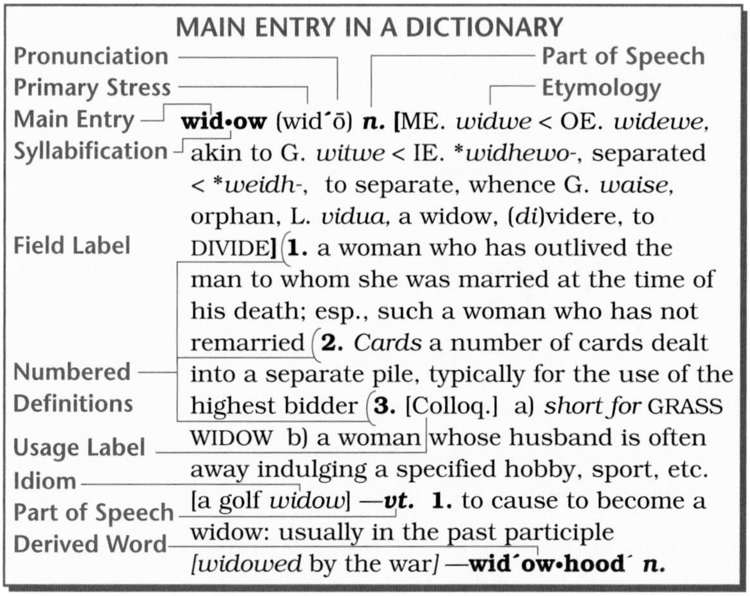

MAIN ENTRY IN A DICTIONARY

Pronunciation — Part of Speech
Primary Stress — Etymology
Main Entry
Syllabification
Field Label
Numbered Definitions
Usage Label
Idiom
Part of Speech
Derived Word

wid•ow (wid´ō) ***n.*** [ME. *widwe* < OE. *widewe,* akin to G. *witwe* < IE. **widhewo-*, separated < **weidh-*, to separate, whence G. *waise,* orphan, L. *vidua,* a widow, (*di*)videre, to DIVIDE] **1.** a woman who has outlived the man to whom she was married at the time of his death; esp., such a woman who has not remarried **2.** *Cards* a number of cards dealt into a separate pile, typically for the use of the highest bidder **3.** [Colloq.] a) *short for* GRASS WIDOW b) a woman whose husband is often away indulging a specified hobby, sport, etc. [a golf *widow*] —***vt.*** **1.** to cause to become a widow: usually in the past participle [*widowed* by the war] —**wid´ow•hood´** ***n.***

- **Syllabification** Dots, spaces, or slashes (/) show how a word is divided into syllables. This can help you when you need to break a word at the end of a line in your writing.
- **Pronunciations** Symbols show how to say a word and indicate which syllable to stress. A heavy mark (´) shows the syllable emphasized most (*primary stress*), and a lighter mark (´) shows one with less emphasis (*secondary stress*).
- **Parts-of-Speech Labels** These labels are abbreviated. They show how a word can be used in a sentence—whether it functions as a noun, a verb, or some other part of speech. Different meanings may fit different uses.
- **Etymology** Etymology is defined as the origin and history of a word. This useful information is provided in brackets after the definition. The etymological abbreviations and symbols are explained at the beginning of a dictionary.
- **Definitions** If there is more than one meaning for a word, each is listed by number. Multiple meanings are often used in a phrase or sentence for clarification.
- **Special Labels** *Usage labels*—such as *slang, dialect,* and *colloquial*—tell you that a certain meaning is not used in formal English. *Field labels,* such as *Bio* (for Biology), show that a meaning is limited in its usage.
- **Idioms** *Idioms* are expressions that contain the entry word, such as *down at the heels.* These may need to be explained because they do not mean exactly what their words say.
- **Derived Words** Words formed by adding a suffix (*-ly, -ness*) are listed at the end of the main entry.

Spelling Tip

Be aware that some words have more than one accepted spelling. All acceptable spellings are listed in dictionaries.

Exercise 12 **Working With Main Entries** Answer the following questions by using a dictionary.

1. Which syllable in *characteristic* has the primary stress?
2. Give the etymology of the word *charade*.
3. Find a slang definition for the word *charge*.
4. Find an idiom for the word *peg*.
5. What is the meaning of *closet* used as a verb?

Using Other Print and Electronic References

In addition to nonfiction books, dictionaries, and periodicals, there is a wide range of other print and electronic references you can use.

Using Encyclopedias Encyclopedias contain facts on a great many subjects. They provide basic information to help you start researching a topic.

Technology Tip

There is a wide range of multimedia encyclopedias on CD-ROM. In addition to articles, photographs, maps, and charts, these CD-ROMs offer audio and video on certain subjects. To use a CD-ROM encyclopedia, type your subject into the keyword search feature.

KEY CONCEPT Use encyclopedias for basic facts, background information, and suggestions for additional research. ■

Volumes and Articles Are Arranged Alphabetically The volumes of an encyclopedia are arranged in alphabetical order. The pages have guide words to show you the first and last subjects covered on each page.

Major Encyclopedias Have an Index Most encyclopedias have an index to help you locate articles. The encyclopedia index entry shown below directs you to the volume and page number of the article. Related articles are also listed.

ENCYCLOPEDIA INDEX ENTRY

Volume
Page Number

Space travel So:560 *with pictures and maps*
See also the reading and study guide on this topic
Air Force, United States (The Air Force in Space) A:185
Altitude A:372b
Astronomy (Space Exploration) A:813
Computer (In Engineering) Ci:742 *with picture*
Cosmic Rays (Effect of Cosmic Rays) Ci:857

Using Biographical References These books provide brief life histories of famous people in many different fields. Biographical references may offer short entries similar to those in dictionaries or longer articles more like those in encyclopedias. Most contain an index to help you locate entries.

Using Almanacs Almanacs are published annually. They contain facts and statistics about many subjects, including government, world history, geography, entertainment, business, and sports. To find a subject in a printed almanac, refer to the index in the front or back. In an *electronic almanac*, you can usually find information by typing a subject or key word.

Using Atlases and Electronic Map Collections *Atlases* and *electronic map collections* contain maps and information based on them, such as facts about cities, bodies of water, mountains, and landmarks. Some also supply statistics about population, climate, products, and natural resources. In *printed atlases*, use an index to learn on which map to look for a particular place. In electronic atlases or map collections, you usually type in the place name, and the computer searches a database for the appropriate map.

Using Thesauruses A thesaurus gives *synonyms* (words with similar meanings) and may list *antonyms* (words with opposite meanings). It is especially useful for writing, when you need to find a substitute for a word. Many *printed thesauruses* arrange words alphabetically. Others arrange words on the basis of themes; you must look up the word in an index to learn where to find its synonyms. With *electronic thesauruses* (included with most word-processing programs), you usually type in or highlight a word, and the computer searches a database.

Using Electronic Databases Available on CD-ROMs or on-line, electronic databases provide quick access to a wealth of information on a broad topic. For example, you could use an electronic database to look at information on a stock's performance over the past several years. Using a search feature, you can easily access any type of data, piece together related information, or look at the information in different ways.

Technology Tip

You can use electronic maps to examine a historical journey, plan the route for a trip, or give local directions.

Exercise 13 **Using Reference Sources** Supply information for each item below, and list the type of reference you used.

1. average temperature of Phoenix, Arizona, in March
2. states that border Lake Erie
3. birthdate of the cartoonist who created Charlie Brown
4. three accomplishments of Harriet Tubman
5. information about malaria
6. three synonyms for the word *inflexible*
7. Ray Bradbury's first published novel
8. two antonyms for the word *discomfort*
9. American League baseball's Most Valuable Player for 1999
10. five states with towns or cities named *Augusta*

31.2

Using the Internet

The *Internet* is a worldwide network, or Web, of computers connected over phone and cable lines. When you go *on-line*, or hook up with the Internet, you can access millions of Web sites where an amazing amount of information can be found. Each Web site has its own address, or *URL* (Uniform Resource Locator). It usually consists of several Web pages of text, graphics, and sometimes audio or video displays.

A number of *search engines* have been established to help you locate a potentially useful Web site. A search engine such as **www.yahoo.com** is a good place to search for broad categories of information.

▲ **Critical Viewing** How can working with another student make it easier to gather information on the Internet? **[Connect]**

KEY CONCEPT Use the Internet to locate many types of information, but judge Web sites for reliability. ■

The Internet is an excellent resource, but it contains Web sites that have not been thoroughly researched or that may contain slanted opinions instead of factual information. Here are some tips for finding reliable information on the Internet:

- If you know a reliable Web site and its address (URL), simply type in the address on your Web browser.
- Consult Internet coverage in library journals (such as *Library Journal*) for lists of reliable Web sites.
- Remember to "bookmark" (or save) interesting and reliable sites that you find while searching the Web.
- Identify the organization or person that set up the site. Is that organization or person likely to have a bias?
- Identify the source of the information. Does the information come from authorities on the topic? Is it backed up by research?
- Is the information up-to-date?

Learn More

For extensive information on using the Internet and critically evaluating Internet sites, see the Internet Handbook on page 575.

Exercise 14 **Using the Internet** On a library, school, or home computer, use the Internet to answer these questions.

1. Who was Allen Funt?
2. How many MTV Awards did Lauryn Hill win in 1999?
3. What are the URLs of four Web sites with information on Lyme disease?
4. Who won the 1998 New York Marathon?
5. What is the URL of a site with a map of Detroit, Michigan?

Section 31.3 Test-Taking Skills

This section provides some tips to help you improve your performance on tests by helping you answer the different kinds of questions they contain.

Strategies for Taking Tests

When you prepare for a test, carefully study the material that the test will cover, and be sure to come to the test on time with all the equipment you have been told to bring—pens, pencils, books, and so on. When you take the test, plan how you will use your time.

KEY CONCEPT Divide your time among previewing the test, answering the questions, and proofreading your answers. ■

LOOK OVER THE TEST (no more than 25% of time)

1. Put your name on your paper.
2. Skim the test to look over the different kinds of questions.
3. Decide how much time you will spend on each section.
4. Allow time for difficult or high-point questions.

ANSWER THE QUESTIONS (allow at least 50% of time)

1. If you can, use scratch paper to jot down your ideas.
2. Answer the easy questions first.
3. For harder items, concentrate on one question at a time.
4. Be sure to follow the directions completely.

PROOFREAD ANSWERS (no more than 25% of time)

1. Check that you have followed directions.
2. Reread test questions and answers.
3. Make sure that you have answered all of the questions.

Exercise 15 **Evaluating Your Test-Taking Skills** Answer these questions about a test you have taken recently.

1. Did you give yourself enough time to study beforehand?
2. Did you focus on the information you needed for the test?
3. Did you look over the test carefully before you began writing?
4. Did you answer all of the easy questions first?
5. Did you allow enough time for the difficult questions or for questions that were worth more points?

Answering Different Types of Questions

If you are familiar with the different kinds of questions that are frequently asked on tests, you may be able to improve your performance on the tests.

KEY CONCEPT Know the different kinds of objective questions and the strategies for answering them. ■

Multiple-Choice Questions This kind of question asks you to choose from several possible responses.

EXAMPLE: The opposite of *martial* is ____.

a. sad	c. enthusiastic
b. peaceful	d. hostile

In the preceding example, the answer is *b*. Follow these strategies to answer multiple-choice questions:

- Try answering the question before looking at the answer choices. If your answer is one of the choices, select that one.
- Eliminate the obviously incorrect answers, crossing them out if you are allowed to write on the test paper.
- Read all of the choices before answering. For multiple-choice items, there are often two *possible* answers, but only one *best* answer.

Matching Questions Matching questions require you to match items in one group with items in another.

EXAMPLE:

____ 1. dredge	a. shy
____ 2. introverted	b. refined
____ 3. genteel	c. dig

In the preceding example, the answers are 1.*c*, 2.*a*, 3.*b*. Follow these strategies to answer matching questions:

- Count each group to see whether items will be left over. Check the directions to see whether items can be used more than once.
- Read all of the items before you start matching.
- Match the items you know first.
- Match the remaining items of which you are less certain.

▼ Critical Viewing Do you think this student is preparing for a test or taking a test? Why? **[Analyze]**

True/False Questions True/false questions require you to determine whether a statement is accurate.

EXAMPLE:
____ Earth is the closet planet to the sun in our solar system.
____ An astronomer is someone who studies stars.
____ A telescope is not used to study the stars.

In the preceding example, the answers are *F, T, F.* Follow these strategies to answer true/false questions:

- If a statement seems true, be sure the entire sentence is true.
- Pay special attention to the word *not*, which often changes the entire meaning of a statement.
- Pay special attention to the words *all, always, never, no, none,* and *only.* They often make a statement false.
- Pay special attention to the words *generally, much, many, most, often, some,* and *usually.* They often make a statement true.

Fill-in Questions Fill-in questions ask you to supply an answer in your own words. The answer may complete a statement or may simply answer a question.

EXAMPLE: Presidential elections are held every ____ years.

In the preceding example, the answer is *four.* Follow these strategies to answer fill-in questions:

- Read the question or incomplete statement carefully.
- If you are answering a question, change it into a statement by inserting your answer, and see whether it makes sense.

Analogies An analogy asks you to find pairs of words with a similar relationship.

EXAMPLE: CEILING : ROOM ::

a. wall : floor	c. roof : house
b. foundation : cement	d. wall : paper

In the preceding example, the answer is *c.* The relationship is *part to whole.* The ceiling is part of a room, and the roof is part of a house. Once you understand analogy relationships (see the chart on the next page), you can use the strategies below to answer the questions.

- Identify how the first pair of words relate.
- If more than one choice seems correct, go back to the first pair, and redefine its relationship.
- If you cannot find an equal relationship between the first pair and a second pair, consider other possible word meanings.

COMMON ANALOGY RELATIONSHIPS	
Relationship	**Example**
synonym (same meaning)	carousel : merry-go-round
antonym (opposite meaning)	enlarge : shrink
function	chauffeur : drive
part to whole	page : book
cause-effect	veterinarian : heal
type	mongoose : mammal

Exercise 16 **Answering Analogies** Identify the relationship between the words in each first pair below. Then, complete each second pair (the first part of it has been provided).

1. NOTIFY : TELL :: SPECULATE : __?__
   a. guess b. invest c. insult
2. SURGEON : DOCTOR :: SEDAN : __?__
   a. drive b. accident c. automobile
3. SHOVEL : HOLE :: GLUE : __?__
   a. loosen b. sticky c. attachment
4. PHARAOH : RULER :: TORNADO : __?__
   a. storm b. hurricane c. summer
5. PERMANENT : TEMPORARY :: PURIFIED : __?__
   a. water b. safe c. polluted
6. HANDLE : CUP :: WINDSHIELD : __?__
   a. car b. protect c. wind
7. STRETCH : RUN :: CHEW : __?__
   a. cook b. swallow c. bite
8. DRIZZLE : DOWNPOUR :: TAP : __?__
   a. drink b. dance c. wallop
9. PILFER : STEAL :: ANTAGONIZE : __?__
   a. remove b. anger c. befriend
10. EMINENT : UNKNOWN :: OBVIOUS : __?__
    a. unclear b. unsafe c. unhappy

Exercise 17 **Answering Test Items** Using a topic you are studying in science class, prepare a short test on the material. Write five multiple-choice questions, five matching questions, five true/false questions, and five fill-in questions. Exchange tests with a classmate, and take the other student's test.

Learn More

To learn more about analogies, see Chapter 30.

Answering Short-Answer and Essay Questions

Some test questions require you to supply an answer, rather than simply identify a correct answer. Identify these questions when you preview the test. Allow time to write complete, accurate answers.

KEY CONCEPT Allow time and space to respond to short-answer and essay questions. ■

Follow these strategies to respond to short-answer and essay questions:

Identify Key Words Whether you are responding to a short-answer question or an essay topic, identify the key words in the test item. Look for words such as *discuss*, *explain*, *identify*, and any numbers or restrictions. If the question asks for three causes, make sure you supply three.

Check Your Space On some tests, you will be given a certain number of lines on which to write your answer. Make sure that you understand whether you are limited to that space or whether you can use more paper. If your space is limited, use it for the most important information that fits the topic.

Stick to the Point Do not put down everything you know about a topic. If the question asks you to identify three kinds of clouds and explain how to recognize them, you will not get extra credit for explaining how tornados move. In fact, including unrelated information may cause you to lose points.

Learn More

Chapter 13, Writing for Assessment, provides in-depth guidance and practice in writing essays for tests.

Reflecting on Your Study, Reference, and Test-Taking Skills

Answer the following questions to consider what you have learned about your study, reference, and test-taking habits and skills.

- Which strategies seem new or unusual? How can using these strategies help me improve my academic performance?
- Which strategies do I already use? Why do I find these most comfortable and useful?

Styles for Business and Friendly Letters

Business Letters

From a letter requesting information about a product to a letter asking for charitable donations, business letters are a common form of formal writing, writing intended for readers with whom the writer is not personally acquainted. Whatever the subject, an effective business letter

- includes six parts: the heading, the inside address, the salutation or greeting, the body, the closing, and the signature.
- follows one of several acceptable forms: In *block format,* each part of the letter begins at the left margin; in *modified block format,* the heading, the closing, and the signature are indented to the center of the page.
- uses formal language to communicate respectfully, regardless of the letter's content.

The **heading** indicates the address and business affiliation of the writer. It also includes the date the letter was sent.

Model Business Letter

In this letter, Yolanda Dodson uses modified block format to request information.

Students for a Cleaner Planet
c/o Memorial High School
333 Veterans' Drive
Denver, Colorado 80211

January 25, 20 – –

Steven Wilson, Director
Resource Recovery Really Works
300 Oak Street
Denver, Colorado 80216

Dear Mr. Wilson:

Memorial High School would like to start a branch of your successful recycling program. We share your commitment to reclaiming as much reusable material as we can. Because your program has been successful in other neighborhoods, we're sure that it can work in our community. Our school includes grades 9–12 and has about 800 students.

Would you send us some information about your community recycling program? For example, we need to know what materials can be recycled and how we can implement the program.

At least fifty students have already expressed an interest in getting involved, so I know we'll have the people power to make the program work. Please help us get started.

Thank you in advance for your time and consideration.

Sincerely,

Yolanda Dodson

Yolanda Dodson

The **inside address** indicates where the letter will be sent.

A **salutation** is punctuated by a colon. When the specific addressee is not known, use a general greeting such as "To whom it may concern:"

The **body** of the letter states the writer's purpose. In this case, the writer is requesting information.

The **closing** "Sincerely" is common, but "Yours truly" and "Respectfully yours" are also acceptable. To end the letter, the writer types her name and provides a **signature**.

Friendly Letters and Social Notes

When you write a letter telling news to a friend or thanking a relative for a gift, you are writing a friendly letter or a social note. A friendly letter is any informal letter based on a personal relationship with the reader. A social note includes a semiformal thank-you note written to someone you do not know quite well. Friendly letters and social notes typically feature the following elements:

- a heading, a salutation or greeting, a body, a closing, and a signature; they generally do not include an inside address
- a comma after the greeting
- paragraphs with indented first lines
- the use of a version of semiblock style, in which the heading, closing, and signature align to the right of center
- informal or semiformal language, often featuring the lively expression of feelings or amusement

How careful you need to be in following appropriate format depends on your relationship with the reader: The less well you know the person, the more careful you should be to follow the correct format. Consult the model below for proper formatting.

The **heading, closing,** and **signature** are aligned, semiblock style, to the right of the center of the page. (In very informal letters, writers may choose to omit their own address in the heading.)

Model Social Note

In this letter, Mayra Gonzalez thanks her aunt for a gift.

A comma is used after the **greeting;** Mayra addresses her reader semiformally.

The first line of each paragraph in the **body** is indented. The writer uses informal language and gives details that are of personal interest.

A friendly letter may use or adapt a **closing** such as "Love," "Yours," and "Best," followed by a comma. As is customary when writer and reader know each other well, Mayra signs her first name only and does not add her name written out.

1111 Main St.
Mayfair, OH
November 11, 20 - -

Dear Aunt Margie,

Well, as you predicted, the trip to the amusement park was a lot of fun. I had a great time! The rides were more thrilling than any I've ever been on before. Even the twins were impressed—I don't think they had a single fight during the entire trip, and you know that's saying a lot!

The only part I wouldn't visit again was the spooky House of Chills. Ugh! I didn't mind the visuals: skeletons, scary pirates, and that sort of thing. But there's one part of the ride that takes place in complete darkness, with very quiet sound effects, and while you sit there wondering what will happen next, a cold, clammy THING runs slithering across your back or your hand! I nearly jumped out of my skin. I wasn't that frightened even when we told scary stories the night the lights went out at your house.

Thanks very much for the tickets and the fun day. We all loved the trip. I hope you'll come to visit again soon.

Your tallest niece,
Mayra

Citing Sources and Preparing Manuscript

The presentation of your written work is important. Your work should be neat, clean, and easy to read. Follow your teacher's directions for placing your name and class, along with the title and date of your work, on the paper.

For handwritten work:

- Use cursive handwriting or manuscript printing, according to the style your teacher prefers. The penmanship reference below shows the accepted formation of letters in cursive writing.
- Write or print neatly.
- Write on one side of lined $8\,^{1}/_{2}$" x 11" paper with a clean edge. (Do not use pages torn from a spiral notebook.)
- Indent the first line of each paragraph.
- Leave a margin, as indicated by the guidelines on the lined paper. Write in a size appropriate for the lines provided. Do not write so large that the letters from one line bump into the ones above and below. Do not write so small that the writing is difficult to read.
- Write in blue or black ink.
- Number the pages in the upper right corner.
- You should not cross out words on your final draft. Recopy instead. If your paper is long, your teacher may allow you to make one or two small changes by neatly crossing out the text to be deleted and using a caret [^] to indicate replacement text. Alternatively, you might make one or two corrections neatly with correction fluid. If you find yourself making more than three corrections, consider recopying the work.

PENMANSHIP REFERENCE

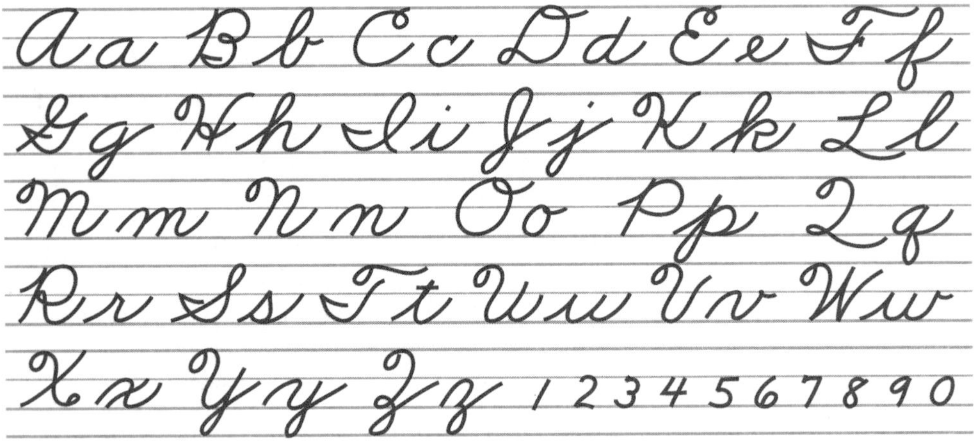

Aa Bb Cc Dd Ee Ff
Gg Hh Ii Jj Kk Ll
Mm Nn Oo Pp Qq
Rr Ss Tt Uu Vv Ww
Xx Yy Zz 1 2 3 4 5 6 7 8 9 0

For word-processed or typed documents:

- Choose a standard, easy-to-read font.
- Type or print on one side of unlined $8\,^1/_2$" x 11" paper.
- Set the margins for the side, top, and bottom of your paper at approximately one inch. Most word-processing programs have a default setting that is appropriate.
- Double-space the document.
- Indent the first line of each paragraph.
- Number the pages in the upper right corner. Many word-processing programs have a header feature that will do this for you automatically.
- If you discover one or two errors after you have typed or printed, use correction fluid if your teacher allows such corrections. If you have more than three errors in an electronic file, consider making the corrections to the file and reprinting the document. If you have typed a long document, your teacher may allow you to make a few corrections by hand. If you have several errors, however, consider retyping the document.

For research papers:

Follow your teacher's directions for formatting formal research papers. Most papers will have the following features:

- Title page
- Table of Contents or Outline
- Works-Cited List

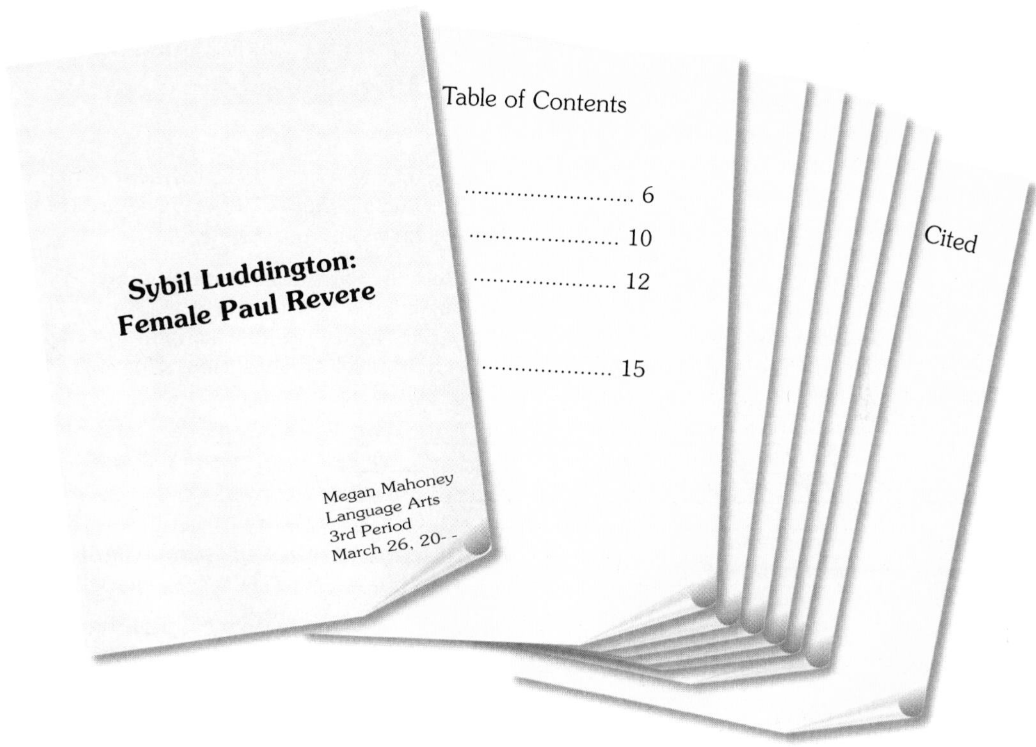

Incorporating Ideas From Research

Below are three common methods of incorporating the ideas of other writers into your work. Choose the most appropriate style by analyzing your needs in each case. In all cases, you must credit your source.

- **Direct Quotation:** Use quotation marks to indicate the exact words.
- **Paraphrase:** To share ideas without a direct quotation, state the ideas in your own words. While you haven't copied word-for-word, you still need to credit your source.
- **Summary:** To provide information about a large body of work—such as a speech, an editorial, or a chapter of a book—identify the writer's main idea.

Avoiding Plagiarism

Whether you are presenting a formal research paper or an opinion paper on a current event, you must be careful to give credit for any ideas or opinions that are not your own. Presenting someone else's ideas, research, or opinion as your own—even if you have rephrased it in different words—is *plagiarism*, the equivalent of academic stealing, or fraud.

You can avoid plagiarism by synthesizing what you learn: Read from several sources and let the ideas of experts help you draw your own conclusions and form your own opinions. Ultimately, however, note your own reactions to the ideas presented.

When you choose to use someone else's ideas or work to support your view, credit the source of the material. Give bibliographic information to cite your sources of the following information:

- Statistics
- Direct quotations
- Indirectly quoted statements of opinions
- Conclusions presented by an expert
- Facts available in only one or two sources

Crediting Sources

When you credit a source, you acknowledge where you found your information and you give your readers the details necessary for locating the source themselves. Within the body of the paper, you provide a short citation, a footnote number linked to a footnote, or an endnote number linked to an endnote reference. These brief references show the page numbers on which you found the information. To make your paper more formal, prepare a reference list at the end of the paper to provide full bibliographic information on your sources. These are two common types of reference lists:

- A **bibliography** provides a listing of all the resources you consulted during your research.
- A **works-cited list** indicates the works you have referenced in your paper.

Choosing a Format for Documentation

The type of information you provide and the format in which you provide it depend on what your teacher prefers. These are the most commonly used styles:

- **Modern Language Association (MLA) Style** This is the style used for most papers at the middle-school and high-school level and for most language arts papers.
- **American Psychological Association (APA) Style** This is used for most papers in the social sciences and for most college-level papers.
- ***Chicago Manual of Style* (CMS) Style** This is preferred by some teachers.

On the following pages, you'll find sample MLA documentation and citation formats for the most commonly cited materials.

MLA Style for Listing Sources

Book with one author	Pyles, Thomas. *The Origins and Development of the English Language.* 2nd ed. New York: Harcourt Brace Jovanovich, Inc., 1971.
Book with two or three authors	McCrum, Robert, William Cran, and Robert MacNeil. *The Story of English.* New York: Penguin Books, 1987.
Book with an editor	Truth, Sojourner. *Narrative of Sojourner Truth.* Ed. Margaret Washington. New York: Vintage Books, 1993.
Book with more than three authors or editors	Donald, Robert B., et al. *Writing Clear Essays.* Upper Saddle River, NJ: Prentice-Hall, Inc., 1996.
A single work from an anthology	Hawthorne, Nathaniel. "Young Goodman Brown." *Literature: An Introduction to Reading and Writing.* Ed. Edgar V. Roberts and Henry E. Jacobs. Upper Saddle River, NJ: Prentice-Hall, Inc., 1998. 376–385. [Indicate pages for the entire selection.]
Introduction in a published edition	Washington, Margaret. Introduction. *Narrative of Sojourner Truth.* By Sojourner Truth. New York: Vintage Books, 1993, pp. v–xi.
Signed article in a weekly magazine	Wallace, Charles. "A Vodacious Deal." *Time* 14 Feb. 2000: 63.
Signed article in a monthly magazine	Gustaitis, Joseph. "The Sticky History of Chewing Gum." *American History* Oct. 1998: 30–38.
Unsigned editorial or story	"Selective Silence." Editorial. *Wall Street Journal* 11 Feb. 2000: A14. [If the editorial or story is signed, begin with the author's name.]
Signed pamphlet	[Treat the pamphlet as though it were a book.]
Pamphlet with no author, publisher, or date	*Are You at Risk of Heart Attack?* n.p. n.d. [n.p. n.d. indicates that there is no known publisher or date]
Filmstrips, slide programs, and videotape	*The Diary of Anne Frank.* Dir. George Stevens. Perf. Millie Perkins, Shelley Winters, Joseph Schildkraut, Lou Jacobi, and Richard Beymer. Twentieth Century Fox, 1959.
Radio or television program transcript	"The First Immortal Generation." *Ockham's Razor.* Host Robyn Williams. Guest Damien Broderick. National Public Radio. 23 May 1999. Transcript.
Internet	*National Association of Chewing Gum Manufacturers.* 19 Dec. 1999 <http://www.nacgm.org/consumer/funfacts.html> [Indicate the date you accessed the information. Content and addresses at Web sites change frequently.]
Newspaper	Thurow, Roger. "South Africans Who Fought for Sanctions Now Scrap for Investors." *Wall Street Journal* 11 Feb. 2000: A1+ [For a multipage article, write only the first page number on which it appears, followed by a plus sign.]
Personal interview	Smith, Jane. Personal interview. 10 Feb. 2000.
CD (with multiple publishers)	Simms, James, ed. *Romeo and Juliet.* By William Shakespeare. CD-ROM. Oxford: Attica Cybernetics Ltd.; London: BBC Education; London: HarperCollins Publishers, 1995.
Article from an encyclopedia	Askeland, Donald R. (1991). "Welding." *World Book Encyclopedia.* 1991 ed.

Sample Works-Cited List (MLA)

Carwardine, Mark, Erich Hoyt, R. Ewan Fordyce, and Peter Gill. *The Nature Company Guides: Whales, Dolphins, and Porpoises.* New York: Time-Life Books, 1998.

Ellis, Richard. *Men and Whales.* New York: Knopf, 1991.

Whales in Danger. "Discovering Whales." 18 Oct. 1999. <http://whales.magna.com.au/DISCOVER>

Sample Internal Citations (MLA)

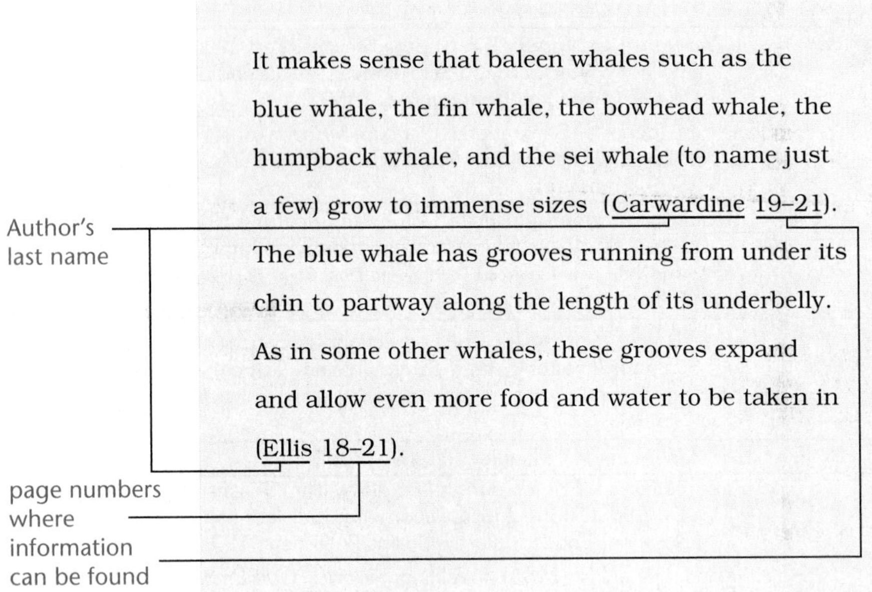

It makes sense that baleen whales such as the blue whale, the fin whale, the bowhead whale, the humpback whale, and the sei whale (to name just a few) grow to immense sizes (Carwardine 19–21). The blue whale has grooves running from under its chin to partway along the length of its underbelly. As in some other whales, these grooves expand and allow even more food and water to be taken in (Ellis 18–21).

Introduction to the Internet

The Internet is a series of networks that are interconnected all over the world. The Internet allows users to have almost unlimited access to information stored on the networks. Dr. Berners-Lee, a physicist, created the Internet in the 1980's by writing a small computer program that allowed pages to be linked together using key words. The Internet was mostly text-based until 1992, when a computer program called the NCSA Mosaic (National Center for Supercomputing Applications at the University of Illinois) was created. This program was the first Web browser. The development of Web browsers greatly eased the ability of the user to navigate through all the pages stored on the Web. Very soon, the appearance of the Web was altered as well. More appealing visuals were added, and sound was also implemented. This change made the Web more user-friendly and more appealing to the general public.

Using the Internet for Research

Key Word Search

Before you begin a search, you should identify your specific topic. To make searching easier, narrow your subject to a key word or a group of key words. These are your search terms, and they should be as specific as possible. For example, if you are looking for the latest concert dates for your favorite musical group, you might use the band's name as a key word. However, if you were to enter the name of the group in the query box of the search engine, you might be presented with thousands of links to information about the group that is unrelated to your needs. You might locate such information as band member biographies, the group's history, fan reviews of concerts, and hundreds of sites with related names containing information that is irrelevant to your search. Because you used such a broad key word, you might need to navigate through all that information before you find a link or subheading for concert dates. In contrast, if you were to type in "Duplex Arena and [band name]" you would have a better chance of locating pages that contain this information.

How to Narrow Your Search

If you have a large group of key words and still don't know which ones to use, write out a list of all the words you are considering. Once you have completed the list, scrutinize it. Then, delete the words that are least important to your search, and highlight those that are most important.

These **key search connectors** can help you fine-tune your search:

AND: narrows a search by retrieving documents that include both terms. For example: *baseball AND playoffs*

OR: broadens a search by retrieving documents including any of the terms. For example: *playoffs OR championships*

NOT: narrows a search by excluding documents containing certain words. For example: *baseball NOT history of*

Tips for an Effective Search

1. Keep in mind that search engines can be case-sensitive. If your first attempt at searching fails, check your search terms for misspellings and try again.
2. If you are entering a group of key words, present them in order, from the most important to the least important key word.
3. Avoid opening the link to every single page in your results list. Search engines present pages in descending order of relevancy. The most useful pages will be located at the top of the list. However, read the description of each link before you open the page.
4. When you use some search engines, you can find helpful tips for specializing your search. Take the opportunity to learn more about effective searching.

Other Ways to Search

Using On-line Reference Sites *How* you search should be tailored to *what* you are hoping to find. If you are looking for data and facts, use reference sites before you jump onto a simple search engine. For example, you can find reference sites to provide definitions of words, statistics about almost any subject, biographies, maps, and concise information on many topics. Some useful on-line reference sites:

On-line libraries
On-line periodicals
Almanacs
Encyclopedias

You can find these sources using subject searches.

Conducting Subject Searches As you prepare to go on-line, consider your subject and the best way to find information to suit your needs. If you are looking for general information on a topic and you want your search results to be extensive, consider the subject search indexes on most search engines. These indexes, in the form of category and subject lists, often appear on the first page of a search engine. When you click on a specific highlighted word, you will be presented with a new screen containing subcategories of the topic you chose. In the screen shots below, the category *Sports & Recreation* provided a second index for users to focus a search even further.

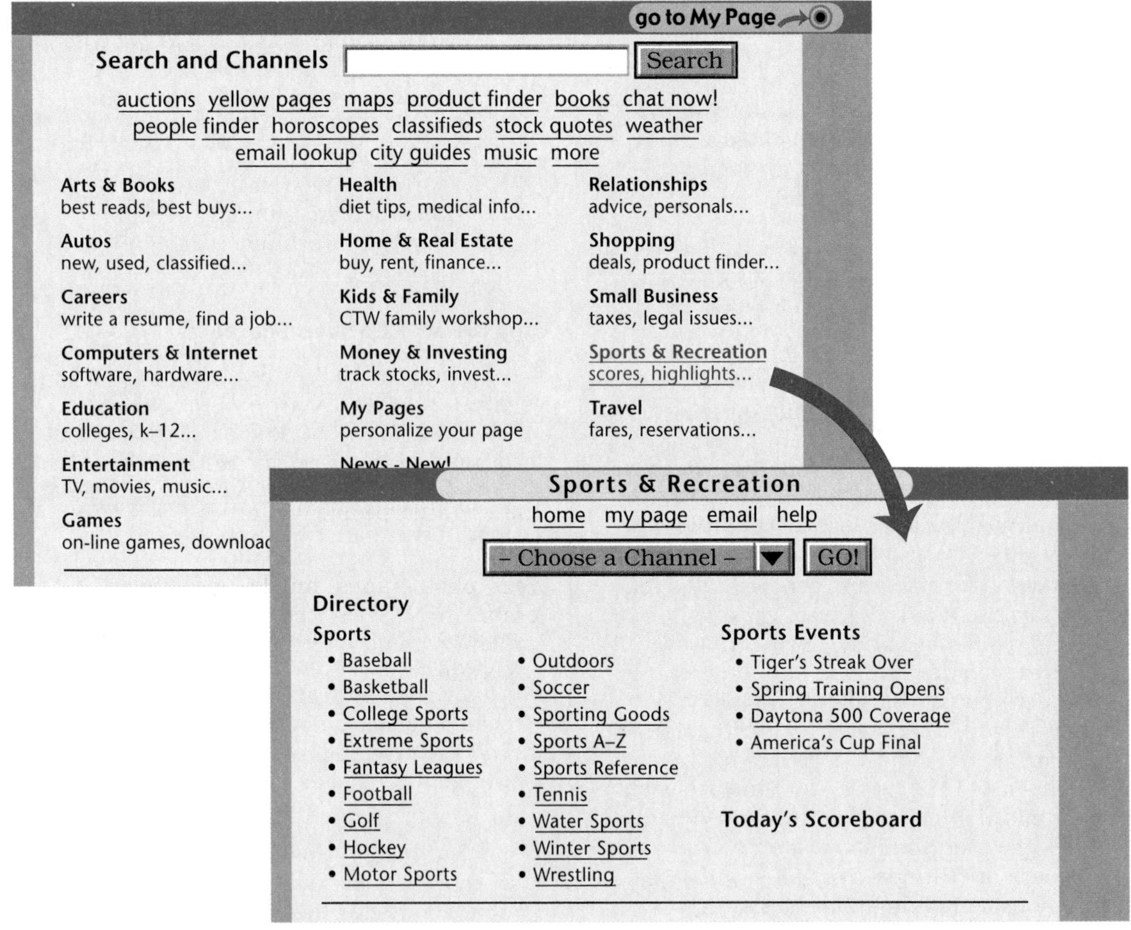

Evaluating the Reliability of Internet Resources Just as you would evaluate the quality, bias, and validity of any other research material you locate, check the source of information you find on-line. Compare these two sites containing information on the poet and writer Langston Hughes:

Site A is a personal Web site constructed by a college student. It contains no bibliographic information or links to sites that he used. Included on the site are several poems by Langston Hughes and a student essay about the poet's use of symbolism. It has not been updated in more than six months.

Site B is a Web site constructed and maintained by the English Department of a major university. Information on Hughes is presented in a scholarly format, with a bibliography and credits for the writer. The site includes links to other sites and indicates new features that are added weekly.

For your own research, consider the information you find on Site B to be more reliable and accurate than that on Site A. Because it is maintained by experts in their field who are held accountable for their work, the university site will be a better research tool than the student-generated one.

Tips for Evaluating Internet Sources

1. Consider who constructed and who now maintains the Web page. Determine whether this author is a reputable source. Often, the URL endings indicate a source.
   - Sites ending in *.edu* are maintained by educational institutions.
   - Sites ending in *.gov* are maintained by government agencies (federal, state, or local).
   - Sites ending in *.org* are normally maintained by nonprofit organizations and agencies.
   - Sites with a *.com* ending are commercially or personally maintained.
2. Skim the official and trademarked Web pages first. It is safe to assume that the information you draw from Web pages of reputable institutions, on-line encyclopedias, on-line versions of major daily newspapers, or government-owned sites produce information as reliable as the material you would find in print. In contrast, unbranded sites or those generated by individuals tend to borrow information from other sources without providing documentation. As information travels from one source to another, the information has likely been muddled, misinterpreted, edited, or revised.
3. You can still find valuable information in the less "official" sites. Check for the writer's credentials and then consider these factors:
   - Don't let official-looking graphics or presentations fool you.
   - Make sure the information is updated enough to suit your needs. Many Web pages will indicate how recently they have been updated.
   - If the information is borrowed, see whether you can trace it back to its original source.

Respecting Copyrighted Material

Because the Internet is a relatively new and quickly growing medium, issues of copyright and ownership arise almost daily. As laws begin to govern the use and reuse of material posted on-line, they may change the way that people can access or reprint material.

Text, photographs, music, and fine art printed on-line may not be reproduced without acknowledged permission of the copyright owner.

Commonly Overused Words

When you write, use the most precise word for your meaning, not the word that comes to mind first. Consult this thesaurus to find alternatives for some commonly overused words. Consult a full-length thesaurus to find alternatives to words that do not appear here. Keep in mind that the choices offered in a thesaurus do not all mean exactly the same thing. Review all the options, and choose the one that best expresses your meaning.

about approximately, nearly, almost, approaching, close to

absolutely unconditionally, perfectly, completely, ideally, purely

activity action, movement, operation, labor, exertion, enterprise, project, pursuit, endeavor, job, assignment, pastime, scheme, task

add attach, affix, join, unite, append, increase, amplify

affect adjust, influence, transform, moderate, incline, motivate, prompt

amazing overwhelming, astonishing, startling, unexpected, stunning, dazzling, remarkable

awesome impressive, stupendous, fabulous, astonishing, outstanding

bad defective, inadequate, poor, unsatisfactory, disagreeable, offensive, repulsive, corrupt, wicked, naughty, harmful, injurious, unfavorable

basic essential, necessary, indispensable, vital, fundamental, elementary

beautiful attractive, appealing, alluring, exquisite, gorgeous, handsome, stunning

begin commence, found, initiate, introduce, launch, originate

better preferable, superior, worthier

big enormous, extensive, huge, immense, massive

boring commonplace, monotonous, tedious, tiresome

bring accompany, cause, convey, create, conduct, deliver, produce

cause origin, stimulus, inspiration, motive

certain unquestionable, incontrovertible, unmistakable, indubitable, assured, confident

change alter, transform, vary, replace, diversify

choose select, elect, nominate, prefer, identify

decent respectable, adequate, fair, suitable

definitely unquestionably, clearly, precisely, positively, inescapably

easy effortless, natural, comfortable, undemanding, pleasant, relaxed

effective powerful, successful

emphasize underscore, feature, accentuate

end limit, boundary, finish, conclusion, finale, resolution

energy vitality, vigor, force, dynamism

enjoy savor, relish, revel, benefit

entire complete, inclusive, unbroken, integral

excellent superior, remarkable, splendid, unsurpassed, superb, magnificent

exciting thrilling, stirring, rousing, dramatic

far distant, remote

fast swift, quick, fleet, hasty, instant, accelerated

fill occupy, suffuse, pervade, saturate, inflate, stock

finish complete, conclude, cease, achieve, exhaust, deplete, consume

funny comical, ludicrous, amusing, droll, entertaining, bizarre, unusual, uncommon

get obtain, receive, acquire, procure, achieve

give bestow, donate, supply, deliver, distribute, impart

go proceed, progress, advance, move

good satisfactory, serviceable, functional, competent, virtuous, striking

great tremendous, superior, remarkable, eminent, proficient, expert

happy pleased, joyous, elated, jubilant, cheerful, delighted

hard arduous, formidable, complex, complicated, rigorous, harsh

help assist, aid, support, sustain, serve

hurt injure, harm, damage, wound, impair

important significant, substantial, weighty, meaningful, critical, vital, notable

interesting absorbing, appealing, entertaining, fascinating, thought-provoking

job task, work, business, undertaking, occupation, vocation, chore, duty, assignment

keep retain, control, possess

kind type, variety, sort, form

know comprehend, understand, realize, perceive, discern

like (adj) similar, equivalent, parallel

like (verb) enjoy, relish, appreciate

main primary, foremost, dominant

make build, construct, produce, assemble, fashion, manufacture

mean plan, intend, suggest, propose, indicate

more supplementary, additional, replenishment

new recent, modern, current, novel

next subsequently, thereafter, successively

nice pleasant, satisfying, gracious, charming

old aged, mature, experienced, used, worn, former, previous

open unobstructed, accessible

part section, portion, segment, detail, element, component

perfect flawless, faultless, ideal, consummate

plan scheme, design, system, plot

pleasant agreeable, gratifying, refreshing, welcome

prove demonstrate, confirm, validate, verify, corroborate

quick brisk, prompt, responsive, rapid, nimble, hasty

really truly, genuinely, extremely, undeniably

regular standard, routine, customary, habitual

see regard, behold, witness, gaze, realize, notice

small diminutive, miniature, minor, insignificant, slight, trivial

sometimes occasionally, intermittently, sporadically, periodically

take grasp, capture, choose, select, tolerate, endure

terrific extraordinary, magnificent, marvelous

think conceive, imagine, ponder, reflect, contemplate

try attempt, endeavor, venture, test

use employ, operate, utilize

very unusually, extremely, deeply, exceedingly, profoundly

want desire, crave, yearn, long

Commonly Misspelled Words

The list on these pages presents words that cause problems for many people. Some of these words are spelled according to set rules, but others follow no specific rules. As you review this list, check to see how many of the words give you trouble in your own writing. Then, read the instruction in the "Vocabulary and Spelling" chapter in the book for strategies and suggestions for improving your own spelling habits.

abbreviate
absence
absolutely
abundance
accelerate
accidentally
accumulate
accurate
ache
achievement
acquaintance
adequate
admittance
advertisement
aerial
affect
aggravate
aggressive
agreeable
aisle
all right
allowance
aluminum
amateur
analysis
analyze
ancient
anecdote
anniversary
anonymous
answer
anticipate
anxiety
apologize
appall
appearance
appreciate
appropriate
architecture
argument
associate

athletic
attendance
auxiliary
awkward
bandage
banquet
bargain
barrel
battery
beautiful
beggar
beginning
behavior
believe
benefit
bicycle
biscuit
bookkeeper
bought
boulevard
brief
brilliant
bruise
bulletin
buoyant
bureau
bury
buses
business
cafeteria
calendar
campaign
canceled
candidate
capacity
capital
capitol
captain
career
carriage
cashier

catastrophe
category
ceiling
cemetery
census
certain
changeable
characteristic
chauffeur
chief
clothes
coincidence
colonel
column
commercial
commission
commitment
committee
competitor
concede
condemn
congratulate
connoisseur
conscience
conscientious
conscious
contemporary
continuous
controversy
convenience
coolly
cooperate
cordially
correspondence
counterfeit
courageous
courteous
courtesy
criticism
criticize
curiosity

curious
cylinder
deceive
decision
deductible
defendant
deficient
definitely
delinquent
dependent
descendant
description
desert
desirable
dessert
deteriorate
dining
disappointed
disastrous
discipline
dissatisfied
distinguish
effect
eighth
eligible
embarrass
enthusiastic
entrepreneur
envelope
environment
equipped
equivalent
especially
exaggerate
exceed
excellent
exercise
exhibition
existence
experience
explanation

extension
extraordinary
familiar
fascinating
February
fiery
financial
fluorescent
foreign
forfeit
fourth
fragile
gauge
generally
genius
genuine
government
grammar
grievance
guarantee
guard
guidance
handkerchief
harass
height
humorous
hygiene
ignorant
illegible
immediately
immigrant
independence
independent
indispensable
individual
inflammable
intelligence
interfere
irrelevant
irritable
jewelry
judgment
knowledge
laboratory
lawyer
legible
legislature
leisure
liable

library
license
lieutenant
lightning
likable
liquefy
literature
loneliness
magnificent
maintenance
marriage
mathematics
maximum
meanness
mediocre
mileage
millionaire
minimum
minuscule
miscellaneous
mischievous
misspell
mortgage
naturally
necessary
negotiate
neighbor
neutral
nickel
niece
ninety
noticeable
nuclear
nuisance
obstacle
occasion
occasionally
occur
occurred
occurrence
omitted
opinion
opportunity
optimistic
outrageous
pamphlet
parallel
paralyze
parentheses

particularly
patience
permanent
permissible
perseverance
persistent
personally
perspiration
persuade
phenomenal
phenomenon
physician
pleasant
pneumonia
possess
possession
possibility
prairie
precede
preferable
prejudice
preparation
prerogative
previous
primitive
privilege
probably
procedure
proceed
prominent
pronunciation
psychology
publicly
pursue
questionnaire
realize
really
recede
receipt
receive
recognize
recommend
reference
referred
rehearse
relevant
reminiscence
renowned
repetition

restaurant
rhythm
ridiculous
sandwich
satellite
schedule
scissors
secretary
siege
solely
sponsor
subtle
subtlety
superintendent
supersede
surveillance
susceptible
tariff
temperamental
theater
threshold
truly
unmanageable
unwieldy
usage
usually
valuable
various
vegetable
voluntary
weight
weird
whale
wield
yield

Abbreviations Guide

Abbreviations, shortened versions of words or phrases, can be valuable tools in writing if you know when and how to use them. They can be very helpful in informal writing situations, such as taking notes or writing lists. However, only a few abbreviations can be used in formal writing. They are: *Mr., Mrs., Miss, Ms., Dr., A.M., P.M., A.D., B.C., M.A, B.A., Ph.D.,* and *M.D.*

The following pages provide the conventional abbreviations for a variety of words.

Abbreviations of Common Titles

Ambassador	Amb.	Lieutenant	Lt.
Attorney	Atty.	Major	Maj.
Brigadier-General	Brig. Gen.	President	Pres.
Brother	Br.	Professor	Prof.
Captain	Capt.	Representative	Rep.
Colonel	Col.	Reverend	Rev.
Commander	Cmdr.	Secretary	Sec.
Commissioner	Com.	Senator	Sen.
Corporal	Cpl.	Sergeant	Sgt.
Doctor	Dr.	Sister	Sr.
Father	Fr.	Superintendent	Supt.
Governor	Gov.	Treasurer	Treas.
Honorable	Hon.	Vice Admiral	Vice Adm.

Abbreviations of Academic Degrees

Bachelor of Arts	B.A. (or A.B.)	Esquire (lawyer)	Esq.
Bachelor of Science	B.S. (or S.B.)	Master of Arts	M.A. (or A.M.)
Doctor of Dental Surgery	D.D.S.	Master of Business Administration	M.B.A.
Doctor of Divinity	D.D.		
Doctor of Education	Ed.D.	Master of Fine Arts	M.F.A.
Doctor of Laws	LL.D.	Master of Science	M.S. (or S.M.)
Doctor of Medicine	M.D.	Registered Nurse	R.N.
Doctor of Philosophy	Ph.D.		

Abbreviations of States

State	Traditional	Postal Service	State	Traditional	Postal Service
Alabama	Ala.	AL	Montana	Mont.	MT
Alaska	Alaska	AK	Nebraska	Nebr.	NE
Arizona	Ariz.	AZ	Nevada	Nev.	NV
Arkansas	Ark.	AR	New Hampshire	N.H.	NH
California	Calif.	CA	New Jersey	N.J.	NJ
Colorado	Colo.	CO	New Mexico	N.M.	NM
Connecticut	Conn.	CT	New York	N.Y.	NY
Delaware	Del.	DE	North Carolina	N.C.	NC
Florida	Fla.	FL	North Dakota	N.Dak.	ND
Georgia	Ga.	GA	Ohio	O.	OH
Hawaii	Hawaii	HI	Oklahoma	Okla.	OK
Idaho	Ida.	ID	Oregon	Ore.	OR
Illinois	Ill.	IL	Pennsylvania	Pa.	PA
Indiana	Ind.	IN	Rhode Island	R.I.	RI
Iowa	Iowa	IA	South Carolina	S.C.	SC
Kansas	Kans.	KS	South Dakota	S.Dak.	SD
Kentucky	Ky.	KY	Tennessee	Tenn.	TN
Louisiana	La.	LA	Texas	Tex.	TX
Maine	Me.	ME	Utah	Utah	UT
Maryland	Md.	MD	Vermont	Vt.	VT
Massachusetts	Mass.	MA	Virginia	Va.	VA
Michigan	Mich.	MI	Washington	Wash.	WA
Minnesota	Minn.	MN	West Virginia	W. Va	WV
Mississippi	Miss.	MS	Wisconsin	Wis.	WI
Missouri	Mo.	MO	Wyoming	Wyo.	WY

Common Geographical Abbreviations

Apartment	Apt.	National	Natl.
Avenue	Ave.	Park, Peak	Pk.
Block	Blk.	Peninsula	Pen.
Boulevard	Blvd.	Point	Pt.
Building	Bldg.	Province	Prov.
County	Co.	Road	Rd.
District	Dist.	Route	Rte.
Drive	Dr.	Square	Sq.
Fort	Ft.	Street	St.
Island	Is.	Territory	Terr.
Mountain	Mt.		

Abbreviations of Traditional Measurements

inch(es)	in.	ounce(s)	oz.
foot, feet	ft.	pound(s)	lb.
yard(s)	yd.	pint(s)	pt.
mile(s)	mi.	quart(s)	qt.
teaspoon(s)	tsp.	gallon(s)	gal.
tablespoon(s)	tbsp.	Fahrenheit	F.

Abbreviations of Metric Measurements

millimeter(s)	mm	liter(s)	L
centimeter(s)	cm	kiloliter(s)	kL
meter(s)	m	milligram(s)	mg
kilometer(s)	km	centigram(s)	cg
milliliter(s)	mL	gram(s)	g
centiliter(s)	cL	Celsius	C

Other Commonly Used Abbreviations

about (used with dates)	c., ca., circ.	manager	mgr.
and others	et al.	manufacturing	mfg.
anonymous	anon.	market	mkt.
approximately	approx.	measure	meas.
associate, association	assoc., assn.	merchandise	mdse.
auxiliary	aux., auxil.	miles per hour	mph
bibliography	bibliog.	miscellaneous	misc.
boxes	bx(s).	money order	M.O.
bucket	bkt.	note well; take notice	N.B.
bulletin	bull.	number	no.
bushel	bu.	package	pkg.
capital letter	cap.	page	p., pg.
cash on delivery	C.O.D.	pages	pp.
department	dept.	pair(s)	pr(s).
discount	disc.	parenthesis	paren.
dozen(s)	doz.	Patent Office	pat. off.
each	ea.	piece(s)	pc(s).
edition, editor	ed.	poetical, poetry	poet.
equivalent	equiv.	private	pvt.
established	est.	proprietor	prop.
fiction	fict.	pseudonym	pseud.
for example	e.g.	published, publisher	pub.
free of charge	grat., gratis	received	recd.
General Post Office	G.P.O.	reference, referee	ref.
government	gov., govt.	revolutions per minute	rpm
graduate, graduated	grad.	rhetorical, rhetoric	rhet.
Greek, Grecian	Gr.	right	R.
headquarters	hdqrs.	scene	sc.
height	ht.	special, specific	spec.
hospital	hosp.	spelling, species	sp.
illustrated	ill., illus.	that is	i.e.
including, inclusive	incl.	treasury, treasurer	treas.
introduction, introductory	intro.	volume	vol.
italics	ital.	weekly	wkly
karat, carat	k., kt.	weight	wt.
left	L.		

Proofreading Symbols Reference

Proofreading symbols make it easier to show where changes are needed in a paper. When proofreading your own or a classmate's work, use these standard proofreading symbols.

insert	I proofred.
delete	Ip proofread.
close up space	I proof read.
delete and close up space	I proofreade.
begin new paragraph	¶ I proofread.
spell out	I proofread 10 papers. sp
lowercase	I Proofread. lc
capitalize	i proofread. cap
transpose letters	I proofraed. tr
transpose words	I only proofread her paper. tr
period	I will proofread
comma	I will proofread and she will help.
colon	We will proofread for the following errors
semicolon	I will proofread she will help.
single quotation marks	She said, "I enjoyed the story The Invalid."
double quotation marks	She said, I enjoyed the story.
apostrophe	Did you borrow Sylvias book?
question mark	Did you borrow Sylvia's book ?/
exclamation point	You're kidding !/
hyphen	online /=/
parentheses	William Shakespeare 1564–1616

Student Publications

To share your writing with a wider audience, consider submitting it to a local, state, or national publication for student writing. Following are several magazines and Web sites that accept and publish student work.

Periodicals

Creative Kids P.O. Box 8813, Waco TX 76714-8813

Merlyn's Pen merlynspen.org

Skipping Stones P.O. Box 3939, Eugene, OR 97403 http://www.skippingstones.org

Teen Ink Box 30, Newton, MA 02461 teenink.com

On-line Publications

Kid Pub http://www.kidpub.org

MidLink Magazine http://www.ncsu.edu/midlink

Stone Soup http://www.stonesoup.com

Contests

Annual Poetry Contest National Federation of State Poetry Societies, Contest Chair, Kathleen Pederzani, 121 Grande Boulevard, Reading, PA 19608-9680. http://www.nfsps.com

Paul A. Witty Outstanding Literature Award International Reading Association, Special Interest Group for Reading for Gifted and Creative Students, c/o Texas Christian University, P.O. Box 297900, Fort Worth, TX 76129

***Seventeen* Magazine Fiction Contest** *Seventeen* Magazine, 1440 Broadway 13th Floor, New York, NY 10018

The Young Playwrights Festival National Playwriting Competition Young Playwrights Inc. Dept WEB, 306 West 38th Street #300, New York, NY 10018 or webmaster@youngplaywrights.org

Sentence Diagraming Workshop

Diagraming is a visual way to explain how parts of a sentence are related. In a diagram, the words from a sentence are positioned on horizontal, vertical, and slanted lines. Each line stands for something different. This section will explain how you can draw diagrams for each of the sentence parts that you learned about in Chapter 19.

Subjects and Verbs

The basic parts of any sentence are the subject and its verb. In a diagram, both the subject and the verb are placed on a horizontal line. They are separated by a vertical line, with the subject on the left and the verb on the right.

S V

EXAMPLE: Cars race.

Cars | race

Names and compound nouns are diagramed in the same way as *cars* in the preceding example. Verb phrases are diagramed in the same way as the verb *race* above.

S V

EXAMPLE: Elizabeth Wilson has been called.

Elizabeth Wilson | has been called

Exercise 1 **Diagraming Subjects and Verbs** Diagram each sentence below, using the preceding examples as models.

1. People grow.
2. Max spoke.
3. Mrs. Rodriguez has changed.
4. Oklahoma State Park has opened.
5. They have been notified.

Adjectives, Adverbs, and Conjunctions

Most sentences contain more than a subject and a verb. Here are the ways to add adjectives, adverbs, and conjunctions to your basic diagrams.

Adding Adjectives Adjectives are placed on slanted lines directly below the nouns or pronouns they modify.

EXAMPLE: A *strong, icy* wind (S) appeared (V).

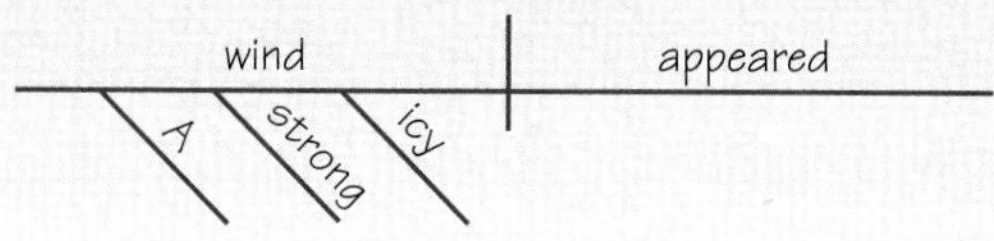

Adding Adverbs Adverbs are also placed on slanted lines. They go directly under the verbs, adjectives, or adverbs they modify.

EXAMPLE: *Quite* nervous (ADJ), Frank (S) spoke (V) *very hesitantly.*

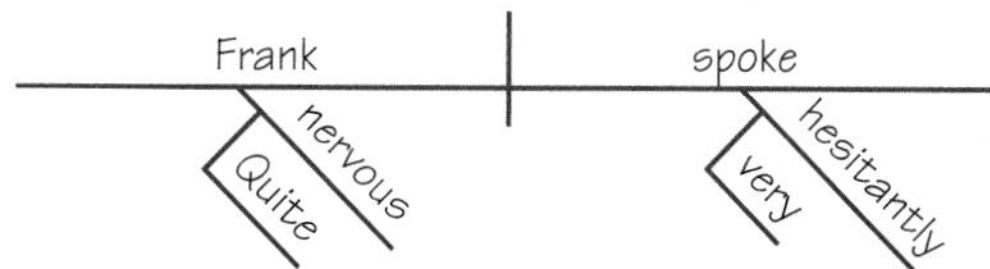

Adding Conjunctions Conjunctions are diagramed on dotted lines drawn between the words they connect.

EXAMPLE: The warm (ADJ) and friendly (ADJ) nurse (S) spoke (V) softly (ADV) but firmly (ADV).

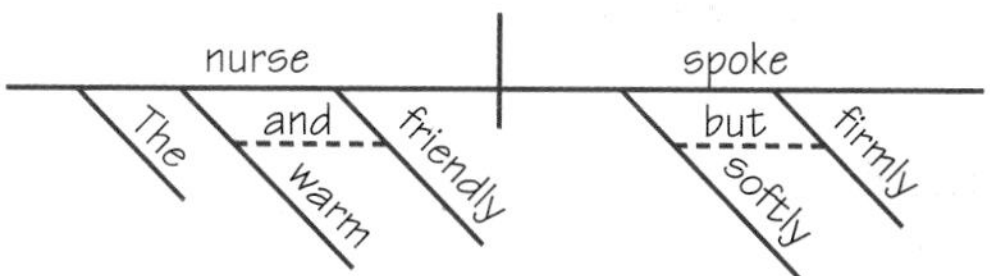

Exercise 2 **Diagraming Subjects and Verbs With Modifiers and Conjunctions** In addition to subjects and verbs, the following sentences contain adjectives, adverbs, and conjunctions. Diagram each sentence.

1. The old woman walked slowly.
2. The instructor spoke rapidly but quite distinctly.
3. The tiny but courageous dog yelped constantly.
4. The red and yellow tulips swayed very gently.
5. Extremely dense smoke was quickly drifting upward.

Compound Subjects and Verbs

It is necessary to split the horizontal line in order to diagram a sentence with either a compound subject or a compound verb.

Compound Subjects A sentence with a compound subject has its subject diagramed on two levels.

EXAMPLE: Father (S) and Mother (S) are arriving (V).

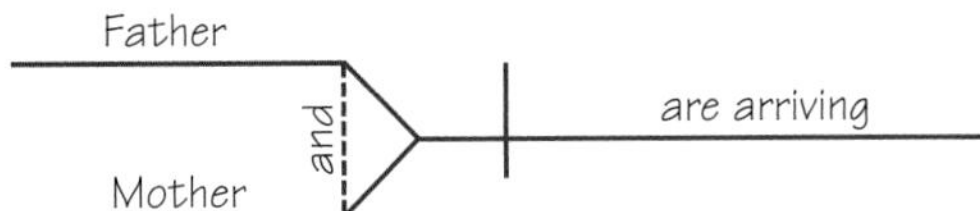

In diagraming compound subjects, place any adjective directly under the word it modifies. If an adjective modifies the entire compound subject, place it under the main line of the diagram. In the following example, *several* modifies the entire compound subject. *Red* and *blue* modify separate subjects.

EXAMPLE: *Several red* balloons (S) and *blue* kites (S) floated (V) overhead.

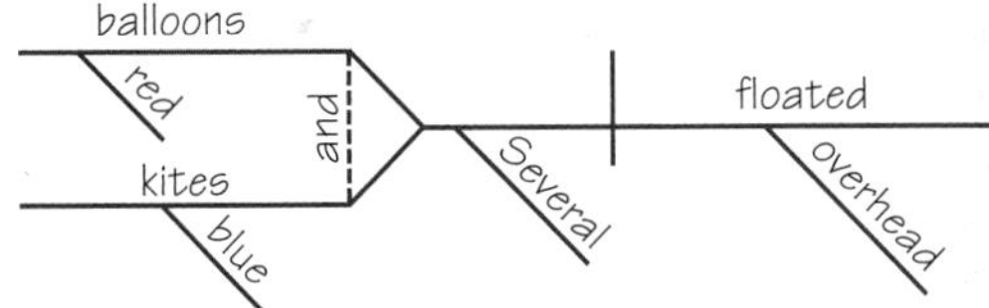

Compound Verbs Sentences with compound verbs are diagramed similarly. In the following example, the adverb *magnificently* modifies both parts of the compound verb.

EXAMPLE: Jeffrey (S) acts (V) and sings (V) magnificently.

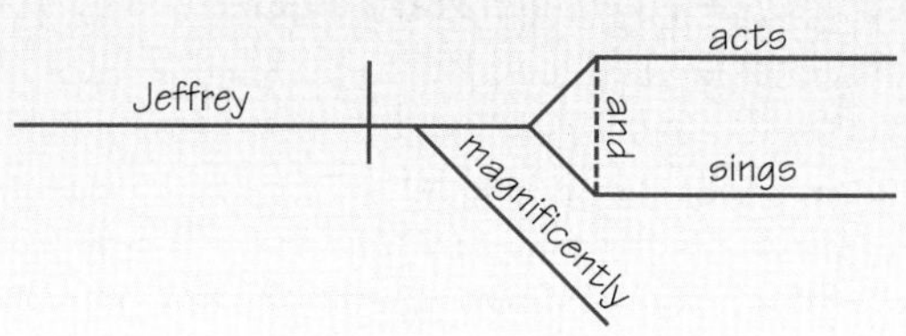

If the parts of a compound verb share a helping verb, the helping verb is placed on the main line of the diagram. If each part of the compound verb has its own helping verb, then each helping verb is placed on the line with its own verb.

EXAMPLE: Betty will (HV) win or lose.

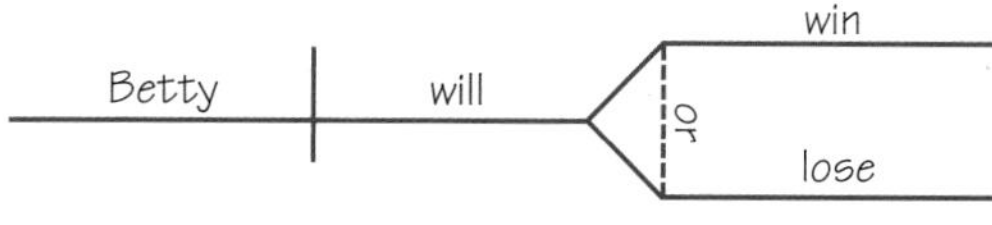

EXAMPLE: This project must (HV) grow or must (HV) shrink.

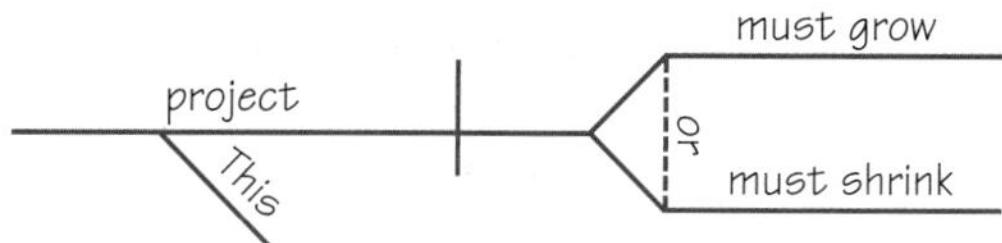

Exercise 3 **Diagraming Compound Subjects and Compound Verbs** Correctly diagram each sentence below.

1. Apples and grapes were served.
2. They can come or can stay.
3. The players, coaches, and parents cheered wildly.
4. The noisy crowd cheered, whistled, and applauded.
5. My brother and sister arrived early and left late.

Orders, Sentences Beginning With *There* or *Here,* and Interjections

Orders, sentences beginning with *there* or *here,* and interjections all follow special forms.

Orders The subject of an order is usually understood to be *you.* The understood subject *you* is diagramed in the regular subject position, but in parentheses.

EXAMPLE: Stop (V) now.

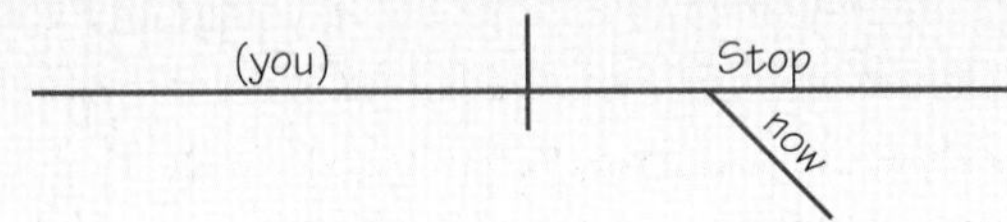

Sentences Beginning With *There* or *Here* *There* and *here* sometimes appear at the beginning of sentences and are mistaken for subjects. They are usually adverbs that modify the verb.

EXAMPLE: *Here* is (V) your watch.

When *there* is used simply to start a sentence, it has no grammatical link to the rest of the sentence. It is therefore placed on a short line above the subject.

EXAMPLE: *There* is (V) an important meeting (S) now.

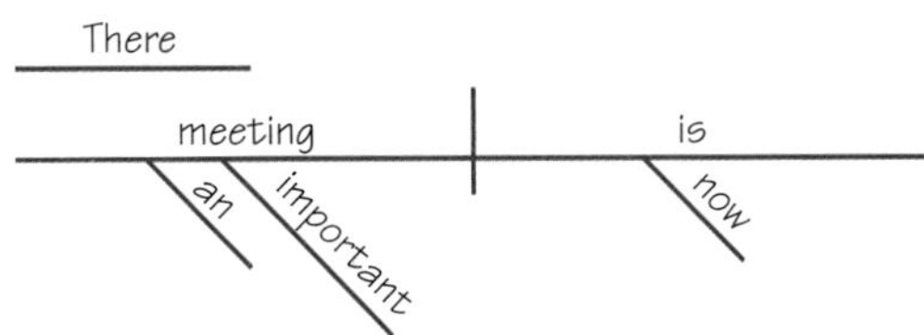

Interjections Like the word *there* when it is used simply to start a sentence, interjections have no grammatical link to the other words in a sentence. For this reason, interjections are also placed on a short line above the subject.

EXAMPLE: Wow! I won. (S: I, V: won)

Wow

I | won

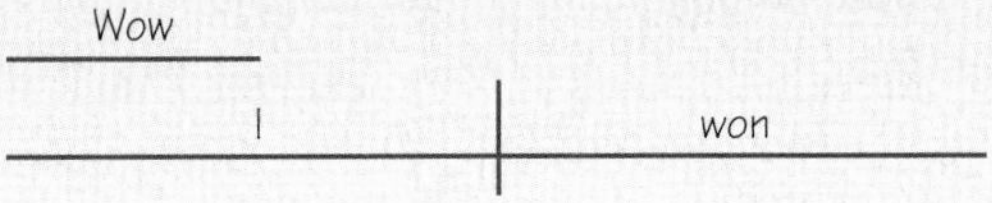

Exercise 4 Diagraming Orders, Sentences Beginning With *There* or *Here*, and Interjections Diagram each of the following sentences.

1. Begin now.
2. Here is my homework.
3. There once was a snake.
4. Whew! That hurt.
5. Gee! Watch out.

Complements

Direct objects, indirect objects, and subject complements are diagramed in three different ways.

Direct Objects A direct object is placed on the same line as the subject and verb. The direct object follows the verb and is separated from it by a short vertical line.

EXAMPLE: Children drink milk. (DO: milk)

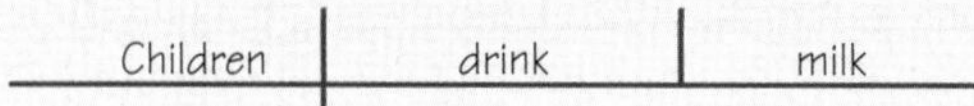

A compound direct object is diagramed in a way similar to that used for compound subjects and verbs. An adjective modifying both parts of the compound direct object is placed under the main line of the diagram. Otherwise, the adjective is placed directly under the word it modifies.

EXAMPLE: I have read five books and magazines. (DO: books; DO: magazines)

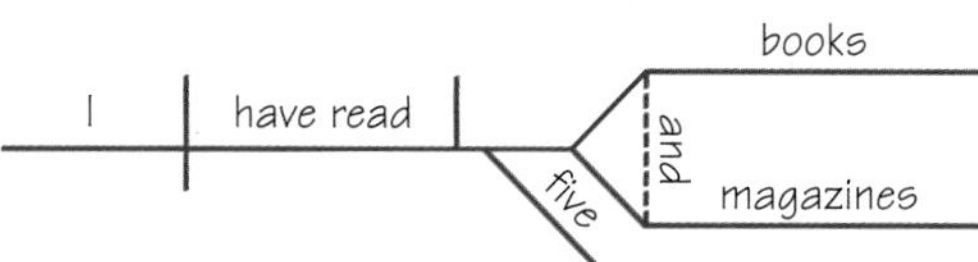

Indirect Objects The indirect object is placed on a short horizontal line extending from a slanted line drawn directly directly below the verb.

EXAMPLE: The teacher gave them the good news. (IO: them)

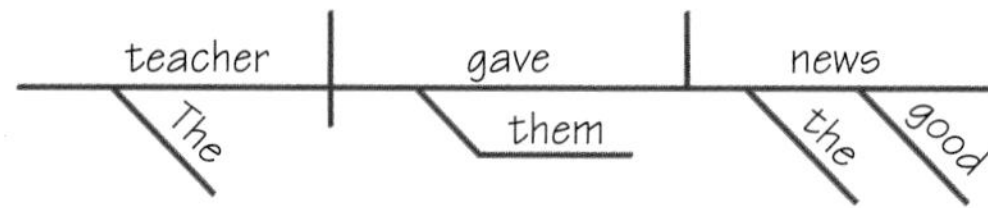

A sentence with a compound indirect object is diagramed in the following way.

EXAMPLE: Mother bought Billy and me new gloves. (Billy = IO, me = IO)

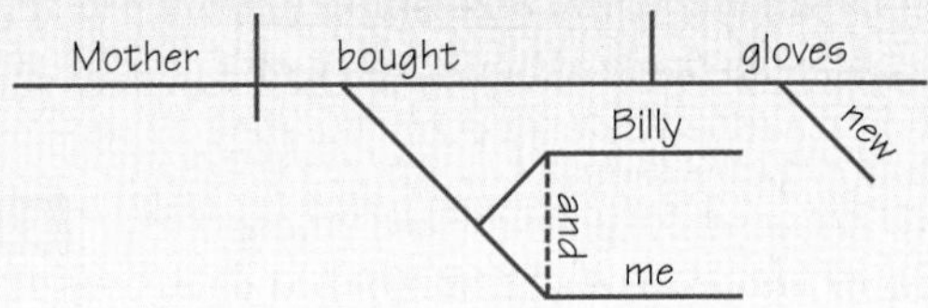

Subject Complements The subject complements—predicate nouns, pronouns, and adjectives—follow linking verbs. All are diagramed in the same way. They are placed after the verb, separated from it by a short slanted line.

EXAMPLE: Julie will be our class president. (president = PN)

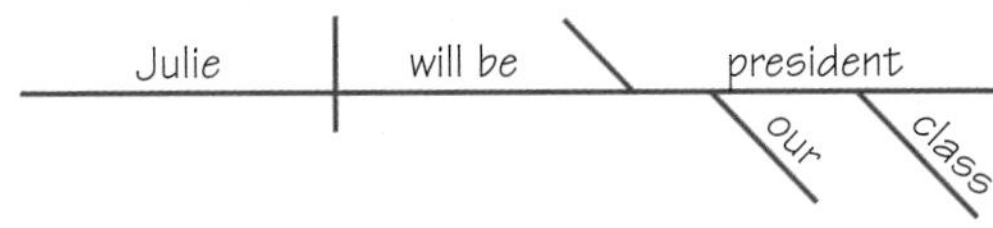

EXAMPLE: Julie seems very intelligent. (intelligent = PA)

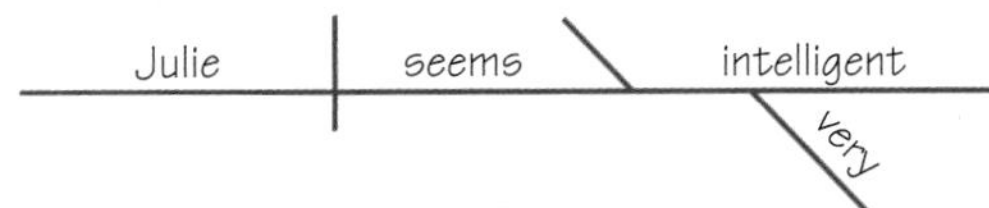

A compound subject complement is diagramed in the same way as a compound direct object, except that the separating line is slanted.

EXAMPLE: Those stamps are old and very valuable. (old = PA, valuable = PA)

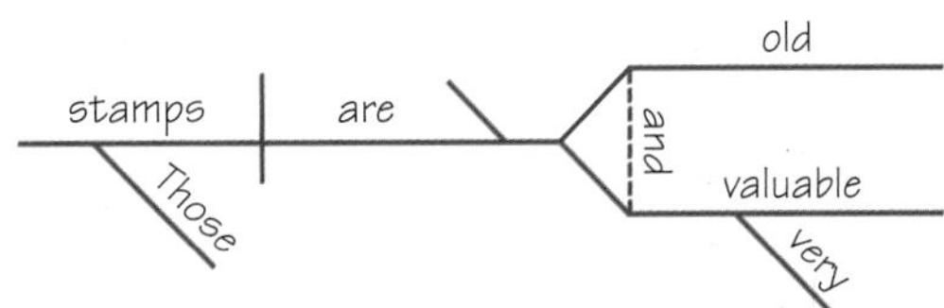

Exercise 5 **Diagraming Direct Objects and Indirect Objects** Diagram the following sentences. Note that some of the objects are compound.

1. My sister owes me a dollar.
2. Our teacher gave Brad and me a new assignment.
3. Father later bought lettuce, radishes, and cucumbers.
4. I will tell my mother the story tomorrow.
5. The gymnast showed us her new routine.

Exercise 6 **Diagraming Subject Complements** Diagram the following sentences. Note that some of the complements are compound.

1. The pool seems quite crowded.
2. The *Silver Streak* is a fine train.
3. Pat is the secretary and treasurer.
4. The river valley was unusually scenic.
5. Our new manager is honest and dependable.

Exercise 7 **Writing and Diagraming Sentences** Follow the instructions below to write five sentences of your own. Then, correctly diagram each sentence. Keep your sentences simple.

EXAMPLE: Write a sentence that contains a direct object.
The actor memorized the entire script.

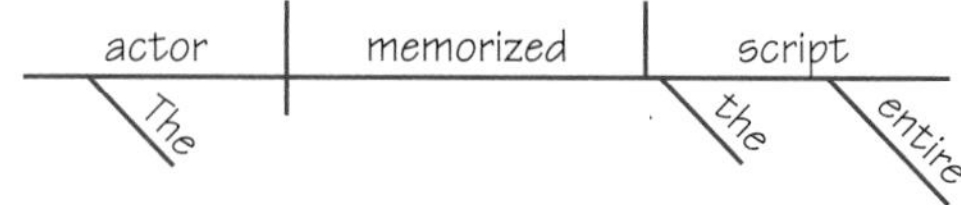

1. Write a sentence that contains at least one adjective and one adverb.
2. Write a sentence with a compound subject and compound verb.
3. Write a sentence that gives an order.
4. Write a sentence that contains a direct object.
5. Write a sentence with a compound subject complement.

Diagraming Clauses

The previous sections on diagraming dealt with different forms of simple sentences. This section will introduce diagrams for clauses in compound and complex sentences.

Compound Sentences

A compound sentence is a combination of two or more independent clauses. To diagram a compound sentence, begin by diagraming each clause separately, one above the other. Then, join the clauses at the verbs using a dotted line shaped like a step. Place the conjunction or semicolon on the horizontal part of the step.

EXAMPLE: Mary (S) slowly opened (V) the package, and then she (S) smiled (V) happily.

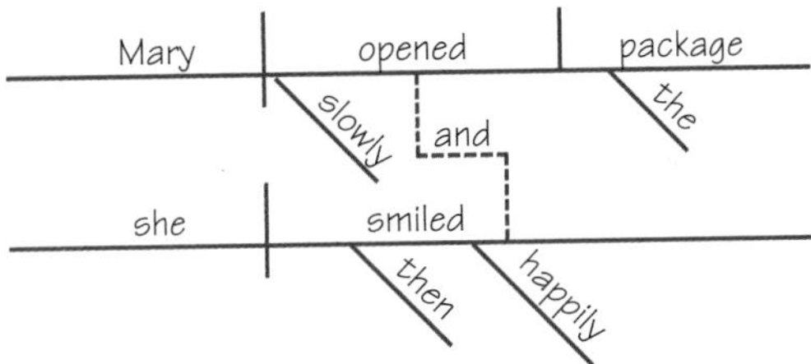

Exercise 8 Diagraming Compound Sentences On your paper, diagram each of the following compound sentences.

1. The roads are safe, but the bridges are icy.
2. Richard left for Boston yesterday; Gregory will leave today.
3. She wrote herself a note, yet she still forgot her appointment.
4. We must paint the fence; otherwise, it may rot.
5. We will give him three guesses; she will then tell him the answer.
6. Mary read the assignment, but she had trouble with the vocabulary.
7. Last winter, we had a great deal of snow; this year, we had very little.
8. She enjoyed the movie, and she recommended it to her friends.
9. We waited for Tom, but he didn't show up.
10. Frances was pleased with the results; everything went according to the plan.

Subordinate Clauses

A complex sentence contains one independent clause and one or more subordinate clauses. In a diagram of a complex sentence, each clause is placed on a separate horizontal line.

Adjective Clauses A subordinate adjective clause is placed on a horizontal line of its own beneath the independent clause. The two clauses are then connected by a dotted line. This dotted line connects the noun or pronoun being modified in the independent clause with the relative pronoun in the adjective clause.

S S V V

EXAMPLE: The person *whom you described* is the principal.

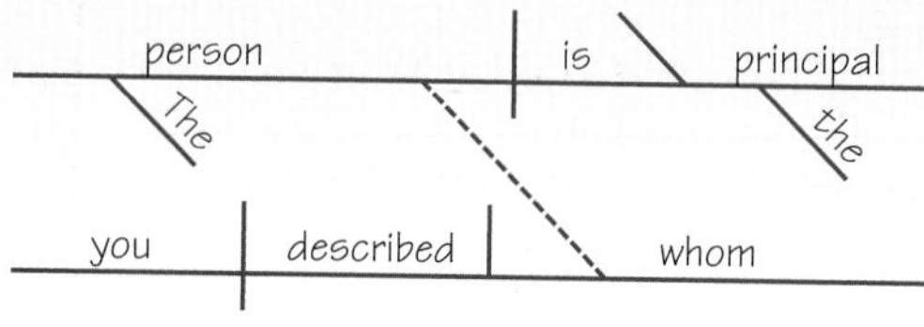

S V S V

EXAMPLE: This is the man *whose car was stolen.*

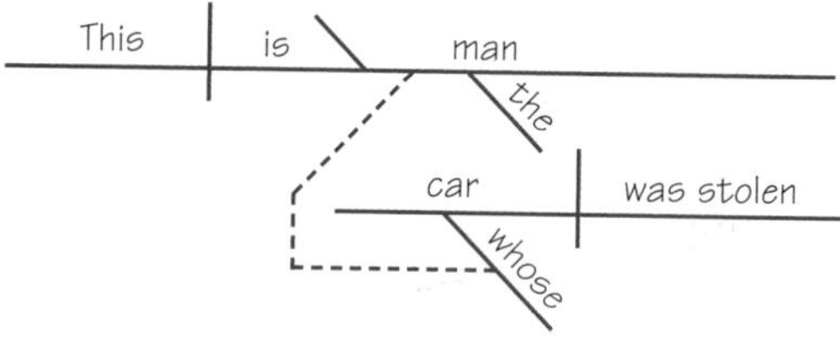

Adverb Clauses A subordinate adverb clause is diagramed in the same way a subordinate adjective clause is. The adverb clause is also written on a horizontal line of its own beneath the independent clause. In a diagram of an adverb clause, however, the subordinating conjunction is written along the dotted line. This line extends from the modified verb, adverb, or adjective in the independent clause to the verb in the adverb clause.

S V S V

EXAMPLE: They left *before the parade began.*

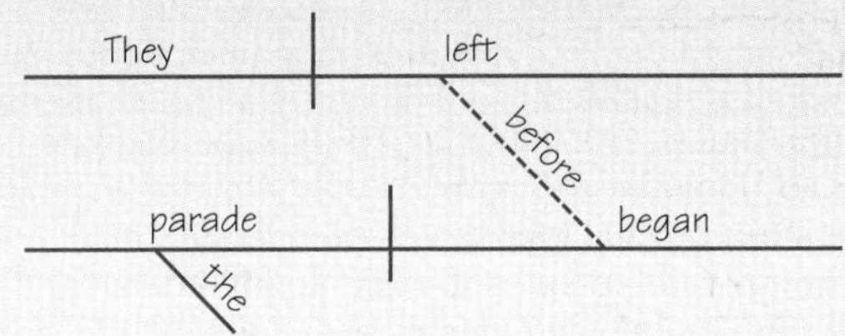

Exercise 9 **Diagraming Subordinate Clauses** Diagram the following sentences, each of which contains an adjective or an adverb clause.

1. I discovered the culprit who had caused the problem.
2. We left the theater before the play began.
3. The milk that I bought is sour.
4. When the judge entered, everyone rose.
5. The plans that they discussed remain a mystery.
6. I visited the town where my grandmother was raised.
7. They were disappointed because they lost the game.
8. This is the author whose work we are studying.
9. The book that you recommended is available in the library.
10. We arrived before the play started.

Exercise 10 **Writing and Diagraming Compound and Complex Sentences** Start with this simple sentence: *Rain fell for two hours.* Expand the simple sentence according to the instructions below to form compound and complex sentences. Then, diagram each new sentence.

EXAMPLE: Form a compound sentence by adding *but* and a second independent clause.
Rain fell for two hours, but we finished the game.

1. Form a compound sentence by adding *so* and another independent clause.
2. Form a compound sentence by adding a semicolon and another independent clause.
3. Add an adverb clause at the beginning to form a complex sentence.
4. Add an adverb clause at the end to form a complex sentence.
5. Add an adjective clause after *Rain* to form a complex sentence.

Index

Note: **Bold numbers** show pages on which basic definitions appear.

A

D

E

H

L

M

P

Q

R

S

U

V

W

Y

Z

Acknowledgments

Staff Credits

The people who made up the *Prentice Hall Writing and Grammar: Communication in Action* team—representing design services, editorial, editorial services, electronic publishing technology, manufacturing and inventory planning, marketing, marketing services, market research, online services and multimedia development, product planning, production services, project office, and publishing processes—are listed below. Bold type denotes the core team members.

Betsy Bostwick, Evonne Burgess, **Louise B. Capuano, Sarah Carroll, Megan Chill,** Katherine Clarke, Rhett Conklin, Martha Conway, Harold Crudup, **Harold Delmonte,** Libby Forsyth, Maggie Fritz, Ellen Goldblatt, Elaine Goldman, Jonathan Goldson, **Rebecca Graziano, Diana Hahn,** Rick Hickox, Kristan Hoskins, Carol Lavis, **George Lychock, Gregory Lynch,** William McAllister, Loretta Moser, Margaret Plotkin, Maureen Raymond, Gerry Schrenk, **Melissa Shustyk,** Annette Simmons, Robin Sullivan, Julie Tomasella, **Elizabeth Torjussen, Doug Utigard**

Additional Credits

Ernie Albanese, Diane Alimena, Susan Andariese, Michele Angelucci, Penny Baker, John Carle, Jaime Cohen, Elizabeth Crawford, Angelo Focaccia, Kathy Gavilanes, Beth Geschwind, Jennifer Harper, Evan Holstrom, Raegan Keida, Leanne Korszoloski, Sue Langan, Rebecca Lauth, Dave Liston, Maria Keogh, Vicki Menanteaux, Gail Meyer, Artur Mkrtchyan, LaShonda Morris, Karyl Murray, Omni-Photo Communications, Kim Ortell, Carolyn Sapontzis, Mildred Schulte, Slip Jig Image Research Services, Sunnyside, NY, Ron Spezial, Debi Taffet

Photo Credits

Cover: Stamp Designs © United States Postal Service, All Rights Reserved; SuperStock; **vi:** *House by the Railroad,* Edward Hopper, AKG Berlin/SuperStock; **vii:** (top) Corel Professional Photos CD-ROM™; **vii:** (bottom) © The Stock Market/Lance Nelson; **ix:** Bruce Forster/Tony Stone Images; **x:** Mary Ellen Lepionka; **xi:** *Will O' the Wisp,* ca. 1900, oil on canvas (triptych), 27x44 in., Elizabeth Adela Stanhope Forbes, The National Museum of Women in the Arts, On loan from the Wallace and Wilhelmina Holladay Collection; **xii:** AP/Wide World Photos/Joel Rennich; **xiii:** © 1999 Richard Laird/FPG International Corp.; **xiv:** Paul A. Souders/CORBIS; **xv:** *Strike,* 1992, Red Grooms, Marlborough Gallery, © 2001 Red Grooms/Artists Rights Society (ARS), New York; **xvi:** Kate DeWitt; **xvii:** M.C. Escher, *Day and Night* © 1998, Cordon Art B.V.-Baarn-Holland. All rights reserved.; **xviii:** © Francis G. Mayer/CORBIS; **xix–xxii:** Corel Professional Photos CD-ROM™; **xxiii:** (top) Corel Professional Photos CD-ROM™; (bottom) New York Convention and Visitors Bureau; **xxiv:** (top) *Zinnias*, 1937, John Hollis Kaufmann, Private Collection/SuperStock ; **xxiv:** (bottom) Corel Professional Photos CD-ROM™; **xxv:** Corel Professional Photos CD-ROM™; **xxii:** (top) Corel Professional Photos CD-ROM™; **xxv:** (bottom) © The Stock Market/Tom Stewart; **1:** *Orange Sweater, 1955,* Elmer Bischoff, San Francisco Museum of Modern Art, Gift of Mr. and Mrs. Mark Schorer; **2:** Peter Cade/ Tony Stone Images; **4:** Ron Chappel/FPG International Corp.; **16:** Mark Richards/PhotoEdit; **18:** Bettmann/Corbis; **19:** (top), (bottom) Getty Images; **23:** Esbin/ Anderson/Omni-Photo Communications, Inc.; **25:** image © Copyright 1998 PhotoDisc, image © Copyright 1998 PhotoDisc, Inc.; **32:** Phil Schermeister/CORBIS; **35:** *Self Portrait,* Emily Childers, Leeds Museums and Galleries (City Art Gallery), U.K./Bridgeman Art Library; **37:** Bachmann/PhotoEdit; **40:** Raymond Gehman/CORBIS; **42:** David Young-Wolff/PhotoEdit; **51:** *The Dory,* Edward Hopper, The Nelson-Atkins Museum of Art, Kansas City, Missouri, Gift of Mrs. Louis Sosland; **52:** Mary Ellen Lepionka; **60:** (top) Rhoda Sidney/PhotoEdit; (bottom) Michael Newman/PhotoEdit; **63:** *House by the Railroad,* Edward Hopper, AKG Berlin/SuperStock; **64:** © The Stock Market/Mug Shots; **66:** *Little Blue Horse,* 1912, Franz Marc, Giraudon, Art Resource, NY; **69:** Van Nuys, Peter Alexander, Courtesy of artist; **73:** © The Stock Market/Jon Feingersh; **74:** David Young-Wolff/PhotoEdit; **82:** *Signing of the Constitution,* Howard Chandler Christy, Art Resource, NY; **85:** *Untitled (Heard),* Barbara Kruger, National Museum of American Art, Washington D.C., Art Resource, NY; **86:** Bettmann/CORBIS; **93:** Horace Bristol/CORBIS; **97:** AP/Wide World Photos/Kevin Winter; **99:** Warren Morgan/CORBIS; **100:** *The Empire of Light, II,* 1950, René Magritte, The Museum of Modern Art, New York. Gift of D. and J. de Menil. Photograph © 1999 The Museum of Modern Art, New York © 2001 C. Herscovici, Brussels/Artists Rights Society (ARS), New York; **103:** (top) *Mexican Men with Burro Carrying Sticks,* Joan Marron-LaRue/Omni-Photo Communications, Inc.; (bottom) *Empire State,* Tom Christopher, Vicki Morgan Associates; **104:** Michael Newman/PhotoEdit; **106:** (left) Steve Hensen/Stock, Boston/PictureQuest; (right) Alon Reininger/Contact Press Images/ PictureQuest; **114:** AP/Wide World Photos/Mark Lennihan; **117:** *Pittsburgh,* 1927, Elsie Driggs, Collection of Whitney Museum of American Art, NYC, Gift of Gertrude Vanderbilt Whitney; **121:** Paul A. Souders/ CORBIS; **122:** © The Stock Market/Bob Shaw; **126:** AP/Wide World Photos; **129:** Paul W. Liebhardt; **130:** © The Stock Market **133:** *Strike,* 1992, Red Grooms, Marlborough Gallery, © 2001 Red Grooms/Artists Rights Society (ARS), New York; **135:** © The Stock Market/C/B Produc-tions; **139:** David Young-Wolff/PhotoEdit; **142:** Hunter Freeman/Tony Stone Images; **145:** PhotoEdit; **146:** CORBIS/-Medford Historical Society Collections; **149:** *Miners in the Sierras,* Charles Christian Nahl, National Museum of American Art, Washington DC/Art Resource, NY; **152–161:** CORBIS/Bettmann; **162:** Joanna Calabro, *Mask Maker,* Venice, 24" x 30" oil on linen. Courtesy of the artist; **165:** *The Girl I Left Behind Me,* Eastman Johnson, National Museum of American Art, Washington, D.C., Art Resource, NY; **167:** CORBIS/Bettmann; **169:** © Team Russell/Adventure Photo; **171:** M.C. Escher, *Day and Night* © 1998, Cordon Art B.V.-Baarn-Holland. All rights reserved; **172:** North Wind Picture Archives; **177:** Robin L. Sachs/PhotoEdit; **180:** *Girl Writing,* 1908, Pierre Bonnard, Barnes Foundation, Merion, Pennsylvania/SuperStock; **181:** image © Copyright 1998 PhotoDisc, Inc.; **187:** Dale Spartas/ Tony Stone Images; **191:** *Snoopy-Early Sun Display on Earth,* 1970, Alma Woodsey Thomas, National Museum of American Art, Washington, D.C./Art Resource, NY; **192:** Corel Professional Photos CD-ROM™; **196:** Courtesy of the Library of Congress; **208–216:** Courtesy of the Library of Congress; **226–249:** Corel Professional Photos CD-ROM™; **250:** Rudi Von Briel/PhotoEdit;

252–289: Corel Professional Photos CD-ROM™; **294–304:** Courtesy of Megan Chill; **308–356:** Corel Professional Photos CD-ROM™; **358:** image © Copyright 1998 PhotoDisc, Inc.; **368:** American Foundation for the Blind, Inc.; **373:** Mary Kate Denny/PhotoEdit; **382:** Courtesy of the Library of Congress; **384:** Corel Professional Photos CD-ROM™; **391:** Silver Burdett Ginn; **394–398:** Corel Professional Photos CD-ROM™; **400:** Courtesy of the Library of Congress; **403–454:** Corel Professional Photos CD-ROM™; **459:** Courtesy of the Library of Congress; **462:** Corel Professional Photos CD-ROM™; **468:** Corel Professional Photos CD-ROM™; **470:** New York Convention and Visitors Bureau; **471–480:** Corel Professional Photos CD-ROM™; **485:** *Emblems,* Roger De La Fresnaye, The Phillips Collection, Washington, DC; **486:** David Young-Wolff/PhotoEdit; **491:** Stephen McBrady/PhotoEdit; **499:** *Zinnias,* 1937, John Hollis Kaufmann, Private Collection/ SuperStock; **500:** David Young-Wolff/PhotoEdit; **504:** David Young-Wolff/PhotoEdit; **506:** Ken Karp/PH photo; **510:** © The Stock Market/Mug Shots; **513:** Tony Freeman/PhotoEdit; **519:** Tony Freeman/PhotoEdit; **521:** Bruce Ayres/Tony Stone Images; **522:** Tony Freeman/PhotoEdit; **526:** Corel Professional Photos CD-ROM™; **528:** © The Stock Market/Lance Nelson; **537:** Pinkerton Security and Investigation Services; **541:** Corel Professional Photos CD-ROM™; **737:** David Young-Wolff/PhotoEdit/ PictureQuest; **548:** Mary Kate Denny/Tony Stone Images; **550:** Tony Freeman/PhotoEdit; **562:** David Young-Wolff/PhotoEdit; **564:** © The Stock Market/Tom Stewart

006